SOCIAL
PSYCHOLOGY
a cognitive approach

EZRA STOTLAND
and
LANCE K. CANON
Both of the University of Washington

1972
W. B. SAUNDERS COMPANY
PHILADELPHIA · LONDON · TORONTO

W. B. Saunders Company: West Washington Square
Philadelphia, Pa. 19105

12 Dyott Street
London, WC1A 1DB

833 Oxford Street
Toronto 18, Ontario

Social Psychology: a cognitive approach

ISBN 0-7216-8608-7

Print No.: 9 8 7 6 5 4 3 2 1

To Patricia Stotland
and to
Avery James and Clifford Crooks Canon

PREFACE FOR PROFESSORS

The social psychologist reader of this book will no doubt be surprised when he scans the table of contents. Traditional chapters on attitude development and change, on group dynamics, on person perception, and so forth, are not to be found. Instead the reader finds chapters with such unfamiliar sounding titles as: Schemas About Interpersonal Relations; Decisions and Actions; and Safeguarding Self-Esteem. Since this book purports to be about social psychology, an explanation of these idiosyncrasies is in order.

These rather unusual chapter titles reflect the fact that the authors have attempted to provide a single theoretical framework around which the diverse areas of social psychology can be integrated. The authors feel that the present state of research and theoretical development in the field borders on the anarchic—with a host of small theories and some middle level theories, each accompanied by a more or less discrete set of related research studies. Each theory and its supporting body of research may make sense within a limited domain but they are seldom integrated with other, neighboring approaches and bodies of research literature. Research on person perception stands apart from research on the risky shift; cognitive dissonance from imitation; multi-motive games from leadership studies, communication studies from frustration-aggression theorizing. This situation bodes ill, since social psychology is not adhering to the scientific value of parsimony. A mature science attempts to limit the number of theories, and, if several middle or lower level theories are needed, they should stand in some orderly, systematic relationship to one another. Social psychology hardly measures up as a mature science in this respect. We have therefore attempted to provide a single framework for the diverse theories and research findings.

We have not, however, ignored theories which differ from ours. We have described them briefly and have attempted to indicate how their concepts and supporting data can be either treated as special cases of our broader framework or shown probably to be weak. Treating them as special cases of our theory has the value of involving greater adherence to the principle of parsimony. Nevertheless, our references to other theories do give the student some idea of the actual diversity of viewpoints in the field.

Another value of our approach is that the student does not have to wander, much like Alice, from one chapter to the next, feeling that each chapter provides its own "wonderland," as if the chapters in the book can be read in any order without undue harm or loss of coherence. We have attempted to have each chapter build at least in part on the material in the previous chapters.

The theory which we have developed is based on the conviction that social psychology can be integrated only by a theory which focuses on intervening processes within the individual rather than on diverse forms of overt behavior. Focusing on overt behavior or problem areas often entails the faulty assumption that for a single effect there is a single cause. There is no reason why all risky shifts, either up or down, need to be generated by the same cause. The history of such research demonstrates the multitude of causes that are possible for the same effect under different circumstances. The same applies to such phenomena as aggression, leadership, attraction, and others. One of the powers of cognitive dissonance theory is that it focuses on intervening processes and thereby provides a framework for understanding a wide range of overt, observable phenomena.

Our theory derives its fundamental concepts from branches of psychology other than social. Thereby we could achieve even more parsimony by tying our theory to theories and data from other branches of psychology. The theory thus gains strength not only because it attempts to integrate diverse areas of social psychology, but also because it relates itself to other areas of psychology. The boundary lines among the fields are fuzzy, in any case.

The non-social psychological approach which we have used is that of cognitive learning. We do not feel that traditional, behavioristic approaches to learning are sufficiently subtle or complex to cope with the phenomena of social psychology. On the other hand, dealing with cognition without dealing with learning is almost a contradiction in terms. Nevertheless, much of cognitive social psychology has been developed completely separate from learning and from history. Yet a discipline which is concerned with cultural and individual differences, with personality development, with change, must perforce deal with learning. The dissatisfaction with the more behavioral learning approaches does not have to apply to more cognitive approaches—and such cognitive approaches to learning, we feel, do recognize the complexity of social psychological phenomena.

Our approach represents just one of the possible ways of applying cognitive learning theories to social psychological phenomena. If ours is not completely successful, we feel that others can improve on it; but we also feel that the cognitive learning approach will, indeed, prove to be the most viable and effective general orientation.

As was mentioned above, one consequence of our theoretical organization in the book is that traditional problem or research areas of social psychology appear in unusual places, under "strange" headings. Aggression is treated in a chapter on defense of self-esteem. Attitude change is dealt with under a variety of headings. Phenomena relating to cognitive dissonance are dealt with in a chapter on decision and action. To assist the professor and the student, we have provided a rather detailed table of contents and an elaborate index. We hope these are adequate aids in the use of this book.

Another point of organization: The first two chapters define the field and describe its methods. The next two chapters describe the theoretical framework, without focusing on social psychology exclusively, since the framework is based on concepts drawn from general psychology. The following chapters spell out the implications of the theory for various areas of social psychology—although the areas are defined in somewhat unique ways. Thus, the professor may choose to assign selectively from among the first four chapters.

We have inserted material in boxes from time to time throughout the text. It has been isolated in this fashion because it involves, to a certain extent, an interruption in the train of thought presented in the main body of the text.

We wish to express our appreciation to Sidney Rosen for reading the bulk of the manuscript in a most helpful and constructively critical manner. We also wish to thank Bibb Latané and George Miller for their careful review of a number of the chapters.

Without the diligence and efficiency of Mrs. Cathy Gosho in typing the manuscript we would never had made it. We also wish to thank Ms. L. Fawcett and Mrs. Sharon Coe for their help.

Special thanks are due to Eileen Wooldridge both for her enthusiastic assistance in proofing portions of the manuscript and for her invaluable personal support and affection.

Patricia Stotland read proof for endless hours. Without her faith and love, the book would never have been written.

We would like to thank the following publishers for permission to quote from their publications: American Psychological Association; American Sociological Association; Appleton-Century-Crofts; Holt, Rinehart, and Winston; Prentice-Hall; University of Washington Press; and John Wiley & Sons.

We would like to thank the following for permission to use their photographs; Scientific American; William Vandivert; Wide World Photos. Inc.; and H. Armstrong-Roberts.

Our special thanks go to Irwin Nash for the use of his compelling photographs.

EZRA STOTLAND

LANCE K. CANON

CONTENTS

Chapter 3

THE ACQUISITION OF SCHEMAS

Chapter 4

THE FUNCTIONING OF SCHEMAS 129

Chapter 5

SCHEMAS ABOUT PEOPLE 165

CHAPTER 1

TOWARD A DEFINITION
OF SOCIAL PSYCHOLOGY

Tradition, as well as the demands of logical progression in the development of a text, suggests that a formal definition of the field of social psychology be provided to give the reader a general orientation to the material which he will find in the pages to follow. However, there is something rather artificial about an attempt to capture the flavor and diversity of this discipline in a one- or two-sentence summary statement. For one thing, as far as practicing social psychologists are concerned, it is probably an irrelevant intellectual exercise, in that it is difficult to imagine such a researcher carefully checking to ascertain that his current work and interests fall within the limits of the domain delineated by such a definition. He is not likely to feel compelled to turn to this sort of broad abstraction as a means for legitimizing his work. Further, the definition is likely to be so broad as to lack any heuristic value; that is, it is improbable that it would have value as a stimulating source of research ideas or ways of conceptualizing and dealing with the issues in social psychology.

But then, even if this broad specification of what social psychology is has limited utility for those directly involved in the field, it may yet function as a useful device in providing a general orientation to the discipline for others. There are several ways in which this sort of definition might be generated. We might, for example, suggest that there is some a priori basis for making a decision as to what social psychology ought legitimately to be and then enumerate these independently derived criteria. Another approach, which seems more appropriate, if indeed the primary utility of the definition is to generate a realistic picture of what social psychology is, involves the development of a quasi-operational definition. The thinking behind such an approach maintains that we mean by a concept nothing more than a set of operations by which the concept is measured or manipulated in some fashion (Bridgman, 1928). Thus, the concept of intelligence would be defined as whatever it is that standard tests of I.Q. test or measure. In a rough analogy to the operationist position, then, we may begin to come to grips with the problem of defining social psychology by taking a look at what it is that social psychologists "do" and how they do it. There is a set of ulterior motives behind our use of this technique. One stems from the fact that this text will not at all times present and deal with the material at hand in terms of the traditional sub-fields within social psychology, and yet the reader should be made aware of the manner in which the discipline has come to be subdivided during its brief history. Thus the section which follows will examine what social psychologists do by briefly outlining these major traditional areas and by then looking closely at a specific piece of representative research. In addition, this sort of exposition will permit the reader to develop a feeling for the diversity of methodological approaches available for the study of the questions which have stimulated research. And finally, since one of the criteria used in selecting the investigations to be discussed was the general "interest value" of the studies, it is our hope that the reader will also come to share some of the enthusiasm and excitement those of us who have chosen social psychology as a career derive from our work.

INTERPERSONAL INFLUENCE PROCESSES

One of the most intriguing sets of issues with which social psychologists have dealt concerns the manner in which persons exert influence over one another. Perhaps this interest derives from the fact that activity aimed at influencing and controlling others is such a ubiquitous phenomenon in the social world—we see it in circumstances as diverse as the relatively structured and formal situation in which an employer dictates the activities of his employees and the informal and often very subtle interplay and exchange of real and promised reinforcements which occur when a young man (lecherous by definition) and a not yet "liberated" woman meet to play out their roles in the dating ritual. Since in our culture an onus is placed on explicitly manipulative activity, and chagrin or discomfort of some sort is one typical consequence of the realization that one has been manipulated, both parties in an exchange are motivated to disguise or deny to themselves and others the influence activity which transpires. As a result the tactics employed often tend to be indirect, subtle, and difficult to investigate and make explicit.

A potential influence situation familiar to the reader involves faculty-student interactions. There is considerable folklore to the effect that "some" students succeed during their academic careers not by means of diligence and innate intellectual ability but rather through the assiduous application of manipulative strategies. There is little doubt that some factors other than testable academic ability and aptitude contribute importantly to academic success as measured by grades, since the available tests often do not correlate highly with grade point average. But is it realistic to imagine that the sophisticated faculty of our institutions of higher learning can really be conned by naive freshmen in this manner? Research by Singer (1964) provides the basis for an answer in the affirmative, distressing as it may be to some. He began with the straightforward hypothesis that a positive correlation exists between students' scores on a personality questionnaire developed by Christie (Christie and Geis, 1970), designed to measure an individual's tendency to be socially manipulative or "Machiavellian," and grade point average (GPA). Appropriate tests were administered to a sample of almost one thousand college freshmen. In anticipation of the criticism that there just might be a relationship between intelligence or academic ability and Machiavellianism so that it could be argued that high scorers on the latter receive higher grades not because of their manipulative ability but simply because they are brighter students, tests of academic ability were also given. No significant correlation was found between these measures, however, and, in addition, Singer employed a statistical technique which permitted him to examine the Machiavellianism-GPA correlation independently of the influence of intelligence. The female reader may find it distressing (or perhaps comforting) to learn that no significant relationship was found for women in the sample. The predicted correlation was found for males, however, and it was especially strong for later-born men. We need to digress briefly here to point out that numerous investigations have shown that there are consistent differences in a variety of traits and abilities as a function of one's ordinal position in the family. That is, first-born and only children appear to differ from later-borns, probably because of some consistently different early life experiences which the first child in a family experiences (e.g., he has no siblings with whom he must compete for parental attention, his parents haven't developed stable ways of dealing with their first child, and he learns to orient toward and depend upon adult or authority figures). (See Sampson, 1969, for a recent review of this literature.) Singer speculates that this difference between first-born and later-born males may result from differences in their ability to carry out manipulative strategies successfully. For example, research has indicated that first-borns tend to become more anxious, are in general more influenceable and dependent on others for evaluation of their opinions, and are more concerned about social correctness than are later-borns. Thus, he argues, while first-borns may express Machiavellian tendencies to as great an extent as do others, they may lack the interpersonal skills required for the effective manipulation of other persons' beliefs and behaviors. So, for later-born males, at least, the evidence indicates that Machiavellianism is a factor in determining the grades students earn.

But what about the women? Are they to be left to struggle in the competition for grades with no resources other than intellect and motivation? Of course not. Singer reasons that the absence of a Machiavellianism-GPA correlation for women may be due to sociocultural factors which make it unlikely for them to behave in an openly manipulative fashion. They may manipulate but are likely to employ attractiveness and appearance rather than deceit and management as tactics. To examine this possibility, faculty members were asked to rate the physical attractiveness of female students from their photographs. A significant positive correlation was found between these ratings and GPA—but only for first-born females. Two questions immediately arise: Why does the relationship hold only for first-borns and does it indicate active manipulatory behavior or is it simply that male instructors pay attention to and learn the names of the attractive girls and then tend to give them an advantage in grading? To look at these issues Singer administered to females in two psychology courses a questionnaire which included questions concerning what might be termed exhibiting behavior. The results indicated that first-born females tend to sit in the front of the classroom, see the instructor after class, and visit him during his office hours more than do later-borns. To bolster the contention further that first-born females use their looks in a manipulative manner, yet another study was conducted to assess the possibility that first-borns are more socially concerned about their bodily characteristics and are actually more knowledgeable about them. If this is the case, the argument that attractiveness is being actively used in the service of grade promotion becomes more tenable. To test this idea, females were recruited to participate in a study of health-related characteristics of students. They filled out a medical questionnaire which asked in part for self-estimates of height, weight, bust, waist, and hip measurements and for a statement of what the "ideal" for these dimensions is. Actual measurements were then taken of these characteristics, but only half of the sample was informed of this in advance of their filling out the questionnaire.

In the unaware portion of the sample, first-born girls distorted their self-ratings in the ideal direction more than did later-borns, but among those who had been forewarned that actual measurements would be made, first-borns were more accurate in their personal estimates. The conclusion, then, seems to be that first-born females are more aware of those dimensions having to do with physical attractiveness, because they can more accurately report on them under appropriate conditions, but that when they don't anticipate an accuracy check they distort their reports in the direction of an ideal. And the implication from all this is that the correlation between grades and good looks is the result of a manipulative maneuver using body rather than Machiavellian activities as a strategy.

In conclusion, Singer comments: "The suggestion that men live by their brains and women by their bodies was made as far back as Genesis. Although not astoundingly new, the implications are rather frightening. . . . The results imply that the poor college professor is a rather put-upon creature, hoodwinked by the male students (later-born) and enticed by the female students (first-born) as he goes about his academic and personal responsibilities. He is seemingly caught in a maelstrom of student intrigue and machination. The picture is bleak. In defense, we can only offer the consolation that when 22 male members of the faculty . . . were administered the Machiavellian scale (they) appeared significantly more manipulative than the students. . . . It is hoped that the academicians are fighting stratagem with stratagem." (Singer, 1964, p. 150.)

Norms, Reference Groups, and Conformity

Another large body of research has been concerned with an understanding of the manner in which implicit and explicit socially derived standards of belief and behavior develop, the impact such norms have on current and aspiring members of groups, and the conditions, both external and internal to the person, which determine the likelihood that he will behave in a manner consistent with what he believes others feel to be correct and appropriate.

Many studies have documented the rather surprisingly great impact which a unanimous group judgment can have on an individual in inducing him to conform to the position taken by the group. We are perhaps less able to maintain an independent stand in the face of unified contrary opinion than we would like to believe. But what if the stakes are raised a bit, so that the consequences of conformity go beyond a belief or attitude change on our part and involve instead the well-being of another person? Milgram (1963, 1965) has provided us with some tentative answers to this question in his work on obedience. The focus here is slightly different in that compliance with the demands of an authoritative individual rather than group consensus is being investigated.

Subjects were recruited, by means of a mailed circular, to participate in a study of the effects of punishment on memory, for which they were paid $4.50. In an admirable departure from the typical use of student populations, the male subjects ranged in age from their early twenties to late forties and were drawn from a wide variety of occupational categories. They arrived to find another participant already present and were informed that a drawing would determine which of them would function as teacher and which as learner in what was to come. The other subject was actually an accomplice of the experimenter and the drawing was rigged so that the naive subject was always given the teacher role. This involved checking on the learner's performance in memorizing a list of paired associate words and administering increasingly severe electrical shocks to him for each error made. This was done by means of a simulated shock generator with thirty clearly marked voltage levels ranging from 15 volts (labeled slight shock) to 450 volts (labeled danger: severe shock). Though the teacher was given a sample shock to demonstrate the operation of the device, no shocks were actually given to the accomplice. His behavior was pre-planned so that it would be necessary for the teacher ultimately to administer the highest level of shock possible if he complied fully with the instructions, which were to give the shocks and advance to the next highest shock level for each error made. Four experimental conditions were set up, varying in terms of the salience or immediacy of the victim to the teacher. In one, the victim operated from an adjacent room and was heard from only when he pounded on the wall at the 300 volt level. After this, he gave no more responses on the memory task; the teacher was told to consider no answer an error and to increase and administer the shocks as usual. In the second condition, verbal protests were audible from the victim. "Starting with 75 volts the learner begins to grunt and moan. At 150 volts he demands to be let out of the experiment. At 180 volts he cries out that he can no longer stand the pain. At 300 volts he refuses to provide any more answers to the memory test, insisting that he is no longer a participant in the experiment and must be freed" (1965, p. 246). The third condition differed from the second only in that the learner was situated in the same room with the teacher and his reactions to the shocks could be seen as well as heard. In the final condition the learner refused at the 150 volt level to cooperate and the teacher was instructed to force the victim's hand onto the metal plate through which the shocks were given. If at any time the teacher questioned what was going on the experimenter told him that he had no choice but to go on. The study was ended when the teacher either refused to give additional shocks or reached the highest, 450 volt, level.

Milgram reports that the situaton was a very "real" and disturbing one for the typical subject, who was quite clearly caught up in the conflict between the demands imposed by the situation and the experimenter and his reluctance to inflict pain on another person. To demonstrate the power of the experimental situation, below is a portion of the transcript from one subject.

"He began the experiment calmly, but became increasingly tense as the experiment proceeded. After administering the 150 volt shock, he began to address the experimenter in agitated tones:

150 Volts Delivered. You want me to keep going?

165 Volts Delivered. That guy is hollering in there. There's a lot of them here. He's liable to have heart condition. You want me to go?

180 Volts Delivered. He can't stand it! I'm not going to kill that man in there! You hear him hollering? He's hollering. He can't stand it. What if something happens to him? . . . I'm not going to get that man sick in there. He's hollering in there. You know what I mean? I mean I refuse to take responsibility. He's getting hurt in there. . . . Too many left here. Geez, if he gets them wrong . . . I mean who is going to take responsibility if anything happens to that gentleman? (The experimenter accepts responsibility.) All right.

195 Volts Delivered. You see, he's hollering. Hear that? Gee, I don't know. (The experimenter says: "The experiment requires that you go on.") I know it does, sir, but I mean — huh — he don't know what he's in for . . .

240 Volts Delivered. Aw no. You mean I've got to keep going up with the scale? No sir. I'm not going to kill that man! I'm not going to give him 450 volts.

"Despite his numerous agitated objections, which were constant accompaniments to his actions, the subject unfailingly obeyed the experimenter, proceeding to the highest shock level of the generator" (1965, pp. 253-254).

Would you care to give your own estimate of the percentages of totally obedient subjects in this situation? Forty psychiatrists were asked to do so, and they predicted that most would not continue beyond the 150 volt level, that only 4 per cent would still be obedient by the 300 volt level, and that only 1/10 of one per cent would actually give the highest shock. Thus, you are in good company if you too made gross underestimates of the degree to which persons will comply with an authoritative order of this sort. Sixty-five per cent of the participants in the first condition described on page 6, 62.5 per cent in the second, 40 per cent in the third, and 30 per cent in the fourth condition were fully obedient; that is, ultimately administered the full 450 volt jolt.

But perhaps the obedience manifested here was largely due to the aura of legitimacy and professionalism provided by the fact that the study was conducted at, and implicitly then under the auspices of, Yale University. Some subjects, in fact, spontaneously mentioned that they had faith in the integrity and benign purpose of the study in view of its sponsorship. To examine this possibility the research was replicated in another city, in a somewhat shabby downtown commercial office building, in a clean though minimally furnished suite of rooms. No university connections of any sort were evident. There was no significant reduction in the percentage of subjects who were fully obedient.

No data pertinent to an explanation of the reduced obedience with increasing salience of the victim were gathered, but Milgram speculates regarding a number of possibilities. It might be the case that only with greater proximity and direct observation of the victim's suffering do genuine empathic responses on the part of the teacher become likely. He may only then really grasp the consequences of his act, and, in addition, "feeling" the discomfort of the victim may in itself be unpleasant and add to the teacher's motivation to discontinue the experience. Also, while the greater proximity permits the teacher to more carefully observe the victim, at the same time it allows the victim to directly scrutinize his tormenter; therefore, it may be less difficult to harm another "behind his back," so to speak. As Milgram notes, the presumed function of blindfolding the person on the receiving end of a firing squad is to reduce his discomfort, but it might just also operate to make the situation less stressful for those who will walk away from the situation. Most persons may also have been negatively reinforced for aggressive behavior directed toward another close at hand who may retaliate, but have not been so likely to have experienced similarly unpleasant reciprocity when the object of aggressive behavior was at a distance. Thus a differential disposition to inhibit aggression in general may exist as a function of the physical proximity of the other person. A related possibility is that the structure of our society does not provide many occasions on which disobedience is reinforced or looked on favorably and so we do not have readily available, easily engaged behavioral patterns upon which to draw when the occasion demands. Reportedly, many participants verbally expressed a strong desire to withdraw from further shock administration, but nevertheless continued as if they were simply unable to put together a plan of action that would allow them to fully extricate themselves. The validity of any of these possibilities can be established only through additional research, of course.

Milgram's conclusions represent generalization considerably beyond the actual data generated in his study, but are sufficiently thought-provoking to deserve repetition. He states that his results "raise the possibility that . . . the kind of character produced in American democratic society cannot be counted on to insulate its citizens from brutality and inhumane treatment at the direction of malevolent authority. A substantial proportion of people do what they are told to do, irrespective of the content of the act and without limitations of conscience, so long as they perceive that the command comes from a legitimate authority" (1965, p. 262).

Attitude Formation and Change

Probably the most extensively treated topic in contemporary social psychology is that of attitude formation and change. In view of the pervasive role attitudes play for the individual in the organization of his behavior and experience this emphasis seems eminently appropriate. Research on the meaning which events, objects, and "things" in general have for persons indicates that one of the most fundamental and pervasive aspects of that meaning involves the evaluation we make of them (Osgood, Suci, and Tannenbaum, 1957). The suggestion is that the basic way in which we orient to things is in terms of our placement of them along a good-bad or approach-avoidance dimension, and this same sort of evaluative dimension is frequently emphasized as one of the defining characteristics of an attitude.

As we have indicated, the term attitude is very widely used in social psychology. Yet, in the past, there has been a wide gap between the usage of the term in research and its definition by theorists. In many research settings it has been used rather loosely to refer to any opinion, any belief, or any feeling, pro or con, that a person might hold about any person, institution, ideology, or object in his environment. In theoretical writings, however, the term has often been limited in its reference to a tendency to react in either a favorable or unfavorable way toward a given person, institution, ideology, or object. Beliefs or opinions which do not involve degrees of favorability are often excluded from the definition. In order to avoid some of these confusions, we will use the term attitude in its broadest sense, referring to any opinion, belief, or evaluation, especially when we describe research in which finer differentiations were not made by the researchers. However, when we discuss more precisely tendencies to react in a favorable or unfavorable way, we will use the term "evaluation" to indicate the more specific usage intended.

Recent research stemming originally from certain implications of Festinger's theory of cognitive dissonance (1957) has raised some interesting issues regarding the relationship between attitudes and behavior. A commonsense analysis would probably hold that attitudes precede and exert a directive influence on behavior. It seems most reasonable to assume that a person searches out, purchases, and consumes a banana split because he likes—has a positive attitude toward—them. However, evidence exists that under appropriate conditions behavior may strongly influence and determine attitudes, that a person's desire to be or appear to be consistent may lead him to develop an attitude that is consistent with his prior behavior. Thus, if a person can be induced in the proper way to go to the trouble of searching out and purchasing that exotic ice cream concoction, he may come to like it because he behaved as he did. The specific conditions under which this sort of effect will occur are still a matter of controversy, as we shall see later in this book.

As a matter of fact, even the theoretical interpretation of this effect proposed by the cognitive dissonance theory position has been the subject of debate, as Bem (1967) has offered an alternative explanation for the phenomenon. This analysis has its roots in a general orientation to psychological research and theory termed radical behaviorism, which studiously avoids the use of hypothetical constructs which refer to non-observable internal states or processes. To account for the current behavior of an organism, emphasis is instead placed on a careful examination of its prior history of rewards, punishments, and activity, with an eye toward constructing an explanation in terms of previously established stimulus-response relationships. Thus Bem is led to note that many attitudes can be thought of as verbalized or verbalizable descriptions of the person's internal state, a self-description, and then to inquire about how an individual develops the ability to generate such statements. His suggestion is that it is learned in just the same manner as is the ability to engage in other sorts of verbal behavior, i.e., the socializing community shapes the behavior by differentially reinforcing and punishing correct and incorrect usage. Of course, precision and accuracy in such training is more difficult where essentially private states are involved. The training agents must rely on externally observable behaviors as indicators of some internal state in order to teach the proper response. Think, for example, of how you might go about teaching a child to accurately indicate when he is fatigued or in pain or likes a particular food. Bem goes on to suggest that an individual may depend on publicly observable behaviors in making self-descriptive statements in much the same way that some other person might; that is, the person may use the same sort of information in analyzing and reporting his own internal states as would an external observer. If, for one reason or another, an individual behaves in a given fashion (eats many banana splits) he may infer a relevant internal state on the basis of his observation of this behavior (I must like banana splits since I eat them often). Though this may not seem to be an intuitively reasonable position to take, there is evidence in support of it. One additional point needs to be made—just as an outside observer would take into account situational factors as evidence relevant to the likelihood that the behavior he sees validly and honestly represents the internal state he is attempting to infer, so does the person who observes his own behavior. To pursue the banana split example, someone who had information indicating that I was being paid to eat them, or believed them to be an excellent aphrodisiac, or had been ordered to eat them by my misguided naturopathic doctor, would not then take this behavior as good evidence regarding my liking for them. Bem argues that I would similarly take into account evidence regarding the credibility of my own behavior in my use of it as a basis for inferring my own attitude.

All this leads to an intriguing study bearing on an issue of considerable social and legal import. It has to do with the circumstances under which persons might be induced to believe a false confession. Working from earlier research which suggested that "saying becomes believing whenever an individual makes statements under conditions in which he expects himself to be telling the truth" (Bem, 1970, p. 62), an experiment was designed to explore the possibility that falsely confessing to some prior action under conditions which have come to be associated with truth-telling might lead to acceptance of and belief in the incorrect statements made.

Subjects, who were told the study had to do with an attempt to discover qualities of the voice which might be used to detect lying behavior, were first given a list of 100 common nouns and another form with 50 words in alphabetical order from the first list. They were instructed to cross out with a pencil all the words on the longer list which were given on the alphabetical guide. This constituted the act about which they would later be questioned. Next, a 50-item informational questionnaire was administered which asked for factual material such as the subject's academic major, preferred brand of toothpaste, opinions on current issues, etc. This information was then used as a basis for asking the subject questions which he was to answer into a tape recorder either truthfully or untruthfully, depending upon whether a green or amber ceiling light was illuminated. For example, the experimenter might ask him what toothpaste he uses. If the red light is on he is to give the correct answer in the form of a complete sentence, e.g., "I use brand X toothpaste." If the green light is illuminated, however, the subject is to make an untrue statement. Half of the questions required true responses and half called for false responses. By this training procedure the colored lights were established as discriminative stimuli, one consistently associated with truthful verbal behavior, the other with untruthful statements.

Finally, to create a situation analogous to giving a confession, the experimenter had the subjects state into the tape recorder that they had or had not crossed out certain of the words with which they had worked earlier. One of the colored lights came on each time the recorder was activated, but the experimenter made no mention that any attention should be given to this. Following each "confession" the subject indicated whether or not he remembered actually having crossed out that word and gave an indication of how confident he was about the correctness of his recall. The situation was arranged so that half the statements made were true and half were false, and within each of these halves the truth light was on for one half of the statements and the lie light for the remaining half.

The finding of greatest interest was that, as predicted, accurate recall of words which had previously been crossed out was influenced by the presence of cues associated with truth-telling. That is, the evidence indicated that a false statement or "confession" (e.g., "I crossed out the word cat," when, in fact, it had not been crossed out) made when the truth light was on tended to be believed by the subjects, who made many recall errors in this situation and indicated that they were much less certain of their memory. Though they were not telling the truth they were misled by the fact that they made the "confession" under conditions in which they had learned to trust their verbal behavior as truthful. Post-experimental interviews provided evidence that the subjects were not aware of the nature of the influence the lights were having on their recall ability.

Bem (1970) points out that his research may have some important implications regarding the real-life situation in which an individual finds himself being interrogated as a suspect or witness in criminal proceedings. The Supreme Court, in the controversial *Miranda v. Arizona* and *Escobedo v. Illinois* decisions in the 1960's, provided guidelines for the conduct of police interrogations which made it mandatory that the suspect be informed of his right against self-incrimination and to have an attorney present, among other things. Many persons, particularly those involved in law enforcement, felt that this represented an unnecessarily severe restriction on effective police work, but the study just described would argue against such a conclusion. For most of us, as honest and law-abiding citizens, the setting of a police interrogation is replete with "truth-telling" cues, so that it is particularly likely that, to the extent that Bem's self-observation hypothesis is valid, one's verbal behavior will strongly influence his attitudes and beliefs. Any errors or inaccuracies that may be introduced in the statements the suspect or witness makes, either because of an honest error on his part or the prompting of the interrogator, may come to be believed and repeated thereafter as truthful.

GROUP DYNAMICS

The cliché which suggests that man is a social animal must be familiar to almost everyone and few would take exception to the proposition that we do, indeed, spend much of our time acting in concert with other people. It is quite natural, then, that one of the important branches of social psychology has as its primary interest the participation of persons in organized social units, or groups. The focus here is on meaningful aggregations of individuals which have at least some rudimentary structure and system of internal regulation and control, on assemblies which actually operate as a unit which has some purpose. Thus, artificial or purely classificatory groupings, such as "all persons over thirty years of age," and aggregates which exist simply because of their momentary physical proximity, such as a group of people waiting to cross a busy street, are not of interest. The assumption underlying this interest in group dynamics is, naturally enough, that there are identifiable qualities and characteristics of organized group behavior which are unique and which cannot be uncovered simply through the examination of individuals in isolation. Another aphorism which suggests that the whole is more than simply the sum of its parts and their attributes, summarizes this commonsense notion. Research in this area has concerned itself with such topics as the communication patterns which develop among group members, factors which may influence the cohesiveness of group participants, the development of cooperation and competition, and the spontaneous development of internal regulatory mechanisms as well as with intergroup relationships of various sorts.

Much is being made currently of the barriers which often exist to inhibit free and open communication among persons. We hear a great deal of talk about the difficulties some parents have in understanding and being able to talk frankly with their children, and currently there seems to be considerable enthusiasm for a variety of techniques, such as "T-groups" and "sensitivity training," whose goal is to "open people up" and make it possible for persons to express feelings and thoughts which are supposedly often held in check under ordinary circumstances. A group of researchers at Yale, led by Argyris (1969), has conducted an extensive series of studies of the nature and quality of the communications among members of a wide variety of small groups in industrial, business, governmental, university, and research organizations. These groups were involved with many different types of tasks, ranging from problems associated with the development and marketing of new products to those having to do with relationships with the White House. And they were "real" working groups, not laboratory-generated, whose members had a past history of associating with each other and the anticipation of further future interaction.

The studies involved non-participant observation for the most part, a technique whereby the investigator does not experiment, does not manipulate or control aspects of the situation, but rather records, as unobtrusively as possible, the natural flow of events and then subjects them to some sort of systematic analysis. Argyris (1965) carefully developed a system of categories and their defining characteristics which can be used to classify the verbal output of group members. These categories were felt to be relevant to interpersonal competence, defined as an "individual's ability to produce intended effects in such a way that he can continue to do so. . . . The higher the interpersonal competence of the individual, the greater is:

1. The awareness of relevant problems.
2. The ability to solve problems in such a way that they remain solved.
3. The probability that the problem-solving process involved has *not* been harmed or negatively influenced (1965, p. 4.)

The categories of behavior are summarized in Table 1.

TABLE 1.   *CATEGORIES OF BEHAVIOR*

Individual		Interpersonal	
Experimenting	i	Help others to experiment	i
	f		f
Openness	i	Help others to be open	i
	f		f
Owning	i	Help others to own	i
	f		f
Zero Line			
Not owning	i	Not help others to own	i
	f		f
Not open	i	Not help others to be open	i
	f		f
Rejecting experimenting	i	Not help others to experiment	i
	f		f

Note: Categories above zero line are hypothesized to facilitate interpersonal relationships, those below the line to inhibit interpersonal relationships. Each category has an idea (i) and a feeling (f) component. Categories positioned closest to the zero line are easiest to perform and those farthest away are the most difficult.

Without going into great detail on the use of this system, let us just note that a given unit of verbal output is basically dichotomized as being either primarily ideational and intellectual (i) or feeling and emotional (f). Owning ideas or feelings refers to "being aware of and accepting responsibility for the behavior"; openness concerns "behavior that enlarges the individual's scope or pushes back his boundaries of awareness and responsibility" and involves encouraging "the reception of new information"; and experimenting refers to "behavior which represents some risk ... the purpose of the risk-taking is to generate new information ... the risk is evaluated in terms of the probability that such exploration could upset the individual's self-acceptance." (Argyris, 1965, p. 7). To give some feeling for how the system might actually be used, we can look at some sample statements. For example, if someone were to say, "I feel like my whole life has been a mess. I'm really frightened and confused at the moment," it would be scored experimenting f; "Give me some more of the details of your theory" would be open i; "I feel nervous" is an example of the owning f category; "It seems to me we should adjourn" fits the owning i category; not helping other to own i would be exemplified by the statement, "Let me explain what you mean, you're bungling it"; and, "For your own good, let's get off this subject" fits the not helping others to experiment i category. Argyris reports that with appropriate training and experience, the interobserver reliability associated with the use of this system is satisfactory. That is, different judges will consistently place a given unit of verbal behavior in the same category.

Study of more than 150 different meetings in 28 different organizations involving close to 46,000 scoreable units of verbal behavior revealed a number of interesting facts about the nature of the communication activity in these settings. In general, a very few of the categories, primarily owning ideas and open to ideas, accounted for the vast majority of the content of the verbal activity that occurred. Only very rarely did persons express feelings or encourage others to do so, or experiment with either ideas or feelings. In 56 per cent of the meetings no feelings at all were mentioned, and in 24 per cent of the meetings they accounted for 1 per cent or less of the verbal activity. Helping others to own up to or be open to the expression of ideas or feelings was found to be similarly infrequent. It was clear that individuals did not say what they believed about even the most important issues if they felt doing so might threaten other members. The general tenor of the interactions was one which encouraged what might be called diplomacy and tact, and discouraged anything other than an essentially impersonal, intellectualized interchange of ideas.

This sort of finding and others led to the suggestion that one of the common characteristics found in the situations studied was a sort of "interpersonal blindness." That is, the atmosphere which pervaded these interactions did much to inhibit the expression of significant feelings and attitudes and to permit the misperception of many situations to go uncorrected. Private interviews with the participants on a variety of topics provided corroborating evidence for this conclusion. For example, a study of 200 influence attempts which were observed in these groups indicated that 134 were not genuinely effective, yet in only two cases was honest feedback provided about the failures. In all the others, the person who had initiated the influence attempt was given information from the others in the group which indicated that he had been successful. Also, in almost 90 per cent of the cases in which the persuasion was effective, hostility was generated in those who had been influenced and yet none of them communicated this to the person involved. Argyris summarizes by saying, "The consequences were relatively ineffective interpersonal relationships. . . . Members seemed to be blind to the negative impact that they tended to have on others (partially because it violated the norms to give such feedback); they were accurately aware of the impact others have upon them, but careful not to communicate this impact openly or directly" (1969, p. 899).

It is Argyris' contention that intra-group communication styles of this sort will be found to be typical of a very wide range of types of groups. He argues that certain ideas or values concerning the nature of effective interpersonal relationships are endemic to all hierarchically arranged, pyramidal organizations; that such a pyramidal structure implies a particular strategy of effective human relationships which stresses rationality, specialization, and control. From this perspective individuals are said to hold the following three basic values about the best way to deal with others:

"1. In any given interpersonal relationship or group, the important behavior is that behavior that is related to the accomplishment of the purpose or task.
2. Human effectiveness increases as people are rational or intellective. Human effectiveness decreases as people focus on interpersonal feelings and/or behave emotionally.
3. The most effective way to tap human energy and gain human commitment is through leadership that controls, rewards, and penalizes, and coordinates human behavior" (1969, p. 899.)

Research by others (Steele, 1968) on the attitudes of, e.g., housewives, teachers, nurses, and students has shown that, indeed, these ideas are widely held. Of course, if they are actually engendered by pyramidally structured organizations this would be expected, since churches, educational institutions, businesses, and governmental agencies all tend to be organized in this manner and would thus tend to reinforce the development and maintenance of these values in persons who come into contact with them. Such values may even be seen as a basic concomitant of the nature of an industrialized, technological society which emphasizes task orientation, relies heavily on specialization and control, and places a great deal of value on rationality.

PERSON PERCEPTION

This field concerns itself with an analysis of the phenomenologically familiar but highly involved and complicated manner in which individuals come to understand other persons. The use of the term "perception" to refer to this sort of activity is, strictly speaking, a bit misleading, as it is clear that persons do not restrict themselves to information which is immediately given them by the various senses in forming impressions of others. To be sure, persons can be viewed simply as physical objects with certain perceivable characteristics, such as height, bulk, color, and patterns of movement, and such information certainly does find its way into the complex calculus by means of which we come to know what another person is like. But we are ordinarily not satisfied to limit our analysis of others in this way and we go beyond the purely physical, perceivable qualities to make inferences about characterstics which are not in the strictest sense observable. As Heider (1958) points out, there is typically a search for invariances or regularities in the observed activity of persons which will permit the inference of what he calls dispositional qualities, i.e., characteristics or traits of a person which dispose or lead him to behave in a given fashion. People are interested in a causal analysis, in establishing why someone acts as he does or is what he is. To simply record another's actions and go no further would not be very helpful in providing a basis upon which predictions might be made regarding his future behavior or in enabling us to be able to deal with him effectively in subsequent encounters. The tendency is to attribute certain motives, intentions, and enduring traits to the person. If we observe that an acquaintance typically avoids looking us directly in the eye, fidgets a great deal, talks hesitantly and little, and blushes easily, we may well come to think of him as shy, and to then believe that he behaves as he does *because* of this trait and that he will act in similar fashion in the future because this is an enduring quality of his. And, we may go further to infer on the basis of other information that he is shy because he is insecure and that he is insecure because . . . and so forth.

Research in this area has dealt with many aspects of the person perception process, such as those factors which influence the accuracy of the judgment of emotional states, the manner in which information is combined to form an impression, the qualities of persons which affect the attribution process and the determinants of the weight or importance given to various types and sources of information. Relatively recently, interest has developed in the systematic investigation of the uses which individuals make of information and messages which are communicated non-verbally. Gestures, postures, limb position and seating arrangements, for example, may all be seen as providing often highly useful information about a person's attitudes toward another with whom he is interacting. One subclass of these variables has been subsumed under the concept of proxemics by Hall (1963), as they all have to do with interpersonal proximity or distance in a broad sense. Such things as the actual physical distance between a communicator and the person he is addressing, the orientation of the two parties toward each other, the amount of eye to eye contact, the "openness" of the arrangement of one's limbs, and the amount of physical contact all fall under this rubric. Though we are seldom consciously aware of their influence, these proxemic variables can have powerful effects. For instance, persons do develop a generally applicable comfortable speaking distance. Interacting in casual conversation with persons of the same sex at distances less than 18 to 20 inches is uncomfortable for most Americans, while persons from Latin American and Middle Eastern countries find considerably closer distances comfortable. Thus Hall reports a strange sort of "dance" going on at an international convention he attended as Americans backed around the room trying to maintain a "natural" distance from their Latin American colleagues, who were attempting to reduce the interpersonal distance to a level which was comfortable for them.

Let us look more closely at what is known about one of these proxemic variables, eye contact. Argyle and Dean (1965) report: there is typically about three times as much eye contact when an individual is listening than when he is talking; persons tend to engage in eye contact at the end of phrases and to avoid it at the beginning of an utterance; there is less eye contact during the discussion of personal topics and when speech is difficult, hesitating, and lacking in fluency; eye contact is greater when the parties involved like one another, are cooperating rather than competing, and is avoided by a person who has recently deceived the other person in the interaction; eye contact can function as a reward, as a reinforcer in certain learning situations, but may also be something which is avoided, as when an individual wishes not to reveal an inner state or wishes to avoid observing the potentially rejecting responses of others.

To account for some of the findings, these authors examine the functions which eye contact might serve. For one thing, it permits an individual to gather information regarding the sort of response his behavior has produced in another and this feedback might logically be most desired just at the end of some statement he has made in order to help him assess its impact. On the other hand, the input from eye contact may only be distracting at the beginning of a speech when attention needs to be given to formulating what is to be said. Further, looking at another person serves to indicate to him that attention is being paid to him and that further interaction can proceed; it also places another person under some obligation to interact, as when one succeeds in catching the eye of a waiter or sales person. Argyle & Dean (1965) also postulate a somewhat more complex function of eye contact in which it is held to be one of a number of factors, such as physical proximity, intimacy of topic, amount of smiling, etc., which determine the overall level of intimacy in interactions among persons. Further, they suggest that an optimum degree of intimacy exists in a given interaction setting and that the various determinants of it will be in an equilibrium state of sorts, such that a shift in the level of any one of them will lead to compensatory changes in the others. This line of reasoning was tested in a simple study in which subjects were asked to participate in a "perceptual experiment" and to stand "as close as is comfortable to see well" a number of objects. One of these was a life-size photo of the face of the experimenter with eyes open, another was the experimenter himself with his eyes closed, and a third was the experimenter with his eyes open. It was found that, on the average, subjects stood eleven inches closer to the photo than to the real person, and six inches closer to a person with eyes closed than to the same person when eye contact was present. A second study varied the distance between the seated experimenter and a subject as they engaged in conversation for a three-minute period. The results showed that as the person to person distance increased from two to six to ten feet, the amount of eye contact on the part of the subjects also increased. Both these studies, then, provided evidence in line with the intimacy equilibrium notion. Variation in one of the several hypothesized determinants of the degree of intimacy was associated with corrective shifts in one of the other factors. Eliminate eye contact and persons find a shorter interpersonal distance to be comfortable; force an increase in interpersonal distance and persons engage in greater amounts of eye contact. Of course, considerably more research would be required to establish the explanation given here as the most appropriate to account for these findings. In any case, these investigations do provide some interesting leads concerning the manner in which non-verbal variables such as eye contact may function to influence, directly and indirectly, aspects of the impression which is formed of another individual.

Issue-Centered Research

Finally, of course, there is much research done in social psychology which doesn't fit nicely under the cover provided by any of the traditional subdivisions of the field. As we argued much earlier, persons who do research are not at all likely to allow themselves to be constrained by definitions and categories which may exist to delineate portions of the total discipline. In the last decade especially there has been a significant movement toward the conduct of non-laboratory, field studies which involve the examination of natural settings (McGuire, 1967; Ring, 1967) and a heightened interest in the investigation of issues which are of interest to society in general as opposed to more parochial problems which are likely to be deemed fascinating only by those who know social psychology well. These trends often lead to studies which cut across the usual divisions, as the motivation shifts from a desire to further our understanding of the dynamics of group interaction or the processes of attitude change or the issues in person perception to an interest in understanding as completely as possible a naturally occurring event. Recent work dealing with the impact of violence in the mass media on individual aggressivity, student activism, "brainwashing" and thought reform, and racial prejudice exemplifies such a problem-centered approach.

Let us take a quick look at a sample of this sort of research. Two social psychologists from the New York City area became intrigued with the circumstances which control the likelihood that an individual will come to the aid of another person who is in distress. Their interest in this problem was specifically stimulated by a news story which reported the murder of a young woman in suburban New York. Her attacker was presumably frightened away after his initial assault when her cries for help brought many people to their windows. However, he returned to her and finished his grisly work—the whole matter reportedly taking almost half an hour. Perhaps the most startling aspect of the case was the fact that subsequent investigation showed that thirty-eight of the victim's neighbors heard the screams and went to their windows to see what was happening—yet none of them came to her assistance or even went so far as to call the police! Unfortunately, this dramatic failure of persons to respond in an emergency is not an isolated case. Darley and Latané, the psychologists mentioned above, uncovered numerous other reports of similar occurrences. And, although each of us may react with shock and a firm belief that we would not hesitate to respond with compassion, we probably also have some notions about the alienation and impersonality of urban life, the "apathy of the masses," and so forth, which make this sort of thing more understandable. Yet it may be too easy to pass the matter off in this fashion. Closer examination of the published accounts of these events suggests that the persons involved may not seem quite so different from us as we might wish to believe. "The thirty-eight witnesses of Kitty Genovese's murder did not merely look at the scene once and then ignore it. They continued to stare out of their windows at what was going on. Caught, fascinated, distressed, unwilling to act, but unable to turn away, their behavior was neither helpful nor heroic; but it was not indifferent or apathetic." (Darley and Latané, 1968, pp. 377–383.) A reaction of helpless fascination to some emergency is not at all unusual, as you perhaps can testify from personal experience or observation—but why?

Darley and Latané reasoned that three critical decisions about what is happening will determine an individual's behavior here. In the first place, he must, of course, *notice* that something is happening; then he must interpret what he notices as an *emergency;* and finally he must decide to accept *personal responsibility* for doing something about it. Thus, failure to intervene could result from factors which adversely influence any one or more of these decisions and the researchers decided to investigate the possibility that the presence of others might be one such critical variable.

In one study (Latané and Darley, 1968), they recruited students to participate in an investigation of reactions to urban living. While they were seated in the laboratory filling out a preliminary questionnaire, smoke began to pour into the room through a wall vent. In a condition where the subject was alone in the room, two thirds of them noticed the smoke within the first five seconds after it began, but, when working with others present, only one quarter of them saw the smoke as quickly. The smoke continued to flow and eventually all persons, whether in groups or alone, did notice it—the point is that the sheer presence of others can retard the process whereby an individual becomes aware of a potential danger. Why should this be so? Well, for one thing, we are taught to respect the privacy of others, to avoid staring at persons whom we do not know, to avoid intruding upon their activity, to not be overly inquisitive. The authors noted that when subjects were alone they often glanced idly about the room as they worked on their questionnaires, but when others were present their attention was more likely to be restricted to their own work.

Once the person is aware of the fact that something a bit unusual is going on, he must interpret the event and give it some meaning. The stimuli associated with many potential emergencies are somewhat ambiguous—those screams next door might indicate an assault or a family argument, a person slouched on a street corner may have suffered a heart attack or he may be sleeping off a drunk, smoke in the room might indicate a serious fire or just a leaky steam pipe. There is ample evidence from other research that we depend, often to a greater degree than we realize, on others for assistance in giving meaning to equivocal situations. However, such socially derived information can be misleading, for often social pressures exist which lead people to disguise or cover up their genuine response to a situation. There seems to be a perhaps unfortunate tendency in our own society to wish to appear cool, calm, and unruffled, and it is thus embarrassing to appear overly concerned or flustered in public. To rush to the aid of a person imagined to be ill only to find him just a bit drunk might elicit ridicule from others. Thus the presence of others in an emergency may lead each person to manifest an air of inappropriate passivity or indifference which contributes to the definition of the situation by all concerned as a non-emergency. "Any individual in such a situation is painfully aware that he'll look like a fool if he behaves as though it were (an emergency)—and in these circumstances, until someone acts, no one acts" (Latané and Darley, 1968, pp. 215–221). Thus it was that 75 per cent of the persons working alone showed sufficient concern over the smoke funneling into the room to leave and search for someone to whom they might report it within four minutes. In that same amount of time, however, the smoke had been reported in only 12 per cent of the three-person groups, even though it became quite unpleasant and irritating. When questioned later about what had gone on, the non-responsive persons gave a variety of explanations for the smoke, none of which suggested that they believed it was due to a fire. By interpreting the situation as non-dangerous they provided themselves with a reasonable explanation for the fact that none of the others in their group was upset and eliminated any reason for taking some action themselves.

To examine the influence the presence of others may have on the last decision in the sequence, the one concerning acceptance of personal responsibility for intervention, yet another experiment was conducted (Darley and Latané, 1968). When the volunteers arrived to participate in a group discussion of the personal problems involved in adjusting to a high-pressure urban university, they were led to a small room equipped with a microphone and earphones. Tape-recorded instructions informed them that in order to promote a candid discussion of this perhaps delicate issue their anonymity would be carefully preserved—they would never meet the other discussants and the experimenter would not listen in. Each person was simply to talk in turn about problems he'd encountered. The first person mentioned a number of difficulties including the fact that he was subject to fairly serious nervous seizures, especially when he felt pressure or stress. The number of others in the group was varied from just this one person up to five other discussants, and they all made their comments in turn. However, there was actually only one true subject and the other comments were all standardized and pre-recorded. When it was the simulated first person's turn to speak once more, an emergency was created in that he was apparently beginning to have an "attack" of the sort he had mentioned earlier. His speech was sporadic and halting, grew increasingly loud and uncontrolled, and he finally pleaded for someone to help him, made a choking sound and then ceased to speak.

Once again the number of bystanders present at the time of an emergency is seen to play an important role in determining the likelihood that someone will intervene. In the two-person groups, in which the subject believed that he alone was aware of the misfortune of the other discussant, 85 per cent of the subjects moved to report the emergency before the victim's speech had ended. Sixty-two per cent of the subjects attempted to help when they had been led to believe that another person in addition to themselves and the victim was present and only 31 per cent intervened in the simulated six-person groups, in which there supposedly were four others and the victim present. The authors interpret this effect in terms of diffusion of responsibility. That is, the knowledge that there are other witnesses to some emergency, each of whom has the potential to aid in some fashion, may significantly diminish the degree to which any given individual feels that it is up to him, and him alone, to intervene. Have a breakdown on an urban freeway and cars by the score pass by without offering assistance, while the same difficulty on an infrequently traveled byway is likely to elicit help relatively rapidly. Is the effect due to urban apathy and rural tender-heartedness? These studies, of course, don't imply that such a hypothesis is false, but do support an alternative explanation: the person on the lonely road may feel greater pressure to stop, for if he doesn't accept responsibility for coming to your aid there may be no one else to do so. There appear to be a number of ways, then, in which the presence of a number of witnesses to some emergency makes it less likely that help will be forthcoming. Something to keep in mind the next time you plan to be the victim of some personal catastrophe. More seriously, a knowledge of these factors and the way they operate may help each of us to respond more appropriately when emergencies do arise in which we have an opportunity to intervene.

Definition by Induction

What conclusions can be drawn from this rather cursory look at the sorts of issues with which social psychology deals? Obviously, our wish to define the field by "pointing," by taking stock of just what some persons engaged in social psychological research actually do, can meet with only limited success, since only a few studies and techniques have been described and since others might well argue with us concerning the degree to which these particular investigations are truly representative of the total range of topics from which we chose. But, then, we argued earlier that the primary utility of attempts at defining the field is to provide the person unfamiliar with the area with a general orientation or "feeling" for it and, hopefully, progress along these lines has been made. Perhaps it would, even so, be beneficial to provide a concise literary definition of a more traditional nature as a way of abstracting and summarizing what has been gained from the direct examination of research. The question then becomes, "What are the common and critical elements in the studies presented?", or, more appropriately, in the work of social psychologists in general?

Focus on the Individual

For one thing, the focal point, the central unit of analysis, in these studies, was the individual, as should be the case with a branch of general psychology. This characteristic, incidentally, serves to differentiate social psychology from other closely related social sciences such as sociology, anthropology, and political science. All may at times deal with some of the same issues and problems, but the others typically espouse an interest in social aggregates "larger" than the individual as the element of primary concern, such as political parties, societies, cultures, or small groups.

Observable Behavior – the Object of Study

And what in the broadest sense is it that is being measured, analyzed, and used as evidence in the search for an understanding of the individual? The intensity of shock he is willing to administer to another, his responses to a questionnaire, his ability to verbally describe with accuracy some previous act are all publicly observable behaviors. While there may be speculation about the internal, private processes and states of the individual, their existence and operation can only be inferred from behavior which is accessible to the psychologist-observer. Indeed, some positions regarding the manner in which psychological research and theorizing should most appropriately be carried out maintain that inference about internal states is an improper and fruitless venture and that the proper focus is on a systematization of the relationships between behavior and other external, manipulable environmental events. The study by Bem (1970) reported earlier exemplifies such an orientation. However, most contemporary social psychologists have not embraced this rather extreme approach and maintain a primary interest in factors within the individual which may mediate, influence, or determine the responses which are made to stimuli impinging upon the person. Thus the greatest involvement is not with the stimuli and the responses as objects of investigation in and of themselves. Rather, the researcher is likely to select particular stimuli to manipulate and responses to record on the basis of his estimate of their utility in helping him understand internal, non-observable properties of the individual. Keep in mind, however, the ultimate dependence upon behavior as the final arbiter of his success in this venture. It is from the observation of overt behavior that his inferences stem and on the basis of which their validity is established or denied.

The Relevant Stimuli – Social in Nature

We mentioned above the experimental manipulation of relevant stimuli and again, if we looked at representative research, it becomes apparent that the stimuli which are being dealt with, while very diverse, may be generally characterized as social in nature. When we speak of a stimulus we are referring to some environmental element which either does affect, or has the potential to affect, the current state of the individual. Social stimuli, then, are ones which stem from other people in a very broad sense. That is, it is clear that not all social psychological research involves the physical presence of another person as the stimulus to which the subject responds, so it would not be correct to restrict our use of the term social in this manner, yet certainly much work in the field does concentrate on the direct impact which interacting persons have on one another. Social stimuli may derive not just from another individual, obviously, but from larger collections of individuals, such as groups, organizations, and institutions. And the actual presence of these other individuals or groups is not a prerequisite to making the situation a legitimate object of social psychological inquiry, because their ability to have an influence on an individual's behavior may be quite evident even in circumstances in which he is functioning in isolation. And finally we find that social psychologists see stimuli which are simply the result of the interaction of persons and of groups as relevant. Here we are referring to the social culture in which the individual functions—such things as the dominant values, rules of conduct, language, beliefs about the nature of the world, and so forth, which are products of the activity of other persons. Thus the picture of social stimuli which emerges includes the explicit and implicit presence of other individuals and groups and the products of their interaction as embodied in the cultural milieu in which the person operates.

The Method of Analysis – Scientific Empiricism

The final common characteristic of the activity of social psychologists to be found does not have to do with the qualities of the objects of investigation but with the nature of the investigative process itself. Thus we find commonalities not only in the content of the studies reviewed but also in the techniques and methods employed. As is the case with other fields of general psychology, the social area is committed to the *scientific* analysis of behavior. Certainly there are other avenues which might be traveled in the search for valid explanations of social psychological phenomena. One might consult relevant literary accounts, or engage in a systematic introspective analysis, or question others concerning their interpretations. But the outcome of such endeavors would not be acceptable, in and of itself, as a valid explanation which could be maintained with confidence. This is not to say that the products of such endeavors are valueless or do not have potential validity, for such research has its origins in just this sort of activity. But before the explanations arrived at in such a manner are put to empirical test they would be considered speculative. We will subsequently discuss in some detail the methods used in scientific investigation, so at this point it will suffice to indicate that in social psychology scientific analysis involves the systematic observation and recording of the behavior of individuals which then may serve as a basis upon which statements may be developed which describe the observed patterns of behavior in more general, summary form. These latter principles should then have utility in predicting the outcomes of other conceptually related situations.

Each of the studies we examined earlier was an exemplar of the first stage of this process in that they all included very careful and controlled observation and recording of some aspect of the behavior elicited in the research setting. They differed, however, in that some were representative of the last-mentioned characteristic of the scientific process while others were initiated from the middle stage mentioned. Bem's study, for example, involved the extension of some principles established by prior research having to do with the way in which behavior and the setting in which it occurs may influence beliefs in a new set of circumstances. The more general summary statements generated from this prior work were used to make a prediction about behavior in a not previously examined relevant situation, i.e., the induction of belief in false confessions. On the other hand, Milgram's study was more explicitly exploratory in nature, representing an attempt to examine some potentially interesting behavior in systematic fashion. Through this search for the stimulus variables which might influence the behavior under observation some more general statements summarizing the relationships would hopefully emerge. Thus this work, too, is ultimately representative of the full range of the scientific method—observation, abstraction, or summarization, and prediction.

An Inductive Definition of Social Psychology

Where does all this leave us? Hopefully with some rough initial grasp of what social psychology is all about in broad outlines. The attempt to extract the elements common to the studies reviewed, which were presented as more or less representative of work in the traditional sub-areas of the discipline, allows us to give a general definition: *Social psychology deals with the scientific investigation of behavior as a basis for developing an understanding of the interaction between explicit and implicit social stimuli and the cognitive and behavioral activity of the individual.*

Perhaps a few additional comments are in order to insure a firm understanding of the implications of our definition. It first simply reiterates some of the points made earlier:

1. that the approach is scientific rather than philosophical, introspective, or literary;
2. that the data employed are derived from the observation and systematic recording of overt behavior;
3. that the focal point of interest is the individual as opposed to larger collectives of persons;
4. that the goal is not just description and cataloguing, but rather a detailed understanding of the phenomena under investigation (a more detailed exposition of just what is meant by understanding in the scientific sense will be given in the next few pages);
5. that social stimuli, including both the actual presence of other persons and their implicit presence as mediated by the influence of the non-human products of social interaction, such as norms, values, etc., are critical; and
6. that the objects of interest are both the behavior of the person and the nature and functioning of certain internal factors called cognitions, which are hypothesized to intervene and influence the relationship between social stimuli and the person's reaction to them.

The phrase "interaction between" makes explicit the point that contemporary social psychology views the relationship between social stimuli and the individual's cognitions and behavior as a two-way street, in that either may play an important role in influencing the other. To attain the goal of genuine understanding of the social behavior of the individual it seems clear that we must have information concerning the ways in which cognitive processes and current behavior affect his reactions to social stimuli as well as an exposition of the reverse relationship in which social stimuli directly influence cognitive and overt activity. Certainly all of us are quite aware of the fact that social stimuli have an impact on our behavior and, as amateur psychologists (or professionals operating outside the laboratory or clinic), may spend more than a little time attempting to analyze this influence. To pick a somewhat perverse example, the unsolicited presence of some person who, it immediately becomes apparent, possesses attributes which are negatively reinforcing for us will very likely lead us to emit a characteristic set of behaviors—behaviors quite different from those which would have occurred had no one intruded upon our immediate environment or if the interrupting person had positively reinforcing qualities. We are likely to do a variety of things in such a situation aimed at maintaining maximum possible physical and psychological distance and at terminating the interaction as rapidly as is feasible.

On the other hand, we are probably less likely to be acutely aware of the influence our behavior has on the social stimuli with which we interact. Although the point being made here is rather obvious—that we are not just passive recipients of the information we receive from environmental stimuli but actively play a role in shaping and creating them—the ways in which this occurs are not obvious, especially to the participants. The influence our behavior may have on the social stimulus may be quite direct in that it actually alters the stimulus itself. In the example above, the avoidance reactions we exhibit are stimuli to which this other person may well respond by altering his behavior. If we respond with anxiety, indifference, defensive maneuvers, or outright hostility to someone, he is likely to react defensively or aggressively himself, no matter how benign or friendly his intentions may have been initially. Since we do not have direct access to information about these positive intentions on his part, as they are private, intrapersonal events and, in our example, never externalized in the form of overt behavior, it is difficult for us to assess the contribution our own behavior has made in shaping the other's responses. What we see instead is evidence that this person does indeed possess some highly unattractive qualities just as we'd anticipated.

A more subtle effect is also very possible in which the social stimulus is in reality not directly altered by our cognitive/behavioral activity. There may instead be an alteration of the stimulus in which the cognitive orientation, the "mental set," of the perceiver leads him to impute a particular meaning to it, to interpret (or misinterpret) it in a given fashion. Thus, as far as the perceiver's idiosyncratic response to it is concerned, the stimulus *has* been altered. Psychologists in other fields have found a distinction between proximal and distal stimuli to be useful and we are making essentially the same differentiation here. The distal stimulus, "out there," at its point of origin in the environment somewhere, might potentially be described objectively in great detail in terms of its measurable physical characteristics. But the proximal stimulus as actually received and perceived by the individual may be quite a different entity. The genuinely color-blind person may not have the capacity to receive and process visual stimuli of particular wave-lengths even though they are present as a demonstrable characteristic of the distal stimulus. Analogously, where social stimuli are involved, the proximal stimulus, the stimulus as interpreted by the individual, as filtered through the influence of his past experience and current cognitive state can rarely be adequately described by referring to the physical qualities of the distal stimulus. Thus even if the person in our example is insensitive to the anxious or hostile reception provided him and perseveres in being polite and positive it may be to no avail. Even if he should make a straightforward pronouncement of his liking for us, it may nevertheless be interpreted in a negative way in view of our initially negative orientation to him. It might be seen as the offensive flattering of a sycophant rather than the welcome admiration of another person who is sufficiently perceptive to recognize our many good qualities.

Cognitions, Behavior and the "Creation" of our Social World

The particular examples we have used to illustrate the reciprocal influence between cognitions and behavior on the one hand and the social stimulus on the other are representative of what Merton (1948) has termed self-fulfilling prophecies. His exposition of this phenomenon highlights the degree to which people may often inadvertently contribute to the creation of circumstances which confirm their prior hypotheses about the nature of the social environment. More broadly, the point is that persons "create" the world in which they live to a greater extent than is typically realized. And, to moralize for a moment—which scientists, including social psychologists, are not supposed to do, since objective research cannot establish the ultimate valididty or invalidity of values—this lack of self-awareness seems unfortunate. We have no royal road to reality, but only the data provided by our "imperfect" sensory receptors which may then be muddled and transformed by myriad, internal cognitive factors as we have suggested. Thus we typically react to our own personal brand of reality and, though we may operate rationally enough given our idiosyncratically flavored premises, these premises may be suspect. Given the racist's faulty but firmly held belief that a particular minority group is inherently incapable of benefiting from a high-level scholastic program, his behavior is quite reasonable when he votes down a bond issue which would improve the schools for these persons. The funds would to him be an obvious waste of money. But the self-fulfilling nature of his prophecy allows him to later point to the fact that relatively few members of this group go on to college as evidence for the validity of his initial belief about their intellectual inferiority. Or we might find the same principles applicable to the increasingly frequent student-police confrontations during campus demonstrations. Some students "know" in advance of their meeting that the "pigs" are *all* brutal, insensitive, and unreasonable and, with this inaccurate structuring of reality to guide their behavior, it makes sense to be similarly obstinate, to forget any efforts to reason with them, to arm and protect oneself, to shout obscenities, which are all they understand anyway, and so forth. And some police officers may be similarly equipped with preconceptions. They "know" that these kids are drug-crazed, irresponsible, violence-prone scum who will respond only to a show of force. When these two types meet it is not terribly surprising that violence results, which can then be used by each as confirmation of those initial beliefs. Many similar instances could be spelled out: the male supremicist attitudes of many men in our culture may lead them to cooperate with the perhaps equally numerous women who share this notion in fulfilling prophecies regarding what is and is not appropriate female behavior by never providing an opportunity for other types of behavior; the beliefs of an employer about the capacities of particular employees; the notion one nation may have concerning the malevolence and aggressive intent of another; and so on. The circular and interactive nature of these relationships should be clear by now—one's cognitive structuring of some situation may predispose him to behave in a particular manner, and this activity operates as a stimulus to the behavior of others in the social environment which may have considerable force in shaping the form that behavior will take; and, to complete one cycle of the sequence, such behavior may be observed and assimilated and thus influence one's cognitions relevant to the situation in question. The important question at a personal level, however, is just how clearly each of us is capable of seeing with some degree of objectivity our own participation in the "creation" of our world.

References

Argyle, M., and Dean, J.: Eye-contact, distance, and affiliation. *Sociometry,* 1965, *28:* 289–304.

Argyris, C.: *Organization and Innovation.* Homewood, Ill., Richard D. Irwin, 1965.

Argyris, C.: The incompleteness of social-psychological theory: examples from small group, cognitive consistency and attribution research. *American Psychologist*, 1969, *24*:893–908.

Bem, D. J.: Self-perception: An alternative interpretation of cognitive dissonance phenomena. *Psychological Review*, 1967, *74*:183–200.

Bem, D. J.: *Beliefs, Attitudes, and Human Affairs*. Belmont, California, Brooks/Cole, 1970.

Bridgman, P. W.: *The Logic of Modern Physics*. New York, Macmillan, 1928.

Christie, R., and Geis, F. L.: *Studies in Machiavellianism*. New York, Academic Press, 1970.

Darley, J. M., and Latané, B.: Bystander intervention in emergencies: Diffusion of responsibility. *Journal of Personality and Social Psychology*, 1968, *8*:377–383.

Festinger, L.: *A Theory of Cognitive Dissonance*. Evanston, Illinois, Row, Peterson, 1957.

Hall, E. T.: A system for the notation of proxemic behavior. *American Anthropologist*, 1963, *65*:1003–1026.

Heider, F.: *The Psychology of Interpersonal Relations*. New York, Wiley, 1958.

Latané, B., and Darley, J. M.: Group inhibition of bystander intervention in emergencies. *Journal of Personality and Social Psychology*, 1968, *10*:215–221.

McGuire, W. J.: Some impending reorientations in social psychology. *Journal of Experimental Social Psychology*, 1967, *3*:124–139.

Merton, R. K.: The self-fulfilling prophecy. *Antioch Review*, 1948, *8*:193–210.

Milgram, S.: Behavioral study of obedience. *Journal of Abnormal and Social Psychology*, 1963, *67*:371–378.

Milgram, S.: Some conditions of obedience and disobedience to authority. In I.D. Steiner and M. Fishbein (Eds.), *Current Studies in Social Psychology*. New York, Holt, Rinehart, and Winston, 1965.

Osgood, C. E., Suci, G. J., and Tannenbaum, P. H.: *The Measurement of Meaning*. Urbana, University of Illinois, 1957.

Ring, K.: Experimental social psychology: Some sober questions about frivolous values. *Journal of Experimental and Social Psychology*, 1967, *3*:113–123.

Sampson, E. E.: Studies of status congruence. In L. Berkowitz (Ed.), *Advances in Experimental Social Psychology*. Vol. 4. New York, Academic Press, 1969.

Singer, J. E.: The use of manipulative strategies: Machiavellianism and attractiveness. *Sociometry*, 1964, *27*:128–150.

Steele, F. I.: Personality and the "laboratory style." *Applied Behavioral Science*, 1968, *4*:25–45.

CHAPTER 2

PERSPECTIVE ON THE SCIENTIFIC APPROACH

Having established for you our own idea of what social psychology *is*, the appropriate next step would seem to be to discuss in more specific terms how it *does* what it does, how it goes about its business of developing a scientific understanding of the interactions between explicit and implicit social stimuli and the cognitive and behavioral activity of the individual. Thus the question to which we now turn is "What is involved in scientific investigation and why is it held to be a more appropriate and efficient way of achieving an understanding of reality than other possible techniques?"

The Basic Paradigm—Variation and Selective Retention

Have you ever really given much thought to just what "science" is all about, to where and how the scientific approach to questions fits into the total scheme of things and enterprises in the world? Probably not. Few of us have, leaving the matter up to the esoteric interests of philosophers of science, even though in our Western society we are surrounded by, and increasingly dependent upon, the products of science and technology. There seems to be a strong tendency upon the part of many to deify science, to think of it as something of almost magical or mystical character, and as being qualitatively very much different from the ordinary, everyday human processes of inquiry about the environment. Although there is certainly nothing approaching complete agreement on the matter, several contemporary philosophers of science have independently developed essentially similar analyses which emphasize the continuity between formal scientific investigation and the manner in which knowledge about the environment is developed in the everyday activity of all individuals. These positions (e.g., Campbell, 1960; Capek, 1968; Popper, 1959; Toulmin, 1967) tend to view all processes of knowledge acquisition as being, at their root, analogues of the natural selection processes which theories of evolution hold to be so critical. For example, Campbell states that "Learning, perception, and other increases in knowledge at the individual level, and increases in the accuracy and scope of scientific knowledge, are part processes of the more general case of increases in the adaptive fit of organisms to environment. . . . Knowing and science are continuations of organic and social evolution and share their basic epistemology" (1969, p. 6). If one is willing to grant that a physical world which is not completely chaotic exists independently of the individual, then the issue boils down to one of developing an efficient and effective match with that reality. And, in the development of that match it is reality itself which must operate as the final arbiter of what is correct and valid and what is incorrect and spurious.

With regard to evolutionary processes we see the constraints imposed by objective reality operating as the criteria against which the adaptive character of some new form of life is "measured." If a new strain, whatever is may be and by whatever means it came to be, provides a good fit with the demands of objective reality then, by definition, the likelihood of its own survival and maintenance will be enhanced. Thus, out of the myriad entrants in this contest for survival only those who can successfully meet the challenges presented by the actual conditions of their environment are selected winners and permitted to perpetuate themselves. At a quite different level we may see the same sort of process run its course. Take, for example, an individual attempting to discover the shortest and most efficient route from his home to his business or school, a trip which he must make almost daily through the intricacies of his urban environment. His search is for the "truth"—for a good fit with reality—much as is the scientists'. The person may have many different possible initial responses in his repertoire which may be tried out and these are roughly analogous to the numerous entrants in the evolutionary contest. Once again reality intervenes as the determinant of which of these approaches will survive, as only certain of them will get him quickly to the location for which he is searching. The survival here involves not genetic repetition but retention in memory. The various strategies which he employs and the routes he takes are not likely to be random or blind, but rather will be very much influenced by the given individual's relevant past experience. Some persons might rely on gas station attendants as useful informants; others might eschew such assistance as worse than useless; some might begin a systematic block by block search; while others will play hunches as to which might be the optimal route to take. Thus, some of these commuters may hit upon the best approach via some brilliant insight into the matter while others require many months of painstaking trial-and-error to discover the solution. And, of course, some may never find the objectively shortest route, though we would expect all to at least closely approximate it. Idiosyncratic variations in the sorts of routes which a person sees as possibilities might, for example, bias the outcome. That is, a dark, unpaved alley might not even be viewed by some travelers as a potential route, yet it might in reality represent a necessary part of the objectively shortest route. In scientific analyses many of the same sorts of effects may be found—intuitive and insightful strategies occur from time to time along with more methodical, incremental advances; the training and theoretical orientation of the investigator strongly influence the manner in which problems are approached and may at times lead him to ignore potential solutions.

However, taking a very broad perspective on these ways of discovering the truth or some approximation to it, it is apparent that the truth which is achieved by both the scientist and the layman is the outcome of both the *systematic selection* of certain responses from a wide range of behaviors on the basis of the adequacy of their match with the constraints imposed by reality and the *retention* of these successful responses in memory.

The necessary elements in either system, then, are:
1. A mechanism for introducing variation
2. A consistent selection process
3. A mechanism for preserving and reproducing the selected variations (Campbell, 1969, p. 7).

In the commuter example the operation of these three elements seems quite straightforward. Variation is introduced in terms of the variety of responses made by the individual as he explores the situation. The selective system which functions involves his sensory receptors and the least time criterion which he has established as a basis for an evaluation of his behavior in the routes he tries. If the physical environment is not changed during the course of his several encounters with it and if the operation of his sensory apparatus and the criterion is not altered in some fashion, then this selective system will be consistent in its operation. Finally, the explorer's memory capacity provides the third characteristic outlined by Campbell, the retention system.

Scientific investigation can be viewed in similar terms: the variety of competing explanations for some phenomenon under study provided by interested researchers; the tests and procedures employed to assess the correspondence of these possible explanations with reality, and eventually to select the most appropriate one; and the retention in both memory and written records of the outcome of the tests conducted and the interpretations made of them.

Immanent and Transcendent Truth

However, this variation-and-selective-retention model needs modification in terms of its implication that comparison with reality is the only criterion by which to judge the validity of some hypothesis. Modern epistemologists distinguish two basic types of truth: a system of propositions has *transcendent truth* to the extent that the propositions are "free from any contradiction with empirical data obtained by observation" (Wolman, 1960, p. 500); they have *immanent truth* if they are free from any inner contradictions. For example, an established mathematical system such as geometry has immanent truth because no two propositions within the system exist which contradict one another. Thus, an important additional way in which the validity of some thesis is checked involves its internal consistency. It must be able to take into account all the available relevant information without including any propositions which contradict one another. These two types of truth complement one another and neither alone necessarily provides all the information we would want to have in order to assert some explanation with confidence.

A Less Optimistic View of Science as a Social System

It all sounds rather neat and perhaps exciting, doesn't it? Competing theories locked in a contest in which only the most fit will survive and in which the only determinants of survival are the internal consistency of a particular explanation and the closeness of fit between it and reality . . . a system that commands respect for its almost cruel objectivity and lack of arbitrariness, with no place for the wishes or human frailties of those who practice the art of scientific investigation to influence the outcome. But, of course, that's not the way things actually happen. For a sharply contrasting view of the scientific endeavor we can look to a position presented by Kuhn in his book, *The Structure of Scientific Revolutions* (1962). He implies that communities of scientists tend to be intellectually ingrown groups which develop theoretical "paradigms," ways of thinking and speaking about the world. These paradigms severely limit concern with problems, issues, aspects of nature which are beyond their scope. This criticism is bothersome and deserves further comment because it concerns the relationship between science and reality testing.

Internal and External Selectors

To deal with the first-mentioned issue we need to look a little more closely at the nature of the selective processes which may operate in the variation-and-selective-retention paradigm which, it has been argued, characterizes all increases in knowledge. If we follow Campbell's analysis further, we see that he dichotomizes these selectors into external and internal ones. The techniques or, if you will, the rituals, of scientific analysis are designed to maximize the selection pressure from external reality, for it is only external selectors whose operation will inevitably lead to valid mapping of reality. However, there are internal selectors whose functioning may well be irrelevant to or inconsistent with adaptive mapping. These factors are characteristics or qualities inherent in the entity (e.g., the social system of science, an individual or animal) which is attempting to discover and accurately describe the nature of the real world. For example, an animal's eating behavior may be strongly influenced by the pleasurableness afforded by the food it consumes rather than by the external reality of the degree to which various foods are nourishing. Thus, adaptive mapping of this aspect of reality is thwarted to the extent that subjectively perceived pleasurableness and nutritive value are not perfectly correlated— and this correlation may be quite imperfect, as in the case of attractive, edible animal poison, for example. At the level of the scientific community, Kuhn, as we have seen, argues that such internal selective processes as the scientific communities' tendency to give more weight and credence to the findings consistent with an established theory than to those which are inconsistent with it operate.

However, as we shall soon see as we describe experimental methodology in more detail, the consistent focus of the investigatory techniques utilized in scientific analysis is on minimizing the role which internal selectors play. It is the case that science only approximates the ideal state in which external selectors alone are operative, and its superiority in this regard is only relative rather than absolute. That is, it is "better" when compared with alternative social systems which also are involved in the search for valid analyses of reality such as religion, philosophy, and literary analysis, but whose explicit ideologies may sometimes emphasize the functioning of internal selectors such as a dependence upon precedent, intuitive insight, personal revelation, and so forth, without the restraints of external selection factors.

Put in a broad perspective, it is notable that certain of the techniques of science designed to reduce the impact of internal selectors are at their base not so different from those employed in certain divination ceremonies. For example, when the traditional food-gathering areas become depleted, certain groups seek advice in finding new locations by constructing an outline map of their immediate territory in a pan filled with sand, allowing it to fill with water, and noting where the first bubbles occur. Several important consequences of depending upon such a procedure are apparent: first, it is one way of introducing variation into the search activity and this is one of the critical aspects of the variation-and-selective-retention sequence emphasized earlier; also, it serves to justify arduous exploration of new sites which might well have gone unexamined otherwise, and, it very nicely prevents any one group member from being held responsible for the frustration or failure that may result. Though such superstitious behavior may seem at first blush to be the antithesis of the scientific approach, there are nevertheless significant similarities. Campbell makes note of this when he suggests that aspects of both approaches are ". . . rationalized as designs to put a question to 'Nature herself' in such a way that neither the asker, his colleagues, nor his superiors can affect the answer. Experiments are such a ritual, as are predictions made and sealed in advance of the event. Along with these go the ideal of objectivity, of 'solid facts' that 'speak for themselves,' . . . of truth uncontaminated by human hope or bias, of truth that stands as it is whether known by man or not" (1969, p. 22). So once again we find reason to argue that at its roots science need not be seen as unique or qualitatively different from other investigatory processes. Where it does differ, however, is in its explicit and consistent emphasis on the use of specific techniques in this search which will maximize the role of external selectors.

Innovation vs. Retention in Knowledge Acquisition Processes

To return to the second general criticism raised by Kuhn—that certain aspects of science as a social system may operate to discourage views which challenge the current orthodoxy—it may be argued that a certain amount of this is an inevitable accompaniment of any system which operates on the basis of the variation-selection-retention process. A little reflection on the matter makes clear the fact that there is a fundamental conflict between two of the elements in this triadic system. The first characteristic mentioned, variation, and the last, retention and reproduction of the selected variations, are at odds with one another in important ways. In the realm of science, if all researchers are busily innovating, introducing useful and necessary variation into the system, then the equally necessary function of retention and refinement of accumulated knowledge is likely to be relatively neglected. The same point is perhaps a little more clearly seen in an example having to do with preliterate societies. We can assume that at a given point in time such a group has accumulated a certain amount of useful knowledge which has been incorporated into its traditions. It is then apparent that each member who is off innovating or trying out some novel transformation of the extant customs will not be contributing to the preservation and modeling for others of whatever adaptation to the environment the group has achieved to date.

How is this basic conflict typically resolved? Examination of the general way in which knowledge is acquired suggests that certain of its characteristics are such as to build in a bias against rapid acceptance of the novel and controversial. The tendency is to favor retention of well-established positions rather than to make the innovator's role an easy one. Such conservatism is in part a function of the psychological make-up of those who investigate. But, it stems also from certain aspects of the investigatory system itself. One of these qualities is socially vicarious learning.

Socially Vicarious Learning and Conservatism

Certainly, one of the signal advantages of membership in some social grouping is the opportunity to engage in vicarious learning—that is, to capitalize on the transmission of the recorded outcomes of other members' trial and error exploration so that one need not directly repeat the exploration oneself. In a world which is itself highly complex and which requires the rapid development and execution of similarly complex behavior patterns on the part of its inhabitants, this dependence upon the accumulated knowledge of society is very great. Successful functioning in the contemporary world in the absence of such vicariously derived knowledge is almost inconceivable. From birth we depend upon others to communicate to us accurate information about our environment, and we very rapidly begin to organize this information into a system of rules and beliefs, which in this book will be termed schemas, about the nature of the world, about the appropriateness or unappropriateness of certain behaviors in a given situation, about the most efficient way of attaining goals, and so forth. Only a small proportion of these schemas or summarizations of information are ones which were initially derived from direct experience and tests of the principles involved. Instead, many were available, ready-made, on the basis of the accumulated wisdom of the culture in which we find ourselves and we become quite dependent upon this process which provides a short-cut alternative to direct

Dependence on vicariously derived information.

trial-and-error induction. Students do not enter school with the notion that there they will be given the opportunity to conduct for themselves all the experiments which led up to the findings ultimately selected as valid and which have then been recorded in their textbooks — most would agree that formal education is a long and laborious enough process when it involves no more than capitalizing on the work others have done in their attempts to provide maps which are valid reflections of reality. To require that everyone repeat all that work for himself would be patently absurd. Rather, the ideal would be to provide the student with a basis for evaluating, in general terms, the adequacy of the various testing procedures others might have used in their search for knowledge, so that he can then make a reasoned judgment for himself concerning which information he wishes to accept or reject.

Of course, it is often possible for the individual to test directly the correctness and utility of the schemas or summary statements which have been communicated to him. If college folklore has it that all professors are absent-minded, he may reject this statement as a valid generalization upon encountering faculty who do not display this trait. Now let's see, where were we? Oh, yes. . . . Thus, even such socially vicarious learning may be made subject to the operation of external selectors as any given individual tests in his own experience the degree of adaptive-fit-to-reality of a variety of principles learned from others. The tremendous economy of the operation is still apparent, however, as the individual is not required to do the great amount of work necessary to produce the summary statement in the first place, but, rather, he may simply test the adequacy of several possible summarizations themselves.

The general point of all this is that we become highly dependent upon relatively broadly stated "rules," summary statements of the painstakingly acquired wisdom of others, or schemas; typically, we, or others whom we trust, have tested their adequacy directly and found them to have adaptive utility; in view of the tremendous economy which they represent we are loathe to give them up even in the face of evidence that there are occasional exceptions to them and, in fact, the argument can be made that it would be maladaptive to do so. Operating on the notion that all professors are absent-minded might lead to the conclusion that waiting more than ten minutes beyond the time for a scheduled appointment with one is fruitless, since he is likely to have forgotten about it completely. Over a series of such interactions, the negative consequences of missing a meeting or two with professors who are exceptions to the rule and who do eventually show up for the appointment may be much less than that resulting from the time which would be wasted were one to wait for the majority who have forgotten about the meeting. Thus, in many cases, there may be good reason for minimizing the impact exceptions have on a general rule. Information which challenges the broad principle may reasonably be suppressed or neglected in the interest of preserving the general element of truth contained in it. There may be built into the system, then, a tendency for the conflict between variation or innovation and retention to be resolved in the favor of retention. If the bit of knowledge involved represents at least a rough approximation of reality, continued acceptance of it even though some exceptions occur may pay off in the long run. Thus the evolutionary system often manifests a conservative bias of this sort. Of course, if the exceptions are numerous and important in their consequences, perseveration will not pay off and the bit of knowledge involved will not survive the selection process which operates.

There is a slightly different approach to this issue which leads to much the same conclusion, i.e., that a certain degree of conservatism and suppression of exception or innovation is an inevitable characteristic of evolutionary-adaptive systems. The search for valid knowledge must be conducted with the tools available at a given moment in time and these tools are usually relatively crude and primitive. They may not permit a very refined sort of analysis, but rather allow us only to approximate reality in our maps of it. It may not be possible to cope with and integrate all the complexities of reality in the descriptions which are generated. As a result, the effort expended involves a search for some regularity or gross lawful pattern amid the distracting complexity which current tools are not sufficiently sophisticated to filter out. Pursuit of a goal of knowing at once everything there is to know about everything which can be known is fruitless. The physical and intellectual limitations of knowing organisms force a more modest tack whereby the ultimate goal is approached incrementally through the development of increasingly precise approximations of reality.

At any given time, then, it seems necessary to make the most out of whatever approximate order can be established and to ignore, for the moment, complexities which are currently too subtle to be systematized. In discussing this issue as it pertains to both science and the perceptual activity of individuals, Polanyi has stated, "The craving to find strands of permanence in the tumult of changing appearance is the supreme organon for bringing our experience under intellectual control. . . . The boundless variety of raw experience is devoid of all meaning, and our perceptive powers can render it intelligible only by identifying very different appearances as the same objects and qualities (1969, p. 114).

An idea which will be developed throughout this text—that individuals in the process of coming to know their social and physical environment develop more or less general rules about the relationships which they observe—is espoused, with an emphasis on the fact that the process involved is one which tends to exaggerate and exploit the stability or regularity which is encountered. There appears to be good reason, then, for arguing that a partial neglect of the apparently unique or irregular aspects of a situation under investigation is required in the interests of progress in the pursuit of knowledge. However, if the irregularities or exceptions are genuine, the neglect must be only temporary. Their incorporation into the map of reality being prepared awaits only the appearance of more sensitive techniques or more sophisticated analysts. The explicit and generally accepted rules which guide the manner in which scientific investigation is conducted are of such a nature as to minimize the impact of *other* potential sources of resistance to innovation. Science, properly done, maximizes the role external selectors may play and minimizes the impact of internal selectors on its findings. It emphasizes quantification, logical exposition, controlled empirical testing, replicability of findings, and intersubjectivity, and, as well, formally rejects the influence which simple authority, precedent, degree of current acceptance, and other such internal selective factors might have. In consequence, a given finding or theoretical position is ideally forced into open competitive comparison with any other relevant findings under conditions which make unsubstantiated belief extremely vulnerable.

Science—Unique in Method

This discussion began with a question regarding the degree to which science was in some sense a unique system: Is science basically different from other systems which are concerned with the mapping of reality, different in such a way that it can legitimately lay claim to some special status among these various systems of exploration? The answer would appear to be "yes and no."

No, science should not be seen as differing in a basic way from other investigatory systems, if you have been convinced by the arguments presented to the effect that all such systems which have the potential for leading to increases in knowledge share the same epistemology—variation-and-selective-retention. Thus, any success science may have in providing a satisfactory analysis of the environment can be viewed as involving, at its root, the very same sort of processes by which a young child comes to be able to cope successfully with his limited world. On the other hand, it was pointed out that a variety of selection factors may be operative in this winnowing process by which one of several competing maps of some aspect of reality is selected as providing the best fit. If science has a unique quality which serves to differentiate it in important ways from its compatriots in the search for knowledge, it is the fact that the investigatory techniques it employs have been carefully chosen to permit external selectors to operate and to inhibit internal selection processes.

METHODS OF RESEARCH IN SOCIAL PSYCHOLOGY

Having extolled the virtues of the scientific approach in general as the most efficient and effective approach to the goal of knowledge acquisition, it is now time to look more closely at just what it entails. Naturally enough, the focus will be on research methodology in social psychology, though much of the discussion will be relevant to research in general. And, the treatment of these topics will be rudimentary and general, as the intent is only to provide the reader with a basic understanding of research technique and its limitations, so that he will be in a better position to evaluate for himself the adequacy of the work which will be discussed in the remainder of the text. Those who wish a more sophisticated treatment of these topics might refer to the excellent reviews by Seltiz, et al. (1959), Aronson and Carlsmith (1968), or Hempel (1966).

Goals — Prediction and Understanding

It has been stated that scientific techniques serve to hasten and sharpen the process of knowledge acquisition, but it will aid the discussion of these methods to first be a bit more precise about just what is meant by "knowledge." Social psychology has prediction and understanding as its interrelated goals. Certainly, simply being able to predict the occurrence of some event does not satisfy the goal of understanding that phenomenon, but it does represent an important first step. Progress toward understanding is typically based initially on the information provided by careful, systematic observation of the naturally occurring relationships among events. When some pattern or regularity is uncovered, prediction is possible on the basis of the assumption that a sequence of events which has consistently occurred in the past will continue to occur in the future. But to be able to predict that breathing into a paper bag will stop hiccups, that a red sky at night will bring fair weather tomorrow, or that the inhalation of the gaseous residue of burning *cannabis sativa* leads to lightheadedness, subjective time distortion, heightened sensory awareness and arrest does not in any sense imply genuine understanding of the processes involved in these relationships.

In science, the traditional mode of knowledge acquisition is the method of hypothesis—some explanation or account of a given relationship is tentatively proposed and then put to empirical test. In this way, then, there is a reciprocity between understanding and prediction. The correctness of a given explanation is established on the basis of its ability to permit accurate prediction of the events under investigation. Understanding provides the ability to predict, and successful prediction serves to increase our confidence in the validity of the understanding.

The Experimental Method

While experimentation is only one of a number of appropriate and valid approaches to the development of understanding, it has, as we shall see, certain advantages which have made it in many instances the preferred technique in social psychological research. The identifying characteristic of an experiment is control by the investigator over the events involved. In contrast with simple observation, where naturally occurring sequences of events are recorded as they happen, in an experiment one set of these events is carefully manipulated in a controlled manner and the effects they have on another set of events are recorded. The hypothesis which guides the conduct of the experiment typically suggests that certain events cause or at least make more likely the occurrence of other events or effects. The presumed causal factors are called *independent variables,* and they are carefully described and measured by the investigator, who introduces them in a controlled fashion into the experiment. The situation is arranged so that their effects on some aspect of the activity, behavior, or current state of the organism being investigated can be precisely measured and recorded; these effects are termed the *dependent variables.* It may help in keeping this terminology correctly in mind to think of the dependent variable as the effect which is a function of, or is *dependent* upon, the operation of the causal, independent variable, while the independent variable is fixed in advance, is *independent* of and uninfluenced by anything which may happen subsequently in the actual experiment.

Advantages of the Experimental Method

One very important advantage of the experiment over straightforward observation of naturally occurring events arises from the fact that with the latter it may be very difficult to isolate the impact of any single variable of interest. Particularly with the issues of interest in social psychology, it is likely to be the case that the variable whose effects are to be assessed is always accompanied by a number of other related variables. Therefore, it becomes difficult to ascertain with certainty that some outcome which is observed to consistently follow the event of interest has been "caused" by it, rather than by one of the other variables that are regularly associated with it under natural conditions. To increase confidence in the designation of some variable as a causal agent, it is necessary to observe its effects in a situation in which it is not so inextricably imbedded in a complex of related events. In an experiment, in which control over the independent variable is established, it is possible to isolate more adequately the potential causal element and by appropriate manipulation to assess the effects of its presence or absence, or of the consequences of its presence in varying degrees of intensity, and so forth.

Of course, there are many variables of interest to psychologists over which control of the sort required for experimental testing is not possible. There may be ethical constraints; for example, one would not want to drastically curtail the interaction a very young child has with other humans to test the effects of such deprivation on subsequent social development. Also, practical considerations such as the expense in time or money necessary for effective experimental manipulation may be prohibitive. And, of course, there may be situations in which it is simply physically impossible to control a variable. Under these circumstances it may nevertheless be possible to discover and observe naturally occurring situations that will permit valid inferences about the variables of interest to be drawn. Thus, in reference to the example above, it might be possible to find children who, for one reason or another, had experienced considerable social deprivation in their early years, and contrast their current behavior with that of a group comparable in all respects other than this deprivation experience.

Correlation and Causality

To illustrate the major advantage experiments have over nonexperimental investigation—their greater ability to provide an adequate test of hypotheses about causal relationships—and to point out some of the difficulties in establishing that one event is causally related to another, we will pursue this example farther. Assume, for the moment, that one of the findings that come out of our naturalistic observations of socially deprived and non-deprived children is that the deprived children exhibit much less tendency to spontaneously orient themselves to social objects, i.e., other persons, in their environment. They appear to be much less interested in and attentive to people than are children who had more extensive interaction with adults in their early years. It would seem intuitively quite reasonable to infer that the early social deprivation is responsible for, or causes, this decreased attentiveness—the deprived children, for one thing, haven't had as extensive an opportunity to learn that other people are frequently the source of rewards and thus that orienting toward them pays off.

What these observations have established is a correlation between sets of events; the presence or magnitude of one event, social deprivation, tends to correspond to or co-vary with the presence or magnitude of another event, reduced interest in social objects. You can see that if this observation is valid, it permits accurate prediction, the first step toward understanding, as was mentioned earlier. But it does not really provide a complete understanding of the relationship. And, as is the case with any purely correlational finding, there are definite problems in drawing inferences about causality.

No reader of this book can doubt that people who like one another tend to be together more than people who don't. Even a short tenure on earth will give anyone a chance to observe this phenomenon. Put more technically, the relationship between liking and togetherness is a correlation, an association between events, entities, states, etc., which occurs in nature. Observation of this correlation does not tell us directly how this correlation came to be; observation in nature often does not give us direct information about the direction of causation generating this observed correlation. Did the liking come first? Or did the togetherness? Or, can either come first and lead to the other? In other words, is the causation mutual, bi-directional? Or is there some third factor, such as similarity of interests, which leads both to liking and togetherness? In these instances, we have ample additional information about the world which would lead us to believe that at least one of the directions of causation did occur. We have all seen a person seek out the company of another he liked. However, this strong presumption that liking can and does precede togetherness does not eliminate the possibility that the causation may also be in the other direction as well. As the song from *Finian's Rainbow* has it, "When you're not with the one you like, you like the one you're with." The most interesting question, then, is to determine whether it is at least possible for causation to work in the less obvious, less commonsensical way (Stotland, 1965).

Often, observation in nature does not permit us to determine whether some directions of causation can and do occur. Often we are not able to observe the temporal sequence of events, although in some cases we might be able to do so. The experimental approach can tell us whether a given direction of causation can occur. The reasons that it can do this will be outlined below. But it is important to notice what an experiment cannot do. It cannot tell us how much the given direction of causation occurs in nature. Perhaps togetherness leads to liking, but not very often or to a great degree. Furthermore, the experimental approach cannot tell us that a given direction of causation does not occur. The reasons for the experimental method's being unable to affirm the negative are partly a matter of the statistical logic underlying research and partly a matter of the difficulty of interpreting the results of research in which no "difference" has been found. The reason for this difficulty will be described later.

One reason why the experimental approach can help to resolve the problem of the ambiguity of direction of causation is that the experimenter controls the perceived independent or causal variables, and has the required information regarding the timing of events. He could put people together to see if liking increased. A second advantage of the experiment stems from the fact that it is possible that some other variable which just happens to be consistently associated with the natural occurrence of the causal variable is actually responsible for the observed relationship. For example, people of opposite sexes who are together for long periods of time are more likely to be married than are those together for shorter periods of time. Thus, the effects of togetherness and the marriage relationship are difficult to separate in nature. In an experiment, it is at least theoretically possible to experimentally prevent this other variable, marriage, from entering the picture, although, obviously, this would be true only for short run experiments. More generally, in an experiment, one goal is to make certain that the manipulations of the independent variable consitute the only differences in treatment of the comparison groups, so that the observed differences can be unequivocally attributed to the effect of the independent variable. To the extent that this requirement of a good experiment is met, the influence of some variable, correlated with the independent variable in nature, is eliminated.

A related and very critical safeguard in experimentation involves the random deployment of subjects to the various experimental conditions. The likelihood of assignment of a given subject to any one of the experimental treatments must be equal. In this way many alternative explanations of the results of the study may be ruled out in advance. Different individuals are certainly not homogenous in their traits and personal characteristics. If they have not been assigned to the several treatment conditions on a random basis, then the possibility exists that any observed differences between them is partially attributable to differences in the kinds of persons who participated in each of the conditions. With random assignment, on the other hand, even though each condition will be heterogeneous with respect to the characteristics of the persons included in it, this heterogeneity will be similar in each of the conditions—the within treatment heterogeneity will be homogenous across treatments. Thus, in the experiment on togetherness leading to liking, subjects could be assigned randomly to the treatments in which they would be together for a long period and in which they would be together for a short period. Any differences in outcome could not then be readily attributed to differences, say, in age, intelligence, etc., because both groups would be about the same in these regards. Sometimes researchers may actually systematically be able to make certain that the two groups are alike in these respects. In any case, any competing explanation of the findings which involves the characteristics of the participants is ruled out if the assignment to treatment conditions has been carried out properly.

It should be clear, then, that the experimental method has certain advantages over other investigatory approaches—the paramount one being its ability to permit the establishment of causal relationships with greater certitude.

However, there is one very important limitation on the value of experimental research in resolving the problem of causation in field settings. This limitation applies to even the best done of studies. It concerns the obvious possibility and, in most cases, probability, that there are many causes for the same event or class of events. For example, receiving a raise in pay may cause happiness because it means greater material wealth, because it gives one a sense of economic security, because it represents a sign of one's employer's esteem, because it raises one's status, and so on. One or more of these causes may function for a given individual for a given raise. Or, one or more of these causes may function for different people receiving the same raise. This may all be obvious, but it points to our not asking what is *the* cause of, say, happiness. There are few events which have or can have only one cause. It is very tempting and indeed very satisfying to be able to say, *the* cause of X is Y, but it is rarely valid. This limitation needs to be borne in mind when we attempt to generalize from a given experimental study. If we do not have a scientific theory to guide us, we often have to rely on our common sense to indicate to us the limitations of generalizability of the causal processes demonstrated by a given study.

On the other hand, this should not imply any denigration whatever of non-experimental techniques. Wholly appropriate, valid, and useful analyses can occur outside the laboratory setting. Investigation by experiment should be viewed as an important tool and not as an end in itself. Observational, naturalistic, or field studies, i.e., ones in which data are gathered in naturally occurring settings and in which the investigator does not intrude by manipulating events, are of very great importance, primarily in terms of their heuristic value. That is, the systematic observation of events as they occur in their natural setting is a most fruitful source of hypotheses about the nature of the relationships among events. These may subsequently be subjected to experimental test, if necessary. In addition, there is an unfortunate and incorrect tendency to equate experimental studies with laboratory studies, when, of course, there is no *a priori* reason why events selected to operate as independent variables cannot be carefully and systematically manipulated in non-laboratory, natural settings. When this is done we have a field experiment, a form of study strongly advocated by Lewin (1951), which is currently becoming increasingly common as psychologists turn their attention more toward issues which have some immediate social significance and relevance to the critical societal problems of the day. Field experiments may be seen as having the potential to combine the advantages accruing to the experimental approach with a more ready and clear-cut generalizability to non-experimental settings.

Internal and External Validity

Obviously, psychologists wish to do more than establish that a given pattern of events occurred in the particular setting studied, with the specific individuals who were examined, at the given time at which the observations were made. The goal is to identify and systematize the lawful relationships which govern social behavior in general. The principles uncovered by experimental study would be of very limited value and utility if their operation could not be extrapolated to circumstances other than those which were involved in a specific study; but, of course, the first step is to demonstrate that they *do* occur in the experiment.

These issues have to do with what Campbell (1957) refers to as the problems of internal and external validity. *Internal validity* is concerned with the question, "Did the experimental treatments make a difference in this specific experimental instance?", whereas the relevant question in establishing *external validity* is, "To what populations, settings, treatment variables, and measurement variables can this effect be generalized?" The importance of both types of criteria should be obvious, and the best investigations are those which are internally valid and also uncover relationships which have a high degree of generalizability to extra-experimental situations.

If a study is to be internally valid, a minimum requirement is that it have some genuine impact on the participants. Aronson and Carlsmith, in discussing what they call experimental realism, suggest that "An experiment is realistic if the situation is realistic to the subject, if it involves him, if he is forced to take it seriously, if it has impact on him" (1968, p. 22). On the other hand, "This realism always tends to lead to great difficulty in understanding precisely what the experimental treatment consists of. Social experiences which are realistic and meaningful tend to be complex, and any two such experiences (treatments) tend to differ on a large number of dimensions. . . . We see this as the basic dilemma of the experimental social psychologist. On the one hand we want maximal control over the independent variable. We want as few extraneous differences as possible between our treatments. We want to specify as precisely as possible the exact nature of the treatment we have administered and its exact effect on the subject. This leads us to try to develop manipulations that are highly specifiable, in which the differences between treatments are extraordinarily simple and clear, in which all manipulations are standardized. . . . On the other hand, if the experiment is controlled to the point of being sterile, it may fail to involve the subject, have little impact on him, and therefore may not affect his behavior to any great extent" (1968, p. 12). Typically, some compromise between realism and control is reached in any given experiment, as both are critical. Without an appropriate level of control unambiguous interpretation of the results is not possible, but in the absence of some minimal degree of realism, as the term is being used here, there is not likely to be any result to interpret.

Although there is no necessary relationship between them, a high degree of experimental realism is also likely to heighten the external validity of a study. The extent to which we may have confidence that some experimentally established principle may legitimately be generalized is increased by demonstrating its operation on heterogeneous samples of persons, in a wide variety of differing experimental contexts, and by means of a multiplicity of different types of observations and measures which all attest to its functioning. Ultimately, however, the question of external validity is an empirical one; that is, the only way really to assess the generalizability of some principle is actually to test its applicability to novel circumstances and situations. Certainly a given finding need not be generalizable to all possible populations and situations to have external validity. Its significance is not necessarily defined in terms of the sheer diversity of circumstances to which it can legitimately be applied, even though the search is for general laws of behavior. Discovering that some result holds only under particular conditions may provide very useful information regarding the dynamics of its operation. Knowledge concerning limiting conditions can be most helpful in developing an understanding of some phenomenon. Thus, the goal is to specify as precisely as is possible what these are.

Though we have earlier suggested that scientific approaches are more likely than other investigative systems to lead to the accumulation of a body of valid knowledge, we were careful to indicate that this superiority is a relative one; that science and, more specifically, the experimental approach in social psychology by no means provides an absolutely certain, infallible set of techniques. The discussion, to this point, has not emphasized the shortcomings which exist, in part because it has been concerned with a general and rather abstract accounting of how research is done. At this theoretical level the discipline is in quite good shape—we know what we want to do and, in broad terms, how to do it. At the more practical level, when it comes to actually conducting an investigation, our footing is a bit less sure, and it is to some of these circumstances on which a study may stumble that we now turn our attention.

Problems of Operationalization

As was mentioned earlier, science characteristically operates by the method of hypothesis in which some tentative way of accounting for or understanding the phenomenon under study is formulated and put to empirical test. The proposed explanation may have come from a wide variety of sources—intuition, "hunch," deduction from an extant relevant theory, induction from previous research findings, common sense, and so on. But no matter what its source, this hypothesis almost invariably involves postulating some variable to be responsible for the anticipated or previously observed effects. "The investigator (wants) to conceptualize some variable which he (feels is) theoretically important and which apparently caused the observed difference in the subject's behavior. We shall refer to this as the conceptual variable" (Aronson and Carlsmith, 1968, p. 13). Thus, an experimenter might suggest that *hunger* is responsible for some observed behavior of a laboratory animal, that *anxiety* leads a person to seek the company of other persons, that involving listeners with a *distracting task* will increase the persuasive impact of a counter-attitudinal message, and so on. The problem arises when it becomes necessary to translate a conceptual variable into concrete experimental operations. It is not the conceptual variable which itself produces any effect in an experiment, but rather some set of manipulations which the investigator has decided adequately represents this variable and this variable alone. But this translation is frequently an imperfect one—the specific operations chosen may produce important effects in addition to those envisioned by the experimenter.

Without belaboring the point by exhaustively analyzing the examples of conceptual variables given above we can, with unfortunate ease, illustrate the multiple meanings which a typical operationalization of each of them might include. Of the many ways to translate the abstract "distracting task" into experimental operations, Festinger and Maccoby (1964) chose to have their subjects watch a humorous and engrossing film while listening to a persuasive communication. Subsequent agreement with the communication may well have been due to subjects' having been distracted by the film and thus less likely to mentally argue against the points being made; but the film was entertaining and funny as well as distracting and, in non-technical terms, the resultant "good mood" might have heightened receptivity to the message. Schachter (1959) induced anxiety by telling persons that they would be undergoing painful electrical shocks later in the experiment and found that this led to a desire to spend a waiting period with certain types of other persons rather than alone. On the other hand, Sarnoff and Zimbardo (1966), using anticipated participation in some potentially embarassing activities, such as sucking on a pacifier, to produce anxiety, found that their subjects preferred to wait alone. Operationalizations of the conceptual variable hunger probably seem to be the least susceptible to multiple meaning of the three we have mentioned and yet there may be ambiguity here, too. If animals are deprived of food to induce hunger, particular characteristics of their subsequent behavior could be due to hunger, but they might also be a function of reduced physical strength or heightened irritability.

This problem is frequently particularly acute in social psychological research as the experimental manipulations employed are often relatively complex, partly in the interests of insuring internal validity, of producing circumstances which will be realistic and involving to the participants. To cope with this problem adequately two complementary approaches are required. On the one hand, a variety of ways of operationalizing the conceptual variable should be employed and these should differ from one another as much as is possible while retaining in common only the original conceptual variable. Confidence that the only common element among them all is really what is responsible for the observed outcomes will be increased if this variety of techniques all lead to the same result. On the other hand, it would be important to demonstrate that a variety of different effects, all consistent with the theoretical properties of the conceptual variable, can be produced by some single experimental manipulation which is an appropriate operationalization of that variable. To illustrate this, our confidence that we have a firm understanding of the concept anxiety and its impact would be heightened if it had been shown that anticipated painful shocks, an expected difficult examination, a forthcoming serious medical operation, and several other different theoretically anxiety-evoking events all were associated with increased affiliation tendencies. Similarly, we would like to have shown that any one of these manipulations, such as the threat of electrical shock, leads to poor performance of a complex task, heightened physiological arousal, and increased desire for and acceptance of rapid, simple solutions to a set of logic problems, as well as a strong wish to be with other persons. Instances of this sort of converging corroboration of conceptual variables, hypothetical constructs, or intervening variables are all too rare in social psychology and this leaves the discipline to work with some unfortunately ill-defined explanatory constructs and experimental manipulations.

Problems of Measurement

Quite similar problems crop up in a consideration of the dependent variables employed in psychological research. Isolating some set of behaviors or responses on the part of subjects which constitute an accurate and unambiguous way of assessing the impact of the independent variable is also a difficult task. The measures used in social psychology are invariably impure in the sense that scores obtained on them are influenced by a number of factors in addition to the one variable whose effect we wish to assess. This sort of measurement uncertainty is not a unique characteristic of psychological instruments. Wilson (1952) has carefully catalogued the imperfections of measuring instruments in science and, to provide an illustration of the general point, let us consider the various forces which affect the operation of a voltmeter. It is influenced not only by the electrical current its designers wish its needle fluctuations to reflect, but also by gravitational effects on the needle, friction in its moving parts, and the laws of inertia. Attempts are made to eliminate the effects of these latter irrelevant forces on the measurement process by minimizing the mass of the needle, keeping its movement perpendicular to the gravitational influences, setting the needle in low-friction bearings, counterweighting it, and so forth. With all these precautions the movement of the needle may reflect with almost complete accuracy the operation of the single variable, voltage. But, "no meter ever perfectly measures a single theoretical parameter; all series of meter readings are imperfect estimates of the theoretical parameters they are intended to measure" (Webb et al., 1966, p. 4). And in social psychology, our understanding of the irrelevant sources of variations impinging on some instrument does not approach in comprehensiveness and depth the sort that is represented in the design of the voltmeter in physics.

The most appropriate response to these difficulties, in addition to striving for ever more pure measures and a complete inventory of the forces influencing a measurement device, is a multi-method approach to measurement. This sort of solution has been advocated by numerous psychologists, including Brunswick (1956), Campbell (1957), and Garner, Hake, and Eriksen (1956), and is just the same as that suggested above in our discussion of the problems of operationalization.

Information provided by any given measurement technique is multiply determined. Thus, the determinants other than those associated with the variable we hope to tap are considered to be sources of measurement error. These sources of error are likely to be substantially different across a number of different test instruments and so the primary common element in them would be the influence of the one variable they were all designed to tap. We would have, then, a series of measures with varying patterns of theoretically irrelevant components, but which are hypothesized to share in the theoretically relevant components. Any single measure could reflect primarily the operation of one or more of these irrelevant components rather than the variable it is designed to tap. We might therefore erroneously conclude that the conceptual variable we believe to have been measured has had an effect. If, however, we find that the predicted effect consistently manifests itself on a number of very different theoretically relevant measures of the presumed causal variable we can be much more certain that this variable is, indeed, responsible for the results. "Once a proposition has been confirmed by two or more independent measurement processes, the uncertainty of its interpretation is greatly reduced. . . . If a proposition can survive the onslaught of a series of imperfect measures, with all their irrelevant error, confidence should be placed in it. Of course, this confidence is increased by minimizing error on each instrument and by a reasonable belief in the different and divergent effects of the sources of error" (Webb et al., 1966, p. 3).

CRITICAL EXPERIMENTS OR CONVERGENT CORROBORATION?

An important implication of the discussion of the difficulties met in operationalizing and measuring variables is that there will be few, if any, critical experiments in social psychology. By critical experiment is meant a single investigation which totally establishes the validity of a given principle or theory, or which decides, once and for all, the superiority of one competing explanation of some phenomenon over another. This sort of certainty is just not in the cards as far as social psychology is concerned. The deck with which we must play is too full of ambiguity and imprecision at the moment. However, this most certainly does not mean that progress is impossible or that principles governing social behavior cannot be uncovered. It simply suggests that reasonable caution is necessary in interpreting and generalizing the results of any given investigation. Almost any study, no matter how carefully planned and executed, will be open to some alternative explanation. Thus, a pattern of consistent results across a series of experiments dealing with the same topic or within the same experiment where a variety of measures or operations are involved must be much more convincing than isolated findings.

We encourage the reader to critically evaluate the research and conclusions reported in subsequent chapters—in fact, the hope of providing a basis for such an orientation has been the *raison d'être* for much of the discussion in this second chapter. This sort of critical acceptance is entirely healthy and, indeed, has guided the authors' selection of material to be included in this volume. A point to be kept in mind, however, is that even though different minor criticisms of each of a series of investigations encountered may be possible, the total picture may nevertheless provide the sort of convergent corroboration which we have suggested is so important. At the same time it is not appropriate to reject the conclusions of a given study simply because this type of redundant confirmation is not available. If the investigation has been properly conducted and carefully controlled such that alternative explanations have been ruled out, it is quite reasonable to tentatively accept the account of the data provided by the experimenters. If the phenomenon investigated is of genuine significance it will undoubtedly merit further exploration and with this comes the possibility of verification or clarification and refinement of the principles initially proposed to account for it.

SOURCES OF BIAS IN RESEARCH SETTINGS

In the last decade an increasing awareness of and interest in the sources of potential bias in psychological experimentation has occurred. A social psychology of the social psychological experiment has developed which involves explicit attempts to document and systematize the ways in which this bias operates. In other words, it has become increasingly clear that an experiment in which a social organism's behavior is the subject of study and which often involves social interaction of some sort between experimenter and subject must be viewed as a social setting which is as fit an object for study as is any extra-experimental social setting. This sort of research suggests that bias may stem from either or both of two general sources—the experimental setting itself and the activity of the experimenter in his relationship with his subjects.

Demand Characteristics and Evaluation Apprehension

"The experimental situation is one which takes place within the context of an explicit agreement of the subject to participate in a special formal social interaction known as 'taking part in an experiment.' Within the context of our culture the roles of subject and experimenter are well understood and carry with them well-defined mutual role expectations" (Orne, 1962, p. 777). Persons who participate in a study as subjects are likely to bring into the situation with them a set of beliefs about the importance of science and research, about what may reasonably be asked of them in an experimental setting, about the appropriateness of adopting a cooperative and unquestioning attitude, about the competence of the experimenter, and so on. Many of these beliefs which have an influence on his behavior throughout the course of the study may be specific to this particular set of circumstances. If they are unique in this sense and do in part determine his activity, including the behavior measured as the dependent variable, then they constitute a source of error or bias. If they do not operate in the extra-experimental world of the subject, they interfere with any attempt to extrapolate from experimental findings to the "real world." The effects of an awareness that this is an experiment and that detailed observations are being made are overlaid on the influence of the experimental manipulations themselves and it is the *combination* of these to which the subject responds. Orne has labeled the totality of these effects the *demand characteristics* of the experimental situation. That they are real, potent, and easily invoked can be simply demonstrated. In a very informal study, a psychologist asked a sample of his colleagues to stop whatever activity they were engaged in at the moment and to do fifteen pushups for him. The typical response was not compliance, but rather questions, about the sanity of the requestor. On the other hand, the same request when prefaced by the comment, "I'd like you to help me out by participating in a little experiment," met with much greater success.

A related issue has to do with what Rosenberg (1965) terms *evaluation apprehension*. It seems reasonable to assume that persons wish to give a favorable impression of themselves to others. This tendency may be even more acute in the setting of a psychological experiment if the subject has the rather naive notion that all psychologists are particularly concerned with assessing the normality or mental pathology of persons. In any case, the subject does know that his behavior is being scrutinized, but often does not know for what purposes the observations are being made or how they will be interpreted. He is thus likely to be apprehensive about the evaluation the psychologist is presumably making of his behavior and therefore to be motivated to discover for himself the "true" purpose of the experiment. He may believe that with this information he can behave knowledgeably and appropriately. In consequence, subjects are often engaged in attempts to outguess the experimenter and, in the process, develop their own hypotheses about the experimenter's hypothesis. Armed with this guess about what the purpose of the study is, the subject can then act in a way which he believes will substantiate the hypothesis so as to gain the approval of the experimenter or to appear mentally healthy or normal; or, if he is a more perverse sort, he may behave counter to the supposed prediction to demonstrate his independence, his aggressivity or his ability to outwit the experimenter. Any of these types of response can play havoc with both the internal and external validity of the results of the investigators.

A completely effective way of dealing with the problems stemming from demand characteristics and evaluation apprehension is yet to be devised, but there are techniques which may moderate their influence. Aronson and Carlsmith (1968) suggest the following: provide the subjects with an intuitively reasonable and acceptable explanation of the purposes of the study which is, however, not related to its genuine purpose; develop experimental manipulations which appear essentially identical to subjects in all conditions so that the hypotheses subjects may generate will not have a systematic effect on the results; attempt to dissociate, from the subject's point of view, the experimental manipulations from the measures taken, on the assumption that he will respond more candidly if he does not see the measurements as part of the experiment; avoid the use of techniques whose intent is blatant and easily deduced by the subject; and conduct the study in other than a laboratory environment.

This last suggestion deserves a bit more amplification as it seems to be one of the most effective solutions. If the subject is not aware that he is participating in an experiment and, in addition, does not know that his behavior is being observed, he is not likely to present the researcher with the problems we have been discussing. What is being opted for here is a subtle form of the field experiment or field study, if manipulations cannot properly be introduced into the setting. Most appropriately, these would be conducted in association with well-designed laboratory investigations of the same phenomenon so that both types of evidence in conjunction would provide strong support for the principles uncovered. The use of unobtrusive measures has been effectively championed by Webb, Campbell, Schwartz, and Sechrest (1966) in their fascinating book on the topic of "non-reactive" research methods.

Although some of the research using "measures that do not require the cooperation of a respondent and that do not themselves contaminate the response" (Webb et al., 1966, p. 2) has been rather rudimentary and trivial, the potential importance of this approach is great. Let us very briefly look at some examples.

Lefkowitz, Blake, and Mouton (1955) studied modeling and conformity behavior in a natural setting by surreptitiously recording the number of persons who violated a "don't walk" traffic signal in Austin, Texas. They found that walking against the signal was more likely when a model (a confederate of the experimenter) first violated the light's admonition and, further, that this sort of conformity was more likely when the model was well-dressed than when he was poorly dressed.

Sechrest (1965) found that a greater number of gross errors (such things as poor spacing, skipping lines, repositioning of hands) occurred when persons were engaged in copying erotic passages of literature than when the task involved material from a mineralogy textbook.

Back in 1922, Moore systematically gathered records of the snatches of conversations he could overhear on a daily walk up Broadway from 33rd to 55th Streets in New York City. Among other things he found that among men conversing with other men only 8 per cent of the conversations were concerned with persons of the opposite sex, while 44 per cent of the women's conversations with other women had men as their central theme. The present authors draw no conclusions from these dated data, but simply present them as grist for the feminist mill.

Feshbach and Feshbach (1963) report that at the beginning of a fear-arousing storytelling experience conducted with young children on Halloween, the diameter of the seating circle was eleven feet. By the time the ghost stories had been completed the circle had spontaneously shrunk to approximately three feet. Such a finding might be seen as related to the earlier-cited laboratory research on fear and affiliation tendencies.

Finally, to demonstrate an archival type study in which written records form the data base we may cite an investigation by Lodge (1963) which used Navy records of jet plane accidents. One of his findings may lead you to select your next airline flight on a quite different basis than you probably have used in the past. It was found that pilots who were taller than the average height of six feet were significantly more likely to have been involved in an air accident than were shorter pilots. Such a correlational study doesn't provide an explanation for the finding, but it might well have to do with the layout of plane cockpits, which have been designed around normal-sized models, and the ease of instrument reading.

With proper motivation and sufficient ingenuity, it should be quite possible to develop more sophisticated techniques for the unobtrusive measurement of many of the relevant variables in social psychology. There is much to recommend the sort of non-reactive research as we have seen.

Unintentional Influence

Recent work by Rosenthal (e.g., 1966) has sensitized social psychologists to the fact that they, as experimenters, must regard their participation in the conduct of a study as a potential source of bias. Numerous investigations have demonstrated that the experimenter may unintentionally influence the results he obtains in a direction supportive of his hypotheses. The process referred to here does not involve or imply deliberate action on the part of researchers to fabricate or alter data or consciously to attempt to induce respondents to behave in the predicted manner. Research has demonstrated, however, that under certain circumstances an experimenter acting in good faith and employing accepted investigatory techniques may subtly and systematically elicit from his subjects the sort of behavior which well substantiates his hypotheses. Typically in these studies there are two groups of experimenters, one half of whom have been given a rationale which leads them to expect one sort of result from the experiment they conduct, while the other half anticipates the opposite outcome on the same task. For example, Rosenthal and Fode (1963) gave one group of experimenters reason to believe that their subjects should give numerically high ratings in response to a series of photographs they were to judge in terms of the success or failure reflected in the faces of the persons depicted. The other group was told they should anticipate low ratings. Although the photographs used were ones which had previously been found to elicit neutral judgments along a success-failure continuum, two groups of experimenters here each obtained results in line with their expectations. A great many studies using this same basic paradigm have been conducted and their cumulative impact at first seemed extremely ominous as some psychologists appeared to conclude from them that bias was a ubiquitous, consistently powerful phenomenon. More recently, however, a more tempered view of this issue has come to the fore, stimulated in part by an extremely thorough re-examination of the research in the area by Barber and Silver (1968). They point out some methodological and statistical problems in many of the investigations purporting to find bias, and counsel against an overly pessimistic and generalized interpretation of the findings.

It seems clear that bias of this sort can at times influence the outcome of an investigation, but we do not yet have clear-cut answers to the questions of just when and under what conditions it will occur or how it is brought about. Canon (1967) has emphasized that it may be most appropriate to view the process, in a sense, as a cooperative venture between experimenter and subject and that certain personal attitudes of both these participants in an experiment will influence the likelihood that bias will manifest itself. We have already suggested that subjects are likely to be actively searching for cues which will allow them to determine what the appropriate and socially acceptable way to behave is. The experimenter may also have a strong vested interest in the outcome of a study. Typically, he has made specific predictions about the way the subjects will behave and has a variety of obvious reasons for wishing to see them come true. Thus, even though he is extremely careful to approach the problem in an open and unbiased manner, he may nevertheless give off very subtle cues in his interactions with the subjects regarding his expectations. His tone of voice or friendliness, a transitory smile in response to a prediction-fulfilling behavior on the part of the subject, more speedy recording of "proper" responses, incompletely disguised surprise when a very unusual response is given, and so forth, may all be difficult to control cues to which the subject may be responsive in his search for the "correct" way to behave.

That such cues, which one is not particularly aware of giving off but which can be "read" by another, do exist is nicely illustrated by the case of Clever Hans (Pfungst, 1911). Clever Hans was a remarkable horse who, by signaling with taps of his foot, could count, add, subtract, multiply, divide, solve problems, answer simple yes or no questions, and read. Ordinarily one might be a bit suspicious of all this, but this was no well-trained carnival animal and his owner did not in any way profit from Hans' fascinating abilities. In fact, the owner was quite willing to allow his horse to be examined by persons seriously interested in discovering the roots of these baffling talents, and it was found that Hans was able to perform well for a variety of questioners—he did not depend on any tricks or intentional cueing from his owner. Two German psychologists, Pfungst and Stumpf, initiated a detailed and systematic study of Hans and, after discovering that he was not clever at all when he could not see his questioners, they were able to uncover his secret. He was simply responding to a postural cue unconsciously given off by most persons when they put questions to him. Hans would begin to tap when his interrogator inclined his head forward and would continue until the person straightened up again. It seems that this is a cue given off by many persons when asking a question in this situation—leaning forward in a gesture of anticipation and encouragement and, knowing the correct answer themselves, leaning the head back again when the proper number of taps had been given. Since Hans would begin tapping in response to such behavior even when no question had been asked, could not give a correct answer unless the questioner himself knew the answer, and could operate properly only when he could see the questioner, Pfungst felt confident he had discovered the reasons for Clever Hans' cleverness. Now, if a German horse can learn to read such subtle signals which are unintentionally provided by an interrogator, it doesn't seem too far-fetched to attribute at least comparable ability to college students participating in a psychology experiment.

We must reiterate, however, that this sort of cue sending and receiving is only one of possibly many ways in which biasing effects may develop and that we currently do not have firm answers regarding the specifics of the process. Preliminary indications are that certain characteristics of the experimenter and of the subjects, such as their anxiety level, relative status, manipulativeness, general demeanor, and need for social approval, may play a role in determining the likelihood that bias will occur. In addition, there has not been a systematic investigation of the characteristics of the experimental situation itself, which may contribute to or deter the occurrence of bias effects. Beginnings in this direction indicate that the greater the ambiguity, non-factualness, and lack of structure in the experimental task, the greater is the possibility that the experimenter's expectations will influence the results obtained. It seems likely that much of the research on this topic has employed experimental paradigms which are particularly susceptible to bias effects and thus generalization from them to studies using other methodologies may not be warranted.

In sum, since we know experimenters can, under certain conditions, have an unintentional influence on their subjects, it behooves us to try to safeguard against this occurrence. But it is easy to blow this potential problem out of proportion and to develop an unwarranted pessimism regarding the degree to which bias may interfere with the conduct of social psychological research. A variety of techniques present themselves as ways of dealing with this issue. They include: seeing to it that the person actually conducting the study is not aware of the experimental condition to which a given subject has been assigned; using automated (video- or tape-recorded) instructions to the participants; having the experimenter run all the subjects in all of the various conditions of the study simultaneously. Attempting to keep the persons who conduct the investigation ignorant of the predictions might appear to be another possibility, but this is not a particularly effective technique as there is a high probability that they, like their subjects, will attempt to discover the hypotheses. A study by Rosenthal, Persinger, Vikan-Kline, and Mulry (1963), in fact, demonstrated that bias effects did occur even when the director of an experiment did not inform his assistants, who actually conducted the study, of his hypotheses. The presumption is that in some unintentional manner the hypothesis was communicated to them, just as they, in turn, communicated it to their subjects.

THEORY—THE ULTIMATE GOAL OF SCIENCE

The discussion in the section above has concentrated on the assets and liabilities of particular investigatory techniques. These various methods supply much of the raw material from which an understanding of social psychological phenomena is constructed. But the goals of science go beyond the prediction and understanding of isolated events and relationships. Theory serves this broader purpose and acts like the mortar which permits the individual building blocks to be fashioned into an integrated, complex structure. There are no shortcuts or standard formulae to provide a guide to the construction of such general explanations. Intuition and careful examination of, and familiarity with, the relevant empirical findings may suggest ways in which the various shapes they present may fit together to form a logical, consistent, and sound structure. And at times the mortar, or theory, may be used generously to fill the gaps between apparently disparate experimental findings. On the other hand, the gaps in a partially completed structure may lead the builder to search for hitherto unnoticed blocks of a particular shape suitable to fill them. That is, a good theory not only will provide for the consistent integration of extant empirical findings but also will permit the prediction of not-yet-observed relationships. It will have both inductive and deductive qualities, in other words.

"Direct empirical measurement is generally agreed to be the fundamental task of natural science. . . . However it is not always possible to answer scientific questions *simply* by means of direct observation and measurement. Many phenomena appear to be too remotely and too tenuously related to the immediately observable variables to permit so direct an approach. Furthermore, there are problems of underlying general relationships between apparently unrelated phenomena that cannot easily be attacked by strictly empirical methods. For these reasons all modern natural sciences have developed a large number of theories or abstract explanatory principles, which are ultimately based upon but by no means entirely reducible to bare empirical measurements" (Marx, 1951, p. 4). It can be seen, then, that theory is not only a goal, but also a very important tool of science. It is used to provide a means for moving beyond the local limitations of specific observations and its use in this fashion serves to remind us of its essentially tentative, provisional nature. We do not expect to find final or absolute laws in science, though there is often a tendency to treat them as such. They are better viewed as currently useful ways of summarizing the functional relationships between variables of interest which may well be replaced in the future by more inclusive or effective ways of integrating events. In consequence, a theory is most appropriately evaluated in terms of its comprehensiveness and parsimony (its ability to account for a wide range of events with few propositions or assumptions), its ability to generate new hypotheses which may be readily tested, and its success in leading to the development of even more comprehensive and consistent theories. It is a common error to believe that, in lieu of or in addition to the above criteria, theories can be evaluated on the basis of some sort of proof that they are "true." However, since it is really only a scheme which specifies what someone believes, on the basis of the information available to him, to be the nature and arrangement of the relationships among a set of variables, a theory cannot be proved—there is no way to ascertain that events not yet observed or investigated will fit nicely into the existing framework provided by some current theory.

On the other hand, theories can be disproved. In fact, this is one of the hallmarks of a scientifically useful theory. It must delineate relationships in such a way that specific predictions may be made which are amenable to empirical test and which are capable of disproof. An explanation which cannot be tested is useless as it provides no means by which it can be properly evaluated. Disproof may take the form of a demonstration that the theory does not adequately account for all the events to which it is pertinent or that it leads to predictions which are inaccurate.

THE PLAN OF THE BOOK

Our brief discussion of the role theory may play in promoting understanding of the phenomena investigated by any scientific discipline should have made the utility of a set of integrated, broadly applicable explanatory principles obvious. From both the scientists' and the students' points of view, the most satisfactory state of affairs would be one in which a relatively small set of assumptions, postulates, and hypotheses exist which provide an adequate way of accounting for a wide variety of social psychological events. In this book we will attempt to create just this sort of framework. The discussion of "what social psychologists do" with which this chapter began provided a sample of the diversity of topic areas into which the field has traditionally been divided. Many critics have lamented the lack of interchange among these subdivisions since the tendency has been to develop theoretical systems which are rather specialized and parochial. Typically, a particular phenomenon or problem is found to be intriguing, a body of research develops in an attempt to fathom its subtleties, and a theory may be generated which provides a good account of the relevant data. Once some satisfactory resolution has been attained, however, investigators have tended to move on to other less-well-explored territory whose mystery piques their interest. This sort of issue or problem-orientation, while leading to very worthwhile and effective understanding of particular problem areas through bursts of intense research activity, has the disadvantage of not stimulating the development of widely applicable theoretical formulations which cut across the traditional subfields. In consequence we have some very useful and well-documented theories having to do with the dynamics of attitude formulation and change, leadership effectiveness, social comparison processes, friendship formation, aggressive activity, and so forth, but relatively few systems which provide ways of integrating these.

Since it is our contention that such an integration is both highly desirable and possible, this book will follow a format unlike that of most social psychology texts. There will not be chapters devoted expressly to each of the several traditional topic areas such as attitude change, group dynamics, interpersonal processes, and the like. Rather, the initial chapters will present a general framework and some data to support its validity drawn from both social psychological research and other fields such as perception, developmental psychology, and general experimental psychology. Thus, some of the early content of the book may, at first glance, seem unusual or out of place in a social psychology text, but its appropriateness should become clear in the subsequent chapters. It will serve both to build the case for the existence of certain psychological processes which we feel are critical to a basic understanding of social psychological phenomena and to describe the nature of the ways in which they operate. Once they have been established we can proceed to show how their functioning manifests itself in a wide variety of types of social behavior. But, again, the framework we develop suggests a particular order in which extant research is most meaningfully discussed which often cuts across the traditional areas. Thus, studies having to do with group dynamics may be presented side by side with attitude change research, rather than in separate, exclusive chapters. Since the interpretation we will make of the implications to be drawn from particular studies may at times differ somewhat from that of those who conducted them, we will, where it seems appropriate, discuss the original interpretation. However, it will be our intent to demonstrate that the analysis we provide is to be preferred in that it serves to account for not only the specific data in question but also is applicable to many other findings in areas to which the originally given interpretation is not applicable. The principle of parsimony which is involved here suggests that the explanation which can successfully encompass the widest variety of data is preferable to perhaps equally valid ways of accounting for some specific body of data which are more limited in their scope. It was pointed out earlier that there are not likely to be many "critical" experiments in social psychology which will yield data which are so unambiguous as to unequivocally establish the superiority of one explanation over another competing one. In view of this, it seems reasonable to give considerable weight to the criterion of parsimony in evaluating alternative explanations.

THE COGNITIVE APPROACH

The title of the book indicates that, of the several very general orientations to social psychology which might be adopted, we have selected one which emphasizes the cognitive activity of the individual in his intercourse with social stimuli. The reader should be aware of the fact that there are alternatives to this very basic question regarding the most appropriate way to approach the study of psychological phenomena. Some of these go so far as to deny that cognitive processes need to be dealt with at all in a scientific psychology. Proponents would argue that we should not concern ourselves with internal, private processes of this sort which they maintain cannot be directly observed or objectively measured and manipulated. Progress toward understanding, they argue, will come by means of intensive investigation of the various relationships between carefully controlled stimuli and the responses associated with them. The arguments developed in support of this position and the cognitive orientation which we favor have become highly sophisticated, subtle, and technical. Thus, to attempt to demonstrate the superiority of one position over the other in a manner that would do complete justice to all the relevant data and the theorizing would involve us in a very long and complicated discussion, much of which would deal with issues only tangentially relevant to social psychology. And, in the final analysis, it may be argued that the differences among the various positions are chiefly a matter of emphasis involving only different experimental methods and interests. It seems more reasonable, then, to simply demonstrate the adequacy and utility of the cognitive orientation by our use of it in dealing with the body of findings that constitute social psychology, and to apprise the reader that rather radically different ways of looking at these data do exist. We, however, agree with Asch when he says, "To limit the investigation to the observation of action alone would be to ignore the paramount fact that the actor is constantly registering in awareness what is happening to him and that this alters his subsequent acts" (1952, p. 68).

Unfortunately, it is somewhat difficult to concisely state what this cognitive approach is and to define just what a cognition is. Scheerer states that cognitive theory deals "with the problem of how man gains information and understanding of the world about him, and how he acts in and upon his environment on the basis of such cognitions" (1954, p. 91). A cognition can be identified as a "centrally mediated process of representing external and internal events" (1954, p. 137). In less technical terms, cognitions are beliefs, thoughts, or items of information which an individual possesses concerning his own internal condition and the nature of the social and physical environment in which he exists. An approach which focuses on cognitive

activity, then, stresses the role which these sorts of perceptual organizations play as mediators between the stimuli which impinge upon the
individual and the response he makes to them. Cognitions are viewed
as an example of what have been called mediating variables in that,
though they may not be directly observed, they are held to shape
and influence in important ways the relationship between an observable stimulus and a measurable response. Their functioning is presumed to intervene between stimulus and response and to be involved
in an important way in determining the meaning which the stimulus
has for the individual, and it is in terms of this meaning that a response
is initiated. Thus there is greater concern with developing an understanding of the nature and operation of internal, cognitive processes
than with a focus on the physical characteristics of the stimuli to which
the individual ultimately responds. It hardly seems necessary to point
out that two persons may interpret identical external events in quite
disparate ways as a function of their different personal histories and
current states. Think of the variety of reactions the long-haired, care-
lessly dressed and manicured street hippie might elicit from a series
of passersby which includes a female, teenage "groupie," a police
officer, an elderly D.A.R. matron, the owner of a local barbershop,
and a bearded graduate student.

THE SCHEMA AS AN ORGANIZING CONCEPT

We have noted in this chapter that all persons, not just the scientists
among us, are engaged in a search for a valid and useful understanding
of the world in which we exist and that there are some basic similarities
in the techniques with which scientists and laymen pursue this goal.
The task for the infant is to create for himself a reasonably orderly
and stable world out of the booming, buzzing, kaleidoscopic and chaotic morass of meaningless stimuli which impinge upon his sensory
receptors. This is no mean task, but, of course, the child typically
has help in the form of protective, supportive, and guidance-giving
adults. Still the infant must make the initial steps pretty much on
his own, as other persons can assist him most directly only after he
has at least developed the ability to recognize them as "things" quan-
titatively different from the cloth that surrounds him or from the slats
in his crib. And their help will be most forceful and efficient only
when he has means of communicating with them in some direct fashion.

From our point of view two assumptions seem necessary to get
the ball rolling. One is that there *are* certain regularities in the infant's
environment; that, in broader terms, there exist more or less lawful
relationships among certain events in the universe. The other is that

the neonate has, or soon develops, the capacity to recognize and respond to such regularities. This is meant to imply only that the sensory apparatus is of a sort which will permit the infant to register or perceive qualities of the stimuli which affect his receptors and that he has some way of storing and later retrieving these impressions. It does not necessarily suggest an innate sensitivity to regularity or a special ability to recognize it. With these not too radical assumptions granted, we can proceed to an analysis of the manner in which persons develop knowledge of the world in which they find themselves, the nature of the information which is likely to be learned, and the ways in which such information operates to influence their behavior, including their interactions with social stimuli.

In broad outline, our basic point is that persons generate relatively abstract and generalizable rules, called schemas, regarding certain regularities in the relationships among events. These schemas may be developed on the basis of direct experience, observation of other persons, and direct communication from others. Whatever their source, once established they serve as a guide to behavior and as a framework which influences the manner in which relevant new information will be assimilated. Since a schema is an abstraction, a general statement detailing the perceived regular co-occurrence of some categorized events, it tends to be relatively permanent and impervious to change even if a few exceptions to it are noted. Though it may initially have been derived from the observation of specific, concrete events, its maintenance no longer depends directly upon them. In the terms used earlier to describe scientific theories, it is conservative, i.e., not subject to rapid change in the face of potentially disconfirming evidence, and, as was pointed out, such conservatism may have considerable adaptive value in the long run. The fact that established schemas influence the way relevant current events will be perceived and interpreted also contributes to their resiliency, as the tendency will be to see events as consistent with them wherever possible.

Although we maintain that persons are not just passive recipients of information but are also actively engaged in an effort to cope with their environment and to develop a valid understanding of it, this does not imply that the schemas which they develop are necessarily conscious and easily verbalizable. If asked to do so, an individual might be able to list in systematic form some of the rules which guide his actions, but this certainly does not mean that he is aware of them in logical, sentence form as they influence his behavior or perceptual activity in a spontaneous situation. For example, a prevalent schema involves the relationship between attraction for other persons and similarity with the characteristics of the persons in question. On the basis of observations of his own and others' behavior, a person may have abstracted a "rule" which suggests a consistent association between the concepts or categories of liking and interpersonal similarity. However, the existence and operation of such a schema does not imply that in each and every occasion where a perception of liking or similarity is involved he will consciously note, "Ah ha, I should like this person since we have so much in common," or, "Since I find this person likeable he must be quite similar to me." He might do so, but the influence the schema may have on his behavior in the situation or on his perception of it in no way depends upon his doing so.

Prior Use of the Schema Concept

The term "silent organization" was used in the 1920s and 1930s to refer to something rather similar in certain of its characteristics to what we have termed a schema. The Gestalt psychologists formulated the concept to refer to a general class of factors with such things as the frame of reference in which judgments of some quality of a stimulus are made, mental "sets," and the generalization of implicit organizing principles from one problem-solving situation to another. In referring to this early work, Scheerer points out that "the common denominator of these silent organizations is that they are not tied to specific individual contents but operate as cognitive structures which have the character of 'typifying schemata,' guiding orientation and action" (1954, p. 110). This description is quite consistent with the manner in which we have conceptualized schemas, but in our usage the term refers to much more than just nonconscious mental sets and frames of reference. An individual may well be aware of the schemas which have been generated in the course of his efforts to abstract some systematic rules about the regularities in his world. Indeed, it is possible to quite consciously invoke or activate a schema as an assist in dealing with some concrete situation which is being faced. For instance, a person upon finding himself in a new work situation thrown together with a number of unfamiliar people might rather self-consciously turn to his schemas relevant to work, meeting new persons, effective behavior in novel surroundings. These might include such schemas as: Persons who talk a great deal are usually leaders, women are easier to get to know than men, an anxiety in a novel situation is lessened by finding some old, familiar elements in it. Self-motivated arousal of such general rules of relationship would perhaps be useful in suggesting successful ways of coping with the situation. On the other hand, it would be highly likely that schemas of this sort would be operative even though they were not intentionally activated by the person, as they can also be brought into play by external factors. A detailed account of the process by which this occurs will come in later chapters, so at this point it is enough to state that stimuli which are associated with some dimension which makes up a part of a schema can serve to activate it. Thus, simply observing that one individual in the work group talks a great deal might arouse the schema mentioned above which relates verbosity and the role of leader. Under these circumstances the individual might not be aware that his attribution of leader status to a given individual was influenced by the operation of the relevant schema.

The term schema has certainly been employed by other psychologists and its use probably began with the British neurologist Sir Henry Head. A portion of his work dealt with bodily posture and muscular coordination. One of the central issues he encountered had to do with the way in which complex bodily movements are integrated. In any such behavior a great many movements must be made in succession and the accuracy of each of them and of the total activity would seem to depend on a very precise record of what had been accomplished by any preceding movements. "For this combined standard, against which all subsequent changes of posture are measured before they enter consciousness," Head "proposed the word 'schema.' " (1920, p. 605). He suggested that they were "organized models of ourselves . . . (which) modify the impressions produced by incoming sensory impulses . . ." (1920, p. 607) and that they were not just static images or memories but were constantly developing in response to incoming sensory experiences.

Bartlett (1932) gave the schema concept a primary role in his theory of memory and referred to it as "an active organization of past reactions or of past experiences. . . . Whenever there is any order or regularity of behaviour, a particular response is possible only because it is related to other similar responses which have been serially organized, yet which operate, not simply as individual members coming one after another, but as a unitary mass" (1932, p. 201). Thus, Bartlett used the term with respect to both cognitive and overt behavioral processes, thus using the term in a more general way than either Head or ourselves. However, Bartlett spoke of an individual's "capacity to turn round upon (his) own schemata and to construct them afresh" and "to go direct to that portion of the organized setting of past responses which is most relevant to the needs of the moment" (1932, p. 206). The latter view much more closely approximates our use of the term.

Numerous other psychologists, including Piaget (1952), Hebb (1949), Lashley (1951), and Allport (1947), have employed the term in one context or another. The common thread in this variety of usages is reference to some sort of internal, integrative process which plays an important part in the determination of behavior and perceptual activity. In the next chapter we will develop in detail our own ideas regarding the specific characteristics of this concept. In order to do this properly it is necessary to draw on material from research in developmental, perceptual, and motivational psychology. Once this is accomplished we can proceed to use this schema as a basis for an integrated presentation of the data and theory which make up the field of social psychology.

References

Allport, G. W.: Scientific models and human morals. *Psychological Review*, 1947, *54*:182–192.

Aronson, E., and Carlsmith, J. M.: Experimentation in social psychology. In G. Lindzey and E. Aronson (Eds.), *Handbook of Social Psychology*, Vol. II, 2nd Edition. Cambridge, Mass., Addison-Wesley, 1968.

Asch, S.: *Social Psychology*. Englewood Cliffs, New Jersey, Prentice-Hall, 1952.

Barber, T. X., and Silver, M. J.: Fact, fiction, and the experimenter bias effect. *Psychological Bulletin Monographs*, 1968, *70*:(6, part 2).

Bartlett, F. C.: *Remembering*. Cambridge, Cambridge University Press, 1932.

Brunswick, E.: *Perception and the Representative Design of Psychological Experiments* (2nd edition). Berkeley, University of California Press, 1956.

Campbell, D. T.: Factors relevant to the validity of experiments in social settings. *Psychological Bulletin*, 1957, *54*:297–312.

Campbell, D. T.: Blind variation and selective retention in creative thought as in other knowledge processes. *Psychological Review*, 1960, *67*:380–400.

Campbell, D. T.: Objectivity and the social locus of scientific knowledge. Draft of Presidential Address to Division 8 of the American Psychological Association, Washington, D.C., September, 1969.

Canon, L.: Relationship of tendencies toward interpersonal manipulation to experimenter bias. *American Psychologist*, 1967, *22*:560.

Ĉapek, M.: Ernst Mach's biological theory of knowledge. *Synthese*, 1968, *18*:171–191.

Carnap, R.: Psychologie in physikalisher Sprache. *Erkenntnis*, 1932, *3*:107–142. Translated in A. J. Ayer (Ed.), *Logical Positivism*. Glencoe, The Free Press, 1959, pp. 165–197.

Feshbach, S., and Feshbach, N.: Influence of the stimulus object upon complementary and supplementary projection of fear. *Journal of Abnormal and Social Psychology*, 1963, *66*:498–502.

Festinger, L., and Maccoby, N.: On resistance to persuasive communications. *Journal of Abnormal and Social Psychology*, 1964, *68*:359–366.

Garner, W. R., Hake, H. W., and Eriksen, C. W.: Operations in and the concept of perception. *Psychological Review*, 1956, *63*:149–159.

Head, H.: *Studies in Neurology*. Vol. 2. London, Oxford University Press, 1920.

Hebb, D. O.: *Organization of Behavior*. New York, John Wiley & Sons, 1949.

Hempel, C. G.: *Philosophy of Natural Science*. Englewood Cliffs, New Jersey, Prentice-Hall, 1966.

Kuhn, T. S.: *The Structure of Scientific Revolutions*. Chicago, University of Chicago Press, 1962.

Lashley, K. S.: The problems of serial order in behavior. In L. A. Jeffress (Ed.), *Cerebral Mechanisms in Behavior: The Hixon Symposium*. New York, Wiley, 1951.

Lefkowitz, M., Blake, R. R., and Mouton, J. S.: Status factors in pedestrian violation of traffic signals. *Journal of Abnormal and Social Psychology*, 1955, *51*:704–706.

Lewin, K.: *Field Theory in Social Science*. New York, Harper and Row, 1951.

Lodge, G. T.: Pilot stature in relation to cockpit size: a hidden factor in Navy jet aircraft accidents. *American Psychologist*, 1963, *17*:468 (Abstract).

Marx, M. H.: The general nature of theory construction. In M. H. Marx (Ed.), *Psychological Theory*. New York, Macmillan, 1951.

Moore, H. T.: Further data concerning sex differences. *Journal of Abnormal and Social Psychology*, 1922, *17*:210–214.

Orne, M. T.: On the social psychology of the psychological experiment: with particular reference to demand characteristics and their implications. *American Psychologist*, 1962, *17*:776–783.

Pfungst, O.: *Clever Hans (the Horse of Mr. von Osten): A Contribution to Experimental, Animal, and Human Psychology.* (Translated by C. L. Rahn) New York, Holt, 1911.

Piaget, J.: *The Origins of Intelligence in Children.* New York, International University Press, 1952.

Polanyi, M.: *Knowing and Being.* London, Routledge and Kegan Paul, Ltd., 1969.

Popper, K.: *The Logic of Scientific Discovery.* New York, Basic Books, 1959.

Rosenberg, M. J.: When dissonance fails: on eliminating evaluation apprehension from attitude measurement. *Journal of Personality and Social Psychology*, 1965, *1*:28–42.

Rosenthal, R.: *Experimenter Effects in Behavioral Research.* New York, Appleton-Century-Crofts, 1966.

Rosenthal, R., and Fode, K. L.: Three experiments in experimenter bias. *Psychological Reports*, 1963, *12*:491–511.

Rosenthal, R., Persinger, G. W., Vikan-Kline, L., and Mulry, R. C.: The role of the research assistant in the mediation of experimenter bias. *Journal of Personality*, 1963, *31*:313–335.

Sarnoff, I., and Zimbardo, P.: Anxiety, fear, and social affiliation. *Journal of Abnormal and Social Psychology*, 1961, *62*:356–363.

Schachter, S.: *The Psychology of Affiliation.* Stanford, Stanford University Press, 1959.

Scheerer, M.: Cognitive theory. In G. Lindzey (Ed.), *Handbook of Social Psychology.* Vol. 1. Cambridge, Addison-Wesley, 1954.

Sechrest, L.: Situational sampling and contrived situations in the assessment of behavior. Unpublished manuscript, Northwestern University, 1965.

Seltiz, C., Jahoda, M., Deutsch, M., and Cook, S. W.: *Research Methods in Social Relations.* 2nd edition. New York, Holt, Rinehart, & Winston, 1959.

Stotland, E.: Experimental social psychology and its neighbors. *Journal of Social Psychology*, 1965, *67*:315–323.

Toulmin, S.: The evolutionary development of natural science. *American Science*, 1967, *55*:456–471.

Webb, E. J., Campbell, D. T., Schwartz, R. D., and Sechrest, L.: *Unobtrusive Measures: Nonreactive Research in the Social Sciences.* Chicago, Rand McNally & Co., 1966.

Wilson, E. B.: *An Introduction to Scientific Research.* New York, McGraw-Hill, 1952.

Wolman, B. B.: *Contemporary Theories and Systems in Psychology.* New York, Harper and Brothers, 1960.

CHAPTER 3

THE ACQUISITION OF SCHEMAS

In the last chapter the fairly obvious point was made that formal scientific disciplines have no monopoly on the interest in organizing, systematizing, and understanding events—each of us is engaged in a life-long process of this sort, a process which seems so "natural" that we are only infrequently aware of engaging in it. Of course, there are many situations in which the goals of learning and understanding are quite explicit, such as those encountered in school or training for a job, but the cliché about not learning the important things in life from books and formal training is quite true. From our daily experience we are constantly developing, testing, modifying, or discarding hypotheses about the nature of the physical and social world, and, on the other side of the coin, these hypotheses influence in important ways the sorts of experiences we have and the manner in which we interpret them. Take, for instance, a situation in which you are just casually rapping over a cup of coffee or a beer with someone whom you have recently met. If the other person and the conversation are interesting it is highly unlikely that you will find yourself being introspective and analytical about the whole thing. You aren't likely to consciously formulate questions such as, "What sort of person is this individual—friendly or unfriendly, open or guarded, higher or lower status than I, similar or dissimilar to me in interests, values, physical characteristics? What sort of interaction are we having—is it pleasant, superficial, lively, personal, or what? What are the important characteristics of the physical setting here—is it brightly lit or intimate, noisy, likely to lead to interruptions by others, comfortable? What does all this information and my past experience in similar circumstances tell me about how I should act, how the other person is likely to behave, and about how we are likely to get along?" Ordinarily you will be much too wrapped up in the content of the conversation you're carrying on to notice that, indeed, questions of this sort are being "asked" and the answers stored and compared with answers to similar questions gleaned from many other such interactions. That is the thesis on which this book will be built. The idea is that general rules and hypotheses—schemas—are being formed on the basis of experience, and that these serve to guide and influence behavior and the meaning we give to the events we perceive.

PERCEPTION AND ATTENTION

If we are to discuss the ways in which people generate ideas about the nature of their environment, it seems clear that a first step must involve some discussion of the manner in which information about it is obtained. Here we will not get into a lengthy exposition of the sensory apparatus itself, as this information, while of very great interest and importance as an area of research, is not particularly relevant to the position which we will develop. Assuming, then, that humans are equipped with a variety of types of sensory receptors which can provide them with information about "what's out there" and about their own internal states, our interest turns to a consideration of one of the critical determinants of what information will actually be processed and analyzed—attention. William James in 1890 noted that "millions of items of the outward order are present to my senses which never properly enter into my experience. Why? Because they have no interest for me. . . . Only those items which I notice shape my mind—without selective interest, experience is an utter chaos. Interest alone gives accent and emphasis, light and shade, background and foreground—intelligible perspective, in a word . . . (Attention) implies withdrawal from some things in order to deal effectively with others. . . ." (1890, p. 403).

The point being made here need not be belabored—it is obvious from a moment's introspection that the perceptual processes *are* selective, that out of the many stimuli which may be impinging upon and affecting our various sensory receptors at any given moment only a relatively small number are actually processed in some manner significant to the person. The term, attention, is used to refer to the ability to react to only some of the information available from the many potential sources that are open to the person. Often this selection seems to be the result of a willful conscious design. In a classroom, we may focus on the speech of the professor and concentrate on following, understanding, and remembering what he is saying. Noises coming from outside the room, the activity of others around us, the pressure of a tight fitting shoe, our own breathing, the hum of the ventilation system, all may fade into the background as we become "absorbed" in this fascinating lecture. It may not often happen, of course; this is a hypothetical example, after all. But what is happening to all those other inputs which have not been selected for attention? Are they simply not processed in any fashion at all? Does our lack of attention to and awareness of them imply that they have no potential for influencing us at all, that we must *decide* to focus on them in order for them to have any genuine impact on us? Evidently not. A perhaps more typical classroom example will serve to make this point. Let's imagine that it's a bright, spring day and a stuffy classroom is just about the last place you'd like to be. As the lecture drones on your attention wanders to an attractive person sitting a few rows away. You may begin to wonder and speculate about what sort of person they really are, how you might get to know them, what a good opening comment might be and soon you're off in a fascinating fantasy world, only vaguely conscious that the professor is still talking, but certainly not aware of his actual words. And then, suddenly, you're rudely returned to the realities of the classroom by the fact that your name has been called. By some misfortune the professor has directed a question to you personally, and you have no idea what the question was, let alone the answer. The point is that there was no decision in the usual sense of the word on your part to direct attention back to the lecturer's comments—some quality of the stimuli to which you were *not* currently attending served to produce a rapid shift of attention back to the lecture. Specifically, in this example, we might assume that the very special meaning and importance which one's own name has was responsible for its ability to attract attention in this dramatic fashion.

Nonattended-to environmental events which are presently stimulating a person's sensory receptors can intrude in the above fashion and bring the person to attend to them. But, paradoxically, how can a person know that a stimulus is "important" enough to deserve or demand attention when he is not attending to that stimulus? The answer obviously must be that these nonattended-to stimuli are undergoing some sort of analysis out of the range of attention. There is no logical reason why some preliminary mechanism cannot exist which conducts an initial analysis of stimuli impinging upon sensory receptors. This rudimentary check could occur quite automatically, screening the inputs so that only those which meet certain criteria proceed through the sensory system to a point at which awareness occurs.

Theories of Selective Attention

A number of theories, based on extensive research, have been propounded to explain how this preliminary screening occurs. We shall not describe the research nor all the theories, but we will present an account developed by Norman (1968), which is an integration of the work of Broadbent (1958), Treisman (1967), and Deutsch and Deutsch (1963). Norman maintained that all the physical stimuli arriving at a sensory receptor are first analyzed by the receptor. This analysis produces a description of the stimulus; or, in more technical language, the analysis extracts from the stimulus a set of values or qualities along certain dimensions. This set of values, which describes the stimulus, is then used by the central nervous system to determine if and where in the person's storehouse of memories, there is something which fits or matches the set of values. In other words, "all sensory signals excite their stored representative in memory" (Norman, 1968, p. 34).

According to Norman, while all of the processes we have just described are occurring, another process is also going on. This second process consists of an analysis of the input which has entered into the central nervous system immediately previously. This analysis reflects our current concerns, our activities, our interests, etc. The analysis establishes a class of events in the outside world deemed to be pertinent to the ongoing analysis. In plainer English, this analysis indicates what sorts of things are relevant to what we are thinking or concerned about. Furthermore, the representatives in memory of these pertinences or relevancies are excited. Thus, this second, more internal process also culminates in the excitation of some representative in memory, just as the more sensory process does. What we then ultimately attend to, notice, etc. is a result of the combination of the two processes, the sensory and internal. All of this, of course, goes on without our being aware of the process. All we are aware of is the ultimate outcome, what we attend to, or notice.

We thus end up with a system that operates very nicely and efficiently, permitting an individual to focus on a manageable portion of his environment. However, this is accomplished without shutting off entirely the possibility that attention will be drawn to generally important stimulus events that have not been a part of the initial focus.

MEMORY PROCESSES

One further aspect of this research and theorizing about attention and the manner in which it functions has important implications for the theoretical orientation which we will develop in this book. All the systems which we have discussed here require a considerable interaction with memory for their operation, and thus we need to discuss briefly what is currently known about memory processes. The most recent theorizing here holds, as did William James in 1890, that there appear to be two memory systems. One, primary memory (cf. Waugh and Norman, 1965), is a small, limited capacity system where temporary storage of current sensory inputs goes on. There is a sharp ceiling on capacity here and new, entering items displace old ones which are then permanently lost. Secondary memory is what we ordinarily refer to when we speak of memory. Here items are more or less permanently stored in a complexly organized and integrated fashion such that they can be retrieved or activated for later use. A great deal of evidence suggests that the organization of the material stored in secondary memory is a critical aspect of its operation and that most of the problems encountered in memorization involve getting the material to be remembered into a form which can be easily integrated into this organized system. The storage of events is, after all, useful only if they can be recalled at the appropriate time, "and the efficient retrieval of stored material requires an involved storage procedure. The proper integration of new material within the old requires the formation of indexes and connecting links in the storage system. If we are to do this organization before material can be efficiently entered into memory, then we require temporary storage buffers to hold incoming sensory material until it can be properly interpreted, for even an efficient retrieval system takes time to operate—sometimes more time than the actual duration of the sensory event" (Norman, 1969, p. 180). Thus, we are led to postulate primary memory as a sort of working storage where newly arrived sensory information is held until it can be properly integrated within the structure of secondary memory. If such an integration is not accomplished there will be no long term storage of the information and it will not be remembered.

To pull these ideas together with our previous discussion of attention, we need only reason that that initial analysis of *all* inputs, which we discussed earlier, involves only the temporary working storage of primary memory. Only those events which are selected for attention by the procedures described earlier will be worked into a state which will permit them to be integrated into secondary, permanent storage. Thus, non-selected items, those not attended to, are not worked over, integrated or stored permanently (Norman, 1966).

The relationship between the organization of material and its integration into secondary memory has important consequences for the schema approach which will be our focus in this book, since schemas are in one sense simply abstract rules or "organizations." It is a common notion that memory is simply a skill which improves with practice, with rote rehearsal, and, while this may be true, it certainly does

not tell the whole story. Unfortunately, psychologists, too, have typically restricted their investigation of memory processes to rote memorization and have only recently become intrigued by the use of mnemonic
devices—"tricks," often personal and idiosyncratic techniques which
can be used to organize material so that it is more easily remembered.
"Memory experts" have always employed them, books on their use
have been written, and they really do work. An anecdote, reported
in a book by Miller, Galanter, and Pribram (1960), illustrates the point
that organizing material in a way that "makes sense," i.e., fits com-
fortably with one's own personalized memory structure, can be a tremendous aid to rapid retention.

One evening we were entertaining a visiting colleague, a social psychologist of broad interests, and our discussion turned to Plans. 'But exactly what
is a Plan?' he asked. 'How can you say that memorization depends on Plans?'
'We'll show you,' we replied. 'Here is a Plan that you can use for memorizing. Remember first that:

> one is a bun,
> two is a shoe,
> three is a tree,
> four is a door,
> five is a hive,
> six are sticks,
> seven is heaven,
> eight is a gate,
> nine is a line, and
> ten is a hen.'

'You know, even though it is only ten-thirty here, my watch says one-thirty.
I'm really tired, and I'm sure I'll ruin your experiment.'
'Don't worry, we have no real stake in it.' We tightened our grip on
his lapel. 'Just relax and remember the rhyme. Now you have part of the
Plan. The second part works like this: when we tell you a word, you must
form a ludicrous or bizarre association with the first word in your list, and
so on with the ten words we recite to you.'
'Really, you know, it'll never work. I'm awfully tired,' he replied.
'Have no fear,' we answered, 'just remember the rhyme and then form the
association. Here are the words:

> 1. ashtray,
> 2. firewood,
> 3. picture,
> 4. cigarette,
> 5. table,
> 6. matchbook,
> 7. glass,
> 8. lamp,
> 9. shoe,
> 10. phonograph.'

The words were read one at a time, and after reading the word, we waited
until he announced that he had the association. It took about five seconds

on the average to form the connection. After the seventh word he said that he was sure the first six were already forgotten. But we persevered.

After one trial through the list, we waited a minute or two so that he could collect himself and ask any questions that came to mind. Then we said, 'What is number eight?'

He stared blankly, and then a smile crossed his face. 'I'll be damned,' he said. 'It's lamp.'

'And what number is cigarette?'

He laughed outright now, and then gave the correct answer.

'And there is no strain,' he said, 'absolutely no sweat.'

We proceeded to demonstrate that he could in fact name every word correctly, and then asked, 'Do you think that memorizing consists of piling up increments of response strength that accumulate as the words are repeated?' The question was lost in his amazement (1960, pp. 134-136).

Of course, the point of this story will be lost unless you spend the few moments required to go through the procedure yourself. It really does work, as you will see.

However, the importance of organization in memory may have other, perhaps less salutary, consequences. As Norman points out, "The requirement that new material be efficiently integrated with old can sometimes cause trouble. Thus, because unfamiliar material is not readily assimilated into memory, we are apt to retrieve what ought to have happened rather than what actually did. When we view a complex event, we may attempt to evaluate it according to previously acquired rules and memories. Thus, we store abstractions and schemata (schemas) rather than images. Much of what we recollect may actually be a re-creation" (1969, p. 181).

Perception and Memory: Constructive Processes

The influence of schemas is not limited to memory systems, however. The available research in the areas of perception, cognition, attention and memory has led a number of theorists to the conclusion that all these processes are most appropriately conceptualized as essentially *constructive* activities. To some, perceptual activity might seem in a rough way analogous to chemical analysis in which unknown substances are carefully, completely and systematically investigated and broken down into all their constituent parts. However, this does not appear to be a satisfactory analogy, as we have attempted to demonstrate in this brief review. Hebb (1949) likens the perceiver instead to a paleontologist who extracts a few critical bone fragments from the background of irrelevant material in which they are embedded and then "reconstructs" the dinosaur in full form which will eventually stand in a museum. Such an approach, based as it is on an examination of recent research and theorizing on topics usually seen as quite distinct from social psychology, is gratifying in its congruence with the schema position which will be developed in this text.

Of course, these schemas, whose effects are so pervasive and important, don't just somehow magically appear. Rather, they develop in a regular and orderly fashion and they have certain characteristics which determine, in part, the way they function. In this chapter, then, the focus will be on the manner in which schemas develop and their nature. Since the processes of acquisition occur in their most clear-cut form in infancy and early childhood, it is on this period of life that we will initially concentrate. You should keep in mind, however, that this concentration on a particular period of life occurs primarily for purposes of exposition—the acquisition of schemas is not confined to any particular time of life.

The previous discussion of attention and memory emphasized the role played by meaning and organization in the functioning of these processes, but meaning and organization are characteristics which can exist only after some minimal amount of experience. After all, there must actually be some past experience before there can be any complex organization of it, and the meaning which events have for an individual presumably also develops on the basis of the quality and nature of his experience with them. When we ask questions about how schemas are acquired in the first place, we are essentially asking questions about how the individual gives meaning and organization to his world. Thus, for the newborn infant, an appeal to the pertinence and meaningfulness of sensory inputs as important determinants of attention is not appropriate. How is attention guided, then? What qualities of stimuli make them interesting and "attention-getting" for the infant?

DETERMINANTS OF ATTENTION IN INFANTS AND CHILDREN

What infants and young children attend to has recently been studied by placing them in semi-naturalistic situations, such as cribs in their own homes which are familiar to them or which have other aspects which are security-giving. Various types of visual stimuli, such as geometrical designs or pictures of people, are presented overhead, sometimes singly, sometimes in pairs, to the infant as he lies on his back in the crib. When stimulus pairs are presented, the infant's eye movements are measured either by direct observation or by means of photoelectronic devices which can detect movements from changes in the amount of light reflected from the eyeball. When somewhat older children are studied, the technique may involve simply instructing the child, for example, to press a lever as long as he desires to watch a given stimulus.

By means of these procedures, it has been found that infants and children prefer to attend to complex or novel stimuli (Frantz, 1966). The complexity of a stimulus refers to the number of distinguishable parts it possesses, the degree of difference among these parts along some qualitative dimension, and the lack of a simple way of integrating the parts involved. Thus, checkerboards are more complex than is a square. Detailed pictures of faces are more complex than ovals with dots for eyes and lines for noses and mouths, and asymmetrical figures are more complex than symmetrical ones. By novelty is meant, for example, an unusual combination of parts of other figures, such as having a horse with a bird's head; or a man with rabbit ears; or it can mean a change from the type of stimuli which the organism has recently been exposed to, such as a shift from horizontal lines to vertical, or a shift from viewing men to viewing women.

Stimulus Change

If we press this distinction between novelty and complexity a little it disappears, so that both can be considered at their root to be instances of change. Obviously, novelty is a matter of change, since novel stimuli must involve a change from what has been experienced in the past by the organism. Complexity is a matter of change on at least two counts. First, as Berlyne (1960) points out, most of the stimuli which an infant or child encounters in his early life are relatively simple. For example, straight lines are more common than jagged ones: tables, cribs, and rooms abound with straight lines. Accordingly, complex objects are novel ones which represent in one fashion or another a change from the infant's typical physical environment. Secondly, complexity may be seen as a matter of change because as the eye scans complex objects, there is more change of stimulation from moment to moment than is the case when simple objects are scanned; there are more parts, more contours and borders, more differences to cause change in stimulation. Compare a hippie to a man in a conservative business suit; or a group of people standing together to a single person. Since the eyes are rarely still for long periods of time, complex objects intrinsically involve change (although change does not necessarily involve complexity).

By viewing both complexity and novelty as involving primarily change in stimulation, it becomes possible to relate the research data on attention to the phenomenon of the orienting reflex, in which Russian psychologists have long been interested (e.g., Sokolov, 1964). They have found that, when a child or an adult is presented with some sudden change of stimulation, such as a sudden, loud noise, or the sudden entrance of a person into a room, there is a total, undifferentiated alerting reaction of the organism, which can most generally be described as a manifestation of an effort on the part of the organism to determine what exactly has happened. Part of this total bodily reaction can be interpreted as a preparation of the organism for further attention and discovery of what is "out there." Who just came into the room? The infant stops what it may have been doing, and becomes highly attentive. This reaction is especially noticeable when children hear sudden loud noises. Thus, the research on the attractions of complexity and novelty and on the orienting reflex can all be construed as reflecting an attentiveness caused by change in the environment.

In short, then, when a child is in a generally familiar setting, changes which occur in any part of that setting tend to cause him to attend to them. It should be emphasized that most studies of reaction to novelty, complexity, and change involve presenting the organism with a combination of *familiar* and unfamiliar stimuli, though not all investigators have stressed this fact in the interpretation of their findings. We feel it to be a critical point. Our argument is that the presence of familiar stimuli is necessary for creating conditions in which novel stimuli will continue to attract attention. This way of looking at the studies of attention in infants and children helps provide an answer to a question that may have occurred to the reader already. It has to do with fear and dread of the strange and unfamiliar. Aren't infants subject to this fear? Don't children act fearful in rooms full of strangers? Aren't they a bit frightened the first day in a new school? How does one predict whether a child will be fearful of or continue to attend to novel stimuli in a situation? The answer we put forth is that some combination of the unchanging and familiar with the new and strange makes the latter attention-drawing. If we look carefully at the studies reported earlier which demonstrated the infant's tendency to direct his attention to novel and complex visual stimuli it seems clear that many of the stimuli in the total situation were "familiar" or unchanging—the crib in which he lay, the blankets and bedding, the manner in which he was handled, and so forth. Some studies, bearing more directly on this issue, have shown, for example, that an unfamiliar stimulus is looked at or visually explored more readily by an infant when a familiar visual stimulus is presented simultaneously right beside it. Accordingly, the child will be less fearful in the room of strangers if the room is in his own house; he probably will be curious about them. He will be curious about the new school if he already knows some of the kids. This issue will be discussed in greater detail in a later section, but for the moment it is important to recognize both the problem involved and the nature of the solution we will develop.

Exploration of the new and novel.

One very important consequence of attention to change is that it greatly enhances the possibilities of the infant's and child's learning about the world. The infant learns by attending to the new and the different, and he seems to have an inborn tendency to do so. Perhaps, in the evolutionary processes, those infants or species which did not have this tendency to attend to the new and changing were "dropped out," since they would on the whole not be very adaptable. Attention to that which is new and changing is almost a necessary condition for survival. Lack of change, in fact, can lead to general apathy and withdrawal. Children who have the capacity to attend to newness and change but who are raised in an unchanging and monotonous environment become developmentally retarded. Children raised in orphanges with highly regularized routines are often found to be intellectually deficient when compared to children raised in families. Some experts maintain that one of the reasons for the poor educational performance of children of poverty-stricken homes is the lack of sufficiently varied stimulation. Animals raised in extremely stimulus-deprived surroundings develop into adult animals quite deficient in attentiveness or the capacity to learn. Of course, animals can be placed into situations of extreme stimulus deprivation, something that seldom occurs in real life with children and which it would be unethical to do experimentally.

Implications of the Tendency to Attend to Change

Now that we have established that in the context of some generally familiar situation, changing, varying, or new stimuli gain attention from infancy on through childhood, two important theoretical implications of this finding require examination. One stems from the very definition of the term "change"—change implies a relationship between what has gone before and what is happening now. A child or infant notices the change in appearance as his father makes "funny faces" or as a resting cat makes a sudden movement. Strange as it might sound, the infant must be seen as having the ability very early in life to react to a relationship—a rather sophisticated early act for such a bubbling, bed-wetting, gurgling, poorly coordinated organism. The relationship involved here is, of course, a very rudimentary one, but the groundwork has been laid for further, more complex developments. Perhaps we have generally underestimated the "intellectual" capacity of infants.

The second implication we wish to draw with regard to the infant's disposition to attend to change is that change implies a change on one or more aspects or dimensions of an entity. The change must be change with regard to shape, size, color, position, intensity, timing, etc., all of which are dimensions of entities. For example, the father's facial features change position as he grimaces. It follows, then, that the infant must have the capacity to perceive in terms of at least rudimentary dimensions. This ability is given simply by the sensory structures where some dimensions are concerned: for example, loudness by the ears; brightness by the eyes; heat and cold by the skin senses. The capacity to perceive in terms of other dimensions may be the result of the brain structure: verticality vs. horizontality; change itself vs. stability, as in the orienting reflex, or in the perception of the degree of familiarity or strangeness of people. Still other dimensions may be learned in ways that will be discussed below.

Dimensions and Positions

The term dimension will be used throughout this text in a quite broad manner. It refers to *any way* in which entities, situations, or objects can vary from one another or can vary over time. Entities, situations, and objects can vary with respect to any of the following, which constitute examples of dimensions: shape, size, degree of hardness, smell, goodness-badness, strength, use, age, degree of activity, sex, type of clothing, kind of activity, type of animal, size of group, amount of conversation, and many others. The point at which any given object falls on such a dimension is called its position on that dimension. On some dimensions the positions which exist are categorical in nature such that a given entity will be located in one of several possible discrete positions or categories identified as belonging to that dimension, such as sex, or type of animal. One very common dimension employed in the classification of objects involves the use to which they may be put. Positions associated with this utility dimension might include categories such as "for eating," "for driving," "for building," "for playing with," "for calling for help," "for teasing," "for talking to," and so forth. On many other dimensions, however, the specifiic positions which objects may hold are distributed in a continuous rather than a discrete fashion along the dimension. Dimensions such as height, weight, hardness, degree of activity, amount of conversation, and age of a person are examples of this type.

Limitations on Information Processing Capacity

The next question to be asked about attention concerns the manner in which it can be distributed. In more concrete terms, this critical question has to do with the number of discrete stimuli or "things" to which an individual can attend at a given moment in time. In

1956, George Miller wrote a classic paper entitled "The magical number seven plus or minus two: some limits on our capacity for processing information." Miller's central point, stated most simply, is that human beings are limited in the amount of information with which they can deal at any given moment. The limitation appears to be mainly an outcome of the structure of the central nervous system, rather than being a function of restrictions imposed by the more peripheral sensory receptors, since the sense organs generally make much more refined discriminations than the brain can process and initiate a reaction to in any given period of time.

Miller (1956) mentions in his paper that he believes there is a "span of perceptual dimensionality." By this he means there is a limit to the number of different dimensions of any object, scene, setting, or display with which an individual can attend and cope. Miller guesses that an adult's span of perceptual dimensionality is probably around 10; he can attend to no more than 10 dimensions at a time because of the structure of his nervous system. For example, if a person were watching a group of people talking to one another, he would probably be able to attend to nine or ten dimensions which might include the following: the ratio between men and women; who was talking; how loud the talk was; whether people seemed calm or excited; whether they seemed friendly or hostile; how much they walked around; who was sitting and who standing; how old the people were; how tall or short they were. A person could not deal with information relevant to more than these listed dimensions. He could not, in our example, also attend to their hair color, manner of dress, topics of conversation, and so on. Of course, he could have attended to some of these dimensions rather than the ones listed earlier. The main point is that ten dimensions, whatever ones they happen to be for a given person in a certain setting, seem to be the limit.

In his discussion of the "span of perceptual dimensionality," Miller does not discuss an issue which might be raised regarding variations in the degree of attention to the various dimensions. For example, an individual may give greater attention to the types of conversation occurring than to the size of the people talking, yet attend in some measure to both. It seems possible that the span of dimensionality might vary with the degree of attention being paid to various dimensions. If an individual is attending very closely to three aspects of a situation, his total span may be less than that of a person who is attending closely to only one. Research on this problem would be useful.

Perceptual Selection

This limited capacity to attend to dimensions leads us to the conclusion that the infant does not perceive any given entity or setting in its totality; that is, in terms of all the dimensions which could be perceived: brightness, color, height, width, number, amount of articulated detail, noisiness, movability, shape, and many others. Only a few of these are attended to at a given moment. The infant, in short, is "selecting" in the sense that he is not responding to the totality of an entity but selecting out a few aspects of it. The infant's selecting involves what have sometimes been called concrete dimensions, dimensions which are tied in closely with the world as directly given to the sensorium.

An objection to the present position might stem from the work of Kagan (1966). He and his associates found a shift with increasing age from what they call a relational way of perceiving to a more analytic way. In the relational mode, two objects are perceived as "going together" because they have some functional relationship with one another. In Kagan's examples, functions such as "wears," "lights," "goes on," "plays" are mentioned. Analytic responses are those in which a child perceives two objects as going together because they have some common attribute: this attribute is abstracted from one object and then the similarity to an attribute abstracted from another is perceived and reported by the subject. Perceiving both apples and oranges to share the attribute "round" would involve this sort of analytic responding. Kagan's own research indicates that the difference between those children who typically make analytic responses and those who give relational responses is in their impulse control and their tendency to study perceived objects closely. Analytic responding is associated with greater control and more patient examination.

However, this distinction does not, in and of itself, necessarily lead to the conclusion that a change in the manner of abstracting is involved. Rather, the observed shift in the manner with which children deal with stimuli appears to involve the willingness or ability to persist at a task long enough to deal with some less obvious aspects of the situation, and thereby make an analytic response. Furthermore, Kagan does not appear to have noticed that all the bonds between the objects in the relational responses appear to be *actions*. Since relational-type responders are presumed to be more impulsive, the actions perceived by these children may simply represent a generalization from the child's own high level of action-orientation. Since children become less impulsive with age, it is not surprising that Kagan finds that they also become more analytic.

Informational Overload and Anxiety

Thus far, two major qualities of the perceptual activity of children have been discussed: the attention to changing or new stimuli and the selection tendency in perception made necessary by the limitation of the number of dimensions to which the child can attend at a given moment. What are the consequences of the fact that both of these tendencies function simultaneously? For example, what can we predict will happen when there is a sharp and clear movement or change of stimulation emanating from some part of the environment which is physically perceivable by the child, but to which he is not at the moment attending? Ten new children suddenly run into the playground in which the child has been playing; if the movement or change is great enough, the child's attention will tend to shift from any object or dimension to which he was originally attending to the area of the movement or change. But, because of the child's limited ability to attend to many dimensions simultaneously, or more generally, because of the child's limited capacity for processing information, he will be pressed to forego his attention to the originally attended-to dimension or object and shift to the changing, attention-getting new one. In short, infants and children are distractable. The child in the playground will stop his game to look at the ten new kids.

But what happens when there is "too much" change, when there are so many aspects of the environment which are markedly changing that the child's attention is being pulled many ways at the same time? Subjectively he may find himself in a kaleidoscope world; the walls are shaking, the floor is vibrating, people are strange and behaving erratically and, consequently, the child's head figuratively spins. Two or three groups of noisy, boisterous children of varying ages, sexes, sizes, and shapes burst into the playground at once. In more technical terms, the child's capacity for processing information is being taxed to its limit, and he is pressed to exceed that limit. There are more attention-demanding changes, occurring along so many different stimulus dimensions, than the child can deal with simultaneously. He is overwhelmed by this blooming, buzzing, confusion, because in this situation he doesn't have the option of simply attending to the maximum number of dimensions of which he is capable and ignoring the rest of the dimensions along which stimulus change is taking place. Each of these changes lays strong and more or less equal claim to the beleaguered child's attention and, in consequence, he cannot efficiently attend to and assimilate the information available from any of them. We assume that any individual, infant or aged, would experience anxiety in such a situation: the celebrity who has questions barraged at him by reporters; a bus passenger plunged into a turbulent city; loud, boisterous conversation bursting in on a TV

"Too much . . . too much."

watcher. Since this assumption is quite important for much that follows, we need to discuss what is meant by anxiety.

This analysis of the reactions to information-overload assumes that one part of the person's system for perceptions of the world has a much greater channel capacity than other parts. The part with the greater capacity is no doubt closer to the sense organs than is the more limited one. Exactly what these two parts are is not certain, but the theoretical models of Treisman and Geffin (1967), Deutsch and Deutsch (1963), and Norman (1966, 1968, 1969) each provide for some sort of sequential system for processing sensory inputs. Thus, each of the theories would suggest a somewhat different way of understanding how the more or less sensitive parts of the system function with respect to each other. Nevertheless, the important point is that they each imply a mechanism for loading a system beyond its capacity. One part of the system simply has more capacity than other parts.

Defining anxiety has been one of the most difficult tasks of psychology, yet one at which psychologists have persisted because the concept is so critical. We will give one definition, but refer the reader to the box on page 91 for a brief critique of other definitions. By anxiety we refer to a state of the person involving physiological arousal and negative affect or feelings. Precise specification of the nature of the various physiological indicators of this state of arousal is difficult for a variety of reasons. The primary obstacle is the fact that the best research available indicates that people vary in the specific ways in which they manifest arousal physiologically. Some change heart rates more than they change blood pressure; others increase their palmar sweating more than they vasoconstrict; and so forth. These individual differences appear to be compounded by the fact that different patterns of arousal seem to occur as a function of the particular situation involved in ill-understood ways. Nevertheless, if we compare groups of people rather than make an attempt to predict the state of the physiology of any particular person, we can capitalize on the fact that most persons manifest a state of arousal by changing in the same direction on a given physiological system, e.g., showing an *increase* in palmar sweating, although there may be individual differences in the magnitude of change. These individual differences may be at the root of another problem, that "different" emotional

Anxiety. Photograph by Irwin Nash.

states, which we can readily distinguish subjectively, such as anxiety as opposed to anger, are not readily distinguishable physiologically. Therefore, researchers sometimes differentiate them on the basis of subjective verbal reports or other forms of communication from subjects about the state of their feelings, such as crying or laughing.

A major alternative definition of anxiety maintains that it is a "residue" of the response to pain. When some stimulus which in the past has preceded pain on one or more occasions is encountered, it will cause the organism to experience anxiety. This definition of anxiety is quite applicable to the situation in which it was developed, but, as Kessen and Mandler (1961) have pointed out, there are many situations in which an individual experiences anxiety without any physical pain having been associated with the eliciting stimului in the past. But, more pointedly, the "pain definition" of anxiety is not really a definition, but a statement of one of the conditions which can give rise to anxiety as a state of the organism. Many other experiences can obviously do so besides pain. Thus, the pain approach is simply not directly relevant to a definition.

Why should a child's being overwhelmed by change, by distraction, so to speak, be assumed to lead to anxiety? Because the overburdening of channel capacity is an instance of a more general type of experience which produces anxiety. This general type involves the realization on the part of an infant, child, or adult that it is unable to engage in some vital activity or to achieve some important goal. The relationship between this experience and anxiety is probably innate. In the present case, the infant is unable to engage in the vital function of processing information because its capacity to do so is overtaxed.

Obviously, anxiety may stem from many sources other than informational overload of the sort just discussed. However, it may well be the case that when examined carefully all circumstances which initiate an anxiety response will be seen to involve the same mediating link which has been emphasized above. That is, a perception that the probability of attaining some important goal is very low may be the common element in all situations which produce anxiety. The issue regarding the source of anxiety has not yet been fully resolved, but considerable data which support this position exist (cf. Stotland, 1969).

The research to test experimentally the proposition that overwhelming the infant with distractions causes anxiety has not and should not be done, for obvious humanitarian reasons. However, an adequate test of the proposition might be developed using infrahuman subjects.

The proposition that overwhelming the organism with change causes anxiety leads us back to a point which we only partially developed. Earlier we argued that fear is the typical response to unfamiliar stimuli when there are no familiar objects or people simultaneously present. As was described on page 81, the presence of familiar objects appears to be associated with the attention-maintaining quality of changing stimuli. When we cited the fear of the totally strange situation, no explanations were given, but some were promised. The first installment of this promise, then, involves the contention that completely strange or changing situations are likely to overburden the organism's capacity to process information and therefore cause anxiety. After the initial attention to the change, the organism may respond by psychological withdrawal from the total situation to escape the anxiety. There are other explanations for the fear of the completely strange situation which will be cited later. These do not contradict the one given here, but simply indicate that the phenomenon is multiply determined.

DEVELOPMENT OF SALIENT DIMENSIONS

If the child can attend only to a limited number of aspects of a situation at a time, to which dimensions will he attend? What are the determinants of this selection? Clearly, the salience of some of the dimensions attended to is innate; for example, a child will attend to sudden, loud noises or the sudden appearance of a person or object; a child will attend to his actions with respect to some object or person. However, the saliency of most of the important dimensions derives from experience. Those innate dimensions on which change occurs more in a child's experience will tend to become more salient as dimensions. A child who perceives a great variation in the warmth of adults will acquire warmth-coldness as a relevant dimension. For a child who experiences a great variety of races of people, the dimension of race will be salient. Further, communications from others also influence the saliency of dimensions. Hearing many discussions of ethnic differences will make such differences salient. Thus, people with different experiences will develop different sets of salient conceptual dimensions, depending on variations of their experience. Obviously, some of these differences are associated with group differences.

Consequences of Differential Attention to Dimensions

Since the child can attend to more than one dimension at a time in any given situation, he may perceive positions or different dimensions simultaneously or very closely in time. He may perceive that the neighbor has a gravelly voice and a beard; that when black people appear on TV his big brother keeps saying, "Damned Negroes"; that when Jim is in a group of children, he talks more than the others; that when he himself asks his mother what "sex" means, she gets angry. If he perceives these positions or dimensions to be associated on a number of occasions he will develop an association or bond between the positions; the position or the dimension will be "linked in his mind." This linkage will tend to lead him to expect to perceive a position on one dimension when he perceives a position on another. When he hears a gravelly voice, he will expect to see the bearded neighbor (and vice versa); when he sees his big brother watching television pictures of black people, he will expect him to say "Damned Negroes. If he sees a group of kids off at a distance with one obviously doing all the talking, he will expect that one to be Jim, and if he reads the word "sex" out loud, he'll expect his mother to become angry. As we shall see in more detail later, these expectations can sometimes influence a person's perception so that he perceives consistently with them. For instance, if the boy with "the big mouth" in the distantly perceived group looks somewhat like Jim, he might be perceived to be Jim.

One implication of the discussion above is that if any person, old or young, perceives a position on one given dimension, his association or the bond "in his head" between that position and a position on another dimension is aroused. Arousal is what leads to the expectation of perceiving something corresponding to the position on the other dimension. The association between beards and gravelly voices is aroused by perceiving the bearded neighbor. In other words, the association or bond can be in either an aroused or a dormant, latent state. When an association of this sort is in a state of arousal, it is the same as a memory that is being recalled, a past situation which is "brought to mind," which is seen in "one's mind's eye." When the bearded neighbor is seen at a lecture, the perceiver might recall his gravelly voice.

Loosely speaking, it is as though the child or older person can simultaneously attend to the present situation and to the present representation of a past situation, the latter being in his imagery or "mind's eye." It is not unreasonable to make the assumption that the memory of more than one past situation can be recalled simultaneously, or be simultaneously in a state of arousal. The child may recall a number of associated past situations at the same time. He may perceive the bearded man talking with a black man and then recall simultaneously the gravelly voice and his brother's saying "Damned Negroes." Clearly, this number is restricted by the limited capacity of the organism to process information. This limitation appears to be reflected in the fact that the individual is not able to attend simultaneously to a present external stimulus situation and to very many aroused memories. We have all noticed that we sometimes shut our eyes or look off into space when we are trying to cope with or think about many memories simultaneously.

CONCEPTUAL DIMENSIONS

Suppose that the child has had some occasions on which he perceived a situation corresponding to one position on a certain dimension, and another occasion in which he has perceived a situation corresponding to another position on the same dimension. Suppose further that memories are aroused, at the same time, of several situations in which the same dimension had been attended to. Our exemplary child might see a bearded and a clean-shaven man talking together, and the perception would tend to arouse his memories of the past occasions in which he saw bearded and clean-shaven men. As Gagné (1962) has pointed out, the individual then is highly likely to perceive that he has used the same dimension in a variety of situations, since the memories of all of them are aroused simultaneously. As a result, he may recognize the dimension *as such*, that is, develop a *concept* of the dimension. This new notion constitutes a radical change from the previous way of perceiving. Up until this point, the dimensions were part and parcel of the perceptual process itself; the child did not step outside of himself and say, "I am attending to beards" or "I am attending to clean-shaven faces." The child just attended unselfconsciously. Now he is, so to speak, taking inventory of his own behavior, not in the formal sense of recording it on some mythical grid, but in the sense of perceiving a similarity in his behavior in a variety of situations. The perceived *similarity* constitutes a conceptual dimension. He now possesses the conceptual dimensions of "beardedness vs. clean-shavedness." Our exemplary child could likewise develop conceptual dimensions such as gravelly vs. smooth voices; angry vs. calm mother or mothers; or talkative vs. quiet boys.

This distinction between the pre-conceptual and the conceptual mode of perception is very much akin to the distinction between concrete and abstract forms of thinking put forth by Goldstein (1939). In one operational measure of this distinction, a person is instructed to sort some blocks into groups in any way he would like to. The blocks vary in size, shape, and color. Some persons can sort blocks into groups according to color, but can do so only by holding two blocks next to each other and comparing them. This is the pre-conceptual or concrete form of behavior. Other people can look at a given block and immediately categorize it and place it in the correct color group without having to compare it directly with the other exemplars of the group. These people, when asked, can indicate that "these are red" and "these are blue." They have the concept of color, with redness or blueness as positions on this conceptual dimension. The first group, who, research indicates, have typically suffered some variety of brain damage, are unable to report the basis of the sorting that they have done. They have no concept of color, although they can use the concrete dimension of color. Similarly, our exemplary child could show that he had the dimension of beardedness by verbally referring to "bearded men"; to "soft voiced men"; or to "calm mothers."

So far we have indicated that the acquisition of conceptual dimensions is an outcome of the child's recalling that he has attended to a perceived or common dimension in a number of situations. There is still another way in which conceptual dimensions can be acquired; it involves the individual's becoming aware of a pattern or configuration among recalled situations. For example, a child may recall a number of instances in which he has tried to get his mother's attention. He may have succeeded on some occasions and failed on others. The child may then perceive this pattern and develop a concept of the irregularity of the behavior of mothers. Further examples of configurationally developed schemas will be given throughout the chapter.

Both routes to the acquisition of conceptual dimensions, via similarity among memories and via configuration, are contingent on the recall of or arousal of memories of previous situations. As indicated above, recall or arousal depends in part on attending to positions on dimensions in a current perceptual situation which are similar to those which have been attended to in the past and thus are contained in the child's repertoire of recallable situations. By this token, children who are presented repeatedly with given sets of dimensions and changes on these dimensions would be expected to develop concepts about them. Indirect evidence supports this expectation, since research has indicated that if an individual has reminders in front of him of previous situations in which he has used a dimension, he is more likely to guess what the dimension is. Thus a child who has a great variety of experiences with a variety of different types of people and who sometimes sees these varied people together, such as at a party, is highly likely to develop conceptual dimensions about people.

Conceptual dimensions may or may not be labelled with language. Most theorists in this area (e.g., Bruner, Oliver and Greenfield, 1966; Vigotsky, 1962) believe that conceptualizing of this sort develops before the child learns to use words, but there is no agreement on whether some conceptual processes continue to function in later childhood and adulthood outside the realm of the verbal, or whether the preverbal conceptual processes become absorbed or replaced by those that have verbal labels. Obviously, this is an exceedingly difficult issue to research.

The Significance of Conceptual Dimensions

Once developed, conceptual dimensions can become part of more complex cognitive structures. By conceptualizing a dimension an individual frees it from its confinement to particular concrete experience. The individual can manipulate a conceptual dimension *as such*, not having to check back to the specific perceptual situations in which it has been used as he does so. This ability is especially important in view of the individual's limited capacity to process information and ideas. Now, instead of having to deal with the many different concrete situations in which a given dimension was attended to, the person need deal only with its conceptualized form. He is then free to relate that conceptual dimension to, say, five or six others to form new associations without overtaxing his capacity. He could, for example, think of putting red together with a given shape of a certain size with a certain material in a given place at a certain time. Our exemplary child can think about how the quiet boys feel listening to Jim without having to think about each of the boys in the group. He might think about black people in general and their relationship to bearded people, without necessarily thinking about the bearded neighbor or about each of the black people he has seen.

This process of manipulating the conceptual dimension freed from its concrete basis is facilitated by the attachment of a label, a word, to the dimension, although labels are not necessary for manipulation to occur. Since the label itself is not tied to the concrete reality and therefore can represent the dimension, manipulating the label is a way of manipulating the conceptualized dimension.

Bruner, Oliver and Greenfield (1966) point out that at a certain developmental stage, words may be seen by the child as a part of the dimension or object. That is, the individual may perceive the word concretely rather than conceptually. However, with experience, the words become detached and can be used to represent a conceptual dimension.

Further, the child can then use the conceptualized dimension in the solution of problems. The necessity for children to have a given conceptualized dimension before they can solve certain problems is reflected in studies of children's responses to relationships. We have already learned that children do respond to relationships from a very early age, but this early ability does not necessarily imply that the child can in any way transfer the consequences of this capacity from one perceptual problem to another. Relationships must be conceptualized first, and can then be used in problem-solving in a variety of circumstances. For example, older children presumably have a concept of relative size; younger children can react to relative size, but they have not yet conceptualized this difference. Thus, children of all ages can rather quickly learn that they will receive a reward if they choose the bigger of two specific boxes. However, older children will tend more than younger ones to generalize this learning to a new pair of boxes, both of which are either much bigger or much smaller than the original ones, especially if the older children can verbalize the dimension of size. This phenomenon of reacting to the relationship between stimuli rather than to their absolute qualities is called transposition. However, since size (or brightness, or loudness) is a relatively simple and salient dimension, even younger children can be induced to conceptualize it if they are given experience with the dimension using a variety of different absolute sizes. If they are presented with a pair of relatively small boxes, one bigger than the other, and also a pair of larger boxes, one bigger than the other, they would then have experienced several different situations in which the size dimension is relevant. Such experience should lead to the conceptualization of this dimension. And research indicates that young children so treated do come to respond to a completely new pair of boxes in terms of their relative size, as would be predicted.

Another instance of the use of conceptualized dimensions for problem solving would be our exemplary child's solving the problem of his mother's irregular reaction to his requests by persisting in making his requests until she breaks down and grants them. He might then apply the same solution in his relations with other "irregular" people he meets, such as teachers, and school bus drivers.

A second consequence of the shift from concrete to conceptual dimensions is that the child can now develop associations between *positions* on given dimensions. This will occur in a manner analogous to, but in a crucial way different from, the development of bonds between changes on directly perceived concrete dimensions discussed earlier in the chapter. These two processes are analogous in that in both cases the bonds develop as the individual experiences instances in which positions on two or more dimensions are correlated, both occurring either simultaneously or successively. For example, after he has developed conceptual dimensions of color, size, and shape, the child may experience a number of small, red, heart-shaped objects. If he recalls several of these experiences simultaneously, he would then perceive that there is an association between certain positions on these dimensions in all of the recalled cases. He would then develop an association between these particular positions on the dimensions involved. Or, after he develops the conceptual dimensions of noise, direction, and change, and after he hears the telephone ring a number of times, he may develop an association among (a) raucousness of noise, (b) starting and stopping, and (c) a given part of the house. Such rudimentary associations between positions on conceptual dimensions we shall term schemas.

To return to our exemplary child for other instances of schemas, suppose he has developed conceptual dimensions of talkativeness-quietness and has also developed a conceptual dimension of groupness, i.e., people standing close to one another rather than being dispersed. If on a number of occasions he perceives people in groups talking a lot and dispersed people not talking to one another, he is likely to recall a number of such occasions simultaneously. He would then develop a schema associating people being in groups with more talking than people being dispersed. Another schema which he might develop concerns race. If he has developed a dimension involving blackness and a dimension of beardedness of men, and if he perceives black men and bearded white men together a number of times, he might develop a schema that "black men and bearded white men are closer to one another than are black men and clean-shaven white ones." (We are assuming that the child has already acquired the dimension of degree of physical closeness.)

The formation of schemas is facilitated by language, since if the individual has labels for the conceptual dimension and for positions on it, it is easier for him to recall the instances in which the association of positions was experienced; recalling the word recalls the situations.

SCHEMA DEVELOPMENT

More technically stated, a schema consists of positions on conceptualized dimensions, and of the relationships among them. A schema may define a class of objects (apples, policemen) since objects can be defined as a specified set of associations between positions or dimensions (apples are roundish, smooth, reddish outside, have stems, and are white inside; policemen are men, dressed in dark blue, with visored caps, badges, guns, clubs, heavy belts, etc.). Or a schema can refer to a class of events, since each event can also be divided in terms of positions on dimensions (thunder is a sudden, very loud, irregular, low pitched sound which occurs outdoors; talking is a movement of the mouth from which articulated words come).

Consequences of the Abstract Nature of Schemas

Schemas differ from the bonds that are established between changes in dimensions attended to, in that the schemas are not immediately tied to the perceived world as the bonds are. This is because the conceptualized dimensions of which schemas consist are themselves not limited to any given object or situation. (The bonds between positions on the concretely perceived dimensions are like the stimulus-stimulus bonds referred to by some theorists. These theorists tend to ignore the development of more abstract dimensions and schemas.)

Thus schemas are open-ended: they can be applied to situations beyond the original ones on which they were developed or used. The child develops the idea not only that the pillows he has experienced are soft, but also that pillows in general are soft. It is not just that mother has been warm and cuddling, but rather that all women are warm and cuddling. Our exemplary child acquired the schema described above as referring to groups in general, not just those he has observed, about black men and bearded men, not just the ones he has seen. Bruner (1964) cites data to show that children who have not yet developed certain conceptual dimensions and schemas have a much harder time generalizing than those who have these dimensions, while there is no difference between these groups in their ability to reproduce a specific concrete situation.

Another consequence of the relative independence of schemas from concrete situations is that a child may have an aroused image of a schema referring to a nonpresent class of objects or people and yet not find that the nonpresence is inconsistent with this image. He can think about black men, bearded men, adult females, etc., without any of them being present. Or he may perceive a situation which violates his schema, and not be as influenced by this contradiction as he would be if a bond were contradicted. After all, if he sees a black man and a bearded white man separately, he can still retain his general schema about their being together, although slightly modified. If our exemplary child observes people shouting at each other from a distance, he is unlikely to change appreciably his schema about groupness and talking. Still another consequence of the relative separation of schemas from concrete situations is that the child will forget many of the particular situations on the basis of which he developed the schemas, and forget many of the details of those specific situations which he does remember. How many of us can remember the first time we noticed water running downhill, or people becoming "red" when angered?

Since schemas are by definition relatively independent of concrete situations as they involve associations between positions on conceptual dimensions, it should be possible to measure the degree to which a child has a schema even in the absence of any concrete example of the objects, entities, or situations to which the schema refers. Certainly, if the child has mastered language skills, it is possible simply to ask him, "If A occurs, will B occur?" Questions of this nature are typically asked of subjects in research on what is called probability learning. In these investigations persons are initially provided with carefully preprogrammed experience having to do with the co-occurrence of a set of stimulus events. In more concrete terms, the onset of a red light might be followed immediately by a green light in 75 per cent of these training trials and by other colored lights in the remaining trials. Ultimately, the subject is asked to predict what will happen in a series of occasions on which a colored light goes on and he can indicate whether he thinks a green, yellow, blue, or other colored light will follow. Children in this sort of experiment exhibit a marked tendency to always predict the occurrence of whatever event most frequently followed the test stimulus in the earlier trials. That is, they do not "probability match" or make predictions that closely follow the actual proportion of times a given event followed another in the early trials. An interesting aspect of this finding is that it tells us that young children's schemas are quite abstract, that they are quite far removed from the concrete reality on the basis of which they developed as they seem not to be influenced by inconsistencies in the situation. This tendency is obviously related to the point made above about schemas tending to be resistant to change. With age, this behavior changes; adults show a much greater tendency to probability match, i.e., to try to take the exception into account.

Schemas and Awareness

The example about probability learning may have given the reader the false impression that schemas are invariably verbalizable, that a person can communicate his schemas explicitly. Just as concepts may or may not have verbal labels attached to them, schemas may or may not. Pre-verbal children obviously have schemas, as do animals. Pre-verbal children can solve simple problems, expect to be fed or cuddled at certain times by certain people, and in many other ways give evidence that they possess schemas. Furthermore, the impression may have been given that schemas, verbalized or not, are conscious phenomena, that a child (or adult) knows that a schema of his is aroused. Again, this is not necessarily the case. Schemas, as Scheerer (1954) pointed out, can take the form of "hidden assumptions," of background assumed but not brought explicitly into awareness. A person may possess the schema of what is technically termed conservation, i.e., that objects retain their volume and weight when they change shape. Yet he may never think about it or recognize it. Of course, it can be "brought to his attention" simply by asking him if he believes thus and so, or by presenting him with a situation which is quite contradictory to the schema. A person may have assumed that Chinese Americans are nonmilitant, but has never said so or thought much about this. However, if he reads of a group of militant Chinese Americans, he might then exclaim, "I always thought of them as being so polite."

Here we face the knotty problem of awareness or consciousness. In much of the research concerned with the question of whether a person is aware of how his behavior is influenced by the setting in which it occurred, the question has been put too simply, because attempts have usually been made to classify people on the basis of some aware/unaware dichotomy. A more useful approach might be couched in terms of degrees of unconsciousness or consciousness. Variation along such a continuum of conscious awareness might be operationalized by such indicators as the spontaneity of verbalizing, as contrasted with the need to probe and remind; the length of time that something remains in awareness, since people sometimes forget what they had been aware of (Verplanck, 1962). The notion of degrees of awareness was implicit even in Freud's writings, as he discusses preconscious memories which are more readily made conscious than unconscious ones.

This discussion of the problem of awareness also implies that the arousal of a schema does not necessarily bring it into full and central conscious awareness, although all schemas of which the person is aware are aroused. The arousal of schemas and of memories which has been discussed above as part of the process of developing concepts and schemas may or may not entail awareness. Many of the processes involved in the development of schemas may go on at the borders of awareness. It would, for example, be the rare and highly precocious child who consciously focused his thought on many examples of conservation before he drew his conclusion that conservation was a general principle; or on many examples of people being close talking more than those dispersed. It is possible that an individual needs to be aware of conceptual dimensions, positions on them, and the instances in which positions were associated in order for him to develop a schema; but no definitive research has yet been done. Perhaps the less aware the individual is of such factors, the greater is the amount of experience with them which is necessary for the development of a schema.

Observed Relationships as a Basis for Schemas

When we first pointed out that the infant and child attend to change, we also indicated that children and even infants can respond to relationships *per se*. In the beginning of life, the relationships that can be attended to are obviously very simple. However, this capacity for responding to relationships is retained and exercised often, so that it becomes quite likely that those dimensions along which such relationships occur in the infant's experience will come to be highly salient. The relationships which are based on the sense modalities which seem innately high in salience, the tactile and proprioceptive modalities, would be most likely to be most prominent for the infant; the infant no doubt early learns relationships having to do with grasping, sucking, dropping, and pulling. Later he will develop conceptual dimensions dealing with the relationships between his own actions and his goals, such as gaining them, or being blocked from them; and of his relationship to others, such as controlling them or being controlled by them. Such conceptual dimensions involving re-lationships could then become part of schemas as they become associated with one another or with conceptual dimensions having to do with objects *per se*. Thus, a given object may come to be schematized as holdable or not, suckable or not, useful for goal attain-ment or not. The fact that schemas often involve relationships of this sort has very great significance, since it means that the child can acquire schemas relating to actions, feelings, processes, events involving other people, and so forth.

Relationships become parts of schemas not only because schemas can be built from dimensions which are themselves relationships. In addition, configurations or patterning of the recalled situations generating the schema may determine some of the relational content of the schema. We have already given an example of relationships as part of a schema: our exemplary child had a schema that his mother responds irregularly to his requests. The relationships in this schema involve the relationship between his requests and his mother's typical response. Another schema entailing relationships is the one this child developed that bearded white men and black men talk to one another. The talking to one another is obviously a dimension of relationships. In another instance, a child may have tried to climb to the top of a tree on several occasions, and in so doing finds that he gets higher and higher on each successive attempt. In recalling these situations, he may perceive the sequential nature of his degree of success, and develop a schema, such as, "I keep going higher and higher on the tree each time I try." The development of such a schema is, of course, dependent on the child's already having acquired a conceptual dimension of sequences in time.

The Degree of Unity of Schemas

Conceptual dimensions which involve relationships serve a special function when they are part of a schema. By their very nature, they tie the other parts of the schema together; they describe the relationships among the positions on the various dimensions. Furthermore, schemas can vary in terms of the number of conceptual dimensions of relationships which tie their various other parts together. For instance, one schema might be that "Dogs chase cats," in which there is only one dimension of relationship, chase. Another person might have a schema "Dogs chase, bark at, and bite cats," in which there are three relationships. The number of relationships among the parts of a schema will be termed its degree of unity (cf. Lewin, 1951; Zajonc, 1954).

As in the case of the development of conceptual dimensions, schemas are more likely to be acquired by a child if there are reminders of his previous experiences present to arouse memories of these experiences. A child who encounters a series of somewhat similar environments is more likely to develop a schema about those environments than a child who does not.

Higher Order Schemas

Let us stop and take an overall look at the child we have "created" through our presentation. He is a child who has the capacity to develop concepts by a process in which prior experiences which are in some fashion similar to a current stimulus situation are recalled, the dimensions common to all of them are observed, and these common dimensions are reified into a conceptual dimension which is somewhat independent of the concrete reality on the basis of which it was formed. By experiencing repeated combinations of correlated positions on the conceptual dimensions, he develops schemas, or associations between various positions on a number of conceptual dimensions. Notice that this process is predicated on the child's having encountered several instances of a given type of experience and then being able to recall these instances.

An additional and critical point is that this process can then be reapplied to the very schemas which emerge from the experiencing of correlated positions on conceptual dimensions. That is, an individual may recall a number of schemas themselves rather than just positions on dimensions, and then develop a still higher order of schemas based on the commonalities among the recalled schemas (cf. Gagné, 1962; Haygood and Bourne, 1965). When an individual develops a higher order of schema, the schemas from which it emerges function much the way that memories of instances of associations between positions on conceptual dimensions do when the schemas themselves were acquired. That is, the various schemas need to be in a state of arousal simultaneously. This simultaneous arousal can stem from a variety of sources, as we shall see later, but for present purposes we can say that this arousal can result from the person's attending to some event or entity which corresponds to positions on the conceptual dimension of the schemas.

This process can be seen with respect to our exemplary child's schema about one boy's talking much more than others in his group. Suppose that every day on his way to school this child also observed a group of men standing together, one of whom talked much more than the others. The group might have been a foreman and a work crew on a construction job. The child would then develop a schema about this group. This schema would not just refer to a series of distinct instances in which the foreman talked to his men, but to the abstraction, "In that group, one man always talks more than the others." Suppose that later the child had observed a ladies' bridge club in his home, in which one of the number always talked more; need we say he would acquire a schema, "One lady in this bridge club always talks more than the others." However, after he has acquired all of these individual schemas, he happens to observe one of the groups, such as the one involving the foreman and his workers. This perception would be likely to arouse not only the schema about the particular group observed, but also the schema concerning the groups of children with one talkative member, and the one having to do with the ladies' bridge club. These other two schemas would be aroused because they share

Thinking: developing a higher order of schema.
Photograph by Irwin Nash.

with the schema about the foreman his positions on such conceptual dimensions as groupness, the talkativeness of one member and the quietness of the other members. Thus, the child will have aroused all three of the schemas simultaneously. This simultaneous arousal then can lead to the development of another schema based on these three schemas. This new schema would be, "Whenever there are groups of people together, one person does all the talking." This new schema is called a higher order schema because it is based on and incorporates other schemas.

Notice several aspects of this example. The higher order schema (H.O.S.) is more likely to develop if the individual can recall, i.e., have aroused, the other schemas which could potentially form the H.O.S., just as recall helps to form conceptual dimensions and the original three lower order schemas (L.O.S.). Thus, if the individual has some reminder of the other schemas, such as a symbol or word, like "group," "talkativeness," or "quietness," it is more likely that they will be aroused. Language facilitates the emergence of H.O.S.s; but it is not necessary for this emergence. Any sort of reminder, such as appearance of a group, could do also.

Another aspect of the example is that the H.O.S.s consisted of the positions on the conceptual dimensions common to all of the "group-talkativeness" schemas; i.e., their being groups, their having one person talk more, etc. Other distinctive characteristics of the individual members are ignored in the H.O.S. The general point here is that H.O.S.s tend to be more general, and less detailed, than L.O.S.s.

Also note that the L.O.S.s corresponding to the various groups function now as units, as totalities, with respect to the emergence of the H.O.S. The person does not need to be attending to every conceptual dimension which goes into the schemas of the particular non-present groups in order to develop the H.O.S. He does not have to attend to its defining color, its size, or any other distinguishing characteristic. Each of the L.O.S.s is taken as a unit when it is being aroused at the same time as other group-talkativeness schemas. The ignoring of the details of each of the group schemas is obviously an outgrowth of the limitation of the individual's cognitive capacity. The ability of people to recall total units has been illustrated in laboratory studies. Asch, Ceraso, and Heimer (1960) had people recall pairs of objects which had previously been presented to them. These pairs differed in the degree to which they constituted a perceptual unit; that is, in the degree to which the members of the pair were bound to one another. One member of what would be a highly unified pair of geometrical figures, for example, might surround the other; or the two figures might be adjacent to one another. Subjects were better able to recall highly unified pairs than those which were less unified. Presumably, the L.O.S. constituted by the unified pairs was recalled as a totality, rather than in terms of its parts. Since recall is one basis for the acquisition of H.O.S.s, recalled units can become parts of an H.O.S. The L.O.S., *as a totality*, can be considered to function for the H.O.S. in a manner parallel to the way a position on a conceptual dimension does for an L.O.S.; that is, the H.O.S. includes the lower order schema of "One boy in a group talks more than others" and this schema is part of the total higher order schema of "When people are in a group, one person does all the talking." Thus, H.O.S.s can be built up out of previously developed L.O.S.s.

The development of the H.O.S. of groups and talkativeness illustrates only one of the two ways in which H.O.S.s can develop. Just as in the case of the development of L.O.S.s and of conceptual dimensions, the patterning or configuration of L.O.S.s can generate a conceptual dimension for an H.O.S. For example, suppose that a child observes some very brutal fist fights between the bigger boys on his block. He develops a schema, "Big boys fight hard." Later he happens to visit another nearby neighborhood and finds that the fights are not as rough, and develops a schema about "that neighborhood" and its fights. Still later, he visits still another, even more distant neighborhood and sees that fights between big boys are more verbal than physical; he develops an appropriate schema. As a consequence of his acquisition of all of these schemas, he may then develop an H.O.S., "The closer you are to my neighborhood, the tougher the fighting."

The process of developing H.O.S.s then can become circular, feeding on itself, leading to the development of more and higher order schemas. The more schemas the child develops, the more opportunities there are for him to develop still more higher level schemas, and those higher level schemas make even more schemas possible. If the child has verbal labels for some schemas, this upward spiraling is enhanced, since the label makes it easier to cognitively manipulate the schemas by simply manipulating the label. However, the reader should not get the impression that we are suggesting that all children are budding "Einsteins" who are trying to integrate all physics into one system. There are definite restraints on this tendency to develop higher order, more all-encompassing schemas, as we shall shortly see.

Each high level schema is based on several lower ones, and the higher level schemas are more abstract, more general, than the lower level ones—thus they can be applied to and are relevant to a wider variety of empirical situations. In fact, the relative abstractness of the concepts involved in the schema can provide an index of its position in a hierarchy of schemas.

One frequently studied higher level schema which we briefly mentioned earlier is termed conservation. It involves the notion that objects can change shape and yet retain the same volume and weight. This abstract schema is derived from such lower level schemas as "water retains its volume when molded into new shapes by new containers." Even these lower level schemas are acquired after the observation of many instances. Younger children often indicate that they believe that an amount of water is greater when it is in a tall narrow glass than when this amount is poured into a shorter, wider one. The necessity for building a higher order schema, such as conservation, from lower order ones, such as in the example just given, is strongly indicated by the general failure of efforts to train children to acquire the conservation schema in a relatively brief, e.g., one hour, session. The children need to acquire the lower order schemas first and only then can they move on to the higher one. Researchers in this area have thus come to the conclusion that it is extremely difficult to get a child to acquire a higher schema unless he is "ready," i.e. has the prerequisite L.O.S.s in his repertoire already.

The difficulty of getting children to form new higher level schemas unless they are ready contrasts sharply with the ease of getting children to "learn" concepts in the so-called concept learning study. In these investigations the subject is given a series of exemplars of a concept, sometimes with negative examples as well. His problem is then to learn to distinguish exemplars from non-exemplars of the concept. The concept which the subject is to "learn" might, for example, be black triangle, and the child would be given several exemplars which differ in size. In addition he might be shown white triangles and black squares. After each presentation of one of these stimuli, he is typically asked to guess whether it is a positive or negative exemplar and is then told whether his guess was right or wrong. This process is repeated either a fixed number of times or until he masters the concept. The reason for the great discrepancy between the ease of learning in these concept learning studies and the effort needed to train children to higher levels of schemas is that in the former studies, it is assumed, and is generally true, that the children already possess the conceptual dimensions, such as blackness or triangularity. The child's task is simply to solve the problem of which of his many conceptual dimensions is applicable in the research setting and how they are associated to form a schema. In order to solve these problems, he needs to use the appropriate dimension, but, of course, in order to do so he also must have a previously developed relevant conceptual dimension. By having the latter, he can then apply this concept to new situations to solve problems without excessive difficulty.

Restraints on the Development of Schemas

If the development of conceptual dimensions and lower order schemas leads to the development of higher order schemas, which in turn can lead to the development of still higher level schemas, where does this cyclical race end? Or does it end? As pointed out above, the process must end, even for an Einstein. The child does not intrude upon the adult world as a precocious spouter of astrophysical systems. So we must ask, what are the determinants of the level of schemas a child (or adult) reaches? To answer this question, we must turn to speculation, but a number of possibilities seem plausible. First, an individual without a wide variety of experience is unlikely to develop a wide variety of conceptual dimensions. With few dimensions, he can develop fewer schemas than someone with many. In short, the sheer requisite raw material may be missing in some cases. Second, developing higher level schemas is contingent, in part, on the perception of some similarity of the concepts in a number of different schemas. Unless such similarity is noted, still higher order schemas may not emerge. It appears plausible to assume that such similarities become more intellectually difficult to perceive as they become more abstract. Perhaps only the poet or the mathematician can react to the similarity between music and mathematics.

Reactions to Informational Overload

A child who is pressed to attend to or process an amount of information close to the limits of his "channel capacity" for coping with it will experience anxiety; and no doubt all children have had at least some experience of feeling overwhelmed by a complex and changing world. The crucial factor is that the child can perceive his own experiences in which his limited information processing capacity, an overload of informational input, and anxiety have occurred together. For instance, a child may be taken to a new neighborhood which is quite different from his own and feel frightened and overwhelmed by all the new things he sees. The child can therefore develop conceptual dimensions which refer to anxiety and excessive information. Obviously, the child does not symbolize these concepts with such terms as anxiety, but it is not necessary that he do so. If he recalls a number of situations in which stimulus overload and anxiety occurred and a number in which low informational input was associated with lack of anxiety, the contrast between the situations provides the raw material out of which may develop schemas about the relationship between the anxiety and excessive information.

So far, our approach has been parsimonious in that we have not had to add to it basically to account for the fact that children learn that certain situations cause anxiety. Let us go on to make one simple, almost truistic assumption, namely, that people are motivated to act to escape and avoid anxiety-arousing situations. Thus, if the child perceives that he is about to encounter a situation which will involve a potentially overwhelming amount of information, he would also expect to be anxious, and would act to avoid that situation, or cope with it in some way. The child may try to get out of going on a trip to a strange new neighborhood. In many instances the child will be unable to avoid such situations; his parents or life experiences in general may not permit him to "stay home." He might be taken for a ride in the car where the strange and changing scene is unavoidable. Perhaps his mother cannot abandon him at home while she goes to the supermarket. He must develop other ways of coping with this source of anxiety. Our discussion has already suggested several ways in which the child might respond in his efforts to deal with such circumstances.

Most simply, the child may learn to direct its attention only to a part of the environment at a time. This may involve the obvious actions of directing his head and eyes in certain ways so as to avoid pressures to attend to too many aspects of the environment. The child may learn to selectively attend; this learning may result from his observing that he is less likely to be overwhelmed when, for reasons of physical inability or interest in one aspect of the environment, he does not move his head and eyes very much. His memories of such occasions may form a configuration or pattern with memories of occasions on which he did shift his gaze, thus leading to a schema of the relationship between selective attention and low anxiety. Perhaps this process of self-direction of attention is the root of the process of selective attention in adults in which the individual avoids attending to information which could cause him anxiety, even when this anxiety is caused by factors other than overwhelming inputs of information. The individual may develop a schema in which selective attention or inattention reduces anxiety and then apply it to a variety of situations in which anxiety might threaten to develop. Munsinger and Kessen (1966b) found that young children, when faced with a complex stimulus, avoid the potential overload of information by the simple procedure of viewing only parts of the total stimulus at a time. Later in life, they may turn off the television when the news is too complicated or too extensive, or just glance over the headlines in the newspaper.

Of course, not all children will learn to avoid anxiety by means of selective attention to the same degree, just as not all adults turn off news broadcasts. Some of the determinants of the degree to which they are likely to learn such a procedure were implied in the previous paragraph: the number of times the child encounters situations in which he might be overwhelmed by stimulus inputs; the number of occasions on which he does not shift his gaze to new and attention-demanding stimuli because of lack of ability or greater interest in some other activity; the number of times his attempts to selectively attend are successful in avoiding anxiety because his self-restricted perceptual environment is not intruded upon by forces beyond his limited control. Notice that each of the factors just cited was introduced by the phrase "the number of. . . ." The reason for this is simply that the greater the number of different occasions on which the raw materials from which schemas are built are encountered, the more likely the child is to develop the relevant schemas.

A second way in which the child can avoid being overwhelmed by the demands on his attention is an outgrowth of the child's developing schemas. As pointed out in the section on schemas, they are relatively independent of the specific details of the situations from which they were developed. By the same token, they are relatively independent of the concrete details of situations in which they are applied. The child may notice a visored cap and badge being worn by a person and say, "That is a policeman," and not have to specifically attend to the stripes and insignia on his arm, the color of his uniform, or his pistol. Once he categorizes that person as a policeman, the details insofar as he has learned them are implied. In other words, by developing schemas and by categorizing objects according to them, the child can cope with more information because some of it is subsumed under some schema, is part of it, or is implied by it. Miller (1956) noted this process and termed it "subitizing." He found that the individual could handle far more information by organizing each item under what we term schemas. The individual deals with the schema *per se* at any given moment, so that he can attend to, say, seven schemas; but each schema contains much information and many details. Thus, the total amount of information the individual can deal with is far greater when he has relevant schemas at hand than when he lacks them. The individual is less likely to experience anxiety if he has schemas under which to subsume his experiences than if he does not. The child is less likely to experience anxiety on the first day of school if he already has schemas about, say, schoolteachers, than if he does not.

The child will develop a high level schema about the relationship between having appropriate schemas and lack of anxiety. This schema can lead to the child's being motivated to acquire schemas, thus adding to and elaborating upon his so-called curiosity motivation. He may then read more, listen more, ask more questions about, say, firemen, astronauts, and politicians.

Schemas and Predictability

The relationship between having schemas and low anxiety can also influence the child's evaluations of certain entities. This occurs when an individual develops schemas about a strange situation, thereby decreasing his anxiety about it. He then should come to evaluate more positively those aspects of the situation which arouse the newly acquired relevant schemas which enable him to make successful predictions about the total situation. Crandall (1967) had adult subjects rate pairs of nonsense syllables for their "goodness-badness," "pleasantness-unpleasantness," etc. The first syllable of each pair, which had, in Crandall's terms, predictive value, was more positively evaluated than the second or nonpredictive syllable. Crandall checked to determine whether this effect could be simply the result of a given syllable's having been first in the pair, regardless of its value for predicting the second one. This check consisted of having subjects also rate syllables which were the first ones in pairs, but which were followed by different second syllables in different trials, so that these first syllables could not be used for predictive purposes. The subjects preferred the predictive first syllables to the non-predictive ones. Thus, a child may say, "I like to play with Joey—I know what to expect from him." Or an adult may say, "I don't agree with what he thinks but at least I know where I stand with him."

Not only are stimuli which arouse schemas and thereby facilitate prediction evaluated positively, but also situations in which stimuli lose their predictive value are anxiety-arousing, and entities associated with this state of affairs are devalued. Carlsmith and Aronson (1965) led adult subjects to expect that a liquid solution they were about to taste was either bitter or sweet. When these expectations were disconfirmed, the solutions were judged to be more unpleasant; bitter solutions were rated as more bitter; sweet solutions were rated as less sweet. Furthermore, if an individual is in a situation in which he can make no predictions, he will find this less pleasant than one in which stimuli occur in a predictable order. Byrne and Clore (1967) presented adults with a ten-minute-long series of pictures in a random, meaningless order, i.e., one in which there was no basis for predicting any subsequent picture. The scenes included pictures of cannibals cooking a missionary, an aerial view of a toy battleship, a talking horse, a flushing toilet, a chess game played with cosmetic bottles, and others. The subjects' feelings after viewing these pictures were compared with those of subjects who viewed a documentary film entitled "Life in Morocco" or who viewed a film depicting the gruesome details of a cataract operation in full color. The subjects who viewed the latter two, or predictable films, felt considerably better than those who viewed the randomly ordered scenes. Notice that the film of the operation was probably as gory as any of the scenes in the random film. This research tells us something about our reactions to the kaleidoscopic tumult of news in a fast-changing world—which may often seem like Byrne and Clore's random order.

Positive Evaluation of the Familiar

An individual is more likely to have developed schemas relevant to familiar entities or situations. It has been found that just allowing a person to become familiar with a situation enhances his subsequently measured ability to make distinctions between parts of it (Epstein, 1967). While he is becoming familiar with the situation, he is obviously developing low order schemas which he can then employ later in solving problems about it, such as the problem of distinguishing parts of it. However, research has not yet unequivocally established that verbal labels for parts of the situation enhance this process of developing schemas and then subsequently making accurate discriminations (Epstein, 1967). In any case, the child tends to like the familiar more than the unfamiliar. Need Linus's blanket be cited? Every parent knows the intensity of fear some children have of strange situations. Research has indicated that infants prefer pictures of faces in which the features are in the usual arrangement to those in which the features are scrambled.

This positive evaluation of the familiar that develops in childhood continues to manifest itself in adulthood. Repeated exposures to pieces of music (Krugman, 1943), geometric figures (Conners, 1964), and nonsense syllables (Johnson, Thomson, and Frincke, 1960; Becknell, Wilson, and Baird, 1963; Zajonc, 1968) lead adults to evaluate them more positively as they become more familiar. This consequence of repeated experience is greatest when the individual has both the capacity and the opportunity to profit from his experience by developing new schemas regarding the entity involved. Munsinger and his associates have demonstrated this in a series of studies (Munsinger and Kessen, 1964; Munsinger and Kessen, 1966a; Munsinger and Kessen, 1966b; Munsinger, Kessen, and Kessen, 1964; Munsinger and Weir, 1967). They found that repeated exposure to geometric figures of varying complexity tended to increase preference for them, with the least increase occurring among the simplest figures. There was little in the way of new schemas which could be developed where the latter figures were concerned. On the other hand, the maximal increase in preference occurred with figures of intermediate complexity which were just too complex to be dealt with in terms of the subjects' available schemas, but which were not so complex and

Satisfaction amid favorite familiar surroundings.

unfamiliar that the person would be unable to develop schemas adequate to cope with them.

Perhaps some of the feelings of nostalgia we have all experienced, of liking for the "good old gang," even love of country, may have some of their roots in the preference for the familiar. The difficulty of changing ideas, group affiliations, ways of doing things, etc. may also simply stem from a "love of the familiar."

Curiosity and Familiarity

If a child encounters an unfamiliar situation or one for which he has no relevant schemas, he can react to the resultant anxiety in one of three ways. He can flee, which he sometimes does; he can attempt to develop schemas about the strange and unfamiliar, and is likely to do so, especially if some other part of the situation is familiar and safe; or, he can attempt to discover that the apparently unfamiliar was really the familiar with some not-very-important changes. If he takes either of the latter two alternatives, he will appear to be curious, to explore, to be interested in the new. These patterns of behavior may thus be seen as efforts to transform the unfamiliar into the familiar, whether by assimilation to previous schemas or by the development of new ones. A good example of this sort of situation would be given by a young child's first trip to a new classroom. He may continually ask the adult who accompanies him, "Who's that?" By being given a name for somebody new, he may be able to understand it as an example of a schema he already possesses; for example, if the new boy is named Joey, and the child already knows a Joey, he has at least the rudiments of a schema about Joeys. The reduction in anxiety when this happens may even cause him to be joyful, feeling delighted at finding the old in the new (Kagan, 1967). Or, learning that the new boy has an entirely new name like "Blue" may facilitate the development of a relevant new schema. This might result from the child's having developed a higher order schema to the effect that names are associated with classes or categories of objects. Therefore, giving someone a name would at least bring up for the child the possibility of developing a schema corresponding to the general impression about the new boy. Thus, the child on his first visit to a new school and on his first encounter with the teacher will be put somewhat at ease by his father's slowly saying, "This is Miss Wooldridge."

Even without the assistance of having a name suggested for the new, a child may develop a schema to correspond to it, and may find great satisfaction in so doing, since he now has developed an additional intellectual tool with which to bring order to his universe.

We indicated above that the child might not engage in these constructive processes of developing new schemas or perceiving the new as a variation of the old, but rather may flee, either physically or psychologically, from the unfamiliar. What, then, are the determinants of the manner in which the child will react to unfamiliar settings? A tentative answer parallels the one given in the opening pages of this chapter in which it was pointed out that children continue to attend to change and newness when in a situation which has many familiar elements, in addition to the new one. Thus, we would predict that the child will be more curious and inquisitive when a familiar parent or other adult, or familiar toy or blanket is close at hand. Arsenian (1943) observed that children are less likely to cry in new situations if they are accompanied by their parents. When adults visit a new strange country, they may feel more curious and adventuresome if they are accompanied by a spouse or a friend. However, a more complete answer to this very important question can be given only after further discussion of other processes and will be introduced in subsequent chapters.

The reader may be a bit puzzled by the apparent contradiction between the existence of positive feelings toward the familiar and the existence of curiosity motivation. However, a close examination reveals that the positive evaluation of the old is the basis for curiosity motivation. That is, the child explores in order to make the new into the old. Furthermore the reaction to the old is an evaluation, a feeling, a "consummatory" state, while the reaction to the new is an act of attention, of moving toward, either psychologically or physically. What the child moves toward may not be the same as what the child evaluates most highly. Likewise, Americans who would like to visit Communist China may nevertheless disapprove of that nation and its politics.

The source of the motivation to attend selectively, to acquire new concepts and schemas, to find that the "new" is really the "old" in disguise, has been explained so far in terms of these activities' enabling the child to avoid being overwhelmed with information, of having his attention divided and subdivided to such an extent that his ability to cope with the informational input is surpassed. However, this motivation has other roots as well. To see them, all that is necessary is to imagine a world in which one's every action has an unpredictable consequence. About all one could safely predict about the consequences of an action would be that they probably would not be the same as those that had followed the action on previous occasions. Just try to conceive of having a car in which the brake pedal sometimes controlled the gas, and the gas pedal sometimes put the brake on; or of the amount of sleep you would get during the night if your only alarm clock worked correctly only about half the time; or if you found that your votes in elections were sometimes counted and some-

A familiar hand helps face the new.

times not (as has happened). It is obvious that adaptation to the world requires at least some minimal predictability of the consequences of our actions.

Some of the child's actions elicit dependable, predictable consequences, while others do not. Shaking a rattle, dropping a ball, hitting a table with a spoon, turning a knob, all have highly predictable consequences. On the other hand, calling Mother, trying to pick up certain objects, crying, throwing a ball, or attempting to catch it, do not have uniform consequences. Further, the child must frequently observe that actions, or entities which can be acted upon, which involve predictable consequences are easier to adapt to than are entities or actions which do not. Actions with predictable consequences lead to fewer frustrations and a higher probability of goal attainment. Thus the child is highly likely to develop a schema that situations in which actions have predictable consequences are easier to adapt to than are those with unpredictable ones. In fact, the child may even develop a schema that anxiety is associated with situations in which the consequences of actions are unpredictable. This schema may underlie some of the anxiety adults feel when in the presence of mental patients.

In addition, the child no doubt acquires a schema to the effect that in those situations for which he has relevant schemas, he is able to predict the consequences of his actions. Since such situations are less likely to be associated with anxiety, the child will have an additional reason for positively valuing the familiar and for negatively valuing the unfamiliar. This motivation adds to the basis for positively valuing the familiar. Obviously, some politicians count on this reaction.

As in the case of motivation based on coping with informational input, motivation based on the predictability of consequences of actions can lead to exploration and curiosity about the world. Since the child has the schema that actions with predictable consequences lead to goal attainment, he will be motivated to learn more and more about the world so as to be able to attain more goals. The development of exploration and curiosity behaviors as a result of this process is, of course, predicated on the child's having developed schemas not only about present goal attainment, but about future attainment as well. The child may gradually come to acquire a schema that future goal attainment is significant, and that learning more and more about the world will enhance such future attainment.

The child will then seek out the new, the strange, the unfamiliar. New toys, puzzles, places, things become attractive as the child seeks to develop schemas about them, to make them familiar. This active seeking out of the new involves more than a rather passive attempt simply to learn about new aspects of the environment that happen to be present. This action-based source of exploratory motivation can involve an active search for the new. In contrast, the motivation to turn the unfamiliar into the familiar which was based on the limited capacity to process information leads the child to react in a somewhat passive way; that is, he seeks to understand a given present situation, but does not attempt to bring into the present those entities which are only dimly perceived.

The next step in this presentation follows from the principle of the previous steps. The child develops schemas about the process of developing schemas. In Harlow's terms (1949) he has learned how to learn. As he observes the ways in which he develops new schemas, the child develops higher level schemas about tactics of exploration or ways of solving problems. He might, for example, learn that solutions to problems of a given type are most efficiently attained by working on a small part of the total problem at a time, although the nature of the specific part may vary from problem to problem. Or he may learn that withdrawing from active work on a given type of problem for a period of time facilitates its solution. The schemas he develops thus rise above any given problem situation and involve what is sometimes called "nonspecific learning" or transfer. Still higher level schemas may develop, such as "problems can be solved" or "persistence pays off." Or, in some cases, just the opposite of these schemas may be acquired. The child may develop additional motivation to acquire schemas about how to solve problems once it becomes apparent that they do indeed facilitate goal attainment and assist him in his efforts to cope adequately with his environment. The child may not only explore but explore ways of exploring; and so on.

Motivational Arousal of Schemas

Without having made it explicit, we have from time to time made an assumption in this section on motivation that probably appeared so natural that the reader may not have noticed it. This assumption is that an individual's motives can arouse a schema. For instance, we have assumed that if an individual is faced with the strange and new, and therefore becomes a bit anxious, his motivation to reduce his anxiety arouses an H.O.S. regarding the formation of schemas about the new. In another part of our discussion we similarly assumed that if an individual is faced with a problem which demands a solution, schemas relevant to problem solution would be aroused. This motivational arousal of a schema may be just a special case of a process which has already been discussed whereby a schema is aroused because the individual attends to some event which corresponds to part of the schema. A higher order schema having to do with problem-solving approaches is highly likely to include as one of its elements a conceptual dimension corresponding to some aspect of the specific problem the person is facing. Especially if the individual has symbolized or attached a verbal label of "strange" to the new, any schema having to do with the way in which he copes with the strange is highly likely to be aroused. In a strange country, an American may seek out other Americans partly because his motivation to reduce anxiety has led to the arousal of a schema about being less anxious when a familiar person is near. Another American may seek to read about the new country because the same motivation has led to the arousal of a schema which suggests that the acquisition of new, relevant schemas is anxiety reducing.

It is important to notice that the schema which is aroused in this way is not necessarily a wish-fulfilling one: that is, the aroused schema does not necessarily or automatically indicate solutions to problems or even imply that there are solutions to problems. Whether or not the aroused schema does suggest an appropriate and effective solution depends on the content of the schema. The American in the strange country may simply think about the others who have found this country unpleasant.

Our analysis in terms of schemas has provided a basis for understanding how the strength of certain motives, i.e., those based on schemas, and their actual form, will vary from person to person, since the particular schemas which any given individual develops are based on his personal experience. Another characteristic of schemas which influences such motives is their independence from concrete situations, which we discussed at length above. Accordingly, motivational states based on schemas would be expected to be quite independent of the concrete situations in which the person is acting. The motivation is based on the schema, rather than on the concrete situation. Accordingly, any motivation based on schemas would tend to be relatively uninfluenced by concrete rewards and punishments in the given situations. For example, the child motivated to seek change will do so even in situations in which there is no immediate material gain to be derived in that situation. Furthermore, the child will be just as strongly motivated to seek change in the next new situation it encounters. The independence of schema-based motivations from influence by concrete situations helps to resolve one of the great puzzles of the psychology of motivation: why certain motives in adults are so strong and persistent that high amounts of punishment or low degrees of goal attainment seem not to reduce their strength appreciably. A person may continue to seek change even when his efforts are unsuccessful in many instances, or when that which he does discover nets him no material gain. Adults have often been known to pursue a goal, such as material success, through many years even when they have made few gains; they may have a schema about the great desirability of money, above all other values in life.

The Development of Social Schemas

Our presentation has come to the point where we now have a conceptual frame of reference which will allow us to introduce material that is more uniquely "social" in nature into our discussion. In this chapter we have so far made only some slight mention of the relationship the child has with his parents and others. Our delay in focusing on interpersonal relationships does not stem from any feeling that they are less important than those topics which have been examined thus far. Rather, it stems from the proposition that an extensive treatment of cognitive learning gives the framework within which interpersonal processes are best understood.

More specifically, as we have seen in some of our examples, the child most certainly does develop concepts and schemas having to do with other people, his relations with them, and their relations with one another. He is highly likely to do so because they are probably the most changing and variable parts of his environment. As compared to crib, toys, home, and even, in some parts of the world, to the weather, parents, brothers, sisters, friends, and relations are rather changeable: they change their dress, tone, and content of speech, physical location, position of their limbs, expression on their faces, etc. It may even be a wonder that the child attends to anything other than the human "stimuli" in his environment. Another obvious reason for his attention to others is that they are the sources of the satisfaction of many of his most critical needs, such as food, closeness and contact, water and warmth, etc.

Accordingly, the child develops conceptual dimensions and schemas about others. He may develop schemas around such concepts as status, liking or disliking, helpfulness, similarity, and communication. As with schemas in general, the degree to which he acquires each of these conceptual dimensions depends in part on the range of variability that he experiences with respect to them. The sex differences, the coming together and separation of people, age differences, difference in power and size, are dimensions along which his experiences obviously vary considerably, so that these dimensions, no doubt, become conceptualized early. He develops such schemas as "Bigger people can do more"; "My parents and brothers and sisters gather together to eat"; "Women and men behave in different ways"; or "Brothers and sisters vary from being very kind to being very nasty." However, families differ in their composition, so as to make the variation on some of these dimensions greater than on others. A child with siblings has more opportunity to develop a concept of similarity-difference among persons than an only child, since he is more similar to his siblings (and they to one another, if he has more than one) than to his parents. An only child experiences less variation on these dimensions; his parents are simply different.

The development of schemas about other people through the family is enhanced by the fact that the same people or situations are experienced in a variety of ways. The necessary repetition of some aspects of family situations and of the people involved in them makes it likely that previous experience with the situations and people will be recalled, so that schemas will be even more likely to develop. These same factors also enhance the tendency to develop higher level schemas about other people, so that there may be considerable upward spiraling of schemas about other people.

The motivational pressures to develop concepts and schemas would be very strong with respect to other people. They are constantly doing new and strange things; new people are constantly encountered. To cope with this high level of information input, the child is strongly pressed to develop concepts and schemas. He can cope with the problem partly through limiting his attention, but the fact that other people are so important for the satisfaction of his needs makes it difficult for him to just ignore all the complexity. The child may even learn to explore and be curious about other people, to try to develop ways of understanding new types of people. At first, the nursery school, full of strangers, may be somewhat frightening, but the child may learn how to approach the other children to find out what they are like. Of course, he is more likely to do so if there is a parent or friendly adult nearby.

Other Persons as Sources of Schemas

One of the main bases for the motivation to develop schemas is that they aid in the attainment of goals. This has already been pointed out, but this basis of motivation is most significant with respect to schemas about others because they are so important for the child's attainment of goals. In fact, one of the most important schemas which a child can learn is that other people are sources of the satisfaction of many needs and are necessary for the attainment of many goals. Furthermore, one of the most important goals which other people can help the child attain is that of the acquisition of dimensions and schemas themselves. The child perceives on numerous occasions that his parents have more information than he does, thereby developing both the conceptual dimension of differential knowledge and a schema that parents do have more relevant information. Since the child is motivated to acquire schemas, he attends to what his parents say, asking them questions, and asking them again and again.

Points well made. Photograph by Irwin Nash.

This process of learning through communication with others is greatly expedited by the relationship between language and the abstract or nonconcrete aspect of conceptual dimensions and schemas. Words refer to categories of objects, entities, and relationships which are themselves defined by schemas. A dictionary definition of a term often can be interpreted as a schema, since it generally does not refer to specific cases but to classes of cases. Thus, words can readily be used to develop schemas, since their meanings are most often nonspecific and abstract.

In most, but not all instances, the child perceives that information he has acquired from his parents and older siblings corresponds to reality as he subsequently experiences it. When a parent says that the days will be getting shorter, they do; that Aunt Susie will be here for dinner, she arrives; that the soup is too hot, it is. The child then develops a schema that there is a correspondence between reality as directly experienced and the specific information and abstract schemas which he acquires from his parents, and siblings, if any. In short, he learns that his parents and siblings are generally right.

This consistency between the directly observed and the socially acquired information is the basis for a most important schema. Of course, if a child grows up in a family in which others are untrustworthy sources of information about the world, the child may acquire very strange schemas about the world of people.

An interesting example of the ways that schemas can be acquired through communication concerns a relatively high level schema which was communicated without any concrete exemplars being given. Haygood and Bourne (1965) instructed some subjects that the "concepts" that they were to learn to identify would consist of the joint occurrence of two attributes, without specifying what these attributes were. These subjects were then given a series of positive and negative instances of a concept which was in fact defined by the joint occurrence of two attributes (i.e., positions on two dimensions) and were instructed to learn and indicate whether new exemplars were or were not exemplars of the concept. These subjects learned faster than those who were given the learning task without the higher order schema of joint occurrence of two attributes.

Much of what we learn about the world is in the form of schemas derived from communication without any direct experience. We learn valuable and useful information about Siberia, Caesar, nuclear explosions, a new government in Pakistan, a strike in a remote mine, mostly through communications from others—rather than from direct experiences.

Another motivational quality that we have mentioned which applies strongly in social situations is the child's high evaluation of the familiar. The child often prefers the familiar friend to the stranger; after he has learned to differentiate parent-adults from nonparent-adults, he has a marked preference for the more familiar parent-adults. In fact, it is the presence of the familiar parents and friends which often permits the child to venture toward the new, the different.

Still another very important schema generally developed by children has to do with their reactions to the communicated expressions about the child's behavior. As any parent knows, there are occasions in which children conform to these expectations and others in which they do not. In most—but obviously not all—cases, the child's needs are more likely to be gratified if he conforms to others' expectations than if he does not. He learns to be obedient at least part of the time. In fact, he learns to conform more or less to the communicated expectations of parents with respect to the arousal of schemas. "You should be attending to this"; "You should be thinking about that." Thus, we see that schemas can be aroused through deliberate, explicit instruction in addition to the earlier-mentioned ways which involved the experiencing of stimuli corresponding to a schema and the operation of relevant motivational states. Of course, the words or appearance of parents and others may arouse the child's schemas more directly; the words may refer to a schema; others' appearance may correspond to a concept that is part of a schema.

POSTSCRIPT: THE ROLE OF PICTORIAL SCHEMAS AND IMAGERY

For the sake of completeness, we will end this chapter with a brief discussion of an omission of sorts which we have made. In looking back over the orientation we have adopted regarding attention, perception, memory and the development of schemas, it is true that we have not dealt extensively with visual, pictorial, or iconic systems. Yet, of course, common experience tells us that they do indeed exist. Persons can call up visual images of past experiences and use this information in a variety of ways, so why have we not made more of this fact in our presentation? This relative neglect can be justified, we feel, on several grounds, all of which boil down to the conclusion that visual imagery plays a much less important role in general than do other forms of representation and storage.

In our earlier discussion of attention and memory, it was noted that much evidence points to the existence of a short-term memory or storage buffer where preliminary analysis of the physiological results of incoming stimuli is carried out. Where the visual system is involved, Neisser (1967) has called this briefly persistent visual image "iconic memory" and research by Sperling (1960) indicates that it lasts for approximately one second. Very loosely translated, this latter research tells us that for this period of time after a briefly presented visual stimulus has actually been terminated we have a very complete record of it with which to work. And what sort of work is done here? Speaking to this point, Neisser concludes that "we must assume that information is quickly 'read' into another, somewhat more permanent, form of memory. On logical, phenomenological, and empirical grounds, the new storage medium must be words. The subject formulates and remembers a verbal description of what he has seen" (Neisser, 1967, p. 36). Thus, the significance of visual or iconic imagery for our purposes may be diminished because much of the time the information it carries is transmitted into nonvisual form for long-term storage. Nevertheless, "it would be rash to conclude that this is the *only* way visual information can be preserved. After all, children and animals also learn from visual experience, obviously without verbalizing it. There are certainly other, more directly visual ways to store information after the decay of the icon" (Neisser, 1967, p. 36).

Dreams, hallucinations, hypnotic imagery, eidetic images, and straightforward recall in visual form of past experiences can all be seen as examples of this phenomenon. There do appear to be wide individual differences in the degree to which visual imagery is used, though there has not been much extensive research into the factors which may be associated with these differences. The available evidence does indicate that the ability to generate vivid and accurate imagery is relatively rare, and there is some suggestion that it tends to diminish with age. For example, Haber and Haber (1964) conducted a careful study of the incidence of eidetic imagery among more than 150 elementary school children. "An image is called 'eidetic' when (1) the subject describes it as having definiteness and clarity comparable to that of external objects; (2) he 'projects' it, i.e., sees it as occupying a particular place in space; (3) he can 'examine' it as he might examine a real picture; and (4) it does not shift its position with eye movements..." (Neisser, 1967, p. 147). In everyday parlance this would be called photographic memory because the person who evidences this ability operates as if he can examine parts of some previously viewed scene and describe them in very great and accurate detail. The Haber study found that 8 per cent of their sample evidenced this capacity, although it seems to be almost nonexistent among adult Americans. Holt (1964) speculates that the decrease of this ability with age may be due to cultural factors such as a factual, skeptical, literal and intellectual orientation which makes the capacity for vivid imagery have little social or survival value. A study by Doob (1964) on imagery among the Ibo tribe in Nigeria lends support to this notion. He found eidetic imagery to be very common among adult rural Ibos, but quite infrequent among members of the same tribe who were living in the provincial capital. Though there may be factors other than cultural ones which are responsible for these differences, the fact that imagery of this sort is not typical among adults is the important conclusion for the point we wish to make here.

In brief, then, we feel comfortable with our lack of stress on purely visual or pictorial schemas because the available evidence leads us to infer that they will not be of very great significance for the social psychological material to which the schema position is to be applied. In any case, there is every reason to believe that their development and operation follow the same principles which have been presented in this chapter.

References

Arsenian, J. M.: Young children in an insecure situation. *Journal of Abnormal and Social Psychology*, 1943, 38:225–249.

Asch, S., Ceraso, J., and Heimer, N.: Perceptual conditions of association. *Psychological Monographs*, 1960, 74:(Whole No. 490), No. 3.

Becknell, J. C., Wilson, W. R., and Baird, J. C.: The effect of frequency of presentation on the choice of nonsense syllables. *Journal of Psychology*, 1963, 56:165–170.

Berlyne, D. E.: *Conflict Arousal and Curiosity*. New York, McGraw-Hill, 1960.

Broadbent, D. E.: *Perception and Communication*. New York, Pergamon Press, 1958.

Bruner, J. S.: The course of cognitive growth. *American Psychologist*, 1964, 19:1–15.

Bruner, J. S., Oliver, R. R., and Greenfield, P. M.: *Studies in Cognitive Growth*. New York, Wiley, 1966.

Byrne, D. and Clore, G. L.: Expectance arousal and attraction. *Monograph of Journal of Personality and Social Psychology*, 1967, 6:(Whole No. 638), No. 4.

Carlsmith, J. M., and Aronson, E.: Some hedonic consequences of the confirmation and disconfirmation of expectancies. *Journal of Abnormal and Social Psychology*, 1965, 66:151–156.

Conners, C. K.: Visual and verbal approach motives as a function of discrepancy from expectancy level. *Perceptual and Motor Skills*, 1964, 18:457–464.

Crandall, J. E.: Familiarity, preference, and expectancy arousal. *Journal of Experimental Psychology*, 1967, 73:374–381.

Deutsch, J. A., and Deutsch, D.: Attention: Some theoretical considerations. *Psychological Review*, 1963, 70:80–90.

Doob, L. W.: Eidetic images among the Ibo. *Ethnology*, 1964, 3:357–363.

Epstein, W.: *Varieties of Perceptual Learning*. New York, McGraw-Hill, 1967.

Franz, R. L.: Pattern discrimination and selective attention as determinants of perceptual development from birth. In A. L. Kidd and J. L. Rivoire (Eds.), *Perceptual Development in Children*. New York, International Universities Press, 1966.

Gagné, R. M.: The acquisition of knowledge. *Psychological Review*, 1962, 69:355–365.

Goldstein, K.: *The Organism*. New York, American Books, 1939.

Haber, R. N., and Haber, R. B.: Eidetic imagery: I frequency. *Perceptual and Motor Skills*, 1964, 19:131–138.

Harlow, H. F.: The formation of learning sets. *Psychological Review*, 1949, 56:51–65.

Haygood, R. C., and Bourne, L. E.: Attribute- and rule-learning aspects of conceptual behavior. *Psychological Review*, 1965, 72:175–195.

Hebb, D. O.: *Organization of Behavior*. New York, John Wiley & Sons, 1949.

Holt, R. R.: Imagery: The return of the ostracized. *American Psychologist*, 1964, 19:254–264.

James, W.: *The Principles of Psychology*, Vol. 1. New York, Henry Holt & Co., 1890.

Johnson, R. C., Thomson, C. W., and Frincke, G.: Word values, word frequency, and visual duration thresholds. *Psychological Review*, 1960, 67:332–342.

Kagan, J.: Developmental studies in reflection and analysis. In A. L. Kidd and J. L. Revoire (Eds.), *Perceptual Development in Children*. New York, International Universities Press, 1966.

Kagan, J.: On the need for relativism. *American Psychologist*, 1967, 22:131–142.

Kessen, W., and Mandler, G.: Anxiety, pain, and the inhibition of distress. *Psychological Review*, 1961, 68:396–404.

Krugman, H. E.: Affective response to music as a function of familiarity. *Journal of Abnormal and Social Psychology*, 1943, 38:388–392.

Lewin, K.: *Field Theory in Social Science*. New York: Harper, 1951.

Miller, G. A.: The magical number seven, plus or minus two: some limits on our capacity for processing information. *Psychological Review*, 1956, 63:81–97.

Miller, G. A., Galanter, E., and Pribram, K. H.: *Plans and the Structure of Behavior*. New York: Holt, Rinehart and Winston, 1960.

Munsinger, H., and Kessen, W.: Uncertainty, structure, and preference. *Psychological Monographs*, 1964, 78:(Whole number 586) No. 9.

Munsinger, H., and Kessen, W.: Structure, variability, and development. *Journal of Experimental Child Psychology*, 1966a, 4:20–49.

Munsinger, H., and Kessen, W.: Stimulus variability and cognitive change. *Psychological Review*, 1966b, 73:164–178.

Munsinger, H., Kessen, W., and Kessen, M. L.: Age and uncertainty: developmental variation in preference for variability. *Journal of Experimental Child Psychology*, 1964, 1:1–15.

Munsinger, H., and Weir, M. W.: Infants' and young children's preference for complexity. *Journal of Experimental Child Psychology,* 1967, 5:69–73.

Neisser, U.: *Cognitive Psychology.* New York, Appleton-Century-Crofts, 1967.

Norman, D. A.: Acquisition and retention in short term memory. *Journal of Experimental Psychology,* 1966, 72:369–381.

Norman, D. A.: Toward a theory of memory and attention. *Psychological Review,* 1968, 75:522–536.

Norman, D. A.: *Memory and Attention.* New York, John Wiley & Sons, Inc., 1969.

Scheerer, M.: Cognitive theory. In G. Lindzey (Ed.), *Handbook of Social Psychology.* Vol. 1. Cambridge, Addison-Wesley, 1954.

Sokolov, E. N.: *Perception and the Conditioned Reflex.* New York, Pergamon Press, 1964.

Sperling, G.: The information available in brief visual presentations. *Psychological Monographs,* 1960, 74:No. 11.

Stotland, E.: *The Psychology of Hope.* San Francisco, Jossey-Bass, 1969.

Treisman, A. M., and Geffin, G.: Selective attention: perception or response? *Quarterly Journal of Experimental Psychology,* 1967, 19:1–17.

Verplanck, W. S.: Unaware of where's awareness. *Journal of Personality,* 1962, 30:130–157.

Vigotsky, L. S.: *Thought and Language.* Cambridge: M.I.T. Press, 1962.

Waugh, N. C., and Norman, D. A.: Primary memory. *Psychological Review,* 1965, 72:89–104.

Zajonc, R. B.: Cognitive structure and cognitive tuning. Unpublished doctoral dissertation, University of Michigan, 1954.

Zajonc, R. B.: Attitudinal effects of mere exposure. *Journal of Personality and Social Psychology Monograph Supplement,* 1968, 9:No. 2, Part 2.

CHAPTER 4

THE FUNCTIONING OF SCHEMAS

Before we go any further, let us take a selective inventory of the cognitive and motivational processes set forth in the last chapter.

I. With regard to general perceptual and cognitive functioning it was pointed out:

    (a) that persons can attend to a limited number of dimensions of the perceivable or imagined world at a given time;

    (b) that attention will be drawn to change and variance, particularly if there are familiar qualities in the total stimulus situation;

    (c) that through the recall of instances in which the individual has perceived in terms of a given dimension, he acquires a conceptualized or abstracted version of that dimension which is somewhat independent of concrete reality;

    (d) that after repeated experiences in which there is an association between particular positions on two or more relevant dimensions, and after simultaneous arousal of memories of these experiences, schemas may develop;

    (e) that schemas themselves can provide a basis for the development of still higher order schemas.

II. On the motivational side, it was noted that:

    (a) the child experiences anxiety if circumstances are such that its attention is drawn to a number of events which are close to, or at, its capacity to process information.

(b) that to avoid such anxiety, the child becomes motivated to develop new dimensions and schemas;

(c) that the child also acquires motivation to generate new schemas, to learn about the new, because such knowledge enhances its ability to attain its goals;

(d) that the child has more schemas about the familiar and can therefore attain his goals and avoid informational overload more effectively in familiar settings;

(e) that this leads him to evaluate the familiar highly and to attempt to transform the unfamiliar into the familiar;

(f) that since the acquisition of such motives is based on the development of schemas, they are relatively impervious to subsequent experiences, as schemas themselves are conceptualized and somewhat removed from the concrete world.

III. Finally, with particular reference to social schemas, it was emphasized that:

(a) the child is highly likely to develop schemas about other people, since they are the most changing and therefore attention-catching entities in the environment and because they are so important for goal attainment;

(b) that among such schemas are likely to be ones to the effect that communications from other people are often valid sources of information — that is, valid sources of other schemas about the world—and that fulfilling people's expectations generally leads to goal attainment.

The image one might glean from this inventory is of a child who is a bit of an intellectual monster—curious, inquisitive, constantly learning, and developing some pretty clear-cut notions about what his parents, brothers, and sisters are all about. He seems to be stuffing his head full of schemas and conceptualized dimensions. Since childhood is the period in which we acquire our knowledge about the world, this stuffing process is natural. Yet the question immediately arises, what is done with all that knowledge? How does it affect the way the child acts, perceives, interprets, and thinks? We will begin to answer these questions in this chapter—much of the rest of the book constitutes the rest of the answer. Since it is the adult who tends to learn less and use what schemas he has more, the focus of the chapter will shift more to adult behavior.

Despite the separation of the discussion of acquisition and functioning into separate chapters, it should not be assumed that they do not affect one another. For example, one of the main themes in the latter portion of the previous chapter was that the individual develops schemas about his own behavior, reactions, and feelings. Thus, the individual does develop higher order schemas about the very way that schemas function. On the other hand, schemas influence what we see and how we interpret what we perceive and this, in turn, determines what additional schemas will be acquired. Thus, the narrowing of our focus to the use, effect, and influence of schemas is primarily for theoretical and expositional purposes. It does not necessarily reflect the actual state of affairs in which schemas influence both perception and the functioning of other schemas and are in turn influenced by perception and by the functioning of other schemas. In reality, this influence occurs in both directions simultaneously in the interacting flow of experience. For our purposes, however, it is convenient to analyze only one part of the flow at a time.

FACTORS INFLUENCING THE AROUSAL OF SCHEMAS

In the previous chapter it was noted that schemas can exist in one of two states in the individual, an aroused state or a dormant state. It is in the aroused state that the schema can have an influence on the functioning of the individual. In fact, in our usage of the term, arousal means essentially being in a state of exerting some sort of influence. In the dormant state, schemas are like a temporarily forgotten memory, an overlooked idea, something simply stored in our warehouse of ideas and conceptions. We also noted that there are two types of events which can bring a schema into a state of arousal: instructions from others and attention to some event which corresponds to a conceptual dimension which constitutes one part of some schema. For the moment let us concentrate on the second of these.

Internal and External Stimulus Factors

In all probability, the reader has visualized the schema arousing event as something out in the world, "out there." This visualization is not incorrect, just incomplete. A schema arousing event can also occur "inside," in the individual's own thinking processes. This should not be so surprising, since we have pointed out that an individual can perceive the functioning of his own schemas just as he perceives his other activities. Accordingly, he may have noticed that a given schema has just come into a state of arousal. This schema may have a position on a conceptualized dimension in common with another. This other schema would then also be brought into a state of arousal. The individual may just have thought about a particular model of a given make of car; he may perceive that he has done so and, con-

sequently, he may think about other models made by the same man-
ufacturer. Or, he may think about a given black person and his schemas
about other black people may be aroused. Alternately, the schema
which he has perceived to come into arousal may itself be a component
of another schema of a relatively higher order, since we found that
schemas as totalities can be incorporated into other higher order schemas. This H.O.S. could then shift from dormancy to arousal. The person
who has just been thinking about dogs may begin to think about animals
in general. A person thinking about the local draft board may begin
to think about the defense establishment.

Conversely, if an H.O.S. has just come into arousal, any L.O.S.s
which have been incorporated into the higher order schema would
come into a state of arousal. A person may think about politicians
as a class, and then come to think of his congressman.

We have just pointed out that schemas that are in a hierarchical
relationship with one another will tend to arouse one another. In
general, schemas which are part of such a hierarchy are more likely
to be aroused and to remain operative if one of the other schemas
in the hierarchy has been activated. In other words, hierarchically
organized thinking tends not to shift freely to new and unrelated
schemas but to focus on the already aroused organization. If we are
thinking about a given problem by subsuming it under some principle,
we may have a rather specific set of schemas functioning—sometimes
to the detriment of any flexibility of thought, or of any ideas not included in that principle. The reader no doubt has experienced
situations in which he did not see the "obvious" solution to a problem
because he was viewing the problem from a given "point of view,"
i.e., H.O.S. Sometimes people may have an H.O.S. aroused concerning
ways to win the war in Vietnam and may thus be unable to think
about how to end the war. Or, some young people may have an aroused
H.O.S. about the generation gap and thus be unlikely to view the
over-thirtys as individual human beings.

Inhibition of the Spread of Arousal

The description just given of aroused schemas activating other
schemas at the same level, or above or below it in some hierarchical
order, raises a simple, basic question: where does this spreading flow
of arousal end? Unless brakes are put on the spread of arousal in
short order, an individual may have an encyclopedia's worth of
schemas aroused.

The answer to this problem also involves the use of a principle
which we enunciated in the last chapter, i.e., the notion that people
are so built, neurologically speaking, that they can react to and assimilate only a limited amount of information at a time. This principle

need only be generalized to apply not only to information coming from the world "outside," but also to stimuli from the world "inside"—from thoughts, ideas, images, and/or internal physiological activity. The channel capacity limitation is properly interpreted to imply that the sum total of information the individual can cope with is limited, regardless of whether it comes from inside or out. This means that if the number of schemas aroused and the number of events attended to are added together, there is a ceiling zone for the sum. Notice that this is not just a matter of separate limits on the number of schemas aroused and on the number of events attended to; this is a ceiling zone for their combined totals. The greater the number of external events an individual is attending to, the lower is the number of schemas which can be active at the same time, and vice versa. When the strobe lights are flashing on stage and the music is wildly booming out, hardly anyone can continue thinking about that math problem, or how to get a job next summer.

We can see many instances of the effects of this ceiling. We are sometimes "lost in thought," which suggests that we are not paying much attention to the world around us. At least some automobile accidents are caused by this type of effect of the ceiling. On the other hand, if a person is extremely bound to the concrete world of events it will be difficult for him to solve certain types of problems—problems which require thought and going beyond the concrete situation. Sometimes, if an individual can withdraw from a given concrete situation for a while and "give it some thought," he is more likely to be able to solve it. Retreats by some religious groups, think tanks, some vacations, may all be efforts to pull away from the pressure of the outside to give the internal, the schemas a chance to function.

When this cognitive activity takes place outside of awareness and over a period of time, the period of time is called the "incubation" period. Another instance of the movement back and forth between thought and attention to the external world occurs when we are engaged in a nonroutine task; we alternate between attending to the outside world of our overt actions and their effects on the environment and the internal, cognitive responses involved in an evaluation of these effects and a decision regarding what next to do (cf. Miller, Galanter, and Pribram, 1960).

We may ask someone a question, and then think about the answer we get, partly to decide whether to ask another question. Sometimes, of course, we do not behave in so rational a fashion and act "on impulse," i.e., our actions are determined by an essentially unreflective response to events outside our skins. The examples just given were not meant to imply that these two modes are mutually exclusive alternatives. We can and do experience mixtures of both; the more of one, however, the less there can be of the other.

Our discussion has assumed that there is a certain interchangeability between information coming from the inside and that coming from the outside. The reasonableness of this assumption receives some nonscientific support from a scene in an early Charlie Chaplin comedy in which Charlie is sitting in a doctor's waiting room right next to a very matronly, very proper-looking woman. Suddenly he hears the rumbling of a stomach, but appears completely baffled as to whether it is his own or the matron's.

Another illustration of this interchangeability comes from a study by Perky (1910) in which subjects were told to look at a screen and to imagine certain objects, such as books or oranges, as appearing on the screen. Unbeknown to them, the experimenter flashed outlines of these objects on the screen at intensities well below the minimum needed for vision. Then she increased the intensities gradually to the point where the outline of the object would be normally easily seen. The subjects reported that they "imagined" the objects only when outlines were at high intensities, but did not realize at all that the outlines were real. The subjects saw actual outlines but thought they were imagining them; they could not tell the difference.

Motivational Influences on Schema Activation

It seems reasonable to expect that anxiety stemming from a schema-based informational overload is less likely to occur than is anxiety from an overload of events to attend to, since the existence of attention-demanding external events is often not something which is under the control of the person. Typically, an individual can more easily arrange to move an active schema into a dormant state, thereby reducing the pressure on his capacity to deal with information, than he can arrange to have an event disappear. Nevertheless, there may be occasions during which such anxiety occurs. In such cases, the individual is no doubt motivated to do one of several things. He may reduce the number of aroused schemas by forcing schemas into dormancy. "I'll just stop thinking about that —it was just too much." "I don't want to think about all those new ideas I heard at the PTA meeting; they're just too much." In some cases a person may develop an H.O.S. which envelops several L.O.S.s, as he develops schemas to cope with complexity in the outside world. "My confusion disappeared when I realized that you could think both about having jobs and about having time to do what you want."

There are still many questions left unanswered by our analysis of the limitation of the number of schemas and events that can be functional at a given moment. One question is how to "count" schemas which are in a hierarchical relationship to one another. If both a higher order schema and a lower order one subsumed under it are aroused, does this situation tax the individual's capacity to process ideas as much as the situation in which two schemas are aroused which do not have any such hierarchical relationship to one another? A person may be thinking about homes in general, as well as a specific home; or he may be thinking about homes and money. Are these two situations equivalent in the degree to which they move the person toward the limits of his cognitive capacity? At the moment, research which might provide the answers to this question has not been conducted.

Several other motivational considerations merit discussion here as they play a role in determining not only the number of schemas which will be operative, but also which specific ones will be selected. In the situations alluded to here the individual is faced with some issue or problem, in the very general sense of the word, with which he must deal. One fairly straightforward effect grows out of an individual's ability to reflect on his own prior cognitive and behavioral activity. On the basis of past experience he may have developed some hypotheses about the most effective general techniques for coping with his environment. Thus he will, when faced with a problem, tend to direct his attention to and attempt to arouse schemas which have been associated with problem solution in the past. This process is a specific example of what is known as "learning to learn." In any case, it can obviously influence what is attended to and what schemas are aroused.

One example of this motivational influence on which schemas remain aroused and which remain dormant is based on the individual's having developed a schema that he solves problems better, attains his goals more effectively, if he thinks about matters relevant to the goal. Thus, when working on a problem, he may restrict the aroused schemas to those which appear to him to be relevant to the problem; he may thereby prevent "free association," the random arousal of schemas which happen to have some similarity to the existing problem. Of course, the schema on which this motivational concentration is based may be invalid in some cases. The solution to some problems may lie outside the realm of what appears to be relevant; thus concentration may in fact be detrimental to the solution of some problems. This may account in part for the ironic tendency of persons to become ineffective in solving certain types of problems when they are especially highly motivated to do so. In some instances, a person who tends more to play around with ideas, who is "looser," may be better able to come up with solutions. Some of the presumed effectiveness of "brainstorming" may stem from the motivation of the participants to let their ideas "come" without much rational guidance.

Another motivation-related factor concerns the individual's general preference for the familiar, his higher evaluation of familiar schemas. The individual may be motivated to keep aroused those schemas which are old, "comfortable" ideas, rather than appeal to less often used, less familiar ideas. Notice that here we are discussing the arousal of schemas by factors other than events in the external world; when the latter events arouse schemas, it is the unfamiliar, the novel, the changing stimuli which are particularly potent, as has been mentioned earlier. When internal factors, such as the arousal of other schemas or the person's motivational state, determine which schemas are to be aroused, the "old schemas" are preferred. How often have we found ourselves thinking in a rut? How often have we listened to others whose patterns of thought seem to follow the same route every time we talk with them? Talk to an Economics major, and everything comes down to dollars and cents. Speak with a Psychology major, and it's all a matter of learning. For a militant, establishment repression is the prime source of the world's ills. Talk to a Minuteman, and it's all a matter of agitation by Marxist agents.

THE OPERATION OF AROUSED SCHEMAS

Thus far in our discussion of how schemas function, we have concentrated on the quantitative aspect of the problem—how many and which schemas can "dance on the head of a" person. We have not yet systematically examined the qualitative question having to do with the effect that one aroused schema has on another already aroused schema. We have defined an aroused schema as one which is influencing the individual's functioning, including in this functioning the arousal of other schemas. Yet, we have not said exactly what aroused schemas do. Let us turn to this issue now and see whether any of the principles we have set forth thus far can again help us.

The Consistency Schema and Its General Effects

We will examine this issue with respect to schemas which are in a hierarchical relationship to one another, an H.O.S. and an L.O.S. subsumed by it. In this examination, we shall encounter one of the

The new sign not seen. Photograph by Irwin Nash.

most significant principles concerning the functioning of schemas with respect to each other, as well as with respect to perception of the world "out there." This principle is that of consistency—i.e., consistency between schemas at one level and those at a higher level, and between schemas and perception. In the last chapter, we noted that H.O.S.s emerge from L.O.S.s; that an H.O.S. can consist of the conceptual dimensions and the associations between positions on these dimensions which are common to a number of L.O.S.s; that an H.O.S. can also include L.O.S.s as total units; and that an H.O.S. can be based on a configuration of L.O.S.s. An individual will very likely be aware of instances in which he has developed H.O.S.s out of L.O.S.s in all of the ways just cited. "After listening to all those professors, I concluded that they don't know about anything which goes on off campus." "After watching all those football fans at all those games, I decided they all go a bit crazy at times."

He may note that he has made a generalization or that he has reacted to a configuration or pattern of related schemas. "I noticed that big dogs are more gentle than small dogs"; "I notice that after there are riots in one city, there are reforms in a number of others."

Since this process, which we refer to as schema formation, is so common, it is highly likely that a still higher order schema to the effect that, in general, higher and lower order schemas in the same hierarchy are consistent with one another, and that concrete experiences are consistent with L.O.S.s, will be developed.

It is important to notice that although the consistency schemas typically are based on observation of the nature of the relationships among specific schemas acquired from L.O.S.s or from perceived situations, the schema itself concerns consistency *per se*. That is, the schema applies whether the consistency is perceived between the events and the L.O.S. or between the L.O.S. and the events; between the L.O.S. and H.O.S. and vice versa.

The student developing the schema about professors knowing nothing about off-campus life may believe that each new professor fits the schema and that the schema fits all the previous professors he has known.

This two-way implication of the consistency schema stems from the two-way process which is involved in the acquisition of schemas. More specifically, suppose that a schema is in the process of being acuired on the basis of a set of observed experiences. While it is in this developmental stage, the individual is likely to experience additional situations which are consistent with it. He will then perceive not only that the schema reflects or is consistent with his concrete experience, but that the relevant concrete experiences are consistent with the schema which is developing. The two-way nature of the consistency thus is perceived from the very onset. Thus, the student who is developing the schema about professors will be thinking about previous professors he has known at the same time that he is watching a new one.

Obviously, the same two-way process can occur with respect to the development of an H.O.S. from L.O.S.s. All this may seem completely obvious and trivial at this point. If you are "underwhelmed" by the revelation that not only are the data on which they are built consistent with the resultant schemas but also that schemas are consistent with the nature of the events to which they are relevant, its significance will soon become more clear. What is important here is not so much that these reciprocal consistencies do exist and are observed, but that an individual develops a very general, broadly applicable principle to the effect that all *his* schemas are valid, correct, accurate, and reliable and, further, that his experiences will be consistent with them.

Communication from Others as a Source of the Consistency Principle

The consistency schema, like any other, can also be acquired directly through communications from other people (cf. Rosenberg, 1960). These communications can take several forms. For one thing, a child may observe that adults frequently talk and act as if they possessed a consistency schema. They say such things as, "That is just what I expected to see," "That idea fits this idea I have," or "I have good reason for believing that." Or, adults may directly communicate to the child that he should have a consistency schema by means of such statements as, "You must have a reason for saying that," "If you say that, you can't believe this."

Since the consistency schema is in part learned from others, people in different subgroups or cultures may acquire it in varying degrees and perhaps in different ways.

On the shores of the Nile, a scorpion asked a crocodile, "Will you carry me on your back to the other side of the river?" The crocodile replied, "How can I be sure you won't bite me while you're on my back?" The scorpion reassured him, "But if I did that, I'd drown—why should I do a foolish thing like that?" "That makes sense to me, hop on my back." When they were in the middle of the river, the scorpion bit the crocodile. As he was dying, the crocodile asked the scorpion, "Why did you do such a foolish thing? It didn't make any sense." Retorted the scorpion, "Why should it make sense? This is the Middle East." McGuire (1966) quotes an Eastern philosopher who argues that if two things are contradictory, they both must be true.

A question might arise whether the consistency schema derived from communications from other people is kept discrete from the schemas acquired from direct experience. Obviously, the answer is that if the individual's experience is such as to lead to the conceptualization of the dimension of consistency in the same way for both types of schema, then they will be combined to form one H.O.S. subsuming both. However, they may remain separate, especially if the communications from other people are not of the type mentioned above.

Once the individual has acquired this high-order consistency schema, it would be aroused by attention to the hierarchical relationship between two other aroused schemas. The person might be thinking of a given politician as an example of politicians as a whole; of a given war as an example of the broader category of wars. If the two aroused schemas in a hierarchical relationship are in fact consistent with each other, then the higher order consistency schema is simply found to be consistent with this consistency. If the politician is known to behave like all others, or if the war has all of the characteristics of other wars, then the higher order consistency schema simply has found another example.

If, on the other hand, the two aroused schemas in the hierarchical relationship are inconsistent with one another, the higher order consistency schema has been violated. If the politician is believed to behave unlike all others, if the war is fought differently from all other wars, then the higher order consistency schema has been found wanting. In consequence, since H.O.S.s develop out of L.O.S.s, we might anticipate some movement toward a change in this general schema to the effect that there is not always consistency between higher and lower order schemas in a hierarchy. To some extent, such changes of this H.O.S. do in fact occur. Some people obviously believe that "nothing is certain." But in most instances the higher order consistency schema is not readily changed or rejected.

Stability of the Consistency Schema

There are several sources of resistance to change of the higher order consistency schema. For one thing, this schema is evaluated highly because it is so very familiar. This familiarity stems from the fact that, as a higher order abstraction, it is relevant to a wide range of instances; in fact, to all hierarchically organized schemas. If the individual has, for some reason, come to verbalize the higher order consistency schema, it is probably even higher in familiarity to him than would otherwise be the case, because the verbal label attached to it makes it easier to recall. It is important to notice that this argument applies not only to the higher order consistency schema, but also to all higher order schemas. In general, they tend to be more familiar than lower order schemas and are therefore evaluated more highly, especially if verbalized.

The higher order consistency schema is then more highly evaluated than are the two aroused hierarchically related schemas that are inconsistent with one another. Therefore, the individual would be more likely to change the two aroused hierarchically ordered schemas in some way so that they once again can be seen as consistent with one another. Thus, he can either come to believe that the politician in question is not "really" a politician or that most, but not all, politicians are phony; or he can come to believe that the war in question really is not a war but a police action, or that not all wars involve major battles.

However, this analysis raises still a further question: which of the two aroused hierarchically ordered schemas will the individual be more likely to change, the higher or the lower? The answer to this question derives from a point made two paragraphs above: higher order schemas are generally more highly evaluated because they are more familiar. Because of processes similar to the one described in the previous paragraph, the H.O.S.s are less likely to be changed to achieve consistency than are the L.O.S.s.

This analysis raises the question of what would happen if the L.O.S. were more familiar than an H.O.S. under which it was subsumed. This odd state of affairs could come about in a number of ways. The H.O.S. may have been acquired through communication from others, rather than from exemplars. The commonality between the two schemas may have been discovered only after the lower order one had been quite frequently aroused. In such cases, the H.O.S. would be more influenced by the L.O.S. than vice versa. For example, the person may change the communicated H.O.S. to conform to the more familiar lower order one.

It would not be difficult to gain an impression from this discussion that changes of L.O.S.s to become more consistent with H.O.S.s involve a deliberate, conscious process; that the person, with goodwill and forethought, makes a decision to change or not to change a schema. This impression of conscious, rational deliberation may be valid in some instances. However, in other cases, the process is not so well thought through. The individual may simply have developed a schema to the effect that H.O.S.s are best not changed, without having the "evidence" immediately in mind; "the old ideas are the best."

With this discussion of the role of awareness and rationality in mind, let us look at some researched examples of the relationship between schemas of different orders and the ways in which L.O.S.s are changed to make them more consistent with H.O.S.s.

The eminent British psychologist F. C. Bartlett is responsible for some of the very best research on memory processes, and his book *Remembering* (1932) records a great many hypotheses, insights, and descriptions that are quite consistent with the most recent work on this topic. One technique he employed was termed the "method of repeated reproduction" which involved having persons read a passage or view some graphic representation and then attempt to reproduce it from memory after various time intervals. One of the most striking and common findings was that the reproduced material evidenced transformations which made it more coherent, rational and "sensible" than the original. One of the stories used was a North American Indian folk tale, and Bartlett reports that "before long the story tends to be robbed of all its surprising, jerky, and apparently inconsequential form, and reduced to an orderly narration. It is denuded of all the elements that left the reader puzzled and uneasy . . ." (1932, p. 86). He suggests that these differences between the original and the version which is remembered are due to "an active bias, or special reaction tendencies, that are awakened in the observer by the new material, and it is these tendencies which then set the new into relation with the old . . . the process of fitting is an active process, depending directly upon the preformed tendencies and bias which the subject brings to his task." (1932, p. 85.) The bias of which he speaks is, in our terms, a higher order schema. In this case the schema would have to do with the expectation that written material, tales or legends, will make sense, be consistent and coherent. Other examples of research which illustrate this relationship are easily found.

Papageorgis (1963) had people learn a series of arguments which contained qualifications on the main thrust of the argument. These qualifications were essentially inconsistent with the main argument. Over a period of 41 days, subjects were observed to be more likely to forget these qualifications than the main arguments. Allport & Postman (1947) found that when an individual passes on a rumor, he will tend to state it in terms which are more familiar to him, to take the rumor and distort it until it fits relevant H.O.S.s which have been aroused. If a person had heard that the Chinese government had sent a diplomatic message to the Indian Government, he might later believe, and tell someone else, that the Chinese had threatened the

Indians. The person's higher order schema that the Chinese threaten to expand, especially in the direction of India, aroused upon receipt of the original message, then led to distortion of the message itself to make it consistent with the H.O.S. Notice what has happened in these cases: the individual has transformed the unfamiliar into the familiar. Thus, the basic motivation for this transformation appears to be much the same as that which was indicated in the last chapter to be the basis for exploratory or curiosity motivation—the transformation of the unfamiliar into the familiar. In the case of the relationship between schemas, this transformation occurs within the person's head, so to speak, while in the case of curiosity, the transformation involves some direct interaction with the environment. Obviously, also, the curiosity and exploratory motives concern the seeking of the new to make it familiar, while the processes we have described here entail making what is already known more consistent.

Temporal Factors in the Operation of the Consistency Schema

So far, we have considered the case in which two or three schemas, hierarchically related, are aroused simultaneously and thereby become more consistent. By this token, two schemas which are relevant to one another could remain inconsistent if they are never aroused simultaneously. But how can they not have been aroused simultaneously if they have some relevance to one another, some common dimensional position or subsumed L.O.S.? The answer stems from consideration, once again, of the limited capacity of the individual to process information. The individual may have reached his ceiling of the number of aroused schemas and the dimensions or events to which he can attend before both of the relevant schemas could be aroused, or he may have been so attentive to events "out there" that only a few schemas could be aroused. Thus, inconsistency can exist between schemas which for one reason or another have not been aroused simultaneously. For example, an individual may be concentrating so very intently on the details of planning a particular action which he would consider immoral that the H.O.S. having to do with moral judgments is not aroused, and he goes forward with his planning. If, however, later the person is reminded of the H.O.S. of morality, or if some other schemas slip out of arousal so that the H.O.S. of morality is more likely to be aroused, then he may change his plans to avoid comitting the immoral act.

More generally, if two inconsistent schemas which have not been aroused simultaneously now are aroused, they are likely to be made more consistent with one another, the more familiar one dominating over the less familiar one.

Sometimes, this process of simultaneously arousing inconsistent schemas can be quite complex. McGuire (1960) gave subjects a questionnaire in which they were to respond by giving the proportion of times that a given event occurred as a consequence of another one. A question might be: "What proportion of high school graduates enter college?" Spaced throughout the questionnaire were questions which were relevant to one another, but the schemas for which were unlikely to be aroused simultaneously because they are aroused usually on different occasions. A question paired with the one above might be: "What proportion of freshmen who enter college ultimately graduate?" The schema relevant to the first question is likely to have been aroused by discussion of high schools; the second, by discussions concerning college. Somewhere else in the questionnaire was a question relating the two other questions; in our example, "What proportion of high school graduates normally graduate from college?" A truly consistent answer to this question would be the product of the two other proportions; if half the high school graduates go to college and half the freshmen ultimately graduate, then one fourth of high school graduates would be expected to graduate college. In most cases, upon first taking the questionnaire, college students were remarkably inconsistent. A person who answered the first two questions with a response of one-half might give one-third as the answer to the last one. If the questions had been placed side by side, the researcher's intent would have been more obvious to the subjects and they probably would have given much more consistent replies. However, by separating them by other questions, these interrelationships were not so obvious. Yet the questionnaires did arouse the schemas corresponding to these questions more or less simultaneously. At some level of awareness, however dim, the individual perceived the relationship between the three and thus an H.O.S. about the probability of the joint occurrence of two independent events being the product of their reported probabilities was aroused. Of course, the person would not state the probability relationships in these mathematical terms, but he no doubt possessed some rough equivalent even though he could not further conceptualize or symbolize this schema.

The individual thus is pressed to bring the three lower order schemas in line with one another, since their being out of line with one another violates the H.O.S. With time, the person should attain more consistency between the three. McGuire found that on a repetition of essentially the same questionnaire a few days later, the subjects were indeed considerably more consistent. In fact, they were almost completely consistent! If one values consistency, this is indeed good news about the human race. The H.O.S. having to do with the rules of combining probabilities had led them to be more consistent, but only when the H.O.S. was aroused along with the simultaneous arousal of relevant lower order schemas.

More generally, this remarkable research indicates that the simultaneous arousal of relevant, but previously not-simultaneously aroused, schemas tends to lead to the activation of an H.O.S. having to do with their relationship to one another. This H.O.S. then influences the lower order schemas in such a way as to make their relationship more consistent with the H.O.S. Again, the H.O.S. itself remains unchanged. Although McGuire did not measure the H.O.S., it is doubtful that any of the subjects tended to reject the schema of combining probabilities as a result of having taken the questionnaire.

Dillehay, Insko, and Smith(1966) repeated this study with more advanced students than participated in McGuire's study and found that their subjects showed less inconsistency when their schemas were initially measured than did McGuire's. There may be several reasons for this: their educational experiences may have provided more opportunities for them to have all three of the potentially inconsistent schemas aroused simultaneously, thus leading them to make them consistent. Since these subjects were enrolled in a social psychology course, they may have "seen through" the purposes of the study and rendered themselves more consistent in the first measurement. In any case, the effects of moving toward greater consistency found by McGuire did not occur to any important degree in the Dillehay, *et al.* study; there simply was less room for improvement.

It is evident from McGuire's research that a few days or so were needed for the individual to do the "intellectual work" of bringing the inconsistencies into line, for the individual to react to the implications that one idea has for another, that one schema has for another. The need for time to see such implications has sometimes led to what has been termed the "sleeper effect"—the delayed reaction one may have to a communication of some sort. This sort of time requirement has also been found in studies dealing with complex messages which contained a number of rather subtly related propositions. As compared to a message in which the intended conclusions were explicitly stated, a "no conclusion" communication, in which the full implications of the propositions were not fully spelled out, had less influence on the recipients when measurements were taken immediately after the message was presented (Hovland and Mandell,

1952). This compares sharply with the powerful delayed effects found by McGuire. Delayed communication effects of this sort were noticed in a study done during World War II to assess the consequences of viewing a movie about the Battle of Britain on American soldiers' attitudes toward our British allies (Hovland, Lumsdaine, & Sheffield, 1953). The immediate consequence of viewing this film seemed primarily to involve the acquisition of a considerable body of information about the R.A.F. and the British war effort in general. No major changes in attitudes toward the British were found to accompany the learning of this information. However, some weeks later there was a marked increase in positive attitudes among those soldiers who had seen the film. Very interestingly, by this time the soldiers had forgotten many of the facts they'd recalled earlier. They had apparently developed a higher order schema to the effect that "The British are O.K.," which was now at least somewhat independent of the specific data on which it was based. Similar delayed effects have also been found by Stotland, Patchen, and Katz (1959), who presented subjects with communications designed to reduce their prejudice toward minority groups by indicating to them that such prejudices are often based on emotional, not-very-rational processes. The implications of this message for the subject's own level of prejudice were not explicitly drawn for them. Measurements of attitudes toward minority groups taken immediately following receipt of the message showed no effect. However, some three or four weeks later, there was a drop in prejudice, provided the subjects had read in the original message a statement pointing out the values of being consistent. It took a while for the subjects to bring the communication about the irrational basis of prejudice in line with the message about consistency. Needless to say, findings of this type should encourage those of us who are disheartened because we appear to have had no influence when we have "tried to explain the truth" to people. They may get the point later.

THE INFLUENCE OF SCHEMAS ON PERCEPTION

In our discussion of the influence that schemas have upon one another, we have implicitly assumed a rather high degree of malleability of schemas. They have been described as elements which can be changed, corrected, added to and subtracted from, even though some of them show more resistance to such alteration than others. The influence of other schemas and of the person's own motives have been the only factors presented as counterforces to flexibility. However, this picture changes as we move down the hierarchy to lower order schemas, toward the concrete level, toward schemas concerning the perception of the world out there. Now, the information the individual is receiving from the perceived world introduces another factor into the situation which can influence the degree to which schemas are changeable. Where very low order schemas are concerned, then, reality considerations place additional constraints on this flexibility. On the other hand, aroused schemas can influence the ways in which the input of information from the world "out there" is interpreted. In short, at the point of perceptual contact with the internal and external environment of the individual there can be mutual influence or interaction between the perceived world and the aroused schemas. For purposes of exposition, we will continue for the time being to examine the influence that schemas have on perception; then we will examine the ways that perception influences schemas after it has been influenced by them.

The consistency schema, which we indicated above is highly likely to be acquired, has as one of its major foci the relationship between lower order schemas and the perceived world, since schemas are constructed in part from the raw material provided by direct experience. If there is any inconsistency between what is perceived and an aroused schema, the consistency schema itself would be aroused. Then, since the essence of this cognition is that there is general consistency between schemas and perceived reality, an individual will tend to perceive in a way consistent with his schema.

This analysis points to the arousal of the consistency schemas as a consequence of the perception of inconsistency, which then leads to perception in a more consistent way. Again, we see the necessity for postulating that the human perceptual apparatus involves a highly complex, multi-level system. Apparently, one aspect of this system can react to perceptual inconsistency, and in so doing produce a more consistent ultimate perception which alone enters awareness. The theoretical models of Treisman and Geffin (1967), Deutsch and Deutsch (1963), and Norman (1966, 1968, 1969), all provide in one form or another for some sort of "preperception perceptual process." It is in this process that the inconsistency is no doubt perceived and reacted to.

A question then arises as to how this consistency will be achieved—through a change of lower order schemas or of the way in which the environment is perceived? In loose terms, the question has to do with whether the schema will be altered to fit the observations which have been made, or whether the observations will be, in a sense, distorted to bring them into line with what the person expects to see on the basis of the schemas which have been activated. The answer stems in part from the fact that when an individual confronts any concretely perceivable situation, it is at least minimally new to the person. Even if it is almost identical to previous situations, it must be new in the sense of its never having occurred in exactly its current state before—obviously. On the other hand, any schema that happens to be aroused is, by definition, older and therefore more familiar. Again, our principles of consistency and preference for the familiar indicate that the schema will tend to have a strong influence over what is perceived and the manner in which these perceptions will be interpreted. If a man with a beard argues for the morality of conventional ways of doing things, someone with a schema that bearded people are unconventional might see him as "kidding." If the police chief campaigns for the legalization of marijuana, a person with a schema that policemen are always opposed to change might perceive the chief to be an "agent provocateur."

The influence of an aroused L.O.S. will be further enhanced if it happens to be a schema which is subsumed under some H.O.S.s: the even greater familiarity of such an H.O.S. makes it even less likely that some change in the relevant schemas will be the avenue by which inconsistency will be reduced. If the person who is observing the marijuana-advocating chief of police also has a schema that all public officials are opposed to change, he would be all the more likely to perceive that the chief is not sincere.

The Effect of Stimulus Ambiguity

In addition, if extant schemas are to influence perceptual activity rather than vice versa, any tendency to form a new schema on the basis of what is attended to in the situation must be overcome. This tendency will, of course, be weak under conditions in which the individual is unable to determine positions on any dimensions he may be able to attend to. Under these circumstances the likelihood that new schemas will be generated on the basis of the current experience will be slight, since their formation is dependent upon the individual's attending to positions on dimensions in the perceivable situation. Thus, the probability that new schemas will be formed is lowest when the perceivable situation is unclear or equivocal; accordingly, in such situations, the influence of the aroused schema on perception would be greater. Such ambiguity and unclarity could be the result of a variety of factors such as the physical inadequacy of the sensory input from the situation (poor light, too much background noise), the fast-changing quality of the situation (a complex football play, a rumble or riot), or the short time in which it occurred (an automobile accident, a quickly uttered radio news report). The equivocality of the perceivable situation could also be the consequence of inadequate information (a conversation in an unknown foreign language), the multiple possible implications of the information available (a drop in the number of people looking for work), or the complexity of the perceivable situation (the Federal Government's budget).

Thus, the perception of unclear or equivocal perceivable situations is subject to relatively great influence from schemas, and the more familiar the schemas, the greater their influence. Research on perception under what are termed impoverished stimulus conditions has shown that when words are presented under conditions of extremely fast exposure, dim illumination, or small size, persons are able to accurately identify those with which they are most familiar more readily than others.

This analysis raises a subtle question, however. Why does the individual not perceive the very unclarity of the situation as a dimension? Why does he not attend to the equivocality? Could not the person just observe that the situation is unclear, that the "truth" cannot be determined with any reasonable degree of certainty and let it go at that? Obviously, in some cases, people do react in this way. On the other hand, there are strong motivations not to react in this way to unclarity and ambiguity, strong motives to perceive in terms of dimensions and schemas, to organize the perceivable world. The most ready way in which the individual can do this is by perceiving in terms of his aroused schemas; developing a new schema would be far more difficult.

Thus, there are strong pressures to perceive the familiar, to perceive in terms of the aroused schema. The next question to be dealt with concerns the specific form of the influence which schemas have on perceptual activity. We will now deal with this question at length.

Determination of Perceived Dimensions

An individual will be predisposed to perceive a situation in terms of the concrete dimensions which correspond to the conceptualized dimensions of the aroused schema. If a person had an aroused schema concerning communications, he would attend to the amount of communication; if concerning power, he would attend to the amount of power. Research by Bruner & Minturn (1955) exemplifies this point. They presented two groups of subjects with a list either of numbers or of letters, thus arousing schemas relating to either numbers or letters.

Then both groups were shown an essentially ambiguous stimulus, a "13." The letter group perceived it as a B; the number group as a 13. Of course, a person can attend to more than one dimension at a time, up to some ceiling, as we learned in the last chapter. Thus, he can attend to all of the dimensions involved in the schema, up to the ceiling. Or if more than one schema is aroused, he could attend to dimensions from several situations.

One implication of this type of influence of schemas on perception is that at different times, the same person might attend to different aspects or dimensions of the same situation, such as power or communication, depending on which schema happened to be aroused. Furthermore, several people with different schemas will tend to perceive situations along different dimensions. Some people may notice the sex ratio at a party; others the topics of conversation. Or, several people who possess the same schemas, but have different ones aroused at a given moment, will attend to different dimensions of the situation. This theme will be developed at length later.

Can there be concrete dimensions attended to which are not tied in with either a schema or a conceptual dimension that is not part of a schema? In other words, can an individual experience new dimensions? Obviously, people do learn new dimensions from other people—teachers, models, experts, parents. We might learn to attend to the degree of detail in a painting; or the counterpoint in music. In all probability, an individual can discover a new dimension himself, but the exact process involved, especially in adults, is a bit mysterious. What are called concept learning studies do not usually answer this question, because they consist mostly of the subjects' guessing which of the dimensions they already possess is relevant to a given problem (cf. Pikas, 1966).

Determination of Specific Perceived Positions on Dimensions

A second type of influence which an aroused schema may have on perception concerns another aspect of schemas—the association between positions on two or more dimensions. If the individual not only attends to one dimension of the schema but also perceives that a given entity or event occupies a particular position on that dimension, he will be predisposed to perceive the associated position on the other dimension of the schema. Let us call these latter dimensions the expected dimension. The particular dimension which is the expected one may vary from situation to situation, since the individual may initially attend to different dimensions of a relevant schema at different times. Whether the individual actually perceives the position on the expected dimension depends in part on whether it is physically possible to do so. If it is not, then the aroused schema exists for the moment partly at the perceptual level, partly at the ideational. For example, suppose that you have an aroused schema about certain types of people whom you believe to have ulterior motives. If you then perceive one of these people, you would expect that he has ulterior motives, even though nothing in his behavior indicates immediately the presence (or absence) of such motives. Thus, the schema remains half at the perceptual level, half at the ideational. The salient point here is that not for a moment would you doubt the existence of the motives. The distinction between what is physically perceivable and what is inferred is often not very important for the person, although it is of considerable interest to the psychologist.

It might also be the case that, although the expected dimension is now physically perceivable, the exact location of a particular entity on that dimension is unclear. The aroused schema may, in this situation, play a role in determining the position which will be perceived. There are many examples of this sort of influence of schemas. Bruner, Postman, & Rodrigues (1951) presented subjects with a silhouette of apples or of oranges, both with the same red-orange coloration. The subjects were then asked to adjust a color wheel until it matched the color of the silhouettes. The subjects who were dealing with apple-shaped silhouettes used more red in making this match than did those who were given the orange-shaped outline. This was taken to indicate that more redness was actually perceived by the subjects when the silhouette was apple-shaped. The same process occurs when a person may barely be able to hear a speech by a person with whom he believes he disagrees. He may then tend to "hear" the speaker contradict many of his ideas.

Another variation of this type of influence of aroused schemas on perception occurs in situations in which the position on the expected dimension is physically clear, but in which the individual does not attend closely to it. He may have attended closely to the dimension whose perception originally aroused the schema, but his attention to the expected dimension may have dropped off.

This sequence of attentional processes may be the result of the physical impossibiliity of perceiving the expected dimension at the same time as the originally perceived dimension, as when we see only someone's head and shoulders in a crowded elevator. We can attend to the dimension of the look on his face and the clothes on his shoulders; this arouses a schema corresponding to a type of person.

We then have an expected dimension about the rest of his appearance as he steps out of the elevator. Or, this sequence of attentional processes may be the result of a very low degree or near absence of attention to the expected dimension. One reason for this lessening of attention to the expected dimension may hark back to what we emphasized so much in the previous chapter: the limited capacity of the individual to process information. The individual may be attending to so many other aspects of the total situation or there may be so many other schemas aroused that attending to the expected dimension as well as to the originally perceived one is beyond him. After all, one of the reasons that people have schemas is to enable them to cope with increasingly great amounts of information. People therefore may not attend to the expected dimension at all times. Yet this dimension is in a state of arousal, along with the rest of the schema. As a consequence, the person may act as if he actually had perceived the expected position on the expected dimension. Thus, if he were later asked to recall what he observed, he would say that he saw an entity corresponding to the entire schema, even though he actually had not attended to the expected dimensions. This process can manifest itself if the individual is asked only a moment later to recall what was observed. Bruner & Postman (1949) flashed pictures of ordinary playing cards to subjects at such rapid exposure speeds that while the color of the cards could be readily perceived, the details of the shape of the figure on them could not. Subjects then identified the cards in terms of color, since it was more readily perceivable than shape. Certain of the pictures presented contained unusual color-figure combinations which do not exist in a standard deck, such as a black ace of diamonds. However, when, for instance, *red* clubs were presented, they were identified as, say, hearts, and the disparity was not noticed. Or, if the figure or design was attended to, it could be seen only in broad outline, because of the short duration of exposure. Thus, a queen with a beard tended to be identified as an ordinary queen, with no reaction to the anomalous beard. A very common instance of this type of inattention has to do with typographical errors. As any person knows who has tried to correct galley proof, especially those of his own writing, it is exceedingly difficult to notice errors of spelling. The general outline of the words, the first few letters of the word, arouse schemas corresponding to the complete intended words, so that errors, especially in the last few letters of the word, may go uncorrected. Postman (1951) showed that people are less likely to notice that a given letter is reversed if it is embedded in a meaningful word than when it occurs in a nonsense syllable. Listening to a friend tell the same story for the umpteenth time, one may not notice the new ending he has for it. Listening to a news report, one may not notice that a "warmonger" made a peace proposal.

Degree of Unity of Schemas

Another influence that schemas have on perception results from the fact that schemas function as units, as integrated wholes distinct from their backgrounds. Thus, aspects of a perceived situation which correspond to the positions on the conceptualized dimensions of the schema will tend to be perceived as a unit, to have a coherence. If a person has a schema about a political group, he may perceive them as a unit, not as separate people. If a person has a schema about meetings, he will tend to see a given meeting as a unity, as an entity. Since the acquisition of schemas is based sometimes on repeated exposures to the same configuration of concrete dimensions, the individual will tend to be more likely to perceive this configuration as a single entity, as a single unit, as he experiences it more frequently (Beach, 1964a; 1964b). The individual will perceive the unit readily, rather than dealing with its parts analytically as discrete entities. The more political parties, the more meetings he has seen, the more will particular parties and meetings appear as units to him.

The greater the number of dimensions of relationship which have been developed to bind together the other dimensions included in a schema, the more unified is the schema. The more orderly the meetings, the better organized the party, the more likely is the person to react to particular parties and meetings as units. The greater the unity, the more the parts are seen as belonging to one another rather than to any other aspects of the situation. Accordingly, the more highly unified a schema is, the greater is the likelihood that the individual will perceive in terms of the positions on the expected dimensions which are specified in the schema. Thus, many of the effects of the schemas described in the previous paragraphs are more likely to occur if the schemas are highly unified. An individual is more likely to extrapolate from what he knows about a person to other, nonpresent dimensions; he is more likely to perceive ambiguous positions on expected dimensions as being consistent with the schema; he is less likely to attend to positions on the expected dimensions. Thus, the person with a unified schema of meetings might be quite likely to expect actually to perceive that meetings have rules, procedures, and goals if these are part of his schema about meetings. Furthermore, the more unified a schema is, the more will the individual perceive in terms of a unit, a total entity, rather than in terms of the dimensions of schemas; he will take the latter for granted.

The perception of a situation in terms of units enables the individual to process more information, since such aggregates may subsume many details. Accordingly, a person who has many schemas would be better able to deal with details and to encompass more aspects of situations than one who does not. The person with the unified schemas about meetings might find it relatively easy to attend to the agenda of a particular meeting.

Adults obviously have more schemas than children and therefore are better able to grasp more aspects of a given situation. An adult is less subject than is a child to having his perception of a situation distorted because he attends only to a part of the situation. Such distortions sometimes take the form of the optical illusion. Adults are less subject to such illusions, Piaget (1955) argues, because they are less likely to "center" on one aspect of the situation. On the other hand, adults show the perceptual constancies more than children do. For example, they are able to compensate for the influence of the small retinal image associated with a distant person by taking into consideration his distance as well, and thereby will judge his height more accurately. They are able to compensate for the unusual retinal image of an object shown at an odd angle by taking the rotation of the object into consideration, and thereby perceiving it in its true shape. Children are less able to engage in these compensations, partly because they are less able to process all of the information that is necessary to compensate for the potentially misleading retinal image.

THE DEGREE OF PROBABILISM OF SCHEMAS

Of course, in some perceptual situations, the expected dimension is not only physically perceivable, but is quite difficult to avoid attending to because of its physical characteristics. It may be too big, too bright, too noisy to escape attention, or there may be so much changing of position on it that attention is drawn strongly to it. Say a person opens a box of brightly wrapped objects, or glances out his window to see a large gathering in the street below. In these cases, an aroused schema might still determine what dimensions are likely to be given attention, but would hardly be expected to determine the positions on them. Even if the person had always experienced boxes with dull wrappings, he could not blind himself to the bright colors. Even if the person had only seen automobiles in the street below, he could not avoid noticing the large collection of people.

The degree of consistency between a given perceived situation and the aroused schema relevant to it is a central concern in the next aspect of the functioning of schemas we will examine—the ways in which perceived situations influence existing schemas. In keeping with our basic assumption that an individual can be aware of the functioning of his schemas, let us assume that the individual can perceive the degree of consistency between a given perception and an aroused schema. He can perceive that the collection of people on the street violates his conception of what happens in streets. The individual can then develop a conceptual dimension concerning this degree of consistency between the schema and the perceived world; accordingly, this dimension can become a part of a schema. Our friend looking out the window might change his schema to the effect that streets are occupied by cars most, but not all, of the time. Let us call the degree to which schemas are believed to have exceptions the degree of probabilism of the schema. The notion of the degree of probabilism of a schema should be distinguished from the schema having to do with the expectation of consistency between schemas and perceived reality. For example, a schema may be highly probabilistic and yet be consistent with reality if reality also is probabilistic. A person may believe that in his area it rains most, but not all, of the time. If it actually does rain on 80 per cent of the days, reality is consistent with his schema. If it rains either 0 per cent or 100 per cent of the time, reality would be inconsistent with the schema.

A question arises as to how exceptional an exception has to be before it is perceived as such. In some cases, any slight deviation might be considered an exception. In other cases, only large deviations along a dimension are seen as exceptions. Beach (1964a; 1964b) has speculated that those variations in definition of exceptions are a result of variations in the goals of the person, of changes in his motivational state. Perhaps there also are stable individual differences in the degree to which people tend to classify objects as similar despite some differences on some dimensions. Pettigrew (1958) has developed a scale to measure this characteristic, which he has termed category width.

It is important to notice exactly what the term probabilistic means. It refers to the degree to which a schema is a matter of probabilities rather than certainties. Thus, a *highly* probabilistic schema is one seen as having a lower probability of being confirmed in every relevant instance than is a schema of *low* probabilism. A schema of *low* probabilism is one of *high* certainty. In short, it is important to distinguish between probability and probabilism; in a sense, they are negatively related.

Preference for Schemas Low in Probabilism

Highly probabilistic schemas pose a problem for the person in view of the motivations with respect to schemas which were cited in the previous chapter. There it was pointed out that an individual is motivated to acquire schemas in part to facilitate the processing of information. Highly probabilistic schemas do so less well in this regard than do less probabilistic ones, because additional information regarding whether the specific situation confronting the individual is an exception or not must be processed. If most but not all professors are believed to be friendly, one has to be on guard for additional information. We also learned that the individual is motivated to acquire schemas in order to facilitate goal attainment. Highly probabilistic schemas serve this purpose less well than schemas of low probability. If a student is trying to ask a professor a question, it would be easier for him if he knew either that all professors were unfriendly or that all were friendly; he could know better how to ask the question. However, if he has a schema that some professors are unfriendly and others not, his waiting to ask a question presents him with additional problems in making a decision. Both of these effects of highly probabilistic schemas are likely to cause the individual some anxiety. His lessened ability to process information and to attain his goals make it likely that at least on some occasions he will be overloaded with information or blocked in attaining goals because of probabilistic schemas. As a result of the person's perception of these effects of highly probabilistic schemas, he will develop a schema that probabilistic schemas are detrimental to him. He will develop motivation to reduce the probabilism of his schemas.

One consequence of this motivation to avoid schemas of high probabilism is that they tend to be less familiar to the person than schemas of low probabilism. Therefore, they are evaluated less highly than are more familiar low probabilism schemas.

The strength of schema-derived motives may vary from person to person because of varying experiences and varying degrees to which the schema underlying the motive is learned. Therefore, some people may have greater tolerance for probabilistic schemas than others. These people are likely to have had fewer experiences than others in which a decision about acting or not acting had to be made; they may have had fewer experiences in which they experienced anxiety as a result of inability to process information. Both of these types of experiences influence the development of motivation to reduce probabilism. For example, an ancient professor hiding in his ivory tower amidst books describing all sorts of theories may develop little motivation to reduce probabilism. On the other hand, the man guarding the door to the tower and checking people to see if they are qualified to enter might develop strong motives to reduce probabilism.

On the other hand, once an individual does acquire a schema-based motive, it is likely to remain with him as a strong motive, irrespective of the gains or pains the motive nets him in any specific situation. This relative imperviousness to influence by direct experience results from the abstract nature of schemas. Thus, the motivation to reduce probabilism may remain with the person even after he no longer has any further experiences from which he originally derived the motivation. He may have a great aversion to probabilistic schemas long after he has been forced to think or act in terms of such schemas. The guardian of the ivory tower door might retain his aversion to highly probabilistic schemas even in the years of his retirement.

Techniques for Reducing Probabilism

How does this motivation to reduce probabilism manifest itself? What can the individual do? First, he can avoid exceptions by arousing another schema for which the instance is not an exception. "I was mistaken; that is not a civilian, but a Vietcong spy."

Second, he can accomplish the same end as in the above instance, but do so in recall or in reminiscence after he has physically left the "exceptional" situation. "I've been thinking about that guy dressed in civilian clothes; I don't think he was a civilian after all; he was a spy." In estimating the average of a set of scores from memory, people have been shown to exhibit a tendency to ignore the extreme "exceptional" scores (cf. Peterson and Beach, 1967). For instance, their estimations are lower than would be the case if they considered the extreme high scores.

Third, the person can find a higher order schema which subsumes both the consistent and the exceptional cases. "Most students don't demonstrate during exam week; those that do are those who don't care about their future." Henle (1942) found that subjects were just as likely to accurately recognize reversed letters as non-reversed ones if they had a higher order schema to the effect that the researcher was going to present some letters in reversed positions.

This latter approach is one which is more likely to be taken by adults than by children, since adults have had more experience in using higher order schemas. Suppose an adult is faced with a random series of events. For example, an experimenter may sound a bell most, but not all, of the time after a light goes on, and ask adults to predict what will occur after each presentation of the light. Most adults will attempt to find some pattern in the series of events, to find some higher order schema which will help to explain the series of exceptions. Thus, they will attempt to develop some system for predicting what will happen after each light, and it often takes the form of the gambler's fallacy, in which they predict that what will occur is what did not occur on the previous trial. Children, on the other hand, just predict that the most likely event will occur; they are not experienced enough to use an H.O.S. Thus, children will turn out to be the better predictors, since they are more likely in the long run to guess correctly. Adults, who are trying to "dope out" the system, will be more sophisticated and make more errors.

Fourth, the individual may reduce probabilism by developing an H.O.S. which does not help him predict specific exceptions, but which permits the prediction that there will be exceptions. We all probably have some H.O.S.s like this about weather forecasts, with all due respect to our local weather bureaus. This tack, of course, turns the exceptions into confirmations of a highly probabilistic higher order schema, but does so at the cost of some of the motivations underlying the avoidance of probabilistic schemas. No one will deny that we would be a lot better able to plan our lives if the weather bureau were better able to predict.

There are many refinements of these techniques of handling exceptions which we will examine in subsequent chapters. Meanwhile, it is important to note that the person obviously will have more opportunity and need to practice these techniques when reality in fact does abound with exceptions. Accordingly, an individual may develop more skill in handling and explaining away "exceptional" cases if he encounters them frequently than if they are rare. Ironically, a schema which encounters more exceptions may then become *lower* in probabilism than the one which rarely encounters exceptions. A professor who belives that most all freshmen are ignorant no doubt has learned how to explain away the knowledgeable ones he encounters. The same professor may be quite disturbed to find an exception to a previously exceptionless scientific law.

However, the techniques that the individual may learn with respect to handling exceptions to one schema may not remain limited to that schema. The individual may perceive his own techniques and develop higher order schemas about how to handle exceptions. He may then develop individually characteristic ways of reducing probabilism which cut across several types of schemas.

Probabilism and the Effects of Schemas on Perception

We have just indicated some of the effects of motivation to avoid highly probabilistic schemas. However, some aspects of the ways that schemas affect perception which we mentioned in the previous section also have an influence on the degree to which schemas become probabilistic. For one thing, an individual often pays little attention to the position of an entity on an expected dimension. Accordingly, he is not likely to attend to any minor deviation from the expected position on the dimension, and may then perceive such situations as being consistent with his schema. A "straight" person might recall that a hippie had a pin with an inverted American flag when in fact it was right side up. This sort of process might even occur when the expected dimension is not physically perceivable, since, in retrospect, the individual may incorrectly recall that he perceived all of the aspects of the situation, since his total schema was in a state of arousal. The "square" might recall that the hippie had long hair, even if it was not possible for him to see it because of a large hat and a turned-up collar. Also, increases in the probabilism of a schema will not develop as a result of the occurrence of an exception if the schema itself is not in a state of arousal.

The individual may perceive instances of the occurrence of the two ways just mentioned in which the relationship between schemas and perception holds probabilism down. He may notice that probabilism is reduced if he does not pay too much attention to detail or if he thinks about certain things only in certain situations. He may then develop schemas relating these ways of acting to reduced probabilism, and these schemas can then be added to the techniques mentioned above which the person is motivated to use to keep probabilism low. A man might learn to think of morality only when he is in church or synagogue. Another may not want to read too many details in the newspapers.

Factors Relating to Change in Level of Probabilism

From a more general perspective it should be noted that highly probabilistic schemas are more resistant to any change in their level of probabilism than are schemas low in probabilism. A schema very low in probabilism can be found to be inconsistent with perception by a relatively small number of exceptions. If a person had a belief that had been at a zero level of probabilism or complete certainty, a single exception could move it toward higher probabilism. If an Arab believed that all Israelis wanted to persecute Arabs, this schema would suffer a serious blow if he saw an Israeli strongly defend Arabs. On the other hand, with highly probabilistic schemas a few confirmations will not have a similarly strong impact, since exceptions are anticipated. A relatively long series of confirmations is likely to be necessary to effect any shift in probabilism in this case.

Another Arab, who believed that most, but not all, Israelis persecuted Arabs, would not have to change his schemas on seeing the Israeli defend Arabs; but he would have to increase the probabilism of his schema if he saw a rather large number of Israelis defend Arabs. On the other hand, certain aspects of the manner in which schemas influence perceptual processes tend to make it more difficult to maintain the low probabilism of some schemas. We have seen that gross and blatant discrepancies from an expected position on a dimension tend to attract attention. We are all a bit startled by the unexpected. We would all notice a priest wearing a beanie. Whether this attention-gaining aspect of exceptions is enough to overcome the just-cited in-attention to expected dimensions is a matter of how much of a change is involved and of how clear and easily perceivable the exception is. If the change is not great or distinct enough, the individual would continue to ignore the dimension in which it occurs.

The relative intractibility of highly probabilistic schemas, the motivations to keep probabilism low, and some features of the influence of schemas on perception indicate the strength of the overall thrust to keep probabilism low. It is as if a schema, once established, has a tendency to become less and less probabilistic with time, as the motivational and perceptual processes have their effects in the ways indicated. The smug "wisdom" of some older people may be an outcome of this process.

The counter-pressures which exist and which tend to force a rise in probabilism are directed mostly at L.O.S.s, since they are the closest to the "real world" and therefore most subject to "exceptions." Nevertheless, as we have seen, even these lower order schemas tend to be less probabilistic than the facts warrant. Furthermore, H.O.S.s build upon the L.O.S.s and thus tend to be no higher than the L.O.S.s in probabilism. In other words, the L.O.S.s act as buffers between the real world and the world of "abstract ideas." The simplification process starts at the level of the L.O.S. In addition, the motivation to keep probabilism low may be even stronger with respect to H.O.S.s than it is where L.O.S.s are concerned, since an increase in the probabilism of an H.O.S. would have the effect of increasing the probabilism of all the schemas subsumed under it. If an individual changed from a firm conviction that money would always be accepted in payment for goods and services to the conviction that it would be accepted only some of the time, he would then have to expect that he would be able to buy food only some of the time and buy clothes only some of the time. Such generalized increases in probabilism would indeed cause anxiety. If an individual has had one or more experiences in which a basic belief (H.O.S.) of his was shaken and consequently many of his other beliefs were disrupted because of their relationship to this central belief, he will thereafter be quite likely to be pro-tective of the low probabilism of his H.O.S.

The impact of this motivation to keep the probabilism of H.O.S.s low would, of course, be felt at each level in a hierarchically ordered set of schemas. The more levels in a person's hierarchy then, the lower would the overall level of probabilism be likely to be. A very ideologically oriented person is often one who thinks in terms of certainties or in terms of schemas of low probabilism. In fact, it is possible that some people who develop such complex multiple-level hierarchies may do so in order to generate a system of interrelated schemas of low probabilism. They may feel less anxious in the "pure," clear-cut world of ideologies and high-level abstractions. Those who disagree with them will often regard them as rigid-thinking fanatics. Of course, such people are quite vulnerable to drastic shifts toward high probabilism should they be forced to recognize that a schema quite high in the hierarchy is inconsistent with some blatant facts.

THE INFLUENCE OF EXTANT SCHEMAS ON THE DEVELOPMENT OF NEW SCHEMAS

An aroused schema plays an important role in determining which aspects or dimensions of a situation will be attended to. Obviously, if the information provided by perception of the situation is consistent with the schema, no new schemas will be acquired. If, however, there is some perceived inconsistency, the schema will tend to become more probabilistic. All of the motivations and processes which we have just described will tend to minimize the shift to greater probabilism; but, if inconsistencies occur frequently enough, and if observed instances of consistency occur infrequently enough, the existing schema may be raised in probabilism to the point where it may no longer really function as a schema. That is, the formerly apparent relationships among positions on given dimensions no longer exist in any stable way for the person. People in the midst of the Great Depression no doubt had many of their schemas shattered.

It is quite possible that in some cases, the various perceived inconsistencies themselves exhibit some regularity, pattern, or consistency. That is, all occurrences of the events which are inconsistent with the current schema may take much the same form. In such instances, the opportunity presents itself to develop a new schema based on the uniformity of the exceptional events. If a child had had a schema that all strangers are dangerous and if he now perceives more and more strangers that are friendly and very few that are not, he might come to acquire a new schema to the effect that strangers are indeed friendly. The important point here is that the dimension of friendliness-dangerousness was present in the original schema the child had, and therefore led the child to attend to this quality of strangers. The new schema thus entails a shift in the particular positions along this dimension which are held to be associated, not the acquisition of an entirely new dimension. The prior schema, then, makes its presence felt in terms of the part it plays in determining the conceptual dimensions, but not the specific positions on them, which will be involved in the new schema.

However, it must be noted that this process of acquiring a new schema out of consistent exceptions to an old one may be inhibited by another aspect of the influence exerted by aroused schemas—the effect of an aroused schema on recall. As was pointed out earlier in this chapter, exceptions to familiar schemas are often distorted in memory to fit the schema. Thus, the number of exceptions and their clarity would have to be higher than one might guess, since the old schema is "working" when the new perceptions are not immediate and clear. This type of distortion and, in addition, the motivations we have discussed, have the effect of inhibiting the acquisition of schemas which, in a sense, violate the person's existing schemas. We will see examples of this in subsequent chapters.

In the last chapter, we pointed out that an individual can develop schemas both through direct observation of situations and by means of communications from others. So far in this chapter, we have emphasized the functioning of schemas which have been derived from the former source. Now we will turn to a discussion of the latter, more social source. It was pointed out that an individual typically develops a higher order schema that thus and such a person or class of people are valid, reliable sources of information, of schemas. Since this is a higher order schema, it is likely to influence lower order schemas to become more consistent with it. "I always thought thus and so, until Daddy told me that it was not true." The H.O.S. having to do with the trustworthiness of certain social sources of information is generally more familiar than many lower order schemas, is thus more highly valued, so that L.O.S.s will be brought into line with it. In the present chapter we have seen that the perception of correspondence between schemas and actual situations tends to be greater than the reality of the situation in fact supports. This applies as well to schemas derived from communications from others. As a consequence, the individual may come to perceive that there is, in fact, a greater correspondence between what he is told and what actually exists than is really warranted by the facts. The reliability of the social sources of schemas thus tends to be self-confirming. The social source will tend to be perceived as more and more reliable over time.

We have also seen that there is great pressure to reduce the probabilism of schemas, and that this pressure is particularly strong with regard to H.O.S.s. These sorts of social schemas are H.O.S.s and therefore highly subject to these pressures. More specifically, an individual will tend to reject possible exceptions to lower order schemas which have been communicated to him. "That is not what he really meant; what he really meant was. . . ."; "What he told me had to do with people like us, not with *them*." Since the individual will tend to reduce the probabilism of all the L.O.S.s derived from a source, the veridicality of the source is thereby protected on all sides.

Furthermore, the individual may be motivated to directly lower the perceived probabilism of the source, especially if that source provides schemas in a wide variety of topic areas. Increasing the probabilism of the H.O.S. having to do with the reliability of this person or class of persons would then require an increase in the probabilism of all of the schemas for which they were responsible.

Such an increase would, of course, be highly discomfiting to the person and to provide protection from this unattractive possibility he can attempt to lower the probabilism of the source directly. "I have to believe in him, since I depend on him for so much information"; "He's got to be right, since I listen to him so much."

References

Allport, G. W., and Postman, L.: *The Psychology of Rumor*, New York, Holt, 1947.

Bartlett, F. C.: *Remembering.* Cambridge, Cambridge University Press, 1932.

Beach, L. R.: Cue probabilism and inference behavior. *Psychological Monographs*, 1964a, 78:(5, Whole No. 582).

Beach, L. R.: Recognition, assimilation, and identification of objects. *Psychological Monographs*, 1964b, 78:(6, Whole No. 583).

Bruner, J. S., and Minturn, A. L.: Perceptual identification and perceptual organization. *Journal of Genetic Psychology*, 1955, 53:21–28.

Bruner, J. S., and Postman, L.: On the perception of incongruity: a paradigm. *Journal of Personality*, 1949, 18:206–223.

Bruner, J. S., Postman, L., and Rodrigues, J. S.: Expectation and the perception of color. *Amercian Journal of Psychology*, 1951, 64:216–227.

Deutsch, J. A., and Deutsch, D.: Attention: some theoretical considerations. *Psychological Review*, 1963, 70:80–90.

Dillehay, R. C., Insko, C. A., and Smith, M. D.: Logical consistency and attitude change, *Journal of Personality and Social Psychology*, 1966, 3:646-654.

Henle, M.: An experimental investigation of past experience as a determinant of visual form perception. *Journal of Experimental Psychology*, 1942, 30:1–22.

Hovland, C. I., Lumsdaine, A. A., and Sheffield, F. O.: *Experiments in Mass Communications*. New Haven, Yale University Press, 1953.

Hovland, C. I., and Mandell, W.: An experimental comparison of conclusion-drawing by the communicator and by the audience. *Journal of Abnormal and Social Psychology*, 1952, 47:581–588.

McGuire, W. J.: Cognitive consistency and attitude change. *Journal of Abnormal and Social Psychology*, 1960, 60:345–353.

McGuire, W. J.: The current status of cognitive consistency theories. In S. Feldman (Ed.), *Cognitive Consistency.* New York, Academic Press, 1966.

Miller, G. A., Galanter, E., and Pribram, K. H.: *Plans and the Structure of Behavior.* New York, Holt, Rinehart, and Winston, 1960.

Norman, D. A.: Acquisition and retention in short term memory. *Journal of Experimental Psychology*, 1966, 72:369–381.

Norman, D. A.: Toward a theory of memory and attention. *Psychological Review*, 1968, 75:522–536.

Norman, D. A.: *Memory and Attention*, New York, John Wiley and Sons, Inc., 1969.

Papageorgis, D.: Bartlett effect and the persistence of induced opinion change. *Journal of Abnormal and Social Psychology*, 1963, 67:61–67.

Perky, C. W.: An experimental study of imagination. *American Journal of Psychology,* 1910, *21*:422–452.

Peterson, C. R., and Beach, L. R.: Man as an intuitive statistician. *Psychological Bulletin,* 1967, 68:29–46.

Pettigrew, T.: The measurement and correlates of category width as a cognitive variable. *Journal of Personality,* 1958, *26*:532–544.

Piaget, J.: *The Child's Construction of Reality.* New York, Routledge, 1955.

Pikas, A.: *Abstraction and Concept Formation.* Cambridge, Harvard University Press, 1966.

Postman, L.: Toward a general theory of cognition. In J. R. Rohrer and M. Sherif (Eds.), *Social Psychology at the Crossroads.* New York, Harper, 1951.

Rosenberg, M. J.: An analysis of affective-cognitive consistency. In M. J. Rosenberg, C. I. Hovland, W. J. McGuire, R. Abelson, and J. W. Brehm, *Attitude Organization and Change.* New Haven, Yale University Press, 1960.

Stotland, E., Patchen, M., and Katz, D.: The reduction of prejudice through the arousal of self-insight. *Journal of Personality,* 1959, *27*:507–531.

Treisman, A. M., and Geffin, G.: Selective attention: perception or response? *Quarterly Journal of Experimental Psychology,* 1967, *19*:1–17.

CHAPTER 5

SCHEMAS ABOUT PEOPLE

In the previous two chapters we have presented in broad, rather general strokes the theoretical framework which will guide our discussion of social psychological phenomena through the balance of this text. However, in developing this position we did not emphasize concrete examples or research findings which were obviously social psychological in content. This was done quite deliberately in that our interest was in developing a framework which transcends narrow, parochial and perhaps artificial boundaries and which draws upon relevant research no matter what its source. Thus, we have employed material taken from studies of basic perceptual and learning processes, developmental psychology, and other disciplines which seemed to have something to contribute.

Now it is time, however, to begin to concentrate on the application of this framework to the social psychological phenomena which will characterize the remainder of this volume. The first topic to be discussed has to do with what has traditionally been called person perception. This concern here is with an investigation of the ways in which we form impressions of other persons and their qualities or traits; the nature of the processes by which we generate and assimilate information about others; and the uses to which we put such information. In approaching this general topic we will employ a procedure which has been used in earlier chapters—that of abstracting one aspect of a very complex naturally occurring event or process, and attempting to develop some general rules and laws about that aspect. In this chapter, then, we will emphasize the processes of person perception in situations in which the other person is seen in relative isolation from his physical or social surroundings, and in which we do not actively interact with him. Such a restriction of focus is not just a useful didactic device, but one which also reflects situations which do occur naturally. That is, there certainly are occasions on which we receive information which more or less exclusively has to do with the characteristics of another person, independent of any context or social setting and where the opportunity for developing a reciprocal relationship is restricted or non-existent. For instance, we might simply read about another person in a novel, newspaper, or laboratory experiment, or be told about someone whom we have not yet met by an acquaintance of his, or intently observe another at a distance. In these examples we are the recipients of various types of information about another individual but do not develop any mutual relationship with him or her. In subsequent chapters more complete interactions will be dealt with in which there is two-way communication and the opportunity for a reciprocal relationship to develop.

This sort of preoccupation or intense concentration on one other person to the exclusion of background and contextual elements or that person's relationships with others who might be present could also be dictated by a precept established earlier. We have already noted that there is a limitation on the number of different aspects of a situation which can be attended to at any given time. Thus, a very intense preoccupation with some other person would tend to lead the perceiver to ignore the surroundings of the other person, physical or social. The concentration on the other person might entail concern with so many aspects of his appearance, personality, speech, gait, opinions, feelings, that there would be little leftover capacity on the part of the observer with which to react to other aspects of the total situation. It is not unusual when watching a movie or play to focus on one character almost to the exclusion of the others, so that when that person is on camera or on stage the others are not really noticed—but we can give a detailed description of the character in whom we were interested.

By the same token, if a perceiver is attending more generally to the total social situation, he will be less likely to make an intensive study of any single other person; his capacity might be already used up. To return to the theatrical example, we can, by way of contrast, focus on the plot of a play so intensely that we notice the characters in the play only very superficially. We view them only in terms of their relevance to the plot as such. In the next chapter, we will examine the processes involved, when the individual focuses on "plots"—but plots will be taken as only one instance of a broader class of entities or events, interpersonal processes, and relationships. What, then, are the factors which determine whether a person will focus on another person in "isolation" or whether he will focus on the social situation? What are the determinants of the degree of attention to persons in isolation as against the social and physical context?

There are a number of consistent and related answers to this question. These answers will not be given all at once, but will be developed throughout this chapter. The reason for the extended presentation of the answers is that they emerge from the application to social psychological phenomenon of different aspects of the framework presented in the past two chapters. The application of this framework to the phenomenon of the perception of persons will be presented by following as much as possible the order in which this orientation has been developed in the previous chapters. By doing so, the usefulness of this framework should be more clearly seen.

Information Processing Capacity for Social Stimuli

It has already been pointed out that an individual might focus on perception of another in isolation because of the general limitation on the number of aspects of a situation to which a person can attend or react. One of the questions which emerges from this application is whether this limitation on channel capacity is the same when the perception of attributes of persons is concerned as it is when the perception of such physical stimuli as tones or clusters of dots is involved. The particular type of channel capacity studied by Miller (1956) and Garner (1962) was the number of differentiations which a person can make on a given dimension of the stimulus, assuming that such differentiations are related to actual differences along the dimensions. For example, if an individual is presented with a series of 15 different tones, he can usually sort them into 7 (plus or minus two) different categories. Miller and Garner have found that this figure of 7 is fairly stable for different types of nonsocial physical stimuli. If the reason for this limit is actually neurological, then it should be the same with respect to perception of persons. Bieri and his co-workers (1966) attempted to determine what the channel capacity was for judgments made about other people. The way in which Bieri usually made his determinations of channel capacity was to have clinical psychologists who deal with maladjusted persons make judgments about the degree of maladjustment of fictitious persons described to them. In a characteristic study, eight different descriptions of fictitious people were presented, one at a time, to the judges. One of the eight was described by just one sentence denoting a particular form of behavior, such as aggression; a second person, by two sentences denoting that form of behavior; and so on, up to a fictitious person described by eight sentences. The judges then rated each of these persons on their degree of maladjustment using a scale which ranged in eight steps from little to a great deal.

The degree to which the judges were able to differentiate meaningfully the eight fictitious persons was measured by a complex mathematical formula. The judge was assumed to have dealt with more information the more he spread his ratings out among all the points on the scale, did such spreading evenly across all eight points, and gave ratings which were correlated with the "actual" degree of maladjustment of the fictitious persons. Bieri found that the amount of information that was processed tended to be slightly lower than the amount other researchers have found for nonsocial stimuli. He found that the information dealt with corresponded to four to six categories, rather than the seven typically found with nonsocial physical stimuli. However, Bieri himself urges caution in drawing any firm conclusions from these data, since most of the studies which he cites have had to do with such dimensions as maladjustment, anxiety, and social withdrawal. It is possible that such "clinical" dimensions differ in some important way from the more garden variety of dimension in the perception of other persons, so that for the latter dimensions the channel capacity may actually be about the same as for physical stimuli. However, the requisite research has not been reported at the time of this writing.

Regardless of what further research does uncover with respect to the magnitude of the "channel capacity" in perceiving other persons in nonclinical ways, the important point is that there is an upper limit on the amount of information a person can deal with, at least as measured in this way. Furthermore, it will be recalled that in the third chapter it was pointed out that in addition to the *degree* of differentiation a person can make on any one dimension, there is another aspect of channel capacity which has to do with the *number* of different dimensions to which a person can attend at any given time. Miller (1956) suggested that an individual could attend to only about 10 dimensions at a time. If we combine both types of channel capacity (the number of different dimensions and the differentiations along each which can be made) we can react to more aspects of the situation than if we have only one dimension. This total improvement is, however, gained at a cost of some degree of differentiation on each dimension. Bieri and his co-workers (1966) also set out to determine whether this powerful tool for processing information was also usable with respect to information about other people. They performed a study along the general lines described above, with the addition that in some instances they provided information about two or three different dimensions instead of just one. However, their results

were quite inconclusive, since the judges did not perceive that variations along the various different dimensions were really independent
of one another. That is, they responded as if they believed that having
a given position on one dimension implied having a particular position
on another. Garner (1962), in his review of the research on this problem,
pointed out the necessity that the independence of dimensions be
perceived if more information is to be processed by increasing the
number of dimensions, even if the variations on the dimensions are
in fact correlated. Again, despite Bieri's pioneering efforts, it can
only be assumed that an increase in the number of dimensions involved
increases the potential for dealing with information about the social
environment.

Cognitive Complexity

Related to this point is a body of research which indicates that
persons do differ in the number of dimensions they typically employ
in dealing with their social environment. Since the acquisition of conceptualized dimensions is an outcome of repeated encounters with
the same situations, the more frequently an individual encounters
a given situation, the more conceptualized dimensions he would be
expected to acquire. The number of conceptualized dimensions
possessed by a person with respect to his perception of other people
has typically been referred to by other investigators as "cognitive
complexity." A cognitively complex person is one who through experience has acquired a relatively large number of conceptual dimensions relevant to the perception of other people.

The use of the term "cognitive complexity" to refer to a trait
or characteristic of an individual would appear to imply that a
cognitively complex person has a greater number of dimensions in
all areas of his experience, not just where perceiving other people
is concerned. However, this point is a rather controversial one.
Schroeder, Driver, and Steufert (1967) have developed a measure
of cognitive complexity which does seem to relate to an individual's
behavior in a wide variety of settings. They reasoned and found
that a cognitively complex person will seek out more different types
of information when attempting to solve problems than will a cognitively simple person, provided the amount of information originally available is neither very great nor very small. For example, in
playing military strategy games, "complex" people sought more
varied forms of "intelligence" about their "enemy" than did cognitively simple persons. Schroeder *et al.* measured complexity by
using any of a combination of tests, such as the Rep Test; a meas-

ure of the number of dimensions which are mathematically necessary to "reproduce" a person's judgment of similarity between objects; the number of different categories into which the person sorts objects; sentence completion tests; answers to test questions especially designed for this purpose, etc., and thus they have some evidence that complexity is general across domains of experience. On the other hand, Crockett (1965) in his review of research on this problem concluded that complexity is specific to certain areas of experience, a conclusion which is more in line with our framework. Nevertheless, a mid-ground is possible: Some people may have such extensive and intensive experience that they become very generally complex. Furthermore, if an individual develops an H.O.S. that complexity in one area of experience is helpful in coping with his social and physical environment, he may apply that H.O.S. to other areas. Whether this mid-ground represents a valid interpretation of the issue must be determined by further research.

The basic idea for measuring cognitive complexity stems from the work of Kelley (1955) who developed the so-called role repertory test or "Rep Test." In its administration an individual is given a list of categories of other people who are important in his life, e.g., mother, father, husband, wife, friend. Then all the possible combinations of three of these categories are formed by the tester and each set is presented, one set at a time, to the person. For example, one set might consist of "friend, husband, father." The person is asked to indicate which two categories in each set he considers more similar to one another than to the third. Next he is asked to state in what way they are more similar to one another than to the third. The "ways" in which the person construes the similarity and difference among the categories are taken as indicators of the dimensions the person uses in perception of other people. This procedure is repeated for all the sets. The number of different dimensions a person uses across all the sets of three is tabulated. A cognitively complex person is one who uses a relatively high number of different dimensions. A cognitively simple person is defined as one who tends to use the same few dimensions in differentiating categories in all the sets. The basic principle of this technique has been used in tests in slightly different ways by Bieri (1966), Crockett (1965), and others, but all the measures get at the number of dimensions.

The effect of experience on cognitive complexity has been most directly studied by Yarrow and Campbell (1963). They measured the cognitive complexity of 8- to 13-year-old children at a summer camp by having them describe one another to the researchers, privately, at the beginning and end of their two-week stay at the camp. Since conceptual dimensions are acquired on the basis of experience, observation, and communication, the children were more cognitively complex at the end of the two weeks than at the beginning. Yarrow and Campbell also found that the dimensions that were used most by the children were those having to do with interactions with one another, such as aggressiveness, friendliness, assertiveness, and submissiveness. These conceptual dimensions refer to those aspects of the other children's behavior that each child would be most likely to attend to, since they were relevant to his own behavior. In fact, the children were even more likely to use these dimensions at the end of the two-week period than at the beginning; they had had more opportunity to encounter instances of these aspects. The significance of sheer exposure to these aspects of others' behavior is suggested by the fact that the children who were more likely to interact with others were more cognitively complex, regardless of whether they were aggressive and assertive or kindly and nurturant. Furthermore, children who were either particularly liked or disliked were viewed more complexly than children who were regarded indifferently; if the children had enough to do with another child to permit the development of a like or dislike for him, they had the chance to become more complex about him. In short, the data from this microcosm of a children's camp suggests that experience of almost any sort with others increases complexity.

One can infer the same relationship between experience and cognitive complexity by comparing the complexity of people who are more likely to have had certain types of experience with those for whom such experience is less likely. Since age obviously gives one more experience with other people, it is not surprising that Yarrow and Campbell found that older children in their summer camp exhibited greater complexity than did younger children. Crockett (1965) reports that college fraternity members are characterized by greater cognitive complexity than non-fraternity students, and it seems quite reasonable to assume that the fraternity members in general have more extensive and intensive interactions with other people and have attended more to other people. Undergraduates and teachers, like people in general, are more likely to spend time with peers than with those higher in status, and therefore have been found to show greater complexity where information and judgments with respect to their peers are concerned. Women school teachers, who work in a setting with relatively few men in it, manifest lower complexity with respect to men than with respect to women. Crockett also reports that the adults he studied tended to view liked persons in a more complex manner than they did disliked, presumably because more time is spent with liked persons. This finding is only superficially contradictory to the earlier reported Yarrow and Campbell results that show high complexity for both those liked and disliked, since in the children's camp setting they studied it is unlikely that the children had much opportunity to avoid their disliked peers because of the counsellor-imposed organization of activities. Obviously, adults in normal circumstances have more opportunity to select their companions and thus to spend relatively little time with persons not well-liked.

Another apparent contradiction exists between the effect of experience on cognitive complexity and the tendency to perceive situations in terms of previously acquired schemas. To the extent that an individual's extant schemas determine how he views and interprets situations, new dimensions or schemas are not likely to be acquired. Thus the degree to which experience does lead to an increase in cognitive complexity depends in part on the number and content of the schemas already in a person's repertoire. If the individual has few schemas that can be aroused in a given situation, or if the schemas are of such a high order as not to specify very much about the exact nature of the situation, then the acquisition of new schemas and dimensions is more probable.

Research on cognitive complexity is so new that many questions about the correlates of cognitive complexity remain unanswered as yet. For example, the failure to find any correlation between cognitive complexity and I.Q. may be a result of the fact that most of the research has been done on college students, who are mostly above average in I.Q. The truth might be that among these people and this restricted range of I.Q.s, there really is no relationship, but that if a sample of persons was studied which was more representative and included lower than average I.Q. persons, a general relationship would show up. This relationship could be visualized as follows; X indicates that there is a large number of people in the box:

| | | *Intelligence* | |
		high	low
	High	X	
complexity			
	Low	X	X

The table shows that in order to be highly complex, a person must be above a certain level of intelligence, but that above that level, it makes little difference how intelligent he is. A similar answer might be given to the possible relationship between cognitive complexity and creativity; people high in complexity might or might not be creative, but people low in complexity might be unlikely to be creative.

Still another type of question arises with respect to the relationship between cognitive complexity and anxiety. One could speculate that cognitively complex people are more anxious because they are confronted with so many alternative ways of perceiving. However, this possibility is probably mitigated by the hypothesized tendency for complex people to have more H.O.S.s, which enable them to process more information.

Determinants of Attention in Person Perception

So far, our concentration has been on what might be termed the quantitative aspects of person perception—how much information about another person can be processed at a given time. Now let us turn to some of the qualitative aspects of this topic. Which people will a person attend to? What aspect of those people selected for "study" will be attended to? A principle that was stated in Chapter Three indicated that an individual is more likely to attend to change, to variation, than to the stable or the unchanging entities in his environment, provided that the change is perceived in the context of some familiar entity or event. It was pointed out that this principle has particular relevance where social stimuli are concerned. Other people act, move, change in appearance from time to time and place to place. They are acted upon, are talked to, are "moved" by events, are changed in appearance by events, and so forth. In fact, a person who does not exhibit at least minimal change over a period of time is likely to be assumed to be ill or dead. At the same time, other people can be familiar in any of several ways, so that change associated with them is highly likely to be attended to. If it is a familiar other person who changes in some fashion, it will nevertheless be the case that many aspects of his appearance, voice, behavior, and so forth will remain the same, by definition. Thus, the change that does occur may be perceived in the context of the familiar and will therefore be attended to. Parents are notorious for their close attention to the changes in their children as they grow and mature; people attend closely to changes in the behavior and fortunes of friends, be the changes desirable or undesirable.

If, rather than a known individual, it is a familiar type or category of person which is changing, attention is still likely to be given even though the familiarity may not be as detailed and extensive as it would be in the case of the familiar other person. Persons may thus be slightly less attentive to such changes than to changes of familiar other individuals. Persons may attend to changes in the behavior of teachers, of store clerks, of foremen, of politicians, and of comedians.

The familiarity which provides the necessary background condition for the observation of social change does not have to reside in the other person; even a strange type of person seen in a familiar context will be attended to. Regardless of the relevant moral judgments, it must be recognized that old-fashioned freak shows at carnivals did not want for customers, but the carnival itself was a familiar event usually occurring in one's own home town, and one usually went accompanied by friends or relatives. If we travel to strange lands, we find the people interesting and even fascinating if we travel with someone familiar. Even the late John Steinbeck in his trip of rediscovery of his own country traveled "with Charley"—his dog.

Suppose, however, we are alone, faced with the changing and unfamiliar behavior of strangers in a strange land. We are isolated in a new country unlike our own. As many travelers can testify, one's experiences under these circumstances are so regular and predictable that they have been given a name: culture shock. The person is forced to attend to the strange, the new, the change because it is all about him—and as a consequence may experience anxiety, become depressed, and strongly desire to have to attend to the new no longer—to go home—or to find someone or something from back home. From personal experience, the senior author knows that even awareness that one is undergoing culture shock does not always help to overcome it.

This account of the determinants of the deployment of our limited attention helps to provide a partial answer to a question which we posed earlier regarding the determinants of how much persons will attend to a social situation as such and how much to the individuals in that situation. The discussion to this point indicates that persons are more likely to attend to individual other people if the social situation is a familiar one or a stable, unchanging one, and if the other people are themselves changing, acting, moving. On the other hand, attention is more likely to be paid to the social situation as such if the individual participants in it are familiar people or categories of people or are relatively unchanging, and inactive, and if the social situation itself is changing. For example, when watching Candid Camera, close attention is typically given to each "victim's" reactions to the same trick situation; the trick situation is initially the same for all the victims, and we watch them in the context of the even more familiar social situation of the Candid Camera show. On the other hand, we are often fascinated by the changing social situations which are encountered by familiar other people. The very length of *War and Peace* may be part of its fascination for readers, since a number of familiar characters may be followed as they encounter a great variety of social situations. Perhaps one of the reasons that culture shock is so overwhelming and repelling is that it typically involves newness both in behavior of individuals and of the social situations in which they are perceived.

Schemas and Implicit Theories of Personality

Conceptual dimensions are based on experience, but become relatively independent of the experience on which they are based. They become part of the individual's way of apprehending the world in general. He tends to use the same dimensions with respect to all types of people, although he will add some with respect to people he has much interaction with, as we have just seen. For example, Yarrow and Campbell (1963) found that, over and above the changes found with experience, each child tended to use the same dimensions at the beginning and end of the two-week period in the camp. A set of dimensions used by a given person may be so characteristic of him that others can fairly accurately match sets of dimensions to the users of these dimensions (cf. Bonarious, 1965).

Our theoretical framework indicates not only that people acquire conceptual dimensions, but also that if the individual experiences association or correlations between particular positions on these dimensions, he will tend to acquire schemas which are representative of such correlations. At the lowest level of schema, an individual can acquire an association between positions which apply only to one person. So-and-so always does thus-and-such when you ask him to do this-or-that. At a higher level of schema, the person may acquire a schema about categories of people, or even of people in general. Higher order schemas which the individual acquires about other people in general are often termed "implicit theories of personality"—which connotes not inaccurately that we are all, in a sense, theorists of personality. Implicit personality theories can be rather simply measured. A person, presented with a trait-adjective which might be applicable to some person, is then asked to indicate what else about the person he can infer. This inference can be indicated by choosing one or more other trait names from among a series of them, or by indicating how probable it is that a given other trait-adjective applies to a person who has that first trait, or by writing a short essay more fully describing the sort of individual who has the given quality. All of these methods have been used in countless studies. What is important to note is that people do not find making such inferences impossible or even overwhelmingly difficult. The reader need only ask himself what other qualities of persons come to mind if all that he knows is that some person is intelligent. The reader might possibly then have thought of him as "industrious, well-educated, and self-sufficient." Or some other very different associated traits may have come to mind. What these traits are is less important than the fact that they are seen as "going together"—we have schemas about people, implicit theories of personality.

Notice that the very notion of having implicit *theories* of personality indicates their abstract nature that, once acquired, they are relatively independent of particular cases. This will become more apparent if the reader tries to remember how he came to believe that intelligent people have the traits which he believes them to have. It is highly unlikely that some one acquaintance will come to mind who has been observed and who possesses the configuration involved in the schema.

Some of the associations involved in implicit theories of personality may be involved with a very high level of schema, applying to all people. However, some of the associations may be particular only to certain classes or categories of people. If a woman does *this*, it means she feels *that*; if a man does *this*, you don't know what it might mean (cf. Koltuv, 1962). In other words, there can be several levels in the hierarchy of schemas about other people.

The specific schemas a person develops are in part an outcome of his personal experiences. There is little research data directly illustrating the effect of experience on schemas, but there is some indirectly relevant data. With more experience, there is a greater basis for developing schemas, so that older children are more likely to draw inferences from their observation of instances of behavior of another person than are younger ones. Gollin (1958) demonstrated this by presenting children with descriptions of four examples of the behavior of a boy, two in which he was rather helpful to others, two in which he was rather hostile. When asked to describe the boy in their own words, older children were more likely to go beyond what was presented and infer other characteristics of the boy. The influence of experience also is illustrated by the fact that most children learn about the apparent differences between the sexes rather early in life. Experience not only leads to the acquisition of schemas, but also to the development of higher orders of schemas. For example, in Gollin's study just described, older children were more likely than younger ones to describe attributes in the boy which explained or accounted in some way for the inconsistency of his behavior—his being sometimes hostile, sometimes helpful. From the perspective of our theoretical framework this would be a reflection of the older children's having acquired higher order schemas which help explain discrepancies in lower order schemas.

Since schemas arise out of conceptual dimensions, an individual would be expected to develop schemas involving those dimensions which he uses most frequently. Koltuv (1962) asked people to indicate which traits were most relevant for their evaluations of other people; not surprisingly, people tended to list dimensions or traits which are relevant for interaction with others: "cruelty-kindness, friendliness-hostility, loyalty-disloyalty," and so on. They listed as nonrelevant such noninteractive dimensions as awkwardness, looks, absentmindedness, originality, formality, speed of reaction. Koltuv also obtained from her subjects a measure of the implications that the presence of one trait has for another. She found that the degree to which a person saw that one trait was related to another was higher for the relevant dimensions than for the nonrelevant. The more frequently experienced or relevant dimensions are more likely to be incorporated into schemas.

In addition to there being a set of associations between positions on conceptual dimensions, we have seen that schemas also have a degree of unity, a quality of being separate and distinct unified entities. In addition to the general tendency of schemas to form into psychological unities, there are strong pressures which increase this tendency with respect to schemas about other people. We generally perceive others as unities, at least with respect to their physical characteristics. All of the parts of a person are proximal and occur together; the person's behavior emanates from his total body. In our culture, we generally say, "He did this," not, "His hands did this." Other people react to the person as a totality—"I told him," not, "I told his ears." Thus, a very high order schema is acquired by people that other people constitute coherent units. (cf. Asch, 1952; Heider, 1958). The acquisition of this schema is enhanced by the motivation to keep probabilism to a minimum. If other people can be perceived as coherent units, then it is less likely that they will be seen to behave in "exceptional" ways. Thus schemas about other people and about categories of other people tend to become reifications, i.e., abstractions which are thought of as being concrete.

Because of this tendency to have unified schemas about other people, we sometimes think of and refer to categories of people as if they were a single person. A classic book compiling research on American soldiers in World War II was entitled *The American Soldier*. We sometimes talk of The Professor, The Student, The Policeman, The Black Militant, or The American Voter. It is not difficult to understand the processes involved, as they were set forth in Chapter Three, but these processes sometimes lead to some rather peculiar ways of thinking about the world, such as assuming that *The* American Voter was excited by some event.

Communications from Others as a Source of Schemas about People

Up to this point we have been emphasizing the acquisition of schemas about people as a consequence of direct observation. However, in Chapter Three it was pointed out that one of the H.O.S.s that people acquire deals with the belief that, to a greater or lesser extent, other people are sources of schemas about the world, and that to a greater or lesser extent, these schemas do correspond to reality. Accordingly, most people acquire an H.O.S. that other people are valid sources of information about other people, to a greater or lesser degree. The qualification about the degree to which this H.O.S. is acquired stems from the fact that, because of the great variability in human behavior, other people, e.g., parents, may be quite mistaken in their predictions and assessments of other people. The child may have observed that on some occasions parents' predictions about other people are simply not borne out. The assumption here is, of course, that the person is in a position to be able to check the schemas against his own perception of reality. This ability to check no doubt varies greatly both with the child and with the particular other people about whom his parents have communicated. A child probably does not have an opportunity to check the parents' (or teacher's) ideas about such people as Asian Indians and Eskimos, and therefore may accept others' ideas about such persons as completely valid. However, if the child has had a chance to check the parents' ideas about Whizzer, who lives down the street, and finds Whizzer really not as bad as his parents say, he may begin to have some doubts about the universal accuracy of his parents' ideas. That is, the H.O.S. about his parents' validity may become more probabilistic even about less accessible groups.

Nevertheless, there are many factors which tend, in varying degrees, to keep the probabilism of the parents' (and other people's) perceived validity low. First, as was pointed out in the previous chapters, the degree of influence that a schema has on perception is a positive function of the equivocality or ambiguity of the perceived situation. Since the meaning of the behavior of other people is often quite equivocal, schemas acquired from parents (and others) may be self-reinforcing; the child or adult may perceive situations in accord with his schemas, even when the facts do not warrant as much accord. Secondly, the validity accorded to parents' (and other people's) communications about persons is no doubt strengthened by their validity in other areas of experience. In other words, the child (or adult) may acquire an H.O.S. that the parent (or other person) is, in general, a source of valid schemas with respect to many areas of experience. Thirdly, the child, or person, may receive essentially the same communication about a given person (or category of persons) from several other people—and he may have acquired a schema which suggests that schemas which are uniformly and consistently communicated by a number of different people are generally valid. Thus, if the parents' communications are duplicated by brothers and sisters, friends and neighbors, there is much basis for the recipient of them to believe in the validity of the communications. A fourth support for the H.O.S. that parents (and others) are sources of valid communications is that at least sometimes the parents are observed to act in ways which are consistent with the schemas they have communicated about other people. This consistent behavior itself conveys to the child the degree of conviction of the parents; and, also, to the extent that the child comes to imitate his parents' behavior, he will also imitate their judgments about Whizzer down the block.

Horowitz (1936) gives us an extraordinary example of the degree to which parental communications can influence a child's schemas, even to the extent of leading him to reject schemas which are based on his own direct experiences. He studied the development of anti-Negro prejudice among white children in the South. He found that up to age five, white children were permitted by their parents to play freely with Negro children; and the white children did not show any strong indication of believing that the Negro children had undesirable traits. However, at age five, the parents customarily informed the children that Negro children were inferior to them and had some very undesirable attributes, and that white children should no longer play with them. Horowitz found that this communication was quite powerful—the whites began to show less tendency to play with the Negro children.

Why was this parental communication so powerful that it overrode the schemas the children obviously had prior to the time of the communication? This question becomes more salient when we compare this type of apparently rapid acceptance with the difficulty that parents sometimes have in, for example, getting "John Jr." to stop playing with "Whizzer." Why the difference? Among the probable reasons are the following: First, the children very likely heard the same communication from other older brothers and sisters, aunts and uncles. Furthermore, their white playmates probably were hearing the same thing from their own parents at much the same time, and then communicating this to the white child in question. Secondly, Negro children may have been warned about continuing to play with white children, may have been told "You are black, stand back." Thirdly, because of the fact that the same dimension of color and the attendant discrimination exists in the adult world as in the child's, it is possible for him to perceive that his parents were making the same discrimination in their behavior as they were expecting their children to make.

Another factor which enhances the strength of the schema regarding the validity of communications from others about people concerns primarily schemas about categories of other people—that is, higher order schemas about others. The strong tendencies which exist to reduce the probabilism of H.O.S.s have already been discussed.

In short, then, there are many factors which determine the degree to which an individual will acquire a schema to the effect that communications from others (especially parents) about people are valid, and which determine the stability or resistance to change of the schemas concerning other people, especially those involving categories of other people.

Schema-Generated Motivation in Person Perception

Up to this point in the chapter, we have shown how people acquire schemas from observation and communication from others, without any great concern with motivation. However, our theoretical framework indicates how some motives can arise from the acquisition of schemas. The first such motive which the framework leads us to involves the seeking of change in order to avoid dullness or apathy. We saw in Chapter Three that an individual is very likely to acquire a schema that change leads to alertness and to general arousal, and that since alertness is associated with goal attainment, the individual becomes motivated to maintain exposure to some at least minimal level of change. This change and newness will be sought only in the context of something familiar. For example, we might be attracted to people who are "fun," "different," "changing," "spontaneous," provided that we meet them in a familiar context, such as our own home, or with a group of other friends.

The motivations which we have just set forth relating to an individual's reactions to other people gives us a broader basis on which to answer our recurrent question: When do we attend to specific other people and when do we attend to total social situations as such? The motivation to seek changeable people in a familiar context would suggest that being familiar with the social situation, the plot, might make us much more interested in new people, changeable people, who could carry out the plot; they would adhere to the plot, but vary in other ways. We would not only attend to them because they involve change, but we might even seek them out. We may search out a new person in a well-structured job; a spontaneous, varied person in a well-defined role. On the other hand, if the people are familiar and knowledgeable to us, we may seek to vary the social situation in some way, play a new game, try a new task, or some such thing.

The second type of motivation stemming from the development of schemas, as indicated by the theoretical framework, is based on the avoidance of anxiety resulting from experiencing too much change, from being overwhelmed by too much information. A child may have had experiences in which he has had to face too many strange people, too many changing people and was anxious as a consequence. An individual is often faced with new groups, with new categories of people, especially when young; from nursery school to kindergarten to first grade; from elementary school to junior high to high school; from high school to work or to college; from work or college to the military. Thus, there are probably many occasions in a person's life in which he is faced with an overload of change, of newness. On the other hand, situations no doubt have been experienced in which familiar people were associated with a lack of anxiety. Thus, an H.O.S. may have been acquired relating situations involving complete strangers and unpredictably changing people to anxiety. However, this H.O.S. does not have to be acquired solely from experiences with other people: it is also quite possible that the individual acquired an H.O.S. relating all sorts of excessive change and strangeness to anxiety. The relationship between strange people and anxiety may then be a relatively lower order schema subsumed under the higher order schema. As we indicated in Chapter Three, there are several ways in which an individual can react as a consequence of this H.O.S.

First, one may simply avoid attending to the new—either psychologically or physically. A sufficient number of experiences may have occurred in which avoidance of the strange reduced anxiety, such that a schema representing this association has been developed. We have already encountered the phenomenon of "culture shock" in which the person becomes anxious in encountering a strange society, especially if he is alone. One reaction to culture shock is obvious: going home, either all the way, or seeking the nearest enclave of fellow countrymen. Another reaction would be to focus on those aspects of the new society which are at least minimally familiar; for Americans, those aspects might be the cars or the restaurants in the new country.

Second, the individual may avoid this sort of anxiety by always having someone with him when he encounters the strange or new. As we have pointed out several times, the new is less anxiety-arousing and may even be attractive, if it is faced in the context of the old.

A third possible way of avoiding or reducing anxiety as a consequence of facing new and changing people, is to acquire conceptual dimensions and schemas about them. Many situations must have been encountered in which having conceptual dimensions and schemas helped to reduce anxiety by enabling the person to process efficiently more information, more newness and change. The teacher in kindergarten is like the teacher in nursery school, and therefore is less frightening; the children in first grade can be viewed as fitting the schema of children in general. In general, then, an individual is highly likely to acquire an H.O.S. to the effect that possession of schemas about other people is anxiety-reducing or avoiding.

This H.O.S. then would lead to motivation to acquire new dimensions and schemas about people. This would lead to such behavior as watching others, both peers and elders, trying to find categories into which to place others, and asking parents to define new categories of people when the old ones don't easily fit. All parents know the phenomenon; and they may know it even to the point of occasional annoyance. One most interesting phenomenon which may in part be a result of this type of motivation to find dimensions and schemas about others is the value one often finds in discovering a strange person's name, or learning the names of a group of strangers. Knowing the name provides at least the rudiments of some sort of schema: "That man with the beret is named Sutton." There may be a point to "name tags" at meetings and conventions. Of course, there are other motivations involved, such as finding it easier to communicate with or about someone whose name we know, but the effect of knowledge even when communication is not possible would be interesting to research to see if people's level of anxiety in a group of strangers drops after one learns their names.

Furthermore, this motivation to acquire schemas can lead to the development of H.O.S.s involving categories of people, rather than single other people. Individuals are likely to have frequently experienced cases in which H.O.S.s involving categories have permitted the processing of greater amount of information than have lower order ones having to do with particular people, since the H.O.S.s enable many individuals to be subsumed as just "examples" of the category; i.e., "He's another_____ ." Such schemas about whole sets or categories of others may sometimes do violence to the individual differences within the category, as we shall see later, and this violence sometimes leads to physical violence as the persons included in some category demand to be seen and dealt with as individuals rather than as indistinguishable exemplars of some broad grouping.

The term "stereotype" is often used to describe what, from the present orientation, would be considered H.O.S.s having to do with categories of people, when the categories have been defined in some socially significant way. We will use the term sparingly here, for several reasons. One has to do with parsimony, since the term schema will not only do as well, but can also be applied to other issues of concern. Second, the term "stereotype" has often implied a negatively evaluated schema, or prejudice. In many cases, sadly, this is true, but it is not necessarily true. Schemas can be evaluated positively, negatively, or neutrally. The negative connotations of some "stereotypes" had best be taken up as a separate issue, as we shall do later. However, it is very important to underscore the point made earlier that many people strongly resent being viewed in terms of H.O.S.s referring to a category; that insults their individuality. However, some people may seek such categorization because the category is itself a positive one or because the anonymity attracts them.

The negative feelings some people may have about being categorized may not be entirely justified, however, in view of an important consequence of the fact that a category is an H.O.S. As such, it is more susceptible to forces to reduce probabilism than are L.O.S.s, those which refer to particular individuals. In the previous chapter we listed some of these pressures: the tendency of L.O.S.s which are subsumed under H.O.S.s to provide a buffer against the potential influence exceptions may have on the higher order schema; the stronger motivation to reduce the probabilism of H.O.S.s; the greater familiarity of H.O.S.s, leading to lessened willingness to change them as a consequence of an exception. Thus, persons come to have beliefs about categories which are characterized by low probabilism, with little recognition of the variations involving individual cases subsumed under the category. This lack of recognition of variation may not be a function of any genuine hostility or prejudice, but may in some cases be more a matter of normal processes of coping with an overload of information or of change.

It is also possible that on some occasions this sort of categorization may actually assist in recognizing the individuality of a specific person. By categorizing, the perceiver takes a large chunk of information relevant to some person and deals with it efficiently as one aspect, one position on some dimension. The perceiver then has "leftover" cognitive channel capacity which may be used to examine more closely other aspects of the person which are not subsumed under the category in terms of which he has initially been perceived. Furthermore, the familiarity of the category would permit the perceiver to attend more to any change, deviation, or newness in these other aspects of the person. A personnel worker may categorize a client very quickly, but then go on to look at those things which are special to that client.

Very little research, if any, has been done to show that the experience of anxiety resulting from change in people, combined with a lack of anxiety when relevant schemas are aroused, leads to the acquisition of motivation to learn more about people. It would be interesting, as a first approximation, to compare a group of children who are very inquisitive about others with a group who are not, to determine if the differences in their experiences approximate the processes indicated here. More experimental research could be done by generating mild anxiety by an overload of change in a perceived person or group of people, and determining whether motivation to acquire schemas about him or them goes up. We may have had the experience of being a bit frightened by a sudden change in the behavior of a friend or relative and then wanting very much to discover some reason for this—to acquire a schema about his behavior.

In addition to the information processing basis of the motivation to acquire new schemas, another basis indicated in Chapter Three is the greater ability an individual has to attain his goals when he has relevant schemas than when he does not. The individual develops an H.O.S. that he is better able to predict the consequences of his actions when he has relevant schemas and is, thus, better able to attain his goals, than when he does not. We can see this process at work in the acquisition of schemas about other people. For example, women are more interested in gaining information about particular men than about women (Nidorf and Crockett, 1964). Women have had relatively dependent roles in American society and therefore have had more need to predict the behavior of others so that they can adapt better. Accordingly, they are more motivated to acquire schemas about other people and are therefore more cognitively complex than men (Crockett, 1965). The previously cited finding that people are likely to develop schemas with respect to relevant interactional dimensions might also be reflected in schemas that have to do with the satisfaction of needs through interactions with others, as well as in the opportunities to perceive others when interacting with them.

The individual has many occasions which provide an opportunity to perceive the processes by means of which he acquires schemas about other people. As a consequence, he can develop an H.O.S. about the ways in which he learns about other people. Such an H.O.S. may be that one learns most by watching; or that more is learned by asking questions, politely; or that trying to provoke or manipulate another person is the best means for learning about him. These techniques are sometimes referred to as "the way I size up a person"; or "the way I get to know a person"; or "testing the limits" by behaving in a given way to see how some other person will react.

Since the individual is more likely to have schemas about familiar other people than about unfamiliar ones, and since familiar people may have often helped him to face the strange and novel without anxiety, he is likely to evaluate them more highly than unfamiliar people. The familiarity does not have to involve a specific person, however. The individual no doubt has acquired many H.O.S.s about categories of people. If another person can be placed in a category, he will be more highly familiar than someone who cannot be so placed; e.g., "I know his type," as against "I just can't figure that sort of person out." Bonarious (1965) reports research which indicates that people prefer to use their own conceptual dimensions and schemas which refer to people than those which are given to them by some researcher. Needless to say, the higher evaluation of familiar other people can also result from the person's having a quite H.O.S. of high evaluation of the familiar which applies to all sorts of entities, not only other people.

THE FUNCTIONING OF SCHEMAS RELEVANT TO PERSON PERCEPTION

We have now completed our application of the theoretical framework to the acquisition of schemas about other people. We can now shift, as we did in Chapter Four, to examining the way in which schemas actually function, to the determinants of their arousal and to the effects they have when aroused. Again, the reader is cautioned that the distinction between acquisition and functioning is made for purposes of scientific analysis, and not because of any assumption that in actuality there is a separation of these two processes. Both can and do occur simultaneously. And, therefore, the scientific analysis of them cannot be made entirely separate. We have already seen that in our discussion of higher order schemas dealing with the validity of communications, it was necessary to involve the notion of probabilism of schemas—a concept which arises primarily out of concern with the functioning of schemas.

Arousal of Schemas in Person Perception

The first general point that was made in the previous chapter about the functioning of schemas indicated that schemas tend to arouse one another, both across levels in the hierarchy of schemas and on the same levels. This point is easily illustrated by means of our own introspections, recalling times when we have been thinking about other people. How often have we said, "So-and-so reminds me of a fellow I knew in the Army," which is a matter of schemas at the same level. Or, "I can think of several people who are of that type," going from an H.O.S. to several L.O.S.s subsumed under it. Or, "I know the type of person he is," jumping from a lower to a higher order schema.

However, a more interesting phenomenon arises because of the limitation on the total number of schemas and outside changes or events that an individual can react to at a given time. As a consequence, when a person's attention is directed to a wide range of external events, he is less likely to attend to internal events. Thus, when we are with a very fast-moving crowd of people, who act, do, and change very much, one may become involved in their activities "before he knows it." The speed of change may so demand attention that no opportunity develops to reflect and examine what is being done. Or, a person may become "glued" to a person who is so changeable, so active, so moving, that not only is little attention paid to anything else, but also not much thinking is done at the moment. Many very persuasive speakers may gain their effectiveness partly because that are so unpredictable, so changing, so "dynamic," that an observer does not have much cognitive capacity left over with which to evaluate critically what is being said. Furthermore, the effectiveness of some of the orators in mobilizing action in their audiences may also be due to the fact that they urge immediate action, so that there is not much time to cerebrate and consider other possibilities, such as not acting. At the end of Mark Antony's speech, his listeners charged directly from Caesar's funeral to seek out and punish his murderers.

On the other side of the coin, a person may be so immersed in his own thoughts, so lost in his own ideas, that he does not attend to people around him. There is the everyday experience of "sneaking up" on a person who is immersed in his own thoughts and startling him when he suddenly discovers you right upon him. A similar case involves the individual who, while he may be talking *to* someone else, does not listen, and may simply be carried away by his own thought processes to the point that the other person comes to exist primarily as an excuse for the expression of thoughts, rather than as a participant in genuine interaction. If you yourself have ever engaged in such self-expressive communication, you know how startling it is should the other person suddenly force his ideas into the "conversation"; it may break your own train of thought and sometimes annoy you.

There may be characteristic individual differences in tendencies to deploy attention outward or inward. These differences were what Jung appears to have referred to as introversion and extroversion. However, research in this area has been somewhat inconclusive, since most of the measures of introversion-extroversion have not been well-validated.

The discussion so far may have given the reader the impression that the individual's attention and schema arousal are passively at the beck and call of changing outside events and similarities between schemas. To some, perhaps large, extent, this passive determination does occur, but, as pointed out in the previous chapter, the individual may be motivated to deploy his attention in some way to solve problems. Thus, an individual may be motivated to evaluate a given other person and may also have a higher order schema that evaluating others depends on attending closely to everything the other person does. The individual would then attend closely to the other. Or, he may have an H.O.S. that evaluation is best accomplished by a balance between attention to the other and thought about what is being seen; he would then simultaneously observe the other and think about his actions, but would probably observe fewer aspects than the first evaluator.

Now that some idea of the factors influencing the arousal of schemas has been given, the next question is simply, what difference does it make whether a schema is aroused or not? What do aroused schemas do that dormant ones don't?

In the last chapter it was pointed out that all of us, to a greater degree rather than a lesser one, develop a quite high order schema about the consistency between different levels of schemas and between schemas and the perceived world. The discussion suggested that efforts to maintain or re-establish consistency in the face of some potential violation of the H.O.S. were more likely to involve some change in an L.O.S. than in the H.O.S. One demonstration of this process with respect to the perception of persons comes from a study (Allport and Postman, 1947) in which the subjects were shown a picture of a scene in a subway in which a well-dressed Negro and a poorly dressed Causcasian who is holding a straight-edge razor in his hand are portrayed. A few moments later, subjects were asked to recall what they had seen. Subjects with anti-Negro prejudice who presumably share some of the "stereotypes" or H.O.S.s about Negroes recalled that the Negro was carrying the razor.

Circumstances conspire against the existence of a situation in which an L.O.S. is inconsistent with some related H.O.S. for any extended period of time, in view of the high probability that both these schemas will have been aroused simultaneously and the resultant strong pressures toward some consistency-producing changes. However, if, for reasons stemming from limited cognitive channel capacity, two related, hierarchically ordered schemas about people had not been aroused simultaneously at some time in the past, then their current simultaneous arousal would lead to their being made more consistent. In other words, a study paralleling the one reported in the last chapter by McGuire (1960) could be done, but has not yet been.

There are a few studies which show the outcome of the processes of making higher and lower order schemas about people consistent with each other—that is, studies simply showing that they are consistent. Anisfeld, Munoz, and Lambert (1963) obtained the evaluations some Jewish high school students in Montreal made of Jews and Gentiles, and found that those who were negatively disposed toward one of these groups tended to be negative to the other as well. Their schemas about Jews and about Gentiles were consistent with an H.O.S. of hostility toward people in general.

One important special case of the influence of higher order schemas on lower order ones concerns the relationship between aroused schemas and newly forming, lower order ones. It was established earlier that aroused schemas can have important influences on what is perceived and on the meaning derived from perceptions, and the more ambiguous and equivocal the situation, the greater will this influence be. Perhaps more than any other object of perception, the actions of other people are equivocal and open to many different interpretations. Why does Joe refuse to go out with Ruth any longer? All sorts of contradictory stories and interpretations fill the air. How many times have we had to say, or have said to us, "I'm sorry, but I misunderstood what you meant?" In a sense, the Mona Lisa's ambiguous smile is on all our faces. Furthermore, other people are often seen in situations in which there is a paucity of clear and unequivocal information: A glimpse at someone in the street, a person far across a meeting room, the driver of the oncoming car. Furthermore, even if a person is close by or easily seen, some potentially significant behavior he emits may last only a fleeting second. Thus, the perception of other people is a domain of experience in which there is a wide and free range of possible influence by familiar, aroused schemas.

One of the bases of the influence of H.O.S.s on lower ones is that the H.O.S.s are more familiar, and familiar schemas in general are more likely to influence perception than are unfamiliar ones, since they are more highly evaluated. This relationship between familiarity and influence on person perception can be illustrated by examining the power of the most familiar schemas of all—those having to do with oneself. When we perceive other people, we are highly likely to perceive them in terms of our self-schemas. There are many examples of this tendency. In studies in which people are asked to predict the responses of another person to a questionnaire of some sort, there is an overall tendency to assume that the other person is much like themselves (cf. Berkowitz, 1960). This is especially likely to be the case if the person doing the predicting has little information about the other person. All of us have had the experience, when trying to puzzle out what someone else might do when we have few concrete clues, of asking ourselves the question, "What would I do in his place?"

One extremely important instance of this application of our self-schemas to the perception of others concerns the fact that we can only perceive our own consciousness, our own decisions, our own direct experiences. We have no direct information at all about other people's awareness or consciousness. Only their overt behavior is available to us; what goes on in their heads, under their skin, is not at all accessible. This is the situation *par excellence* for the influence of self-schemas in the perceptions of others. We therefore perceive that others are aware, are conscious, have thoughts, feelings, goals, intentions (cf. Heider, 1958). We perceive that the other person perceives. This impression is often so direct, so powerful, and so immediate that we are not aware of the basis on which we judged that the other person was perceiving, thinking. In fact, a very significant determinant of our reaction to other people is our perception of their intentions and feelings—even though we have no direct knowledge of them. Their overt behavior is interpreted in terms of what it signals to us about what goes on inside them, which we perceive in terms of our own self-schemas, a good deal of the time.

One consequence of our perception of others in terms of our self-schemas derives from our tendency to perceive ourselves as the source or cause of our actions. We tend to hold ourselves responsible for our own actions. We do not, for instance, generally tend to trace back the causes of our actions in terms of a sort of infinite regress sequence, going back, for example, to early childhood events and concluding that the reason we are doing such and such is because our parents treated us in a particular way. We generally stop much short of this sort of historical analysis (cf. Heider, 1958). Further, we do not generally attribute our behavior to a complex and detailed list of factors, such as our physical state, other people's behavior, our goals, situation constraints, and so on. Rather, we usually are satisfied with a much less rigorous account of the causes of our actions. Thus, in viewing others, we tend to hold them responsible for their actions, to see them as having decided to do what they did and deserving the blame or credit. Of course, we may sometimes look at the causes of our behavior in a complex fashion, or some people may tend to do so characteristically. In those instances, other people would likewise be viewed as not being responsible. As we shall see below, there are other schemas that can be involved as well.

Much more technical and detailed discussions have been developed regarding the processes by which characteristics are attributed to persons and of the sorts of information which are typically employed in order to make such attributions. Following the lead of Fritz Heider in this area, these theorists, e.g., Jones and Davis (1965) point out that persons tend to be seen as rather unique entities in the environment in terms of their casual significance. That is, people are appropriately viewed as being very important sources of activity, change, and movement—they make significant things happen—and, thus, it becomes particularly critical that a person be able to understand other persons' "true" nature so that he will be able to understand, predict, and perhaps control the entities which play such an important role in determining what happens in his world. Heider suggests that this involves a search for "dispositional" qualities, basic, enduring, underlying traits which dispose an individual to act in a particular fashion under particular types of conditions. Since any direct access to the existence of such traits is difficult, persons can only infer their existence on the basis of observation of overt behavior which directly or indirectly implies them. That is, "honesty" cannot be seen directly in another person, only behaviors which might be termed honest or dishonest. But in making predictions of another's future actions, it may be important to assess the likelihood that he possesses a general trait of honesty whose existence can then be assumed to make honest behavior on his part more likely. These attribution theories, then, have dealt in a complex way particularly with the conditions which make it more or less likely that inferences about predispositional traits will be made on the basis of specific information or observation regarding some other person. Both the complexity of these theories and the fact that a great body of supportive data has not yet been generated to confirm their predictions leads us to mention them only briefly at this point.

A very interesting example of the arousal of self-schemas having to do with motives, intentions, and the like concerns the attribution of these qualities to inanimate objects—a process called animism. To a greater extent than is realized, persons engage in animistic thought. Automobiles are thought of as loyal and helpful when they last a long time, or nasty and hostile when they go wrong. Haven't we all been angry at a car at one time or another? Logically speaking, is it not a bit odd to be angry at a hunk of metal? Yet, when such machines are found to be harmful or capricious, self-schemas of intentions are aroused. This process bespeaks the abstract nature of the conceptual dimension involved in schemas. They can become so independent of their roots in our own experiences of ourselves that they very easily can be applied to machines (or oceans, or mountains, or rivers).

The familiarity of a schema is not, of course, the only factor which determines how likely it is to influence perception. A more basic determinant involves simply the aroused or dormant state of the schema. Even the most familiar schemas, such as self-schemas, are not always aroused, but when they are, their influence may be strong. Lundy (1957) conducted an experiment which, from our point of view, dealt with certain of the consequences of explicitly arousing self-schemas. He got people together in pairs, telling one member of each pair that in their subsequent ten-minute conversation about vacations or about their school, they were to focus on themselves. The other half were told to attend closely to the other person. After the conversation, the members of the pairs were given the task of predicting how the other person would respond to a questionnaire. The group for whom self-schemas had been aroused tended to predict that the other person would respond to the questions in much the way as they themselves had. The other group tended to be more accurate than was the first group in their predictions.

Another way in which the influence of aroused self-schemas has been shown deals with the influence an emotional state may have on the perception of others. For instance, if an individual is frightened, he is, by definition, aware of his fright; he has an aroused self-schema of the type "I am afraid." Feshbach and Feshbach (1963) investigated the effect of frightening young boys by telling them of a dangerous study in which they were about to participate and by showing them frightening appearing equipment which they believed would be used in the study. While they were awaiting the start of the study (which never actually took place), they rated pictures of other people on a variety of qualities. As compared to a group of less frightened subjects, these boys judged the pictured people to be more fearful.

Of course, self-schemas are not the only ones which can influence the perception of others. Other schemas relating to other people can also be achieved. A very interesting example in which either of two nonself-schemas was aroused by instructions comes from a study by Kelley (1955). He informed half the members of a class that the speaker they were about to hear was "cold," the other half that he was "warm." Both groups actually observed the same speaker at the same time. During the speech, the "warm" instruction subjects spoke up to the speaker more than did the "cold" ones, presumably because they perceived him to be a more supportive person. This interpretation is supported by the results of a post-speech questionnaire in which the "warm" subjects ascribed many other related attributes to the speaker, while the "cold" ones gave a picture of an indifferent, unhelpful person. However, the difference between the two groups was not a matter of a "halo effect," since the differing attributes were limited to those traits that were related to warmth and coldness. Thus, for example, there was no differentiated attribution of such traits as intelligence.

The likelihood that a schema about oneself will be aroused is obviously less, the more alternative schemas the individual has. Thus, a person who has many schemas is less likely to view another in terms of his self-schemas than is a person who has few other schemas. One determinant of the number of a person's nonself-schemas about others is his cognitive complexity; that is, the number of conceptual dimensions he typically uses in perceiving others. More complex people can be assumed to have more schemas simply because they have available for their use a greater number of different dimensions which can form parts of schemas; with a greater variety of dimensions, a greater variety of schemas can be formed. Accordingly, people of high cognitive complexity are *less* likely to perceive others as being similar to themselves than are people of low cognitive complexity (cf. Bieri, 1955; Crockett, 1965). Furthermore, since they have more different schemas, highly cognitively complex people are more prone than are lows to see differences between other people (cf. Bieri, 1955).

We have just seen instances in which schemas were aroused either by direct instruction or by giving the person a certain type of powerful experience. However, higher order schemas about others can be aroused simply by the information one has about a particular person; i.e., through perceiving the individual as holding a given position on a given dimension, so that any higher order schema involving that position and dimension is aroused. Even in cases in which no other information about the person is available, the "expected" dimension on the aroused higher order schema will predispose the perceiver to view the other person as having a given position on that dimension. There are many examples of this phenomenon. Heider (1958) has described the ways in which people often take a given observation about the behavior of another and immediately draw a wide variety of inferences about what that person is likely to do under all sorts of circumstances. Thus, a great many personality traits may be ascribed on the basis of a very limited observational base. If the stimulus person does something good, for example, he may become a nice guy—one who in general does good things. The good act may arouse a schema to the effect that good people do good things. If a person is observed to successfully complete a difficult task, it may be assumed that he is a very able person in a variety of circumstances. His achievement arouses a schema which suggests that able people accomplish difficult acts. Though there may be only one instance to work with, persons often make such a generalization with complete confidence. Jones and de Charms (1957) showed experimentally that if a person fails at a task which is relevant to the perceiver and if this failure is seen as a result of his not having tried hard enough, he comes to be seen as a less dependable person in general.

Even the physical form of an action or of a person can arouse schemas which lead people to make inferences about unobserved aspects of the person. Ekman (1965) found that people could make accurate guesses as to what others had said just by observing their body and head movements. Veness and Brierley (1963) had someone speak in a given passage in either a cold or warm tone of voice. Persons who listened made quite different judgments about the speaker's personality, depending on his tone. Secord and his co-workers (Secord and Muthard, 1955; Secord, Dukes, and Bevan, 1954) have shown that people can draw inferences about personality characteristics on the basis of facial cues alone. Women who have certain skin textures, degrees of fullness of lips, and degrees of facial tension are judged to be more sexy than other women. Furthermore, people whose faces are seen to be very extreme or eccentric are judged to have extreme or eccentric personalities. The dimension of extremity is so abstracted from its concrete roots that quite diverse specific situations can be perceived as being relevant to very general schemas.

If a person is believed to have certain qualities or characteristics which permit his being classified as "belonging" to some pre-established category, then additional characteristics which are assumed to be associated with that category will be also ascribed to him. For example, for some people, evidently, knowledge of another person's occupation has vast implications for his other attributes (cf. Triandis and Fishbein, 1963). Or, identification of someone as being black is viewed by many people as implying that he possesses a number of other attributes. Secord, Bevan, and Katz (1956) found that if a person is identified as being a Negro from his photograph, he is then perceived to have the presumed traits involved in the perceiver's stereotype of the Negro, regardless of whether his features were extremely negroid or only slightly so.

This same sort of process is involved in an often-used experimental setting in which subjects are given written or verbal descriptions of the traits presumably possessed by a fictitious person. Asch (1952) read subjects either of the following sets of adjectives as descriptions of a particular person:

a. intelligent, skillful, industrious, *warm*, determined, practical, cautious

b. intelligent, skillful, industrious, *cold*, determined, practical, cautious

Subjects were then asked to describe this person in their own words. Asch reports the following two descriptions as being typical of those who heard the "warm" description (p. 263):

"A person who believes certain things to be right, wants others to see his point, would be sincere in an argument and would like to see his point won."

"A scientist performing experiments and persevering after many setbacks. He is driven by the desire to accomplish something that could be of benefit."

Those hearing the "cold" set of adjectives gave descriptions like the following:

"A very ambitious and talented person who would not let anyone or anything stand in the way of achieving his goals. Wants his own way, he is determined not to give in, no matter what happens."

"A rather snobbish person who feels that his success and intelligence set him apart from the run-of-the-mill individual. Calculating and unsympathetic."

Asch also had his subjects respond to a checklist of adjectives by indicating those which they would attribute to the person who had been described. The checklist responses also show differences as a function of the warm and cold variation in the original description. Asch wrote (p. 276): "A remarkably wide range of qualities is embraced in the dimension warm-cold. It has references to temperamental characteristics (e.g. optimism, humor, happiness), to his relations to the group (e.g., generosity, sociability, popularity), to strength of character (persistence, honesty). It even includes a reference to physical characteristics, evident in the virtually unanimous characterizations of the warm person as short, stout, and ruddy, and the opposed characterisations of the cold person."

Wishner (1960), following up on Asch's work, had the students of 10 laboratory sections of introductory psychology rate the instructors in their sections on 53 scales concerning personality traits. Wishner then measured the degrees of relationship between all the possible pairs of scales, among these scales being that of "warm-cold." He then presented to other subjects descriptions of a person who was shown as either "warm" or "cold." These subjects then rated the person on various scales. Wishner found that only those scales which had been related to the warm-cold scale in the first study were rated differently by the subjects presented by "warmth" than those presented with the "cold" in the second study. In other words, the subjects' reactions to particular people described as warm or cold were consistent with the higher order schemas they had about warm-cold.

These data should not be taken to mean that all trait adjectives are as powerful in their effect as are "warm" and "cold." They vary greatly in their power. In other words, for many people, some adjectives are parts of schemas which have many dimensions and thus have a wide-ranging influence, while other adjectives are not parts of such schemas. (Asch has given the name "central" to the more powerful adjectives, like warm-cold.)

The reader may have been expecting a section in this chapter on the determinants of the accuracy of perceptions of other people. The reader has a right to expect such a section, since the problem of accuracy is so important in everyday life. In fact, for a number of years, a great many social psychologists devoted much research energy to this problem. However, all this energy was useful primarily in pointing out the difficulty of such research. The techniques that were generally used involved asking subjects to predict how another person would answer some questionnaire. This simple technique was, however, loaded with pitfalls, as was pointed out by Cronbach (Cronbach, 1955; Gage and Cronbach, 1955). First, the tendency already mentioned to generalize from self to others, and thus to simply indicate that the other person would respond as the subject himself would, plagued the researchers, since an individual would appear to be more accurate if the other person happened to be like him, in fact, or like him in his way of responding to questionnaires. Second, a person would appear to be more accurate if he simply had a tendency to make better predictions about the "average" person. On an *average* basis, such a person would score high in accuracy, but without necessarily paying attention to particular people, and might therefore be quite incorrect in *specific* predictions. Third, both of these tendencies often interact in misleading ways with other factors related to the accurate perception of other people. For example, if an average person has a tendency to assume that people he likes are similar to himself, and if he likes many people, he would tend to score as an accurate judge of others. These problems, among others, led to a shift away from concern with the accuracy of perception to more concern with the way in which we perceive others; i.e., with the process of perceiving. From studies of these issues, we may be in a better position later to return to the problem of accuracy. Nevertheless, Cline (Cline and Richards, 1960) and his associates at the University of Colorado have persisted in researching the accuracy problem, but have used more sophisticated methods. For example, instead of predictions of others' answers to questionnaires, the subjects predict (and post-dict) the behavior of some other person in everyday situations. The other person's actual behavior is determined by very intensive research to provide a baseline for judging accuracy.

Primacy Effects in Impression Formation

Thus far, we have examined the cases in which the individual has no information about the expected dimension of aroused schemas; i.e., the positions that the perceived person has on dimensions other than the one about which the perceiver has some information. He has to guess or infer, although these guesses and inferences are perceived by him to be veridical perceptions. Another type of perceptual situation that shows the influence of aroused schemas is one in which it is physically possible for the person to perceive aspects of some situation which are relevant to the expected dimensions, but do not attend closely to them. The aroused schema is sufficient to give the perceiver "knowledge" of the expected dimension, so that he does not have to attend closely; after all, one of the main reasons for the acquisition of schemas is to economize in the deployment of attention. The first information an individual has about another will often arouse a higher order schema. This schema then guides perception and interpretation of the subsequent information, so that the individual may well attend to it less. However, at the same time that this schema is thus influencing attention, the individual is developing a lower order schema about the person being described. This L.O.S. may involve the notion that the person exemplifies the schema aroused by the first information received.

This set of circumstances has been called the "primacy" effect in person perception, since it is the first information secured about another person which appears to determine the effects of subsequent information received about him. Another way of describing the effect is simply in terms of the strong influence which first impressions have. From this discussion, it should, however, be clear that not all impressions of others evidence the impact of primacy effects. No such influence would be anticipated if the initial information which the perceiver receives about another is not part of a schema, or, if it is part of a schema, if the schema does not have many dimensions.

Asch (1952) devised a simple method for demonstrating primacy effects by varying the position in which a given trait-adjective describing another person was presented in a list of adjectives, when all the other adjectives remained in a fixed order. He found that when he presented certain adjectives, such as warm or cold, early in the sequence, the picture that the subject obtained of the fictitious person was different from the one obtained if these adjectives were placed later in the list. If they were placed early, they aroused the relevant higher order schema. The subsequent adjectives were then less well attended to, giving the schema free rein. If the same adjective was placed late in the sequence, some earlier adjective or set of adjectives were highly likely to have already aroused some related schema.

Asch did not interpret his work in terms of schema theory, or in terms of any theory based on learning. He assumed that the primacy effects were the result of an overall "direction" which the earlier adjectives in the list initiated. The meaning of subsequent adjectives may be reorganized, changed to fit the thrust of this organizational direction. Asch's central point was that the impression gained of the other person was organized and integrated, rather than an amalgam of discrete parts and a repetition of what had been learned.

There are several reasons for rejecting Asch's position. First, Wishner's (1960) work suggested that the meanings of adjectives did not change as a result of primacy effects. As was mentioned above, the relationships among adjectives remained the same in different contexts. If, as Asch would have it, the meanings of adjectives changed in different contexts, one would expect the implicative relationships among them to change as well. Second, although Asch himself pointed out that not all adjectives generated primacy effects and that primacy effects influenced only some of the conclusions drawn about a person, he did not explain how some adjectives came to be more powerful than others. Obviously, some form of cognitive learning is the answer. Third, Asch's general argument was directed primarily against approaches to learning which emphasize discrete connections between stimuli and responses. The orientation espoused in this text emphasizes the learning of more abstract and more integrative processes. The processes involved in developing organized perceptions of other people can be learned. The more complex and original kinds of organization which Asch reports he sees in some of the descriptions of other people which his subjects developed can be seen as the outcome of a very high order schema whose arousal leads to the development of such original and complex organization tendencies. This H.O.S. would be of the same type as "learning to learn" schemas.

Primacy effects have been observed not only when individual adjectives have been used, but also when paragraphs describing the fictitious person have been presented. Luchins (1957) presented a short paragraph describing someone as either extroverted or introverted, and then gave the same subjects a second paragraph which presented the opposite trait from the first. The subjects were then asked to write their own paragraphs describing the person, and a primacy effect was found. The fictitious person initially described as introverted (or extroverted) was ultimately described by the subjects as introverted (or extroverted).

One of the most common ways in which primacy effects have been studied in experimental contexts which use trait adjectives to communicate information about the characteristics of the stimulus person has been to use adjectives of varying degrees of social desirability. The order of presentation of desirable or undesirable traits can then be varied systematically. For example, the desirable traits might be presented first, and then the undesirable ones, or vice versa. After reading or listening to the list of adjectives, the respondent is simply asked how much he believes he would like or dislike the person being described. In a particularly well-designed study of this type, Anderson (1965) presented subjects with a list containing either desirable or undesirable adjectives. Inserted in each list was a block of three adjectives which were opposite in desirability to the other adjectives in that list. The block of "opposite" adjectives was inserted at all possible positions in the larger list of adjectives. Anderson found that the earlier in the list this opposite block was inserted, the greater was the influence on the subjects' ratings of the likability of the person.

Primacy effects have been found not only with respect to the evaluation of particular other people but also with respect to categories of people. Bossart and Di Vesta (1966) had subjects listen to a series of six paragraphs describing unfamiliar people, each paragraph containing four adjectives which were either high or low in desirability. The order of presenting the desirable or undesirable paragraphs was varied and a primacy effect was found.

These data dealing with primacy may seem to be in contradiction to the so-called recency effect that has often been found in studies of learning. The recency effect refers to the tendency for subjects to be able to recall the very last thing they were attempting to learn

better than those immediately preceding it. However, the contradiction is more apparent than real, because primacy effects have
been found in studies of learning as well as recency effects; the first
and last syllables in a list of syllables to be memorized tend to be
learned more easily and rapidly than do those in the middle of the list.

Procedures for Reducing the Primacy Effect

If such primacy effects are the result of a relative lack of attention
to the information presented, then these effects should be overcome
by arousing some higher order schema which would lead the person
to attend more to the later information. Anderson, who has been the
foremost proponent of the attentional explanation of primacy effects,
has shown how such higher order schemas do eliminate primacy effects. More concretely, Anderson and Jacobson (1965) presented sets
of three adjectives to subjects, each set describing a fictitious person.
Each set contained two desirable (or undesirable) adjectives and one
undesirable (or desirable) adjective, the order of presentation varying
among sets. Some of the subjects were simply told in advance that
all of the adjectives were equally important; i.e., the experimenter
aroused an H.O.S. to the effect that "all of the information is equally
important." Accordingly, no primacy effects were found in the
judgments of likability of the described people; subjects' judgments
of the likability of the described persons were simply a function of
an average of the desirability of the individual adjectives used to
describe that person. Anderson and Hubert (1963) instructed their
subjects to change their ratings of likability as new information was
accumulated—and also eliminated any primacy effect.

Luchins (1957) similarly found that simply instructing the subjects
not to "go on" first impressions, but to wait till all the information
was in, eliminated primacy effects in a study in which the subjects
were given two paragraphs describing a fictitious person as either
extroverted or introverted, the order of the paragraphs being
systematically varied.

If a person is given a whole series of sets of adjectives, each
describing a different person, and each set has a mixture of desirable
and undesirable adjectives, then the person would be likely to develop
an H.O.S. to the effect that each set contains both "good" and "bad"
characteristics. This H.O.S. would then lead him to attend to all
the information, not just the first received. Accordingly, the primacy
effect would be reduced. This sort of reduction in the primacy effect
was found by Anderson and Barrios (1961), who gave their subjects
some 60 sets of adjectives and found that the primacy effect was steadily
reduced.

The same elimination of the primacy effect can be achieved by simply asking the subject to give his impression of the other person after the presentation of each adjective in the list. The subject then must pay attention even to the latter adjectives (cf. Stewart, 1965). Similarly, the primacy effect can be eliminated by stopping the presentation of adjectives in the middle of the series and having the subjects rate the fictitious person on a series of simple rating scales (Briscoe, Woodyard, and Shaw, 1964). The subjects were then presented with more adjectives, and made their final ratings. These last ratings were not as determined by the initial adjectives as were those of subjects who did not make ratings halfway through.

What we have learned about primacy effects can be summarized readily: In general, people tend to manifest primacy effects because the first information they receive about another tends to arouse schemas such that little attention is given to any subsequent information. However, primacy effects are easily eliminated by the arousal of any H.O.S. which directs the person to attend to the latter information; the arousal of these H.O.S.s can be self-generated or induced by instruction from others.

Much of the research we have just described concerning the determinants of the primacy effect has been done by N. Anderson and his associates. However, their approach to this area of research does not stem from schema theory. Instead they use a theoretical model called the weighted averaging model. They assume that an individual reacts to the degree of favorableness of a series of bits of information about another person by averaging their degrees of evaluation. Thus, six bits all of a given degree of favorableness would lead to the same overall evaluation as two bits of that same degree. However, not all the bits are equally weighted; some are more important than others and thus are given more weight in the averaging. For example, a primacy effect is reflected in a heavier weighting given to the first adjectives presented. However, Anderson's model does not have any basis for predicting which adjectives will be weighted more; it can only describe the effects of weighting. The present approach leads to more direct prediction as to when the early and late presented adjectives will have more effect.

In more concrete language, persons tend to be greatly influenced by first impressions—but, we can keep an open mind about the other fellow if we are forced to or force ourselves to.

The Unity and Coherence of Impressions of Others

As was mentioned earlier, schemas about other people tend to have a unitary quality, to form entities that are internally coherent and distinct from the surroundings. This tendency is a reflection of the tendency of all schemas to exhibit this unitary quality, and also of an H.O.S. to the effect that schemas do, or ought to, show such unity. People vary in the degree to which they have this H.O.S. In any case, let us see how this unifying tendency is manifested in the perception of other people.

The power of the H.O.S. to form coherent, unified schemas about particular other people appears to be very great. For example, persons will rate the desirability of trait adjectives differently when told they refer to a single person than when they are presented simply as separate adjectives. Wyer and Dermer (1968) found that in the former case, the subjects tended to rate adjectives as being more similar than in the latter case.

Kastenbaum (1951) presented subjects with three similar re-cordings of telephone conversations, but varied the tone of voice so that one sounded warm, one cold, and one neutral. The subjects were first told that three different people had been recorded, and that they were to write down their impressions of each of them. Next, they were told that, in fact, the same person had made all three re-cordings, and that they should now write a single description of that person. The subjects found great difficulty in doing so, and expressed their negative feelings about the task. In contrast, another group of subjects who had listened to the same recordings but who were told from the beginning that all the recordings were made by the same person, had no difficulty writing descriptions of that person. Somehow the three schemas formed by the first group had independent coher-ences, a kind of life of their own that could not be simply abolished by fiat. The schemas were almost reifications, with respondents react-ing as if they were real objects or entities.

Recency Effects in Impression Formation

In Kastenbaum's study, subjects had developed three more or less unified schemas before they were asked to make them into one. What happens if an individual is in a situation in which he is receiving information about another person in sequence, but this sequence is interrupted in the middle by his taking time out to form a coherent picture of this person? More particularly, what happens if, after this coherent picture has been formed, the additional information about the other person is inconsistent with the previous information? We might reason that this new information would present a clear-cut change from the developed picture of the person and would therefore attract attention. The attention paid to the new information might then lead to a change in the newly developing and acquired schema about the person. Further, because of the special attention given this new information, it might well have more of an influence on the schema than did the original information. In other words, a recency effect would occur.

The process described in the previous paragraph was demonstrated in a study by Rosenkrantz and Crockett (1965). They presented their subjects with a series of eight anecdotes about a fictitious person, presenting four positive ones and then four negative ones for half the subjects, and vice versa for the other half. Half of each of the two groups of subjects wrote up general descriptions, responded to an adjective checklist, and in other ways recorded their impressions of the stimulus person between the blocks of positive and negative adjectives, and again at the end. The very request made by the experimenters for the subjects to give an essay-type description of the person would tend to arouse the H.O.S. mentioned above regarding the expectation that other people are more or less unified in their characteristics. The final evaluations made by the subjects were more in line with the second set of adjectives than with the first. Rosenkrantz and Crockett themselves state that the subjects who wrote the descriptions between the two blocks of information had a chance to consolidate their impressions of the person by writing the descriptions, and that the second set of adjectives then came as a greater surprise to them, and they therefore attended to it more and were more influenced by it.

In the Briscoe et al. study (1964), there was a slight but dependable recency effect. Subjects in their study simply filled out some rating scales between the two blocks of information about the stimulus person, so that the amount of consolidation or unification would be expected to be less than that which occurred in the Rosenkrantz and Crockett study, and the recency effect they found was, indeed, small. Furthermore, this line of reasoning would suggest that, if the interruption in the middle of the sequence is of a sort that does not lead to unification of the schema about the person, recency effects will not occur. Such non-unifying interruptions can involve simply giving the person a task not connected with perception of the person (cf. Briscoe et al., 1964). Furthermore, if there is no interruption to give the person a chance to develop a coherent schema, the contrast between the first information and the later information may well not be sufficiently sharp to gain the latter greater attention. Thus, primacy effects would result, as we have already seen.

It is important to note in considering this set of studies that the subjects' schemas about the other person were rather new and developing; that is, they were not highly familiar. Therefore, they were more readily changeable than schemas which are well established or familiar.

Briscoe *et al.* found that interrupting the flow of information about the other person with a completely irrelevant task did not eliminate the primacy effect. Luchins (1957), on the other hand, did find that he could eliminate the primacy effect by a similar procedure. The difference in these results could have resulted from a number of factors. There might have been inadvertent communications from the experimenter in the Luchins study, since he personally gave the subjects their nonrelevant tasks. In Luchin's study, the interrupting task, arithmetic problems, was more involving than was the cancellation task used by Briscoe *et al.*, so that the Luchin's subjects were more likely to return to the perception task as if it were an entirely new one.

The H.O.S. which suggests that other people are coherent and unified entities and which underlies some of the processes described in the previous paragraphs, is acquired through experience as are all schemas. Consequently, people would be expected to differ in the degree to which they acquire it. Furthermore, this H.O.S. may itself be subsumed under a still higher order schema to the effect that "things in general are coherent." Such individual differences are illustrated in a study by Gollin (1953) in which subjects were presented with a written description which suggested a kindly prostitute; that is, someone who has both desirable and undesirable qualities. Subjects were then asked to describe her. Some gave an integrated, coherent description by seeing her prostitution as, in part, an act of "kindness." Others achieved unity by simply writing about either her prostitution or her kindliness but not both. Still others presented both the desirable and undesirable, with no attempt to integrate the two. Interestingly enough, Gollin found that these differences were associated with other differences in the way the subjects looked at a quite different situation. It was found that subjects who judged such "isms" as Buddhism, capitalism, etc., to be representatives of a larger class of social ideologies tended to be the same ones who developed an integration of the inconsistencies in the first task. On the other hand, those who indicated that they viewed the "isms" as being discrete ideologies were less likely to have developed an integration of the two descriptions given in the earlier task. This finding suggests that for many people, the perceived degree of coherence of other people was just a special case of their perception of the world in general.

In contrast to the approach taken here, Fishbein has recently argued that the degree to which one person positively (or negatively) values another is a direct function of the number of positive (or negative) attributes he believes the other to have. This view is contrary to the present approach, since it does not recognize the possibility that the initial information received about another person often, if not always, arouses an H.O.S. which leads the person to attribute qualities to the other consistent with the H.O.S. Fishbein's approach adheres to a model of human behavior that implies that larger units of behavior, such as overall evaluations, are simple summations or unorganized agglomerations of smaller units of behavior. This position, then, would hold that a perceiver simply *adds* up, rather than averages, the positive and negative attributes he believes another person to have in order to arrive at an overall evaluation. This implies, for example, that if additional negative items of information are given about another person, the general evaluation of that person will invariably become more negative. On the other hand, the position on this matter developed by Anderson would not necessarily predict such an outcome. As was mentioned earlier, his contention is that the process involved here is most appropriately described in terms of an averaging; not of an additive model. From this point of view, then, adding additional negative information could actually, under certain circumstances, lead to a more positive evaluation. That is, if the additional negative items were *less* negative than the average of the items of information the perceiver already has about the person, they should be integrated into the total impression by averaging and they would pull the impression in a more positive direction. To use a highly simplified hypothetical example, let us say that the original evaluation of some person could be represented as —5 on some relevant scale, and an additional characteristic evaluated as a —1 attributed to him. An additive model would predict that the resultant new impression would be $-6 (-5 + -1)$, whereas the averaging approach would suggest a -3 as the new overall evaluation $\frac{(-5 + -1)}{2}$.

The data which Fishbein cites in support of his theory have to be viewed in the light of the finding by Podell and Podell (1963) that people do not evaluate a stimulus person more positively because of his having been characterized by more positive attributes unless they have been exposed in the research study to a number of stimulus persons who have been assigned varying numbers of positive attributes. This variation would then com-

municate to the subject the experimentally used range on the dimension of "good-bad." He then can evaluate the person with
respect to this range. In research by Fishbein and Hunter (1964),
subjects were presented with lists of trait-adjectives, all positive,
but varying in the degree to which they were positive or desirable.
The subjects always received the most positive adjectives first,
then the next most positive, and so on. However, the length of
the lists of adjectives was varied. Fishbein and Hunter found that
the longer the list, the more positive was the evaluation of the
person given. Fishbein's approach appears to imply a simple additive effect, each additional adjective, even the later one, adding
a "unit" of positivity or negativity. In contradiction, Anderson
(1968) found that people do not simply view another person as "one
unit" more favorable with each additional positive trait-adjective
attributed to that person. More particularly, he found that if three
extremely favorable adjectives are presented, the subjects' final
evaluation is more positive than if the subjects first received these
adjectives and without a break received three only moderately
positive adjectives. The results were parallel when negative
adjectives were used. Thus, the date with respect to Fishbein's
thesis are contradictory.

More generally, Rosnow, Wainer, and Arms (1970) point out
that the effect of additional information about another person may
depend on how much overlap in meaning there is between the
additional information and the information the person already has.
For example, learning that a person believed to be "cruel" is also
"mean" would be a situation involving rather great overlap between the old and the newly added attributes. Their data suggest
that an additive process becomes more likely as the evaluative re-
dundancy or overlap of attributes decreases. Fishbein would have
to take this overlap in meaning as a factor determining the effects
of the additional information on overall evaluation.

We are now ready to provide still another answer to the question
that was posed at the beginning of the chapter, concerning the determinants of the degree to which an individual will attend either
to separate persons in a social situation or to the social situation *per
se*. One of the functions of schemas is to enable the person to process
more information at a given time. Therefore, if the individual has well-
developed schemas about the separate individuals in a situation, greater attention can be paid to the social situation as such. Thus, in the
perceptual situations in which an individual evidences a primacy effect, he would be more likely to be able to attend to the social situation.
If the primacy effect is eliminated so that the individual attends to
later information which comes to him about another person, he will

be less able to notice the interactions among the people present. Similarly, the more unified and coherent are an individual's schemas about the other people in the situation, the more likely he is to attend to the social situation *per se*, since his unified schemas provide efficient ways of rapidly processing information about the particular persons with whom he is involved. By the same token, if the individual has a well-developed schema about the social situation, the plot, he can give greater attention to the individual people, the characters.

Following our theoretical framework, we can now turn to the problem of what happens when familiar and aroused schemas about other people run headlong into an exception, so that positions on expected dimensions of the schema are clearly contradicted by some blatantly obvious aspect of the social environment. Notice all the qualifications that are included in the previous sentence. In order for contradiction to occur, the schema must be a familiar one, not one which is in the process of being acquired, as in the case of the L.O.S. about particular other people which we discussed in the previous paragraph. The schema must be aroused; what are logically and physically real contradictions may not be reacted to as such by the person unless a relevant schema is aroused. And the contradiction must be so blatant that it demands attention because it represents a substantial change from the schema itself. Still another qualification concerns the degree of probabilism of the schema; highly probabilistic schemas are harder to contradict than those of lesser probabilism. At the same time, an individual is highly motivated to keep probabilism to a minimum, especially with respect to schemas about other people, since they are so important for the attainment of his goals. Thus there is strong motivation to minimize the degree to which exceptions to a schema increase its probabilism. The great strength of the motivation to perceive others as constant and stable has been most profoundly articulated by Heider (1958) and is shown in studies by Podell (1961) and Levy (1967) in which subjects indicated they liked other people less who were described as having both desirable and undesirable traits than those who were described as having only traits of intermediate desirability. When a person has both desirable and undesirable traits, predictions which a perceiver might make about his behavior would be more probabilistic than if it were known "where he stood." Thus, Levy found that his subjects were less confident of their ratings of the likability of the more variable person. This motivation to keep the probabilism of schemas about other people low provides us with another reason why we tend so strongly to make inferences about other people on the basis of limited information. This tendency was illustrated on pages 185 to 196, but there it was attributed mostly to the functioning of the tendency to perceive particular people in a manner consistent with higher order schemas. Now, we see that in addition to the movement toward consistency, persons are motivated to extrapolate from limited information in order to reduce probabilism or maintain it at low levels.

In "everyday life" familiar schemas about other people can be at all levels of order, since we have L.O.S.s about old friends as well as H.O.S.s about whole categories of people. However, there are stronger pressures on H.O.S.s than on L.O.S.s to remain low in probabilism, both from motivational pressures and from the outcomes of the ways in which schemas function. Thus, H.O.S.s would in general have a lower level of probabilism. This difference between higher and L.O.S.s is apparently reflected in a study by Koltuv (1962). She had people ascribe traits to familiar and unfamiliar other people, and for each subject she computed the coefficients of correlation between all pairs of traits. If a person was highly certain that the presence of one trait implied the presence of another, the correlation would be high. Thus the magnitude of the correlations can be taken as an index of the absence of probabilism in the schema relating the traits. Koltuv found that an individual is more likely to apply to a stranger than to a familiar person an H.O.S. about categories of people. He would have an L.O.S. about the familiar person. Thus, the low probabilism of the H.O.S. was reflected in higher correlations between traits attributed to strangers than to familiar people. H.O.S.s about categories of people would therefore be fairly vulnerable to exceptions. In general, more probabilistic L.O.S.s can better tolerate exceptions, since the exceptions "fit" the schema. If John is not always witty, we don't stop calling him a witty person; we recognize that his "wittiness" is probabilistic. Bob is generally kind, but he can be tough "when he has to be." Nevertheless, even relatively probabilistic schemas can be contradicted by a run of exceptions; if John has not cracked a joke in a month, we may conclude that he has lost his touch. Furthermore, even L.O.S.s can be low in probabilism, although, in general, this is less likely than is the case with H.O.S.s. For example, a child may view a given teacher as invariably mean. If the teacher were to do him a single good turn, he would be quite surprised.

In research, it is easier to examine the reactions to clearly perceived exceptions to H.O.S.s, to familiar categories of people, simply because many people share the same schemas about categories of people; they have stereotypes. The reactions of college students to violations of their stereotypes about factory workers have been investigated in a study by Haire and Grunes (1950). (The date is important in this study, since this particular stereotype may have changed since that time or have become more probabilistic. The college student reader can no doubt make a better guess about the amount of change than the authors can.) In any case, the students were presented with a trait-adjective description of a factory worker and were then asked to describe him in their own words. However, half the students read lists which included nothing about the worker's intelligence. These students gave quite uniform descriptions of the worker, many of them saying he was not intelligent. The other half of the students read the same adjectives, except that "intelligent" was now added to the list, thus providing a direct contradiction to their schemas about factory workers. They handled this problem in a quite variable fashion. Some aroused a new schema which would redefine the meaning of "intelligent" or give it different shades of meaning; e.g., he was witty and lively; he was a foreman; he's intelligent compared to other factory workers; intelligent refers to the raw or innate quality, not the present ability. Others found higher order schemas which explained why an intelligent man worked in a factory: he lacked drive; he lacked education; he lacked opportunity for advancement. Others found a type of H.O.S. to take care of the exception: they simply rejected the idea that he was intelligent and the researchers who gave the description thereby were being accused implicitly of having erred. Regardless of which of these tacks a college student takes, the H.O.S. about factory workers would remain unchanged.

Another instance of the way people protect their higher order, familiar schemas comes from a study in which subjects were told of a member of the upper social class who was a member of the Communist Party (Pepitone and Hayden, 1955). The subjects appeared to handle the problem by redefining either the meaning of his membership in the Party or in the upper class.

"His political views are at variance with the whole capitalistic pattern. He probably professes to be a socialist to ally himself with his workers, but he is probably a Republican at heart."

"He is a man of principle and firm conviction. This must be so, otherwise he would not belong to both the National Association of Manufacturers and the Socialist Party (sic). . . . There is good in both and he stands by the principles of both despite recognizable conflicting differences."

Another way of handling exceptions to familiar schemas has been pointed out by Secord and Backman (1964). An individual may accept an increase in probabilism of his category ("Maybe they're not all alike"), but make up for this by establishing some subcategories or subtypes; within each subcategory, however, the probabilism is low. "There are two types, those who know their place and those who don't."

The intellectual dexterity which is shown in these examples is impressive as well as it often is humorous. And, as we have repeatedly pointed out, the individual is quite likely to perceive and be aware of his own performance in explaining away exceptions. Thus, he may well develop H.O.S.s about his techniques for reducing probabilism or maintaining it at a low level in the face of exceptions. Since he is motivated to keep probabilism low, he will tend to apply these techniques to other situations involving exceptions, both to the same H.O.S.s and to others as well. The individual may develop generalized ways of handling exceptions.

The tendency to develop H.O.S.s about how to handle exceptions to a given H.O.S. has a rather ironic consequence. If an individual has had a good deal of experience with exceptions to an H.O.S. about other people, he may simply develop and apply better techniques for handling exceptions, rather than increasing the probabilism of his H.O.S. about other people. The person who actually faces a rather variable environment of people may become most adept at keeping probabilism low (cf. McGuire, 1966). This adeptness may in some cases be increased by motivations to keep probabilism low because people facing many exceptions may well also be people who have to act in some way with respect to the other person or persons. As we have seen, one of the roots of the motivation to keep probabilism low is the need to make unequivocal decisions and to act, so that people who both have to face exceptions and to act may become most adept at keeping probabilism low. In consequence, the official who has to "meet the public" and make decisions (the prison guard, the salesman) may all have quite "clear" ideas about the public, prisoners, and potential customers.

The resiliency of H.O.S.s about categories of people, this resistance to change by exceptions, can cause some serious problems in society. In those cases in which reality is, in fact, much more variable than the low probabilism of the H.O.S. allows for, an individual may guide his behavior and make decisions which simply do not conform to reality. The existence of such H.O.S.s may well be a major source of difficulty, conflict, and in some cases, hatred among groups of people. The members of one group will react to another as if the members of the second group were made of the same mold, when there really is no mold. This reaction is an insult to individuality and to their perception of their own group's variability. Of course, if the members of a group do attribute the same characteristics to themselves as do others, and also view their group as being as homogeneous as others do, then less conflict would arise. In some cases, there appears to be some agreement between groups about each other's characteristics (Abate and Berrien, 1967). However, the research which shows such agreement seldom concerns itself with the question of the relative probabilism of the schemas of the two groups. Let us be clear about what we are saying. The argument here is not that general differences between groups do not exist; it is obvious that they do and research has often spelled out the differences in great detail. Our first problem is whether the schemas about the differences correspond to the actual differences. The second problem is the degree of conformity within these groups. Some groups may be highly unified; others may be quite diverse. Yet, the pressures to reduce probabilism are such as to lead an individual not to distinguish between homogeneous and heterogeneous groups.

The problem of the resistance of H.O.S.s about categories to change or to increase in probabilism is compounded when the individual has acquired his H.O.S. by means of communications from others. The H.O.S. about the validity of the sources of his information is itself of low probabilism. Thus, the individual acquires schemas of low probabilism from sources of low probabilism. It is small wonder then that we often have fairly firm ideas about groups with which we have never had contact. Katz and Braly (1933) showed that most well-educated collegians felt they could reasonably describe almost all the nationalities in the world with a maximum of five adjectives per nationality.

What happens, however, when people who have a schema about another group which is based primarily on communications from others actually contact members of the other group? More specifically, what happens to their schemas? This type of contact is different from the frequent, regularized contact with another group which we cited a few paragraphs above. In the latter cases, the individual has developed techniques for keeping probabilism low. The contacts we are discussing now are new, even though the schemas are old. The individual probably has not developed many techniques for handling this sort of exception, so that they may have a stronger impact on him. Furthermore, he is likely to attend to the exceptions, since they represent a change, perhaps even a surprise, which is perceived in the familiar context of a schema derived from communications from other people. Thus, we would expect to find that the increased attention to unanticipated exceptions that may occur in direct contact would lead to changes of stereotypes, to increases in probabilism. One problem is in trying to find empirical research examples of this: in real-life situations, the contacts with the other group take place in a context in which both groups have goals which may be similar to each other's, or which may be different, which may involve cooperation, or may involve competition in which these goals may be achieved or not; or the contacts may involve interaction, or just observation; or they may involve similarity of status, or differences. Since all of these factors can have effects which are either independent of, or interact with, the effects of contact in itself, it is almost impossible to draw any general conclusions about what happens to the schemas as a result of the contacts *per se*. Furthermore, most of the research on the effects of contact between groups has concerned the effects on evaluation of the other group, but little has been done on changes in the probabilism of the stereotype.

The significance of the context in determining the consequences of contact between groups is illustrated by contrasting two studies of the effects of contact. The first (Deutsch and Collins, 1951) was a comparison of the attitudes of white housewives toward black people in two public housing projects, one in which blacks and whites were segregated into different buildings, one in which the two groups were randomly assigned to apartments. Both the black and white people in the two projects were of the same socio-economic group, the working class, and had therefore many of the same problems in life. Their relationships were not competitive, at least not obviously so in the housing project itself. Neither group had any prior claim to the project, since both groups were admitted at the same time. Finally, the integration or segregation of the housing projects was apparently sanctioned by a respected power, the Federal Government. In this context, it was found that white housewives in the integrated project were considerably more positive about Negroes after having lived in the project for a considerable period than were those in the segregated project; and the closer a white woman's apartment happened to be to a black's, the more positive she was. Before we jump to the perhaps happy conclusion that contact makes for more positive H.O.S. about the other group, we must ask whether any or all of the contextual factors, such as common status, non-competition, support from an authority, were significant in determining the effects of contact on the feelings of the whites. Further, we must ask what the actual attributes of the black group were and how homogeneous they were. There was no data gathered on either of these points.

This study in the housing project stands in contrast to the results of a comparison of Americans who varied in the amount of contact they had with Greeks (Triandis and Vassiliou, 1967). The Americans with maximal contact were those working in Greece in jobs which required direct contact with Greeks. Those with minimum contact were simply students at the University of Illinois. The researchers found that the maximal contact group had a poorer opinion of Greeks than did the minimal group. Further, the maximal contact group thought better of themselves than did the minimal—it appears that the discrepancy between their self-evaluations and their evaluations of others increased as a result of contact. On the other hand, Greek students studying in America thought more poorly of their own country than did Greek students in Athens. Triandis and Vassiliou explain these findings in terms of the values common to both nationalities: material success, high standards of living, "the good life"; with increased contact both the Americans and Greeks could not help but perceive the American's greater achievement of these values. Again, the motivations and context of the contact appear critical; the results of contact can be diametrically opposite, depending upon the contact context. In neither of the studies just cited was it possible to study actual change of a stereotype—the subjects were examined only after their contact. Obviously, this makes for some ambiguity in interpreting the results, since we cannot be certain that the groups that had contacts were not different from the other groups in some imperceptibly relevant way. Furthermore, in neither of the studies was there much concern for the change of content of the H.O.S.; the focus was on the perhaps more socially significant problem of the groups' evaluations of each other.

One of the few relevant studies in which an actual change of the content of stereotypes was observed was done in Lebanon in 1951-1952 by Prothero and Melikian (1955), who administered the measures devised by Katz and Braly to students and businessmen in May, 1951, before any large influx of Americans to Lebanon. The measure consists of having subjects list adjectives which describe a given nationality. Americans were viewed as rich, industrial, democratic, materialistic, mercantile, and practical. Then, between May, 1951, and December, 1952, there was a great influx of Americans —Point IV workers, U.S. Information Agency workers, diplomats, and, most importantly, sailors from the 6th Fleet who were given one week's leave. The fleet was in the week before the Katz and Braly measure was administered to a group comparable to the first. On the second measure, none of the originally attributed traits was dropped—the H.O.S. maintained itself! However, a number of traits were added: sociable, superficial, jolly, simple. This study suggests that H.O.S.s about categories of people don't lose any of their parts in the face of direct contact with members of the categories. Instead, new attributes are simply added, especially those that don't contradict the already existing ones. Prothero and Melikian themselves point out that the new did not contradict the old. Nevertheless, the reader is cautioned about overgeneralizing from this research—after all, we don't know the exact context in which all of these contacts occurred; we don't know how much the Americans actually had these attributes; and we don't know how homogeneous the Americans actually were.

References

Abate, M., and Berrien, F. K.: Validation of stereotype: Japanese versus American students. *Journal of Personality and Social Psychology*, 1967, 7:435–438.
Allport, G. W., and Postman, L.: *The Psychology of Rumor.* New York, Holt, 1947.
Anderson, N. H.: Primacy effects in personality impression formation using a gen-

eralized order effect paradigm. *Journal of Personality and Social Psychology,* 1965, 2:1–9.

Anderson, N. H.: Application of a linear-serial model to a personality-impression task using serial presentation. *Journal of Personality and Social Psychology,* 1968, 16:354–362.

Anderson, N. H., and Barrios, A. A.: Primacy effects in personality impression formation. *Journal of Abnormal and Social Psychology,* 1961, 63:346–350.

Anderson, N. H., and Hubert, S.: Effects of concomitant verbal recall on order effects in personality impression formation. *Journal of Verbal Behavior,* 1963, 2:379–391.

Anderson, N. H., and Jacobson, A.: Effect of stimulus inconsistency and discounting instructions in personality impression formation. *Journal of Personality and Social Psychology,* 1965, 2:531–539.

Anisfeld, M., Munoz, S. R., and Lambert, W. E.: The structure and dynamics of the ethnic attitudes of Jewish adolescents. *Journal of Abnormal and Social Psychology,* 1963, 66:31–36.

Asch, S.: *Social Psychology.* Englewood Cliffs, New Jersey, Prentice-Hall, 1952.

Berkowitz, L.: The judgmental process in personality functioning. *Psychological Review,* 1960, 67:130–142.

Bieri, J.: Cognitive complexity-simplicity and predictive behavior. *Journal of Abnormal and Social Psychology,* 1955, 51:263–268.

Bieri, J., Atkins, A. L., Briar, S., Leaman, R. L., Miller, H., and Tripodi, T.: *Clinical and Social Judgment.* New York, Wiley, 1966.

Bonarious, J. C. J.: Research in the personal construct theory of George A. Kelly: Role construct repertory test and basic theory. In B. A. Maher (Ed.), *Progress in Experimental Personality Research, Vol. 2.* New York, Academic Press, 1965.

Bossart, P., and di Vesta, F. J.: Effects of context, frequency, and order of presentation of evaluative assertions on impression formation. *Journal of Personality and Social Psychology,* 1966, 4.538–544.

Briscoe, M. E., Woodyard, H. D., and Shaw, M. E.: Personality impression change as a function of the favorableness of first impressions. *Journal of Personality,* 1964, 35:343–356.

Cline, V. B., and Richards, J. M.: Accuracy of interpersonal perception—a general trait? *Journal of Abnormal and Social Psychology,* 1960, 60:1–7.

Crockett, W. H.: Cognitive complexity and impression formation. In B. A. Maher (Ed.), *Progress in Experimental Personality Research,* Vol. 2. New York, Academic Press, 1965.

Cronbach, L. J.: Processes affecting scores on "understanding others" and "assumed similarity." *Psychological Bulletin,* 1955, 52:177–193.

Deutsch, M., and Collins, M. E.: *Interracial Housing.* Minneapolis, University of Minnesota Press, 1951.

Ekman, P.: Differential communication of affect by head and body cues. *Journal of Personality and Social Psychology,* 1965, 2:726–735.

Feshbach, S., and Feshbach, N.: Influence of the stimulus object upon complementary and supplementary projection of fear. *Journal of Abnormal and Social Psychology,* 1963, 66:498–502.

Fishbein, M., and Hunter, R.: Summation vs. balance in attitude organization and change. *Journal of Abnormal and Social Psychology,* 1964, 69:505–510.

Fishbein, M.: An investigation of the relationships between beliefs about an object and the attitude toward that object. *Human Relations,* 1963, 16:233–239.

Gage, N. L., and Cronbach, J.: Conceptual and methodological problems in interpersonal perception. *Psychological Review,* 1955, 62:411–422.

Garner, W. R.: *Uncertainty and Structure as Psychological Concepts.* New York, Wiley, 1962.

Gollin, E. S.: Forming impressions of personality. *Journal of Personality,* 1953, 22:32–48.

Gollin, E. S.: Organizational characteristics of social judgment: A developmental investigation. *Journal of Personality,* 1958, 26:139–153.

Haire, M., and Grunes, W. F.: Perceptual defenses: processes protecting an organized perception of another personality. *Human Relations,* 1950, 3:403–411.

Heider, F.: *The Psychology of Interpersonal Relations*. New York, Wiley, 1958.

Horowitz, E. L.: The development of attitudes toward the Negro. *Archives of Psychology*, 1936, No. 194.

Jones, E. E., and Davis, K. E.: From acts to disposition. In L. Berkowitz (Ed.), *Advances in Experimental Social Psychology*, Vol. 2. New York, Academic Press, 1965.

Jones, E. E., and de Charms, R.: Changes in social perception as a function of the personal relevance of behavior. *Sociometry*, 1957, *20:*75–85.

Kastenbaum, A.: An experimental study of the formation of impressions of personality. Unpublished master's thesis, New School for Social Research, 1951.

Katz, D., and Braly, K. W.: Racial stereotypes of 100 college students. *Journal of Abnormal and Social Psychology*, 1933, *28:*280–298.

Kelley, H. H.: The warm-cold variable in first impressions of persons. *Journal of Personality*, 1950, *18:*431–439.

Kelley, H. H.: Salience of membership and resistance to change of group-anchored attitudes. *Human Relations*, 1955, *8:*275–290.

Koltuv, B. B.: Some characteristics of intrajudge trait intercorrelation. *Psychological Monographs: General and Applied*, 1962, 76 (No. 33, Whole No. 552).

Levy, L.: The effects of variance on personality impression formation. *Journal of Personality*, 1967, *35:*179–193.

Luchins, A. S.: Primacy-recency in impression formation. In C. I. Hovland (Ed.), *The Order of Presentation in Persuasion*. New Haven, Yale University Press, 1957.

Lundy, R. M.: Assimilative projection and accuracy of prediction in interpersonal perception. *Journal of Abnormal and Social Psychology*, 1957, *52:*33–38.

McGuire, W. J.: Cognitive consistency and attitude change. *Journal of Abnormal and Social Psychology*, 1960, *60:*345–353.

McGuire, W. J.: The current status of cognitive consistency theories. In S. Feldman (Ed.), *Cognitive Consistency*. New York, Academic Press, 1966.

Miller, G. A.: The magical number seven, plus or minus two: some limits on our capacity for processing information. *Psychological Review*, 1956, *63:*81–97.

Nidorf, L. J., and Crockett, W. H.: Some factors affecting the amount of information sought about others. *Journal of Abnormal and Social Psychology*, 1964, *69:*98–101.

Pepitone, A., and Hayden, R.: Some evidence for conflict resolution in impression formation. *Journal of Abnormal and Social Psychology*, 1955, *51:*302–307.

Podell, J. E.: A comparison of generalization and adaptation level as theories of connotation. *Journal of Abnormal and Social Psychology*, 1961, *62:*593–597.

Prothero, E. T., and Melikian, L. H.: Studies in stereotypes: V. Familiarity and the kernel of truth hypothesis. *Journal of Social Psychology*, 1955, *41:*3–10.

Rosenkrantz, P. S., and Crockett, W. H.: Some factors influencing the assimilation of disparate information in impression formation. *Journal of Personality and Social Psychology*, 1965, *2:*397–402.

Rosnow, R. L., Wainer, H., and Arms, R. L.: Personality and group impression formation as a function of the amount of overlap in evaluative meaning of the stimulus elements. *Sociometry*, 1970, *33:*472–484.

Schroeder, H. M., Driver, M. J., and Steufert, S.: *Human Information Processing*. New York, Holt, Rinehart, & Winston, 1967.

Secord, P. F., and Backman, C. W.: Interpersonal congruency, perceived similarity, and friendship. *Sociometry*, 1964, *27:*115–127.

Secord, P. F., Bevan, W., and Katz, B.: The Negro stereotype and perceptual accentuation. *Journal of Abnormal and Social Psychology*, 1956, *53:*78–83.

Secord, P. F., Dukes, W. F., and Bevan, W.: Personalities in faces: I. An experiment in social perceiving. *Genetic Psychology Monograph*, 1954, *49:*231–279.

Secord, P. F., and Muthard, J. E.: Personalities in faces: IV. A descriptive analysis of the perception of women's faces and the identification of some physiognomic data. *Journal of Psychology*, 1955, *39:*269–278.

Stewart, R. H.: Effect of continuous responding on the order effort in personality impression formation. *Journal of Personality and Social Psychology*, 1965, *1:*161–165.

Triandis, H. C., and Fishbein, M.: Cognitive interaction in person perception. *Journal of Abnormal and Social Psychology*, 1963, *67:*446–453.

Triandis, H. C., and Vassiliou, V.: Frequency of contact and stereotyping. *Journal of Personality and Social Psychology*, 1967, 7:316–328.

Veness, T., and Brierley, D. W.: Forming impressions of personality. *British Journal of Social and Clinical Psychology*, 1963, 2:11–19.

Wishner, J.: Reanalysis of "impression of personality." *Psychological Review*, 1960, 67:96–112.

Wyer, R. S., and Dermer, M.: Effect of context and instructional set upon evaluations of personality-trait adjectives. *Journal of Personality and Social Psychology*, 1968, 9:7–14.

Yarrow, M. R., and Campbell, J. D.: Person perception in children. *Merrill-Palmer Quarterly*, 1963, 9:57–72.

CHAPTER 6

SCHEMAS ABOUT INTERPERSONAL RELATIONS

In the last chapter we saw how schemas about individual other people are acquired and what effects these schemas have on a person's perception of others, as the latter are viewed as if they were in a kind of vacuum. Such perceptual focusing on a person "in isolation" sometimes occurs because that is all we have to attend to—a new character presented in the first chapter of a novel and described only in terms of his personality, a stranger walking down a street alone. But a question was raised in the last chapter: when will a person focus his attention on a single other individual when the latter is physically in a crowd, when he is interacting with other people, when he is not alone walking down the street? Or, conversely, when will the person attend more to the relationships among the people he observes, to the plot, the conversation, the interaction? To be sure, the answers to these complementary questions need to be put in terms of degree rather than in terms of two distinctly different foci of attention. The answer should be given in terms of degree of focus on the individual, and of degree of focus on the plot, with many shades of gray possible between the two extremes.

In the chapter on the perception of persons, we gave some of the answers to this question. A person will be more likely to attend to those aspects of the situation which are new or changing when there is some familiar aspect present. Thus, if a familiar person is encountered in a strange or changing set of relationships with other people, the perceiver is likely to attend more to the changing or strange relationships. We think little about the character of the familiar detective as he unravels a "plot" of new and original intrigue. On the other hand, if the plot is a familiar one, like the perennial triangle, then we are more likely to focus on the personalities of the people involved. We notice their individual characteristics more in the context of the familiar plot, and thus are more likely to develop schemas about them. Of course, if their attributes, behaviors, or anything else about them appears to be nothing more than a reflection of the social interactional situation, there would be nothing individual to attend to—no change from the plot would be entailed. A clerk might not attend to the personality of a customer who behaves just as all other customers have behaved. But if the customer should differ from the others, the clerk would be quite likely to attend to him, notice his idiosyncrasies, and develop some sort of schema about him as a person (cf. Jones and Davis, 1965).

In addition to the factors mentioned above which determine the degree of attention to relationships between people, the individual may attend to interpersonal relationships because he has been directed to do so by some important other person. In more technical language, the other person directs us to arouse a schema regarding interpersonal relationships: "Look at the way they are talking to each other"; "Isn't that an interesting conversation?"; "See how they clutch each other"; "Notice the way they aggravate one another." Or, conversely, the request may entail looking at a particular person in isolation: "Notice the way he pronounces 'the'?"; "His gait is rather peculiar, isn't it?" Or the other may direct us to arouse a higher order schema about interpersonal relationships: "Try to get an impression of how people react to him"; "Pay attention to the way they get along with each other." We all find it difficult, if not impossible, to avoid doing what the requestor asks us to do—"Now that you have pointed this out to me, it is very hard not to notice it." The reason for the power of these directions from others is twofold. One is that schemas concerned either with interpersonal relations or with isolated people can be aroused by direction from others, like any other schemas. The aroused schemas then direct attention. Second, the very content of the communication arouses the schemas referred to by that content. As a result of hearing the person giving the directions mention "conversation," a person's schema about conversation is likely to be aroused; or, hearing about "his lisp" might very well arouse schemas about lisping. We would attend either to the conversation or to the lisp; if we attend to the former, we attend to interaction; if to the latter, to the person in "isolation."

Another process which can determine whether we attend to the interaction or to the person in isolation has to do with the effects of higher order schemas. Suppose a person has an aroused H.O.S. which apparently has the following meaning: "It is important to attend to the characteristics of individuals." This person would then be more likely to do so. Or, a person might have aroused a H.O.S. about the importance of interaction *per se.*

Closely tied to the effects of H.O.S.s is the effect of motivation on the degree of attention to the "plot." An individual who is motivated to learn about a given person because he might later have to work with him, or hire him, or a person who is trying to write a description of another, would be more likely to attend to the individual in himself. A judge at a debating match who is motivated to attend to the interplay of the arguments or an offensive quarterback trying to outguess the opposition would attend more to the plot, and less to personality.

We have noted repeatedly that familiar schemas are preferred to strange ones, even when the latter catch our attention. The same preferences occur also with respect to schemas about social interaction. An individual who has been in a given occupation for a long period of time often develops a fondness for his way of relating to the people with whom he comes into contact on the job. Any behavior by others which deviates from his pattern is not only readily noticed but disparaged. Sociologists have pointed to bureaucrats as people who are most likely to show this kind of rigidity. They may develop a technique for handling all comers, so that someone dealing with them may feel unhappy because he is not recognized as an individual. More precisely, if he does something that shows that he is different, he will be noticed, but not liked. Furthermore, if the occupation also entails making decisions about other people, the person may be motivated to reduce the probabilism to assist in coming to decisions. A bureaucrat might believe that *all* people who answer certain of his questions in a given way are lying, that there are few exceptions, if any; and that, therefore, he should reject any requests these persons make. The low probabilism of such schemas, of course, increases the impersonality of relationships the bureaucrat has with the public; in our terms, the arousal of such preferred schemas of low probabilism decreases the tendency to attend to the other person as an individual.

The bureaucrat example should not mislead the reader into thinking that only bureaucrats are subject to this process. Any person who repeatedly encounters the same social situation may develop schemas about it which are also highly preferred. A fixed pattern of race relations may be preferred by some partly because it is familiar—although there are obviously other reasons for such preferences. A routinized pattern of flirtation, a routinized way of talking to service station attendants, a routinized way of talking to neighbors, a routinized way of some counselors talking to students may all exemplify this same process.

This is not to argue that all people become as rigid as the bureaucrat described above; we have pointed out that there can be strong motivations to attend to the new, even to seek it. However, the degree to which such motives develop will vary from person to person because of the factors which we have already indicated. In any case, the behavior of the above described bureaucrat has to be viewed as a tendency which is always present, but which can be overcome by other motivations and experiences.

Now that we have looked at some of the determinants of when an individual will attend to interpersonal processes, the next question obviously is, how much is included in the interpersonal situation to which the individual attends? For an answer, we return to a familiar concept, the idea of dimension capacity, the maximal number of dimensions to which an individual can attend. Interpersonal situations are like any other in that there is a limit to the number of aspects of the situation to which a person can attend. Should the individual approach this limit, he will become increasingly anxious. Thus, he will tend to avoid situations which involve too many people, too much interpersonal activity, or excessive informational input from other people. Slater (1958) had people get together four times in groups varying in size from 2 to 7 members. The people preferred groups of 5 members, rather than the maximum of 7. Furthermore, members of the larger groups evidenced more complaints, among which were ones to the effect that the groups were too disorderly and that there was insufficient control of procedures. Their complaints obviously reflect in part an aversion to conditions involving more information than could be efficiently assimilated. One might, of course, ask why the members did not prefer the smallest groups. There probably were several reasons for this, and Slater himself indicates one of them: that the subjects were quite polite, restrained, and superficial in their relationships in the smaller groups. If Slater's explanation is correct, then one would expect that if people get to know one another better so that they could feel free to be more blunt, open, and free with one another, they would prefer smaller groups. Accordingly, Tagiuri (1958) found that in a variety of groups which remained together for an extended period of time, such as groups of naval cadets, summer camp groups, seminars, and semi-therapeutic groups, people tended to pair off in cliques of *two* people. Thus, when obstacles to free interaction between people are low, people appear to choose smaller groups.

In addition to avoiding large groups, people may reduce the amount of information they have to process by developing schemas in which a collection of discrete individuals is regarded as a single unit: the individual reacts to the collectivity as a single entity, group, or unit and thereby reduces the total number of aspects of the situation that could demand attention. Thus, persons refer to clubs, gangs, teams, organizations, cliques, institutions, "establishments" and nations, for example. The peculiarity of this way of looking at such collections is strikingly brought home by statements such as "That company fired him," when, of course, it really was a decision of a number of people in authority, rather than the whole company. Or, we might hear "That country declared war," when it was only the government (sic) that did.

One of the major factors pressing a person toward attending to a high number of dimensions and thus tending to make him more anxious is the amount of change in the environment, since changes attract attention. Thus, an individual will be very likely to be motivated to avoid high degrees of change in his social relationships. Ziller (1965) has presented a very insightful analysis of the reactions of organized groups to changes in their membership. He points out that groups generally tend to be averse to too rapid turnover in membership and that all sorts of processes are used to avoid the negative aspects of excessive change. For example, the established members of a group may pay little attention to the personalities of new members; instead, they may simply attend to their formal positions as newcomers in the group. In fact, Ziller points out that in some groups there is a regularized process for the introduction of newcomers. Initiation procedures, "hazing" of new members, "cooling off" periods, are exemplars of such processes. An H.O.S. is developed which concerns the very process of accepting a newcomer. The H.O.S. itself does not change; it is stable, so that the amount of attention demanding change is reduced.

As has been pointed out repeatedly, the arousal of a familiar H.O.S. allows an individual to approach the new and changing with less anxiety. Thus, the presence of any aspect of the group which is stable and familiar to the members will reduce the anxiety they feel in response to *any* type of change in the group, not only those involving group membership. The most effective way of keeping the anxiety over great change to a minimum is to make the process of changing a regularized, routine procedure. In that way, any time there is a change in the group, a familiar procedure or aspect of the group has to be attended to. For instance, all of the familiar procedures of parliamentary rules are involved in any new measures established by formal groups. In some groups, the leader may always be involved in enunciating a new policy or change of procedure. At an informal level, there may be familiar and routinized channels of communication which are used to tell people about changes in the group's processes.

In addition to regularizing procedures, other aspects of the group may function to keep the anxiety over change low. Members of groups with unchanging membership, with unchanging procedures, with familiar symbols, such as insignias, uniforms, and titles, may all be more capable of facing change in the relationships among members than those without these.

As pointed out in Chapter 3, the changes to which people attend take place along dimensions or aspects of entities or situations; and repeated experience with changes along a given dimension has many effects: the dimension will tend to become salient for the person; he will learn of the range of discrete positions that is possible on the dimension; and he will tend to conceptualize the dimension. Throughout much of this chapter, we will be giving examples involving many dimensions of interpersonal relationships, their salience, the learned range of variation on them, and their conceptualization. Most of these examples will involve schemas which are well learned early in life; but at this point, it is important to note that adults also can acquire new conceptual dimensions. Zajonc and Wolfe (1966) found that people who were high in the hierarchy in a firm had widespread formal interpersonal contacts in the firm. The variety of their experiences in the organization led them to describe it by citing more aspects of it than did those with less wide experience; that is, the former persons had acquired and conceptualized more dimensions about interpersonal processes in the firm. An individual may acquire new dimensions relevant to interpersonal processes through the variety of his experiences. He may then retain and notice aspects of interpersonal processes which would otherwise be unnoticed. This is essentially what anthropologists do when they write about their homelands from a new perspective after having studied previously unfamiliar societies.

In Chapter 3, it was pointed out that as people experience correlations between positions on their conceptualized dimensions, they acquire schemas reflecting these correlations. We also learned that people tend to evaluate highly those entities or schemas which are familiar. In the last chapter, we saw one example of this high evaluation of familiar schemas in the tendency for people to stabilize their choice of friends in a group (Campbell, 1964; Bloom, 1964). Partly this tendency results from the high evaluation of familiar friends, but it may also reflect a wish on the part of group members to avoid any change in the pattern of interpersonal relationships. Once having become accustomed to knowledge that, for example, A likes B, members may subtly apply pressure to assure the continuation of this relationship. In addition, the aversion to strangeness, especially in groups which do not have a well established role of "newcomer," may be in part a result of such a new member's potential for changing established patterns of relationships among those already in a group. The members no doubt have experienced situations in the past in which the introduction of a new member to an established group led to a change in the way people related to one another. A new person may establish new patterns of friendship; he may have new ideas about what the group should do; he may relate to the members in new ways.

Pleasure in finding the familiar in initially strange situations may be one of the bases of the enjoyment some find in rather esoteric literature—since the types of schemas reflected in the plots may be international, if not universal. Shibutani (1961) makes this point eloquently:

"Even a cursory glance at the folklore and literature of the world reveals a remarkable similarity in plots, in spite of the diversity of language, costume, and setting. Indeed, the bulk of world literature seems to revolve around a handful of recurrent themes. The experiences of men, though infinitely varied, are endlessly duplicated; the stories all begin in situations that most people understand either from their own experiences or from living side by side with other human beings and noticing what it is like to endure them. A beautiful girl forces an infatuated man to defile himself to demonstrate his love and then rejects him as degraded. An evil man outsmarts himself through his avarice and attains success at some terrible cost, realizing only when it is too late that he has struggled in vain. It is precisely because such events take place everywhere that novels can be translated from one language into another and be appreciated in spite of the change of literary style. The fact that *Carmen* can too easily be transposed into *Carmen Jones* is an indication of the secondary importance of the cultural setting in comparison to the plot and characterizations. Great classics in one culture are usually hailed in another; European writers credited with extraordinary insight into human nature—Balzac, Dostoyevsky, Pascal, La Rochefoucauld, Shakespeare—are appreciated elsewhere for the great "truths" that they reveal. Although the Japanese are reputed to be an unemotional people who are content to have their marriages arranged for them by parents and matchmakers, it would be difficult to find a more passionate tale of romantic love than Koyo Ozaki's ever popular *Konjiki Yasha;* nor do they fail to appreciate the sacrifice of Marguerite in Alexandre Dumas' *La Dame aux Camelias.* An American reading Vergil's *Aeneid* discovers that human nature has not changed in 2,000 years. Thus, in spite of the innumerable divergencies in time, place, and culture, there is apparently a limited set of experiences that are universal" (p. 398).

Equivocal Interpersonal Situations

We saw in Chapter 4 the way in which the motivation to perceive the familiar combines with the H.O.S. to the effect that there is consistency between schema and reality. This motivation operates to produce a tendency to perceive ambiguous or equivocal situations in terms of aroused, familiar schemas. Any social situation which is new to a person is to some extent equivocal; he may not know very much about the people in it, or how they relate to one another, or exactly how they will relate to him. Therefore, in new social situations, the tendency to perceive in terms of established schemas which are aroused should be quite prevalent. Leik (1963) reports that when a man and woman first meet, they are likely to behave consistently with the more traditional differences in the male and female roles, with the man attending to things material and to other problems of relating to the physical environment, and the woman attending more to interpersonal or emotional issues. As they get to know one another, this adherence to the stereotyped roles declines and less distinction is made between the two roles. Even some situations which are familiar may continue to be equivocal and thus to be susceptible to this sort of effect. For example, Smith, Bruner and White (1956) have shown that people view the equivocal world of international relationships in terms of their schemas about social relationships. Persons who believe that anger or a show of force is the appropriate response to everyday frustration caused by others are also likely to believe that America should take this type of aggressive stance with respect to its relationship with the Soviet Union. Those who believe in "turning the other cheek" in every day life feel America should do the same.

Of course, even the familiar schemas would not affect the perception of equivocal or ambiguous situations unless they were in a state of arousal. These schemas may be aroused by the individual's attending to some part of a new or equivocal situation which arouses a familiar schema. What aspect of the situation is attended to depends on a number of factors: the relative salience for the perceiver of the dimension which corresponds to the part; the amount of change or movement in that part; its sheer physical prominence; and others. For example, in the meetings between men and women described above, an individual is highly likely to attend to the sex difference, a salient dimension for most people, and then to have the relevant schemas aroused. In perceiving international relationships, the individual may attend to a new threat from the Soviet Union because it represents a change from the immediate past; it is literally "news." Thus any schemas he might have with respect to reactions to threats may be aroused.

Once a schema is aroused, an individual will tend to perceive in terms of the other dimensions of the schema, i.e., the expected dimensions of the schema. The reader may notice that the process is much like the one described in the last chapter as leading to the primacy effect in the perception of persons.

THE PROBABILISM OF INTERPERSONAL SCHEMAS

One of the most important factors to consider in examining the relationship between schemas and the perceivable world is the motiva-

tion to keep the degree of probabilism of schemas low. It is this motivation which, in part, determines the individual's reactions to exceptions,
to contradictions with his schema. Accordingly, the strength of this
motivation is of critical importance. One of the sources of this strength
stems from the fact that people often have to decide between mutually
exclusive courses of action and often cannot just modulate their
behavior to correspond to the probabilities involved. A boy needs
to decide whether to ask a particular girl out or not; a taxi driver
whether to stop for a given customer or not; a hostess whether to invite a specific person or not. In such cases, the individual is motivated
to keep the probabilism of his schemas low so that he can act with
apparent certainty and clarity. Many schemas about social relationships
are relevent to decisions about actions. The boy may choose to ask
a particular girl for a date because of how well he expects to get
along with her; the hostess may choose to invite some individual
because she expects that he will have something in common with
the other guests. Social schemas are thus, in general, susceptible to
this source of motivation to keep probabilism low. However, they
will differ in the degree of relevance for action. Some schemas may
seem to a person to be more "important" and critical than others.
These are likely to be those involving actions, and therefore those
associated with strong pressures to keep probabilism low.

Another factor which keeps the probabilism of schemas about interpersonal processes low is that these schemas are typically of higher
order. It is because they are higher order schemas that we can discuss
them here, since they refer to common aspects of a great variety of
situations and are therefore rather widely held, as we shall see. However, one consequence of their being higher order schemas is that
they are even more subject to the pressures to keep probabilism low,
since we saw in Chapter 5 that H.O.S.s are particularly subject to
such pressures. Furthermore, as H.O.S.s they are protected from exceptions by the lower order schemas which act as buffers between
them and the more exception-laden reality.

The motivation to keep low the probabilism of these H.O.S.s has
many occasions to express itself, since they are likely to be aroused
in all sorts of social situations. There are many occasions on which
an individual will attend to the degree of similarity between himself
and another person; or to the degree of liking between himself and
another. Furthermore, in many of these situations the schema is likely
to be contradicted, since human interaction is rarely as completely
regular as the schema would have it. As a consequence, the individual
is rather likely to have many occasions in which he has to find ways
to minimize the influence of the contradictions on his schemas. Thus,
he is likely to develop some techniques for doing so, which he applies
in a number of situations for a number of schemas. For example,

a person might tend generally to reclassify the exceptions as being related to schemas different from the one which was initially aroused. Or, the person might develop a standard higher order schema which explains away the exceptions, such as "Similar people like one another, except when they are too similar."

In addition to the techniques for handling exceptions which we have already mentioned, there are some which are particularly appropriate with respect to schemas having to do with social relationships. These additional techniques are an outcome of the fact that it is possible sometimes to change the actual social situation: two people can sometimes be separated or brought together; or one can try to change one's attitude to another; or one can change one's behavior toward another person. In comparison, it is much more difficult to change the overall personality or character of another person. Thus, one technique a person might use to cope with exceptions to schemas about social relationships is to change the actual situation from one that contradicts the schema to one which confirms it.

One of the general effects of schemas is to lead a person to perceive situations as being consistent with them or to act so as to make them consistent. This effect obviously leads to a minimization of the number of exceptions encountered to these schemas. This minimization, in turn, tends to reduce any tendency to raise the probabilism of the schemas, and, in fact, might work so as to keep it considerably lower than reality might be expected to dictate. This tendency to keep probabilism low is also enhanced by the person's avoidance of situations which present blatant and intractable exceptions. In short, the schemas tend to be self-stabilizing.

Another factor leading to the stabilization of schemas, and to the reduction in their probabilism, concerns communications from other people. Once a number of people have acquired a given schema through their own direct observations, they are likely to attach verbal labels to the dimensions involved and to the relationships observed between positions on these dimensions. Since language abounds in words describing dimensions of interpersonal relationships, the verbal labels are readily available. Accordingly, each individual will be able to communicate with others about given social situations by means of the verbal labels of his schemas. Thus, it is likely that people will acquire schemas not only from their own direct experiences but also by communications from others.

These communications will reduce the probabilism of these schemas for a number of reasons. First, the communications themselves are often phrased in terms implying low probabilism: "Don't you think those guys like each other because they have a lot in common?", "I think people like people who like them." Second, when an individual develops an H.O.S. on the basis of a number of communications from other people, its probabilism will be low simply because it is an H.O.S. Third, when the person combines the H.O.S. based on communications from others with the H.O.S. based on his own observations, the still higher order schema emerging from the combination would have still lower levels of probabilism.

COMMON INTERPERSONAL SCHEMAS

Throughout the balance of this chapter, we will examine a number of H.O.S.s which are rather widely held in American society. In examining each one, the basis in people's experience for the acquisition of the schema will be shown. Then research which demonstrates the effects of this schema on perception and on overt behavior will be cited. In many instances, the research will indicate cases in which the schemas lead to ways of perceiving which are not necessarily supported by the facts at hand. Two people may be seen as liking one another when there is no direct indication that they do; they may be perceived as alike when there are no grounds at all for doing so. This is not to say that reality is being contradicted, rather things are read into reality, equivocal cases are interpreted consistently with schemas, and more is imputed to relationships than is warranted.

In reading about these schemas, it should be kept in mind that it is not being suggested that they are the only schemas held by people. Rather, those which will be discussed are those on which at least noticeable amounts of research have been done, so that the acquisition and functioning of schemas may be illustrated by reference to systematic research as well as to anecdote. One probable reason that these particular schemas have been researched is that they are indeed prevalent in American society. However, we do not say that these are necessarily the only ones which are prevalent, or even among the more prevalent. Moreover, there are no doubt differences between subgroups of Americans in the schemas they hold: rural vs. urban, black vs. white, rich vs. poor. The differences between subgroups of the American population result from differences in their experiences and the differences in the salience of various dimensions.

A research technique to get at the everyday experiences of people from which they acquire schemas has been suggested by the work of Barker and Wright (1955) in which the hour-by-hour experiences of children in a small town were traced and systematically recorded. If such work were expanded and if some measures could be obtained of the dimensions the children attended to in these situations, a complete social psychological geography might emerge.

Some idea of the number of as yet relatively unresearched schemas about interpersonal processes—which we do not discuss in the rest of the chapter—is gained through a study by Stotland, Thomson, Reed, and Katz (in press). They measured people's schemas about interpersonal processes by administering a questionnaire which consisted of items as follows: on each page was a picture of some interpersonal situation, such as two secretaries talking. Below the picture was a caption which described the relationship between the two people in terms of a salient dimension of the picture, such as conversation, e.g., "Two secretaries are talking to each other at lunch." The subject was then asked to guess what position the two people in the picture had on some other dimension of interpersonal relationships, such as liking. "How much do they like each other?" Each subject's answer to this question was compared with his answer to a parallel picture and question combination in which two secretaries are sitting near each other at lunch but are not talking. If a subject guessed that the two secretaries who talk to one another like one another more than in the instance where they are not talking, this was taken as a sign of this subject's having a schema relating talking and liking. Five such pairs of picture-question combinations were presented to each subject, to provide a broader measure of the schemas. In another type of picture-question combination used in this research, the two people pictured differ along some dimension such as amount of talking. The subject then is asked to guess the position of each person on some other dimension: "How much does A like B?" and vice versa. This type of picture-question combination gives an indication of schemas involving two people at different positions on a dimension.

This research indicated that many of the schemas described in the balance of the chapter are rather widely held among American college students. Some of those which are perhaps a bit surprising are as follows: If one person talks more than another, they will tend to differ in their opinions even about matters they are not talking about; if two people are similar in opinions, they are more likely to help one another than if they are "different"; if one person likes another more than he is liked by the other, they will differ in their opinions; if two people influence one another, they will also help one another. Further research might well indicate that these schemas have the same sort of effects as those more fully investigated ones which are described in the balance of the chapter.

The reader may ask why more emphasis has not been placed here on the motivation to develop new schemas, to seek change to keep one alert. The answer is simply that very little research has been done on the manifestation of these motives in social situations. However, we can point to a few examples. Ziller (1965) has pointed out that this motivation sometimes leads to changes in the structure of groups, when, of course, there is enough familiar and stable to permit the change to be approached. Thus, members of groups may "reorganize" to give themselves a "fresh start," even when the new organization may not be essentially different from the old. The change itself may rejuvenate the organization. Another example comes from the popularity of books in which familiar authors or types of authors of some prestige and familiarity present new viewpoints on everyday processes of interpersonal relationships: books on oneupmanship, books on the "Games People Play," books on an anthropological view of our society. Needless to say, research is needed to determine the conditions which enhance this exploratory motivation with respect to interpersonal schemas, to show the balance between the familiar and the new.

Schemas Involving Physical Distance and Movement

It is obvious that physical distance between people is one of the dimensions of social interaction. Each of us learns early in life that two people cannot communicate easily with one another if they are very far apart; that two people cannot help one another readily unless they are close, especially when the help is of the type children need; that two people can often express their feelings toward one another more readily if they are close to one another, especially if the feelings are positive; that one person can learn more about another person if they are physically close than if they are apart.

Schemas Relevant to Interpersonal Distance

Since the physical distance between two people is attended to in a wide range of situations, the distance dimension is highly likely to figure importantly in schemas having to do with still other dimensions of social interaction. One other dimension with which distance is frequently involved is the degree of liking one person has for another. Many situations are encountered in which people like the persons close to them more than they do those who are distant. The experienced correlation between positions on these two dimensions

The crowd manifests its disagreement via interpersonal distance.

provides the basis for acquiring a schema. Lott and Lott (1965) report that in the college and boarding school samples they investigated, people came to like those persons who were seat neighbors in class more than those who were more distant; that clerical workers in large firms preferred the people who work closer to them; that sorority girls liked those who lived in the same house as themselves more than those who lived in a different house run by their sorority; that bomber crewmen preferred those whose position in the plane was closer to their own. It is small wonder that people develop schemas about closeness and liking. In fact, closeness is often taken as a synonym for mutual liking. However, the generality of this tendency should not blind one to the fact that people differ in the amount of exposure to these instances and therefore differ in the degree to which they will acquire this schema. Further, the absolute distance involved in liking situations may differ in different people's experiences, so that the particular nature of their schemas would also differ.

We do not have to look far to see why there should be so many instances on the basis of which the closeness-liking schema is acquired. People who are repeatedly close to one another become familiar with one another, and we have already seen that the familiar is preferred. People who have freedom to choose with whom they will be close will obviously choose someone they like. In noncompetitive situations, being close often provides more opportunity for helpfulness. People who are members of the same family or team or clique tend both to like one another and to be close in view of the fact that the nature of their membership groups requires that they be close. It is small wonder, then, that there are so many instances of closeness being correlated with liking.

The closeness-liking schema has some interesting effects on perception. Using a technique developed by Kuethe (1962), Little (1965) gave his subjects paper silhouettes of people, two at a time. The people were described to the subjects as being either friends, acquaintances, or strangers. Then the subjects were asked to place the silhouettes on a felt board. The subjects placed the silhouettes described as friends closer together than they placed the "acquaintances," who in turn were placed closer together than were the "strangers." This study by Little also strongly indicates that in everyday life, people may underestimate the interpersonal distances in situations involving friends, or overestimate the distance between non-friends; and that people tend to assume that two people who happen to be physically close to one another also like one another more than do two people who don't happen to be close, even when there is no reasonable or factual basis for making this assumption.

Motivational pressures exist both to avoid perceiving con-

One message typically communicated by such close interpersonal proximity is: "These people like each other."

tradictions to schemas and to avoid creating situations which are contradictory to schemas. One way in which contradictions can be avoided
is by guiding one's own behavior so that it is consistent with the
schema. Thus, in situations in which there is a choice, persons will
tend to move closer to people whom they like, or to try to induce
liked others to move close by; and vice versa for people who are
disliked. This might occur even without the operation of the pragmatic
factors which lead to the occurrence of exemplars of the schema, such
factors as enhancing communication or help through closeness.

Another schema with which physical distance is involved concerns the relationship between men and women. Again it is obvious
that people usually have both perceived and experienced instances
having to do with the closeness of men and women. This hardly
needs documentation. However, people do differ in the particulars
of their experience with even this almost universal phenomenon.
Thus, some people on the basis of their experience will acquire
schemas which represent closer physical relationships between
men and women as typical and expected than will other persons.
People who view closer male-female relationships as typical have
probably perceived more instances of association between men and
women and would therefore be more inclined to associate the
words "man" and "woman." In accord with this presumption,
Kuethe (1964) found that people who tend to place or replace
silhouettes of men and women closer on the felt board in the
technique described above were more likely to say "man" when
asked to state the first word that occurred to them on hearing
"woman" and also to say "woman" on hearing "man."

Schemas Involving Movement

Thus far in our consideration of interpersonal schemas involving
distance, distance has been viewed statically without concern for
movement and change of distance. Yet movement is very much a part
of social interaction, since, obviously, people change distances between themselves in the course of action and interaction. The dimension of movement is also highly likely to be a salient one for the simple
reason that it involves change. If it is a familiar person who moves,
or if the movement takes place in a familiar setting, then there is even
greater likelihood that attention will be paid to the movement.
Persons therefore are quite likely to acquire schemas which involve
the concept of movement in one form or another. A quite simple
example is the notion that people typically face the direction in which
they are moving. Some of the effects of this schema on perception
have been shown by using the Kuethe techniques involving silhouettes

and a felt board. In the study by Lewitt and Joy (1967), the silhouettes of two men walking, two children pedaling tricycles, two men riding bicycles, and two men driving cars were placed by the experimenter on the felt board. For half the subjects the experimenter placed the figures facing each other, for the other half, facing away from each other. All the subjects were then told to remove the silhouettes and then to replace them on the board. The subjects replaced the silhouettes which were initially facing one another closer together than they did those facing away. The schema involving the correlation between facing and movement led them to "see" movement on the basis of the direction of facing.

A more interesting type of schema has to do not only with the simple direction of movement of people, but with the patterns of movement—whether the movement is in a straight line or a crooked one; whether the movement is at a steady pace or a varying speed; whether the movement is continuous or staccato-like; and so on. Further, a pattern of movements may involve two or more entities: do they move simultaneously, successively, in overlapping periods of time; do they move toward or away from each other; do they touch or not? Aside from parades, military formations and the like, it is clear that most everyday movements of people tend to be in irregular patterns, which are related in complex ways to the movements of other people. Such patterns of movement attract attention not only because they are movements and therefore involve change, but also because often the nature of the movement *itself* is changing. The speed and direction of movement of people change, for example.

It is likely that patterns of movement will be represented in schemas about people, since certain patterns are likely to be regularly associated with certain forms of interaction. The pattern of movement in a chase, for example, or in an embrace, are fairly uniform. Accordingly, when people attend to any set of objects, even those which are abstract and inanimate, which move in a complex pattern and have some of the characteristics mentioned above, they tend to perceive these objects as if they have human qualities and are interacting with one another. Needless to say, the perceiver does not hallucinate the objects to be people, but, at the ideational level, he imputes human qualities to them. Heider and Simmel (1944) presented subjects with a movie whose "characters" consisted of four geometric shapes: an open rectangle with a doorlike structure, two triangles, and a small circle. The rectangle remained stationary, but the other shapes moved about in irregular patterns. The subjects were asked to "write down what happened in the picture." Most of the subjects described the situation in animistic terms, as if the figures had human qualities. The two triangles were frequently reported to be fighting; one triangle is shut up in the "house" and tries to get out; one triangle is chasing the other two figures; the figures move the door. In about 50 per cent of the cases, the subjects saw the two triangles as men fighting over the "circle-woman"!

Marek (1963) followed up on this work of Heider and Simmel by using 12 different films rather than one, thus providing a broader basis for determining exactly which patterns are associated with which types of social interaction. For example, he reports that an object which maintains a general overall direction of movement, "despite considerable obstruction," appears to observers to be attempting to achieve a goal by going around obstacles. Similarly, a succession of movements by the same object typically suggests to the observer a capacity for anticipation and planning.

People who have attended more to others are more likely to have schemas relating patterns of movement to social interaction than those who have attended less. Thus, Marek (1963) found that children who were given the greatest amount of attention by their parents and thus had ample opportunity to observe the movements of other people were much more likely than other children to perceive human interaction and qualities in the movements of the figures in the 12 films just described.

The Liking-Help Schema

The conceptual dimension having to do with the degree of liking or disliking of other persons figures importantly in schemas about interpersonal relationships. Obviously, the reason for the involvement of the liking dimension in so many schemas is that expressions of liking are so frequent in social life and such a basic quality of any orientation or involvement with people. The sheer number of words used to express high and low liking in the English language is overwhelming. The amount and pattern of likes and dislikes among teenagers is a constant source of conversation among them. Young children often communicate primarily in terms of how much they like or dislike one another. One of the general concerns of most of us is just how attractive or well-liked we are, and how we can bring others to like us more.

In all probability, the previous paragraph did not tell the reader anything of which he was not already aware. Not only is this sort of awareness important as a further reflection on the universality of the use of the liking dimension, it is also an indication that the term "liking" does not in itself cry out for definition. The reader, unless he is a specialist in the study of language or of interpersonal relationships, probably took the meaning of the term as given, as well understood, as obvious. Nevertheless, in presenting a systematic social psychology, the authors cannot rest on this "obviousness"; we must look at the issue of defining liking. Further, clarification will also help to answer another question that is perhaps not quite so obvious—the question of why liking is such a prevalent conceptual dimension.

A Definition of Liking

We will define a person as liking another person or object if the first person experiences positive affect or emotion because he perceives the second person or object, or a symbol of the latter. A person dislikes another when he experiences negative affect or emotion because of the perception of the second person or object, or a symbol of the latter.

The involvement of emotions in liking and disliking has been demonstrated in a number of studies. Westie and de Fleur (1959), for example, first obtained a measure of their white subjects' evaluation of blacks by means of a questionnaire. Then they were shown photographs of black people and of whites. The subjects who had previously indicated dislike for blacks showed more of a galvanic skin response in reaction to these stimuli than did subjects who liked them. (The galvanic skin response, or GSR, is a commonly used indication of general autonomic emotional arousal, especially of a negative sort.) Cooper (1959) found a similar pattern of results while using blood pressure as an index of emotional response when subjects were shown pictures of people of different races. The whites who indicated that they did not like Negroes showed more of a rise in blood pressure. Likewise, Poirier and Lott (1967) measured the amount of people's negative feelings toward others who were not members of their group. A variety of instruments was used to give measures of physiological arousal. While the subjects were working at what they believed to be the primary task in the experiment, either a black or a white person came into the experimental room purportedly to adjust the attachments of the physiological instruments. The more anti-black a person was, the more he manifested GSRs when the black came in to make the adjustments than when the white did.

What causes an individual to experience positive or negative affect because of the presence of another person? In other words, how, basically, does a person come to like or dislike another? The roots of liking can be understood by recognizing that, even when interpersonal relationships are not centrally involved, an individual often experiences positive affect when his goals are attained, when his needs are met, and negative affect when his goal attainment is blocked, his needs unsatisfied. Not surprisingly, Carlsmith, Collins, and Helmreich (1966) found that the more they met a person's need for money, the better he said he felt. Furthermore, experiencing of positive or negative affect leads the individual to like or dislike the objects associated with the affect. Staats and Staats (1958) gave subjects electric shocks while they observed some nonsense syllables, and no shock while observing others. The subjects later evaluated nonsense syllables which had not been associated with shock more positively than those which had been associated with shock.

Since goal attainment or the frustration resultant upon failure to attain desired ends causes positive or negative affect, goal attainment or frustration influences the liking or disliking of objects or entities. Accordingly, if some other person or object is present when goals are attained and absent when they are not, or if he or it is perceived as instrumental to their attainment, then the individual will tend to develop a schema that a given person or object is associated with need satisfaction. In short, the individual will like him or it. Conversely, if the other person or object is present when goal attainment is blocked and absent when goals are attained, he or it will be disliked (cf. Rosenberg and Abelson, 1960).

The relationship between the degree to which another person satisfies one's needs and the degree of liking for him is illustrated in the following studies. Nunnally, Duchnowski, and Parker (1965) had subjects play a spin-wheel game in which a pointer stopped on one of three nonsense syllables. One syllable was associated with gaining two pennies, another with losing one, and a third with neither gaining nor losing. After playing the game the subjects indicated greater liking for the syllable associated with monetary gain. Jones and de Charms (1957) led some subjects working in a group to believe that they would be rewarded exclusively on the basis of their own individual efforts and others to assume that reward was entirely contingent upon the success of the total group of which they were part. The experiment was arranged so that one of the participants in every group did fail on his task. The subjects tended to judge this person more negatively on a variety of measures if they were dependent upon him for successful attainment of their goal, i.e., when their rewards depended on group success. This was especially true when the subjects were led to believe that the person in question had failed as a result of not trying hard enough, rather than because of some lack of ability. Our liking for someone who satisfies our needs is illustrated in a study by Aronson and Cope (1968), which showed that liking is high for a person who punishes our "enemies," even when that person is, and will remain, ignorant of us and our "need" to perceive our enemy in pain.

Since we have a great many needs, and since much of life consists of actions designed to satisfy them, it is not surprising that the degree of liking, the level of evaluation is a pervasive dimension of most experience. The prevalence of this dimension is also related to the nature of need satisfaction in early childhood.

The schema which holds that needs that are not immediately met are often met in the not-too-distant future is less prevalent among children than among adults. Furthermore, the needs which the child experiences most strongly are, in fact, those which cannot be put off for very long: needs for food, water, warmth, etc. Accordingly, for children, the satisfaction of needs is often a more pervasive and attention-demanding concern than it is later in life. As a consequence, we tend early in life to like or dislike very intensely.

With this early start in life involving so much concern for liking and disliking, it is small wonder that adults also are so prone to like and dislike, especially when the self-strengthening qualities of schemas are considered.

The Evaluative Dimension

The early-acquired dimension of liking and disliking begins as a simple dimension of positive and negative affect, but soon communications from others and observations of them lead to extension and elaborations. It becomes elaborated into the dimension of good-bad, of positive and negative evaluation. This extension appears to occur in part as a result of the child's perceiving that his parents say that something is "good," when it is associated with positive outcomes for the child, such as gaining praise or love from them, becoming healthy and strong, having fun, and so on. A "good boy" is one deserving of rewards; one is punished for playing with the "bad" neighbor. On the other hand, parents say something is "bad" when it is dangerous or painful for the child, or when it will lead to disapproval from them. Thus, the simple dimension of like-dislike is extended to include the dimension of good-bad. The dimension that emerges probably is most aptly called the dimension of evaluation.

The fact that adults evaluate cannot help but be perceived by the child. As we shall see later, the child has a strong tendency to imitate his parents, so that he too is likely to come to be an evaluator. Furthermore, evaluations are directly communicated to the child as a means of controlling him: "Doing that isn't nice"; "That was very nice of you"; "Tom is a good boy." Children will acquire this conceptual dimension, with its verbal labels, from their parents.

Despite what we have just been saying about the prevalence of evaluation as a conceptual dimension, the dimension may not occur in any simple way in schemas which have received a great deal of varied attention from public discussion, direct experience, private discussion, mass media, and other sources. The simple dimension of like-dislike may then be replaced by a more complex set of dimensions. This possibility is indicated in research by Woodmansee and Cook (1967). They presented white adult subjects with a very long and varied series of questionnaire items having to do with blacks. Instead of finding through factor analysis that the dimension of evaluation was an important or dominant aspect in terms of which judgments were being made, a series of dimensions or factors was uncovered such as: derogatory beliefs, local autonomy, gradualism, ease in interpersonal relations, acceptance in close contact, and integration-segregation.

Since liking is so prevalent and widely used a conceptual dimension, it is highly likely to become involved in many schemas for many people. We have already seen how liking and closeness are correlated for many people; the ubiquity of this schema would be expected on the basis of our analysis of the meaning of liking as being grounded in need satisfaction. However, even more basic to that explanation of the meaning of liking is its relationship to the helpfulness of another person.

The relationship between liking and help is one of the most pervasive of our experiences. We like those who help us and dislike those who harm us. The frequent occurrence of this relationship is not only attested to by our individual experience, it has also been documented by research. Deutsch (1949) divided a college class into groups which met regularly over the semester. In half the groups, the students were told that they would be given a single grade for the entire group; thus, the better the performance by the group, the higher the grade of each member. In this situation, then, good performance by each member was helpful to all. Other groups were told that each student would receive a separate grade, depending on how well his contribution to the group compared to the contributions of others. Under these circumstances, good work by one student was potentially harmful to the others. Needless to say, the individual students in both groups tried to do as well as they could. Deutsch found that the students in the helpful group came to like one another more than did those in the competitive group. Feldman (1968) measured the degree to which cabinmates in a children's summer camp rated each other as contributing to the welfare of the group, the cabins varying in their average levels of rated contribution. Also obtained were the self-ratings of liking for other members of the group. Feldman found that those cabins in which the contributions were higher were also those in which the liking was greater.

Once an individual has acquired the schema of liking helpful people, it affects his perceptions of various situations, since these are likely to be perceived consistently with the schema. If he likes someone, the assumption that that person is helpful will be made, even if there is no factual basis for doing so, unless, of course, there is clear information to the contrary. Thus, in the study by Stotland, Thomson, *et al.* mentioned earlier in this chapter, it was found that people tended strongly to perceive that liking people leads to helping them and vice versa; while disliking leads to not helping them, and vice versa.

This schema will not only affect perception, it will also influence behavior in interesting ways. Swingle (1966) had two people play a competitive game against each other. The task required each subject to press one of four colored levers as quickly as possible after the other participant in the game stated a color name aloud. The other participant learned which color was to be named by him by observing which one of the four lights in a panel, which only he could see, was activated. The first subject would gain a point each time he was able to press the correct lever within one and one-half seconds from the time the light went on; thus his success was dependent on his partner's cooperation in rapidly reporting the correct color. At first, each player's partner was made to appear cooperative as he did send the color names quickly. Later, in half the cases, the partner appeared to be slacking off, since the subjects began to do poorly. In the other half of the cases, the partner appeared to continue to be cooperative and helpful, since the subjects continued to gain points. For half the subjects in each of these conditions the partner was someone whom he had known previously and considered to be a friend. When the partner was a friend and yet began to be less cooperative, the subject actually began to press the levers more slowly. These subjects indicated that they thought their partner was simply "goofing around," and that he really was not trying to hurt them. In response to this situation they lowered their involvement in the task, so that their partner's slowness would do them no real harm. On the other hand, if the partner was perceived to be a disliked person, the subjects did not slow down their lever pressing when the partner became uncooperative. "I dislike him; he was trying to hurt me, and I'm not going to suffer because of him," seemed to be their approach. Furthermore, if the disliked other was very cooperative, the subject also appeared to withdraw from the situation by slowing down his lever pressing. The individual here might be pulling away from a situation which is inconsistent with his schema. In contrast, if a friend is cooperative, the subject works even harder at lever pressing. In short, Swingle's study shows some of the ways in which people's actions are guided by the schema—liked people are helpful—and if the situation contradicts this schema, they attempt to withdraw from it or perceive it in a different way.

That helping implies liking for another person and vice versa is a widely held assumption or schema in our society.

Not only does the schema suggest that liking implies help, it also entails an assumption that helpfulness implies liking. Lerner, Dillehay, and Sherer (1967) told some subjects that they were to engage in a highly competitive game in which they were to attempt to trap their partners; other subjects were instructed that they were to play a cooperative game in which they would probably share rewards with their partners. Then all subjects heard the same interview which each of them was led to believe has been conducted with their partner-to-be, who turned out to be a relatively unattractive person. However, those subjects who expected to cooperate with him judged him to be more attractive than those who expected to compete.

In short, there is some evidence which shows the effect of this schema. However, additional research could be carried out to test the propositions that situations consistent with the schema are more pleasant than those that are not; that situations inconsistent with the schema are distorted in meaning, thus making them harder to recall accurately; that individuals will try to make a liked person more cooperative if he is not already very cooperative and to make a disliked person less cooperative.

Data having to do specifically with interpersonal processes are not available to illustrate the tendency of L.O.S.s which are inconsistent with the H.O.S. to change toward greater consistency. However, Rosenberg (1968) has shown how this tendency functions with respect to matters of public policy. During the Algerian revolt against French rule, subjects were first asked to indicate their degree of approval for American support of French policy. Next, they indicated how likely they thought it was that each of a series of general goals or values would be achieved or fostered by the policy. They then indicated how important each of these goals, such as world peace, was to them. A general index was constructed by multiplying each subject's ratings of the importance to him of each of the goals by the ratings of his estimations of the probability that the policy would help achieve each goal, and by summing the products. Some subjects were found to be consistent in that, for example, they liked and approved of the French policy in Algiers and rated it as helpful in achieving general goals which they felt to be important, while others showed inconsistency. Two weeks later, the questionnaire was re-administered. The previously inconsistent subjects were found to have changed their ratings toward consistency, while the consistent ones had not changed. Similar results were found with respect to Yale University undergraduates' attitudes toward admitting coeds.

Liking-Interaction Schema

In our discussion of the meaning of "liking" as a reflection of need-satisfaction, it was pointed out that liking often entails relating to the liked person or other entity. This is because it is often necessary to have some sort of direct relationship with another person for needs to be satisfied, i.e., for the other person to be helpful. Thus, it is often the case that interaction is associated with liking. Some aspects of this relationship were discussed earlier in the examination of the relationships between physical distance and liking and between helping and liking.

Experience appears to provide us with numerous examples of the relationship between liking and interaction. Most preadolescent boys in America have had a "bunch of fellows" with whom they spent a lot of time; obviously they interacted with and liked one another (Campbell, 1964). Clerical workers in a large firm who had more interaction with one another because of the organization of their work were more likely to like one another than were those who had less interaction (Homans, 1950). Bomber crewmen whose jobs brought them into some kind of interdependent relationship liked one another more than did those who did not have to interact (Lott and Lott, 1965). Festinger, Schachter, and Back (1950) found that in a housing project for married students, those whose apartments opened on to the main street were less liked than those whose apartments faced on to the courtyard in which most of the interacting among neighbors occurred. Students who lived closer to the stairs and the laundry room and therefore had more opportunity to interact with others in the project who came to use these facilities were also more popular.

The acquisition of this schema over time is reflected in some research by Horowitz (1936). He asked Southern white children to rank other children whom they knew in order of liking. Also, he showed the children pictures of various play situations and a series of pictures of children of their acquaintance. They were then asked to indicate which children they would want to play with in each situation. Both white and black children were included in the rankings test and the "show me" test. With age, the degree of correlation between the two tests increased, although the black children were increasingly rejected on both tests.

What was just pointed out in the previous paragraph needs to be qualified in an important way. Not only do we interact with people who are helpful to us and thereby liked by us, but we also interact with people who are harmful to us. In fact, interaction with another person is sometimes necessary for harm to result. In order for someone to rob you, he has to be quite close to you and has to interact with you. Two people who are fighting are obviously interacting. How then can we argue that a schema relating interaction and liking is at all prevalent?

The first reason is that in general, when given a choice, people will avoid harmful interactions, obviously. To the extent that people have the free choice of continuing or not continuing interactions with others, there will be far more examples of interaction with another for helpful than for harmful reasons (cf. Newcomb, 1947). Some people may have lived in a society or a sub-group in which such free choice was not in fact available. Such people would be less likely to acquire the schema; or, if it is acquired, it would be highly probabilistic. The second reason that we assume that, in general, people will interact with those whom they like is that interaction with another makes him more familiar, and familiar people are more highly evaluated.

We would expect that the acquisition of a schema relating liking and interaction would have a number of effects: perceiving high liking should lead to the perception of high levels of interaction and vice versa. This was illustrated in the study by Stotland, Thomson, *et al,* in which people tended generally to perceive that liking and interaction were associated. We would also expect that people would experience feelings of discomfort in situations in which the two were not related; distortion in meaning to make such inconsistent situations fit the schema better; efforts to enhance interaction with liked people and to like people with whom one interacts. Research illustrating these effects, however, is not abundant. Lott and Lott (1965) cite data which show that people in groups who talk more, who interact more with others, are assumed to be liked more by the others. It would be plausible to assume that at the point that the person monopolized the floor, this assumption would no longer be made, since the person is no longer genuinely interacting with others but is dominating them. Darley and Berscheid (1967) told some coeds that they would be assigned to another coed with whom they were to talk about dating and sex and then had them indicate which traits they liked in partners. Next, the coeds rated the likeability of their partners-to-be, based on a description given them by the experimenter, and of another person with whom they did not anticipate any interaction. They tended to rate their partners-to-be as more likeable than the other person, even though the descriptions on which these judgments were based gave them no basis for doing so. This tendency to rate someone with whom interaction in the future is expected as likeable may be so strong that even an "objectively" negative partner-to-be may be perceived so positively that should there later be a free choice of which person to work with, the "objectively" negative one will be selected in preference to a more positive or attractive person (Berscheid, Boye, and Darley, 1968).

Even after interaction has actually taken place, the schema may influence the perception of another person. Bieri (1953) had students take a questionnaire measure of the degree to which a frustration would lead them to be angry with others, with themselves, or with no one. The subjects then chatted with another student for 10 minutes on each of the following topics: taking a vacation together and their psychology course. Then each privately guessed how the other had filled out the questionnaire. These students guessed that their partners in conversation were more similar to themselves with respect to their reactions to frustration than did a comparable group which had not conversed.

Similarity-Liking Schema

The next schema to be examined involves another widely used conceptual dimension of interpersonal process: the degree of similarity between people. Why is similarity so prevalent as a conceptual dimension? The answer stems from the nature of the functioning of schemas. It was pointed out in Chapter 4 that in general familiar schemas are more likely to be aroused and thereby to influence perception than are unfamiliar ones. Thus, familiar schemas about other people are more likely to be aroused than less familiar ones. The sheer frequency with which familiar schemas about other people are aroused provides the basis for the individual's developing a conceptual dimension about the similarity between a presently perceived person and the schema about a previously encountered person. Thus, people are highly likely to develop a conceptual dimension about the similarities *per se* between people. "He's just like the guy I work with"; "She's just like all the girls from Newark"; "He looks just like his grandfather."

Sources of the Similarity-Liking Association

The schema involving similarity and liking usually takes a form which suggests that high liking and high similarity are associated, as are low liking and difference. This schema can refer both to an individual's perception of his own relationship with other people and to his perception of other people's relationships to each other. "I like him—we agree in our ideas about the war in Vietnam"; "He comes from my home town." "I don't like him; we're always disagreeing"; "I just can't stand people who insist on looking at the world that way." With respect to the perception of other people: "They are great friends; they seem to agree on everything"; "They won't last long—they're always quarreling." Why do types of situations referred to in these examples occur frequently enough for people to acquire the higher order schema of similarity and liking being associated positively? There are a number of reasons that have been set forth by researchers on this issue. Needless to say, there is no reason for assuming that any one of them is the "only reason"—they all may contribute to the occurrence of situations in which liking and similarity are linked.

The tendency to prefer familiar schemas to unfamiliar ones provides one such source. In perceiving another person we often arouse a schema about ourselves and then view the other person in terms of this schema. Examples of this process were given earlier, and it was shown that, when there is uncertainty about the proper interpretation of another's behavior, a tendency exists to predict that the other person will act as we ourselves would if in the other's situation. If there is no blatant contradiction to this prediction, we are likely to continue to perceive the other as similar to ourselves, i.e., see the other in terms of the familiar schemas about ourselves. The other would then at least be liked because of the familiar that is seen in him. Of course, if he behaves in a "strange" way, or in a way that we don't understand because it does not fit any of the schemas we have about our own behavior, then there will be a tendency to feel less positively toward him. We have seen examples of this reaction earlier in this chapter. This process has, to this point, been described from the point of view of the perceiver. However, an individual may observe the outcome of this process between two other people as well: he may perceive that two people like one another and that they resemble one another and that they have, without blatant contradiction, been able to view one another in terms of their schemas about their own behavior.

A second reason for the occurrence of this association is a very close cousin to the first. In general, an individual is better able to predict the behavior of another person who is similar to himself than that of a person who is different (cf. Newcomb, 1959). This greater ability to predict is, of course, part of the basis of the preference for familiar schemas about "anything" referred to in the previous paragraph; but, even if there were no such general preference, there would be a preference for people whose behavior can be accurately predicted. And, clearly, similarity of the other to oneself provides a basis for accurate prediction.

A third basis for the development of this schema concerns communication between people. As Newcomb (1959) has pointed out, communication is more easily and effectively carried out with people who have the same understandings about the world, who make the same unspoken assumptions about things so that we do not have to "explain everything." Runkel (1956) has shown that students who use the same dimensions as their teachers in viewing material related to a course are likely to receive higher grades. Notice this does not necessarily mean that the teachers and students agreed on the position of any given idea on a dimension. For example, they may agree or disagree concerning whether the UN is basic to world peace. All that seems to be necessary is that, say, the criteria for making that judgment be agreed upon. Of course, if they agree on the judgment they are quite likely to be even better able to communicate easily and to like one another more; but the basic point is that communication is enhanced if the parties involved use the same dimensions. And, when communication is more effective with certain other people, need satisfaction by means of communication is also likely to be made more efficient—some of the students Runkel studied obviously found this to be the case!

A fourth source stems from the fact that persons will be better able to meet their needs in concert if similarity and its concomitant, more effective communication, exist; and thus they will like one another more. Clearly, if there is agreement between two people about "what the facts are" or what is important in a given situation, it will be relatively easy for them to agree, if they have to, on some course of joint action through which each will satisfy his needs.

It is important to notice that the bases of the liking-similarity relationship discussed above all concern similarities of purposes, goals, opinions, attitudes, and values. Joint decision making, communicating, and predicting another's behavior are all facilitated by these types of similarity. Thus, the similarities that occur in conjunction with liking are not of just any type, but of the broad class which involves purpose and attitudes. The situations on the basis of which people acquire the related schemas then would concern mostly this particular class. The bulk of the research that is described below concerns just such similarity of purpose and attitudes. Before we proceed to describe some systematic documentation of the occurrence and effects of the liking-similarity schema, one other implication of the list of reasons described above for the development of such a schema must be considered. It is that the content of similarity differs somewhat for each of these reasons. For example, liking based on ability to communicate may refer to slightly different kinds of similarity than liking based on ability to predict another's behavior. In the case of communication, the similarity may be with respect to their knowledge about a given area of possible conversation; in the second, it may be in the actions the other person takes. No doubt, in all everyday situations, both bases for liking occur, but they may occur to different degrees. If two people meet at a party, the agreement with respect to moon shots, for example, is no doubt more salient than in a work situation in which two people need to be able to coordinate their efforts. Therefore, it is possible that an individual can acquire several different

L.O.S.s under the H.O.S. concerning liking and similarity. Each of these L.O.S.s might refer to different types of situations and therefore to somewhat different bases of similarity. To return to our example, a person may have one L.O.S. about parties and another about work.

Instances of the relationship between similarity and liking have been amply documented by researchers (cf. Lott and Lott, 1965). For example, husbands and wives who describe themselves in a similar way tend to be happier in their marriage than are those who do not (Tharp, 1963). Families in which there is agreement with respect to the goals of family life and to the relative importance of types of communication and political beliefs are happier than others (Levinger and Breedlove, 1966; Byrne and Blaylock, 1963). People who are from similar backgrounds with respect to social class, religion, and race are more likely to be happily married than those from different backgrounds.

A study of a children's summer camp demonstrated that those who lived in cabins in which there was a high degree of agreement about what behaviors were acceptable tended to like their cabinmates more than did children in cabins which did not develop such agreement (Feldman, 1968). Anderson (1939) found that among younger children, friendship choices were based on similarity of chronological and mental age, and of physical size, all of which bespeak similarity of interests. Among older children, more direct measures of similarity of interests are correlated with liking. High school students tend to have close friends only among those who are of the same socio-economic class or of a socio-economic class only one step higher or lower among the five levels of classes studied by Hollingshead (1949). Kahl and Davis (1955), in a study of the "man in the street," found that people choose their closest friends from among those at the same socio-economic level, i.e., the same income, education, type of home. Izard (1960) found that friends tend to value the same goals in life. Newcomb (1961) very intensively studied a group of students who lived in cooperative-like houses on the University of Michigan campus. He found that after a few weeks, students had chosen as friends those who agreed with them on their general goals in life. Festinger, Schachter, and Back (1950), in the housing project study mentioned earlier, measured the degree to which the couples living in each courtyard liked one another by asking them to list their friends. The degree of liking was indicated by the degree to which couples in a given courtyard chose others in that courtyard rather than people outside of it. Also, the researchers obtained a measure of the couples' attitudes about a community problem in the housing project. They found that courtyards with a higher degree of agreement regarding the community problem were also those in which there was a higher degree of mutual liking. This finding is rather remarkable when one considers that the people throughout the whole housing project tended to be quite homogeneous—all veterans, all married, all about the same age, all students at M.I.T. Seashore (1954) found that in a large factory, those groups of workers who liked one another more tended to agree more about how hard to work than did groups with less liking.

Consequences of the Similarity-Liking Schema

It is small wonder, then, that the similarity-liking schema is so prevalent. What then are some of the effects of having this schema? One is simply that an individual will tend to anticipate that he will like others who are similar to himself. Byrne and his associates have done much work to show this effect (Byrne, 1961; Byrne and Blaylock, 1963; Byrne, Clore, and Worchel, 1966; Byrne and Griffitt, 1966; Byrne, Griffitt, and Stefaniak, 1967; Byrne and Nelson, 1965; Byrne, Young, and Griffitt, 1966). These studies have shown that people predict that they will like more those who are of the same social class, share the same attitudes about political and social matters, or describe themselves in similar ways. One way in which this high liking of the similar person is reflected is in the ascription to him of desirable attributes such as a high degree of personal adjustment, high I.Q., great knowledge of current events, and high moral standards of behavior. Remarkably, Byrne found that a very high level of agreement on political and social issues could lead even a racially prejudiced white to indicate that he is attracted to a black. Anderson and Coté (1966) found that French-Canadians were more attracted to Anglo-Canadians if they shared some beliefs. Byrne and Griffitt (1966) found that even among elementary school children agreement on attitudinal issues led to assumptions of greater liking.

Predictions are also made in the other direction implied by the schema, from liking to similarity. For example, Secord and Backman (1964) found that friends tend to believe that they share the same needs. Berkowitz and Goranson (1964) led pairs of students to believe that they would like one another since they each had the personality traits desired by the other, and led others to believe that they would not like each other. Later in the study the former group indicated that they believed the attitudes of the pair-mate toward fraternities to be much like their own, while the latter group tended to believe that their pair-mates' attitudes were different. Levinger and Breedlove (1966) found that the more happily married a couple is, the more likely they are to exaggerate their degree of agreement on such things as their goals in family life and the importance of family communication. Tharp (1963) not only found the same sorts of results as did Levinger and Breedlove, but also discovered that happily married couples, more than less happily married ones, exaggerated how much they believed they would resemble one another in their self-descriptions. Newcomb (1961) found that at the beginning of their stay in the campus residence he studied, students perceived that the people they initially liked shared their values in life and also shared their choices of others in the house as friends. There was, in fact, no relationship between agreement and liking during these early days of living in the house. The persons involved had not lived together long enough to discover who really agreed with them. Taylor (1967) asked college students how much they liked a prominent sophomore in their school, and then obtained a measure of the degree to which the students agreed with that sophomore about having coeds at their college. The results indicated that the more they liked the sophomore in question the more they thought there was agreement between them on this issue.

Not only do people make predictions about their own degree of similarity to liked others which are consistent with this schema; they also make consistent predictions about this relationship in other people. The Stotland, Thomson, *et al.* research cited earlier showed that people tended strongly to associate similarity and liking. Miller, Campbell, Twedt, and O'Connell (1966) found that in a college dormitory, pairs of friends were perceived by others to be more similar in their self-ratings than they actually were, and more similar than were pairs of non-friends.

To take this effect one step further, there is evidence that individuals will tend to perceive consistently with this schema even when there is potentially contradictory information in the situation. For example, Brewer and Brewer (1968) brought together pairs of people who either agreed or disagreed about capital punishment and asked them to discuss the issue. Some of the pairs had been led to believe that they would like one another, and others that they would dislike one another. After the discussion, the subjects were asked to judge one another's feelings. In the high expected attraction pairs, the subjects in the disagreeing groups minimized the amount of disagreement. In the low attraction pairs, the subjects in the agreeing groups tended to perceive less agreement than there actually was.

Thus, the influence of this schema is indicated not only in the predictions that people make about social situations which are seen to be relevant to liking or similarity dimensions but also in their reactions to situations which are contradictory to the schema. Burnstein (1967) has shown that one way in which the impact of such exceptions may be reduced is simply by assuming that the situation is only temporarily in contradiction to the schema. He presented subjects with descriptions of a number of different hypothetical social situations involving two people. These situations differed with respect to how much each person was described as liking the other and with respect to their supposed attitudes toward the political candidates Goldwater and Johnson. Subjects were asked whether the feelings that the two people had about one another and about the two candidates would be likely to change. The changes predicted were ones which would have led to higher levels of agreement between people who liked one another and disagreement among those who disliked each other. The subjects, in other words, were predicting that the described situations would become consistent with their schemas, that the inconsistent circumstances described would be only temporary states of affairs.

The pressure to modify situations to conform to schemas is also reflected in an individual's memory of situations. Over even short periods of time, an inconsistent situation may be remolded to become more in line with the schema. One effect of this remolding is to make it more difficult for a person to learn about situations which are inconsistent with his schema. If there are several opportunities to observe the situation, memory of it may be distorted in the time periods between the observations thus necessitating a greater number of observations before the true state of affairs is accurately learned. Zajonc and Burnstein (1965a, 1965b) presented subjects on a number of trials with the names of pairs of people and with information about their likes and dislikes and about whether or not they agreed with one another. The subjects' task was to memorize and be able to repeat the information given them about who liked and who disliked whom. A greater number of repetitions of this information was necessary for subjects to learn the names associated with two people who *liked* one another and *disagreed* than to learn which people liked one another and agreed. In addition, the errors that were made while learning about the first schema-inconsistent type of situation consisted mainly of incorrectly "remembering" the two people who supposedly liked one another as also agreeing with each other. Even in the short intervals between trials it appears that memories were distorted to fit the schema.

Cottrell, Ingraham, and Menfort (1971) failed to replicate the Zajonc and Burnstein results in a similar study. The difference in results may be attributable to the fact that in the latter studies there was a one-minute interval between repetitions of the list of associations the subjects were to learn. During this interval, the subjects' schemas may have had a chance to lead to errors.

Cottrell *et al.* do not appear to have had an interval in their procedure, but presented lists again immediately after the first presentation.

Another sort of reaction to a situation which is contradictory to a schema involves heightened attention to that situation. Such response is especially likely if the contradiction is so blatant as to be unavoidable. This greater attention to a discrepant situation might continue in memory even after the situation is not physically present, as the individual attends to the L.O.S. corresponding to the situation. Attention to this L.O.S. would be given not only because it represents a clear change from a strongly established schema, but also as a consequence of efforts to resolve the discrepancy, such as by finding some H.O.S. to "handle" it. Such continued attention to descrepant situations is illustrated in a study by Gerard and Fleischer (1967), who presented their subjects with short stories in which a person who liked another also agreed or disagreed with him about a third person. Later, the subjects were asked to tell the experimenter "what comes to mind." The stories in which a person liked someone with whom he disagreed were more often mentioned than were those in which there was agreement between persons who liked one another. Notice that these results do not contradict the other studies having to do with distortions or recollections since the present one was not concerned with the accuracy of memory or learning. Tendency to most strongly recollect the discrepant stories is not due to their being viewed as more pleasant. On the contrary, the reason for the maintenance of the L.O.S. corresponding to the discrepant situation in an aroused state is that it represents an unpleasant, incongruent state of affairs which calls for some sort of resolution, since situations discrepant from schemas tend to be negatively evaluated. In fact, in the Gerard and Fleischer study just described, the subjects were also asked to rate the degree of pleasantness of the stories which had been presented to them. As would be expected, the discrepant situations were evaluated as less pleasant than those which conformed to the schema. Jordan (1953) also found that situations which were discrepant from the similarity-liking schema were rated as less pleasant than were those which were consistent with it.

Suppose a person is presented with a complex pattern of relationships among a number of people such that some pairs of people like each other and are similar; some like each other and are dissimilar; some dislike each other and are similar; and others dislike each other and are dissimilar. When such a complex set of relationships is presented and the individual has little time to study it, it is very difficult for him to determine the average overall degree to which the relationships conform to the schema. In such cases, the individual is unlikely to evaluate the group in terms of the degree of adherence to the schema. A study showing this effect of massive input of information is reported by Singer (1966) to have been done by Carrier and Singer.

Since such discrepant situations are more unpleasant, direct efforts to alter them in a schema-consistent direction may develop in addition to the tendencies already mentioned to distort the perception or memory of them. That is, there may be attempts to increase the amount of agreement with someone who is liked, or to change the characteristics or opinions of someone who is liked so that they actually are similar to one's own. Back (1951) asked students to describe the type of person they liked, and to describe themselves. Later, he assembled the students in pairs, telling some of the pairs, randomly selected, that they were the type of people who should like one another according to the descriptions, while he told others, also randomly selected, that they would probably not like one another. The subjects were then given an opportunity to talk about stories each had written based on some pictures shown them by the experimenter. The subjects in the high liking groups attempted more than did those in the low liking groups to convince each other that their own story was better than the other person's and that the latter should change his story to make it more similar. Similar results were obtained by Gerard (1961) who found that groups of people who had been led to like one another tried hard to influence one another in order to reach some common understanding of a controversial issue, regardless of their degree of disagreement. They tried harder than did groups of people who were led either to feel indifferent or hostile toward one another.

Of course, an individual can also change a situation to conform to his schema by changing his own position to be more similar to that of some other liked person's (cf. Allen, 1965). Thus, in Back's study, when the subjects wrote their own stories privately after their discussion of it with the others, those who liked one another altered their stories to be more like the other person's than did those subjects who did not like one another. In Gerard's study just described, the subjects who had been led to like one another did, in fact, change their opinions to be more like the group's to a greater extent than did those who were led not to like one another; this difference occurred primarily when the people had initially disagreed to a high degree. McGuire (1957) had a speaker make himself either liked or not liked by an audience by predicting the occurrence of an event which was either very desirable or undesirable from his listeners' point of view. If he had made himself liked, he was later better able to convince the audience about a matter which was unrelated to the predicted event than if he had not made himself liked. Moreover, an individual might even shift his opinions to be more like those of a person even before he meets the person, if he is led to believe that he will like him (McCleod, Harburg, and Price, 1966).

Kelman (1958) found that college students agreed privately with the opinion of an attractive person more than did students who heard the same opinions uttered by a less attractive person. This difference was especially marked when the students were reminded of the person from whom they heard the opinions. The effects of this schema can even sometimes cause an individual to change his conception of himself. Kipnis (1961) found that male college dormitory residents who initially perceived that their overall evaluations of themselves were either higher or lower than their evaluations of their best friends shifted their self-evaluations to be more like their ratings of their friends over a six-week period. The potential strength of the liking-similarity schema is shown here in the fact that self-evaluations were shifted in a *negative* as well as a positive direction in order to more closely match the friend's position.

Not only are opinions and beliefs subject to the influence of the schema, level of performance on a task also is. Thus, Schachter, Ellertson, McBride, and Gregory (1951), and Berkowitz (1954) showed that when a group of people who like one another are working on a task together and agree to work fast or to work slow, the individual members of the group will conform to the agreed-upon rate. If the members of the group do not like one another, they are less likely to perform in conformity with the agreed-upon rate. The similarity-liking schema can be assumed to underlie these changes of performance level because the group members are highly likely to believe that their fellow group members are themselves performing in line with the decided-upon level of performance. If the members did not so believe, if they felt that the others were not adhering to the group's decided-upon rate, they probably would have been highly unlikely to adhere to it themselves, even if they liked one another.

The fact that a person will change his perceptions and evaluations of himself in line with the liking-similarity schema has one very important consequence which merits further discussion. This effect has to do with cases in which a person alters his perceptions and evaluations of his own ability to engage in a given action. An individual will tend to believe that he has the same level of ability as someone whom he likes has; that he, too, can engage in the same activities as can the person he likes. This effect helps explain why it is that, at times, simply observing another person engage in some activity will lead the observer to immediately believe that he also can do it, while at other times the conclusion will be that only the other fellow can do it and he himself cannot. It is likely that this difference in reaction is, in part, a result of different degrees of liking for the other. There are, of course, other factors which can determine whether or not a person comes to believe that he, too, can engage in activities which others are seen to accomplish. Furthermore, the effects of the liking-similarity schema on a person's schemas about his own abilities can take a variety of forms. For instance, a person might have previously believed that he could engage in a given activity, but not at the level of proficiency of the other person. You may have believed that you could dive only from the lower boards until you see a good friend dive from the higher ones; you then feel you might be able to do so yourself. Or, the activity might be a completely new one. You may never have dived at all, but now feel you can because you saw your friend do so. Or, a person might come to believe that he will be able to engage in the activity in the future, although not at present. Other aroused schemas may indicate that a delay is to be expected. Your friend might have started his swimming and diving lessons four weeks before you did.

To return to the main theme about reactions to discrepancies from the schema, it needs to be pointed out that, if some of the processes which have just been described—conforming, persuading, perceptually "distorting"—fail to be effective in changing a situation which is discrepant with a schema so that it becomes more consistent, an individual may attempt to flee or avoid such situations.

As a final point, Hollander (1960; 1961) has brought attention to a very interesting effect of the functioning of this schema. Suppose a person has repeatedly indicated that he is similar to other members of a group both by his words and his actions. He has done so to such a degree over so long a period of time that the other group members have come to like him to a quite high degree. This high liking is obviously also a result of the fact that he is quite familiar, an "old timer." Such a person might be so well liked that he can even afford to differ from the other group members in certain respects without losing very much standing in the group. He has built up what Hollander has called "idiosyncrasy credit." He is so well liked that he can be different in certain respects without seriously jeopardizing his status in the group. Of course, if he carries this to some extreme, if he becomes different from the group in many important respects, then he may use up all of this "credit" and have to "negotiate a loan."

The Liking-Liking Schema

Above, the similarity-liking schema was examined from the point of view of only one of the persons involved in the relationship, as if the other person were only someone the first would like or be similar to. Obviously, both of the people involved in a given relationship must be considered if the types of situations from which people acquire their schemas are to be fully understood. If both of the people are aware of the similarity between them, then the effects of the similarity-liking schema would lead them to like one another. Since it is likely that people often learn of such mutual similarity in goals and attitudes, similar people will be very likely to come to like one another. In a parallel fashion, the above discussed relationship between closeness and liking acts both ways; both people would come to like the other as a consequence of closeness. And, similarly, two people who are interacting with one another will tend to like one another.

And, in addition to the above reasons for mutual liking to occur, this effect is likely because, in general, people prefer to be liked rather than disliked. Being liked implies that the other affirms one's values, is more ready to help, more ready to cooperate, more ready to meet one's needs in general. Another person's high evaluation of an individual leads the latter to a higher evaluation of himself. Since people prefer to be liked, they would also come to evaluate highly the source of this liking. Thus, mutual liking develops.

Tagiuri (1958) studied the friendship choices made by a wide variety of groups—naval cadets, persons attending summer camps and seminars, semi-therapeutic groups—and discovered that mutual liking occurred much more frequently than would be expected by chance. Lott and Lott (1965) also found that being accepted by others leads to liking them more. Accordingly, people will tend to acquire a schema to the effect that liking tends to be mutual.

The acquisition of this schema obviously is a function of time and appropriate experience—so that, for instance, older children would be more likely to have acquired it than would younger ones. This effect of age was shown in a study by deJung and Meyer (1963), who asked children from 5th to 12th grades whom among their peers they would most prefer to have with them in each of a variety of social situations. Then each child was asked to guess how each other child in his class would rate him. The children in the upper grades were more likely to guess that their preferences would be reciprocated than were those in the lower grades.

Notice that, to this point, the positive positions on this schema have been emphasized: the experiencing of mutual dislike has not been mentioned. The reason for the less frequent observation and study of mutual dislike probably is that people in American society have a tendency to avoid expression of dislike—politeness demands a covering up of many negative feelings that people may have. Thus, who dislikes whom may simply not be very obvious, aside from the difficulty of observing mutual dislike. Tagiuri (1958) found that people in his groups were less accurate about guessing mutual dislike than in guessing mutual liking. Data from a study by DeSoto and Kuethe (1959) indicate that, when making judgements in the abstract, people believe that "hating," and "disliking," occur less frequently than does "liking." Rosenhan and Messick (1966) asked the participants in their study to guess whether a picture of a smiling or angry person would be presented next in a series of pictures. Some subjects were actually shown 70 per cent angry faces, but even so tended to guess that an angry face would be shown substantially less than 70 per cent of the time. Other subjects were shown smiling faces 70 per cent of the time and guessed that they would be shown a smiling face 70 per cent of the time. Further, this tendency to cover up dislikes has the effect of reducing the opportunities the disliked person has for gaining information regarding the distaste others have for him, so that he may not respond with dislike to the person who, in fact, dislikes him. Furthermore, people tend to avoid the company of others whom they dislike, so that negative evaluations may not even have a chance to be expressed.

The existence of the schema concerning mutual liking leads people to perceive consistently with it. DeSoto and Kuethe (1959) presented people with abstract descriptions of some of the relationships which they were to assume existed between specified people and asked them to guess about certain other relationships. The subjects predicted in general that if one person likes (or trusts, or confides in) another, the latter will reciprocate the feeling. In actual groups, in which the true degree of liking between people is often ambiguous because of the complexity of social life, this schema also determines perception. Tagiuri (1958), as was mentioned above, found that people in a wide variety of groups perceived more mutuality of positive choice than there actually was, both between themselves and other people and between pairs of other people. Not surprisingly, there was a noticeable trend for people to perceive that others, whom they disliked, disliked them; but, as would be expected from the discussion of the previous paragraph, people did not tend to perceive mutual dislikes between pairs of other people.

Since people tend to assume that liking is reciprocated, it should be more difficult for them to learn about nonreciprocated liking. After exposure to an interpersonal situation about which they are learning, memories of the situation would be expected to evidence distortions in the direction of mutuality, thereby causing errors. DeSoto (1960) investigated the ease or difficulty with which persons could memorize various sets of specified relationships between people. It was found that relationships with reciprocated liking or reciprocated "confidences" were learned more easily than were those in which the liking or confiding was one-sided.

There are no doubt other effects of this schema, such as discomfort at perceiving nonmutual liking, or even nonmutual disliking; lack of full attention to the expression of feelings of one of a pair once the positive feelings of the other are recognized; or action to make someone change his feelings for another to make this mutual.

The Similarity-Interdependence Schema

Now that we have examined a number of schemas involving the degree of liking between people, we turn to schemas involving similarity. The first one with which we shall deal is the similarity-interdependence schema, which suggests that if people are interdependent with regard to one another they are similar to one another and vice versa. One qualification having to do with the nature of the interdependence which is involved in this schema must be made—the schema does not refer to cases involving negative or antagonistic interdependence of the sort which might exist between, for example, two prize fighters or two competitors in general.

The relationship between similarity and interdependence is partly an outcome of the relationship between each of these dimensions and liking. Since there are prevalent schemas associating liking and similarity on the one hand and liking and interdependence on the other, then an H.O.S. relating similarity and interdependence would tend to develop frequently. A person who has both of the liking schemas in question is quite apt to frequently have them aroused simultaneously, leading to the acquisition of an H.O.S. relating similarity and interdependence. In addition, there are more directly experiential reasons for the individual's acquiring this schema. In order for people to interact in a mutually helpful way, it is almost a necessity that they have at least some common understandings, if only for purposes of communication. If they have some shared goals, their interaction would be even more helpful to both of them. Joint decisions would be easier to reach; they would understand one another's behavior better and therefore would be better able to predict this behavior. If such similarities do not exist, then it is quite likely that the interdependence relationship would no longer be helpful and, given a chance, the participants would quit it. Thus, as a consequence, persistent, visible interdependent relationships will tend to involve similarity.

Since the interaction between two people in an interdependent situation is relevant to their need satisfaction, they are quite likely to attend carefully to the interaction; and since the similarity between them is so functional in this sort of interaction, it is quite likely that they will attend to it, also. Then, the association between similarity and interdependence will lead to the acquisition of the corresponding schema.

Consequences of the Similarity-Interdependence Schema

What are some of the influences of the possession of this schema? To repeat, the research by Stotland, Thomson, *et al.* also showed that people tend to perceive that persons who help each other are more similar than people who don't. Another effect of this schema is to lead people to predict that people with whom they are interdependent will be similar to themselves. Stotland, Cottrell, and Laing (1960) had subjects work on individual tasks in a group setting in which they could not communicate about non-task matters nor could they see more than the tops of each other's heads. Some of the subjects were in groups in which the tasks were so arranged that a good deal of interchange of materials useful for each of them was required, while others were in groups in which there was little interchange or necessity for it. The subjects in the high exchange groups guessed more than did those in the low exchange groups that the other members of their groups had filled out a personality questionnaire much the way that they themselves had. Another effect that has been documented is that an individual will perceive that a person with whom he is to cooperate is more similar to him than is someone with whom he is about to compete. In a study by Lerner, Dillehay, and Sherer (1967), the subjects were told that they were going to compete with someone or cooperate with him, or do neither. The subjects then overheard an interview with this person, and subsequently predicted how he would fill out a questionnaire. They indicated that they believed the person with whom they were to cooperate was more similar to themselves than was the person with whom they were to compete. Rosenbaum (1959) showed this effect after the subjects had actually competed. He had his subjects discuss a topic and told them that either they would get a reward for their individual contributions to the discussion, or they would get a reward for cooperative contributions, on the basis of the overall quality of the group discussion. After the cooperative discussion, the subjects perceived each other as more similar than after the competitive one.

Although no research has indicated that people find situations which do not conform to this schema to be unpleasant, Lerner and Becker (1962) have shown that, given a choice, people prefer those situations which are consistent with this schema. Each subject was first shown questionnaires about values presumably filled out by two strangers, with one of them indicating substantial similarity to the subject's views on these matters and the other indicating dissimilarity. The subjects were then told either that they would be playing a game of "winner take all" or that they would be playing a game in which both could win. Given a choice of partners between the two strangers, the subjects tended to choose the similar one in the "both win" game and the different one in the competitive game.

If a person is already in a situation of interaction and has some control over his own behavior, he is inclined to behave in a way similar to others with whom he is interacting or has interacted. Stotland and Cottrell (1962) had subjects work in groups in which they could not communicate with one another. Although each subject worked on his own individual task, all the subjects had certain materials which could be helpful to one of the others in the successful completion of his project. Further, a helpful exchange of these materials with that person was carried out since he also had material that was useful to the others. After the individual tasks had been completed, in half the groups the subjects with whom the others had exchanged material were selected to do additional work at a table while being observed by the others. For the remaining half of the groups, one of the subjects with whom none of the others had exchanged materials was selected to work on this task. In half of each of the groups, the selected subject did very well at the task, while in the other half, he did poorly. The other subjects then worked on this task themselves. Those who had observed the "high exchange" subject perform well performed well themselves; those who had seen him perform poorly, performed poorly themselves; those who had observed a "non-exchange" subject were unaffected by his performance. This task was one requiring considerable attention for good performance, so that it was rather easy for the subjects to control this attention so as to be in line with the schema.

All the research cited involves the subject's bringing similarity into line with interaction; it would be very interesting to show how subjects vary in the amount of helpful interaction they expect to have with someone similar to them, as contrasted to someone different, and how they behave in line with these expectations.

Another possible widely held schema is that similarity is associated with closeness. We have just seen that similarity is associated with interaction, and interaction and closeness are obviously associated. However, data to indicate the widespread acquisition of this schema are sparse. Kuethe (1962) found that silhouettes of men are placed closer together on a felt board than are rectangles.

The Similarity-Groupness Schema

The term "group" is a remarkably elusive term, despite the fact that it is used so ubiquitously. Psychologists, sociologists, and laymen have their own definitions which are somewhat different. In the context of the present chapter, we shall be using what we assume is the rather loose, common, nontechnical definition used by laymen. Obviously, if we are to examine the schemas which people have, it is the lay definition which is significant. This approach defines a group as a collection of people who interact with one another, who like one another, who tend to be close physically and psychologically to one another. But we have already seen that interaction and liking both imply similarity for most people, and closeness may do so as well. Thus, as part of their schemas in which they define groups, most people have the attribute, similarity. Clearly, all the reasons that have been given above for the "natural" occurrence of the relationship between interaction and similarity and liking and similarity apply to those collections of people called groups. And there is ample experience consistent with this relationship. For example, Tannenbaum and Bachman (1966) found that women who were highly active in their local chapters of the League of Women Voters were more alike in their attitudes than were those who were less active. Thus, most people would have a schema in which the "groupness" of people implies that they are similar.

Consequences of the Similarity-Groupness Schema

What are some of the expressions of the possession of this schema? First, people will tend to perceive more similarity between people perceived as a group than between the same people not so perceived. Wyer and Dermer (1968) had subjects rate the desirability of sets of adjectives, some of them being presented as descriptions of a different person, some of them being presented as a "group." The latter, rather ambiguous instructions, had the effect of making the ratings of the desirability of the various adjectives more uniform. It would be very interesting to do a study to show this process with respect to actual groups of people—to show that people predict that the members of a group are more alike than they actually are, and perceive that this prediction is borne out. Many members of groups might be quite surprised and angry at such a derogation of their individuality.

This prediction of similarity among group members will influence an individual's perception of himself. Wolfe, Stotland, and Zander (1960) assembled coeds in either of two conditions. In one, the high unity condition, the coeds sat around a large table, were addressed as members of a "group," picked a name for themselves, were told about a task in which they were to work cooperatively, since performance of the group task required two different jobs, and were shown a work flow chart. In the other condition, the low unity one, the girls sat far apart along the walls of a room, the term "group" was never used in addressing them, they did not pick a name, nor did they see the flow chart. However, they were given the same group task with the same two jobs. Actually, all of the girls in both conditions worked only on one of the two jobs, the other being "dummied in," unbeknownst to them. After the girls had completed the task, half the high unity group and half the low group were told that they had done poorly. Then the subjects rated themselves on a variety of abilities. The subjects in the failing high unity groups rated themselves lower than did those in the failing low unity groups on a variety of abilities, some quite closely related to the group task, some having no direct relationship at all. Thus, the subjects perceived themselves to have the same general level of ability as the group in which they worked, to the extent that they felt themselves to have been part of a genuine group. There was no difference between the two successful groups. However, the subjects were given an additional task on which they evaluated their abilities and performances. On this additional task, the subjects in the high unity failing groups again rated themselves lower than did those in the low unity failing groups. In addition, in the two successful groups, the high unity had higher self-evaluations than did the low unity participants. In short, then, the more a collection of people constitutes a group, the more they are perceived to share the same level of ability on both group-relevant and non-relevant attributes!

If an individual is told that he is part of a group, he will feel some pressure to make himself similar to the others in it. Deutsch and Gerard (1955) assembled groups of students to make judgments about the relative lengths of sets of visually presented lines. Each subject was led to believe that he was the last to publicly announce his judgment of each of the sets of lines presented. Each subject heard that the other subjects were making judgments on some of the sets which were discrepant with the evidence of their own senses. That is, on some trials an "obviously" shorter line was judged by the others to be the longest one. Some subjects were told that they constituted a group whose effectiveness in performing the judgmental task would be compared to that of other groups, while other subjects were not told anything about their being a group. The "group" subjects were more likely to agree publicly with the erroneous judgments of their groupmates, even though such agreement was not actually in the best interests of the group.

The avoidance of the unpleasant state which exists when group members differ and disagree may underlie not only the studies just mentioned, but also a rather peculiar effect of decreasing the size of a group (cf. Thomas and Fink, 1963). In small groups, people are less prone to express their disagreement with other members than they are in larger groups. The reason for this effect may be that disagreeing with someone in a small group will reduce the overall degree of similarity among the members more than will disagreeing in a large group. In a large group, the agreement among the other members may provide a protection from creating a situation which is contrary to this schema. No doubt, other processes are at work to generate this effect, but the similarity-group schema is undoubtedly more than a minor reason for the effect.

One would also expect that this schema would lead people to try to "homogenize" their group, to make it more uniform. The prevalence of uniforms, insignias, codes, standards, and so forth, may reflect in many instances an effort to keep the group similar in appearance. Or, homogeneity may be achieved by ejecting the deviant members of the group. In a classic study by Schachter (1951) the college student subjects who were assembled in groups designated as such exhibited a tendency to reject people who differed from the group's opinion, even when the opinions were not relevant to the purposes of the group.

Schemas About Generality of Similarity

The fact that people who are alike in one aspect are usually alike in others as well is one of the most obvious facts of social life. If two children are of the same age and sex, it would be unusual if they were not also at about the same grade in school. If two men are equally wealthy, they are highly likely to live in certain neighborhoods rather than in others. If several people have just loudly registered their feelings about the war in Vietnam, one would probably be right in guessing their feelings about the Department of Defense. In fact, H.O.S.s which refer to categories of people are often defined in terms of common attitudes and opinions believed to be held by these people. Since we use categories in thinking about the world of people, we must also be making the assumption that similarities between people tend to be general. That is, we are quite likely to have an H.O.S. that people who are similar in one respect tend to be similar in others; people who are different in one respect are likely to be different in others.

One way in which the possession of this schema is evident is in predictions made about the attributes of others. If a person perceives that two people are similar in one respect, he will tend to perceive that they are similar in others as well. One particular instance of this type of prediction occurs when a person perceives that someone is similar to himself in one way, and then predicts that the other has additional attributes in common with himself. A.J. Smith (1957; 1960) did two studies in which he had people fill out a questionnaire, the Allport-Vernon Scale of Values, in which they indicated which broad values were important for them. Then he presented these subjects with questionnaires in which half the questions had been answered by someone else. For some subjects, the answered questions indicated a high degree of agreement with their values; for others, the answers indicated low agreement. Then all of the subjects predicted what the answers would have been to the remaining questions. Those subjects who had received questionnaires with values similar to their own predicted that the remaining questions would also indicate similar values, and vice versa for the subjects receiving the low similarity questionnaires. Burnstein, Stotland, and Zander (1961) introduced a "deep-sea diver" to some groups of grade school boys as someone who had grown up in the same neighborhood, gone to the same school, swam in the same hole, and whose father had worked in the same type of factory. Other boys learned that the diver was different in all these respects. All the boys then guessed the diver's preference in nonsense drawings. The boys who believed the diver to be similar to themselves guessed he would like the same nonsense drawings as themselves, more than did those with the "different" diver. Stotland, Natsoulas and Zander (1961) found that coeds who found that they agreed with another coed in preferences between pairs of nonsense syllables and pairs of short phrases of music also felt that this other coed shared their preferences in girls' names.

When an individual changes his perception of himself, he then changes perception of similar other people. On the basis of their ostensible physiological reactions to pictures of nude men, Bramel (1963) indicated to some male college students that they had homosexual tendencies. They then listened to a man tell stories which he made up to describe what was going on in some pictures of scenes from life. If the man was described as a fellow student, the subjects, when later given an opportunity to do so, attributed more homosexuality to him than if the man was described as a criminal.

Predictions can also be made in the reverse direction, so that a person would be expected to guess that he himself has the same attributes as another similar person. Obviously, such generalization from the other to oneself is more likely to take place if the individual has little direct knowledge from his own experience about his own position on the dimension referred to by the attribute. Chapman and Volkman (1939) told some children how a group of children like themselves had performed on a given task and asked them how well they expected to perform. They tended to predict that they would perform like the similar group. In the Burnstein *et al.* study, boys other than those described above were also told that the deep-sea diver was similar or dissimilar to themselves in background. The diver then told the boys about some of his preferences related to his work, such as diving in the morning rather than the afternoon, walking on sandy rather than pebbly bottoms. The boys then made predictions of their preferences if they became divers. They predicted that they would share more of the similar diver's preferences than the dissimilar one's. Hertzman and Festinger (1940) informed college students of the level of performance on mathematics problems of college students like themselves, of high school students, or of mathematics experts. For some subjects these performances were above their own previous levels, for some below. The students tended to shift their predictions of their performances, either up or down, toward the level of other college students, but were unaffected by information about the other two groups' performances.

In addition to affecting a person's predictions about his future behavior, the generality of similarity schema can also influence an individual's current perception of aspects of himself. This influence can occur when there is not even the remotest possibility of the person's perceiving that there is an actual basis in the immediate situation for assuming that the similarity to the other person is general. Stotland and Hillmer (1962) had subjects assembled in large groups to work on some rather simple paper and pencil tasks. The subjects had been told that each of them would work on a different set of tasks, the assignment of the tasks being completely random and arbitrary. After completing the tasks, each subject read about a student who had participated in the same study previously and who had worked either on the same tasks as the subject, or on an entirely different set of tasks. Then half of each of these two groups of subjects read that this other student had been found, quite separately from his work on the task, to be very high or very low in clerical ability. Then all of the subjects worked on a clerical task and evaluated their performances. Subjects who had read about the student as having been arbitrarily assigned the same task as themselves tended to evaluate their performances on the clerical task consistently with the other student's level of ability. The students who read about someone who had worked on different tasks were uninfluenced by his level of clerical ability. (The subjects' actual performances did not differ between these conditions.) Thus, the subjects' perception of their own performance levels were influenced by the generality of similarity schema.

Dabbs (1964) presented subjects with transcripts of interviews with a soldier, in which he expressed his attitudes toward the Army. To half the subjects, he appeared as a "coper," a person who actively tried to determine his own life course; to the rest, he appeared as a "non-coper." Subjects who had been found to be copers themselves were more likely to accept the coping soldier's attitudes as their own than were subjects who had been found to be non-copers, and vice versa when the soldier was a non-coper. Stotland, Natsoulas, and Zander (1961) had coeds choose between pairs of lines of music, and then hear the choices made by two other coeds, one of the other agreeing more with the subjects' choices than the other. Next, the subjects made private choices between pairs of nonsense syllables, after hearing the choices of the other two coeds. The subjects' choices here agreed more with those of the coed who had agreed in the musical selections.

The effects of this schema on memory are also evident, as individuals recall better material which fits the schema than that which does not. Rosekrans (1967) showed boys a film of another boy performing a war game. The boy was described to them as being either very similar to themselves in background or very different. The boys were then asked to reproduce the filmed boy's ways of playing the war game. The boys who had observed the similar boy recalled his activity better than did those who had observed the boy who differed from them. Those who observed the similar boy had no doubt imagined themselves performing as he did, and thus had enhanced their ability to recall what he had done.

This schema also has the effect of leading a person to change aspects of himself to be consistent with it; that is, people tend to model themselves on other people who are similar to themselves in ways other than on the dimension in the actual modeling. Obviously, not all types of overt behavior are equally susceptible to the influence of this schema—in some cases, the person's behavior is determined by many other factors, such as ability, other goals he might have, the degree to which his behavior is under his own control. But there are many instances in which these other factors are relatively insignificant.

For example, Brock (1965) had paint salesmen try to induce a customer to purchase either a more or a less expensive type of paint. To half the customers, the salesman said that they themselves had very successfully used about the same quantity of paint as the customer needed; to the other half, they said they had successfully used twenty times as much. The salesmen were more successful in influencing the brand purchased if they said they had used the same quantity as the customer needed. Linde and Patterson (1964) found that paraplegics and normals publicly accepted one another's judgments of the relative lengths of lines more when they were in homogeneous groups than when they were in mixed groups of normals and paraplegics.

We have presented data to show that similarity is generalized even when there is no apparent basis for assuming that similarity is general in a given instance. Nonetheless, when there actually is some relevant, logical basis for generalizing similarity, people will do so more than they will when there is no such basis (cf. Berscheid, 1966). The reason for our emphasis on the cases in which there is no basis is that they are simply more interesting and compelling.

In the study by Rosekrans described above, the boys were found also to *spontaneously* play the war game in a manner more like that of the similar boy than that of the different one. Stotland and Dunn (1962) used much the same procedure as was used in the Stotland and Hillmer study to lead subjects to perceive themselves as similar to or different from another person. This other person was then described as being either very good or very poor at clerical tasks. The subjects' own subsequent performances on a clerical task were consistent with the similar other person, but not with the different one. Hollander, Julian and Haalund (1965) assembled subjects in groups and had them observe a series of trials in which three illuminated lights went out, one after the other, in a relatively rapid sequence; the subjects' task was to judge which of the three was the first to be turned off. On the first 20 trials, each subject was led to believe that he was the first person in his group to announce his judgment and that the others either agreed with him on every one of his choices or that they agreed with his judgment on only a portion of these trials. On the next series of trials, the subjects were all led to believe that they were the last person to make a judgment. Those who had been agreed with more often on the first 20 trials tended to agree more frequently with the judgments the others indicated on the latter series of trials. Chalmers, Horne, and Rosenbaum (1963) found the same effect of subjects' agreeing publicly with the judgments of those who had previously agreed with them, even when only the subject and one other person were involved.

Some forms of action in real life settings are also susceptible to the influence of this schema. Rosenbaum and Blake (1955) approached students in a university library to ask them to volunteer to participate in a psychological experiment. If a student had just observed another student consent to participate, he was much more likely to volunteer himself than if he had not. For our male readers, a study by Bryan and Test (1967) should have much meaning (and, indirectly, for our female readers too). These researchers had an undergraduate girl stand near a parked 1964 Ford with an obviously flat tire visible to oncoming drivers. A quarter mile back up the road, they sometimes arranged to have a man helping fix a flat tire for another woman in distress. Under these conditions, many more men stopped to help the coed further down the road than did when there was no prior similar model.

Not only is altruistic behavior influenced by this schema, but emotionally laden behavior also is. Bandura and Menlove (1968) had some children who were afraid of dogs watch other children get closer and closer to dogs, some of which were fearsome. Later, the first group of children actually approached dogs more closely than did those who did not observe the fearless children approach the dogs. Geer and Turteltaub (1967) showed the same sort of effect on adults by having some who were afraid of snakes observe others behaving calmly around snakes. The practical implications of these two studies are obvious and important.

So far in our examination of the effects of the schema that similarity is general, we have seen how an individual may come to believe that he can engage in a given activity when he perceives that he is similar in some way to another person. However, in some cases the primary similarity which is involved may simply be the ability to engage in the same activity as the other, rather than similarity in opinions or background or status or some other broad class. However, the "problem" may be that while the person is aware of his ability and of its similarity to another's ability he may not yet have the schema which indicates that he too can engage in it in the same situation as that in which the other has been observed to engage in it. Let us examine the consequences for an individual of perceiving another person engage in the activity in a given set of circumstances. When he observes the other person acting in a particular way, a schema about his also being able to engage in that same activity is aroused. He would then perceive the similarity between his own ability to engage in that action and the other person's. Such perceived similarity then would arouse the higher order schema that similarity is general. Therefore, this higher order schema will lead the individual to acquire a schema to the effect that he, too, can engage in the activity in the same situation as the other. In short, one set of circumstances which leads the person to acquire the schema that he can act as someone else does in a given situation is the observer's having both a schema that he has the ability to engage in the given activity and a schema that similarity tends to be general. Thus, if the person has never engaged in the action himself, he may be somewhat less able to acquire the schema about his engaging in a given action (Walters, 1968). The individual could then possibly acquire the schema of "he can—I can't."

The process leading to "he can—I can" has been illustrated in the work of Grosser, Polansky and Lippitt (1951) who placed two children in a room with toys which they were prohibited from taking. One of the children had been secretly instructed to start playing with the toys anyway. When he did, the other followed suit. Likewise, Walters and Parke (1964) found that just showing a child a film of another child violating his mother's instructions not to play with some toys increased the probability that the observing child would violate similar instructions coming from the experimenter.

One qualification needs to be made about what has just been pointed out. An individual may have a schema that, although he is unable to act at the present time as some similar other person does, he may at some later time acquire the ability to do so; or that one day he might be in situations in which he may be permitted to act in a given way which is currently prohibited. This is especially likely to be the case when young people are observing their elders. Thus, the observer can acquire the schema that he will later be able to engage in a given form of behavior, but cannot at present. Furthermore, even if he does not acquire this schema at the time of observation, he might do so later when he does acquire more abilities and does move into certain situations. He might then reminisce about how, for example, his father acted in given situations and then develop the notion that he, too, can act in this fashion.

In some cases, a schema referring to the action of some person may be subsumed under an H.O.S. which involves a broad conceptual dimension of activities, such as work or play. The specific activity in question is only an example or subtype of this general category such as factory work or playing baseball. This broad H.O.S. might be aroused by the observation of the other person engaging in the specific activity. Under these conditions, the observer might then be likely to acquire a schema which indicates that he can engage in the larger class of activities, not just the particular activities of the other person. This whole process of observing another's activities, generalizing to oneself, and then acquiring a schema about a class of activities larger than the other person's specific actions is illustrated in a study by Geen and Berkowitz (1967). Some students were given an unsolvable puzzle while another student (an accomplice of the experimenter) completed his puzzle in view of the other naive students; others went through this same experience but, in addition, the successful accomplice disparaged them for failing at the task. Still other students were given a solvable puzzle. Obviously the group of students who were ridiculed for their failure were highly motivated to be hostile toward the accomplice, but were not clear about the appropriateness of exhibiting hostile behavior in this experimental setting. Then certain of the subjects were shown a film of a prize fight in which one fighter rather brutally thrashes the other. Finally, under a plausible pretext, all of the subjects were given a chance to administer electric shocks to the accomplice. The subjects who had been insulted and who had seen the film administered greater shocks to the accomplice. From the point of view of schema theory, the observation of physical aggression in the film had aroused a schema about all sorts of aggressive behavior, such as insults; the observation of the film pointed up the possibility of aggression in that situation; and the provocation of the accomplice provided the motive to behave in line with the schema.

If a person has no opportunity to gain information regarding the actions of other similar persons, his ability to generate and maintain stable schemas about what actions and performance levels are possible for him may be impaired. Festinger (1954) found that people who were unable to gain information regarding the performance levels of other people similar to themselves on a task had quite variable expectations of their own performances from trial to trial as compared to persons who were able to compare themselves to others who were working on the same task. Data from an investigation by Radloff (1966) indicated that people who were working on a task which required them to track a moving object were much more variable in their evaluations of their performances if they were told they were much better at the task than any of the others who had worked at it; so much better that there were few, if any, people who were similar to them in ability. On the other hand, if they were told that they were close to the average level of performance of other college students, they were relatively stable in their evaluations.

The previous discussion has shown how the generality of similarity schema functions with respect to an individual's perception of his similarity to other people. However, very little research has been done which might demonstrate the expected negative evaluation of situations which are incongruent with this schema, situations in which an individual discovers that he is different in one respect from people with whom he is similar in other ways; nor has research shown the actions an individual might take in order to change some other person or himself to conform to the schema should discrepancies be encountered.

IMPLICATIONS OF DISCUSSED SCHEMAS FOR PARENT-CHILD RELATIONSHIPS

In this chapter research relevant to the acquisition and functioning of a variety of common schemas about interpersonal processes has been examined. The discussion of the ways in which they have been acquired and the manner in which they function has given more concrete meaning to the more abstract discussion of schemas in the earlier chapters. Some aspects of the functioning of these schemas have been shown to lead people to draw inferences about interpersonal processes which do not have any substantial degree of support in reality.

In other cases, we have seen the ways an individual's perception of himself and evaluation of his own abilities, actions, performance levels, and beliefs may be influenced by schemas involving liking, similarity, interaction, groupness, proximity and interdependence. These influences on self-perception and evaluation are also likely to manifest themselves in a dramatic fashion in children, since a growing child is particularly likely to frequently be faced with situations in which he does not have well established schemas about possible actions—he often will find himself facing new places, new people, new jobs, unfamiliar games, new classrooms, and so forth. If a child is highly likely to acquire schemas about his own actions through the interpersonal schemas we have cited, then it follows that he will often develop schemas about his own possible actions in which these actions are like those of others who are similar to him, whom he likes, whom he is close to, or whom he interacts with. If we know, then, to whom the child is similar, whom he likes, whom he is close to and interacts with, we should be able to predict fairly well what actions he will believe he can engage in. As we pointed out above, he will then actually tend to engage in these actions.

Obviously, on the whole, it is likely that children will like their parents, be close to them, and interact with them. This is what family life is all about. Furthermore, the child usually perceives himself to be similar to at least one of his parents. Thus, we would expect that children tend to act in ways similar to their parents in many respects. Obviously, there are many reasons beyond these for the similarity of parents and children, such as the parents' encouragement of similar behavior or the similar environmental experience of the parent and child. Nevertheless, it is no doubt the case that the schemas about interpersonal processes do generate more of the similarity between parent and child. The variety of actions which are similar between parents and children is legion. More aggressive parents produce more aggressive children (Eron, Walder, Toigo, and Lefkowitz, 1963; Lefkowitz, Walder, and Eron, 1963; McCord, McCord, and Howard, 1961). Thus, if a parent severely punishes a child for transgressions, even for hostility, the child will tend to be more aggressive and hostile when he is out of the house than the child who is not punished severely. Kagan (1958) found that boys who were more angry and aggressive, saw their fathers as quite punitive, angry and aggressive, and bossy at home. Maccoby (1961) found that boys who were more likely to enforce rules were those whose parents were quite strict, but were warm to them. Hyman (1959) has amply documented the point that children share their parents' economic and political attitudes and party affiliation. Even more subtly, Blum (1959) found that children of cognitively "rigid" parents are themselves more rigid than other children. In this study, rigidity was measured by presenting subjects first with a picture of, say, a cat, and then with a picture of a cat that has a few doglike features, and then another picture even more doglike, and so on until they are presented with a picture of a dog. The subjects are asked to describe what they see. The more the subjects continued to see a cat, as it changed into a dog, the more rigid they were defined as being.

Obviously, if a child does not have a parent to whom he is similar and close, he will be different from one who does. Lynn and Sawrey (1959) studied the effects on their sons of the absence from the home of seagoing fathers. As compared to boys whose fathers were home, these boys had difficulties in getting along with other boys, no doubt because they just did not know how to be a male; in fact, they varied between extreme forms of overly masculine behavior to overt feminine behavior.

The kaleidoscope of schemas which have been examined in this chapter must have impressed the reader as attesting to the complexity and subtlety involved in interpersonal situations. Since the focus was primarily on only those schemas which have been researched, in actual fact, these interpersonal schemas are probably even more varied!

References

Allen, V. L.: Situational factors in conformity. In L. Berkowitz (Ed.), *Advances in Experimental Social Psychology*, Vol. 2. New York, Academic Press, 1965.

Anderson, C. C., and Côté, A. D. J.: Belief dissonance as a source of disaffection between ethnic groups. *Journal of Personality and Social Psychology*, 1966, 4:447–453.

Anderson, J. E.: The development of social behavior. *American Journal of Sociology*, 1939, 44:839–857.

Aronson, E., and Cope, V.: My enemy's enemy is my friend. *Journal of Personality and Social Psychology*, 1968, 8:8–12.

Back, K. W.: Influence through social communication. *Journal of Abnormal and Social Psychology*, 1951, 46:9–23.

Bandura, A., and Menlove, F. L.: Factors determining vicarious extinction of avoidance behavior through symbolic modeling. *Journal of Personality and Social Psychology*, 1968, 8:99–108.

Barker, R. G., and Wright, H. F.: *The Midwest and Its Children*. Evanston, Illinois, Row-Peterson, 1955.

Berkowitz, L.: Group standards, cohesiveness, and productivity. *Human Relations*, 1954, 7:509–519.

Berkowitz, L., and Goranson, R. E.: Motivational and judgmental determinants of social perception. *Journal of Abnormal and Social Psychology*, 1964, 69:296–302.

Berscheid, E.: Opinion change and communicator-communicatee similarity and dissimilarity. *Journal of Personality and Social Psychology*, 1966, 4:670–680.

Berscheid, E., Boye, D., and Darley, J. M.: Effect of forced association upon voluntary choice to associate. *Journal of Personality and Social Psychology*, 1968, 8:13–19.

Bieri, J.: Changes in interpersonal perception following social interaction. *Journal of Abnormal and Social Psychology*, 1953, 48:61–66.

Bloom, B. S.: *Stability and Change in Human Characteristics*. New York, Wiley, 1964.

Blum, A.: The relationship between rigidity-flexibility in children and their parents. *Child Development*, 1959, 30:297–304.

Bramel, D.: Selection of a target for defensive projection. *Journal of Abnormal and Social Psychology*, 1963, 66:318–324.

Brewer, R. E., and Brewer, M. B.: Attraction and accuracy of perception in dyads. *Journal of Personality and Social Psychology*, 1968, 8:188–193.

Brock, T.: Communicator-recipient similarity and decision change. *Journal of Personality and Social Psychology*, 1965, 1:650–654.

Bryan, J. H., and Test, M. A.: Models and helping naturalistic studies in aiding behavior. *Journal of Personality and Social Psychology*, 1967, 6:400–407.

Burnstein, E.: Sources of cognitive bias in the representation of simple cognitive structures: balance, minimal change, positivity, reciprocity, and respondent's own attitude. *Journal of Personality and Social Psychology*, 1967, 7:36–48.

Burnstein, E., Stotland, E., and Zander, A.: Similarity to a model and self-evaluation. *Journal of Abnormal and Social Psychology*, 1961, 62:257–264.

Byrne, D.: Interpersonal attraction and attitude similarity. *Journal of Abnormal and Social Psychology*, 1961, 62:713–715.

Byrne, D., and Blaylock, B.: Similarity and assumed similarity of attitudes between husbands and wives. *Journal of Abnormal and Social Psychology*, 1963, 67:636–640.

Byrne, D., Clore, G. L., and Worchel, P.: Effect of economic similarity-dissimilarity on interpersonal attraction. *Journal of Personality and Social Psychology*, 1966, 4:220–224.

Byrne, D., and Griffitt, W.: A developmental investigation of the law of attraction. *Journal of Personality and Social Psychology*, 1966, 4:699–702.

Byrne, D., Griffitt, W., and Stefaniak, D.: Attraction and similarity of personality characteristics. *Journal of Personality and Social Psychology*, 1967, 5:82–90.

Byrne, D., and Nelson, D.: Attraction as a linear function of proportion of positive reinforcement. *Journal of Personality and Social Psychology*, 1965, 1:659–663.

Byrne, D., Young, R. K., and Griffitt, W.: The reinforcement properties of attitude statements. *Journal of Experimental Research in Personality*, 1966, 1:266–276.

Campbell, J. D.: Peer relations in childhood. In M. L. Hoffman and L. W. Hoffmann (Eds.), *Review of Child Development Research*. New York, Russell Sage, 1964.

Carlsmith, J. M., Collins, B. E., and Helmreich, R. L.: Studies in forced compliance: I The effect of pressure for compliance on attitude change produced by face-to-face role playing and anonymous essay writing. *Journal of Personality and Social Psychology*, 1966, 4:1–13.

Chalmers, D. K., Horne, W. C., and Rosenbaum, M. E.: Social agreement and the learning of matching behavior. *Journal of Abnormal and Social Psychology*, 1963, 66:556–561.

Chapman, D. W., and Volkmann, J. A.: A social determinant of the level of aspiration. *Journal of Abnormal and Social Psychology*, 1939, 34:225–238.

Cooper, J. B.: Emotion in prejudice. *Science*, 1959, 130:314–318.

Cottrell, N. B., Ingraham, L. H., and Menfort, F. W.: Retention of balanced and unbalanced cognitive structures. *Journal of Personality*, 1971, 39:112–131.

Dabbs, J. M.: Self-esteem, communicator characteristics, and attitude change. *Journal of Abnormal and Social Psychology*, 1964, 69:173–181.

Darley, J. M., and Berscheid, E.: Increased liking as a result of anticipation of personal contact. *Human Relations*, 1967, 20:29–40.

de Jung, J. E., and Meyer, W. J.: Expected reciprocity: grade trends and correlates. *Child Development*, 1963, 34:127–139.

de Soto, C.: Learning of social structure. *Journal of Abnormal and Social Psychology*, 1960, 60:417–421.

de Soto, C., and Kuethe, J. L.: Subjective probabilities of interpersonal relationships. *Journal of Abnormal and Social Psychology*, 1959, 59:290–294.

Deutsch, M.: An experimental study of the effects of cooperation and competition upon group process. *Human Relations*, 1949, 2:199–232.

Deutsch, M., and Gerard, H.: A study of normative and informational social influences upon individual judgments. *Journal of Abnormal and Social Psychology*, 1955, 51:629–636.

Eron, L. D., Walder, L. O., Toigo, R., and Lefkowitz, M. M.: Social class, parental punishment for aggression, and child aggression. *Child Development*, 1963, 34: 849–867.

Feldman, R. A.: Interrelationships among three bases of group integration. *Sociometry*, 1968, 31:30–46.

Festinger, L.: A theory of social comparison processes. *Human Relations*, 1954, 7: 117–140.

Festinger, L., Schachter, S., and Back, K.: *Social Pressures in Informal Groups*. New York, Harper, 1950.

Geen, R. G., and Berkowitz, L.: Some conditions facilitating the occurrence of aggression after the observation of violence. *Journal of Personality*, 1967, 35:666–676.

Geer, J. M., and Turteltaub, A.: Fear reduction following observation of a model. *Journal of Personality and Social Psychology*, 1967, 6:327–331.

Gerard, H. B.: Disagreement with others, their credibility, and experienced stress. *Journal of Abnormal and Social Psychology*, 1961, 62:559–564.

Gerard, H. B., and Fleischer, L.: Recall and pleasantness of balanced and unbalanced cognitive structures. *Journal of Personality and Social Psychology*, 1967, 7:332–337.

Grosser, D., Polansky, N., and Lippitt, R.: A laboratory study of behavioral contagion. *Human Relations*, 1951, 4:115–142.

Heider, F., and Simmel, M.: An experimental study of apparent behavior. *American Journal of Psychology*, 1944, 57:243–259.

Hertzman, M., and Festinger, L.: Shifts in explicit goals in a level of aspiration experiment. *Journal of Experimental Psychology*, 1940, 27:439–452.

Hollander, E. P.: Competence and conformity in the acceptance of influence. *Journal of Abnormal and Social Psychology*, 1960, 61:365–369.

Hollander, E. P.: Some effects of perceived status on response to innovative behavior. *Journal of Abnormal and Social Psychology*, 1961, 63:247–250.

Hollander, E. P., Julian, J. W., and Haalund, G. A.: Conformity to process and prior group support. *Journal of Personality and Social Psychology*, 1965, 2:852–858.

Hollingshead, A. B.: *Elmtown's Youth*. New York, Wiley, 1949.

Homans, G. C.: *The Human Group*. New York, Harcourt Brace, 1950.

Horowitz, E. L.: The development of attitudes toward the Negro. *Archives of Psychology*, 1936, No. 194.

Hyman, H.: *Political Socialization*. Glencoe, Illinois, Free Press, 1959.

Izard, C. E.: Personality similarity, positive affect, and interpersonal attraction. *Journal of Abnormal and Social Psychology*, 1960, 61:484–485.

Jones, E. E., and Davis, K. E.: From acts to disposition. In L. Berkowitz (Ed.), *Advances in Experimental Social Psychology*, Vol. 2. New York, Academic Press, 1965.

Jones, E. E., and de Charms, R.: Changes in social perception as a function of the personal relevance of behavior. *Sociometry*, 1957, 20:75–85.

Jordan, N.: Behavioral forces that are a function of attitudes and cognitive organization. *Human Relations*, 1953, 6:273–287.

Kagan, J.: Socialization of aggression and the perception of parents in fantasy. *Child Development*, 1958, 29:311–320.

Kahl, J. A., and Davis, J. A.: A comparison of indices of socio-economic status. *American Sociological Review*, 1955, *20*:317–325.

Kelman, H. C.: Compliance, identification, and internalization: three processes of attitude change. *Journal of Conflict Resolution*, 1958, 2:51–60.

Kipnis, D. M.: Changes in self concepts in relation to perceptions of others. *Journal of Personality*, 1961, *29*:449–465.

Kuethe, J. L.: Social schemas. *Journal of Abnormal and Social Psychology*, 1962, *64:* 31–38.

Kuethe, J. L.: Social schemas and reconstruction of social object displays from memory. *Journal of Abnormal and Social Psychology*, 1962, 65:71–74.

Kuethe, J. L.: Pervasive influence of social schemata. *Journal of Abnormal and Social Psychology*, 1964, 68:248–254.

Lefkowitz, M. M., Walder, L. O., and Eron, L. D.: Punishment, identification, and aggression. *Merrill-Palmer Quarterly*, 1963, 9:159–174.

Leik, R. K.: Instrumentality and emotionality in family interaction. *Sociometry*, 1963, 26:131–145.

Lerner, M., and Becker, S.: Interpersonal choice as a function of ascribed similarity and definition of the situation. *Human Relations*, 1962, *15*:27–34.

Lerner, M. J., Dillehay, R. C., and Sherer, W. C.: Similarity and attraction in social contexts. *Journal of Personality and Social Psychology*, 1967, *5*:481–486.

Levinger, G., and Breedlove, J.: Interpersonal attraction and agreement. *Journal of Personality and Social Psychology*, 1966, 3:367–372.

Lewitt, D. W., and Joy, V. D.: Kinetic versus social schemas in figure grouping. *Journal of Personality and Social Psychology*, 1967, 7:63–72.

Linde, T. F., and Patterson, C. H.: Influence of orthopedic disability on conformity behavior. *Journal of Abnormal and Social Psychology*, 1964, 68:115–118.

Little, K. B.: Personal space. *Journal of Experimental Social Psychology*, 1965, *1*:237–247.

Lott, A. J., and Lott, B. F.: Group cohesiveness as interpersonal attraction: a review of relationships with antecedent and consequent variables. *Psychological Bulletin*, 1965, 64:259–309.

Lynn, D. B., and Sawrey, W. L.: The effects of father-absence on Norwegian boys and girls. *Journal of Abnormal and Social Psychology*, 1959, 59:258–262.

Maccoby, E. E.: The taking of adult roles in middle childhood. *Journal of Abnormal and Social Psychology*, 1961, 63:493–503.

Marek, J.: Information, perception, and social context I. *Human Relations*, 1963, *16:* 209–231.

McCleod, J. M., Harburg, E., and Price, K. O.: Socialization, liking, and yielding of opinions in imbalanced situations. *Sociometry*, 1966, 29:197–212.

McCord, W., McCord, J., and Howard, A.: Familial correlates of aggression in nondelinquent male children. *Journal of Abnormal and Social Psychology*, 1961, *62:* 79–93.

McGuire, W. J.: Order of presentation as a factor in "conditioning" persuasiveness. In C. I. Hovland (Ed.), *Order of Presentation in Persuasion*. New Haven, Yale University Press, 1957.

Miller, N., Campbell, D. T., Twedt, H., and O'Connell, E. J.: Similarity, contrast, and complementarity in friendship choice. *Journal of Personality and Social Psychology*, 1966, *3*:3–12.

Newcomb, T. M.: Autistic hostility and social reality. *Human Relations*, 1947, *1*:69–86.

Newcomb, T. M.: Individual systems of orientation. In S. Koch (Ed.), *Psychology: A Study of a Science*. Vol. 3. New York, McGraw-Hill, 1959.

Newcomb, T. M.: *The Acquaintance Process*. New York, Holt, Rinehart, and Winston, 1961.

Nunnally, J. C., Duchnowski, A. J., and Parker, R. K.: Association of neutral objects with rewards: effect on verbal evaluation, reward expectancy, and selective attention. *Journal of Personality and Social Psychology*, 1965, *1*:270–274.

Piaget, J.: *The Moral Judgment of the Child*. New York, Collier, 1962.

Poirier, G. W., and Lott, A. J.: Galvanic skin response and prejudice. *Journal of Abnormal and Social Psychology*, 1967, *5*:253–259.

Radloff, R.: Social comparison and ability evaluation. *Journal of Experimental Social Psychology Supplement*, 1966, 1:6–26.

Rosekrans, M. A.: Imitation in children as a function of perceived similarity to a social model and vicarious reinforcement. *Journal of Personality and Social Psychology*, 1967, 7:307–315.

Rosenbaum, M. E.: Social perception and motivational structure of interpersonal relations. *Journal of Abnormal and Social Psychology*, 1959, 59:130–133.

Rosenbaum, M. E., and Blake, R. R.: Volunteering as a function of field structure. *Journal of Abnormal and Social Psychology*, 1955, 50:193–196.

Rosenberg, M. J.: Hedonism, inauthenticity, and other goals towards expansion of a consistency theory. In R. P. Abelson, E. Aronson, W. J. McGuire, T. M. Newcomb, M. J. Rosenberg, and P. H. Tannenbaum (Eds.), *Theories of Cognitive Consistency: A Sourcebook*. Chicago, Rand McNally, 1968.

Rosenberg, M. J., and Abelson, R. P.: An analysis of cognitive balancing. In M. J. Rosenberg, C. I. Hovland, W. J. McGuire, R. P. Abelson, and J. W. Brehm (Eds.), *Attitude Organization and Change*. New Haven, Yale University Press, 1960.

Rosenhan, D., and Messick, S.: Affect and expectation. *Journal of Personality and Social Psychology*, 1966, 3:38–44.

Runkel, P. J.: Cognitive similarity in facilitating communication. *Sociometry*, 1956, 19:178–191.

Schachter, S.: Deviation, rejection and communication. *Journal of Abnormal and Social Psychology*, 1951, 46:190–207.

Schachter, S., Ellertson, N., McBride, D., and Gregory, D.: An experimental study of cohesiveness and productivity. *Human Relations*, 1951, 4:229–238.

Seashore, S. E.: *Group Cohesiveness in the Industrial Work Group*. Ann Arbor, University of Michigan, 1954.

Secord, P. F., and Backman, C. W.: Interpersonal congruency, perceived similarity, and friendship. *Sociometry*, 1964, 27:115–127.

Secord, P. F., and Backman, C. W.: *Social Psychology*. New York, McGraw-Hill, 1964.

Shibutani, T.: *Society and Personality*. Englewood Cliffs, New Jersey, Prentice-Hall, 1961.

Singer, J. E.: Motivation for consistency. In S. Feldman (Ed.), *Cognitive Consistency*. New York, Academic Press, 1966.

Slater, P. E.: Contrasting correlates of group size. *Sociometry*, 1958, 21:129–139.

Smith, A. J.: Similarity of values and its relation to acceptance and the projection of similarity. *Journal of Psychology*, 1957, 43:251–260.

Smith, A. J.: The attribution of similarity: the influence of success and failure. *Journal of Abnormal and Social Psychology*, 1960, 61:419–423.

Smith, M. B., Bruner, J. S., and White, R. W.: *Opinions and Personality*. New York, Wiley, 1956.

Staats, A. W., and Staats, C. K.: Attitudes established by classical conditioning. *Journal of Abnormal and Social Psychology*, 1958, 57:37–40.

Stotland, E., and Cottrell, N. B.: Similarity of performance as influenced by interaction, self-esteem, and birth order. *Journal of Abnormal and Social Psychology*, 1962, 64:183–191.

Stotland, E., Cottrell, N. B., and Laing, G.: Group interaction and perceived similarity of members. *Journal of Abnormal and Social Psychology*, 1960, 61:335–340.

Stotland, E., and Dunn, R. E.: Identification, "oppositeness," authoritarianism, self-esteem, and birth order. *Psychological Monographs*, 1962, 76(9, Whole Number 528).

Stotland, E., and Hillmer, M.: Identification, authoritarianism, and self-esteem. *Journal of Abnormal and Social Psychology*, 1962, 66:334–342.

Stotland, E., Natsoulas, T., and Zander, A.: Generalization of interpersonal similarity. *Journal of Abnormal and Social Psychology*, 1961, 62:250–256.

Stotland, E., Thomson, S., Reed, T., and Katz, A.: Social schemas of American college students. *Human Relations*, in press.

Swingle, P. G.: Effects of the emotional relationship between protagonists in a two-person game. *Journal of Personality and Social Psychology*, 1966, 4:270–279.

Tagiuri, R.: Social preference and its perception. In R. Tagiuri and L. Pettrullo, *Person Perception and Interpersonal Behavior*. Stanford, Stanford University Press, 1958.

Tannenbaum, A. S., and Bachman, J. G.: Attitude uniformity and role in a voluntary organization. *Human Relations,* 1966, *19:*309–322.

Taylor, H. F.: Balance and change in the two-person group. *Sociometry,* 1967, *30:* 262–279.

Tharp, R. G.: Psychological patterning in marriage. *Psychological Bulletin,* 1963, *60:* 97–117.

Thomas, E. J., and Fink, C. F.: Effects of group size. *Psychological Bulletin,* 1963, *60:*371–384.

Walters, R. H.: Some conditions facilitating the occurrence of imitative behavior. In E. C. Simmel, R. A. Hoppe, and G. H. Milton (Eds.), *Social Facilitation and Imitative Behavior.* Boston, Allyn & Bacon, 1968.

Walters, R. H., and Parke, R. D.: Emotional arousal, isolation, and discrimination learning in children. *Journal of Experimental Child Psychology,* 1964a, *1:*163–173.

Walters, R. H., and Parke, R. D.: Influence of response consequences to a social model on resistance to deviation. *Journal of Experimental Child Psychology,* 1964b, *1:* 280–296.

Westie, F. R., and DeFleur, M. L.: Autonomic responses and their relationship to race attitudes. *Journal of Abnormal and Social Psychology,* 1959, 58:346–347.

Wolfe, D. M., Stotland, E., and Zander, A.: Unity of group, identification with group, and self-esteem. *Journal of Personality,* 1960, *28:*463–476.

Woodmansee, J. J., and Cook, S. W.: Dimensions of verbal racial attitudes: their identification and measurement. *Journal of Personality and Social Psychology,* 1967, *7:*240–250.

Wyer, R. S., and Dermer, M.: Effect of context and instructional set upon evaluations of personality-trait adjectives. *Journal of Personality and Social Psychology,* 1968, *9:*7–14.

Zajonc, R. B., and Burnstein, E.: Structural balance, reciprocity, and positivity as sources of cognitive bias. *Journal of Personality,* 1965a, *33:*570–583.

Zajonc, R. B., and Burnstein, E.: The learning of balanced and unbalanced social structures. *Journal of Personality,* 1965b, *33:*153–163.

Zajonc, R. B., and Wolfe, D. M.: Cognitive consequences of a person's position in a formal organization. *Human Relations,* 1966, *19:*139–150.

Ziller, R. C.: Toward a theory of open and closed groups. *Psychological Bulletin,* 1965, *64:*164–182.

CHAPTER 7

DECISION AND ACTION

In the previous two chapters the commonly acquired schemas concerning other individuals, their interrelationships, and the relationships between others and ourselves were examined. It is time now to become a bit more self-centered, in the literal sense of the term, and examine a set of schemas which is relevant both to our own and other people's decisions and actions. There are several ways in which schemas influence the decisions persons make and the actions they take. For one thing, some schemas when aroused can play a role in determining an individual's goals in a given situation. An individual may have an aroused schema which indicates that thus and such an object is desirable. He would then become more likely to act in ways which will make that object his own. Or, an individual may have an aroused schema that some activity is pleasant and enjoyable; he will then tend to act so as to be able to engage in that activity. An individual may have acquired a higher order schema to the effect that being with other people is pleasant—and therefore will have being with others as one of his goals. Since these schemas are of a high order, they are relatively persistent and immune to change. For example, a few unpleasant experiences with others may not have any particular effect on the schema which summarizes the perception that being with others is pleasant.

Since at least some goals that people have are derived from their

schemas, the arousal of certain schemas would increase the likelihood that an individual would act to attain any goal indicated by
the schema. Atkinson (1964) has shown that people who demonstrate on tests that they have a schema that high achievement
is very desirable are likely to work hard to achieve a goal, provided
that this schema is aroused. The schema can be aroused by informing a person that a given situation is competitive, or that it involves evaluation of the person. People who do not possess this
schema, or possess one which indicates that high achievement is
not so desirable, do not work as hard in such competitive situations.

There are some schemas concerning the specification of desirable goals which are very widely held. For example, no student
can doubt that most of his compatriots have a schema which
suggests that attaining high grades is desirable. Thus, the arousal of
this schema would lead most students to become quite interested
in gaining information which would help them attain high grades.
Cohen (1957) aroused this schema among college students by telling them that a new academic policy would influence their grades
and by describing the nature of this change. For other students, he
reversed the order, telling them about the policy first and then telling them that their grades would be affected. The first group
attended more closely than did the second to the description of the
policy. Another parallel example comes from a study by Peak (1960)
in which students, immediately after taking a quiz in class, were
asked to evaluate a teaching policy which was described to some
as instrumental to, and to others as likely to frustrate, their goal of
getting good grades. Not surprisingly, these students evaluated the
two policies differently. However, other students who evaluated
these same two policies two weeks after a quiz, when the schema
about the desirability of good grades was less likely to be aroused,
did not evaluate the two policies as differently as did the first group
of students.

There are, however, more subtle ways in which these generally
held schemas about the desirability of certain goals can be aroused
in social situations. For instance, suppose a person is playing a
game with another person in which he has a chance to take
advantage of the other. In such a situation, Marlowe, Gergen, and
Doob (1966) found that people are more likely to avail themselves
of the opportunity to take such an advantage if the other person is
perceived to be very egotistical. The perception of the partner in
the game as egotistical may have aroused schemas in most of the
subjects which suggest that egotistical people are "undesirable",
and that it is not unfair to take advantage of undesirable people. On
the other hand, the study showed that if the other person was described as "self-effacing," a positive and desirable trait in most per-

sons' eyes, the subjects were much less likely to take advantage of him.

Certain aspects of the extensive research using the "prisoner's dilemma" game may also be seen as illustrating the influence of aroused schemas on goals and actions designed to attain goals. This is a game involving two people in which both stand to gain moderately if they trust each other to cooperate; on the other hand, if one of them does make the trusting response the other may gain a relatively large reward and simultaneously penalize his opponent by choosing an alternative, exploitative or competitive response. Finally, if they both are competitive, they will both lose. More concretely, the game might be set up as follows:

Person I	Person II
A +2	A +2
B +3	A −1
A −1	B +3
B −1	B −1

The left-hand number in each box indicates I's gain or loss if their joint choices lead to that box; the right-hand, II's gain or loss. If both choose A, the trusting choice, they both make +2. If I chooses B, the competitive choice, and II chooses A, then I makes +3 and II loses 1. Likewise, if I chooses A and II chooses B, the latter will make 3 and A will make −1. If both choose the competitive choice, B, they both lose. The matrix above and the explanation accompanying it are typically shown to both participants in the game. The problems facing the players then have to do basically with the strategy each wishes to follow over the series of trials to come. If a player chooses option A this suggests he wishes to trust his opponent to also select A, so that both will make some, but not a great deal of money. However, the other player can select B, under these conditions, thereby exploiting his opponent's trust, winning a greater amount for himself and simultaneously penalizing his opponent. Obviously over a series of trials, patterns of trust or attempted exploitation can be built up or torn down as each player attempts to hit upon a strategy which will allow him to achieve a satisfactory outcome.

When this game is played for small stakes, like imaginary tokens or pennies, then the vast majority of people make competitive choices in most instances. In other words, each player hopes to gain a competitive advantage over the other, rather than to accumulate a large number of tokens or pennies. The schema of "It's desirable to be ahead of the other person" appears to be aroused in most people. However, if the stakes are raised, if people are playing for dollars rather than pennies, the schema about the desirability of gaining large amounts of money is aroused. From the rules of the game, it is clear that the surest way to do so is for both partners to make cooperative choices. Consequently, there is a marked rise in the proportion of cooperative choices when the stakes are raised (Gallo, 1966; Kelley, 1968; McClintock and McNeil, 1966).

Not only are our goals influenced by our schemas, our decision to act to gain these goals is guided by schemas about the consequences of possible actions in a given situation. We act in ways which we believe will bring us to the achievement of our goals. Miller, Galanter, and Pribram (1960) have presented an excellent theoretical description of the way in which an individual guides his behavior toward his goals. After aroused schemas have indicated the appropriate goals in some situation and the most likely means to attain them, the individual then begins to act in accordance with these schemas. He is then in a position to perceive the possible consequences of his initial actions. If they are consistent with the aroused schemas, he continues to act; that is, if he perceives that his actions have the expected and desired effect of moving him toward his goal, he will continue this series of actions. If, however, he perceives that the consequences of his initial actions are not consistent with his schema and are unlikely to lead to goal attainment, additional schemas involving the conceptual dimension of frustration are likely to be aroused. Among such schemas might be one concerning problem-solving: "When one means to attaining a goal fails, other means will often be found by doing thus and such." The individual then shifts to seeking other more appropriate means and actions in that situation. For another person with a different set of past experiences involving initial failure to attain goals, high frustration may be part of a schema which suggests withdrawal rather than persistence: "If one means to attaining a given type of goal fails, then others are likely to fail as well." This individual might then just give up. As Miller, Galanter, and Pribram point out, some of the means to attaining a goal may involve a series of subgoals or steps. Each of these subgoals may have a corresponding L.O.S. about means to attain them, which is subsumed under higher order schemas about their relationship to the final goals.

An individual's decisions about what specific actions are most appropriate for goal attainment are also guided by his schemas. This point may also be illustrated by some of the research on the prisoner's dilemma game. As the game is set up a competitive gain for one party depends on the other person's making trusting or cooperative choices. Thus, if the other person is consistently cooperative, a player who is motivated not just to gain rewards but to do better than his opponent will choose competitively in most instances. However, if the other person has also indicated by his choices that he, too, will make competitive choices, then the best competitive strategy will be to make at least some cooperative choices so as to induce the other person to make some as well. More specifically, if an opponent has started his game by making competitive choices, and has thus indicated that he can and will do so, and then shifts to mostly cooperative choices, it is best to make at least some cooperative choices to reduce his tendencies to revert to competitive choices. Thus, people tend to play more cooperatively with those who have been competitive than with those who have been consistently cooperative (who, it seems, invite exploitation) (Bixenstine and Wilson, 1963). On the other hand, if a person's opponent is expected to have few opportunities in the future to be exploitative himself, then the person will feel less need to make cooperative choices in order to encourage him to make at least some cooperative choices. Thus, Marlowe, Gergen, and Doob (1966) found that subjects who did not expect much more interaction with their opponents were more competitive than those who did. If a person perceives that his opponent will match choice with choice (i.e., that Person II will make a cooperative choice when Person I does and a competitive one when Person I makes that choice) it is obvious that both stand to gain more by choosing cooperatively (Sermat, 1967).

Another example of the person's supporting a line of action because it is instrumental to the attainment of his goals comes from the area of evaluation of public policy. Rosenberg (1956) administered a questionnaire to students to measure which goals of American foreign policy were important to them, and also measured their evaluations of a policy of allowing Communists to address public meetings. Some days later, he presented arguments to them which suggested that this policy regarding Communist speakers would either facilitate or hinder the attainment of the foreign policy goals which they had earlier indicated were important to them. Post-communication measures indicated that the students had shifted their evaluations of the speaker policy in a direction consistent with its perceived helpful or harmful effects on their goals.

THE INSTRUMENTAL ROLE OF INTERPERSONAL SCHEMAS IN GOAL ATTAINMENT

Certain of the schemas about interpersonal processes which we discussed in the last chapter may play a definite role in guiding behavior. These often subtle schemas about interpersonal processes can also indicate means appropriate to the attainment of certain types of goals. By examining some of the instances in which they do, we can see how forms of action that do not seem to have any obvious reason are often guided by these less obvious schemas.

The Similarity-Interaction Schema

For example, a person who has as one of his goals a perception of himself as similar to another person might very well attempt to interact with him. One reason that an individual might desire to view himself as similar to another is that the other is of higher status. If one interacts with a person of higher status, one might feel a bit higher oneself.

Kelley (1951) demonstrated this process in a study in which subjects were assigned to either a high- or low-status position in a team effort. The high-status people sent written messages to the lows in another room. The notes instructed the latter on how to arrange some bricks according to a plan. Some of the low-status people were told that if they performed well, they might be promoted to the higher-status position, while other low-status people were told that they could never be promoted. Both groups of low-status people were permitted to send messages to the highs about any topic they desired. The low-status people who envisioned the possibility of eventual promotion took the route of working well in order to attain the desired higher status. Since this avenue of advancement was blocked for the "permanently" low-status subjects, they took the alternate route involving interacting more with their high-status partners. They sent a relatively high number of messages to them which frequently concerned matters other than their task. As Kelley put it, they engaged in "substitute upward locomotion." By concentrating more on non-task matters, they were avoiding reminders of their lower status.

Needless to say, the permanently low-status subjects did not go so far as to hallucinate that they were in the more desirable position. What they did accomplish was to generate a perception of themselves as perhaps not quite so low-status as they had initially been led to believe. Their reactions were not factually realistic, yet they were psychologically realistic in that the arousal of the similarity-interaction schema led to an enhanced self-perception. One might ask how this self-perception could be maintained in the face of its conflict with reality. The primary reason has to do with the fact that the similarity-interaction schema is an H.O.S., and as such is relatively immune to change on the basis of a single exception. Furthermore, there was a certain factual ambiguity in the degree of difference in status between the two groups. Thus, perception of the degree of difference could be brought more in line with the H.O.S. by simply perceiving the difference as small. This tendency of people to seek to interact with those above them in status has been found in more "natural" situations as well. Hurwitz, Zander, and Hymovitch (1968) assembled people, who were of high and low status in their community, in group discussion meetings. The participants all were told of each other's relative positions in the community. It was found that the lower status people talked more to the highs than to other lower status people. The highs exhibited a strong preference for conversing only with one another!

If an individual uses this schema on a number of occasions, he is likely to develop an H.O.S. based on his experiences in using it. This H.O.S. would be to the effect that interaction with higher status people leads to a more desirable self-image. He might then tend to engage in this sort of behavior on many future occasions. We have all encountered people whose actions are characteristically guided by this schema—although, in reality, many other benefits in addition to a more positive self-evaluation are likely to accrue to a low-status person as a result of such interactions.

On the other side of the street, persons may exhibit tendencies to avoid social interaction with others from whom they are motivated to appear different. Such persons may be avoided because they are believed to be of lower status, or because they have some sort of stigma. Of course, if the conversation or other interaction is of a sort which emphasizes the difference between the two, then there would be little tendency to avoid contact. Thus, a person might not avoid and might even seek out situations in which he gives orders or advice to the other person, and thus at least appears to be different, to be of higher status. The reader will recall that the high level of interaction between the lower and higher status subjects which Kelley found in his laboratory situation involved communication about things other than the task around which their status differences were centered. Thus, in order for the interaction-similarity schema to be effectively employed in such a way as to enhance a person's self-perceived status, the communication involved in the interaction must deal with topics and content which are not directly related to the basis for the status difference.

The Generality of Similarity Schema and the Self-Concept

In addition to the similarity-interaction schema, research has pointed to other instances in which schemas about interpersonal processes have provided the means for attaining goals. Another such schema, which was also discussed in the previous chapter, has to do with similarity between two or more people being general, the implication that if two people have a given trait in common, they will have others in common as well. Thus, if a person is motivated to perceive himself as possessing a given attribute and if another person is perceived to possess that attribute, one route the person can take to enable him to perceive himself as having the former attribute is to establish other similarities to this person. These latter similarities will lead him to perceive himself as "possessing" those desired attributes as well. Obviously, this avenue will be taken primarily when the person cannot establish the observed attribute directly. For example, Zajonc (1955) found that children prefer to wear a cap worn by a TV hero of theirs. Lippitt, Polansky and Rosen (1952) observed the degree to which boys in a summer camp imitated one another under circumstances in which the person imitated could have no knowledge that he was being imitated, e.g., snapping a twig from the same bush as they hike down a trail. The boys tended to imitate those who were higher in status in the camp group in view of their superior fighting ability, knowledge of campcraft, skill in manipulating adults, and other traits. Lippitt, et al. report that they had the feeling from their observations that after imitating a high status camper, a boy felt that in some magical way he had closed the gap in status between himself and the other boy. Burnstein, Stotland, and Zander (1961) presented grade school boys with a deep sea diver who was described as either very expert or mediocre in ability. The diver then told of his tastes with respect to when and where to dive; the boys said that if they became divers they would share the high-status diver's tastes. The boys had been told that the tastes and preferences involved did not in any way influence diving performance. Bandura, Ross, and Ross (1963) presented children with a scene in which one adult clearly gave the appearance of being more powerful than did another since, for example, he was providing the latter with food, and presumably had control over certain important resources. Each adult then engaged in some very unusual idiosyncratic patterns of behavior as the children continued to watch. When later given an opportunity, the children were more likely to imitate the more powerful adult.

Outside the laboratory setting, this tendency to view similarity among persons as very general may lie behind at least some of whatever success there has been through "prestige suggestion" advertising: "If the great man uses X after-shave lotion, perhaps I will feel, or be, greater when I use it." Some persons may attempt to establish some sort of similarity to more powerful people than themselves even when this power is used in an extremely hostile way toward them. Bettelheim (1943) and Cohen (1953) report that in the Nazi concentration camps during World War II some of the inmates picked up and wore scraps and odd pieces of the guards' uniforms, imitated their gait, and even played some of their sadistic games. By so doing they no doubt felt more powerful themselves. It is interesting that the prisoners who engaged in this type of behavior were those who seemed particularly to admire power.

Processes of Identification and Imitation in Children

The process of acquiring similarities to prestigious, powerful, or admired others in order to enhance one's self-evaluation appears to be very important in the psychological development of the child. It should be noted that a number of the studies reported above were done with children. Kagan (1958) and Whiting (1959) have both pointed out that this process may underlie a child's identification with the same sex parent. The child establishes those similarities that he can between himself and the adult; these often include such things as gait, ideas, mannerisms, opinions, and patterns of speech. And this may be done so as to perceive that he has more of the other desired qualities and advantages of the adult which are not currently available to him in any direct fashion, such as power over others, love relationships, and various interpersonal and physical skills. These perceptions of oneself as having such power may be exhibited only on certain occasions; and their expression may be delayed until the child has grown to the point at which he has the "right" and the ability to act in a more adultlike fashion.

This is illustrated in a study by Hoffman (1961), who asked children who they would want to be like when they grew up. If a boy's father was dominant over his mother, he was more likely to want to be like him than if his mother was dominant. If his mother was dominant, he was more likely to prefer to be like her. The boys were doubtlessly motivated to acquire the attributes of power or dominance. Since they could not possess them immediately, they could resort to establishing similarities to the dominant parent in ways that were open to them. Hetherington (1965) had children watch their parents make choices between 20 pairs of objects; then the children made their own choices among the same objects. Boys were more likely to imitate the choices of the more dominant parent. Thus, it is not surprising that Hetherington also found that sons of dominant fathers were more masculine in their preferences for objects even when these preferences were measured separately from the measure of their imitation of their parents. Notice that all of these data pertain to the parents' dominance over each other, rather than to their dominance over the child. Girls show some of these same effects, but to a lesser degree than boys, probably because power is a less desirable trait in girls than in boys in American culture. On the other hand, there is some evidence that girls prefer to be like and imitate the warmer of the two parents.

Differentiation From Low-Status Others

In contrast to the effort to increase similarity with a high-status person is the effort to decrease similarity with, or increase difference from, a low-status person. By so doing, the person enhances his perception that he is different from the lower status or stigmatized person in more ways than just with respect to the similarity he is attempting to decrease. Novak and Lerner (1968) had college students predict how a normal person, a crippled child, and a schizophrenic would fill out an attitude questionnaire which they themselves had filled out previously. The students ascribed less similarity between their own responses and the schizophrenic than between themselves and the normal adult or crippled child. In the world outside the laboratory we have all seen conspicuous distinctions that some groups maintain between themselves and certain other groups, which the former hold in low regard. Perhaps some of the motivation for doing so is the motivation to perceive themselves as different from and, by implication, better than, the other groups in more general ways than just those conspicuous distinctions.

Just as in the case of the similarity-interaction schema, people will tend to develop a higher level schema based on the way that the schema about similarity being general influences their feelings of status. That is, they will tend to develop a schema which suggests that finding similarities between oneself and a higher status person leads to a rise in evaluation of one's own status, while finding similarities between oneself and a lower status person leads to a decrement. Accordingly, people may like higher status people who are similar to themselves and dislike lower status people who are similar to themselves. To show the high-status effect, Jellison and Mills (1967) had some housewives describe themselves on a questionnaire. They then were told about another woman who had described herself as similar to or as different from themselves. Half the women receiving each type of self-description of the other woman then learned that by a lucky chance, the latter had just won a trip to Paris in a contest; the other half learned that nothing "special" had happened to the woman lately. It was found that the subjects indicated greater liking for the lucky woman who was similar to themselves than for the different lucky woman or for either of the unlucky ones. We have all seen, and perhaps experienced, the great feeling of affection, even adulation, that may develop for a similar person who has just achieved a high level of status. An astronaut is not just an astronaut, he is an American as well and Americans feel very positively toward him. He has made them "even prouder to be an American."

The dislike of similar low-status people is shown in another part of the study by Novak and Lerner (1968) in which they presented college students with a description of another college student which indicated that he was either similar to them in attitudes or different. The other college student was also described either as someone who had had a "nervous breakdown" recently, or as someone who had not. The subjects were found to be much less willing to interact with the similar person who had had the nervous breakdown than with the different person who had had a breakdown, or with a "normal" person. This dislike of a similar, stigmatized person may underlie some of the intense hostility sometimes shown toward a member of a group, clan, or family, who has "disgraced" the name. The resentment may be even greater than toward a person of another group who has done something wrong: "We don't expect anything better from *them.*"

Another schema about interpersonal processes which is much used by people to help them attain goals is the similarity-liking schema which suggests that people who are similar to one another with respect to attitudes, beliefs, and goals like one another more than people who are not. Thus, if an individual is motivated to perceive that he is of higher status, he might attempt specifically to make friends of people of higher status so as to feel similar to them. Bechtel and Rosenfeld (1966) told some college coeds that they had some information which indicated that they were of average status in their dorm, and then told them of other coeds who were either of average status also or of higher status. When asked which girls they would prefer as friends, they chose the higher status girls. Undoubtedly, we have all seen this phenomenon in everyday life, a prime example being the name-dropper who builds up his esteem in his own eyes by reminding himself of his perhaps only perceived friendships with important persons. Glidewell, Kanter, Smith, and Stringer (1966) report that children also like people more who are above them in status than those at the same or lower level.

The Similarity-Liking Schema and Social Acceptance

On the other hand, an individual may use the similarity-liking schema in order to attain the goal of perceiving himself as being liked by others. This process is clearly demonstrated in a study by Walster and Walster (1963), in which introductory psychology students were told that they would be meeting in discussion groups, but could choose their group from among the following kinds of groups: other introductory psychology students (who were strangers); married high school students; researchers; graduate students in psychology; factory workers. Some of them, in the control group, simply made their choice immediately. Some of them were told that it was important for them to get the other participants to like them; that is, their schemas about the desirability of being liked were aroused by instructions. These students tended more than the first group to choose groups which were similar to themselves, such as other psychology students. They no doubt felt their similarity would enhance the likelihood that friendships could be established. Still other students were told that they would probably not be liked by the others; again, their schemas about liking were aroused. This latter group of students also preferred to meet with people who were similar to themselves. Finally, still other students were told that they would be liked by the other group members, since they would be introduced to them as someone whom they would like. These students had no need to use the similarity-liking schema, since they believed that the goal of being liked had already been accomplished and thus were much more willing to join groups of people dissimilar to themselves than were the other groups of students.

Another way in which an individual can gain liking from others by using the similarity-liking schema is to change toward greater agreement with them, to make himself conform closely to their beliefs, attitudes, and preferences. Thus, when the schema corresponding to the desirability of being liked is aroused, people will be more prone to increase their agreement with others if they are not already liked by them. Dittes and Kelley (1959) found that people who felt they were only moderately accepted by an attractive group changed their judgments to conform more to those of the group than did those who were more fully accepted by the group. The moderately accepted group's schema about the desirability of being liked was aroused simply by being told that they were only moderately liked, so that they went on to use the means available to them to gain liking, which was conformity. Myers (1962) gave a group a series of tasks, but by instruction reduced the importance of doing well on the tasks. Members of attractive groups who felt rejected by the others in it conformed more than those in groups which were less attractive or in which the members felt accepted. Furthermore, if people are concerned about the possibility of expulsion from an attractive group, they will conform more closely (Zeff and Iverson, 1966).

Another way in which the schema about the desirability of being liked can be aroused is through the perception that some other person has a high degree of power relative to one's own. If the other person likes you, presumably he will be more likely to use his power in a helpful way; if he does not, he might harm. Jones (1964) has documented the various tactics which people use in order to communicate their agreement with another on whom they are dependent. He points out that people perceive that it is important to convince a more powerful person of the sincerity of their agreement with him. If they are not convincing in their affirmations of agreement, then the powerful person might not perceive them as really being similar and may therefore not come to like them. One way in which a person can convince another that he is sincere is not to agree with him on all occasions. However, the subtlety of the tactics which people use to convince others of their sincerity may go well beyond this example. The need to appear to be sincere in order to gain acceptance from others may be so strong that an individual actually shifts his private opinions, i.e., those not communicated to others, to conform to their beliefs. Thus, Kiesler (1963) found that such private beliefs are shifted to conform to the group's more if the person is only moderately accepted by an attractive group than if he is highly accepted. The moderately accepted person is attempting to become "sincere." However, in the communication of his areas of agreement he may not become so extreme as to destroy his credibility.

The schema about the desirability of being liked can also be aroused when the person draws the attention of others to himself simply by his saying something in their presence. Thus, a person might avoid disagreeing with another person if he has to do so in a face-to-face situation, whereas he might maintain his independence in an anonymous one (cf. Deutsch and Gerard, 1955; Asch, 1952).

Thus far we have discussed the arousal of the schema that liking is desirable and have assumed that such a state customarily leads to the arousal of the schema that similarity is associated with liking. However, the arousal of this latter schema would depend, in addition, on the number of other schemas already aroused and on the individual's having acquired the similarity-liking schema. Thus, the degree of conformity to groups would be increased if people were reminded of the similarity-liking schema. Walker and Heyns (1962) did just this and found that, in fact, conformity to attractive groups was higher than in a condition in which the subjects were not thus reminded. Needless to say, if they had been reminded of other schemas that are related to liking, these other schemas would also have guided their behavior.

Of course, if an individual has little expectation that he can gain the liking of a group, he will not employ the similarity-liking schema. People who are highly rejected by groups, especially but not exclusively, from unattractive groups, are not particularly likely to conform. In the Dittes and Kelley (1959) study, people who felt highly rejected by the group did not conform to it. The private conformity which Kiesler (1963) found in his people who felt moderately rejected by a group was not found among those who were rejected more extremely.

So far we have examined cases in which an individual employs the similarity-liking schema to increase his acceptability to members of a group or to another person. In contrast, an individual may be motivated to feel rejected by a given group. This may occur when he is hostile to them and seeks an excuse to provoke a disagreement with them in order to have an occasion for expressing his hostility. Or, it may occur when an individual is motivated to demonstrate to a third party that the other dislikes him. In these cases, a person might provoke an argument, emphasize a difference, "anticonform" by appearing negativistic and contrary. The individual is not just indifferent to the other person or group. He seeks their dislike by proclaiming his different attitudes, beliefs, and values.

The Proximity-Similarity Schema

Still another schema which an individual might employ to attain goals is the one relating physical closeness and similarity. Benoit-Smullyan (1944) gives us a vivid description of how this schema is employed in everyday life:

"The fact that a man of high prestige is also a center of attraction has particular sociological interest. This attraction results from the fact that prestige is *contagious*. Those who associate with people of high prestige, participate in that prestige; even fleeting contact confers some prestige. ('Shake hands with the man who shook the hand of the President.') Prestige contagion is a common-place phenomenon. . . . Those who regularly associate with a person of high status, come, in some mysterious fashion, to 'participate' in the prestige, at least to the extent of raising their own. For this reason even menial offices rendered to a king tend to enoble, and the servants of the great assume a supercilious demeanor. *Per contra*, close association with those of markedly lower prestige and status tends to degrade. These facts explain in large part the ceaseless struggle of those in low prestige to lessen the physical, or *a fortiori* the social distance separating them from persons of high prestige; and the no less determined efforts of those of high prestige to avoid physical and *a fortiori* social propinquity with those of lower prestige. Prestige contagion and prestige participation explain the various manifestations of the nearly universal phenomenon of social climbing and snobbery" (p. 157).

In the previous pages, we have examined the ways in which a number of the schemas about interpersonal processes are employed by a person to attain goals of either perceiving himself to have certain attributes or of having another person react to him in a given way. The schemas we have examined are only a few of those which we described in the previous chapter and were selected mainly because systematic research has been done which demonstrates the ways in which people employ the schemas. The other schemas described in the last chapter are also used in an instrumental way, although research has not yet as extensively documented their use. For instance, a person may employ the schema that liking is generally reciprocated by seeking to gain another person's affection by proclaiming his own. Any lover knows this from experience. Or, the schema that helping and liking are associated may be employed by a person's helping another whose liking he seeks. Or, an individual may seek to sit close to another to communicate his liking for the other, even when they cannot verbally communicate or interact in any way. This list of examples can obviously be lengthened almost indefinitely.

Differentiation of Instrumental from Basic Effects of Schemas

These examples involving the instrumental employment of schemas about interpersonal processes raise a fine theoretical point. How does one distinguish empirically between these instrumental usages and the effects of the interpersonal schemas on the perception of interpersonal situations as described in the previous chapter? How does one distinguish between situations in which a person perceives a given condition as consistent with a schema and situations in which such perception enhances a person's status in his own eyes? Even more pointedly, how does one distinguish between situations in which a person changes his own (or other's) behavior in order to make it consistent with a schema and situations in which a person changes his own behavior to, say, communicate agreement with a group he seeks to enter?

As a first answer to these questions, we must recognize that any specific action by a person can be motivated in several ways at the same time. An individual may be motivated both to perceive a situation consistently with his schemas and to attain another goal. A person may conform to a group because he likes them and is motivated to perceive himself consistently with the similarity-liking schema. He may also, at the same time, conform to the group because he seeks to gain the group's liking. There is nothing contradictory in having more than one goal for an action. In fact, it is probably true that most actions in life have more than one goal. We often eat to satisfy hunger, to enjoy the taste of the food, and to relate to other people in a warm and friendly way.

A second answer to these questions is that in some cases, especially, but not exclusively, in laboratory studies, the different bases for action and perception can be examined in a more purified state. In some such states, it is unreasonable often to assume that one or the other of the types of motives is having any appreciable effect. For instance, if an individual is asked simply to make a prediction about how A and B feel toward each other, knowing only that they have different attitudes, his predictions are hardly likely to be based on his wanting to be liked by either A or B. Further, if an individual is asked how much he likes another person whom he can never meet and who can never ever know of his existence, no question can be raised about his being motivated to gain this person's liking.

On the other hand, if an individual increases his degree of agreement between himself and another person when he perceives that the other will learn of the agreement as compared to a situation in which the other cannot learn of the agreement, then this increase can be attributed in large part to an effort to gain the other's liking. Or, if an individual who believes that similarities between people tend to be general starts to increase his perception of differences between himself and a stigmatized other person, one can assume he is motivated to avoid perceiving himself as also having the stigma. In short, then, the two types of processes may occur simultaneously, but they can be sorted out from one another under certain circumstances.

Another point of interaction between the instrumental use of the interpersonal schemas and the more basic influences of schemas themselves is that their instrumental use often creates more instances consistent with them. Sometimes by bringing himself into more agreement with a group which he likes in order to gain their esteem, an individual creates more exemplars of the schema. By so doing, he tends to reduce or counter any tendencies there might be to increase the probabilism of the schema. For example, if an individual is faced with a situation in which he perceives himself to hold different values from a group which he likes, this perception might tend to increase the probabilism of the liking-similarity schema. However, his efforts to conform to the group soon counter this tendency by showing that the contradiction was temporary. In fact, a person might develop an H.O.S. to the effect that such violations of the schema are in fact temporary. However, the contradictions of some schemas are not so easily escaped or avoided. A boy who imitates the talk of a football hero to enhance his self-perceived status may perceive himself as being a better athlete; but if he cannot avoid seeing that he remains, in fact, a poor athlete, the schema is contradicted. In such instances, the schema about similarity being general needs to be quite low in probabilism to sustain the boy's belief in his enhanced athletic prowess. He might then be full of self-believed alibis about why he dropped that football. Or, in some instances, his sense of his own increased athletic ability may, in fact, lead him to play harder and thereby vindicate his new belief in himself. This latter, rather important point will be discussed more fully in Chapter 10.

At this point, it will be useful to back off for a moment and see where we have gone in this chapter. The reader will recall that we plunged into the discussion of the use of interpersonal schemas to gain certain ends because they were interesting and patent examples of the more general process in which actions are guided by schemas. It was pointed out earlier in the chapter that people usually have good reason for the actions they take—that most action is based on some schema which defines the means to attain some goal. And the goal itself may in some cases have been based on the arousal of a schema.

Schemas Concerning Morality as a Basis for Action

The discussion to this point has emphasized one broad basis for particular behaviors: reasons for actions generally involve an individual's perception that they will facilitate his attainment of some positively valued end state or goal. However, there is, in addition to this means-goal type of reason, another which concerns the moral basis of action and restraints from acting. Communications from others establish the moral conceptual dimension of actions, with the extremes defined in terms of moral goodness or moral badness. "It is naughty to do this"; "You were a bad boy because you threw that stone"; "So and so was wrong to steal that." Or, conversely, "That was very good of you to give me that"; "Joe was very kind to help Jim with that." It is important to recognize that the moral dimension has two poles—that morality not only prohibits but directs. For instance, moral standards indicate that it is better to help someone who needs help than not to do so; that it is just to give a person what he has worked hard to attain; that giving up something of your own to help another is morally good. We will see some of the effects of these positive aspects of morality later. Parents and others morally evaluate the child's behavior as a means to control it, and, at the same time, to establish in the child the persuasive dimension of moral judgments for actions, in addition to the more general means-goals aspect that we have discussed thus far.

Several questions about the use of the moral dimension to control the child's behavior arise. One is, why do moral judgments control the behavior of children as well as that of adults? This question will be tackled later when we discuss the self-concept. Another question is, where do the moral dimensions come from? The answer to that question had better be left to sociological, historical, or theological investigators.

The moral conceptual dimension, being one which is based on communications from others, is at first assimilated into the child's already acquired conceptual dimensions and schemas (Piaget, 1962). Only gradually does the distinctive quality of the moral dimension emerge for the child, as he encounters more instances in which this dimension is not readily perceived as being just another way of referring to means-ends reasons for acting or not acting. For instance, if a desired toy can be obtained by theft, the parents' telling the child that it is improper and wrong to steal provides a situation in which this dimension is almost directly counter in its implications to the goal-means kind of reason for action. Thus, Kohlberg (1964) found that the acquisition of a distinctive moral dimension increases with age. Accordingly, at first children confuse morality with the goal of maintaining good relations with parents. Still later they begin to see morality as being authoritative prescriptions and proscriptions from parents and other authority. Some children then develop even higher order schemas regarding morality as it becomes subsumed under other such higher order schemas as agreements between people, as respect for individual rights, as laws democratically assured. But, of course, the attainment of these H.O.S.s about morality is contingent on the acquisition of other H.O.S.s about the relationships of people in society. Thus, a child who does not have these other schemas cannot acquire the more complex schemas about moral behavior. Turiel (1966) attempted to teach children the more complex schemas concerning morality, but found that he could not do so if the child was not already fairly close to acquiring them.

Once the moral conceptual dimension has been acquired, the individual can include it among the reasons upon which he decides to act, or chooses to act in a given way. Thus children who have a better knowledge of this dimension are less likely to violate moral stipulations by, for example, cheating (Kohlberg, 1964). The acquisition of moral conceptual dimensions thus has a double effect of leading the individual both to evaluate his actions along this dimension and to guide his actions to stay within the bounds of the moral prescriptions. Thus, people who have acquired this dimension are more likely both to act morally in most instances and to evaluate their behavior along a moral dimension, which means that they will sometimes feel guilty because of their violations. Brown (1965) reports a study by McKinnon in which only 25 per cent of the people who cheated on an examination said they sometimes felt guilty, while those who did not cheat said they often felt guilty. Apparently, the innocent feel guilt and the guilty feel innocent.

Berkowitz and his associates (Berkowitz, 1957; Berkowitz and Daniels, 1963, 1964) have shown in a series of studies how the more positive aspects of the moral schema affect our behavior. These studies have shown that when another person depends on you, you will try to help him by working harder than you would if the other person did not depend on you. This altruistic behavior occurs even when the other person cannot help in return and cannot even find out that he has been helped by you. This was demonstrated by having a subject believe that he was helping to test supervisory skill of another subject as the other supervised him in some task. The subordinate subject could help the other by speeding up his production, and did so even when the other could neither see him nor find out who he was. Berkowitz also showed that individual differences in altruistic behavior are correlated with scores on a questionnaire dealing with a person's sense of social responsibility, i.e., the degree to which he has acquired a schema about the positive value of actions helping other people. Further, Berkowitz showed that if this schema was aroused by having a person receive a favor from another person, he was more likely to act in an altruistic way toward a third person.

Thomas (1957) showed the same sort of altruism among a group of telephone company operators. They were assembled in groups to make objects out of paper, the process involving five steps. In some of the groups, the subjects worked in teams of two, one taking on two of the steps, the other, the remaining three. In other groups, the subjects each worked on all five steps by themselves. The subjects in the first type of group worked faster. The subjects filled out a questionnaire afterwards in which they indicated how much responsibility they felt for the other group members; the more responsible the subjects felt, the harder they worked.

An argument can be made that the individual's behaving in a moral way is but a special case of means-goals action. For example, the goal in certain situations might be to think well of oneself, to conceive of oneself as a moral person, and thereby keep self-esteem high. Nevertheless, it is useful to distinguish moral from other goals because they often come into conflict. In any case, the main point of this part of the chapter is that moral judgments are related to a person's decision to act in a given way or not to do so.

HIGHER ORDER SCHEMAS REGARDING THE RATIONALITY AND REASONABLENESS OF BEHAVIOR

So far in this chapter, we have seen how an individual's behavior is directed toward the attainment of goals, some of which are based on schemas, how the actions an individual decides to take are often based on schemas, and how the conceptual dimension of morality enters into this process. However, schemas are involved in this process in an additional way as well—a way which is very important for understanding some rather peculiar forms of human action which will be described later in this chapter.This way concerns the individual's developing an H.O.S. concerning the manner in which his actions are guided by schemas. He is likely to develop such H.O.S.s because he perceives his own actions and is aware of the ways in which his schemas guide them. The individual obviously has many experiences almost from the beginning of life in which he attends to his own actions because they involve change. The familiarity of his own body, his arms, his voice, and so on, makes his attention to actions all the more likely, since familiarity of this type operates to reduce the amount of anxiety associated with the new and different. Likewise, the person will attend to the aroused schemas which guide his choices of goals and means. The very fact that these schemas provide the bases for decisions about acting obviously indicates that the individual attends to them. Therefore, the person is highly likely to acquire an H.O.S. that his behavior is guided by schemas. Personally and phenomenologically this H.O.S. often takes the form of beliefs that decisions to act are based on reason, that reasons are the basis of action.

There are certainly other reasons for an individual's attention to the relationship between schemas and action. The individual can also come to attend to his own actions because he is directed to do so by others. Early in life a person may be questioned about the basis of some given action, or, in some cases, be even told about the reasons for his actions by others. Parents will ask a child why he did something, often after he did something "naughty." Sometimes parents will tell the child why he did something naughty, without waiting for the child to give an explanation. As the person grows older, he may be questioned by siblings, friends, and enemies with respect to his motives, both for good and bad actions, and with respect to the basis in reality for his choice of action. Accordingly, he will become more likely to attend to the reasons for his actions and to provide more of a basis for the acquisition of the H.O.S. about having reasons for actions.

This probing of an individual's motives by older people provides an additional basis for the acquisition of this H.O.S. The communication and probings of others indicate to the child that he should have an H.O.S. that actions have a "reasonable" basis. The putting of the question to the child indicates that the adult world believes that he is expected to have reasons for any of his actions. They are telling him that he is expected to have a schema that actions and decisions have reasons.

Once this H.O.S. about his own behavior is established on the basis of observations of his own actions, it provides a basis for perception of other people as behaving in the same way. He may assume that because he is behaving in a rational, ethical way, others do as well. We saw this process of generalizing from self to others in Chapter 5. Thus, when the person has acquired this H.O.S. with respect to himself, he will tend to perceive others as acting according to it and therefore will perceive more exemplars of this process in others.

Furthermore, we can often observe this process in others when they communicate their thinking as they are acting, when they tell us how they are planning to act and why they stopped or changed a course of action. Our observations of other people and communications from them can thus provide an additional basis for acquiring an H.O.S. about the rational and ethical basis of behavior.

The reader, like many of the rest of us, may have the impression sometimes that other people are behaving without good reason. We've all said at one time or another, "He's nuts!" And sometimes we may have been right. But at other times, we may have been very wrong, since the individual may have good reasons for his behavior which may not be apparent to the bystander. The social psychologist Asch (1952) has often properly faulted his colleagues for interpreting experimental studies as suggesting that people are mechanical, unthinking creatures. He has sometimes repeated their studies, but with the simple, additional step of asking the subjects just why they did what they did. And, more often than not, they were able to give logical, coherent, reasonable answers. Action may then be reasonable and proper from the point of view of the actor, even if it is not from the point of view of the observer. This is not to say that if another person believes that an action is reasonable and proper, that makes it so. There are honestly held false beliefs and sincerely worshipped false gods.

In sum, then, individuals are highly likely to acquire an H.O.S. which implies that their own and other people's decisions and actions are guided by good, realistic, rational and ethical reasons from a variety of sources: communications from others that they have reasons for their actions, observations of one's own actions, perceptions of others as conforming to this H.O.S., and communications from them that imply that they adhere to this schema.

This schema, as stated, suggests that there are few exceptions to our behaving in this rational and proper way. Clearly, any rational look around the world and at ourselves would certainly give us the impression that there are many exceptions. People often appear to be irrational and sometimes immoral in their actions. Sometimes our own behavior may be somewhat inexplicable to us. However, our concentrating our attention on the exceptions may be the result of the fact that these *are* exceptions to the general rule, contradictions to our schemas, and therefore attract our attention. Furthermore, these schemas about actions and decisions are of a rather high order—and as such, are of low probabilism—so that, in the long haul, the exceptions would have little influence, although they might attract momentary attention.

We can now turn to our examination of the influence that the possession of this schema has on an individual's perceptions and actions. Before we do so, however, we need to become a bit more precise about the specific forms that this H.O.S. takes. The specific schemas we shall see under this overall higher order schema imply such beliefs as: "Persons choose things they like and reject things they don't like"; "One voluntarily chooses to receive communications when the communication has some value"; "We choose actions which have more important facts supporting them over those which have less important ones supporting them"; "We choose actions which cause less pain, work, suffering, than those which cause more"; "We choose to suffer, work, sacrifice only in order to achieve goals whose values are so great as to justify and make worthwhile the sacrifice, suffering, or work"; "We choose to make statements because we believe them to be true." These specific schemas may sound very banal and truistic; in fact, we agree that they are. But this very fact indicates how widely accepted, how universally acquired they are. The influence of these schemas on our perceptions and actions, however, is hardly truistic or banal. Some of the effects which we will define in the following pages are, to put it mildly, odd. Much of the research which will be cited as a demonstration of the consequences of these schemas is work originally done to test the predictions of Festinger's (1957) theory of cognitive dissonance. This theory and its ramifications has probably stimulated more research, controversy, and discussion than any other position in contemporary social psychology and represents a well-established and integrated system. As will be made more explicit at the end of this chapter, the schema position which has been developed in this book makes very similar predictions and statements about human behavior as does dissonance theory—but the schema theory is viewed as a more general approach going beyond the areas of interest to which the dissonance position has traditionally been applied. So let us proceed.

Post Choice Justification of Decisions

The first specification of the H.O.S. we shall examine is that a schema guiding an action is aroused immediately prior to the action as well as during the action itself. In ordinary language, we usually—not always—know what we are going to do prior to the point at which the action is actually initiated. Schemas which concern goals, as well as those which concern means, are aroused just prior to any given action, as well as during it. The first effect of this specific schema we shall consider concerns a situation in which the individual has a goal of making a choice between or among two or more objects, courses of action, people as friends, etc; that is, he has not yet made the choice but is anticipating that he will. Since the schema implies that decisions to act in a given way are based on good reasons, he is also motivated to have good reasons for making the choice. If he does not have them when he chooses, he will be violating the schema, as well as possibly making a mistake. It sometimes happens that the individual does not perceive that he has enough information about the various alternative courses of action to develop good reasons for any of them or against any of them. In these cases, the individual will be motivated to seek information which will enable him to develop reasons; he will therefore seek information about all the alternatives equally if he is equally ignorant about them. Jecker (1964a), for example, found that if an individual expects to choose one of two people to be his partner in a game, he is equally interested in information about each of them. Lowe and Steiner (1968) had girls choose between two men with whom they would have dates. Before the choices were final, the girls were interested in gaining both positive and negative information about each of the two men. After the choice was made and the girls now had the goal of the date itself, they sought information about the negative aspects of their "date," presumably to give them more guidelines for their later actions.

If an individual perceives that he has enough information to provide good reasons for a choice, he will be less motivated to gain information. Thus, if two objects are almost equal in desirability, the individual will be more apt to seek information about them than if one of the objects is much higher in desirability than the other (Mills, 1965a). Furthermore, the individual will avoid information which might undermine the good reasons he has already for his choices. Mills and Jellison (1968) first had subjects rate products in terms of their desirability. Then they told the subjects that they could choose between one of them and a product they had previously valued considerably higher in desirability. Before they had to make their choice, the subjects either were given a chance to read some advertising which concerned the less valued of the two products or were given a chance to read information about some other product which was valued almost the same as that product. In the first case, reading the advertisement about the product which they had judged to be relatively undesirable might undercut the reasons they had for rating it relatively low in desirability, so that they would not be able to reject it for good reasons in favor of the more desirable object. Accordingly, the first group of subjects spent less time reading the advertisement than did the second. In the latter case, they were not expecting to have to choose between the advertised object and the more desirable one, so that there was no reason for avoiding positive information about it.

Now that we have seen how an individual is motivated to act consistently with the schema before he makes a choice to act in one way or another, we can turn to an examination of the effects of the schema on the person's perceptions, evaluations, and actions, after he has made his choice of action. An L.O.S. which becomes relevant to decisions and actions after a person has made a decision is the simple notion that liking something is a good reason for choosing it. Thus, the L.O.S. is that "One chooses things he likes and rejects things he does not like." Or, the schema can be stated in the reverse form: "A person likes what he chooses and dislikes what he rejects." The effects of this schema are obvious and pervasive. When we observe another person make a choice, we automatically assume that he likes what he chooses, without any further information. If we perceive someone choose something that we have reason to believe he does not like, we feel uneasy and upset. We may seek to find reasons so that his behavior can be restored to consistency with our schemas. "He must be buying that for someone else." If we are still unable to do this, anxiety is likely to increase. Part of the anxiety some people feel around mental patients may be that some of their behavior may not be subsumable under any schema. The same might apply to our own behavior. If an individual chooses to do something which he "knows" he doesn't like, he might feel very uneasy and seek reasons—sometimes going to a psychology text.

Suppose an individual has had to make a choice between two objects which were almost equal in desirability. In such a situation, as in many of those described in the rest of the chapter, the individual is put in a position of having to make a choice in the absence of sufficiently strong and clear-cut reasons for choosing one alternative over another. He may have to choose "prematurely" for a number of reasons: both alternatives might "disappear" if he does not act soon; the store might be about to close. He may perceive that others expect him to make some choice immediately. He may realize that the time and cost which will be incurred by waiting before making a choice are too great. He may perceive that not choosing indicates that he is a weak or vacillating person. This list may obviously be extended. The main point here is that these are reasons for engaging in an act of choosing, but are not reasons for choosing one alternative rather than the other. Thus, regardless of which alternative he chooses, the person may perceive himself as coming close to contradicting the schema, if not actually doing so, since he has had to reject something he does not dislike discernibly more than the thing he has chosen or vice versa. In short, he has little good reason for making the particular choice he did make. One way in which he can change the situation to become consistent with the schema is to change his degree of liking for the objects in question. Brehm (1956) demonstrated this process by first asking subjects to rank a series of objects suitable for gifts in order of their desirability. Then he presented two of the objects one of which they could choose as a gift actually to be sent to a friend of theirs. Half the subjects were presented with choices between objects they had ranked very close in desirability. The other subjects were presented with a choice between objects which they had ranked quite far apart. Finally, he had all the subjects rerank all the potential gifts, including the two between which the subjects had chosen. Brehm found that on these final rankings the subjects who had been given a choice between the two closely ranked objects tended to raise the rank of the chosen object and lower the rank of the rejected one. They were revising their "likings" for the two objects to make them more consistent with the schema and with their actual choice behavior. On the other hand, the subjects who had made a selection between objects that were quite divergent in the original ranking did not tend to raise the rank of the chosen object nor demote the rejected one in attractiveness. The initial difference in desirability between these two objects was sufficient to provide good reason for the choice, so that no change was demanded.

The reader will recall that the schema about the reasons for actions we choose to take applies both to ourselves and to others. The generality of this schema has been demonstrated in a very clear way by Bem (1967); he simply described the Brehm study to college students, having some of them read about the condition in which the objects between which the subject made his choice were close in rank, and having others read about the other condition. The subjects then guessed what final rankings would be made by "real" subjects. Their guesses were remarkably close to what Brehm actually found, showing the differences between the two conditions. Thus, the individual brings his perceptions of other people in line with the schema: "If they made the choice of X, they must have liked X much more than Y."

The theoretical approach used by Bem to explain his findings stems from the learning theory approach of B.F. Skinner. Bem and Skinner argue that, when a child is taught the correct way of verbally describing his own private feelings, the only way the teachers, his parents, and other adults, often can determine his private feelings is to examine the physical context or experience of the child. For example, the adults know the child feels pain when he is burned; if the child says, "It hurts me," the adults respond in such a way that the child learns to associate his pain and the statement. Thus, the child learns to associate objective situations of being burned with feelings of pain. Therefore, when he is in doubt about whether he feels

Sour grapes. Photograph by Irwin Nash.

pain, he might observe that he has just been burned and therefore conclude that he is in pain. Likewise, if a person is in
doubt of whether he likes something or not, he might observe
whether he has chosen it or not. If he has, he concludes he must
like it. And, likewise, he will conclude that someone else likes
something the latter chooses; the process is much the same in
making the judgment about oneself as about another person.

Obviously, Bem's approach has many parallels to the present one. However, his does not explain why people will seek
to change situations to conform to the "associations," nor why
people experience anxiety when the "associations" are violated.

This process of changing the level of liking for an object after having chosen or rejected it may be seen as the result of effort to find reasons for the choice when there were insufficient reasons before the choice had to be made. Accordingly, if sufficient reasons were available at the time of the choice, the individual would not be motivated to find additional ones for his choice after having made it. Several ways of making reasons available at the time of choice have been shown to have the effect of reducing the tendency to shift evaluation of objects after a choice. One way shown by Brehm and Cohen (1959) is simply to make the chosen and the rejected object so alike with respect to actual attributes that the individual can readily perceive that he is not losing very much by rejecting one of the objects, since the other is highly likely to have many of the same desirable qualities. Children were given a choice between two toys which were very similar or between two toys which were about equal in desirability but were quite different. The children were found to increase their evaluations of the chosen toy and lower their evaluations of the rejected one only in the case of the relatively different toys.

Another way to provide children in advance with reasons for making a choice is to invoke a threat that if they make a given choice they will be severely reprimanded by an adult. More specifically, Aronson and Carlsmith (1963) placed children one at a time in a room with a variety of toys. The adult experimenter then told the children that she would have to leave for a few minutes and that they should not play with a certain rather attractive toy. To half the children, she said she would be very angry if she found that they had played with the toy, thus providing a very clear reason for not playing with the toy. To the other children, she said, very mildly, simply that they should not play with the toy. This communication from the adult provided a less good reason for not playing with the attractive toy; enough of a reason to keep from playing with it, but certainly less than that provided by the fear of the adult's anger. Then each child was left alone with the toy for a few minutes. Most children did not, in fact, play with the toy. Finally the children were asked to indicate how much they liked each toy. As compared to their ratings of their liking of the toy prior to being left alone with it, the children who had been threatened by the adult did not change their liking; they had been provided with a good enough reason for not playing with the toy. The other children, however, lowered their ratings of the toy as compared to their prior ratings. They had chosen not to play with the toy, but had initially had fewer reasons for doing so. They found reasons to justify their behavior by saying that they "really" did not like it very much anyway. Pepitone, McCauley, and Hammond (1967) repeated this study and found that the non-threatened children actually played less with the previously forbidden toy when they were subsequently given permission to do so. Sour grapes in the research laboratory! Freedman (1965) repeated this procedure and found that, one month later, the children were averse to playing with the "forbidden" toy if the adult had not strongly threatened them for playing with it. In the month-later test, a different experimenter was used and the children were expressly told that they could play with the toy in question. Despite the length of time, the new experimenter, and the explicit permission, the children who had not been threatened for playing with the toy continued to avoid it!

Freedman also found that he could provide good reasons for not playing with the toy by having the adult remain in the room with the child, rather than leaving the child alone after the original admonishment not to play with it. Under these conditions even when the adult did not threaten the children, it was found that the children did not devalue or reject the forbidden toy.

If a child does not play with the forbidden toy simply because it is not physically available, then the child has not actually made the choice not to play with the toy. Then he would feel no motivation to devalue the forbidden toy. This was demonstrated in a study by Turner and Wright (1965) in which they repeated the same threat—no-threat variation as in the above studies; but they also had a condition in which the toy was simply removed by the adult without explanation when she left the room. In the latter condition, the children did not show the usual tendency to devalue the forbidden toy.

Consequences of a Decision to Listen to Counter-Attitudinal Communications

Getting back to the adult world, we find another very interesting situation in which people make re-evaluations of ideas, objects, and people in order to find, after the fact, acceptable reasons for their having made a certain choice. This situation is that of choosing to expose oneself to a persuasive communication which the individual expects to be in opposition to his own present attitudes and beliefs. On the face of it, the choice to do this would seem to have little justification. After all the feeling might be, "They're wrong; what's the use of listening to them?" Nevertheless, a person may feel considerable pressure to choose to expose himself to a non-supportive communication for one of the many reasons indicated earlier: he may have had to choose between two equally undesirable alternatives; social pressures, such as from an experimenter, might be on him to make some sort of choice; etc. As was pointed out above, none of these reasons provides support for the actual alternative chosen, only for the act of choosing. However, one way of justifying the choice of agreeing to listen to the opposition is to raise one's evaluation of the opposition and its ideas. That is, it is reasonable for a rational and open-minded person to expose himself to counter-attitudinal information to the extent that this material is logical, important and significant. Thus, the schema which suggests that persons have good reasons for their choices and their behavior would be expected to lead an individual to seek to justify a decision to listen to a speech which he knows supports a position counter to his own. And he may well do this, then, by seeing those arguments as logical and objective, and this may then actually lead him to be persuaded by them. Thus Brehm and Cohen (1962) gave people a choice of whether to read some material which opposed their own beliefs or to leave the experiment. Since there were pressures on the subjects not to leave the research, they had a difficult choice to make; neither alternative was very attractive. Nevertheless, most all chose to stay and thus to expose themselves to the contrary information. Some subjects were given material which opposed their own position to a great degree, while others were given material which did so to a lesser degree. The researchers found that the subjects tended to agree with whatever position was advocated; that is, the more discrepant the communication from their own original positions, the more the subjects shifted away from their original beliefs. On the other hand, subjects who were exposed to the same communications without having been put in the position of choosing to examine the material changed their attitudes less, the more discrepant the communication was from their original attitudes.

A parallel process was shown in an ingenious study by Jones and Brehm (1967). They had college students listen to a tape recording of a speech about intercollegiate sports. Sometimes at the beginning of the tape, the speaker announced that he was impressed by today's students; other times he announced that he was decidedly unimpressed. Thus, the speaker was an attractive one to some of the students, and a negative one to others. Half the students listened to the tape after having been given a choice; they were told that they did not have to listen unless they chose to, because the tape contained some potentially objectionable material. It was found that in the choice condition the negative speaker persuaded the students to his position more effectively than did the positive speaker. The students listening to the negative speaker had the problem of finding some reason for having listened to such a speaker; an obvious source of justification was to evaluate the content of his speech more highly, to see his arguments as important, cogent and logical. Those who listened to a positive speaker had less of a problem of finding reasons to justify their behavior and so did not have to raise their evaluations of the content. On the other hand, another group of students listened to the tape ostensibly by accident while in a waiting room. These students, who were not faced with the problem of finding reasons for their having heard the communication, agreed more with the positive speaker than with the negative one.

Re-evaluation of the Importance of Supportive and Nonsupportive Information

Another specific schema subsumable under the general H.O.S. that the choice of some action is based on good and sufficient reasons is that "The facts that one takes into consideration in making a choice are the important ones." Suppose a person has had to make a choice between two people who were different in their attributes, but about equal in their overall desirability; in such a case, there would be little to provide the person with reasons for his preferring one over the other. One way of restoring this situation to consistency with the schema is to perceive the "facts" which are supportive of the choice as being more important than those which are not supportive of the choice. To demonstrate this process, Davidson and Kiesler (1964) had subjects first rank a list of traits in terms of their importance as a basis for making judgments about other people. Next the subjects had to indicate which of two men they thought should be hired for a job, the two men being described as about equally desirable with respect to these traits, even though the men had different traits. After making their choices, the subjects reranked the importance of the traits and were found to now rank the traits possessed by the man they had chosen higher than they had when they first ranked them. Interestingly enough, this new ranking of the traits appears to have considerable stability in that it will even be subsequently applied to choices other than the one which led the subjects to shift their rankings (Penner, Fitch, and Weick, 1966).

Additional, Choice-Relevant Information

The effects of the two specific schemas—having to do with the relative desirability of chosen and unchosen alternatives and the relative importance of reasons for making a choice—that we have looked at in the above paragraphs were generated by the person himself, without any assistance which might come from additional information about the objects of his choice. People changed their liking for the objects, or ιε-εvaluated the importance of various pieces of information, on their own, partly because the conditions of the studies were such that no additional relevant information was provided the subjects. Suppose, however, that such information had been made available. The individual then might seek out this information in order to generate additional good reasons for his choice, if he did not already have adequate reasons. Mills (1965) demonstrated this seeking of information in an ingenious study in which he had coeds rank various toilet and beauty aids in order of preference. He gave some of them a choice of keeping either their second or their third-ranked objects, and gave others a choice between the eighth- and ninth-ranked. The subjects would have few good reasons to support whatever choice they made under these circumstances, since the objects in each pair were almost equal in desirability. A last group of subjects was given a choice between the second- and ninth-rated objects; these subjects obviously had good reasons for their selection. Then all of the subjects were asked whether they would like to read advertisements for the various objects. Mills found that when the choices had involved items similar in attractiveness, in which there would be little basis for finding very strong reasons for choosing one object over the other, the subjects were much inclined to prefer to read favorable advertisements about their chosen object and to ignore the material concerning the rejected one, regardless of whether the objects had been high or low in the initial ranking. It is very important to note how this preference for supportive information contrasts with the person's information-seeking actions before he has made a choice. The reader will recall that before the choice, the evidence seems to indicate a rather rational and objective seeking out of information with respect to both sides. After making a difficult decision, actions with regard to information appear to shift sharply, and support is sought rather than information. However, if considerable relevant information has been accumulated before the choice situation is encountered, it may be easier to find sufficiently strong supportive reasons after making a choice without an appeal to additional information. The backlog of choice-relevant information provides a ready-made source of reasons which adequately justify a given decision (cf. Festinger, 1964).

A study by Mills, Aronson, and Robinson (1959) which was later replicated by Rosen (1961) has often been cited to indicate that people do not necessarily seek information to support a preferred action after they have chosen it. Students in a classroom situation were asked to indicate which of two types of examinations they would prefer to take in their course, essay or "objective" questions. After they had made their choice, the students were given a choice of reading material about why each type of examination was superior. And, contrary to the Mills data, the subjects preferred to read the information which opposed their choice. However, this finding need be interpreted as contradicting Mills only if it is assumed that the information is relevant only to the choice the students had just made about examination forms. Obviously, these students expected to take very many more examinations, and, psychologically, they could very well perceive themselves as being in the situation prior to making their choice. As we saw earlier in the chapter, this is a situation in which people tend to look at all sides of an issue.

Individuals probably experience a number of instances in which they have had to make choices with little reason for preferring one of the alternatives, and have had to find reasons "after the fact." They will probably experience many instances in which finding reasons "after the fact" is sometimes not easily accomplished, since the information that they had before and after the fact is often not basically different. In some cases they might not even be able to find a sufficient basis to establish reasons for their choices, so that they might be left with unresolved contradictions between the schema which suggests that there are good and sufficient reasons for choosing a given line of action and the actual choices they have made. In other instances, reasons that were found might be undermined later. In terms of this discussion, then, we would expect individuals to be motivated to avoid situations in which they have to make choices with little reason; or if such choices have been made, to exhibit tendencies to establish reasons for this choice which are unlikely to be contradicted by subsequent information. The results of a study by Walster, Berscheid, and Barclay (1967) clearly give experimental support to this presumed tendency. They gave children a difficult choice to make between a pair of toys which were close in attractiveness as shown by an earlier ranking of the toys in order of preference. The children were then told that they were soon going to hear a talk about one of the toys which had been involved in their selection, but not about the other. The children tended to develop reasons for their choice by appropriately changing their evaluation of the latter toy; however, they presumably perceived that there was a possibility that any immediate re-evaluation of the former toy might later be undercut by the talk so there was no change in its rated attractiveness.

An individual can avoid the problems inherent in the attempt to justify the particular selection made in a difficult choice situation by denying that a choice has been made in the first place. The possibility of developing the perception of not having made a choice will be made more likely if there is some ambiguity in the choice situation itself. For example, in some situations, the individual may have indicated which of two objects he prefers, but the possibility may still exist that he still will receive the non-preferred object or even both objects. The person may then focus his attention on this indeterminacy and perceive that, in fact, he has not really made a choice. In such instances, he would then not be motivated to find additional supportive reasons for his preference, since he has not yet really chosen or committed himself to just one of the options involved. Accordingly, Jecker (1964*b*) and Allen (1964) found that if a person believes that there is at least some possibility that he will receive both the more preferred and the less preferred objects, he will not tend to increase his liking for the first and decrease his liking for the second. In these studies, girls indicated their preference between pairs of records which were almost equal in desirability. However, in one condition the experimenter told them there was a chance that there would be enough records for them to receive both. When asked to re-rank these records, the girls did not raise the ranking of the preferred record nor lower the ranking of the less preferred one. On the other hand, girls who were told that they definitely would receive only their preferred record did shift their rankings consistently with their choice.

Schemas Concerning Effort Expenditure and Discomfort

Another schema which may be subsumed under the H.O.S. which suggests that people, ourselves included, have good reasons for their actions and their choice of behavior summarizes the notion that people prefer to do those things which cause less pain, suffering, and work for themselves over those things which cause more pain, suffering, and work. Thus, the assumption is made that people will buy from the lowest bidder, that people will take the shortest, easiest route between two places, that people will prefer the more efficient machine to the more costly one. If we perceive that someone's behavior grossly violates this schema, for example, by spending more than necessary to purchase an object, by overtipping, or by "making things hard for himself," we will at first feel somewhat anxious. However, we often overcome this anxiety by assuming that there is some other goal that the person has, for which the increased sacrifice is necessary and reasonable.

Consequences of a Choice to Undergo Pain or Stress

A person might sometimes make a choice of some course which will cause him pain or discomfort because the alternatives are even more painful to him. However, sometimes the alternatives are so nearly equal in "undesirability" to the painful choice that the individual is not left with good reasons for having made this choice. One possible way in which a person can react to this failure to confirm the schema is by reducing the perceived degree of pain, inconvenience, discomfort, or effort which has been incurred. In this way the choice to voluntarily submit to what is initially perceived to be an unpleasant experience comes to represent a less blatant contradiction to a schema which involves the notion that persons do not choose to engage in behaviors which are truly self-damaging, self-defeating, or deemed unpleasant without ample justification. By minimizing or denying the magnitude of the inconvenience or discomfort which has been experienced, the choice and the subsequent behavior in line with that choice cease to be irrational, unreasonable, or, in our terms, inconsistent with a relevant schema.

Notice that the observation of human behavior that is summarized in this schema is not that persons never choose to undergo unpleasantness, but rather that they do so only in conjunction with strong and compelling reasons. One factor which has figured importantly in experimental investigations in this area may be conceptualized as relevant to this notion of justification; it has to do with whether or not persons are given a choice as to whether they will submit to unpleasantness. The absence of choice, being forced by compelling circumstances to accede to a request to experience discomfort, is not incongruent with the schema. Thus, marked differences in persons' responses to unpleasant circumstances would be anticipated as a function of the presence or absence of prior perceived choice.

For example, Watts (1966) told subjects that they might later participate in a study which would involve painful electric probes of their tongues. Then, some of them were given a choice as to whether to take an unpleasant oral anesthetic while others were simply given the anesthetic without being asked to explicitly choose to submit to it. Those who chose to take the anesthetic rated it as less unpleasant than did those who simply were given it.

In a stimulating book on the topic of the influence which cognitive factors may have on motivational states, Zimbardo (1969) presents other studies having to do with hunger, pain, and thirst. The general procedure is similar to that of the investigation reported above. Some subjects are asked to choose to undergo an unpleasant state of affairs, such as additional food or water deprivation or painful electrical shocks, and are given only minimal reasons for doing so. In contrast, other subjects are not given an opportunity to choose or refuse, or are given many strong reasons for undergoing the discomfort, such as money or a talk explaining how important and useful their participation will be. Results indicate that the first-mentioned subjects who willfully commit themselves with little justification differ markedly from the others in three broad areas of post-discomfort measurement. First, at a personal and subjective level, they report feeling less hungry (Brehm, 1962), or less thirsty (Brock and Grant, 1963; Mansson, 1969), or less pain (Zimbardo, 1969) than do other subjects who have undergone objectively equivalent discomfort. Thus, as we have suggested, it seems to be the case that a person in this situation avoids a contradiction to his schema by "reasoning" that the unpleasant state of affairs really wasn't so unpleasant after all, so that his actions were not unreasonable, in the final analysis. But this effect appears to go beyond just feeling less hungry or less discomforted as these same subjects behaved overtly as if they actually were less thirsty by drinking less when given an opportunity to drink as much as they would like following a period of water deprivation (Mansson, 1969), and as if they were less hungry by ordering less food for an anticipated meal (Brehm, 1962). And finally, there is evidence that there were actually physiological differences on measures that are ordinarily close correlates of the subjective states of hunger and pain and of the objective circumstances which induce them. Brehm, Back, and Bogdonoff (1964) found a lower concentration of plasma-free fatty acids in the blood stream of these subjects and this measure has usually been found to be a reliable correlate of length of fasting. Zimbardo, Cohen, Weisenberg, Dworkin, and Firestone (1969) report that subjects who made a choice to endure painful shocks showed a decrease in galvanic skin response (GSR), an electrophysiological measure of stress, compared to others given shocks of the same intensity but no choice. In fact, the GSR for the former subjects was very similar to that of control subjects for whom the shock intensity had actually been lowered by over 20 volts. These last two studies need to be interpreted with some caution, but they do suggest that it may be possible for individuals not only to alter their subjective impression of some drive state such as hunger or pain, but to functionally alter the drive itself.

These results have some very interesting implications regarding the ability of people to sustain pain and suffering. Obviously, a person who chooses to do so is in a better position to sustain pain than one who does not. Ironically, this is more true of people who choose to suffer despite a lack of good reasons for doing so. Those who choose blindly are the ones who are most likely to say, with casual fortitude, "Didn't hurt a bit!" And they may not be lying or "fooling themselves" when they say it.

The schema whose effects we have just examined implies that an individual will choose the least painful route to a goal. However, if the individual does choose to undergo some pain or suffering, or to work hard, he must have some reason for doing so, some goal to achieve by his suffering or efforts. This is the gist of the next schema we will examine as a specific case under the general schema of having good reasons for actions. Thus, if an individual chooses to act in a way that involves pain, great effort, etc., but has just barely sufficient reasons for doing so, he will seek to establish more and better reasons, to find some goal or reward in the situation which is sufficient to justify his actions or suffering. We do not ordinarily work hard or suffer pain for insignificant or problematic goals. Thus, the more suffering, work, or effort an individual has chosen to undergo or to engage in, the more important and the more real the goals ordinarily have to be.

In many cases in which an individual works or suffers, a series of actions on his part are necessary. Work usually involves a number of steps, or the creation of a number of units. At each step in such a work sequence an individual implicitly or explicitly makes a decision as to whether to continue on to the next act or unit. In this way, many types of work may involve a series of decisions or choices on the part of the person. The fact that some people do quit before fully completing a project when a job becomes too demanding bespeaks the reality of these choices. The same may be true of some forms of suffering, in which an individual has a series of options as to whether to undergo pain or not. Thus, in these respects, the individual who is working hard or suffering is often in a situation in which he is making choices and therefore needs to have reasons for them. Notice that in this respect, work and suffering are different from the processes discussed above with respect to the effects of one act of choosing a given line of action. In the studies to illustrate these processes, usually the subjects engaged in one act of choosing, not a series. Thus, to demonstrate the effects of choice, it was necessary to systematically vary the degree to which a person had a choice of acting or not. On the other hand, in the studies to show the effects of work or suffering, such systematic variations of choice have not been found necessary because usually a series of trials or difficult acts is required of some of the subjects. Because a series of painful or effortful tasks is required, the subject is almost automatically put into a situation in which he has at least some choice.

Effort and the Perceived Likelihood of a Future Event

Suppose an individual works on a task but is not certain as to whether there is any objective or purpose to his work. The harder he works, the more he needs to believe that there is in fact a goal to his work. Yaryan and Festinger (1961) told subjects that some of them would later be selected to take a test for which some preparation was needed. For some of them the preparation involved the arduous task of memorizing a long set of complex symbol relations; others prepared for the possibility of future participation by simply glancing over this same set of materials in order to acquaint themselves with it. After having worked on their respective tasks, all subjects were asked to estimate the likelihood that they would actually participate in the test that was to come for only some of the subjects. Those who had expended relatively great effort in preparation for this possible future event indicated that they believed it more likely than did those whose preparation had been relatively minimal. Arrowood and Ross (1966) repeated the study and found that it was not even necessary for the "high effort" subjects to actually work on the preparatory task for them to judge that they would be rather likely to take the test. All that was necessary was for them to expect that they would be working hard.

Evaluation of Goals as a Function of Effort Expenditure

The increased value which is taken on by objects for which an individual has worked hard has been shown in a study by Lewis (1964). Here, first grade boys in a high effort condition had to turn a handle, to which a two-pound brake was attached, 18 times to obtain a colored poker chip. In the low effort condition only three turns of the crank, with no braking force involved, was necessary to obtain a chip. All the boys worked at this task till they had accumulated 20 chips. Then they were faced with a learning task in which chips of the same color as those for which they had worked earlier were used as the positive reinforcement for a correct response. The results here clearly showed that there was a direct relationship between the degree of effort previously associated with getting the chips and their reinforcement value in the later learning situation. Lewis also ran this study with 6th grade boys, but with these older subjects he did not obtain any significant differences. He suggests that this was due to their greater strength and stamina—the supposedly high effort condition really didn't involve any substantial effort for these bigger boys.

Another example employing a very different operationalization of the effort variable, comes from the work of Aronson and Mills (1959), whose subjects were Stanford University coeds taking introductory psychology. At Stanford, students chose which of several studies whose descriptions were posted they would like to participate in to complete a requirement for their psychology course. Some of them chose the Aronson and Mills study, which was described as having to do with informal discussions of sex-related material. Thus, they perceived that they had chosen this study. When the coeds arrived for the study, the experimenter told them that they would have to take a test designed to measure their emotional maturity and ability to actively participate in a frank and open manner in the subsequent group discussions of college sexual behavior. The test consisted of reading aloud to the male experimenter a series of words. The girls were again asked if they wished to continue with the study. For one group of girls, the "initiation" into the discussion group was severe—the words they read were extremely vulgar and included slang terms for sexual acts and portions of the anatomy, so that they were presumably embarrassed in front of the male experimenter; i.e., they underwent an effortful, unpleasant experience in order to participate. For other girls, in a mild initiation condition, the words, while generally related to sex, were quite mild and neutral in tone. These girls suffered little, if at all. And, still other groups were not given any test to get into the group. All of the girls were then informed that they had been admitted to the group and that a meeting was now in progress. They were told that they could listen in on the meeting this time, through headphones, although they would be able to join it at a subsequent meeting. The discussion which they heard was actually a staged and prerecorded one, deliberately designed to be quite dull and uninteresting as it dealt with the physiology of sex in a dry manner. The girls then were asked to indicate how interesting they thought the group discussion had been and how interested they were in participating in future meetings. The groups which had earlier undergone the embarrassing, effortful test or initiation rated it as more interesting than did the other groups.

Gerard and Mathewson (1966) also investigated the influence which suffering or discomfort encountered in the pursuit of some goal may have on the eventual evaluation of that goal. However, their study involved a much improved experimental design which took into account a number of objections and alternative explanations which had been raised in response to the Aronson and

Mills experiment. That is, a number of ways of accounting for their results can be developed. For example, the severe initiation condition, which involved having the girls read some very explicit sex-related words, might have led to a great deal of sexual arousal such that they were very anxious to join the group in order to pursue a discussion of sex; or the obscene material might have intrigued them and led them to anticipate that the groups would eventually settle down to a discussion on this level. A sort of "relief" hypothesis is also possible—perhaps the obscene words made the initiates very anxious and the dull discussion they actually heard put to rest their fears that the discussions would be filthy, so that it was rated as attractive. Or one might propose a "contrast" explanation which would hold that any experience following the highly unpleasant severe initiation would be seen as more pleasant in contrast to it. One last way of accounting for these results espouses a sort of "afterglow" notion. A strong sense of accomplishment might have accompanied being told that one had successfully passed the difficult or severe initiation test and this self-satisfaction and pleasure may have generalized to affect judgments about the overheard group discussion.

The Gerard and Mathewson experiment took these possibilities into account and permitted an assessment of the degree to which they might have contributed to a tendency to overvalue an experience for which one has suffered. Electric shocks, either mild or severe, were used as the "initiation" rather than a "test" whose content was similar to the discussion group topics (which had to do with cheating in college this time) to rule out the "arousal" explanations. Also, to assess the "contrast" and "relief" notions, some subjects were not told that the shocks were part of a test which they had to pass in order to gain group membership. These two explanations would maintain that it would make no difference whether or not the shocks were seen as an initiation procedure. Finally, some subjects who were led to see the shocks as part of an entrance test were not told whether or not they had passed before they rated the attractiveness of the purposefully dull discussion they heard. In this way the "afterglow" hypothesis could be assessed.

The results strongly supported the "suffering leads to liking" explanation only and ruled out each of the alternative explanations discussed above. Thus, the interpretation offered for the original Aronson and Mills data appears to have been the most adequate one, and our confidence in its legitimacy is considerably enhanced by the findings of this subsequent investigation.

Raven and Fishbein (1961) had subjects participate in what they understood to be an investigation of extrasensory perception.

Their task was to indicate when, if ever, a word was flashed on a screen before them, the flashing being accomplished by a person in another room who was attempting to mentally project a list of words. Some subjects were given painful electrical shocks each time they reported that they did not see any message or word at the appropriate time. The female subjects who thus suffered for their belief in the nonexistence of ESP indicated on a post-test that they had come to believe less in its existence than did those who did not undergo shock. These results were not found among the men in the sample, who evidently viewed the study as a test of their masculine ability to withstand pain.

The effects of suffering and hard work extend beyond evaluating more highly something which is worked for in a direct sense. This high evaluation may in addition have the effect of leading the person to evaluate more highly certain aspects of the object or situation other than the immediate goal of the individual. An example of this type of effect comes from a study by Zimbardo (1965) in which subjects read a persuasive message aloud as part "of a study of verbal behavior," while listening to their own voice being played back to them either with a moderately long or a short delay. It is known from other work with delayed auditory feedback that the moderately long delay period used by Zimbardo makes it very difficult to read aloud with any fluency. Persons under these conditions typically find themselves stuttering, hesitating, repeating, and, in general, being unable to smoothly string together series of words. The subjects who were in the moderately long delay condition and who thus found the speech reading task to be difficult and effortful were found to have shifted their opinions toward those espoused in the passage they read more than did the short delay subjects.

Since the schema about the appropriate nature of the relationship of hard work to goal magnitude exists in the abstract, it should not be necessary for a person actually to engage in hard work for this schema to function. All that should be required is that he perceive that he has chosen to commit himself to work at a given level in order for the effects of the schema to manifest themselves. Wicklund, Cooper, and Linder (1967) told subjects that they were to participate, if they chose to, in a study of the relationships between heart rate and recall. They were to run in place while listening to a speech, falsely attributed to Senator Eugene McCarthy, opposing the deferment of college students from the draft (although the Senator's position on this was not known to the researchers). Other students were informed that they would listen to this speech while sitting down. Before they actually started the study, the subjects who expected to run were found to have become more opposed to the deferment of college students than were those who expected to sit—a truly non-intellectual way of changing a person's beliefs! These researchers also found that if persons are asked to give up more time than they expected in order to listen to a political speaker whose position was known, they indicated greater favorability to the position advocated in it than did those who were not asked to give up more time! "I must believe it since I've chosen to inconvenience myself in order to listen to this point of view, (since I wait to hear only things that are worthwhile)."

So far, we have seen how individuals tend to enhance the attractiveness of goals which are associated with hard work, suffering, waiting, or other difficulty, in order to develop appropriate reasons or justification for undergoing these hardships. If, before they start working, suffering, or waiting, they have ample reasons for doing so, they will be less likely to need to find additional ones to enhance the size of the goal to find it more acceptable. Gailon and Watts (1967) told some subjects that they should do some work to prepare for a test they would actually take, while others were told that they had only a fifty-fifty chance of taking the test. The first group had a better reason for the preparatory work and thus did not raise their evaluation of the work as did the fifty-fifty group. Freedman (1963) assigned subjects to a very boring clerical task giving them either a good or a poor reason for doing so. Those who were given the poor reason evaluated the task more positively; they found a good reason—fun. Freedman also found that if he gave the subjects the good or poor reasons *after* they had completed the task, the reverse occurred: the subjects hearing good reasons were more positive about the task than those hearing poor reasons. Subjects had by this time already made a decision to work on the boring task and all had done so for the same, presumably weak, reasons which must have been given by the experimenter. The hearing of the good or poor reasons at the end of the task did not influence their finding of good reasons. If anything, they may have been annoyed at having been duped into working on a poor study, or pleased that they had worked on a good one. These evaluations of the task may have reflected their annoyance or pleasure.

Effort Expenditure as a Function of Perceived
Over- or Underpayment

We have seen the ways in which a schema relating hard work, suffering, and sacrifice to important and real goals influences an individual's evaluations of his own behavioral goals. But we have pointed out on several occasions that this schema is general; like the other schemas subsumed under the H.O.S. of having reasons for actions we choose to take, it applies to other people as well as ourselves. Thus, if one person perceives that another is acting, working, or sacrificing without good reasons, the perceiver will be disturbed. How often have we seen someone working hard for nothing and been troubled by the situation. Sometimes we walk away, but at other times we stay and try to rectify it. One way we can do this is to provide good reasons for the other's sacrifice, work, or suffering, if we cannot stop the sacrifice. One special circumstance in which people can provide good reasons for another's sacrifice is when the other is a provider of desirable things, such as money, or, for children, candy. Suppose that the other's suffering takes the form of giving more desirable things than is reasonable. Then the person in question can provide more reasons for the other's actions by doing something in return. For instance, Adams (1965) reports a study in which children were given from one to six small candies each time they pressed a plunger. The harder they pressed the plunger, the more they got. After they had pressed the plunger a number of times, the experimenter then began to give them 25 candies on each trial, regardless of how hard they pressed. The children reacted by pressing the plunger much harder than they had before. Since the reason the experimenter had been giving them high reward in the first trials was because they had pressed the plunger harder, the children evidently presumed that they could provide more of that reason when he gave them more candies.

This peculiar effect of overpaying people has also been found in adults. Adams (1965) points out that workers who were overpaid for each hour's work worked harder than those who were paid reasonable wages. Some subjects were given a job proofreading, being told that their backgrounds indicated that they were not fully qualified; nevertheless, they would be given the same pay as those who were. These subjects did an exceedingly careful job of proofreading, even finding "mistakes" that were not real mistakes, as compared to other subjects who were told they were qualified and received the proper pay, or to still other subjects who were told they were unqualified and were given lower pay. In another study, people who were hired at a high rate of hourly pay to do interviewing for which they were told they were not fully qualified produced more interviews per hour than people who received the same pay, but were told they were qualified. By working harder, the former gave their employer good reason for having made the sacrifice of hiring them.

On the other hand, a person can bring the situation back into line with the schema by reducing the employer's sacrifice. It would be too much to expect that people will return their wages. However, when a person is paid by the number of units he produces and perceives that he is overpaid for each of the units, he can reduce the employer's sacrifice by producing fewer, but better units (cf. Adams, 1965).

Still another effect of this schema may be more direct. The individual might return money to a partner who has contributed equally to a joint goal, but who has taken less than his share of the proceeds. Leventhal, Allen, and Kemelger (1969) found this to be the case.

However, if a person is in a situation which is inconsistent with this schema, he may choose to devalue the situation. If an individual perceives that his contribution to his job, his sacrifices for it, are in line with what he gets from it, then he will feel satisfied; if they are not, he is likely to feel less satisfied. Notice that this proposition means that a person's degree of satisfaction with his job may not be a matter of how "objectively" well off he is, but how well off he believes he is as viewed in terms of his contribution. During World War II, Stouffer *et al.* (1949) found that soldiers in the Infantry, in which there were few promotions, were more satisfied with the promotion system than were soldiers in the Air Corps, in which promotions were frequent. These results were explained by the tendency of the Air Corps men to expect that they would receive the just compensation of promotion for their efforts, just as others in their outfits had received. The frequent promotion of the others provided the standard for defining what just compensation for their efforts or contributions was. In the Infantry, the infrequent promotions of others provided a lower standard of how much a soldier should receive for his efforts. This phenomenon of the use of other people's progress as a basis for evaluating one's own has been termed "relative deprivation" when the evaluation indicates that the person is worse off than others. The group to which he compares himself is called the "reference group," e.g., the people who have made the same contributions to a job as the person perceives himself to have made.

Patchen (1961) studied workers in a large oil refinery, asking them to which group they compared their wages. Among those who compared themselves to those who made more money, some workers mentioned ways in which the others had contributed more to their jobs, such as in education, seniority, age, skills, responsibility, or having worked harder. These workers were more satisfied with their wages than were those who perceived that they were the equals of those who made more money, with respect to individual contributions to the work. However, comparisons with others are not essential for a person to be upset if his sacrifices and contributions don't match his benefits. Likewise, Adams (1953) found that the morale of an outfit in the Air Force was higher, the greater the consistency among the men's ages, ranks, flying time, education, reputed ability, length of service, combat time, and positional importance. In a national sample survey, Jackson and Burke (1965) found that people whose occupation was inconsistent with their education and the status of their racial-ethnic group reported more symptoms of physiological stress than did those whose occupation was consistent.

These peculiar effects of overpayment may sometimes lead a person to do favors for another so as to place the other under some pressure to "work harder" in return. This process is sometimes accompanied by proclamations of how much of a sacrifice the favor was, so as to increase the pressures. Also, at least some actions which appear to be motivated by gratitude may in fact be an effort to restore the situation to consistency with the schema.

Another way in which the schema about the relationship between effort and goals can influence us is by leading us to overvalue our efforts if we observe that they achieved some goal. "If we achieve an important goal, we must have worked hard for it." Research has not yet been done to demonstrate the way in which we overvalue our own efforts, but Lerner (1965) has shown how this schema affects our perceptions of other people. Subjects were given a chance to listen to two people meet, talk about themselves, and then work on some anagrams. The subject-observers were told that each of the people whom they observed had drawn a number and whichever had drawn the "lucky" number would be paid at the end of the anagram task, while the other fellow would not. The workers were ostensibly not informed about the lucky number until the end of the task, nor were the subjects. After the winner was designated, the subjects judged that he had worked better than had the other person, when, in fact, there had been no difference in the quality of their work.

The schema which suggests that a person's sacrifice and suffering is for a purpose commensurate in value to the degree of sacrifice applies even when work is not involved, even when the sacrifice involved is, for example, simply a matter of giving of a favor, or of money. If another person gives you much money, or if he gives you a considerable portion of his money, you will give him a substantial amount of money in return. Pruitt (1968) showed this in a study in which two subjects were playing a game in which they were given a certain amount of money and could send it to a partner, to whom it would be worth 1.5 times what it was to the sender. Each subject first received money from the other person, with full knowledge of how much the other had. Then the subject sent money from his own resources back in return. It was found that the greater the proportion of his partner's money the subject received, the greater the proportion of his own money he returned to the partner. This was found to be the case even when the amounts received were actually the same. If the partner had sent the person a given proportion of a small amount of money, the person sent him more in return than if he had sent the same proportion of a larger amount of money. In other words, if the other person sacrifices when he has little to begin with, we return more than if he sacrifices the same proportion of larger resources. The fairness of Pruitt's subjects is indeed impressive; let us hope that they were not unique, but representative.

Attitude-Discrepant Behavior

Another schema that is subsumed under the broad schema regarding having adequate reasons for our chosen actions is one which summarizes the belief that a person's public statements are congruent and consistent with their real, private beliefs and opinions. Obviously, we do not tell the truth under all circumstances and some people often do not. But, most of the time, we do not say things that are contrary to our beliefs. Because of the pressures to reduce the probabilism of H.O.S.s we tend to minimize the number of exceptions to this schema, so that persons generally do have this sort of schema. Its effect on the perception of other people is seen in a study by Jones and Harris (1967), in which college students were asked to judge how much a writer of a pro- or anti-Castro essay agreed with what he wrote. In general, the students judged the writer as agreeing. The schema was apparently so strong that when students were asked to judge the true belief of debaters in a formal debate, who had the position they were to espouse and defend arbitrarily chosen for them, they tended to perceive the debaters as agreeing with their debating positions.

Suppose an individual chooses to say something which he does not believe. He might choose to do so because of pressure from other people, such as peers, experimenters, professors, or the offer of monetary or other rewards. But these reasons may not be perceived by him to be so strong and compelling as to provide completely adequate justification for such behavior. However, if the pressure which induces the person to make public statements contrary to his private beliefs is overwhelming, then its very magnitude provides the person with "good reasons" for lying; in that case, he may perceive that he has violated the "truth" schema, but at the same time his actions are consistent with the H.O.S. of having good reasons for actions. The pressure then provides the good reason.

On the other hand, suppose the pressures are just great enough to give the person some reason for speaking against his beliefs, but not so great that they provide good reasons for lying. In that case, the individual is faced with a contradiction to the truth schema as well as to the H.O.S. about having reasons for actions. One way he can resolve this dilemma is to bring his beliefs in line with what he has chosen to say. Raven (1958) led subjects to believe that other members of a group they were in disagreed with their judgments of how to best treat a juvenile delinquent. Some subjects did not shift their publicly stated opinions under this pressure at first, but had an opportunity to do so after writing a short interpretation of the juvenile's case. Some of these subjects did shift toward the group after writing the interpretation. Those who did wrote interpretations—before shifting—which supported the group's position. Apparently, the pressure from the group had led them to decide to shift toward the group, but they felt they could not do so until they had written out some ideas in support of the group. They needed to believe what they said, so they found reasons for changing what they believed.

The Role of Perceived Choice

Suppose a person is given a choice between speaking out against his beliefs and some other negative action which is almost as repugnant to him. Then if he chooses to "lie," he will violate the schema about the congruence between private beliefs and public statements. He can bring his actions into line with the schema by reducing the extent of his lie, by actually coming to believe what he has said. On the other hand, if the individual has no choice of whether or not to make counter-attitudinal statements, then the relevant schema has not been violated. Such action would be consistent with the overall H.O.S. that persons have reasons for their chosen actions. If one is required by superior forces or situational demands to act in a fashion inconsistent with one's actual beliefs or opinions, the force itself and the absence of any opportunity to refuse provide ample and sufficient reasons to justify the action.

Brock (1962) had some non-Catholics write essays on why they would want to be Catholic, but gave them a choice: "If you don't want to write on this topic, you can leave the experiment." Others were simply instructed to write the essays as a requirement of the experiment. The first group tended to become more pro-Catholic than did the second. Davis and Jones (1960) had subjects insult another subject very grossly, but without the latter's being able to see who was insulting him. Some of the insulters were simply instructed to do so because it was part of the study, since the researchers were interested in studying the effects of being insulted. Other subjects were told they could either praise or insult the other subject, but that, for experimental reasons, the researcher would prefer that they choose to make insulting remarks. The subjects given the choice were more likely than those who were not to come to believe the derogatory things they said. However, these subjects did not come to believe their insults if they were told that they would have a chance to tell the person insulted that they really did not mean what they said; this opportunity to speak to the insultee made the insults less of a lie, since they could subsequently "undo" them. Accordingly, the insulters perceived less that they were in violation of the schema, and did not come to believe their lie.

The perception of another person is also influenced by the degree to which the other person is seen as having freely chosen to make some statement. In the Jones and Harris study (1967) mentioned above, some of the subjects were told that the person had written the pro- or anti-Castro essay of his own choice, while others were told that he was instructed to write on one side or the other. The first group saw the essay writer as believing what he wrote more than did the second. This effect was in addition to the findings reported above that just learning that the person had written the essay led to believing that he was "sincere."

A Negative Relationship Between Reward and Attitude Change

At the beginning of our discussion of the schema about telling the truth, we pointed out that if a person has some "compelling" reason for publicly misrepresenting his feelings or ideas, he is less likely to have to shift his beliefs to be consistent with his utterances. His public utterances are then consistent with the H.O.S. of having reasons for chosen actions. One type of strong justification for speaking publicly against one's beliefs is money. If an individual is offered a sufficiently large amount of money to speak or write against his beliefs, the money provides the good reason. Cohen (1962b) asked subjects how much freedom of choice they felt they had if they were given various amounts of money to speak against their beliefs. The subjects reported that they felt they had less freedom of choice when large amounts were offered, i.e., the reason for speaking out against their beliefs was sufficiently strong when the money offered was great that they felt it was a compelling reason. On the other hand, if the amount of money offered is small but nevertheless large enough to get the person to make counter-attitudinal statements, the reasons for doing so are not quite so compelling. The person can then resolve the contradiction to his schema by perceiving that he did tell the truth. In plainer English, people who are induced to lie for a small amount of money are more likely to come to believe their lie than those who are induced to do so by a large amount.

An example of this peculiar relationship comes out of a situation in the late 1950's at Yale University. At that time, when university student bodies were considerably less political and involved in off-camp issues, rather benign and frivolous annual "riots" were a spring tradition in the Ivy League schools. True to form, an occasion for such a spontaneous and unplanned event presented itself on a sunny St. Patrick's Day in New Haven as the parade wound itself directly through Yale's campus. A recent snow coupled with the appearance of the mayor in an open car and city police marching in precise formation proved to be too great a temptation for certain of Yale's finest, and a blizzard of snowballs greeted the entourage. For a variety of reasons—generally strained "town-gown" relationships, the especial significance of the day and this event for the Catholic members of the police force, and the fact that many of the snowballs had somehow turned to iceballs by the time they were thrown—the reception provided by the students was not taken in the lighthearted vein in which it was given. The police stoically maintained their ranks through the melee around them, but once out of the campus area they regrouped and returned to dole out retribution for the insults administered to them. Numerous arrests were made, many backsides were bruised by truncheons, and, in general, the Yale population was shocked and outraged by the ungentlemanly treatment afforded them by New Haven's finest. Subsequent editorials in the student newspaper deplored the alleged brutality and indiscriminate violence of the police, and campus opinion held that it was the police, not the students, who had rioted. Taking advantage of this situation, Cohen (1962a) had his graduate student assistants approach students in their dormitories with a request to assist them in gathering a variety of opinions regarding the police action. It was explained that no trouble had been encountered in eliciting anti-police statements, but that the experimenters also had a need for essays which would present strong and persuasive arguments sympathetic to the police position. In consequence, the experimenters were willing to pay for such essays. Four incentive conditions were used—50¢, $1, $5, and $10. After writing the essays, the subjects were given an opportunity to indicate their actual opinions on the matter, and it was found that there was an inverse relationship between the amount of money paid for the counter-attitudinal, pro-police essay and the respondent's ultimate favorability to the pro-police position. From our point of view, advocating a position antithetical to one's true attitude is schema-discrepant behavior and is thus anxiety arousing or noxious. To avoid such an unpleasant state of affairs, one of the options open to the person is to alter his private opinion to bring it into line with his public utterances. To the extent that the Yale students' came to accept as their own the pro police position they took, there was nothing discrepant or inconsistent about their behavior. But also, the more sufficient and compelling the initial reasons for engaging in the counter-attitudinal activity, the less this behavior would be schema-discrepant and thus the lower would be the necessity to justify it by coming to privately accept the public statements made.

The same "reverse" effect of money was found by Festinger and Carlsmith (1959), who first had their subjects work for about an hour on a quite boring clerical task. Then the subjects were asked to stand in for an absent experimenter who was to tell the next subject to come to participate in the study that the task was quite interesting. The subjects were offered either $1 or $20 to do so, with an additional explanation in the latter case that the money was given with the understanding that they might be called again if the experimenter was absent again. After the subjects had misinformed the next "subject" (actually a trained assistant), the subjects were asked by a non-experimenter representative of the psychology department to evaluate the task. The subjects who had been paid $1 thought more highly of it than those paid $20. In fact the $20 group had about the same negative opinion of the task as a group of subjects who had worked on it but had not misrepresented it. Again, for reasons that will be presented below, the reader should note that the task of lying here was not very elaborate or complex, so that the $1 and $20 groups did not differ in the "quality" of their performances as liars. This study was essentially repeated by Carlsmith, Collins, and Helmreich (1966) with the same results, indicating the absence of any effect of the amount of money on the performances in the lying situation.

If another person misrepresents the truth about something for a small amount of money, we also tend to perceive that he now believes what he is saying. "Since he is saying that for so little incentive, he must believe what he says; that is the only reason he could have for saying that!" Bem (1965) gave his subjects a detailed description of the procedures and the circumstances in the Cohen (1962a) study about Yale University students writing the essays in favor of the New Haven police for the varying amounts of money. He then asked them to estimate precisely how the participants in that study felt about the police at the end of the study. Essentially, then, this question asked the subjects to predict the results of the Cohen study, since the primary dependent variable used in it was ultimate attitude toward the police. Bem's subjects did, in fact, accurately predict that the Yale students who wrote for 50¢ were actually more favorably disposed toward the police after writing the essay than were those who wrote the essay for $10. Bem similarly told students about the Festinger and Carlsmith (1959) study in which the subjects described a boring task to another person as having been interesting for either \$1 or \$20; again the students predicted the results accurately. The effects of the schema about telling the truth are thus general; both with respect to ourselves and other people: if a "lie" is told for little incentive, we believe that the person has come to believe his lie. In that way the schema can be maintained.

Importance of the Timing of the Offered Reward

The reader should note that in the studies described above an important point was that the subjects made their choice of whether to write the attitude-discrepant essays or make the utterances with full knowledge of how much money they would make by so doing. The amount of money involved entered into their choice and, as we have argued, could then play a role as a more or less adequate justification for the decision to behave in a manner inconsistent with their private beliefs. In this way it could have an effect on their beliefs. However, if a person learns that he will receive a reward of money, or of approval, only *after* he has already made his decision and is committed to the counter-attitudinal activity, then the effects of the reward would not be expected to have the above described result of leading the person to believe his statements (cf. Scott, 1957; Wallace, 1966).

Conditions Yielding a Positive Relationship Between Reward and Attitude Change

A situation in which an individual is offered money to decide to make statements against his beliefs has to be distinguished also from one in which the giving of a monetary reward is perceived to be something the donor chose to do independently of the person's decision to make a statement against his beliefs. The latter condition, then, is one in which the person is given a large or a small amount of money to do something which he had already decided to do. In this case, the individual will apply the schema that people sacrifice only for some goal to his perception of the other person. Thus, if the donor is giving the person a large amount of money, the person can keep the situation consistent with his schema by giving him a large amount of "return for his money." Examples of this phenomenon were given earlier, in the studies of children pushing plungers harder and of adults working harder when they were paid more, even when their excess effort would have no effect on their pay. Likewise, a person who has been paid a large amount to make statements against his beliefs can keep the situation consistent with this schema by making more or better statements against his position. Rosenberg (1965) had subjects arrive at his office to participate in a study, but told them that his research was running somewhat behind schedule. He then suggested that the subject might wish to participate in a study being done in another department, since he understood that the researcher was paying persons for their participation and that it wouldn't take much time. In this other researcher's office, the subjects were offered 50¢, $1, or $5 for writing essays on why their university (Ohio State) football team should not go to the Rose Bowl even though it had just won the Big Ten championship. (This issue was a very real one on the campus, since the faculty had incurred a great deal of animosity from the students by voting not to go to the Rose Bowl when they won the championship. The student body was strongly in favor of their team's being permitted to play in the Bowl game.) The students returned to Rosenberg's office after writing the counter-attitudinal essays and were given a fairly long questionnaire to fill out. Among the many items were a few critical ones which assessed their attitudes toward Ohio State's participation in the Rose Bowl. The results indicated that the more money students had been paid, the longer and more persuasive were their essays. Further, the more they had been paid to write against going to the Rose Bowl, the less favorable they were to having the team participate.

Rosenberg's primary reason for developing this particular experimental design was to deal with a criticism he makes of several earlier studies dealing with the relationship between the amount of money offered for counter-attitudinal behavior and attitude change. He argues that subjects may experience "evaluation apprehension," a feeling that their normalcy, adjustment, or adequacy is being evaluated in psychological experiments. Thus, if they are offered very large amounts of money he feels they may become suspicious, may believe that they are being bribed to change their opinions and will thus wish to show that they aren't the sort of person whose integrity can be so easily bought. In consequence, they change their opinions less in the direction of the attitude-discrepant essays or statements they have made the more they have been paid. His design, which physically, and presumably psychologically, separated the attitude measurement from the essay-writing activities, was intended to eliminate such suspiciousness.

One important effect of this high production of statements which results from high payment is that the statements may convince the individual himself. He obviously uses arguments which he thinks are good; they obviously must have some consistency with his own set of schemas about the issue in question. Thus, the more statements he makes, the more likely he is to come to change his attitudes. In the Rosenberg (1965) study mentioned above, the longer the essays the subjects wrote against having OSU go to the Rose Bowl, the less they believed it should. Rosenberg (1966) also reports that in a study by Carlsmith, Collins, and Helmreich (1966), the better essays a subject wrote describing a boring task as being fun, the more he later gave indications of feeling that he really enjoyed the task. These findings are, of course, open to the interpretation that the subjects who wrote the longer essays were those who were, to begin with, less strong in their opposition to the statements. However, the feelings about football were very strong at OSU and the task was a very boring one indeed; it is unlikely that many subjects had really been equivocating about their stands before going into the experiment. Furthermore, it would be a surprising world indeed in which we were uninfluenced at all by arguments, especially our own!

This discussion of the effects of increased rewards leans heavily on so-called incentive theory. The term "incentive" would suggest that the money is an incentive to greater production. However, the procedure in the relevant studies does not involve telling the subjects that the harder he works, the more he will be paid. Therefore, incentive theory does not clearly indicate why the individual produces more when paid more.

Since the giving of more money under certain conditions leads to more production, which in turn leads to greater change of our attitudes, then the more money that a person is given for producing argumentative statements, the more he should change his beliefs toward his statements. This conclusion sounds at first to be quite contrary to the data discussed earlier which indicated that a low amount of money led to more change. The solution to this puzzle apparently is that in the first set of studies, the subjects were making choices to participate in counter-attitudinal activity on the basis of the amounts of money offered, and thus it could figure as sufficient or insufficient justification for their decision. In the Rosenberg study, they had committed themselves to the schema-discrepant behavior before they learned of the money which would be involved. The money's impact was thus manifested more in terms of its influence on the number and quality of the arguments produced than as a reason for their initial decision to agree to engage in attitude-discrepancy activity. That is, the payment when given after agreement to participate is most relevant to the schema which indicates that others should be compensated in accord with the degree of their sacrifice or effort. The relevant cognitions might then be, "He paid me a great deal to do something I'd already decided to do. It's only fair that I do the very best job I can in making up these arguments."

Situational Determinants of the Attitude Change-Reward Relationship

In the studies of the effects of the size of a donor's "gift" to the subjects, it was generally possible and likely that the subjects could vary the number and quality of arguments in their statements. However, in some situations this variation might not be quite so possible. If the length of time available for writing the arguments is too short, the subjects may simply not be able to produce more arguments or better ones that demand time to formulate. Thus, Rosenberg (1968) found that if the subjects were given only 50 seconds to write arguments, those who received more money did not differ significantly in their production from those who received less. However, if the subjects were given 2½ minutes in the same study, the greater the amount of money given, the more and better arguments they produced and the more they thereby convinced themselves.

Rosenberg (1968) interprets his study by assuming that the subjects had free choice to participate or not. However, the extent of their freedom of choice is not made clear because the "pitch" used to "recruit" the subjects is not reported. Furthermore, Rosenberg reports that the results are not changed by including in the sample of subjects those who did not report after the study that they perceived that they had high choice. Furthermore, in the short time condition, the absence of any significant difference in either argument production or change of belief between those who were paid much and those paid little is inconsistent with the results cited above for situations with high perceived choice. In short, Rosenberg himself has given us reason for presuming that the amount of choice was fairly limited in his study.

Besides lack of time, another factor which might limit the effect of size of payment on argument production is that there may be only a limited number of arguments that can be made. How many arguments can be made to support the position that sugar tastes good? Or, the subjects may be so familiar with the arguments on the "other side" that they all can very easily reel them off. There is no great benefit to the donor to hear the hackneyed arguments again. Or, the donor may not indicate that more or better arguments are what he is looking for. Instead, he might just ask the subjects to produce some arguments.

In situations such as these, the person who has received a large sum from a donor will have to find some other way to compensate him for his sacrifice. One way is to perceive that the arguments and statements made are quite valuable; "You're getting your money's worth; aren't these good statements!" As a consequence of this exaggeration of the value of the arguments, the individual might convince himself that there might be some truth to the arguments he is making and come to believe them more. Rosenberg (1965, 1968) compared those subjects who wrote long essays against OSU's Rose Bowl participation for $5 to those who wrote equally long ones for $1, and found that the former group changed their opinions more toward the statement they made. Elms and Janis (1965) found that when the donor was a legitimate, favorably evaluated agency in the eyes of the writers, the more the agency paid for attitude-discrepant essays the more the subjects agreed with what they were writing, even though they did not in this study write more for the high paying donor. (This absence of effect of money on length of essay is probably due to some of the factors mentioned in the previous paragraph.) In both the Rosenberg study and the Elms and Janis study, the amounts of money given for the statements became known to the subjects some time after they had decided to, and had begun to, participate in the study, and thus were not involved in the subjects' choices—the money was a "donation." However, the same effect of high payment can result if a person is not given very much choice as to whether to write the statements or not. A researcher may strongly indicate that he expects the person to participate regardless of the amount of money involved. Thus, in a study by Carlsmith, Collins, and Helmreich (1966), the experimenter gave some quite plausible reasons why he needed the subject to write some ways of describing a boring task as interesting: "At this point the director seated himself beside the subject, stated that he had a problem and that the subject might be able to help. He remarked that, as the experimenter described, some subjects in other conditions read an essay describing the task as fun, interesting, exciting, and enjoyable. But he further commented that the experimenters were unhappy with this essay. The director felt that the essays were unsatisfactory because they did not sound like they had been written by high school students and that they did not have the perspective of someone who had taken the experiment. The experimenters had decided to write a new description of the task and felt that the best way to proceed would be to ask a few of the subjects to write positive descriptions of the task. He emphasized that no other subjects would read these essays because he would merely use them as sources of phrases and ideas for an essay which he, the director, would write. He then added that, since they were 'in a bind,' he could pay the subject 50¢ ($1.50, $5) to write a 5- or 10-minute description of the task (p. 7)." As a consequence, the $5 subjects were found later to agree more that the task was in fact interesting and fun than were the $1 subjects.

The importance of the subject's perception of whether he or the donor is making the choice is most clearly demonstrated in a study by Linder, Cooper, and Jones (1967). They repeated the Rosenberg type of study, but before some of the subjects went to the "other researcher" they were told, "You can participate in the other fellow's research or not." Other subjects were simply instructed to go. Among the latter subjects, the more the other researcher paid them, the more they believed what they wrote, even though the money did not influence the size or content of the essays. Among the free choice subjects, however, the opposite relationship between magnitude of monetary incentive and attitude change was found: the more they were paid, the less they came to accept the position they took in their essay—again with no influence in the length or content of the essays.

SCHEMAS INVOLVING MORAL AND JUST BEHAVIOR

The last schema whose influence we will examine in this chapter is one which suggests that one does not choose to do what is considered to be morally wrong and one does choose to do what is adjudged by society to be right and just. Earlier in the chapter we examined some of the reasons why people acquire this schema, despite the obvious fact that there are many people who do wrong and do not do right. Now let us see how this schema influences people's perceptions and actions.

Suppose an individual is given a choice between walking out of an experimental study or administering shock to another person when he makes errors while learning a task. Brock and Buss (1964) gave some subjects this choice, finding that most all chose shock. Other subjects were not given a choice, but were simply instructed to administer the shock. The level of shock that the subjects administered was either quite painful or mild. Then the subjects who had been giving the shocks were asked to evaluate the severity of a shock now administered to them. The subjects who had been given the choice evaluated the shock as less severe, especially if they themselves had administered painful shock. They were restoring the situation to consistency with the schema by simply minimizing the strength of the shock. If they had not been given a choice, no such minimization took place.

The Evaluation of Others in Light of the Morality Schema

Reducing the intensity of the perceived pain inflicted on another is not the only way that a person can restore a situation to consistency with the schema. The individual might perceive that the other person deserved the shock; in the Brock and Buss study, the subject might have perceived the other as being deliberately non-cooperative. Inflicting pain might then not be quite so wrong. Lerner and Matthews (1967) showed this process. Their subjects came to the laboratory two at a time and were told that they would each be in either a painful or nonpainful part of the study. The subjects determined which conditions they would be in by drawing lots from a bowl. Some subjects were told that they were drawing before their partners, and whichever condition they happened to draw, their partner would get the opposite one; i.e., they were responsible for their partner's fate. Needless to say, all of the subjects "happened" to draw the slip indicating no pain for themselves and, therefore, pain for the other. A second group of subjects was told that the other subject had drawn first and that they would be in the nonpainful and the other subject would be in the painful condition. A third group were told that each subject determined his own fate in the study independently of the other. They would simply get what they drew; again, they all drew the nonpainful condition. All the subjects then gave their first impressions of the other person. The subjects in the first group, who felt responsible for the other's painful fate, described the other more negatively than in the last conditions in which their fates were independent. "Since I chose to give her pain, she must be deserving of it." The subject whose fate was decided positively by the other felt she was a relatively attractive person. Minimization of the pain inflicted on the other and justifying it are not the only ways that a person can restore a situation to consistency with the schema. He can try publicly to give reasons for his wrongdoing, or try to compensate the other (Berscheid and Walster, 1967; Walster and Prestholdt, 1966).

The perception of other people's actions is also influenced by this schema. Suppose we see that a person who appears to be normal and old enough to make knowledgeable choices inflicts pain on another person. This apparent violation of the schema can be rectified by perceiving that the victum deserved what he was getting. Lerner and Simmons (1966) had subjects observe a "Dr. Stuart" do a study in which pain was inflicted on another subject (although, in fact, no pain was inflicted). Subjects who were asked to evaluate the action at the midpoint in the study were more negative toward the victim than those who thought the study was over. The first group was anticipating more violation of the schema, and therefore was more motivated to attempt to reduce the degree of violation by saying that the victim deserved her fate. The implications of this study are obviously quite frightening: a human tendency to justify pain-giving if it is done by a responsible person. Perhaps in some cases there is justification, but certainly not in all.

The process of finding reasons for having made difficult choices also occurs with regard to the schema about moral action, just as it has been found to occur for all the other schemas we have been examining. After an individual has made a difficult choice between an ethical act and a non-ethical one and has chosen the former, he still may perceive that he does not have very good reason for his having made the choice, since the non-ethical action might have gained him considerable rewards. One way out of this contradiction to the schema about good reason for chosen actions is for the individual to increase his perception of the degree of immorality of the rejected alternative. Mills (1958) measured the attitudes of sixth grade students toward cheating before and after participating in a contest. The contest was so arranged that the students had an opportunity to cheat, but for some the stakes in the contest were higher than for others. When the temptation to cheat was great because the stakes were high, the students who did not cheat became more severe in their moral condemnation of cheating. On the other hand, students who did cheat became less severe in their condemnation of cheating, especially if the stakes were low. Since there was less good reason for cheating in the latter case, the subjects had to find good reasons for their choice by reducing the condemnation of cheating.

THE SCHEMA APPROACH AND THE THEORY OF COGNITIVE DISSONANCE

Most of the studies we have cited in the last half of this chapter were actually performed to test predictions derived from Leon Festinger's theory of cognitive dissonance (Festinger, 1957; 1964). The basic concept of importance to this theory is the cognitive element which is defined as things which one might know about anything: "The sky is blue; I just ate a cracker; he just told a lie; water flows downhill." When cognitive elements are seen as relevant to one another by someone who holds them, they can have one of two relationships with one another: they can be consonant or dissonant: They are consonant when they are consistent, when one follows from the other, when one implies the other. "I just stepped on a sharp object. I feel pain in my foot." They are dissonant when the opposite of one of them follows from the other, when they are inconsistent. "I found Smith to be a boring person. I just told Jones that Smith was a fascinating individual." The theory does not spell out the specific meaning of the critical phrase "follows from" as completely as we might like, but it is clear that more is involved than purely logical consistency or inconsistency. Festinger (1957) states that, in addition to logic, cultural mores, past experience, and very general cognitions may form a basis for the development of the inconsistency or consistency which is involved. Aronson (1966) has suggested that it may be most useful to think of dissonance as involving the violation of an expectation. For instance, take the cognitions "The sky is completely blue and cloudless; I feel many raindrops on my head." These two elements are obviously dissonant. If the sky is clear, I do not expect to feel rain. Rain does not "follow from" my observation of clear skies.

Given a set of relevant cognitive elements, the total dissonance in that set is a function of the ratio between the total number of elements and the number which are dissonant where each cognitive element is multiplied by the importance the individual attaches to it. The more of the latter, the greater the total dissonance. The greater the total dissonance, the more the individual experiences a state of tension and discomfort. The individual is motivated to reduce tension by reducing the dissonance involved. He can do this by increasing the number of consonant elements or by reducing the number of dissonant elements. For example, it is dissonant for an individual to choose to eat bitter food. If for some reason he does choose to do so, he can reduce dissonance by judging the food not to be bitter (eliminating a dissonant cognition) or by developing good reasons, strong justification, for having eaten it (adding elements consistent with his behavior).

In the present chapter, we have cited many studies which we have interpreted in terms of the individual's seeking to find "good reasons" for his actions. These studies, for the most part, were originally seen as involving dissonance reduction because of the individual's having only poor and insufficient reasons for his actions. The poor reasons are dissonant with his actions. Another parallel between dissonance theory and the present schema approach involves the distinction made in the more recent version of dissonance theory between the nature of actions made before and after decisions are made (Festinger, 1964). Dissonance theory, as do we, postulates that people seek information in a balanced and unbiased fashion before making a choice, but seek to bolster their reasons for having made a choice after it once has been made. The present approach is also consistent with the refinements of dissonance theory suggested by Brehm and Cohen (1962), who emphasized the importance of perceived choice or volition and commitment to a decision as necessary conditions for the development of a state of dissonance. The schema interpretation of what is "consonant" is quite compatible with the Aronson and Carlsmith (1962) and Aronson (1968) definition of consonance as resulting from the occurrence of the expected and of dissonance as resulting from the occurrence of the unexpected.

Thus, there is a very general correspondence and compatibility between this elegantly simple and most stimulating theoretical position and our own. The many ingenious and skillfully executed experiments conducted by persons intrigued by dissonance theory have been of invaluable assistance in sharpening and refining the principles we have attempted to establish in the schema approach. Of course, we feel that the present system has certain advantages, else there would be little point in developing a schema analysis of these investigations. Let us then examine some of the differences between the two—differences which do not imply that dissonance theory is invalid in any sense, but which rather suggest that the schema position is broader in the scope of behaviors and situations to which it may legitimately be applied and also, at times, better able to specify the critical causal elements in a given situation. First, the schema approach indicates what cognitive elements an individual might have, while dissonance theory does not delve into the problem of what determines what certain cognitive elements an individual has. The chapter in the present volume concerned with attention and cognitive learning gives a basis for predicting what "elements" a person might have.

Second, dissonance theory does not indicate clearly what relevance between elements consists of. The schema approach implicitly defines the relevance of cognitive elements as involving their being part of the same schema.

The schema approach indicates what "dissonance" consists of: a violation of a schema. Dissonance theory has had a difficult time defining dissonance with great specificity. This is partly because it has defined dissonance at one point by using such almost synonymous terms as failure to follow from, opposite, and obverse, which do not really clarify the issue. The use of synonyms to define a term in science is not in itself an unacceptable procedure. However, to use this procedure, the synonyms should clarify the meaning of a term by communicating clearly; such clear communication can occur only if there already is an understanding common to the author of a theory and his audience of the meaning of the set of synonymous terms. This has not been found to be the case for "dissonance." When such lack of common understanding occurs, the usual solution in science is to translate the term into a combination of other, more so-called "primitive" terms which are in fact understood in a common way by the author and the audience. Thus, dissonance could, for example, be defined as a "violation of expectations" (Aronson, 1968), if "violation" and "expectations" are commonly understood terms. Dissonance theory, in its classic presentation, was not clearly translated into such a combination of primitive terms.

Festinger did make some attempt to define dissonance by pointing to various types of cases in which it could occur. One type was logical inconsistency, in which a person simply perceives that two of his beliefs are logically incompatible. However, if we assume that knowledge of what constitutes an illogical belief is learned, then this type of dissonance situation is simply a special type of situation in which higher order schemas about logicality are violated. Festinger also describes a type of dissonance in which an individual perceives a contradiction between behavior expected by society and the actions of a given person. Obviously, the individual's perception of the contradiction depends on his having learned what behavior is expected. In short, even Festinger's own examples of dissonance are translatable into learning, and therefore into terms of schema theory.

The schema approach does not require that the motivation to reduce dissonance stand in isolation from other areas of concern in psychology and from other types of motives. Dissonance theory simply asserts that people are motivated to reduce dissonance, just as they reduce thirst and pain.

Dissonance theory is ambiguous as to whether the individual is motivated to reduce inconsistency whenever it exists. The question of whether an inconsistency must be consciously perceived and felt before an individual will act to reduce it isn't directly faced. The schema approach would maintain that the individual is so motivated only if a schema is aroused and a contradiction to it is perceived.

Dissonance theory does not indicate the conditions under which an individual will seek out inconsistency, such as when he seeks change, surprise, contradictions, unexpected circumstances. For example, magicians' shows are full of apparent inconsistency, yet people seek them out and find them pleasant. Persons often enjoy surprise; we often seek change and novelty. We have already indicated in previous chapters some of the conditions under which the person will seek the new, the different, the little understood. We shall indicate other reasons in subsequent chapters.

And finally, dissonance theory, while recognizing the existence of individual differences with respect to cognitive elements, relevance, dissonance, motivation to reduce dissonance, etc., does not have a systematic way of dealing with these differences. Since schemas are learned and since learning experiences differ among people, the schema approach can systematically treat these differences. We have not done so in this chapter, partly because there is little relevant research data, partly because whatever data there is on individual differences in schema acquisition is best treated in a later chapter.

BEYOND DECISION AND ACTION—THE EFFECTS OF SELF-RELEVANT SCHEMAS

The main theme of this chapter is that the individual develops schemas about the way he acts, the way he makes his choices about how to act, and the effects that these schemas have. Needless to say, schemas having to do with choices and actions are not the only ones which the individual can develop about himself. He can develop schemas about other aspects of his own experience. And these schemas can also have effects like those having to do with choosing and acting. Let us finally examine some of these schemas.

Suppose an individual expresses a given opinion, attitude, or belief a large number of times, either to other people or to himself as he thinks about the opinion and related matters. A person might do this during an election campaign, as he expresses his opinion about the candidates, reads about them, watches them on TV. Or, he might have a series of arguments with someone about the relative merits of two baseball teams. In such cases an individual will come to acquire a schema to the effect that he has a given opinion or attitude. He comes to think of himself as being a person who holds thus and such opinions. As in the case of other schemas, the individual will tend to bring or keep his subsequent actions in line with it. This effect is illustrated in a part of a study by Deutsch and Gerard (1955), which will be described in more detail in a later chapter. In it, subjects in groups were presented with the problem of making judgments of the relative length of curved lines. Some of the subjects were instructed to record their private judgments on a "magic pad" before they learned of the judgments made by the other group members. (A "magic pad" is one on which everything written can be immediately and permanently erased by simply raising a plastic cover. Thus, the subjects' recordings of their judgments were not known even to the experimenter.) Subsequently, the subjects learned of the judgments of other group members, which were, on some trials, made to appear quite discrepant from the actual relative lengths of the lines. The subjects then were required to announce their own judgments to the other group members. If a subject had recorded his private judgment on the magic pad, he was less likely to be influenced to conform to the erroneous judgments of his peers than if he had not gone through this procedure. Writing his private judgment on the pad was seemingly effective in encouraging the subject to develop low order schemas, "My judgment is 'A' is the longer line"; since he had to write his judgment down, he had to formulate a judgment in advance of hearing the others', and then had before him the visible representation of that schema.

Sherif (Sherif and Cantril, 1947; Sherif and Hovland, 1961; Sherif, Sherif, and Nebergall, 1965) has described a special relationship, called ego-involvement, that sometimes occurs with respect to a person's attitudes and beliefs. With ego-involvement, a person knows that he holds certain attitudes and beliefs and also believes that they are related to his self-esteem, his evaluation of himself.

A person might value himself highly because he holds given attitudes, or value a given attitude highly because it is his. This latter evaluation of the attitude is a likely outcome when the attitudes are controversial, when the person has had to defend his positions against attack in arguments. In such cases the individual would be even more prone to resist changing his attitudes than in the

Deutsch and Gerard study. (The whole problem of self-esteem will be treated fully in Chapters 10 and 11.)

Another type of schema, closely allied if not overlapping with the ego-involved ones which we have just discussed, stems from an individual's membership in certain groups. An individual may, for example, have a schema that he is a member of a certain religious group. Part of this schema may involve an adherence to certain beliefs. Thus, when this schema is aroused, the individual will indicate that he adheres to these beliefs; when this schema is not aroused, he will be less likely to adhere to these beliefs. Charters and Newcomb (1958) assembled some college students in groups according to their religious affiliation: Protestants, Catholics, Jews and others were assembled in "mixed" groups. When students were in groups with their co-religionists, the experimenter gave an introduction to the research which indicated to the subjects that they were all of the same religion. Nothing regarding religion was mentioned in mixed groups. All of the subjects, in all four types of groups, were then given questionnaires to measure attitudes which were related to their groups. For instance, birth control and Catholicism. It was found that students, especially Catholics, were much more orthodox in their attitudes in the co-religionist groups, in which their religious schemas had been aroused, than in the mixed groups. Kelley (1955) similarly found that when Catholics were reminded that they were Catholics, they were much more resistant to anti-Catholic messages.

At a completely different level of concern is a study by Valins (1966) in which he capitalized on the fact that most college students have a schema that when they are emotionally aroused by something they like, their heart rate will change. If they perceive that their rate is changing while they are looking at something, they will conclude that they like this "something" quite a bit. Valins presented 10 slides of semi-nude females to male college students while hearing sounds which were supposed to be their heartbeats. For five of the slides, the "heart rate" did not change. For the other five, heart rates increased for half the subjects and decreased for the other half. The subjects rated the slides for which there was a change in heart rate, either up or down, as much more desirable than the non-change slides; this difference was obtained immediately after viewing and in a disguised interview conducted four to five weeks later. Also, when given a chance to take some of the pictures with them, the subjects chose the "change" pictures.

The same sort of process also occurs with respect to negative reaction. If an individual perceives that he is physiologically aroused in a way that suggests negative affect, then he assumes that there must be something he doesn't like or is afraid of. Bramel,

Bell, and Margulis (1965) told subjects that they would be able to observe their own states of fear, as physiologically manifested, by reading a galvanometer which was attached to their skin. Some subjects were then shown slides of scenes of Russia and slides of a horse and a landscape. Others were shown movies of Russia and some neutral material. Some of the subjects were led to believe that they were highly fearful while watching the Russian material. On a pretest, other subjects were not given any information about their physiological state while the Russian material was being presented. Then the subjects were given a questionnaire about their attitudes toward Russia. The subjects who learned that they were fearful of the Russian material increased their rating of the danger of Russia to the United States over their ratings prior to the experiment.

Most subjects come to the psychological laboratory expecting that they will be tired at the completion of the research session; that is, they have a schema to this effect. Thus, to be consistent with this schema, they would have to be fatigued at the end of the session. Walster and Aronson (1967) told subjects that they were to participate in a study of the relationship between visual thresholds and eye fatigue. After a long period of adaptation to the dark, some subjects were told they would be given three tasks to measure visual thresholds, others that they would be given five tasks. At the completion of three tedious or difficult tasks, the three task subjects reported that they felt much more tired than the five task subjects, who expected two more tasks.

One of the most striking examples of the way that a schema about one's own behavior and feelings can influence a person comes from the work of Bem (1966). He created the schemas in the laboratory, in contrast to the researchers just cited, who capitalized on schemas the subjects brought with them to the laboratory. The study was a relatively complicated one involving several subparts. In general, it involved first having subjects engage in some specific activity (crossing out certain specified words in a longer list of words), the details of which they would later be asked to recall. Then, in a separate part of the experiment, an association was built up between certain distinctive external stimuli (a red or a green light) and truthtelling or lying. Next the participants were instructed to make either correct or false statements about the activity they had engaged in during the very first part of the study (they lied or told the truth about which of the words they had crossed out). And, although their attention was now not explicitly directed toward them, the "lie" and "truth" cues which had earlier been built up were present at this time. Thus, any effect which these truth-telling or lying cues had on the subjects could be assessed by finally asking them to recall the specific nature of those initial responses (to indicate which of the words they had actually crossed out). In this ingenious and complicated study, then, Bem could determine, for example, whether lying in the presence of cues which have in the past been associated with telling the truth makes one more likely to believe that lie. And this is precisely what the resultant data indicated.

Bem goes on to speculate about some of the intriguing implications of this finding with regard to the issue of inducing belief in false confessions. If one is willing to generalize far beyond the confines of the laboratory setting in which the data were initially gathered, it can be seen that a variety of cues present in many interrogations are ones which are, for most persons, at least, associated with truth telling. A police station, uniformed officials, recording of one's statements, and so forth, are likely to be stimuli which our experience and schemas indicate are tied up with truthfulness. Thus, a determined and skillful interrogator who could confuse or undermine our initial recollection of some set of circumstances might be in a position to lead us to believe the responses he elicits from us in such a setting. Whether these extensions of the initial finding are correct or not, the study does establish the principle that a schema relating certain typical behaviors and the settings in which they typically occur can dramatically influence our perception and recollection of past actions.

References

Adams, J. S.: Inequity in social exchange. In L. Berkowitz (Ed.), *Advances in Experimental Social Psychology*, Vol. 2. New York, Academic Press, 1965.

Adams, S.: Status congruency as a variable in small group performance. *Social Forces*, 1953, 32:16–21.

Allen, V.: Uncertainty of outcome and post-decision dissonance reduction. In L. Festinger (Ed.), *Conflict, Decision, and Dissonance*. Stanford, Stanford University Press, 1964.

Aronson, E.: The psychology of insufficient justification: An analysis of some conflicting data. In S. Feldman (Ed.), *Cognitive Consistency*. New York, Academic Press, 1966.

Aronson, E.: Expectancy vs. other motives. In R. Abelson et al. (Eds.), *Theories of Cognitive Consistency*. Chicago, Rand McNally, 1968.

Aronson, E., and Carlsmith, J. M.: Performance expectancy as a determinant of actual performance. *Journal of Abnormal and Social Psychology*, 1962, 65:178–182.

Aronson, E., and Carlsmith, J. M.: Effect of the severity of threat on the devaluation of forbidden behavior. *Journal of Abnormal and Social Psychology*, 1963, 66:584–588.

Aronson, E., and Mills, J.: The effect of severity of initiation on liking for a group. *Journal of Abnormal and Social Psychology*, 1959, 59:177–181.

Arrowood, A. J., and Ross, L.: Anticipated effort and subjective probability. *Journal of Personality and Social Psychology*, 1966, 4:57–64.

Asch, S.: *Social Psychology*. Englewood Cliffs, New Jersey, Prentice-Hall, 1952.

Atkinson, J.: *An Introduction to Motivation*. New York, Van Nostrand, 1964.

Bandura, A., Ross, D., and Ross, S. A.: Vicarious reinforcement and imitative learning. *Journal of Abnormal and Social Psychology*, 1963, 67:601–607.

Bechtel, R. B., and Rosenfeld, H. M.: Expectations of social acceptance and compatibility as related to status discrepancy and social motives. *Journal of Personality and Social Psychology*, 1966, 3:344–349.

Bem, D. J.: An experimental analysis of self-persuasion. *Journal of Experimental Social Psychology*, 1965, 1:199–218.

Bem, D. J.: Inducing belief in false confessions. *Journal of Personality and Social Psychology*, 1966, 3:707–710.

Bem, D. J.: Self-perception: An alternative interpretation of cognitive dissonance phenomena. *Psychological Review*, 1967, 74:183–200.

Benoit-Smullyan, E.: Status, status types, and status inter-relationships. *American Sociological Review*, 1944, 9:151–161.

Berkowitz, L.: Effects of perceived dependency relationships upon conformity to group expectations. *Journal of Abnormal and Social Psychology*, 1957, 55:350–355.

Berkowitz, L., and Daniels, L. R.: Responsibility and dependency. *Journal of Abnormal and Social Psychology*, 1963, 66:429–436.

Berkowitz, L., and Daniels, L. R.: Affecting the salience of social responsibility norm: effect of past help on the response to dependency relations. *Journal of Abnormal and Social Psychology*, 1964, 68:275–281.

Berscheid, E., and Walster, E.: When does a harm-doer compensate a victim? *Journal of Personality and Social Psychology*, 1967, 6:435–441.

Bettelheim, B.: Individual and mass behavior in extreme situations. *Journal of Abnormal and Social Psychology*, 1943, 38:417–452.

Bixenstine, V. E., and Wilson, K. V.: Effects of level of cooperative choice by the other player on choices in a prisoner's dilemma game. Part II. *Journal of Abnormal and Social Psychology*, 1963, 67:139–147.

Bramel, D., Bell, J. E., and Margulis, S. T.: Attributing danger as a means of explaining one's fear. *Journal of Experimental Social Psychology*, 1965, 1:267–281.

Brehm, J.: Post-decision change in the attractiveness of alternatives. *Journal of Abnormal and Social Psychology*, 1956, 52:384–389.

Brehm, J. W.: Motivational effects of cognitive dissonance. *Nebraska Symposium on Motivation*. Lincoln, Nebraska, University of Nebraska Press, 1962.

Brehm, J. W., Back, M. L., and Bogdonoff, M. D.: A physiological effect of cognitive dissonance under stress and deprivation. *Journal of Abnormal and Social Psychology*, 1964, 69:303–310.

Brehm, J. W., and Cohen, A. R.: Re-evaluation of choice alternatives as a function of their number and qualitative similarity. *Journal of Abnormal and Social Psychology*, 1959, 58:373–378.

Brehm, J. W., and Cohen, A. R.: *Explorations in Cognitive Dissonance*. New York, Wiley, 1962.

Brock, T. C.: Cognitive restructuring and attitude change. *Journal of Abnormal and Social Psychology*, 1962, 4:264–271.

Brock, T. C., and Buss, A. H.: Effects of justification for aggression and communication with victim on postaggression dissonance. *Journal of Abnormal and Social Psychology*, 1964, 68:403–412.

Brock, T. C., and Grant, L. D.: Dissonance, awareness, and motivation. *Journal of Abnormal and Social Psychology*, 1963, 67:53–60.

Brown, R.: *Social Psychology*. New York, Free Press, 1965.

Burnstein, E., Stotland, E., and Zander, A.: Similarity to a model and self-evaluation. *Journal of Abnormal and Social Psychology*, 1961, 62:257–264.

Carlsmith, J. M., Collins, B. E., and Helmreich, R. L.: Studies in forced compliance: I. The effect of pressure for compliance on attitude change produced by face-to-face role playing and anonymous essay writing. *Journal of Personality and Social Psychology*, 1966, 4:1–13.

Charters, W. W. and Newcomb, T. M.: Some attitudinal effects of experimentally induced saliency of a membership group. In E. Maccoby, T. M. Newcomb, and E. L. Hartley (Eds.), *Readings in Social Psychology* (3rd edition). New York, Holt, Rinehart & Winston, 1958.

Cohen, A. R.: Need for cognition and order of communication as determinants of opinion change. In C. I. Hovland (Ed.), *The Order of Presentation in Persuasion*. New Haven, Yale University Press, 1957.

Cohen, A. R.: An experiment on small rewards for discrepant compliance and attitude change. In J. Brehm and A. R. Cohen (Eds.), *Explorations in Cognitive Dissonance.* New York, Wiley, 1962a.

Cohen, A. R.: The effect of volition. In J. Brehm and A. R. Cohen (Eds.), *Explorations in Cognitive Dissonance.* New York, Wiley, 1962b.

Cohen, E. A.: *Human Behavior in the Concentration Camp.* New York, W. W. Norton, 1953.

Davidson, J. R., and Kiesler, S.: Cognitive behavior before and after decisions. In L. Festinger (Ed.), *Conflict, Decision, and Dissonance.* Stanford, Stanford University Press, 1964.

Davis, K. E., and Jones, E. E.: Changes in interpersonal perception as a means of reducing cognitive dissonance. *Journal of Abnormal and Social Psychology,* 1960, 61:402–410.

Deutsch, M., and Gerard, H.: A study of normative and informational social influences upon individual judgments. *Journal of Abnormal and Social Psychology,* 1955, 51:629–636.

Dittes, J. E., and Kelley, H. H.: The effects of different degrees of acceptance upon conformity to group norms. *Journal of Abnormal and Social Psychology,* 1959, 53:100–107.

Elms, A. C., and Janis, I. L.: Counter-norm attitudes induced by consonant versus dissonant conditions of role-playing. *Journal of Experimental Research in Personality,* 1965, 1:50–60.

Festinger, L.: *A Theory of Cognitive Dissonance.* Evanston, Illinois, Row, Peterson, 1957.

Festinger, L.: *Conflict, Decision, and Dissonance.* Stanford, Stanford University Press, 1964.

Festinger, L., and Carlsmith, J. M.: Cognitive consequences of forced compliance. *Journal of Abnormal and Social Psychology,* 1959, 58:203–210.

Freedman, J. L.: Attitudinal effects of inadequate justification. *Journal of Personality,* 1963, 31:371–385.

Freedman, J. L.: Long term behavioral effects of cognitive dissonance. *Journal of Experimental Social Psychology,* 1965, 1:145–155.

Gailon, A. K., and Watts, W. A.: The time of measurement parameter in studies of dissonance reduction. *Journal of Personality,* 1967, 35:521–534.

Gallo, P. S.: Effects of increased incentives upon the use of threat in bargaining. *Journal of Personality and Social Psychology,* 1966, 4:14–20.

Gerard, H. B., and Mathewson, G. C.: The effects of severity of initiation in liking for a group: A replication. *Journal of Experimental Social Psychology,* 1966, 2:278–287.

Glidewell, J. C., Kanter, M. B., Smith, L. M., and Stringer, L. A.: Socialization and social structures in the classroom. In L. W. Hoffman and M. L. Hoffman (Eds.), *Review of Child Development Research,* Vol. 2. New York, Russell Sage, 1966.

Hetherington, E. M.: A developmental study of the effects of sex of dominant parent on sex-role preference, identification, and imitation in children. *Journal of Personality and Social Psychology,* 1965, 2:188–194.

Hoffman, L. W.: The father's role in the family and the child's peer group adjustment. *Merrill-Palmer Quarterly,* 1961, 7:97–105.

Hurwitz, J. I., Zander, A., and Hymovitch, B.: Some effects of power on relations among group members. In D. Cartwright and A. Zander (Eds.), *Group Dynamics,* 3rd edition. New York, Harper & Row, 1968.

Jackson, E. F., and Burke, P. J.: Status and symptoms of stress: additive and interaction effects. *American Sociological Review,* 1965, 30:556–564.

Jecker, J. D.: Selective exposure to new information. In L. Festinger (Ed.), *Conflict, Decision, and Dissonance.* Stanford, Stanford University Press, 1964a.

Jecker, J. D.: The cognitive effects of conflict and dissonance. In L. Festinger (Ed.), *Conflict, Decision, and Dissonance.* Stanford, Stanford University Press, 1964b.

Jellison, J. M. and Mills, J.: Effect of similarity and fortune of the other on attraction. *Journal of Personality and Social Psychology,* 1967, 5:459–463.

Jones, E. E.: *Ingratiation.* New York, Appleton-Century-Crofts, 1964.

Jones, E. E., and Harris, V. A.: The attribution of attitudes. *Journal of Experimental Social Psychology,* 1967, 3:1–24.

Jones, R. A., and Brehm, J. W.: Attitudinal effects of communicator attractiveness when one chooses to listen. *Journal of Personality and Social Psychology*, 1967, 6:64–70.

Kagan, J.: Socialization of aggression and the perception of parents in fantasy. *Child Development*, 1958, 29:311–320.

Kagan, J.: The concept of identification. *Psychological Review*, 1958, 65:296–305.

Kelly, G. A.: *The Psychology of Personal Constructs*. New York, Norton, 1955.

Kelley, H. H.: Communication in experimentally created hierarchies. *Human Relations*, 1951, 4:39–56.

Kelley, H. H.: Salience of membership and resistance to change of group-anchored attitudes. *Human Relations*, 1955, 8:275–290.

Kelley, H. H.: Interpersonal accommodation. *American Psychologist*, 1968, 23:399–410.

Kiesler, C. A.: Attraction to the group and conformity to group norms. *Journal of Personality*, 1963, 31:559–569.

Kohlberg, L.: Development of moral character and moral ideology. In M. L. Hoffman and L. W. Hoffman (Eds.), *Review of Child Development Research*. New York, Russell Sage, 1964.

Lerner, M. J.: Evaluation of performance as a function of performer's reward and attractiveness. *Journal of Personality and Social Psychology*, 1965, 1:355–360.

Lerner, M. J., and Matthews, G.: Reactions to suffering of others under conditions of indirect responsibility. *Journal of Personality and Social Psychology*, 1967, 5:319–325.

Lerner, M. J., and Simmons, C. H.: Observer's reaction to the innocent victim: compassion or rejection. *Journal of Personality and Social Psychology*, 1966, 4:203–210.

Leventhal, G., Allen, J., and Kemelger, B.: Reducing inequity by reallocating rewards. *Psychonomic Science*, 1969, 14:295–296.

Lewis, M.: Effect of effort on value: an exploratory study of children. *Child Development*, 1964, 35:1337–1342.

Linder, D. E., Cooper, J., and Jones, E. E.: Decision freedom as a determinant of the role of incentive magnitude in attitude change. *Journal of Personality and Social Psychology*, 1967, 6:245–254.

Lippitt, R., Polansky, N., and Rosen, S.: The dynamics of power: a field study of social influence in groups of children. *Human Relations*, 1952, 5:37–64.

Lowe, R. H., and Steiner, I. D.: Some effects of the reversibility and consequences of decisions on post decision information preference. *Journal of Personality and Social Psychology*, 1968, 8:172–179.

Mansson, H. H.: The relation of dissonance reduction to cognitive, perceptual, consumatory, and learning measures of thirst. In Zimbardo, P. G., *The Cognitive Control of Motivation*. Glenview, Illinois, Scott, Foresman and Company, 1969.

Marlowe, D., Gergen, K. J., and Doob, A. N.: Opponent's personality, expectation of social interaction, and interpersonal bargaining. *Journal of Personality and Social Psychology*, 1966, 3:206–213.

Marsten, A. R.: Imitation, self-reinforcement, and reinforcement of another person. *Journal of Personality and Social Psychology*, 1965, 2:255–261.

McClintock, C. G., and McNeil, S. P.: Reward and score feedback as determinants of cooperative and competitive game behavior. *Journal of Personality and Social Psychology*, 1966, 4:606–613.

Miller, G. A., Galanter, E., and Pribram, K. H.: *Plans and the Structure of Behavior*. New York, Holt, Rinehart and Winston, 1960.

Mills, J.: Changes in moral attitudes following temptation. *Journal of Personality*, 1958, 26:515–531.

Mills, J.: Avoidance of dissonant information. *Journal of Personality and Social Psychology*, 1965a, 2:589–593.

Mills, J.: Effect of certainty about a decision upon post decision exposure to consonant and dissonant information. *Journal of Personality and Social Psychology*, 1965b, 2:749–752.

Mills, J., Aronson, E., and Robinson, H.: Selectivity in response to information. *Journal of Abnormal and Social Psychology*, 1959, 59:250–263.

Mills, J., and Jellison, J. M.: Effect on opinion change of similarity between the communicator and the audience he addressed. *Journal of Personality and Social Psychology*, 1968, 9:153–156.

Myers, A.: Team competition, success, and the adjustment of group members. *Journal of Abnormal and Social Psychology*, 1962, 65:325–332.

Novak, D. W., and Lerner, M. J.: Rejection as a consequence of perceived similarity. *Journal of Personality and Social Psychology*, 1968, 9:147–152.

Patchen, M.: A conceptual framework and some empirical data regarding comparisons of social rewards. *Sociometry*, 1961, 24:136–156.

Peak, H.: The effect of aroused motivation on attitudes. *Journal of Abnormal and Social Psychology*, 1960, 61:463–468.

Penner, D. D., Fitch, G., and Weick, K. F.: Dissonance and the revision of choice criteria. *Journal of Personality and Social Psychology*, 1966, 3:701–705.

Pepitone, A., McCauley, C., and Hammond, P.: Change in attractiveness of forbidden toys as a function of severity of threat. *Journal of Experimental and Social Psychology*, 1967, 3:221–229.

Piaget, J.: *The Moral Judgment of the Child*. New York, Collier, 1962.

Pruitt, D. G.: Reciprocity and credit building in a laboratory dyad. *Journal of Personality and Social Psychology*, 1968, 8:143–147.

Raven, B. H.: Social influence on opinions and the communication of related content. *Journal of Abnormal and Social Psychology*, 1958, 58:119–128.

Raven, B. H., and Fishbein, M.: Acceptance of punishment and change of belief. *Journal of Abnormal and Social Psychology*, 1961, 63:411–416.

Rosen, S.: Post decision affinity for incompatible information. *Journal of Abnormal and Social Psychology*, 1961, 63:188–190.

Rosenberg, M. J.: Cognitive structure and attitudinal affect. *Journal of Abnormal and Social Psychology*, 1956, 53:367–372.

Rosenberg, M. J.: When dissonance fails: on eliminating evaluation apprehension from attitude measurement. *Journal of Personality and Social Psychology*, 1965, 1:28–42.

Rosenberg, M. J.: Some limits of dissonance: Toward a differentiated view of counterattitudinal performance. In S. Feldman (Ed.), *Cognitive Consistency*. New York, Academic Press, 1966.

Rosenberg, M. J.: Hedonism, inauthenticity, and other goals towards expansion of a consistency theory. In R. P. Abelson, E. Aronson, W. J. McGuire, T. M. Newcomb, M. J. Rosenberg, and P. H. Tannenbaum (Eds.), *Theories of Cognitive Consistency: A Sourcebook*. Chicago, Rand McNally, 1968.

Scott, W. E.: Attitude change through reward of verbal behavior. *Journal of Abnormal and Social Psychology*, 1957, 55:72–75.

Sermat, V.: The effect of initial cooperative or competitive treatment upon a subject's response to conditioned cooperation. *Behavioral Science*, 1967, 12:301–313.

Sherif, M., and Cantril, H.: *The Psychology of Ego-Involvement*. New York, Wiley, 1947.

Sherif, M., and Hovland, C. I.: *Social Judgment*. New Haven: Yale University Press, 1961.

Sherif, C. W., Sherif, M., and Nebergall, R. E.: *Attitude and Attitude Change*. Philadelphia, W. B. Saunders, 1965.

Stouffer, S. A., Suchman, E. A., DeVinney, L. C., Star, S. A., and Williams, R. M.: *The American Soldier: Adjustment During Army Life*. Princeton, Princeton University Press, 1949.

Thomas, E. J.: Effects of facilitative role interdependence on group functioning. *Human Relations*, 1957, 10:347–366.

Turiel, E.: An experimental test of the sequentiality of developmental stages in the child's moral judgments. *Journal of Personality and Social Psychology*, 1966, 3:611–618.

Turner, E. A., and Wright, J. C.: Effects of severity of threat and perceived availability on the attractiveness of objects. *Journal of Personality and Social Psychology*, 1965, 2:128–132.

Valins, S.: Cognitive effects of false heart-rate feedback. *Journal of Personality and Social Psychology*, 1966, 4:400–408.

Walker, E. L., and Heyns, R. W.: *An Anatomy for Conformity*. Englewood Cliffs, New Jersey, Prentice Hall, 1962.

Wallace, J.: Role reward and dissonance reduction. *Journal of Personality and Social Psychology*, 1966, 3:305–312.

Walster, E., and Aronson, E.: Effect of expectancy of task duration on the experience of fatigue. *Journal of Experimental Social Psychology*, 1967, 3:41–46.

Walster, E., Berscheid, E., and Barclay, A. M.: A determinant of preference among modes of dissonance reduction. *Journal of Personality and Social Psychology*, 1967, 2:211–216.

Walster, E., and Prestholdt, P.: The effect of misjudging another: Overcompensation or dissonance reduction? *Journal of Experimental Social Psychology*, 1966, 2:85–97.

Walster, E., and Walster, B.: Effect of expecting to be liked on choice of associates. *Journal of Abnormal and Social Psychology*, 1963, 67:402–404.

Watts, W.: Commitment under conditions of risk. *Journal of Personality and Social Psychology*, 1966, 3:501–515.

Whiting, J. W. M.: Sorcery, sin, and super-ego: a cross-cultural study of some mechanisms of social control. In M. R. Jones (Ed.), *Nebraska Symposium on Motivation*. Lincoln, Nebraska, University of Nebraska Press, 1959.

Wicklund, R. A., Cooper, J., and Linder, D. E.: Effects of expected effort on attitude change prior to exposure. *Journal of Experimental Social Psychology*, 1967, 3:416–428.

Yaryan, R. B., and Festinger, L.: Preparatory action and belief in the probable occurrence of future events. *Journal of Abnormal and Social Psychology*, 1961, 63:603–606.

Zajonc, R. B.: Some effects of the "space" serials. *Public Opinion Quarterly*, 1955, 18:367–374.

Zeff, L. H., and Iverson, M. A.: Opinion conformity in groups under status threat. *Journal of Personality and Social Psychology*, 1966, 3:383–389.

Zimbardo, P. G.: The effect of effort and improvisation on self-persuasion produced by role-playing. *Journal of Experimental Social Psychology*, 1965, 1:103–128.

Zimbardo, P. G.: *The Cognitive Control of Motivation*. Glenview, Illinois, Scott, Foresman and Company, 1969.

Zimbardo, P. G., Cohen, A., Weisenberg, M., Dworkin, L., and Firestone, I.: The control of experimental pain. In P. G. Zimbardo, *The Cognitive Control of Motivation*. Glenview, Illinois, Scott, Foresman and Company, 1969.

CHAPTER 8

OBSERVATION AND COMMUNICATION AS SOURCES OF SCHEMAS

The pattern of the last three chapters has been essentially the same. We have shown how people acquire particular schemas about other people, about social situations, and about the self. We have seen how these schemas influence thought, perception, and action with regard to other people, social situations, and ourselves. Nevertheless, in these chapters we did not pay very much attention to the processes by which schemas are acquired. In contrast, we paid most attention to the content of the schemas, what the schemas actually were. We described the events, situations, and circumstances which an individual could observe or learn about through others. We pointed out why such circumstances and events were likely to occur, and, therefore, why certain schemas were likely to be acquired by many people. In the present chapter, we will begin to bring the presentation into better balance—we will focus on aspects which we previously tended to go over lightly. These aspects concern primarily the processes of acquiring schemas, regardless of the specific content of the schemas concerned.

CHAPTER ORIENTATION

The processes by means of which people acquire schemas have already been set forth in broad strokes in the third chapter; in general, it was pointed out that schemas may develop through direct observation of events and of the relationships among events or by means of communications from others. However, there are many different ways of observing the world, and many ways of receiving communications from others. We will examine some of these different ways in this chapter.

In the process of doing so, our discussion will lead us to three primary areas of research in social psychology. Initially, a case will be made to support the contention, touched upon earlier, that the absence of relevant, detailed schemas regarding some situation being faced by an individual is distressing and anxiety arousing. Not knowing how to act appropriately or how to "make sense" of one's current environment is pretty obviously an unpleasant state of affairs. Thus, each of us is very likely to develop a higher order schema which represents a summary of many specific observations to the effect that having schemas pertinent to a given set of circumstances is associated with relatively low levels of discomfort and anxiety and vice versa. As a consequence, we are likely to be strongly motivated to develop such useful schemas. Careful attention to the nature of the events which confront us is one obvious way to accomplish this goal, and the broad outlines of this process have been discussed in considerable detail in earlier chapters. Now, however, we will concentrate on a particularly significant type of "event" whose careful scrutiny is a most important source of information and schemas—other persons. Chapter 5 presented a detailed explication of the ways in which schemas guide and influence the perception of others and the impressions of their attributes which one develops, but the interest in this chapter will be in the ways in which others can be used by an observer as sources of schemas regarding the anticipated or current situations in which he finds himself. Thus, data from the recent extensive interest in the processes, determinants, and consequences of imitation and modeling behavior will be examined from the perspective provided by the schema approach. Theorizing about the role of imitation has long been of interest to personality and social psychologists, and the concept of identification with significant other persons is an important aspect of classical Freudian theory. However, the name most closely associated with more contemporary research on the topic is that of Albert Bandura of Stanford University. His careful and extensive work on this topic has been most influential in giving the notion of imitative behavior the prominent position it currently holds in social, learning, and developmental psychology, and we will draw heavily on his research.

Of course, the development of schemas via an interpersonal medium may involve a rather more direct operation. Rather than simply providing a model from which we may learn, others may communicate information in schema form to us. In some cases, persons may very actively attempt to press their interpretations of reality upon us, while in other, probably more common circumstances, we are likely to seek to elicit from others information regarding their schemas, their ways of selecting, systematizing, and organizing the important elements of some situation. In the discussion in Chapter 2 of the parallels between the scientific method and the ways in which each of us as ordinary individuals attempts to make sense of our world, the importance of communications from others was emphasized. As a short cut to knowledge, we frequently depend upon the accumulated wisdom of others like us rather than actually empirically testing every "hypothesis" by our own experience. Progress in developing an understanding of events would be slow indeed if this option were not available. Books, talks with presumably more experienced persons, films, and so forth have become critically important sources of information on topics ranging from the action of falling bodies in physics to the appropriate way to behave on one's wedding night where a quite different class of falling bodies is involved.

Here the discussion will lead us to research on conformity behavior in which a dependence upon schemas derived from the activity of our peers is typically involved. The classic work of Solomon Asch (1952) and the multitude of experiments following his seminal investigations of the great impact which peer group influence may have will be examined. Additionally, we may give added weight to the structuring of situations which particular other persons provide—other persons whom we identify as having special knowledge, experience, or access to information, who are "experts," in other words. Now, with this rough description of where the schema approach will take us established, let us begin to fill in the details.

ANXIETY AND THE ABSENCE OF RELEVANT SCHEMAS

In the previous three chapters, we have, to a certain extent, treated the individual as a rather passive recipient of information, as a *tabula rasa* on which experience and other people wrote. To some large extent this implication is accurate, but it is at the same time incomplete. The individual may also actively seek out information. In the first chapters, we set forth a number of reasons for this active search for information. It was pointed out that when an individual confronts a situation for which he has no relevant schemas or only schemas which lack very great specificity about a current situation, he will experience anxiety. This is especially the case if this situation is not experienced in the context of some other adjacent or broader circumstances about which the individual does in fact have well-established, specific schemas.

Informational Overload

There are several bases for this relationship between the absence of relevant schemas and anxiety. One derives from the tendency of people to experience anxiety when they have too much information "coming at them"—when there is too much change along too many conceptual dimensions. Too many things may be going on simultaneously and this places demands on the individual's information-processing ability which may exceed its capacity. On the other hand, if the individual does have some schemas which relate changes on various dimensions relevant to the situation at hand, then the attendant anxiety will be lower because he can respond to whole "chunks" of information as perceptual or conceptual units which simply exemplify a given schema. However, if the only available pertinent schemas are of a relatively high order, they are less likely to enable the person to process adequately and completely the information present in the perceptually complex and changing situation which is being referred to here: the very broad and general nature of such schemas makes it less likely that they will be relevant to the specific changes on specific dimensions of perception of a given concrete situation. Thus, the existence of low order, rather specific relevant schemas are likely to be a prerequisite for low anxiety in the presence of complex, rapidly changing situations.

Goal Attainment

A second reason why the absence of specific schemas leads to anxiety has to do with an individual's actions which are designed to achieve goals. It is obvious that if the individual does not know what the consequences of his actions will be in a given situation, he will be very hard put to attain his goals, to meet his needs in that situation. Thus, without schemas explicit enough to indicate what the consequences of specific actions he may be contemplating will be, the individual will experience anxiety, since he will be unable to act decisively or with any assurance that his behavior is appropriate.

Higher Order Schemas

Anxiety may also arise as a result of a higher order schema to the effect that not having lower order schemas relevant to one's current situation leads to anxiety. Most people have no doubt encountered many situations in which they have experienced anxiety as a consequence of the absence of pertinent specific schemas, and have experienced less, or no, anxiety in situations in which such schemas were present in their repertoire. On the basis of such experiences, the individual acquires an H.O.S. about the association between schemas and anxiety. Thus, once such an H.O.S. has been acquired, anxiety may well result simply from the failure to find extant schemas relevant to a given situation, even though no particular action is called for, even though the person is not currently motivated to achieve some goal.

To this point, we have ignored one factor which was mentioned earlier as reducing the impact which the absence of specific situation-relevant schemas may have in producing anxiety—that factor has to do with the presence of at least some familiar elements in the current situation. If some aspect of the situation is familiar, for example, if there are familiar people around or if the person encounters the "newness," the "strangeness," in a large setting which is familiar, anxiety will be low. This effect of "something old" will have to be borne in mind by the reader throughout much of the discussion which follows, because in much of the research that is relevant to these problems, the presence or absence of something old has often not been measured or studied. In most cases, the degree to which something old is a factor is apparently held constant across the different conditions or situations examined within a single research study.

Relevant Research

So far, the discussion has been quite abstract; let us get down to cases. As we have just pointed out, an individual may well experience anxiety in situations in which he does not have specific schemas, even when this lack does not directly affect his actions. In a laboratory study by Raven and Rietsma (1957), some subjects were prevented from developing schemas about the way their particular tasks fit in with the total functioning of their group. These subjects were instructed that their job was to cut triangular squares out of a paper sheet, but were only told that the group was producing some vaguely defined "product," which was "sometimes flat, sometimes hollow." These subjects also overheard the instructions the experimenter gave to other members of their group, but these instructions, too, were very unclear. Other subjects were told clearly that the group was producing model houses, and they overheard the experimenter give clear instructions to the other group members. The subjects who received the vague communications felt more negative about their tasks and about the experiment in general. Thus, even if a person knows in very specific terms what he is to do, he may feel upset and anxious if he has no schema that provides for an integration of his actions with other aspects of the total situation of which he is aware. Of course, if he did not know exactly what to do and, in addition, did not have any clarity at all about the broader context involved, he would feel even more anxious.

Notice that in this laboratory situation, the subjects no doubt did have higher order schemas to the effect that the group had a goal, that the experimenter had some purpose in the situation. But these H.O.S.s did not subsume specific enough L.O.S.s to prevent anxiety. For example, the subjects had no clear idea of the specific goal in the project or what the purpose of their participation was.

Even when a person's fate in a situation is inevitably bad, anxiety will be greater if he has no specific schemas about some pertinent aspects of the unpleasant situation. In other words, even information about how bad "bad" is reduces anxiety. For example, Elliott (1966) found that persons who had been given a sample shock while awaiting a series of electrical shocks reported they felt better during the waiting period and were observed to have less heart rate acceleration than did people who were not given a sample shock. This difference was found both when the sample shock was strong and when it was mild. The sample shock provided a basis for the development of a very specific, pertinent L.O.S. concerning the intensity of the shock they were to receive.

On the other hand, if an individual has only a general H.O.S. about how he can act in a given situation to change his fate, he will be anxious. For example, a student going to see a counsellor has an H.O.S. that the counsellor needs to know something about him, but he is unlikely to have an L.O.S. about exactly what things he can tell the counsellor, nor about the order or manner in which they should be discussed. He does not know how the counsellor will react to what he says. Whether and how to talk about grades, or teachers, or social life? In a study by Dibner (1958), some students in their first sessions with a college counsellor got no particular guides from the counsellor as to what to say. The counsellor only expressed general interest in what the student was about to say. Other students received from the counsellor clear guidance about what to tell him; the counsellor simply asked clear questions of the students. The first group of students reported that they felt more tense and anxious in the interview than did the second. Furthermore, the first group showed more anxiety physiologically than the second; the former showed more drops in the electrical resistance of their skin, which are usually taken to be signs of physiological arousal.

In the counsellor-student relationship studied by Dibner, the students in the condition of ambiguity lacked specific schemas both about the counsellor's behavior and about the consequences of their own actions; in fact, the two are inextricably combined. In most social situations in which people lack specific enough schemas, they lack both types. The person doesn't know how he can act nor how the other is going to respond. Anxiety which stems from this lack of specific schemas appears to be remarkably prevalent in American society. Kahn, Wolfe, Quinn, Snoek, and Rosenthal (1964) found that about one third of the male hourly and salaried workers in America reported that they were disturbed by the ambiguity present in their work situations. These workers felt anxious about their lack of clear knowledge of what they would have to do to get ahead; a lack of clear knowledge of what was expected of them or of how they were evaluated by their supervisors. The workers' ratings of the ambiguity of their situations correlated .51 with their ratings of their feelings of tension and .41 with their feelings of futility. Clearly, the degree of ambiguity had much to do with the way they felt about their jobs. Of course, in such a field study, one could argue that the perception of ambiguity was the result of the tension. But, in view of the laboratory studies cited above, it would be easy to argue that at least a large part of the relationship was a result of the effects of ambiguity itself. It is small wonder, then, that people frequently say, "If I only knew where I stood" or, "If I only knew what they want." The reader, as a student, no doubt has been in classes in which the professor did not indicate what the student's job was to be; and no doubt the reader felt anxious in such classes. The research of Kahn et al. indicates, however, that such ambiguity is not limited to classrooms; perhaps the profs who are ambiguous are advertently or inadvertently preparing the student for "life"—which, after all, is part of the job of an educator.

Schema-Motivated Information Acquisition

As we pointed out above, most people experience situations with specific schemas and no anxiety and other situations with few or no specific schemas and anxiety. As a consequence, people develop a higher order schema to the effect that having specific schemas about specific situations is anxiety-reducing or -avoiding. It is important to note that value is placed not just on having a specific schema, but on having veridical, accurate knowledge, not just fantasy beliefs.

After all, the instances from which the individual acquired the H.O.S. about the value of specific schemas involved the person having a schema which actually enabled him to accurately predict events, or to process the actual input of information from the situation. A pipe dream about "if only" usually does not serve either function.

Thus, H.O.S.s can be aroused and have effects even in situations in which the person does not have to act to attain any goals and in which his fate will not be influenced by any newly acquired knowledge. Hence, the individual will come to evaluate schemas positively; he will be motivated to acquire information when available, to learn about new things, to be curious. In other words, when confronted with a new situation about which he has no specific schemas, the person will seek to learn about the situation, especially if there is something familiar near at hand. If there is no familiar context, the resultant anxiety may be so great that the person will attempt to flee the situation to escape the anxiety. Nevertheless, as we shall see, the high evaluation placed on information is a factor that influences much of our behavior. We seek information even when it seems to be of no practical value to us.

Lanzetta and Driscoll (1966) found that when given a choice between asking for information about their fate in the laboratory and not asking, subjects preferred to do so regardless of whether their fates involved either receiving a shock or receiving no shock; receiving a reward or no reward; or receiving a shock or a reward. The information they received could in no way determine which alternative they were to receive. Jones (1966) told some of his subjects that they would be shocked any time after 15 seconds after a previous shock; others that they would be shocked some time after 30 seconds; and still others that shock would come some time after 45 seconds. The 15-second group thus had less knowledge of exactly when they would be shocked, since the period of possible shock began in 15 seconds rather than 45 seconds. The 15-second group asked more for information about when to expect to be shocked and about its intensity than did the other groups.

This same sort of process of seeking schemas can be observed when the schemas refer to oneself in general, what sort of person one is, one's attitudes, needs, traits, etc. A growing child will often seek to acquire schemas about himself from any available source; he may simply ask his parents about himself or he may test himself by looking for challenges. Erikson (1950), who is a very astute observer of young people, has commented that they often seek an "identity." They may even seek to acquire a negative schema about themselves, such as "juvenile delinquent," because it gives them an identity, which is preferable in their eyes to not having any. There are some unusual and extreme circumstances in which even adults, whom we would expect to have a well-developed set of schemas about themselves, find that these schemas are not relevant to their immediate environment. These adults exhibit an intense, and to the objective observer, often "irrational" drive to establish relevant schemas, preferring some even quite strange ones to none at all.

Schein (1951) reports that prisoners of Chinese communists who were subjected to brainwashing also sought to find identities after their old identities were destroyed. This destruction involved placing them in a prison environment which had none of the usual supports for their way of thinking about themselves—no work, social amenities, or other supports, which had provided a setting in which they could act in accord with their previously held schemas about themselves. In these situations, Schein reports, the prisoners desperately sought to find some new definition of themselves. But the possibilities of finding a new schema were severely limited in the prison. Nevertheless, they often found a new identity, a new set of schemas about themselves, even when it was an identity that would otherwise be acceptable only to the guards or the prison interrogators. In Chapter 7 we described the observations of Bettelheim (1943) of concentration camp inmates who imitated some of the behavior of the guards. Some of the motivation behind the imitation of the extremely brutal guards was no doubt to find a new identity in a situation in which the old pre-captivity ones were no longer relevant.

Summary

It should be noted that the people whose behavior has been described in the research which has been discussed acquired the schemas for one or more of at least three reasons. One is simply that they may happen to be attending to that aspect of a situation which presents new information, to the aspect in which they perceive something for which they do not have a specific schema. They may be attending to this aspect because, in fact, it is new or changing, or because they have been directed to do so. These are the factors which we have been emphasizing in the last three chapters. The second reason is that they seek them to reduce or avoid anxiety. A third reason is that they have acquired an H.O.S. in which high value is placed on information itself, and are therefore motivated to acquire it. Notice that this last, motivational reason for acquiring schemas is based on a higher order schema and therefore is general. The value of information in any particular situation does not have to be demonstrated, because they are positively motivated to acquire schemas as a consequence of their high evaluation of information. In any situation—"natural" or contrived by researchers—all sets of factors, the simply attentional and the actively seeking, no doubt have an influence on the behavior of people. How much each factor contributes to the end result no doubt varies from situation to situation, depending on a variety of influences, such as the degree of anxiety the person has experienced in the situation. For our purposes, it is not necessary to determine exactly how much each is contributing—just to know that all no doubt are contributing.

OBSERVATION OF OTHERS AS A BASIS
FOR THE DEVELOPMENT OF SCHEMAS

We have now discussed the observational and motivational bases for acquiring schemas. As we mentioned in the opening paragraphs of this chapter, we need next to be concerned with the specific ways in which people acquire these schemas. We will organize this examination of the specific ways by first looking at those ways of acquiring schemas which entail observation. We will concentrate on observation of other people, especially other people who have about the same level of capability of understanding reality. Next, we will turn to the acquisition of schemas through communication from these people. Finally, we will examine the effects of communications of people whom we perceive as better equipped than ourselves to understand some particular aspect of the world. In examining these various routes to the acquisition of schemas, we will present research which is pertinent, but we will not be able to present research examples from all aspects of experience. The research has not been done. We will therefore try to fill this gap by citing everyday experiences. Thus, this procedure will appear somewhat like an uneven inventory.

Schemas Developed by Means of Observation

To begin with observational ways of acquiring schemas, the most obvious way is simply to look, to inquire, to observe, to find out what in fact is the case. There is no need to document this. However, in some cases, such looking and inquiring is not possible. The evidence is not available—we don't see the other side of the moon or the insides of our own bodies. The individual may simply "not know what to do", what specific actions are possible and what their consequences are. In such cases, it is often possible for an individual to acquire specific schemas about what behavior is possible in a given situation and what its consequences will be by observing the actions of others in that situation. The individual can then acquire a schema about possible actions and consequences in the situation. These schemas

Close observation and active modeling. Photograph by Irwin Nash.

can then serve the purpose of reducing anxiety due to the lack of schemas about actions in that situation and can themselves guide action in that situation. Because of their importance, we turn now to a detailed examination of the processes of acquiring such schemas and the consequences of such acquisitions.

It is obvious that we do not acquire schemas pertaining to possible actions of our own from observing actions of any and all other persons. We are not likely to assume that we can dive from watching an experienced diver, nor that we can orate from watching a skilled orator. There are circumstances, conditions, which are necessary for the schema to be acquired. The conditions necessary for the acquisition of these schemas are very important to examine, since their acquisition sometimes leads to actions guided by such schemas. Such actions are what people often refer to as imitation. Thus, by understanding the conditions which determine the acquisition of these schemas, we can know something of the conditions determining imitation.

Perspective on the Nature and Significance of Imitation

At this point it will be useful to pause for a moment in order to develop some perspective on the nature and importance of the discussion of imitation. The term imitation has a long history in which it has been used as an explanation of all sorts of human behavior. A French social philosopher, Tarde (1903) went so far as to use imitation as the basis of a whole theory of how human society develops and changes. He assumed that human beings are imitative "by nature," that people just tend to imitate. To be sure, he did put certain qualifications on this proposition, such as people being more likely to imitate other people in the same group as themselves. Nevertheless, the overall thrust of his theory was toward the universality of imitation. Likewise, in everyday life, we often use imitation as an explanation of many types of behavior: we say that so-and-so is behaving like thus-and-such because he imitates his older brothers; that the audience started booing because they were imitating one member of the audience; that a new style is catching on with teenagers because they are imitating a rock group; and so on.

What is singular about these uses of the term imitation is that it is used as if it helped to explain something. But nothing really is explained by using the term. All we have done is describe something that happens; the teenagers acting in the same way as some rock musicians can be described as an example of imitative behavior. We categorize the behavior, but we do not know anything more about why it occurs, what its determinants are, or what conditions are necessary for it to occur. When we say something about these whys, whats, and wheres, we have begun to explain it.

Our concern with imitation grew out of an interest in the ways in which people reduce anxiety resulting from a lack of pertinent schemas relevant to their own possible actions. However, we will sometimes go well beyond this original purpose in an examination of imitation. One very important point that the reader should be alert to as he examines the determinants and effects of imitation is that there are a number of different causes or conditions that can lead to imitation. Imitation is a type of behavior, like most complex behaviors, which can have a number of roots, some of them quite complex. Therefore, it is inappropriate to ask what is *the* cause of imitation. What we can ask is what is the main cause in a given situation; and what are the causes in different situations.

After this long introduction to the problem, we are going to ask the reader's indulgence once more while we defer our answer to these questions we have posed for a few pages in order to face an issue that has to be faced before we can examine the data relevant to the answers to the problem we just set forth.

The Relationship Between Schema Acquisition and Overt Action

One final point must be made before our examination of research on imitation begins. It will be important to distinguish between circumstances in which the observation of another person's actions leads to the acquisition of a schema about one's own possible actions, on the one hand, and a perhaps more complete process on the other which involves actually engaging in imitative action. This distinction must be made not only because it is an important one theoretically, but also because most studies which have dealt with the acquisition of schemas on the basis of observation of others have used the observer's *actions* as the primary index or measure to indicate whether or not a schema has been acquired. Yet it seems quite possible that schema acquisition can occur quite independently of any related overt activity on the part of the observer. Therefore, before we can effectively examine studies which relate to the conditions which lead to the acquisition of the schema, we must look at the relationship between the schema and overt action.

The distinction between acquisition of a schema and action guided by it is clearly shown in a study by Bandura (1965) in which children were shown an adult engaging in hostile behavior. Some of the children were shown the film under conditions which led them to imitate the aggressive behavior of the adult, and some under conditions which did not lead to actual imitative behavior. However, when Bandura asked the latter children to describe the behavior of the adult, they gave as accurate descriptions as the first group did. They acquired a schema at least about the other's actions, even when they did not act like the other. Mischel and Liebert (1966) found that a child can communicate to another child a schema regarding the appropriate behavior in a given situation which the former child acquired from observation of an adult (cf. Bandura, Ross, and Ross, 1961).

Whether or not a person goes on to act in line with the schema based on his observations of others depends in part on the individual's goals, his motivations. He may not be motivated to attain a goal which would be attained by acting like the other person, and thus will not act. Later, if he does come to be motivated to attain that goal, the schemas which he obtained from observing others can then come to guide his behavior. This process is especially pertinent for a child's observations of his parents. He may acquire many schemas about possible actions that he can take, which he is not motivated to take at that time, but which he will become motivated to take as he grows older. For example, he may observe his father's affectionate behavior toward his mother, and act "imitatively" only years later when he is married. Or, as implied in the case of the example just given, he may simply not have the opportunity or ability to engage in the action at the time he observes the other person. Later, when he has the ability and the opportunity, the belated imitation may emerge.

Interpersonal Schemas and Imitation

In Chapter 6 we cited a number of schemas about interpersonal processes which involved similarity, such as the one concerning the generality of similarity. Since they do involve similarity, one would expect that they could have an influence in leading to the acquisition of schemas regarding the possibility of imitating others' behavior. We will review a number of these to show their relevance for the present problem, but it should be borne in mind that the issue of significance here is not whether any given individual will attempt to reduce anxiety by means of these schemas; the point is rather that the arousal of them provides this as one of perhaps several possible modes available for anxiety reduction.

For instance, the situation in which the individual does not have usefully specific schemas. He may perceive that he is similar to another person in age, or sex, or neighborhood background. Then, on the assumption that similarities between persons tend to be quite broad, he may conclude that it is possible for him to engage in many of the same activities which he observes this other person carry out. A city boy who is on his first camping trip may be uncertain about what activities in this strange setting are appropriate, useful, enjoyable, or possible for him. He may see other, perhaps more experienced, boys climbing trees—something he has never done. He may then come to believe that he too can climb trees, and thus his anxiety about not having some schemas to guide his actions would be reduced. Observing the activities of less similar others such as much older boys or camp counsellors would be much less likely to lead to the acquisition of such useful schemas.

Another schema that can have a parallel effect concerns the relationship between liking and similarity. A person may observe someone he likes engage in a given activity in a situation new to the observer. This could be an activity that the person had never engaged in—but now he may acquire the schema that he, too, can engage in this activity, based on this schema which implies that liking and similarity are associated with one another. Other examples based on the schemas relating interaction and similarity, proximity and similarity, could be quite easily developed, but there is no point in our spelling them out here.

If a person is not in a position to observe the actions of similar, or liked, or close persons, he will tend to be relatively less able to acquire schemas about what he can do, schemas which will assist him in evaluating and interpreting his own capacities. Festinger (1954) found that people who were unable to perceive how well other people similar to themselves were doing on a task had quite variable expectations of their own performance from trial to trial as compared to others who *were* able to compare themselves to others who were working on the same task. Radloff (1966) found that people who were working on a task which required that they track a moving target were much more variable in their evaluations of their own performances if they were told they were much better at the task than many other people, so much better that there were few, if any, people who were similar to them in ability. If they were told that they were close to the average level of performance of other college students, they were relatively stable in their evaluations.

In the course of life for most people, there must be many occasions in which they have observed some of the effects we have just set forth of the absence of any schemas about how to act. An individual is likely to have perceived a number of occasions, especially in his childhood, in which he experienced anxiety as a consequence of not having any schemas indicating what he was to do. Likewise, he must have experienced situations in which he acquired schemas about his possible actions as a consequence of his observations of similar, liked, or close other people, and thereby experienced a diminution of his anxiety. Thus, individuals are highly likely to develop an H.O.S. that having such people at hand is a way of reducing whatever anxiety may be due to the absence of schemas concerning what actions are possible and appropriate. Therefore, if the individual finds himself in a situation in which he does not know "what to do," he is highly likely to seek out other people, especially if they are similar to him or are people he likes.

Schemas Regarding the Consequences of Observed Behavior

In our discussion of a person's similarity to other people, we emphasized the way in which this similarity enables the person to acquire schemas about possible actions and thus reduce his anxiety. This discussion was not intended to give the impression that these effects are the only ones which result from the observations of another's actions. It is only one special case. In addition to reducing any anxiety the individual might have been experiencing because of an absence of schemas about his own possible actions, the acquisition of this schema can also indicate goals that can be attained by acting in a given way, or what pains or deprivations can be avoided by acting in a given way. In other words, the schema can include not only the actions themselves but also the degree of desirability or un-desirability of the consequences of the actions. If the goals are sufficiently important for the individual, he will then go on to act like the other person, to imitate him, if he gets an opportunity to do so.

There are many examples of imitation that are based on this process of acquiring schemas which include the desirability of the consequences of actions as well as the actions themselves. Bandura, Grusec, and Menlove (1967a) let children observe an adult play a bowling game and reward himself with gift certificates only when he obtained a superior score. In addition, in the presence of some other children, the experimenter did nothing. Then all the children were given a chance to bowl. They were more likely to reward themselves only for their superior performances if they had observed the experimenter praise the adult. Notice that in this study, the child has acquired a schema about high standards of self-reward which were not dependent on the experimenter's praising him for this behavior. The schema that such behavior was desirable or led to praise was thus of a sufficiently high order that it was not necessary for the experimenter to praise the child for the latter to act in accord with the schema. No doubt, if the experimenter persisted in not praising the child, the schema might have changed.

On the other hand, the individual may acquire a schema which suggests that some observed behavior leads to undesirable consequences. Bandura (1965) had children observe an adult "beat up" a Bobo doll with a mallet (a Bobo doll is an almost person-sized doll which usually stands upright and, if hit, bounces back to the upright position), punch it, and exclaim hostilely at it. Then another adult was seen to either punish the first adult by "bawling him out" and spanking him, or praise him or do neither. The children then were given a chance to play with the Bobo doll. Those who had observed the adult being punished following his aggressive interaction with the doll were themselves less aggressive than were those who saw him being praised or who saw him neither praised nor punished. The lack of any significant difference between the "praise" condition and the "neither" condition probably was the result of the "fun" that the children saw in playing with this big, soft doll by hitting and banging it about, which was great enough to motivate them to act accordingly; the praise may well have been superfluous as far as making such activity seem attractive is concerned.

Notice that in the examples we have given thus far, observers have acquired schemas which include information about consequences of acting in a given way. We have assumed, without being explicit about it, that the observer has a schema or a conceptual dimension of the action itself. That is, he is in some sense an observer of what it is that he is doing; he may become aware of the fact that he is engaging in imitation. He is especially likely to conceptualize matters in these terms if he has imitated the other person with respect to a number of different types of actions. He might then develop a conceptual dimension of imitative actions, since the imitation *per se* would be common to all of the different types of actions. Suppose also that in each case the individual has found that the imitative actions have led to desirable consequences. Each time he imitated some other person, he might have received praise, food, or some other satisfying, rewarding element, regardless of what the specific actions involved were. As a consequence, he would develop a schema to the effect that imitating this type of person "pays off." The imitative actions might then become general, regardless of what the other person did. This process, in a very rudimentary form, was first demonstrated by Miller and Dollard (1941) in a classic study. They had a child observe another child choose between two boxes and always get a candy out of the box he chose. The first and observing child then also was given a choice between the boxes. If he chose the same box as the other, he received a candy himself. This procedure was repeated a number of times with each pair of observing child and "leader." Not surprisingly, the children began to imitate the leader regardless of which box he chose. The "variety of actions" which we mentioned above is very limited here—just choosing one or another of two boxes. But the study does illustrate the point.

Suppose that an individual has developed a schema which indicates that imitating a given person pays off; but, in addition, let us assume that the observer has a conceptual dimension regarding the class or type of person like the one he has been imitating. He might then develop a schema that all people of this class are worth imitating. Or, in fact, he might have acquired this schema from imitating a number of different people in that category and having found that it paid off in all these instances. A child might, for example, acquire a schema that imitating adults pays off, because adults usually do things which are effective in attaining goals.

Review

In summary, then, different degrees and directions of generality of imitative behavior may result from an observer's discovery that a given other person's actions have a desirable outcome; who will be imitated and to what extent he will be imitated is dependent on the schemas of the observer. If his aroused schemas concern only the actions of the other, then the imitation will be limited to those actions in a given situation. If the aroused schemas also include the imitative action itself as conceptualized by him as imitative, then the individual might develop a schema that imitative actions *per se* pay off. If the aroused schemas include not only imitative behavior as such, but also imitation of a given other person, the observer would then come to imitate that person, if it "paid off." Or, if the aroused schema included imitating a whole class of other people, then, the imitative actions would be general indeed. Furthermore, if the schema about the value of imitative behavior is of a high enough order, the degree to which imitative actions pay off or not on specific occasions may be insufficient to change it (cf. Winch, 1962).

Needless to say, the individual can just as readily acquire a schema that non-imitation pays off, or that imitation leads to undesirable consequences, or that "doing just the opposite" pays off. There is no need to spell out all the possibilities—they parallel those we have just set forth.

The reader should clearly note that we are not arguing that imitative action is the result only of the pay-off, or that looking at the pay-off is sufficient to explain it. We have already pointed out a number of other bases for acting like another person, in addition to some sort of tangible reward. Further, in our discussion, we have pointed out that the acquisition and arousal of the conceptual dimension of imitative behavior occurs before the acquisition of schemas about the pay-off. The individual cannot learn that imitating another person or type of person pays off unless he has observed that he has imitated this other person or type of person. Of course, the individual can imitate a given action of another person or type of action of the other person without having the conceptual dimension of imitation. In that case, the imitative behavior will be limited to that action only.

Broad Pressures Toward Imitative Behavior

In this chapter, we have pointed out a number of bases or sources of motivation to engage in imitative behavior. We have seen that people may make their behavior similar to others' because they are similar to them in some other way, because they like them, because they interact with them. We have seen how people increase their similarity to others to try to reduce anxiety, to try to feel more like them, and to try to get the other person to like them. We have seen how people imitate others because such imitative behavior pays off in some way. This accumulation of different motivations all pointing in the same direction suggests that the accumulated pressures to make oneself similar are often very strong.

These pressures are so strong that children and some adults will imitate others when these others are not even present, i.e., in play and games. Children obviously often model their games after the adult world: playing house, playing "mothers," playing soldier, or "cops and robbers", cowboys and Indians. Many of the toys that children like are often those which are replicas of the tools of the adult world: tractors, guns, cars, telephones, utensils, clothes. The toy departments of stores are often microcosms of the adult world. The children's motivations for imitative play are probably very complex, although not studied as much as they should be (Piaget, 1951; Sutton-Smith, 1966). But there is little doubt that children engage in imitative play for many combinations of the reasons cited in the previous paragraphs.

This is not to argue that all play is based on imitation. There are many other motivations for playing than just imitation. In fact, we shall examine some of them, such as the motivation to feel a sense of competence and mastery, in later chapters. Nevertheless, even in play which is motivated by factors other than the imitative ones mentioned above, the forms of play are influenced by schemas about actions which have been acquired by observing others, especially adults. We pointed out earlier in this chapter that the individual, under certain conditions, is likely to acquire schemas about possible actions he can take in certain situations. These schemas can then guide the person's behavior even when he is not particularly motivated to imitate. These schemas about possible actions might, for example, guide behavior which is motivated primarily by the desire of two people to relate to one another. Two children want to play together; playing house is an easy way to keep playing together. Or, some boys are motivated to compete; playing cowboys and Indians is a convenient way to do so. Or, a child is motivated to feel some sense of mastery over the environment; playing "builder" is one way of doing so.

Again, we are not stating that all children's play is modeled on the adult world; clearly, much of it is spontaneous or guided by the games of the children's world, such as tag or kick the can.

ENRICHMENT OF SCHEMAS VIA IMITATION AND ROLE PLAYING

Prior to engaging in actual imitative behavior, a person's schemas about another's actions are most directly based on observations of the other's overt behavior, on direct communications from that person regarding his actions, and on communications from still other persons about the model. Information from each of these sources may often be inaccurate or incomplete. We cannot observe everything that another person does; we cannot observe all of what he does in all its details; we do not always attend to the specific dimensions of another person's behavior which are most important to him. When we receive communications from or about the other person, the messages involved may be ambiguous, or understood in ways somewhat different from that which the communicator intended; the communication may be incomplete or garbled. Thus, imitative behavior may often be guided by schemas which are fallacious or inadequate.

When the individual does begin to act imitatively, however, the schemas based on observations of the other may be enriched in many ways. The person now is forced to attend to those aspects of his own actions or of the environment which are important for the imitative actions. He is forced to attend to the details. More importantly, he is highly likely to have to engage in the same sort of thinking, problem-solving processes as did the model, since they may be demanded by the action itself. These are processes which could not be directly observed before and whose richness and detail could be only inadequately communicated; the person literally adds new dimensions to his schemas about this form of action. For instance, in many situations, the actor will now experience the emotions associated with these actions, emotions that he previously might not even have known about or might have erroneously or inadequately understood. In short, then, playing at someone else's actions, or imitating him even when "play" is not involved, leads to the acquisition of new dimensions to the schemas about these actions and to lower order schemas subsumed under these actions.

Emotionality and Empathic Responses

The potential consequences of this embellishment of schemas about actions is very strikingly illustrated in a study by Janis and Mann (1965). Some adult subjects actually enacted the role of a patient who goes to a doctor with a cough and is told that he has lung cancer, and needs an immediate operation. The enactment includes a discussion of the effect of smoking on cancer. Other subjects just listened to tape recordings of such enactments. As compared to the latter subjects, the actors reported that they felt more scared of having cancer, became more negative toward cigarette smoking, and believed more in the data showing the relationship between smoking and cancer. Two weeks later, the actors dropped from an average of 10.5 cigarettes daily to 4.8 daily. Eighteen months later, this difference between the two groups of subjects in their smoking habits was still in evidence (Mann and Janis, 1968).

One of the processes that no doubt was involved in the effectiveness of this procedure is that, in some limited form, the individual experienced the fearful emotions of a person who actually was being given the information about his dangerous illness. This experiencing of emotions similar to another's can occur even when enacting his role symbolically in imagination only. Stotland, Sherman, and Shaver (1971) told subjects that one of them, and only one, was to undergo a treatment from a diathermy machine (which is a machine that can generate heat within a person's arm, or other parts of the body, by means of radio waves, and is used therapeutically). Three conditions were created by telling subjects that this treatment would be painful, neutral, or pleasant. Some of the subjects were instructed that when the other person was undergoing the treatment they were to imagine how they would feel if they were in his position. Others were instructed to imagine how he felt undergoing the treatment; these subjects no doubt imagined how they themselves would feel in his situation in order to understand how he felt. Still other subjects were told to engage in neither of these activities of the imagination, but just to watch the person's physical motions very closely while he underwent the treatment. After these instructions were given, the person (an accomplice) appeared to undergo either a painful, neutral, or pleasurable treatment. Both groups of subjects who had been instructed to imagine how the treatment felt were more physiologically and subjectively aroused during the painful treatment than were those who were instructed only to look at the other's movements. On the other hand, none of these groups showed much emotional arousal when the other person received the "neutral" treatment. When the other received the supposedly pleasurable treatment, the "imagination" subjects showed more tendency to empathize than the "look at" subjects. In general, then, the "imagination" subjects empathized with the other person, i.e., experienced some of the same emotional responses as would a person actually experiencing the treatment.

If a person is undergoing a painful experience, another person who has schemas about that experience which include the conceptual dimension of pain is more likely to empathize with him. That is, the latter is more likely to experience some of the feelings of the former when he places himself imaginatively in the other's position. The conceptual dimension of pain can become a part of the schema about the former's fate sometimes as a consequence of the second individual's previously having expected to be in the other's position and, therefore, having symbolically placed himself in that position in anticipation of actually being in it. In another study, Stotland et al. informed some people that they would soon undergo a painful "heat treatment." Other subjects were told that someone else would undergo the treatment. Then, the first group was told that a mistake had been made in reading the schedule and that they would not undergo the pain. Then both groups of subjects observed someone undergo this painful treatment. The subjects who had expected to suffer themselves were more likely to empathize with the person undergoing the heat treatment; that is, they showed more emotion both physiologically and subjectively.

Consequences of Empathy

What the consequences of this greater understanding of the other person's actions, thoughts, and feelings will be depends, of course, on what it is about the other person that is better understood. In the Janis and Mann studies, what was understood better was the fear of death from lung cancer. In the Stotland et al. study, the subjects better understood the other person's pain and anxiety. In a study by Johnson (1967) the consequences are quite different. He presented subjects with information about a law suit in which the two sides were incompatible; other subjects were given the details of a compatible suit. Then each was assigned one of the sides in the suit. Some of the subjects then were told to take the part of the opposition, temporarily, and argue its side until they judged that their opponent understood the position they were arguing. Other subjects did not enact this reversal. The subjects who reversed and did a good job of it were more likely to understand the incompatibility of the positions than the subjects who did not reverse, when the sides were actually incompatible. When the sides were compatible, the good role reversers also understood this fact better than did the non-role reversers.

The studies by Janis et al., Stotland et al., and Johnson together illustrate that what happens as a consequence of enacting another person's role depends both on the content of his role and the motivations of the person (cf. Turner, 1956). An individual may learn to avoid another's fate, to perceive that he understands how another feels, to learn how different the other person's ideas are. For example, an individual may come to avoid being in the presence of another person who is undergoing a painful experience with which he might empathize; or, another individual might empathize with the person and then act to reduce the other person's and, therefore, his own pain. Or, if the other person is experiencing joy because of some success, enacting his role even imaginatively might lead to the person's being envious. The reason we point this out is that it is sometimes thought that enacting another person's role somewhat automatically guarantees more positive behavior toward the other person; in some cases it might, but in others it might lead to more and more specific schemas about the other. This understanding will, of course, reduce anxiety, as we have pointed out all through this chapter, but other factors may determine how the person acts toward the other person.

Imitation and the Understanding of Others

In most cases, the additional dimensions and L.O.S.s which are added to an observer's extant schemas about the actions in question will correspond closely to those of the person whose behavior is being imitated. Of course, this correspondence does not necessarily occur; but if both the actor and the observer are initially relatively similar with respect to their schemas, especially those which are relevant to the actions, then the additions which develop when the observer actually engages in imitative behavior are likely to correspond fairly closely to those of the model. Under these circumstances, the observer will come to have a set of schemas about these actions which he can use to rather accurately understand the other person's behavior. More precisely, suppose an individual is motivated to predict another's behavior as accurately as possible. One way in which he can do this is to arouse the schemas having to do with the other person's actions. If these schemas have been embellished and enriched by his having engaged in actions similar to those of the other person, then, on the whole, we would expect the predictions to be more accurate. Allport (1924) showed pictures of faces expressing varying emotions to subjects and asked them to guess what the emotions depicted in the photographs were. After the subjects had been instructed to try to imitate the expressions depicted in the pictures, those who had been poor at making predictions improved greatly.

A person is likely to observe occasions on which he has developed a more accurate understanding of some other person by imitating his behavior. On that basis, he is likely to develop an H.O.S. to the effect that imitation leads to more accurate and differentiated schemas about other people. A person faced with new and strange behavior on the part of some other individual about which he had no relevant schemas might experience some anxiety as a consequence. He might then try to reduce this anxiety by imitating the other's behavior, in accord with schemas about imitation leading to the acquisition of more differentiated schemas. Berger (1966) had subjects watch another person perform hand signals for the blind. While actually observing, the subjects tended spontaneously to practice the signals they were observing.

An increased understanding of another person's actions can also lay the groundwork for better, more complete, or more appropriate communication between people. If one has more detailed information about how another feels, thinks, and acts, communication may well be facilitated. Feffer and Suchotliff (1966) had subjects make up stories about various scenes and then had them retell the stories from the points of view of the various characters in the story. The qualities of the retold stories were measured in terms of the degree to which the subjects "refocused" from the point of view of each character without losing the continuity of the story. People who did better on this test did better in a verbal charade game played later. The study simply illustrates that people who are better able to enact other people's roles and actions and who therefore would be expected to have more highly elaborated and accurate schemas about their behavior are better able to communicate with them. Likewise, Marshall (1961) had some kindergarten children enact some dramatic plays in which they played roles other than their own real ones. The children who talked more in these dramatic presentations were the preferred playmates in that kindergarten. Part of the other children's liking for them may well have been based on their ability to communicate more effectively. A study which clearly shows that imitating the other person's actions leads to better communication has not been run at this writing, although there can be little doubt of the results of such a study.

Empathy and Altruism

Another very important possible consequence of acquiring well-elaborated and detailed schemas about other people's experiences has to do with a person's concern about the welfare of some other, his motivation to help the other person. This would be especially likely to occur if part of the elaborated schema included a conceptual dimension representative of the other's emotional experiences, thus facilitating the person's empathy with the, say, painful experience of the other. He might become motivated to help the other out of the pain and thus reduce his own empathetically based discomfort. Or, if he experiences empathy a number of times when other people are suffering, he might be motivated to prevent the pain of others. Accordingly, if children are induced to empathize with others, they are more likely to behave in a moral way. The studies by Stotland, Sherman, and Shaver (1971) have shown that people can be induced to empathize with the experiences of another by imaginatively rehearsing the experiences of the other; therefore, children can be led to empathize with others by symbolic means, by communications from their parents, rather than only by undergoing the actual experience of the other. Thus, children who are led to empathize in this way might very well be more likely to behave morally and altruistically.

This process is well illustrated by a study by Hoffman (1963), in which he asked parents of three-year-olds to describe in great detail what happened the day before. On the basis of these reports he categorized the parents' disciplinary techniques into three categories: One, explaining to the child what the negative consequences would be of his engaging in a prohibited act; two, simply telling the child it was wrong for him to engage in the act; three, explaining the consequences to other people of engaging in the act, telling the child of the other person's needs. Hoffman found that the children induced to empathize with others by the third technique were more helpful to and considerate of others. Likewise, Hoffman and Saltzstein (1967) used a projective test and teacher ratings to measure how guilty seventh grade children felt as a consequence of their own transgressions, and how much responsibility they assumed for rectifying the consequences of a transgression. It was found that children of parents who explained the consequences to others of violations of standards were more likely to experience guilt and take responsibility than were the children of parents who used the other techniques of discipline.

A question raised by Hoffman's research, as well as some of the other work cited above, is why the children behaved altruistically and morally as a consequence of their empathizing. As pointed out above, there are many possible consequences of empathizing. The answer probably is simply that the schema about other people's experiences was acquired in a context in which the parents were directly informing the child how to act, what to do about the consequences to the other. The parents did not, for example, tell the child to avoid thinking about the consequences because it would make him feel bad.

Needless to say, such parentally induced empathy with others is not the only basis of moral behavior. As we saw in the previous chapters, the moral dimension of action is acquired early in life, as the child learns that certain acts are good and others are bad in the eyes of others who are powerful and important to him. And the schemas about the actions which incorporate the moral dimensions may guide actions. However, it is possible that both sources of moral judgments about actions may contribute to the same broad schemas regarding appropriate and moral behavior as the child grows older. In fact, Piaget (1952), the great Swiss psychologist and astute observer of children, has argued that as the child develops, he shifts from moral judgments which simply declare that certain acts are good or bad, regardless of cause or consequence, to more concern with the consequences of actions; and, finally, to more concern with motivations of the person who transgresses. Both the shift to concern with the consequences and to concern with others' motives may be a result of wider experiences which provide a basis for empathizing both with the transgressor and with his victim.

OBSERVATION OF OTHERS AND THE
LABELING OF EMOTIONS

Thus far we have been indicating some of the ramifications of an individual's observing and imitating others when faced with a situation in which he has no satisfactorily specific L.O.S.s about his own and other people's possible actions. Another, perhaps less obvious, set of circumstances in which these same processes may operate has to do with having no specific schemas about one's own bodily sensations. Suppose an individual finds that he has certain sensations coming from various parts of his body, but also finds that he has no basis for knowing just what it is that is causing them. They might indicate that he is sick, or emotionally aroused, or under the influence or drugs or alcohol. In this case, he might attempt to acquire the absent L.O.S.s, which would assist him in his efforts to understand and appropriately label these ambiguous "feelings" by observing another person whom he believes is probably experiencing the same bodily sensations and then assuming that his own sensations have the same cause. "Now I know what's the matter with me; you ate that x and feel ill, so I must be feeling ill, since I ate it, too."

This process of turning to others to find out what the reasons are for one's own internal state is illustrated in a fascinating study by Schachter and Singer (Schachter, 1964; Schachter and Singer, 1962). It was originally stimulated, in part, by the observation these researchers made that their extensive review of the research on the physiology of emotions failed to turn up evidence for general distinct patterns of arousal being associated with different felt emotions. That is, for most of us, most of the time, there is no difficulty in identifying what emotion we're experiencing. Anger seems very different and distinct from love or joy and the possibility of confusing these seems remote. Yet this subjective distinctiveness on an experiential level is apparently not paralleled by similar distinctness at a physiological level—the best available evidence indicates that there are no generally found, identifiably different, specific patterns of physiological arousal which underlie the various emotional responses that persons feel. If this is the case, the manner in which we come to label and experience different emotional responses as different is raised. The Schachter and Singer work investigated the possibility that social factors, the observation of similar others, might be one source of information that is used in leading persons to label a given broad pattern of physiological arousal in a given way. Their subjects were told that they would be participating in a study of the effects of various drugs on vision. They were given an injection of what was ostensibly "Suproxin," which was described to them as a "mild and harmless" chemical agent whose influence on visual acuity was being investigated. The injection which some of the subjects received was actually a shot of saline solution—a placebo, which is completely neutral in terms of its action on the physiology of the body. Other subjects were actually given a shot of epinephrine, a substance which causes palpitations, tremor, and sometimes a feeling of flushing and fast breathing. The subjects who had received epinephrine were also given one of the following types of information about the effects of the shot: The *epinephrine-informed* subjects were told that the Suproxin would cause the symptoms which, in fact, are caused by the epinephrine they had been given. The *epinephrine-ignorant* subjects were told that there would be no side effects from the Suproxin. The *epinephrine-misinformed* were told that there would be side effects, numbness, itching, and headache, but these are not, of course, the actual symptoms which come as a consequence of receiving epinephrine.

Next, all of the subjects were told that there would be a twenty-minute wait before the visual test began so that the Suproxin could take effect. Meanwhile, they would wait in a room with another subject who had also just received Suproxin—i.e., they were similar to this other subject. In half the cases, this other subject (who was an accomplice) acted in a very euphoric way: doodling, playing "basketball" with a piece of crumpled paper and a basket, making a paper airplane and flying it around the room, making and using a paper slingshot, playing with a hula hoop. In the other half of the cases, both the subjects were given long questionnaires to fill out while waiting. Some of the questions were quite insulting, such as asking about the promiscuity of the subject's mother. The accomplice made comments from time to time about the questions, his comments becoming increasingly angry, until he finally left the room in a fit of great irritation and anger.

The subjects were then given a believable rationale for filling out a questionnaire just before taking the visual tests, and in it they were asked to answer items concerning their current mood since it might affect the tests which were to come. Among subjects who had been with a euphoric accomplice, those who were in the *epinephrine-informed* condition reported less that they felt good or euphoric than did those who had been given no information or had been misinformed. In other words, when the subjects had bodily sensations which they could not readily explain, about which they had no specific schemas, they reported feeling euphoric, like the accomplice. They came to believe that the bodily sensations, which they were actually experiencing because of the epinephrine injection, were caused by their euphoric mood. When the subjects had been given accurate information in advance about why they felt these sensations, they did not turn to the behavior of the accomplice to provide an explanation. Furthermore, the subjects' actual behavior while waiting paralleled their verbal reports of their feelings, as judged by hidden observers who rated their activity while they were with the model. These behavior ratings indicated that subjects in the uninformed and misinformed groups acted in a more happy, euphoric way, following the lead of the accomplice, to a greater extent than did the informed subjects. The subjects who received the placebo were not very different in the reports of their feeling or in their behavior from the informed subjects. It was found that a few of the uninformed and misinformed subjects doped out the real reasons why they were experiencing these bodily sensations; these subjects were much less influenced by the accomplice's behavior than were those who did not. This is as would be expected, since they also had satisfied their need to understand and interpret their state of emotional arousal—they did so, however, in a way which the experimenters had not expected, by seeing through the deception employed. Among the subjects who had waited with an angry accomplice, the results paralleled those just described for the euphoric condition.

In sum, then, this remarkable study showed that when a person lacks appropriate schemas for understanding the causes of some emotional reaction he is experiencing and perceives another person who is in a similar situation as himself, he generalizes this similarity to include the cause of his bodily sensations. He thereby acquires specific schemas about the reasons for his bodily sensations. It is as if we turn to others to find out why we feel as we do.

Let us take a look at another interesting example of turning to similar other people to find out about oneself. Take an individual who is in an emotional state and does know the cause. Suppose too that the individual also has a schema that he can have emotional states of which he is only partially aware; possibly he read enough Freud or the many writings inspired by him to believe that he may have unconscious feelings. Obviously, many college students have this schema about unconscious emotional states. Thus, when he experiences certain bodily sensations, he might take them as signs that there may also be some causes for it beyond those which he is consciously experiencing and aware of. This will be most likely to occur when the actual emotional cues are equivocal or weak, or few in number. He may feel "butterflies" sometimes; his headache may be fleeting; he's not certain his palms are sweaty. He believes some emotion is occurring, but he does not know what it is. In such cases the individual is highly unlikely to have a schema which clearly indicates to him which or how much of an emotion he is experiencing; anxiety may ensue. One way out of this uncomfortable state of affairs is to turn to other people who are in a situation similar to his own in order to see if he can determine what emotion they are experiencing.

Gerard (1963) told some subjects that they were soon to receive an electric shock. Dummy apparatus was attached to them for the ostensible purpose of measuring their emotional states. They were each shown a dial connected to the apparatus which indicated their emotional states. For some subjects, the needle on the dial was quite variable, for others it was quite stable, indicating different degrees of "emotional stability." All of the subjects were then asked whether they would like to wait for the shock alone, or with other subjects who were in the same experiment. The more variable the needle readings had been, the more likely the subjects were to prefer to wait with other subjects. That is, the less clear a basis they had for inferring how frightened they "really" were, the more likely they were to avail themselves of an opportunity to observe another similar subject, so that they could better "find out" how anxious it was appropriate to be. They could then generalize to themselves from someone similar to themselves.

Social Comparison Processes

Turning to observe similar others to find out something about oneself does not occur only when that something is an emotional state. The process also manifests itself when an individual lacks information about his ability level, when he does not have schemas which will assist him in making an evaluation of the level of adequacy of his performances. Singer and Shockley (1965) gave some coeds a test, alone, one at a time, that ostensibly measured their ability to overcome the influence of optical illusions, detail camouflage, etc. Some of the subjects were told that no standards of performance on the test had yet been established. Others were told that their performance had been better, the same as, or poorer, than that of other people who had taken these same tests. All the subjects were then asked whether they wanted to meet other subjects who also had taken the test. The coeds who had been told that there was no standard, i.e., who had not been given a basis for evaluating their ability, indicated more desire to meet other subjects than did those who had been informed of their standing regardless of what their standing was. Probably at least some of children's seeking of friends is part of an effort to find similar others so as to be better able to determine their levels of ability. After all, as children grow they face many new kinds of possible activities, with little basis in their own experience for judging their ability levels.

Much of the research dealing with the use of others as a basis or frame of reference with which to judge one's own abilities, attitudes, and beliefs stems from a theoretical position developed by Festinger (1954). In it he proposes that individuals have a strong need to evaluate or measure their abilities and attitudes. At times, this can be accomplished by reference to direct, physical, or objective measurement. One might, for example, take a standardized test of one's abilities in English composition or mathematics, or might time himself in the 100 yard dash. Then, by referring to others' test scores or to the "record book," he could obtain some very good notion of his relative standing and thus be able to place an evaluation on the adequacy of his own performance. However, where many of the psychologically most significant attributes or qualities of a person are concerned, there is no such objective or physical referent to which he can turn as a basis for evaluation. And yet the desire or need to evaluate the adequacy and appropriateness of these qualities is still great. How does one evaluate the "correctness" of his belief in a Supreme Being, the reasonableness of his fearful reactions to a thunderstorm or earthquake, the appropriateness of his opinion that man's human nature is basically selfish, or the adequacy of his ability to accurately "size up" and understand other people? The answer, of course, is a complicated one, but it seems clear that such judgments are at least in part based on social comparison processes, that the ideas held by others on such points figure as very important items of information whether we realize this at a conscious level or not. For this purpose a person is likely to seek others who are rather similar to himself with regard to the ability or opinion in question, since those who are very dissimilar do not provide information which is very useful for a precise evaluation. Comparison with very dissimilar persons would only indicate that one is better than, say, a complete novice, or worse than an established expert. Experiments like those of Schachter's and Gerard's have been inspired by an extension of Festinger's theory to the area of an individual's evaluation of his own emotions. This sort of extension was first made by Schachter (1959) in studies which indicated that certain subjects expecting to be in a quite frightening experiment which would involve receiving painful electric shocks preferred to be with others who were also waiting for the experiment to waiting alone or with persons who were not going to receive shocks. Detailed analyses of the data from this series of studies on the psychology of affiliation indicated that, indeed, the desire to be with similar others was predicated on a desire to use them as a basis for determining the appropriateness of the person's own reactions. Being able to see just how frightened others are at the prospect of being shocked assisted in judging the propriety of one's own reaction.

It is obvious that there is a distinct parallel between Festinger's and Schachter's work and theorizing and the approach used here. On the other hand, there are several points of variance. The first is that these earlier theories seem to foster a tendency to view the motivation to gather comparison information as the only reason for fearful people's desire to be with other fearful people. The schema approach, as we shall and have seen, suggests that there are many motivations involved in preferring to be with other people in a fearful situation. A second point of difference is that Festinger's theory assumes that an individual is motivated not just to evaluate himself but to evaluate himself very precisely. This assumption appears to be a gratuitous one, since people probably vary in the degree of precision they are motivated to attain. Some may care little about such precision.

The present theory indicates that the observed preference to be with others who are facing the same danger is based at least in part on the motivation to use the schema about similarity being general as a way of acquiring information about how to act or feel in a given situation. However, this motivation is seen as only a special case of a broader approach, while Festinger's theory does not relate social comparison theory to any broader system.

We have thus seen how the schema of similarity between people being general has provided a vehicle for an individual's acquisition of schemas about his own bodily sensations. This schema is but one which can mediate our acquisition of schemas about ourselves through our observation of others. Many of the other schemas about interpersonal relationships which we mentioned in Chapter 6 can also lead to the acquisition of schemas about oneself. For instance, being physically close to another person who is sad may lead us to believe we are sad when we have been unsure as to how we feel. There is, however, little research evidence to demonstrate these other effects.

COMMUNICATION FROM PEERS AS A BASIS
FOR SCHEMA FORMATION

We can turn now to a discussion of the next mode of schema acquisition which was set forth in our plan for this chapter—that of communications from other people whose capacity to understand the world we judge to be about the same as our own. As was pointed out in Chapter 4, we generally assume that other people are in some basic ways very similar to ourselves "under their skins" or "inside their heads." We assume, for example, that other people have the same capabilities for perceiving the world as we ourselves do, since they have the same eyes, ears, and other senses, unless physically handicapped, since they have at least a minimal capacity to reason, and since they have at least a minimal capacity to remember. As a consequence of this very elementary assumption we make about other people's capabilities, we also assume that other people, given the opportunity, will perceive the real world as we do. We make this assumption not only because other people are known to have basically the same sensory and intellectual organs as we ourselves do, but also because there is much evidence to support it. If we walk around a hole in the street, we see that other people walk around the same hole. If we hear thunder and feel drops of rain, we see that both we and other people start hurrying for shelter. In short, then, we acquire a very high order schema to the effect that what is real will be perceived in the same way by all people who are physically capable of doing so. "If the other fellow is directing his eyes in a given direction, he will perceive much the same things as I would in his position."

Because it is based on universal experience, this schema is held by almost all people. And because it is so consistently supported, there may even be a tendency for it to be aroused in situations in which it is not applicable. This over-application of the schema is most noticeable in children. Piaget (1955) has pointed out that children have a tendency to believe that other people see the real world in the same way as they themselves see it, even when the other people are physically not in a position to do so. For instance, if a child is on one side of a mound of earth and is asked what a child on the other side sees, the child will tend to report that the other sees the same things as he himself sees. It is important to note that this schema is generally very low in probabilism. We don't just assume that *most* people will see the wall in front of them—we assume that *all* will see it. We will return to this important point later.

Conformity to Peer Group Judgment

Suppose that an individual is faced with a real situation about which he does not have specific schemas. He may then employ this schema about the universal equivalence of perception of the real world—that other people see the world in similar ways—as a means of acquiring the missing specific schemas. The individual would thus attend to communications from other people to learn how they perceive this chunk of reality. And these communications provide the basis for the individual's acquiring an L.O.S. about that aspect of reality. Sherif (1936) performed some classic studies in such a situation. He brought three people, one at a time, into an already darkened room in such a way that they had no clear idea of how large the room was. He then told them that from time to time a tiny light would go on somewhere off in the distance, and that after a moment or so, it would move for two seconds. The subjects' job was to judge how far it had moved. (In fact, the light did not move; for neurological reasons, a pinpoint of light viewed in an otherwise darkened room will be seen to move. This phenomenon has been termed the autokinetic effect.) Since the subjects did not know how large the room was, they could not estimate how far away the light was, and therefore could not make an accurate judgment about the distance the light had apparently moved. The light was turned on for brief periods of time over a long series of trials and on each trial each subject in the group stated aloud his estimate of the distance he "saw" the light move. Sherif found that as the trials progressed, the distance estimates given by subjects in each group gradually began to converge. The subjects moved toward greater unanimity in their judgments. According to the schema about the real world being seen the same way by all, this development of similar judgments implies that the judgments corresponded to reality. To be sure, there is a certain "irrationality" to this perception, since all the subjects were actually equally incapable of judging how far away the light was and thus of judging its "movement." The reason for the subjects' acceptance of others' judgments is probably a result of their expectation that the experimenter would not give them an impossible task to perform. Sherif found that after having been part of such a "converging" group, subjects continued to make judgments within the narrow range of distances established in the group even when they were subsequently separated from the group and were alone. In fact, Bovard (1948) and Rohrer et al. (1954) found that 28 days and even a year later, people who had been through a "Sherif-like" experiment still made judgments in line with the ones that their group had previously established.

To avoid any misunderstanding of what happened in the Sherif experiments, we must point out that the group affects the judgment an individual makes of the distance between himself and the light, not the actual visual sensory experience of movement of the light (cf. Linton, 1955).

This process of converging in judgments depends on the subjects' belief that the light does, in fact, move. If the light's movement is not perceived as real, then the schema relating agreement and reality is not aroused and the convergence of the group members would not occur. Asch (1952) reports a study in which he told the subjects that the movement of the light was purely "subjective," an effect of processes "in their heads" and thus not real. Much less convergence was found in these groups. The subjects who did converge were found either to have forgotten Asch's words to them, or not to have believed them! Likewise, Crutchfield (in Krech, Crutchfield and Ballachy, 1962) found that people are more likely to agree privately with what they perceive to be the unanimous judgments of a group about a matter of fact than about a matter of opinion.

Many studies since the classic one by Sherif (1936) have shown that when the person is wanting for a specific schema about an aspect of a situation about which the group agrees, he will tend to believe that what the group agrees upon is true. If a person is unsure of the solution to a problem, of the number of peas in a jar, of the number of stones in a mosaic, he will tend to move to the group norm. If he has a schema about the solution of the number of pieces, he is less likely to conform. The consequences of a discrepancy between a person's schema when he has one and the schema the group apparently agrees upon will be discussed in the next chapter.

The studies of a group's influence on its members which have been done since Sherif's study and which will be cited below have not usually followed his methodology. Sometimes subjects learn of other people's beliefs by means of lights on a panel, sometimes by listening to speakers, sometimes by written communication, sometimes by messages that members of thus and such a group tend to believe X. Sometimes the subjects are alone when they learn of others' beliefs, sometimes in groups. These differences are not pertinent for our purposes here, although they no doubt are for other purposes. Furthermore, the materials these studies deal with range from lengths of lines to evaluations of the men in the Kremlin. For reasons that we will discuss shortly, this difference does not present serious problems. On the contrary, the variety of methods and materials used in these studies should lend support to the proposition that the effects found are not limited to any one study or situation.

Limitations on Peer Group Influence

This observed convergence on a single definition of reality as established by the group, even when there are just two people in a group, obviously implies that the farther apart the group members are before they learn of each other's judgments, the more they will have to change their positions. Interpreted slightly differently, this suggests that sometimes the greater the magnitude of a change in a position which is advocated in a communication, the more the recipient of the persuasive communication will change in response to it. However, there are limitations on this relationship between extremity of advocacy and movement. The limitations stem from the fact that, in most cases, the individual has some high order schema even about the ambiguous, uncertain aspect of reality that is involved in most of these studies. As we have pointed out a number of times, the individual turns to others for the lower order, more specific schemas, but not necessarily for related H.O.S.s. For instance, the individual may turn to the group for assistance in ascertaining the number of stones in a mosaic; but he has some broad idea of the feasible range of reasonable judgments. He knows that, for instance, the number is not less than 25 nor greater than 100,000. If the group members make judgments within that range, the individual reacts as he does with the Sherif-type situation and gravitates toward some judgment that is more or less at the center of the range of judgments made in the group. Thus, when the group makes judgments within the range of believability as defined by the H.O.S., the greater the difference between an individual's judgment and the judgments of other members of the group, the more the individual will change. If the divergence between the individual's judgments and the other people's is so great as to be out of the range of believability the individual will begin to question whether his schema applies; perhaps these other people are not, like himself, competent perceivers of the world: they might be stupid, "nuts," phony, physically handicapped. He, therefore, begins to perceive that the schema is not relevant and no longer considers their judgments in making his own about reality. As a consequence, there is a diminution in the ability of the group to influence an individual's judgments when the discrepancy between his and the group's judgments goes beyond some point.

This decrease in the amount of influence at the point where "too much" is demanded by the other group members can be viewed in conjunction with the earlier-mentioned direct relationship between the amount of change advocated and the magnitude of actual change which occurs within the range of believability. As the amount of discrepancy between a person's judgment and the group's starts from zero and then increases, at first he changes more and more, and then the amount of change drops off. This has been found by Koslin, Stoops, and Loh (1967), Bochner and Insko (1966), Aronson, Turner, and Carlsmith (1963), Insko, Murashima, and Saiyadain (1966); in studies employing the number of objects in a display, the quality of poems, such bits of reality as the number of hours of sleep needed each night, judgments of verticality, and others. Sherif, Sherif, and Nebergall (1965) report the same sort of effects for judgments about political affairs.

Interpersonal Influence

If the underlying motivation behind the convergence is to establish agreement so that the people involved can come to believe in the validity of their judgments, can come to have a specific schema about reality, then they can attempt to establish this agreement by changing the judgments of others toward some common one. In other words, the schema "all normals perceive the world accurately and similarly" can be employed in the reverse form for the individual to establish the accuracy and validity of his perceptions. To wit, "Only if we agree in our perceptions are they (is mine) valid." Accordingly, the individual may attempt to change others to agree with him. This attempt to influence others might even have occurred in Sherif's situation, although this is not clear from his data. Festinger, Gerard, Hymovitch, Kelley, and Raven (1952) had a number of college students make guesses about the outcome of an actual labor-management dispute. The subjects then publicly announced their guesses, which tended to converge on a modal judgment. The subjects agreeing with the modal judgment then tended to direct their communications to the disagreeing participants in order to try to change their minds.

The type of conformity which we are discussing here is motivated in a different way than the type discussed in Chapter 6. In that chapter, the motivation involved an effort to bring the social situation into line with the schema that similarity and liking are associated. Sometimes such conformity is an effort to gain acceptance from other members. In the cases discussed in the present chapter, the motivation is primarily an effort to "ascertain" some fact about reality. To be sure, both types of motivation may be present in any given situation, but for theoretical purposes it becomes necessary to distinguish them. On the other hand, it would be foolhardy to simply observe a conforming person in "real life" and just decide on the basis of superficial observation which motive predominated.

Notice that in the above situation the subjects were unable to ascertain for themselves the actual outcome of the labor-management dispute. Thus, in order to develop a specific schema about the outcome, they had to rely on the establishment of agreement among the people who were in their group.

Secord and Backman (1965) have argued that the same sort of process occurs with respect to the schemas a person has about himself. Suppose an individual has some doubt about the accuracy of his judgments about some aspect of himself; he thinks he is intelligent, but is not sure. One way in which he can establish the psychological reality of his intelligence is to get other people to indicate that they too believe he is smart. Of course, he has to be subtle about his approach; he might gently fish for compliments or he might act as if his own ideas are good and try to convince others of their worth.

Not surprisingly, after an individual has experienced a situation in which the reality of his beliefs has been undermined by learning of discrepancies with others, he will feel quite positively toward people who do agree with him (Worchel and Schuster, 1966; Hakmiller, 1966).

In the course of life for most people, there must be many occasions on which they have observed some of the effects of schemas about interpersonal processes we have set forth in this chapter. Especially in his childhood, an individual is likely to have frequently experienced anxiety as a consequence of not having any schemas indicating what he was to do or what was real in a given situation. Likewise, he must have experienced situations in which he acquired schemas about his possible actions as a consequence of his observations of similar, liked, or close other people, and thereby reduced his anxiety. Thus, the individual is highly likely to develop a higher order schema that having such people at hand is a way of reducing anxiety. Therefore, if the individual finds himself in a situation in which he does not know what to do, or what is real, he is highly likely to seek out other people, especially if they are similar to him or are people he likes.

There may exist another consequence of this schema relating unanimity to reality which would be interesting to research. It is that something which on the one hand we "know" is not concretely and physically "real" may appear to be real and true when and if other people also "see" it. For instance, the constitution under which Britain is governed is not written, and yet is very real to the British; they know that others also believe it "exists." Abstract principles, such as justice and truth, are considered to be real in some sense if many people agree that they exist. The unwritten rules of a child's game are very real to them because of the degree of agreement about them. Piaget (1951) has pointed out that children assume that the rules of their games are perceived to have as much concrete reality as the toys with which they play. He attributes this perception to a tendency on the part of children to assimilate the perception of rules to their previously acquired schemas about physical reality; there is only one type of reality in the child's world: material, or physical, reality. His interpretation is obviously quite close to the present one.

If this social definition of reality actually does occur, it would have a very important consequence for the problem of this chapter. The reader will recall that the basic issue faced at the beginning of the chapter involved the anxiety stemming from a lack of specific schemas about some aspect of reality. Up to this section in the chapter we have implicitly limited our discussion to material reality. But the discussion in this section suggests quite dramatically that such a limitation is too restrictive. What is real psychologically may, and often does, go beyond physical, concrete, material reality. It would imply that in certain circumstances, at least, we need not be overly concerned with a distinction between material reality and "abstract" reality; between "factual" statements and "opinion" statements; between beliefs and attitudes. The reason for not making these distinctions would be that they may not be psychologically present or meaningful to the persons being studied, however present they are to some objective observer.

Nevertheless, there are obviously differences among people in the point at which they draw the line and judge certain ideas as subjective, as being truly matters of opinion. These individual differences and their situational determinants cry out for research.

One consequence of making the non-physical real through unanimity concerns situations which are real and are known to be, but which are perhaps not real enough. We have a very successful experience, and it does not become "really" real to us until we tell someone about it; we rush to tell our spouses or good friends. The death of someone may appear more real and final at the funeral than in the privacy of our own sorrow; one explanation for the existence of funeral rituals is that they help the living fully "realize" what has happened. One reason for telling a joke is to make it more real to ourselves: "I have to tell that joke—it's funny to me each time I tell it." A joke becomes funnier to us in the telling, and we sometimes break up into laughter before we can give the punch line. The beauty of a sunset may be more real to us if we see others admiring it; we may seek out others to admire the beauty with us.

SCHEMA DEVELOPMENT FROM OBSERVATION
AND COMMUNICATION IN A NATURAL SETTING

Thus far in our examination of the ways in which people acquire schemas about reality and about themselves, we have examined how observations of others and communications from them influence schema development and lead to the acquisition of L.O.S.s. In natural situations, observations and communications often occur together, interacting and influencing one another. Let us see how this occurs in certain natural, real life situations. For example, what happens to groups of strangers who assemble to form a committee; to a number of people who have been hired at the same time and have been formed into the same work section; to a group of new draftees who have been assigned to bunks in the same part of a barracks; or to a group of freshmen who happen to room in the same wing of a dormitory. In all these instances, the people do not know one another, they have no lower order, specific schemas about one another. Further, exactly what they are to be doing as a group is not very clear; the situation is so new for them that they have only the highest order of schemas about what they are there for. The company, Army, or other organization has defined only the general objectives of the group. Even more to our present point, the members of the group do not have any L.O.S.s about how they should relate to one another, about who does what under which circumstances. Of course, something in the situation might arouse one of the schemas about interpersonal processes which we mentioned in Chapter 6, such as the relationship between liking and similarity; if such a schema were aroused, the amount of anxiety experienced in such a setting would be mitigated. Or the members might have schemas about categories of people in the group—instructors, students, Spaniards, or others. Further, if the group is similar in certain obvious respects to other groups in which the individual has participated, he should be less anxious. Or, if the group meets in a familiar setting, or under familiar rules, such as Roberts' Rules of Order, anxiety will be lessened. But, in the cases we are describing, it can sometimes happen that the members know so little about each other and their interrelationships that there is little in the situation to arouse any of the above schemas. Sometimes people will have a schema about how to act when meeting strangers, when making new acquaintances. Such schemas will, of course, reduce anxiety, but in some cases, they may prove inadequate, may guide behavior only up to a very rudimentary point and then be useless to guide it beyond that point. Two young people out on a blind date may have some schemas about how to act when first meeting, but may be tongue-tied after the initial "ritual"; anxiety ensues. In short, such situations are clearly ones which tend to generate anxiety.

The negative effects of a lack of detailed schemas about another person in a group setting have been illustrated in a study by Smith (1957) in which he had groups of people play the parlor game of Twenty Questions, in which the group could address no more than 20 questions to the experimenter in an effort to determine what object, person, idea, he had in mind. In some groups, three legitimate subjects were faced with two other subjects (actually trained assistants) who remained completely silent, with no explanation being given for their silence. In other groups, the silence of the two was explained via their answers to a questionnaire as reflecting their "usual role" of listeners. In still other groups, there were no silent members. Smith found that having a silent group member reduced the group's effectiveness in the game, especially if no explanation was provided to account for his silence. Likewise, the members of groups in which there were no silent members, or in which the silence of the two "subjects" was explained, indicated on a post-experimental questionnaire that they felt more satisfied with the group.

Let us consider the cases in which anxiety-reducing factors are minimal. How will the group members cope with their anxiety? One way in which their anxiety can be reduced stems from the members' previous experiences with groups, and social situations in general. The members no doubt have experienced situations before in which anxiety was associated with a lack of schemas relevant to their own and other people's actions; and the members no doubt experienced situations in which an absence of anxiety was associated with group members having well-defined expectations about one another's behavior. Thus, it is highly likely that the group members possess schemas of a negative association between anxiety and having schemas. These schemas can then guide the actions of the members in the direction of acquiring schemas about their own and others' actions in the group; about a system of expectations regarding who does what under which circumstances; a set of schemas referring to the interaction among the people in the group. If such a set of schemas is acquired by the members of a group, the group no longer is schema-less and anxiety will be reduced. The members will then have schemas which refer to their own behavior, what they "do" in the group, what they are expected to do in the group, and a set of schemas about what the other members of the group do. These schemas are quite likely to be integrated into an H.O.S. that indicates where each person fits in the interaction among group members. One person might be the source of information; another might be the joker or clown; another might do the hard work; another might be the person who has "all the ideas." These schemas can refer not only to the allocation of "jobs" in the group but also to the evaluations which the members make of one another, who likes whom, and who dislikes whom; which persons are friendly to others outside the group, and which are not. Secord and Backman (1965) have pointed out that one of the most important consequences of the stabilization of actions in a group is that the schemas that individual members of the group have about themselves are supported. That is, if an individual came to the group holding the schema that he is a good "idea" man, the consistently positive response of the other members of the group to his ideas will tend to support this schema. Of course, if another idea man has beaten him out, the person might decide to quit the group to avoid the resultant anxiety.

The reader should not get the impression that we are saying that people in groups set up formal tables of organization about the various activities of the members. Such schemas about who does what have been found in the most informal or casual groups. In fact, in many groups, these schemas may not be verbalized very much by the members to one another under ordinary circumstances; but should a member do the unexpected, violate the schema about what he is to do, both he and the other members of the group would be sure to be somewhat anxious; they might then recognize the schema they had.

How the various jobs within the group are sorted out is a result of a number of factors. Some people are obviously better able to perform certain jobs than are other people. In the beginning of the group, the person who does certain things better than others will perceive that this is so, and so will the other members of the group. If he is motivated to participate in the group, he will continue to act in these relatively effective ways. Thus, he and the others will acquire a schema that *this* is what he does, and does well. Or, another person might not be more able to act in certain ways, but he might have more need to do so. He might be motivated to be the wisecracker because he may need to perceive himself as having a good sense of humor. Thus, this person would gravitate toward the "job" of wisecracking. Or, the allocation of jobs may be sheerly a matter of accident, of who happens to have a deck of cards with him or who happens to have a cousin who worked in this company before. Or, after a while, the members of the group may deliberately determine what the most efficient organization of work or play is, and assign jobs accordingly. The point of this discussion is not the obvious one that people differ in their abilities or goals. The point is that these differences in need and ability lead to a certain

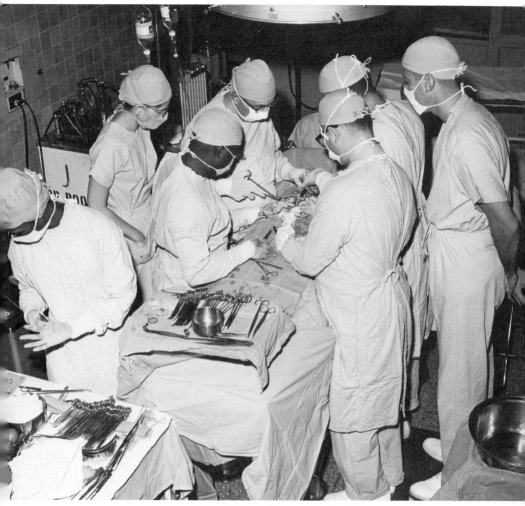

Formalization of role requirements.

stabilization of actions in the group, provided the jobs that need to be done in the group do not change very radically.

The members of the group may acquire schemas about one another and about how they interact with each other, through means other than observational processes. In addition, they communicate with one another. They talk about one another's behavior, both directly with the person talked about and with others. Through this communication, the members soon learn that the other members of the group share schemas about one another to a greater or lesser degree. Since they have no doubt observed more or less the same behavior in the group, the schemas they have acquired are generally quite similar. They may discover that they have all separately recognized that John is the idea man. This communication, however, has additional effects. As we have seen, the individual group members will tend to come to an agreement in their schemas about one another, since the communication is about something which is real—each other's behavior. They will tend to come to an agreement about how much of an idea man John is, about how funny the clown is, about who gets along with whom. These agreed-upon schemas about the jobs that each member of the group has can be referred to as social roles.

An Example of a New Group Developing Schemas

The process by which group members develop schemas about one another and their patterns of interaction has rarely been studied in its pure form. A study of such development was one of the few positive outcomes of a tornado which struck Topeka, Kansas, in 1966 (Taylor, Zurcher, and Key, 1970). A sociologist became non-professionally and deeply involved as a member of a volunteer aid crew and later reported his experiences, as well as comments from his fellow crew members. For example, the authors report on the occurrence of just the sort of process described above as follows: ". . . toward the end of the work day, a rudimentary division of labor began to develop. When a job was nearing completion, Contactman would scout in advance of the truck, spot homes endangered by debris, and speak with the owners about the crew's helping them. Monsterman drove the truck and operated the power winch. Climbers I and II scrambled on rooftops and up trees, setting the hook of the winch. Sawman I moved in with his power saw when rapid cutting was needed. Roper I, who had joined the crew late Friday afternoon, affixed guide or hauling ropes when necessary" (1970, p. 87). And, apparently, these developments were subjectively felt by the participants in the work crew themselves, as one of them is reported to have said ". . . I think we learned a way of working, you know, like the guy who could drive, the Monster. There was the driver, and there was the guy who could kind of size up the situation, and another guy sort of assumed the task of talking with the people in the house. I think certainly very specific roles emerged that were quite appropriate to what we had to do. It's interesting, I still don't know the names of the guys. . . . It didn't seem important to ask. . . . It seems irrelevant " (1970, p. 92).

One consequence of the growing agreement about each other's behavior may be that the shared schemas become more real to the group members. As was discussed in the box above, schemas about which people are in agreement among themselves may take on an additional quality of reality. They conform to the H.O.S. that reality is perceived unanimously by similarly able people. Thus, the group members acquire schemas about one another which are reacted to as if they were concrete objects: John's job in the group is to give ideas; Hank's job is to clown; Jenny's job is to smooth over ruffled feathers. The jobs are reacted to as "things." This perception of the "jobs" that people have are sometimes referred to as social roles.

In addition to the social roles, the group members communicate about the ways in which they relate to one another, the patterns of interaction, the social structure or system. "We do thus and such first; then we do that"; "We kid around a while and then we play cards." These schemas also take on an aura of reality, of "thingness," just as in the case of social roles, as the group members communicate with one another about these matters.

COMMUNICATIONS FROM EXPERTS AS A SOURCE OF SCHEMAS

So far in this chapter we have emphasized the individual's acquisition of information through observations of and communications from his peers, the "Twenty-million-Frenchmen-can't-be-wrong" approach. We now turn to the next item on our agenda for this chapter—an examination of the role that communications from experts has in our acquisition of schemas about the world. There are many aspects of the environment, of the world, which we believe that we can perceive, but only if we have special training or experience or skill. These may be seen as necessary in order to obtain the information in the first place, or in order to interpret the significance of obtained information. Anyone can examine an X-ray, but only someone with radiological training can tell us what it means. In fact, much of our first information about the world came from experts with greater training, experience, and skill than ourselves, namely, our parents. And throughout our lives we encounter many instances in which we have to rely on experts for knowledge about the world: teachers, craftsmen, doctors, electricians, professors, lawyers, mechanics, and many others. In this world of increasing specialization and of complexity of knowledge, we come more and more to live in a world which can adequately be described to us only by experts. Thus, it is small wonder that many people acquire a schema which indicates that specialists in given areas of experience are reliable sources of schemas about their areas of specialization.

In many instances, people assume that an expert is someone like themselves, who sees reality as we all do, but who simply has had more experience or training and can thus know about aspects of reality inaccessible to the rest of us. In a sense, then, we trust the expert because we assume we could also see the world as he does if we had his training or experience. He is then like us, and the expert schema and the schema about peers are mutually supportive, rather than contradictory. Nonetheless, in other cases, experts are not accepted on this basis. We may assume that a person has a special gift to see a special aspect of reality. The poet, the great writer, the philosopher, the priest, the mystic, may all be perceived as being expert in ways that the rest of us could not attain even with training because we lack some inborn knack, gift, talent, or other trait. In these cases, the individual has a special set of H.O.S.s which provide a basis for assuming that a given writer or mystic sees parts of the world that we cannot. These H.O.S.s may, for example, constitute a theory of literary genius, or a theology about mystic relations with the supernatural.

Types of Experts and Opinion Leaders

The term expert should not be limited to those who have some "official" or formal designation as such because of the jobs they have, such as mechanic or doctor. The term also applies to those people who just happen to be better informed about certain areas, regardless of their vocations. Katz (1965) reviews much research which indicates that a great deal, if not most, of the time we turn to such people in everyday life, people whom we may call "opinion leaders." The person who reads more about politics is asked his opinion about candidates, and others accept them. Women turn to young, unmarried women for ideas about fashions. Younger housewives turn to older ones for ideas about shopping. As Katz points out, these experts are often of about the same social status as the people who listen to them. However, what distinguishes these experts is that they either have direct experience in the area of their expertise, or they turn to still other experts to become better informed. They often do the latter by reading magazines and newspapers, watching TV, or by using other sources of information. Thus, these are experts' experts (and so on?).

Low Probabilism of the "Expert" Schema

The number and variety of experts that many people encounter in life, and the frequent reliability of the information obtained from them, tend to make this schema one of low probabilism, the number of instances compatible with it being legion. Furthermore, as pointed out earlier, as a high order schema its probabilism is kept low for several other reasons. One type of reason which is especially significant is that L.O.S.s subsumed under it are kept consistent with it, so as to reduce the number of exceptions. More concretely, we tend to perceive situations in line with the communications of experts, and thus provide ourselves with additional support for the schema. If an expert tells us that a given painting is beautiful, we may find the beauty in it; if an expert tells us a given poem is second-rate, we may quickly find its flaws. And then we will have more instances in which the expert was right. Another factor strengthening this schema stems from the fact that the needs that are met by some of these experts are so strong that there is strong motivation to perceive them as being veridical. Think of the anxiety we would experience if we lost much of the typical confidence in the professional competence of doctors; think of the anxiety we would experience if we had to drive a car repaired by a mechanic of dubious ability. To avoid such kinds of anxiety, we need strongly to keep the probabilism of schemas about the utility of experts low. Still another factor tending to keep the probabilism of this schema about experts low is that it is not independent of the schema we discussed earlier in this chapter about reality being perceived similarly by similarly competent people. In most cases, most of our friends, peers, and colleagues share the same beliefs about the same experts. Thus, we come to believe in the reality of the expert.

Our belief in experts may be so low in probabilism that when receiving communications from them we may come to accept what they say without attending very much to the reasons that they give for what they say (McGuire, 1969). A doctor's conscientious explanation of why a given medication has an effect on this tissue rather than that may pass us right by, but we will still use the medication. A lawyer may tell us about torts (and retorts), but we may just accept his advice. Of course, an additional reason for our acceptance of this information from the expert is simply that we do not have the schemas to grab hold of more than a limited amount of information which he communicates to us. The power of experts is indicated in the following study. Bochner and Insko (1966) gave subjects communications from a peer or from a medical expert, who advocated the position that only very little or no sleep per night was actually necessary for people. The subjects rejected the idea of so little sleep when it came from a peer and disparaged the peer. However, the researchers found that the less sleep advocated by an expert, the less sleep the subjects thought necessary. An expert does not completely lose his influence, under at least these circumstances, even when he makes outlandish proposals. Similar results were obtained by Aronson, Turner, and Carlsmith (1963), who had their subjects make ratings of poems.

In the face of all we have just said, we now have to place some qualifiers on our discussion. Notice the variety of sources which influence the probabilism of the schema regarding experts: our experience in testing their knowledge, our need for the information they give, the support that they have from our peers. All of these factors influencing the probabilism of this schema could vary in their influence on a given person or group of people because of idiosyncratic variations in their experience. For instance, some people may have lost out in all of their dealings with lawyers; some may have had many experiences with inept but expensive plumbers. These instances may have been so frequent as to weaken the schema about experts, or the somewhat lower order schemas about particular types of experts, such as lawyers or plumbers. For other people the needs satisfied by experts may be of lesser importance. The senior author recalls a witty and dedicated Scotsman arguing in Speaker's Corner in London that, as a matter of personal integrity, one should die of one's own diseases and refuse all medication. Or, one may have been in a group such as Christian Scientists, in which some types of experts (medical doctors) are rejected.

Source vs. Content Orientation to Expert Information

At several points in our discussion thus far, we have mentioned the degree to which a person attends to the content of the communication from an expert. For instance, we have just seen how a person who has less confidence in experts is more likely to attend to the reasons they give for the conclusions they make than a person whose schema about experts is so strong that he accepts them implicitly. This distinction between reacting to the expertness of the expert and reacting to what he says has been described as "source vs. content" orientation. In source orientation, the person's aroused schemas contain dimensions which concern the expert; in content orientation, the dimensions of the aroused schemas concern the content of the message. As we have implied, people may differ in their tendency to be source or content oriented (cf. McDavid, 1959).

Despite the ability of people to focus on the content or source, there is a considerable amount of interaction between the two. If an individual focuses on the source, for example, the schemas about the source may then determine how the content is perceived. The perception of the content is made consistent with schemas about the source. On the other hand, if schemas about content are aroused, the perception of the source will be influenced by the content schemas. Let us examine some of the complex ways in which source and content affect one another.

Denial of Reputed Expertise

One of the most straightforward ways in which a schema about a source can influence perception of content is for the schema to hold the source as a non-expert—a false expert, a source which claims to be an expert but really is not. Thus, Hovland and Weiss (1951) showed that Americans are less likely to accept a communication if it is attributed to a Russian newspaper than if it is attributed to a reliable American one, like The New York Times. For reasons that will become more evident later, it should be noted that this effect of perceived disrespectability of the source was measured immediately after the communication was presented; below, we will see how this effect may change with time.

Sometimes our schemas about an expert's being misleading are aroused by our perception that he has a vested interest in presenting a given point of view. On the other hand, if an expert presents an argument which is obviously not in his best interest, persons tend to believe that they can be more assured of his objectivity and are therefore likely to be more convinced by him. Mills and Jellison (1967) had subjects read a speech that was supposed to have been given by a political candidate in which he advocated increasing taxes on truckers. The subjects were told that he had given the speech either to truckers or to railroad men. The subjects were more influenced by his speech when they believed he had spoken to a group of truckers; presumably, it took honesty and courage to tell the truckers they should be taxed more. Walster, Aronson, and Abrahams (1966) found that even a person of low prestige or expertness is believed more if he argues against his own self-interest. On the other hand, if the expert's bias or self-interest is perceived to overlap with that of his audience, then the audience might be more accepting of his communication. Mills (1966) found that if a speaker indicates to his audience that he likes them, they will be more accepting of what he says when he says that he is trying to influence them than when he says he doesn't care whether they believe him or not. When he says he likes them and that he would like to influence them, he presumably is trying to help them: they evidently accept the help. On the other hand, Mills found that if a speaker said that he disliked his audience, they rejected his ideas more if he said he was trying to influence them—thus suggesting his harming them—than if he did not say this. In short, we tend to be more accepting of communications from honest experts than biased ones, unless we happen to share the latter's bias.

Perceived Objectivity and "Overhearing" a Message

Another way in which we believe we can learn what an expert's honest beliefs are is by having access to his private ideas. What does a lawyer say to his partner when neither client, judge, nor jury are present? On the basis of our experience, we no doubt have the schema that people, including the lawyer, will be more candid and fair in private than in public. A number of studies have indicated that if we eavesdrop on such private communications, we will tend to believe them. Walster and Festinger (1962) escorted students from an introductory psychology course through the psychology laboratory and led them to believe that they were overhearing some graduate students talking against cigarette smoking. Some of the introductory students were led to believe that the graduate students actually knew they could be heard, while others were told that the graduate students did not know that they were being overheard. The smokers among the psychology students were more influenced if they thought they were really eavesdropping. Brock (1965) found that when a student "overheard" a telephone conversation in which a member of the psychology department advocated a reduction in tuition rates, he was less likely to be convinced by the argument if the conversation was obviously going to be heard by students than if it were "entirely" accidental that he overheard the conversation.

The individual obviously has many experiences in his life in which he has agreed with valid experts and disagreed with invalid ones. Thus, he is highly likely to acquire a schema corresponding to this experience. And, as in the case of the schemas we examined in the previous three chapters, the individual will tend to perceive the world consistently with these schemas. Kelman and Eagly (1965) varied the credibility of the source of messages. Their subjects tended to perceive the messages from highly credible sources as being more supportive of their own points of view than they actually were. Likewise, Manis (1960) found his subjects tending to minimize the extent to which the expressed views of high prestige communications deviated from their own opinions.

Suppose that an individual and an expert are in a high degree of agreement; they are members of the same ideological group. The individual then has a schema that he is in agreement with this expert and that he tends to agree with valid experts in general. There are therefore strong forces in him to perceive that he, the expert, and the ideology are in agreement. If he is then confronted with a statement that appears superficially to suggest that the expert now rejects the ideology, one course the individual can take is to reinterpret the statement so that it is less or not at all divergent from the ideology. On the other hand, the individual will develop a schema that he disagrees with false experts and a schema that he disagrees with a given false expert. He will then interpret, at least somewhat, any equivocal or ambiguous statement consistently with these schemas. Examples of how this process of perceiving consistently with these schemas occurs come from research reported by Asch (1952). He had some American college students read the following statement: "I hold that a little rebellion, now and then, is a good thing, and as necessary in the political world as storms are in the physical." Half the students were told the statement was made by Jefferson, half by Lenin. Then both groups were asked to give their interpretation of the statements. The difference between the two sets of interpretations is dramatically illustrated by the following examples, although the amount of "reinterpretation" needed is greater with respect to Jefferson than Lenin (pp. 421–422).

JEFFERSON

Thomas Jefferson meant to imply that when institutions no longer represented the people, those institutions can be overthrown. Jefferson, however, was a bit rash when he made the statement. He certainly did not believe that every twenty years there had to be a political revolution, and his political career was moderate, and not as fiery as his words. His over-zealous statement only meant to imply that the mass of people should be allowed to participate in the government.

Jefferson did not mean both a

LENIN

Lenin based his statement on the Marxian dynamic concept of society. He implied that the world is ever changing and that rebellions were necessary, now and then, to ensure the progress of society. He also implies that individuals can influence their destinies by their own actions.

Lenin is justifying the Russian Revolution and probably all revolutions as a potential source of good.

I believe that Lenin here meant rebellion in the sense of outright revolution within a country, not against aggressors. I totally disagree social and political revolution. A political revolution, to him, probably meant little more than a change in the bureaucracy. However, many who have used this quotation have inserted a much different meaning.

Jefferson wanted an America for Americans. He did not want the abuses which came from the control of the English. Therefore he attempted to justify the American Revolution. But he did not mean that revolution itself was a good or necessary thing. It depends on the circumstances and on foreign influences.

In order for the conditions of the people to be improved, there must be some agitation now and then so that attention will be focused on need for reforms and change.

Jefferson probably meant rebellion as an upheaval in personal political opinions within a party, rather than a revolutionary turnover of one party by another.

I think Jefferson meant the word "rebellion" to be forcing an issue before an apathetic administration.

"A little rebellion" is a necessary thing in order to keep the politicians on their toes and to remind them that they are servants of the people.

By "little rebellion" Jefferson might have meant what we would now call third parties.

By rebellion he means alertness and the exercise of political rights.

that it is essential "now and then." However, I do believe that political factions are necessary. . . .

A statement like the one quoted would be expected to come from a man like Lenin, with his revolutionary ideas.

Lenin was probably vindicating the Russian Revolution. He meant that a Revolution is not bad but good and necessary. It is necessary as it removes evils and cleanses as a storm does the physical world.

Lenin may have been speaking his own words, the words he believed, or he may have been speaking such words in order to justify a program. That is all we can assume. We cannot state clearly what the utterance meant to its author. By trying to we inject our own feelings.

I don't think such a statement is consistent with the philosophy of Lenin. He would rather apply it to specific historical conditions. In other words, I don't think he made it.

This does not seem to be an abstraction from Lenin, since it would not be likely or consistent that Lenin would speak of "a little rebellion, now and then." The entire statement seems too diffuse and abstract.

The "Sleeper" Effect

Throughout this whole discussion of the effects of false and valid experts, we have not made much of the basic proposition with respect to information with which we began. That is, it was pointed out that people tend to develop an H.O.S. which stresses the value of having specific schemas about a given situation which is being confronted. When the individual's schemas about a particular source indicate that the source is a reliable one, then the schema about the source and the schema regarding the utility of specific information work hand-in-hand to foster ready acceptance of the communication involved. In the cases which we have just described, however, the two schemas are working at cross-purposes. The schema to the effect that a source is unreliable will act to deter the individual from accepting information from that source and thus from acting in accord with the H.O.S. about the value of having specific schemas. "I would like to accept what you say about this situation because I don't know much about it myself, but I really don't trust you."

However, suppose that an individual has heard some expert, whether judged to be false or valid, make a statement only one time, or a very limited number of times. Under such conditions, the individual is much less likely to form a strong relationship between the source and his communication than if several occasions were experienced in which the expert made these statements. Suppose further that the person does not know very much about the topics to which the communication refers and therefore has at least some motivation to accept the information because it clarifies some ambiguity. Then, in view of the utility of the information, a condition may be created such that he is likely to accept the information contained in a communication without necessarily remembering who said it. How little of what we know about the world is identified by us as to source! Notice that this process of separating the source of information from its content can occur regardless of whether the source of information was a valid expert or a false expert. Thus, the individual may come to accept information from a false expert if he is highly motivated to gain information. Of course, this process which may lead to the acceptance of ideas from false experts cannot take place in the situation in which the communication is received, since the association between the source and the statement is too apparent there. However, if the individual leaves the situation so that the schema about the false source is hardly likely to be aroused, then the individual does come to accept the information from the false source.

This process was shown in a study by Hovland and Weiss (1951). They had some students listen to a message about a new drug, attributing the message to a medical journal for some students and to a mass circulation journal for others. They gave other students a message about atomic submarines attributing it either to Robert Oppenheimer (the man who helped lead America's development of the A-bomb) or to Pravda, the Russian newspaper. Still another group of students received a message about a shortage of steel, some thinking it came from an economist, others from an extremely right-wing columnist. The immediate effects of the communications from the "false experts" were like those in the studies cited above: less acceptance of the message from them than from the valid experts. Notice, however, that all three messages concerned topics about which students would hardly be expected to have a large fund of information; and notice also that the association between the message and the source was experienced only once. It is not surprising, then, that some weeks later the students markedly increased their acceptance of the messages from the false experts. An instance of what has come to be called the sleeper effect. The effects of the messages from the valid experts had dropped somewhat over time, so that the degree of acceptance of the messages from the false and valid sources was not appreciably different.

Suppose that the person is reminded of the connection between the false source and the message some weeks later, after he has come to accept the false message. Then, the individual will once again reject the message, since he no longer can conveniently forget or ignore the connection between the two. This was demonstrated in a study by Kelman and Hovland (1953), who also found the same sleeper effect as did Hovland and Weiss, but were able to eliminate it by simply reminding the subjects that they had received a message on the topic in question from a false expert.

In Chapter 4, sleeper effects were also discussed. In the cases discussed there, the effect was the reverse of the present one in that the communication had no immediate effect, but did have an effect after the messages were digested by the subjects. Obviously, the cause of the sleeper effect was also different from the present one. There has been, however, some speculation that in one of the studies illustrating the previously mentioned form of the sleeper effect, the underlying dynamics were not very different from the presently cited ones of rejection of the source. In that investigation, soldiers were shown the film, "The Battle of Britain" by the Army in order to improve their attitudes toward the British. There is little doubt that many of the soldiers resented this effort to change them, since their attitudes toward the Army were less than positive. They may have considered the Army much like a false expert and may have thus rejected its film. However, given the low level of knowledge about the Battle of Britain, they tended over time to cut the bond between the source and the message and then to accept the implications of the message. It is not unlikely that both this false expert process and the reaction-to-implications process functioned in this setting. This provides a good example of how more than one process may validly explain the same effect, especially in natural settings.

The Judgment of Controversial Issues

In our discussion of the relationship between the source of a statement and its effects, we have concentrated thus far on valid and false reports. We have not said very much about interrelationships between source and content when experts are not exclusively involved. For instance, we have not said very much about situations in which both peers and experts may be involved. Let us now turn to one particular type of situation in which both peers and experts are likely to be sources of messages, situations of controversy, those in which groups of peers and experts disagree with other groups of peers and experts.

Suppose an individual is involved in a controversy of some sort: he is a member of a group that is undergoing an attack; he is involved in an election campaign, or in a referendum on an issue about which he has strong convictions. Many such controversies arise because some choice is soon to be made by a community, usually—but not always—an election in which people vote for or against some candidate or proposition. Many such controversial issues are discussed in public as if there were only two possible positions, being for or against a given policy, e.g., being for or against the war in Vietnam or the busing of school children. Furthermore, an individual may not only have observed the public controversy, he may also have had discussions, nay, arguments, with people on the opposing side, again a situation in which there is a polarization of views into pro and con. Or, the individual may have heard experts, i.e., leaders, argue strongly for or against the positions on the "other side." In short, controversy ordinarily involves views crystallized into pro and con, into two camps, with little room for the moderate middle, who see justice on both sides. "You're either for me or against me."

If an individual is somehow involved in such a controversy, he will soon acquire a schema that statements made in such situations are of two sorts, pro or con. The existence of moderate, balanced, compromising, or even noncommittal statements is denied. Thus, when people involved in such controversies are presented with a series of statements whose positions in the controversy would otherwise be judged to range by a series of small steps from one extreme to the other, there is a tendency to perceive that the statements are in either the pro or the con category.

All of this was nicely illustrated by a laboratory experiment done by Atkins and Bieri (1968). Their subjects were people who were either very strongly pro- or very strongly anti-religion. Some of each type was introduced to another person, a peer (actually a trained assistant) who maintained just the opposite opinion from the person. The two were then asked to argue about religion for a few moments. Other subjects did not meet another person or otherwise engage in any argument. Then all of them were presented with three statements selected from a series of statements which ranged by steps from extremely pro-religion, through a moderate position, to extremely anti-religion. They were then asked to indicate how pro- or anti-religion they thought each statement was. The subjects who had been involved in an argument were more likely than the others to classify all the statements as being only either pro or con. Those just emerging from the argument saw the statements in terms of the schema they had just acquired from the argument or of a schema about the polarization of views about religion which they had previously acquired and which were aroused by the argument.

Similar results have been obtained in more natural settings. Manis (1960) found that students who were either strongly pro-fraternity or anti-fraternity judged statements about fraternities as being extremely pro or con; they did this more than did students who were neutral; that is, who were less likely to be involved in campus controversies about fraternities. Zavallini and Cook (1965) had subjects who varied in their positions on one of the most controversial issues in American society in the 60's when their study was conducted, the issue of the civil rights of Negroes. These subjects were also asked to make judgments about the positions represented by various statements. The subjects who were favorable to the Negroes placed the statements in either of the extreme categories. Those who were less favorable, but who were not extremely anti-Negro, were less prone to place statements in extreme positions. Sherif, Sherif, and Nebergall (1965) report that South Texans who were extremely anti-Mexican-American were more prone than neutral or uninvolved Texans to place statements about Mexican-Americans in extreme categories. These authors also report that members of the League of Women Voters who were heavily involved in a controversy over fluoridation of drinking water were more extreme in their judgments of statements than were women who were not involved (or as well-informed as the League members).

Assimilation and Contrast Phenomena

Research on the issues we have just examined was instigated by the work of Hovland, Harvey, and Sherif (1957) and carried on mostly by Sherif. Their interpretation of results similar to the ones just described is different in some respects from the one given here. Sherif interprets the tendency to place statements in extreme categories as a result of the perceptual processes of assimilation and contrast. Assimilation refers to the tendency to exaggerate the perceived similarity of two objects which are already similar to some degree. Contrast refers to the tendency to exaggerate the difference between objects which are, in fact, somewhat different. Thus it has been found in the psychological laboratory that the more different two objects are, the more likely they are to be contrasted rather than assimilated. Sherif and his colleagues argued that the same occurs for statements of positions in a controversy. A person who is at one extreme, who is usually a more involved person, thus will assimilate to his own positions those which are close to his own and contrast those which are more distant. Those in the middle, the less involved people, will be less likely to assimilate and contrast, partly because they have less well-defined positions, partly because they have less "room to contrast."

However plausible the Sherif and Hovland argument is, the results have not borne them out very well. Although both contrast and assimilation have been found, they have frequently not been found to occur within the same study (Sherif, Sherif, and Nebergall, 1965). Some studies find contrast effects, while others give evidence of assimilation. If anything, assimilation seems to occur more frequently than contrast. Sherif does not have any convenient method for explaining these shifts. On the other hand, the present approach suggests that the irregularity of results is an outcome of the particular issue being studied and the nature of the controversy. In some controversies, the line of demarcation between the two positions may be closer to the "logical" middle, in other cases the line may be perceived closer to one extreme than the other. Statements on one side of the line would be assimilated; on the other, contrasted. Thus, to predict where the point of contrast and point of assimilation occur, it would be necessary to closely study the arguments used by both sides in a given controversy. To complicate matters, the lines may shift through the course of a controversy or over time independently of the controversy, as in the case of the shifting meanings of Hawks and Doves in the Vietnam War.

Disagreement Among Experts and Information Selection

So far, in our discussion of experts, we have considered the situation in which there is one expert per issue or "chunk" of reality. "Our family doctor tells us what is the matter with us."

"The history professor knows about the American Revolution." However, there are many situations in which we not only expect more than one expert, such as two doctors or two history professors, we also expect that there will be disagreement between or among the experts. Political opponents, opposing lawyers, and debaters are special kinds of experts whom we expect to disagree with other experts. If a person has more allegiance to one expert rather than to the other, then this situation is not very different from the ones we have been examining up to now. However, there are special cases in which we have acquired a schema that the truth emerges only after both sides of an issue are heard. Probably legal trials are the most common examples. Accordingly, if an individual is presented with information relevant to just one side of a legal contest, he will be motivated to get information and arguments from the other side; in so doing, he will learn the truth, he expects. This process was demonstrated by Sears (1966) in a study in which subjects received a synopsis of the trial of a juvenile who was charged with killing her father. Some subjects read no summation of the case. Others read the closing statement of either the prosecutor or the defense attorney. Still other subjects read both closing statements. The subjects were then asked to indicate which of several different kinds of additional information they wanted about the case. The subjects who had read the closing statements of only one of the attorneys showed more preferences for the other attorney's closing statement than did the subjects who received either no summation of the case or both attorneys' positions. The subjects who received no summation at all showed the most preference for an "overview" of the case; the two attorney subjects showed little preference for the overview.

This schema about trials is apparently so strong that if an individual believes he is getting new information about the side opposite to the one he may have already voted for, he will tend to accept this information simply because he believes it is new. More concretely, Sears and Freedman (1965) had subjects read about a murder trial and vote for acquittal or prosecution. Then the subjects were given two articles to read, one favoring the prosecution, one the defense. Before reading these articles, however, some of the subjects were told that the information was new, derived from a legal seminar about the case which had access to new information. Other subjects were told that the information was old, but consisted of the comments of legal authorities who were asked to comment on the case. Despite the fact that all the subjects read the same two articles, those who were told it was new changed their opinions about the case more than the other subjects. This outcome could have resulted from either or both of two processes: more intensive reading of the "new" articles, or more readiness to accept the "new" information. In any case, the individual's actions were consistent with the schema about learning about two sides of an issue.

References

Allport, F.: *Social Psychology*. Boston, Houghton-Mifflin, 1924.

Aronson, E., Turner, J. A., and Carlsmith, J. M.: Communicator credibility and communication discrepancy as determinants of opinion change. *Journal of Abnormal and Social Psychology*, 1963, 67:31–36.

Asch, S.: *Social Psychology*. Englewood Cliffs, New Jersey, Prentice-Hall, 1952.

Atkins, A. L., and Bieri, J.: Effects of involvement level and contextual stimuli on social judgment. *Journal of Personality and Social Psychology*, 1968, 9:197–204.

Bandura, A.: Influence of models' reinforcement contingencies on the acquisition of imitative responses. *Journal of Personality and Social Psychology*, 1965, 1:589–595.

Bandura, A., Grusec, J. E., and Menlove, F. L.: Some social determinants of self-monitoring reinforcement systems. *Journal of Personality and Social Psychology*, 1967, 5:449–455.

Bandura, A., Ross, D., and Ross, S. A.: Transmission of aggression through imitation of aggressive models. *Journal of Abnormal and Social Psychology*, 1961, 63:575–582.

Berger, S. M.: Observer practice and learning during exposure to a model. *Journal of Personality and Social Psychology*, 1966, 3:696–701.

Bettelheim, B.: Individual and mass behavior in extreme situations. *Journal of Abnormal and Social Psychology*, 1943, 38:417–452.

Bochner, S., and Insko, C. A.: Communicator discrepancy, source credibility, and opinion change. *Journal of Personality and Social Psychology*, 1966, 4:614–621.

Bovard, E.: Social norms and the individual. *Journal of Abnormal and Social Psychology*, 1948, 43:62–69.

Brock, T. C.: Commitment to exposure as a determinant of information receptivity. *Journal of Personality and Social Psychology*, 1965, 2:10–19.

Dibner, A.: Ambiguity and anxiety. *Journal of Abnormal and Social Psychology*, 1958, 56:165–173.

Elliott, R.: Effects of uncertainty about the nature and advent of a noxious stimulus (shock) upon heart rate. *Journal of Personality and Social Psychology*, 1966, 3:353–356.

Erikson, E. H.: *Childhood and Society*. New York, Norton, 1950.

Feffer, M., and Suchotliff, L.: Decentering implications of social interactions. *Journal of Personality and Social Psychology*, 1966, 4:415–422.

Festinger, L.: A theory of social comparison processes. *Human Relations*, 1954, 7:117–140.

Festinger, L., Gerard, H. B., Hymovitch, B., Kelley, H. H., and Raven, B.: The influence process in the presence of extreme deviates. *Human Relations*, 1952, 5:327–346.

Gerard, H. B.: Emotional uncertainty and social comparison. *Journal of Abnormal and Social Psychology*, 1963, 66:568–573.

Hakmiller, K. L.: Need for self-evaluation, perceived similarity and comparison choice. *Journal of Experimental Social Psychology Supplement*, 1966, 1:49–54.

Hakmiller, K. L.: Threat as a determinant of downward comparison. *Journal of Experimental Social Psychology Supplement*, 1966, 1:32–39.

Hoffman, M. L.: Parent discipline and the child's consideration for others. *Child Development*, 1963, 34:573–588.

Hoffman, M. L., and Saltzstein, H. D.: Parent discipline and the child's moral development. *Journal of Personality and Social Psychology*, 1967, 5:45–67.

Hovland, C. I., Harvey, O. J., and Sherif, M.: Assimilation and contrast effects in communication and attitude change. *Journal of Abnormal and Social Psychology*, 1957, 55:242–252.

Hovland, C. I., and Weiss, W.: The influence of source credibility on communication effectiveness. *Public Opinion Quarterly*, 1951, *15*:635–650.

Insko, C. A., Murashima, F., and Saiyadain, M.: Communicator discrepancy, stimulus ambiguity, and influence. *Journal of Personality*, 1966, *34*:262–274.

Janis, I. L., and Mann, L.: Effectiveness of emotional role-playing in modifying smoking habits and attitudes. *Journal of Experimental Research in Personality*, 1965, *1*:84–90.

Johnson, D. W.: Use of role reversal in intergroup competition. *Journal of Personality and Social Psychology*, 1967, *7*:135–141.

Jones, A.: Information deprivation in humans. In B. A. Maher (Ed.), *Progress in Experimental Personality Research*, Vol. 3. New York, Academic Press, 1966.

Kahn, R. L., Wolfe, D. M., Quinn, R. P., Snoeck, J. D., and Rosenthal, R. A.: *Organizational Stress*. New York, Wiley, 1964.

Katz, E.: The two-step flow of communications: an up-to-date report on a hypothesis. In H. Proshansky and H. Seidenberg (Eds.), *Basic Studies in Social Psychology*. New York, Holt, Rinehart, & Winston, 1965.

Kelman, H. C., and Eagly, A. H.: Attitude toward the communicator, perception of communication content, and attitude change. *Journal of Personality and Social Psychology*, 1965, *1*:63–78.

Kelman, H. C., and Hovland, C. I.: "Reinstatement" of the communicator in delayed measurement of opinion change. *Journal of Abnormal and Social Psychology*, 1953, *48*:327–335.

Koslin, B. L., Stoops, J. W., and Loh, W. D.: Source characteristics and communication discrepancy as determinants of attitude change and conformity. *Journal of Experimental Social Psychology*, 1967, *3*:230–242.

Krech, D., Crutchfield, R., and Ballachey, E. L.: *Individual in Society*. New York, McGraw-Hill, 1962.

Lanzetta, J. T., and Driscoll, J. M.: Preference for information about uncertain but unavoidable outcome. *Journal of Personality and Social Psychology*, 1966, *3*:96–102.

Linton, H. B.: Dependence on external influence: correlates in perception, attitudes, and judgment. *Journal of Abnormal and Social Psychology*, 1955, *51*:562–567.

McDavid, J., Jr.: Personality and situational determinants of conformity. *Journal of Abnormal and Social Psychology*, 1959, *58*:241–246.

McGuire, W. J.: The nature of attitudes and attitude change. In G. Lindzey and E. Aronson (Eds.), *Handbook of Social Psychology*, 2nd edition, Vol. 3. Reading, Massachusetts, Addison-Wesley, 1969.

Manis, M.: The interpretation of opinion statements as a function of recipient attitude. *Journal of Abnormal and Social Psychology*, 1960, *60*:340–344.

Mann, L., and Janis, I. L.: A follow-up study on the long-term effects of emotional role playing. *Journal of Personality and Social Psychology*, 1968, *8*:339–342.

Marshall, H. R.: Relations between home experiences and children's use of language in play interactions with peers. *Psychological Monographs*, 1961, *75*: No. 5 (Whole No. 509).

Miller, N. E., and Dollard, J.: *Social learning and imitation*. New Haven, Yale University Press, 1941.

Mills, J.: Opinion change as a function of the communicator's desire to influence and liking for the audience. *Journal of Experimental Social Psychology*, 1966, *2*:152–159.

Mills, J., and Jellison, J. M.: Effect on opinion change of how desirable the communication is to the audience the communicator addressed. *Journal of Personality and Social Psychology*, 1967, *6*:98–101.

Mischel, W., and Liebert, R. M.: Effects of discrepancies between observed and imposed reward criteria on their acquisition and transmission. *Journal of Personality and Social Psychology*, 1966, *3*:45–53.

Piaget, J.: *Play, Dreams, and Imitation in Childhood*. New York, Norton, 1951.

Piaget, J.: *The Origins of Intelligence in the Child*. New York, International University Press, 1952.

Piaget, J.: *The Child's Construction of Reality*. New York, Rutledge, 1955.

Radloff, R.: Social comparison and ability evaluation. *Journal of Experimental Social Psychology Supplement*, 1966, *1*:6–26.

Raven, B. H., and Rietsma, J.: The effect of varied clarity of group goal and group path upon the individual and his relation to his group. *Human Relations*, 1957, *10*:29–44.

Rohrer, J. H., Baron, S. H., Hoffman, E. L., and Swander, D. V.: The stability of auto-kinetic judgments. *Journal of Abnormal and Social Psychology*, 1954, *49*:595–597.

Schachter, S.: *The Psychology of Affiliation*. Stanford, Stanford University Press, 1959.

Schachter, S.: The interaction of cognitive and physiological determinants of emotional state. In L. Berkowitz (Ed.), *Advances in Experimental Social Psychology*. Vol. 1. New York, Academic Press, 1964.

Schachter, S., and Singer, J. E.: Cognitive, social, and physiological determinants of emotional state. *Psychological Review*, 1962, *69*:379–399.

Schein, E. H.: *Coercive Persuasion*. New York, Norton, 1951.

Sears, D. O., and Freedman, J. L.: Effects of expected familiarity with arguments upon opinion change and selective exposure. *Journal of Personality and Social Psychology*, 1965, *2*:420–426.

Secord, P. F., and Backman, C. W.: An interpersonal approach to personality. In B. Maher (Ed.), *Progress in Experimental Personality Research*. Vol. 2. New York, Academic Press, 1965.

Sherif, M.: *The Psychology of Social Norms*. New York, Harper, 1936.

Sherif, C. W., Sherif, M., and Nebergall, R. E.: *Attitude and Attitude Change*. Philadelphia, W. B. Saunders, 1965.

Singer, J. E., and Shockley, V. L.: Ability and affiliation. *Journal of Personality and Social Psychology*, 1965, *1*:95–100.

Smith, E. E.: The effects of clear and unclear role expectation on group productivity and defensiveness. *Journal of Abnormal and Social Psychology*, 1957, *55*:213–217.

Stotland, E., Sherman, S. E., and Shaver, K. G.: *Empathy and Birth Order*. Lincoln, Nebraska, University of Nebraska Press, 1971.

Sutton-Smith, B.: Role replication and reversal in play. *Merrill-Palmer Quarterly*, 1966, *12*:285–298.

Tarde, G.: *The Laws of Imitation*. New York, Holt, 1903.

Taylor, J. B., Zurcher, L. A., and Key, W. H.: *Tornado: A Community Response to Disaster*. Seattle, University of Washington Press, 1970.

Turner, R. H.: Role taking, role standpoint, and reference group behavior. *American Journal of Sociology*, 1956, *61*:316–328.

Walster, E., Aronson, E., and Abrahams, D.: On increasing the persuasiveness of a low prestige communicator. *Journal of Experimental Social Psychology*, 1966, *2*:325–342.

Walster, E., and Festinger, L.: The effectiveness of "overheard" persuasive communications. *Journal of Abnormal and Social Psychology*, 1962, *65*:395–402.

Winch, R. F.: *Identification and Its Familial Determinants*. Indianapolis, Bobbs-Merrill, 1962.

Worchel, P., and Schuster, S. D.: Attraction as a function of the drive state. *Journal of Experimental Research in Personality*, 1966, *1*:277–281.

Zavalini, M., and Cook, S. W.: Influence of judges' attitudes on ratings of favorableness of statements about a social group. *Journal of Personality and Social Psychology*, 1965, *1*:43–54.

CHAPTER 9

CONTRADICTIONS OF SCHEMAS

In the previous chapter, the reasons behind an individual's acquisition of a schema to the effect that having specific schemas relevant to the situations he encounters were examined. It was shown how this schema may lead the person to seek new information, to learn. We saw that the individual accordingly develops schemas about peers and experts as sources of information about the world. Let us take our discussion one crucial step further. Life does not allow us to sit back smugly, surrounded by a nice set of schemas that explain everything, schemas derived from peers and experts. As has been pointed out, everyone on occasion will encounter situations which either do not fit their schemas well or are blatant contradictions to them. Many instances of such contradictions have already been mentioned in passing. However, the significance and consequences of such contradictions have not yet been dealt with in appropriate detail. We need to do so not only because of the general issues we are discussing in this chapter, but also because there is one very special issue with respect to these schemas. That issue is, "What constitutes a contradiction?"

POTENTIAL CONTRADICTIONS AND HIGHER ORDER SCHEMAS

This becomes a critical issue because reality is often so complex that frequently it is not altogether clear whether or not a given schema has been directly contradicted. For example, one aspect of reality may support a given position; another aspect of the same reality might contradict it. The controversies which raged in the mid and late 1960s over whether we were "winning" or "losing" the war in Vietnam, and over the rate of progress of black Americans, are examples of the complexity of many aspects of reality. This complexity may also have another effect. The schemas that the individual acquires may begin to match the complexity of the situations. The individual may develop a sophisticated, knowledgeable view of the war in Vietnam which considers many of the complexities and apparent inconsistencies in the real situation. In such cases, it may be that the individual is prepared for every apparent inconsistency and can deal with any that turn up without changing his relevant schemas very much. More specifically, the individual may be ready in advance for the apparent contradictions and thus will be not be affected by them.

Preparation for Contradictions

Some of the ways in which relatively abstract or higher order schemas can be developed which can be used to deal with potential contradictions and, in a sense, make them non-contradictions is very well illustrated in a series of studies by McGuire (1964.) He hypothesized that it might be possible to "inoculate" persons against future strong attacks on their beliefs and attitudes by first presenting them with relatively weak statements arguing against a position they held. McGuire reasoned that this process might be a very rough analogue to the way in which chemical inoculations operate—the introduction of weak toxins into the bodily system leads to the development of hitherto absent defenses which are then effective in warding off quite strong attacks by the disease processes involved.

He first measured his subjects' adherence to what are called "cultural truisms"—schemas which are very widely held in a society and rarely if ever questioned, e.g., "It is better to be healthy than sick"; "Brushing one's teeth daily is desirable"; "Children should be educated." Next, the subjects either made up arguments in defense of these truisms or read prepared arguments defending them.

In some cases, the arguments the subjects read or were asked to make up were supportive; i.e., they simply gave reasons why the truism should be considered to be true, e.g., "It is better to be healthy than sick because one is often in pain when one is sick." In other cases, the arguments were refutational, i.e., they were specifically intended to refute possible counterarguments. For example, "It is not true that being sick once in a while is good because it gives one a deeper appreciation of health. Being sick can also have the effect of making one bitter and angry." A few days later, the subjects were presented with arguments strongly attacking the truisms. Some of the issues raised in these persuasive communications were the same as those which had been previously dealt with in the refutational condition and some were new arguments. McGuire found that unless the person had previously received either the supportive or refutational treatment, he was readily influenced by these attacks on the truisms. However, the refutational treatment was much more effective in allowing the person to defend against the subsequent counterarguments than was the supportive treatment. The persons in the refutational condition were ready to chew up the later attacks which came their way. What is most interesting is the fact that the prior refutational defense was clearly superior to the supportive preparation, even when entirely new counterarguments were used.

This last result indicates that the refutational treatment led the person not only to acquire arguments with which to meet the specific attack on the truism; it also led the person to acquire higher order schemas to the effect that the truism, this widely held and rarely questioned belief can, indeed, be attacked, and also that it can be defended against these attacks. Thus, when confronted with entirely new arguments attacking the validity of the truism, the person was less surprised by the attack and also more likely to find an adequate defense against it. The schema just mentioned would lead him to anticipate that such defenses could indeed be found or invented.

McGuire chose to work with cultural truisms in order to achieve better control in this research. However, there seems to be good reason to expect these findings to have applicability where other sorts of beliefs, opinions and attitudes are concerned. There is little doubt that in our everyday lives all of us have had a number of experiences in which we were confronted by attacks on our ideas and yet were able to resist these attacks either because we had pre-established counterarguments or refutations or because we developed some on the spot in response to attempts to undermine some current belief. As a consequence, schemas about our abilities to withstand attacks on our ideas would be expected to develop.

The acquisition of this schema has important consequences which we will discuss later in this chapter.

Primacy Effects

In the chapter on the perception of other persons, we pointed out that there is a strong tendency for the first information that an individual receives about another person to determine how the other person will be perceived—the primacy effect. A question then arises as to whether or not there is also a primacy effect when one is receiving information about aspects of reality other than people. More specifically, if an individual first receives information which supports one side of an issue or defines reality in a given way, would not the schemas based on that information be more influential than others stemming from contradicting information which might be received later? Our first impulse would be to say yes, since the reasons given for the primacy effect were not particular to the perception of other people, but stemmed from the general functioning of schemas. Yet, research on this problem has not consistently uncovered evidence for a primacy effect. The probable reason for this is indicated in McGuire's work and some related considerations. As was pointed out in the discussion above, the content of the communications about reality is often quite complex; in most of the research on this problem, the issues investigated have been controversial, public ones. In such cases, the schemas the individual initially holds will be likely to dominate over contradictory information received later, provided that the initial schemas subsume lower order schemas whose content is relevant to the later contradiction and sufficient to meet and defeat it. This conclusion is suggested but not proved by McGuire's work; it is possible that his findings are limited to cultural truisms. Nevertheless, McGuire's work suggests the importance of the logical power of the "prime" arguments to "meet and defeat" the subsequent counterarguments. The primary and subsequent arguments may be intrinsically different in logical consistency, in empirical support apparent to the subjects in the studies, etc. In much of the research on primacy effects, little care has been taken to consider this factor of the logical relationship among schemas. The first messages that are received on an issue are equated in length and style with the second messages, but these characteristics are rather superficial.

The failure to find consistent evidence for a primacy effect in circumstances where the information in question does not deal with the characteristics of some other person is not necessarily inconsistent with the evidence for primacy effects where person perception is involved. The explanation given for the latter phenomenon emphasized that the schemas aroused by the initial information lead the person to pay less attention to the subsequent information, to consider it less important. Such ignoring of later information has not been found in research which deals with the perception and interpretation of events other than persons for a number of reasons. First, the later-presented information is typically introduced in such a way that it is very difficult to ignore—a new speech, a new article, or other new information. And the subjects are usually explicitly instructed to read or listen to it. Furthermore, there are other schemas and other motivations which lead a person to pay attention to the later messages. These other factors relate to the individual's schemas that some issues are controversial and that in certain situations it is particularly appropriate to examine both sides of an issue as, for example, in the case of jury trials, before conclusions can legitimately be drawn.

This discussion implies that under certain "ideal" conditions, primacy effects can be found—when the first arguments are just as strong, or logical, as the second, when the attacks and refutations are equally strong in both messages, when the individual has the clear option of paying little attention to the second arguments and feels no pressure from his sense of fairness to listen to them. Clearly, such a combination of conditions is not likely to occur often in "real life," and may, indeed, be very difficult to establish in a controlled laboratory situation.

There have been a number of attempts to bring some order into the research on primacy effects where complex issues are involved. One by Miller and Campbell (1959) is based on principles of learning and argues that whether a primacy effect will be found or not depends on the length of time intervening between the presentation of the first and second pieces of information and on the time interval between the second information and the final measurement of the subjects' opinions after exposure to the two pieces of information. On the basis of knowledge of the rates of forgetting of any newly learned material, and on the assumption of a primacy effect as a general tendency, they predicted and found a primacy effect if the two messages were presented close in time and if there was a relatively long interval between the second message and the attitudinal measurement. They made this prediction on the basis that immediately after the subject has been exposed to the second message, he will remember more of it than of the first message and will therefore be more influenced by it. Later, when most of what was learned from both messages has been forgotten, the hypothesized general tendency toward a primacy effect will hold sway. Despite the ingenuity of this argument, the results which support it were not replicated by Wilson and Miller (1968), so that a question must be raised about their thesis. Further, their argument assumes a primacy effect—which is what we have to explain in the first place.

Development of Counterarguments

Let us return to McGuire's research. The subjects who received the refutational treatment not only were given an opportunity to prepare for attacks against their beliefs but were also at one and the same time informed that their beliefs could be subjected to attacks. The individual then would be motivated to develop arguments in defense of his point of view even in advance of the confrontation with an actual attack. Thus, these subjects not only acquired schemas about the possibility of refuting attacks, they also acquired a schema that their truisms were attackable and needed to be defended. Thus, the individual begins to develop defenses against possible attacks, even attacks which he has not yet encountered.

One of the effects of indicating directly to an individual that his beliefs are going to come under fire was shown clearly by Brock (1967). Students were told that they would soon be reading arguments in favor of raising tuition—a forewarning that a direct attack on their belief that tuition should be held low would be made. While awaiting the presentation of the written arguments, the subjects were asked to write down their thoughts. This data indicated that they were actively engaged in a process of developing arguments in favor of keeping tuition low. The higher the level of tuition that they expected the coming arguments would demand, the more counterarguments they thought of. And, the more counterarguments they thought of, the less they were influenced by what they subsequently read.

Active and Passive Preparation

The reader may recall that in McGuire's work some of the subjects learned to refute arguments by reading refutations prepared for them, while others were simply told that they were to make up refutations themselves of the arguments that might be used against the truisms. The latter subjects thus not only acquire a schema that arguments in defense of the truisms can be found, but that they themselves can find them. Therefore, when they have received the news that their beliefs are going to be attacked, they are more likely to act on their own, to take the initiative in finding the counterarguments. Watts (1967) had subjects either read arguments in favor of a particular point of view or write arguments for eight minutes defending that point of view. The latter, active, group continued on their own to discuss the issue and to look up reading material about it, while the group that read preprepared refutations did much less of this. Thus the process of actively defending their beliefs had some long-range consequences.

This continued "intellectual" activity obviously is going to lead to additional consequences. The individual should become increasingly able to defend his position against an attack, since he is building up a reservoir of defenses and is learning some things about efficient ways to develop defenses. Thus, with time, he should become increasingly able effectively to defend his beliefs. Watts (1967) found that this activity minimizes the probability of the person's changing his beliefs over a period of time; McGuire's work suggests that the people who were asked to actively write arguments in defense of their beliefs became better able to defend them after a period of time.

McGuire is also very concerned with a comparison of the effectiveness of the passive treatment which involves simply reading ready-made arguments with that of writing original arguments in favor of the opinion items. However, it is exceedingly difficult to develop any general conclusions on this issue from his research because of some of the unique qualities of the cultural truisms used in his research which are not shared by other varieties of opinions and beliefs. As McGuire himself points out, the arguments against truisms which the experimenter gives are usually completely new to the subjects, since the cultural truisms are, by definition, widely held, seldom challenged beliefs. In consequence, the subjects found it very difficult at first to defend against the counterarguments; what the subjects wrote was simply not very good, effective, or persuasive. It is small wonder, then, that McGuire sometimes found that the reading of pre-made defense arguments or passive treatments were superior to the active argument conditions in protecting the person from subsequent attacks. This differential would probably not occur if material other than truisms were used, as McGuire himself points out. The point is that the active treatments have a different effect on the person's subsequent behavior than do the passive ones, not that the active is necessarily superior to the passive.

Furthermore, if a person has enough time to think of good arguments with which to defend his position, he will be better able to do so. Freedman and Sears (1965*b*) conducted a study in which an audience, consisting of secondary school youngsters in their teens, was told 10, two, or zero minutes in advance that they would be listening to a speaker who would argue vehemently that teenagers should not be permitted to drive. Then all of the subjects listened to the speaker. The 10-minute warning group was least persuaded by this talk, the zero-minute group the most.

Suppose an individual has for a long time held a belief which he understands to be controversial, one which he expects is going to be attacked. He would have ample time to consider the arguments against his position and, in his own mind, to refute them. Further, he probably has had considerable opportunity to try out his defenses and thereby to improve upon them. Through all of this, he becomes exceedingly resistant to change of his belief. The outcome of this process is reflected in research by the finding that people who hold extreme, that is, controversial, beliefs are generally both better informed than those with less extreme beliefs and are more resistant to influence. This process may also explain the rigidity of older people with respect to controversial issues about which they are very concerned.

The reader might recall that we introduced this section on McGuire's work by raising a question as to what actually constitutes a contradiction to a schema. It can be seen now that what might otherwise be viewed as contradictory information may not, in effect, be so because the individual is ready to demolish its validity. A contradiction is only a contradiction if the individual facing such information or arguments cannot counter it. To sum up, then, potentially contradictory information may be dealt with by being ready with counterarguments; or the reality that might be construed as presenting a contradiction may be so complex and equivocal as to be perceivable in several different ways, including a non-contradictory way; or the schema in question may be high enough in probabilism to be undisturbed by contradictions.

SCHEMAS REGARDING ABILITY TO COPE WITH CONTRADICTIONS

Some of these same factors which reduce the tendency to experience contradictions can be seen at work in the way that people in social groups acquire schemas about each other's behavior and about the way that people in the group interact with one another. Earlier, the manner in which people communicate about these matters, lending an additional air of reality to their shared schemas, was discussed. However, the issue of contradictions to these schemas was not faced in that discussion. In fact, the occurrence of contradictions in such circumstances is minimized by the fact that social behavior is often quite complex and multifaceted. As was pointed out above, when schemas refer to complex portions of reality, contradictions to them are often not readily perceived. The schemas may match the complexity of reality in such a way as to minimize the perception of contradictions. John is a complex person; Mary is moody; he did that only because he had to; we usually do that first, but we were tired that evening, so we didn't. Another way of making much the same point is to say that these schemas are often of high probabilism—and thus hard to contradict directly. The person may acquire a schema which indicates that he can cope with the contradictions and vagaries in other people's behavior; that "human nature is variable" so that he will not be overwhelmed by it.

Selective Exposure to Contra-Decisional Information

An individual's having a schema that he can cope with the opposition to his ideas also may lead him to have no particular motivation to avoid confrontation with the opposition. He believes he can cope with the opposing arguments and the potential contradictions. During the Goldwater-Johnson campaigns, Lowin (1967) mailed to Democrats and Republicans post cards offering them brochures about the two candidates. The material which would be included in the brochures was represented to the recipients by a few sample statements. Some of these statements presented strong arguments which would be difficult to refute, others presented weak arguments, easy to refute. The return rate of actual requests for the brochures indicated that people chose to have brochures which would present strong arguments favoring their own side or weak arguments for the opposition. They avoided strong arguments for the opposition and weak arguments for their own side.

As a matter of fact, there is little conclusive evidence to indicate that people consistently make decisions to expose themselves mainly to information and publicity in favor of their own positions and to actively avoid the opposition (Freedman and Sears, 1965a). The absence of such evidence has only recently been recognized by social psychologists, and has come as a bit of a surprise, since communications and attitude researchers had for years been assuming that the available evidence did support the seemingly reasonable contention that people will avoid exposure to information which purports to undercut or argue against a belief or attitude which they hold. In general, then, there is support for the contention that individuals will prefer to expose themselves to supportive information, material which is consistent with a decision or choice recently made or an opinion or attitude currently held. However, the seemingly reasonable corollary assumption that persons will strongly avoid information which is contra-decisional or which presents arguments against some opinion which they hold is much less well supported by research findings.

Confidence and Utility

A study by Canon (1964) attempted to clarify some of the ambiguity surrounding this issue by identifying certain of the variables which will be significant determinants of persons' willingness to approach counter-attitudinal information. Instead of assuming a *general* tendency to prefer supportive and avoid discrepant information this investigation examined the possibility that certain situational and personal characteristics will operate to create special circumstances in which one or the other tendency will predominate. The variables selected for study were the recipient's confidence in his ability to successfully deal with and refute the contradictory information available to him and the utility or usefulness which that information has for him. By manipulating the success that the participants encountered in the decisions they made regarding the best solution to a series of written problems, high and low confidence groups were created. That is, in one group the subjects were consistently informed that the solution they selected in each case was the correct one and thus should have become relatively confident of their ability to do well, to cope with the situation, while the other subjects received feedback which indicated poor ability on their part to deal with the type of problems in which they were working. On the last problem in the series none of the subjects was told whether or not he had chosen the best solution. Instead, some of them were led to believe that they would have to defend their choice in a debate with an expert on these matters who would make a forceful case in favor of the solutions they had rejected. Others were told they would simply be asked to write an essay supporting the solutions they had chosen. Then all subjects were asked to indicate which of a number of articles dealing with the problem in question they would like to examine as an aid to their preparation for the debate or essay. The various article titles indicated that they were either supportive of the choice the subject had made or antagonistic to it. It was reasoned that the contra-decisional articles would be of relatively high perceived utility for those in the debate condition, since knowing what arguments the opposition may muster in support of its position would be useful for someone who knows he will soon have to face up to those arguments in a face to face discussion, while one could write a forceful essay without even mentioning opposing views.

As predicted, strong preference for supportive information and avoidance of discrepant articles was found in the low confidence, low utility condition, whereas highly confident persons for whom contra-decisional material was particularly useful preferred to expose themselves to information which did not support the choice they had made.

A replication of this study by Freedman (1965) provided strong support for the predicted influence of the ability variable but not for the anticipated influence of confidence, while data gathered by Clarke and James (1967) paralleled the findings of the original study with regard to both confidence and utility.

Thus, considerable support exists for the contention that persons who have been led to develop a schema which indicates that they can effectively cope with potential contradictions to their beliefs and attitudes will typically deal with such contradictions by confronting them directly, anticipating that they can be "defused" and perhaps actually turned into additional supportive material. For example, one may look with delight and relish upon the opportunity to hear the latest pronouncements from some extremist political candidate, since the ability to counter any arguments he may present is anticipated in view of the confidence one has in the superiority of one's own chosen candidate. And the expected easy refutation of the opposition's arguments will only further bolster confidence in the validity of the position already taken.

Applications of these principles can be used to account for some of the earlier failures to uncover evidence for avoidance of attitude discrepant information. For example, Mills, Aronson, and Robinson (1959) and Rosen (1961) gave students a choice of objective or essay exams in a college course and then noted their preferences for articles giving arguments in favor of one or the other types of exam. From the perspective developed here, avoidance of articles favoring the type of test not selected by any given student would not be expected. An experienced college student would be expected to be quite confident of the correctness of the decision he made regarding the sort of exam he prefers and does best on, and no amount of expert opinion about which type of test is, in some sense, objectively the best should shake that confidence. The student knows from extensive and perhaps painful experience which test is best for him. On the other hand, getting information about the non-preferred exam may be seen to be a good strategy. Since students rarely have the sort of choice they did in these studies, having to take the non-preferred type of test in future classes is likely and information regarding them may, thus, be rather high in utility. Schemas regarding one's ability to deal with the opposition and the usefulness of non-supportive information, then, seem to play a significant role in determining a person's reactions to contradictory material.

However, the issue is not quite as simple as we may be making it sound here. There are many other factors which can lead to "selective exposure" to information.

Other Factors in Voluntary Exposure to Information

First, much of the research suggesting that people expose themselves only to information with which they agree was apparently the result of many factors in addition to a motivation to seek out supportive material only. For example, let us say a study revealed that the vast majority of persons who choose to expose themselves to a campaign against racial prejudice are persons who initially agree with the position developed in the campaign. This might be used as evidence for selective exposure—it suggests that persons will seek out and expose themselves to information which supports their current opinions and are unlikely to expose themselves to contradictory information. But if we look more closely we may discover that people less prejudiced against minority groups tend, in general, to be better educated. Then, if better educated people are more likely to attend to information campaigns in general, it would be expected on this basis alone that less prejudiced people would be more likely to attend to a campaign against prejudice. The initial finding would then be most appropriately interpreted as an outcome of the effects of education, rather than of "selective exposure" and avoidance (cf. Freedman and Sears, 1965a). Social class, ethnic background, and other demographic or more or less historical, non-motivational characteristics can also be shown to have similar effects.

Secondly, the discussion above indicates that there will be little selective exposure to supporting arguments only, if the individual has a schema to the effect that he can cope effectively with the opposition. However, not all people have this schema, and all of us have schemas in support of which we may not have very many arguments or subsumed schemas. Thus, in the last chapter, we saw in research by Mills (1965a; 1965b) that people will, indeed, avoid information which they fear will undercut the rationale they had in support of choices they had just made. The objects of concern in

Mills' research were different choices between gift objects, choices that would be hard to defend. Thus, the subjects avoided the contrasting information. Another example comes from research by Brock and Balloun (1967), who did not give their subjects very much time to muster counterarguments to defend themselves. They had smokers and nonsmokers listen to tapes of speakers which were either pro-smoking or anti-smoking. The messages were made somewhat difficult to understand by a great deal of static, which the listener could reduce for short periods of time by pressing a button. Subjects tended to eliminate the static more, thus enabling them to better understand, for those speakers favoring their beliefs about smoking than for those opposing them. Since the arguments in the speeches were immediately given, with no time to prepare rebuttals, the subjects may have avoided listening very closely to them.

Third, there may be some definite practical reasons for attending to information, even information which contrasts with one's own current position. One might be preparing for a debate (Jones and Aneshansel, 1956; Canon, 1964), or for other less formal reasons, anticipate having to defend one's views rather openly.

Also, in some situations the individual may have an H.O.S. which suggests that the truth cannot be determined by listening only to one side of the issue. Even though an individual has already indicated his choice of one side in a controversy, he may be interested in the opposition for reasons of open-mindedness and fairness (McGuire, 1969). And certain situations such as those involved in a jury trial or a scholarly investigation call for an unbiased approach to all the available information.

In addition, an individual is likely to acquire a schema which indicates that information is valuable in general. This schema is especially important when situations about which the person has few specific schemas are involved.

In short, then, in magnificent hindsight, there are many reasons for doubting that there is a general tendency to avoid information which one expects will contradict one's point of view.

SOCIAL CONSENSUS AND CONTRADICTIONS

Thus far in our discussion of contradictions to schemas we have dealt with situations in which the schemas have concerned relatively complex aspects of reality. This complexity, as we have seen, permits the development of equally complex higher order schemas with many schemas subsumed under them. This complexity may operate to permit the refutation of counterarguments, the elimination of a potential contradiction. On the other hand, in some areas of experience, contradictions to schemas may be so blatant, clear, and simple, that they cannot easily or readily be explained away. Anxiety results. This negative state can occur even when the contradictions involved have positive implications. For example, Baron, Robinson, and Lawrence (1968) gave college students a so-called test of social sensitivity in which they were to judge the emotional states of people portrayed in pictures. Some of the subjects were told they were correct on each trial, some on 33 per cent of these trials. Then, after a number of trials, the experimenter changed the proportion of trials on which they were told their judgments were correct. The "better" group now found that they were doing somewhat, considerably, or extremely worse; the other group found that they were doing somewhat, considerably, or extremely better. At the end of the study the subjects rated their mood. It was found that the greater the change in the proportion of right answers, the worse the subjects said they felt, regardless of whether the change was in a direction which indicated better or poorer performance.

What happens when the individual is faced with a clear-cut, unavoidable instance in which the schemas about peers and experts being good sources of information about the world are contradicted? How such instances can occur becomes evident when we examine a bit more closely what these schemas imply. Let us first examine schemas about peers. An important schema indicates that if the person is in a position to perceive a given segment of reality as are other people who are similar to him, he will perceive that reality to be the same as do others. If he and his friends look at the same car while standing next to one another, they will see it in much the same way. Thus, the schema will be contradicted if he sees the car as red when they see it to be blue. In such instances, the individual experiences anxiety.

It is important to recognize that the issue here is limited to those instances in which the contradiction is clear. If the question involved was whether the car has two or four coats of paint, then a disagreement would not violate the schema. As we learned from Sherif's (1936) work, the individual in such ambiguous cases tends to change his and other people's perceptions toward increased agreement among them. Such changes of perception of a situation to conform to the schema are possible when the shifts do not themselves contradict the schema. But in the case of the red or blue car, not much "compromise" is possible and the individual is highly likely to be quite disturbed by such a state of affairs.

He experiences anxiety because the schema about reality being similarly perceivable by similar people has been violated. However, the level of anxiety in such cases is quite high, partly because this schema is at a quite high level. Violating it implies that many of the schemas subsumed under it may be wrong. That is, the individual may doubt the truth of many things that he has believed are true because others believed them. Obviously, there are many things we believe about the world because other people also believe them. Another reason that a violation of this schema causes much anxiety is that it is a schema of very low probabilism. As we saw earlier, schemas of low probabilism are more readily violated than are those of high probabilism. This low level of probabilism results first from the high level of this schema—we saw earlier that higher order schemas tend to be low in probabilism. Furthermore, in point of fact, this schema is seldom violated; when it is night time, there is little disagreement about the fact.

Participant's responses to the "incorrect" judgments of others in an Asch conformity experiment.

Pressures Toward Social Consensus—Conformity

The degree of anxiety caused by a violation of this schema is illustrated by a simple, ingenious, and classical series of studies done by Asch (1952). He assembled groups of approximately 12 college students in a small college classroom to make almost trivial judgments about the relative lengths of lines. On a card, he showed them a line and on another card, he showed them three other lines. The subjects' job was to indicate verbally which of the three lines was of the same length as the first (one always was of this same length). On each of 20 presentations of sets of lines, each of the students announced which he saw as the line of the same length. The differences between these lines were sufficiently obvious that errors in judgment were very rarely made under ordinary circumstances. In short, this was a situation in which any sighted person would have no difficulty seeing what was real.

Asch, however, contrived the situation so that, after the first two presentations, all the subjects except one publicly made erroneous judgments. These accomplices had been instructed in advance to make the errors; the one exception, who was completely unaware of the deception, was seated so as to be the last person to make his judgment. When the subject was confronted with the gross violation of his schemas, he became upset, tense, anxious. Others (Gerard, 1961; Steiner, 1964) have performed studies much like Asch's and have found that the subjects show this anxiety in their physiological reactions, such as decreases in the electrical conductivity of their skin.

Redefinition of the Situation

The individual does not simply sit in such situations suffering this anxiety. He attempts at first to redefine the situation so as to make it consistent with the schema and thereby reduce anxiety. How he tries to do so is vividly illustrated in the descriptions Asch (1952, pp. 462-465) gives of his subjects' reactions. These effects generally take the form of perceiving that not all the subjects had equal access to the reality of the length of the line, so that the schema would not apply. In reading this description, it is important to note that these effects are generally unsuccessful, since the contradiction is so clear-cut.

b. *Effort at re-establishing equilibrium.* The immediate reaction of most critical subjects is one of varying degrees of puzzlement or confusion. A few stop the proceedings at the first or second disagreement to inquire if they have understood the instructions correctly; others less bold make similar inquiries of their immediate neighbors. None are prepared for the fundamental disagreement; instead they look for a more obvious source of misunderstanding. The subjects are not yet fully in the conflict; they are in fact resisting it as a real possibility by searching for a simpler explanation. They hope that the early disagreements were episodic and that they will give way to solid unanimity. As the disagreements persist, they can no longer cling to this hope. They now believe that they are perceiving in one way, the group in another.

c. *Localization of the difficulty in the critical subject.* Most subjects see a disturbance created, not by the majority, but by themselves. They do not call upon the majority to justify its judgments; most simply try to defend the validity of their own reactions. The subject assumes the burden of proof. He, not the majority, becomes the center of the trouble; it is he who is disrupting the consistent trend. Nearly all speak in terms of "the group contradicts what I see," not in terms of "I contradict what the group sees." In the same direction is the reluctance of many subjects to assert definitely that the majority is in error. It is noteworthy that the experimenter, too, despite full knowledge of the situation, at times perceives things in the same way, with the subject as the creator and center of disturbance.

d. *Attempts at solution.* Once the realization has taken hold that there is a basic disagreement, the subject makes an effort to overcome the difficulty by explaining it somehow. The doubts and tensions that the disagreements engender are conditions that support the flourishing of hypotheses, all designed to bridge the inexplicable gap. Some actually help to diminish the tension. Subjects may feel that the other members of the majority are conformists, following the first subject who for some reason is inaccurate. Others may mention that some in the group are wearing glasses. Most hypotheses are, however, *ad hoc* and half-hearted. Quite frequently a subject will say that the disagreements are the result of the different positions of the observers, overlooking the inconsistency of this proposal. Still others vaguely refer to psychological illusions, or propose that the group was judging on the basis of criteria other than length. As a rule, the subjects do not take their hypotheses, which fluctuate considerably, too seriously.

As soon as he becomes concerned to know why *he* is wrong and, as soon as he begins to respond to the urgencies of the situation, he becomes less free to look at it with a detached eye and to arrive at a solution that to an outsider seems relatively simple.

e. *Centering on the object of judgment.* In their eagerness to locate the source of the difficulty the subjects now look with greater care and become more attentive and scrupulous in observing and comparing. They act to increase the clearness of their perceptions and judgments. The more the subject is out of step with the group the more anxiously does he turn to the situation itself. That one effect of group opposition is to direct the person back to the situation and to induce a heightened objectivity is a trite observation. It has, however, been neglected in psychological discussion. A particularly interesting example of this tendency is the desire expressed by a few of the more spontaneous subjects to see the lines again and to measure them. Some suddenly jump up and approach the cards. It is as if these subjects were trying to eliminate the last possibility of indirectness involved in viewing the lines from a distance. A few, indeed, asserted that they would stick to their view until they were able to measure the lines. It is probable that in a less formal situation many more might have insisted on a close-up view of the cards or on the most direct test of superposition. In this behavior these subjects are showing that they are not accepting the group as the final arbiter in the matter.

g. *Longing to be in agreement with the group.* Most subjects miss the feeling of being at one with the group. In addition, there is frequent reference to the concern they feel that they might appear strange and absurd to the majority. One of the strongest subjects reported: "Despite everything there was a lurking fear that in some way I did not understand I might be wrong; fear of exposing myself as inferior in some way. It is more pleasant if one is really in agreement."

Perception of Self or Group as "Expert"

As we pointed out above, the brazenness of the contradiction between a person's own perception of the length of the lines and the group's judgment is such that his efforts to reduce anxiety by finding "explanations" is not very successful. Asch's description of the subjects' behavior gives ample evidence of the subjects' lack of belief in their own "explanations." Thus, the individual is left with his anxiety. Another tack he can take to reduce his anxiety at this point is to reject either himself as a source of information about the immediate reality before him, or to reject the group as a source of information. That is, he can split the sense of the schema about unanimous perception of reality in two—either the group is accepted as a valid source of information because it is unanimous, or the person accepts the information provided by his own eyes because his senses provide such obvious evidence. To be sure, no matter which of these tacks the individual takes, he can not eliminate anxiety, since his schemas are being violated by both these tacks. Taking either course does have the compensatory value of making the situation fit another schema we have been discussing in this chapter—the expert schema. If he accepts the group, he makes it more expert; if he accepts himself, he makes himself more expert. Thus, by accepting one or the other (or rejecting one or the other) he may come to believe that his schemas have been violated somewhat less; he just had the wrong schema aroused when he first encountered the group—he "might have known" that they were "better" or "worse" than himself. Of course, such a solution to the problem is still not entirely satisfactory; in fact, no solution is, except for insight into the true purpose of the situation.

The question then arises as to what factors determine to what extent an individual will perceive the group as expert and how much he will see himself. In some of the Asch situations, the individual is confronted with a large number of people, 11, who are unanimous in their judgments of the lengths of lines. Therefore it is difficult for the person to perceive himself as the expert and to reject the group. In fact, Asch (1952, pp. 463-464) reports that characteristically, the subjects began to doubt themselves.

f. *Growth of self-doubt.* Despite all efforts the disagreement persists. The subjects search for a principle of explanation, but they are deprived of the possibility of finding it. Nothing can be clearer or more certain than that the materials contain the relations perceived. There is something wrong, but they cannot say what it is. At this point doubt sets in for many. Some begin to fear that their senses may be deceiving them, and their consternation deepens. It is to this factor that we trace the poignancy of many reactions. Some of the most confident and independent subjects become shaken. One of these reported developing the feeling that he was either very right or very wrong. Another declared: "To me it seems I'm right, but my reason tells me I'm wrong, because I doubt that so many people could be wrong and I alone right." The responses of many others go in the same direction: "I would follow my own view, though part of my reason would tell me that I might be wrong." "From what I saw I thought I was right, but apparently I must be wrong. I began to doubt that my vision was right." "What I said appeared to me to be right, but I don't know who is right." "Now the whole class is disagreeing with me and it is possible that I may have been wrong." Some of the staunchest subjects admitted to feelings of doubt. "A little doubt came into my mind, but it was before my eyes, and I was determined to say what I saw. Even though in your mind you know you are right, you wonder why everybody else thinks differently. I was doubting myself and was puzzled."

Factors Influencing Conformity to Group Judgment

This self-doubt, and its complement, perception of the group as expert, may become so great that the individual may begin to conform to the group, to publicly state, for example, that a line that is shorter than another is really the same length. In fact, Asch found that over 30 percent of the subjects' answers were erroneous ones in agreement with the group! Interestingly enough, in subsequent studies on the same problem, the percentage appears to remain around 30! Furthermore, 58 percent of the subjects made two or more conforming judgments in a series of trials. Asch has, in a small way, created an Orwellian world in which long is short; the frightening possibility of black being seen as white, good as bad, looms before our imaginations. The reader should not forget that the subjects were students at colleges which are generally considered to have quite high standards. Let us therefore examine in more detail some of the factors involved in this conformity to falsehood.

In the first place, the reader should recall that there are many reasons why an individual would publicly state that the erroneous group judgment was correct. Asch himself interviewed the subjects afterward and found that many of them said they publicly agreed with the group because they were afraid to "make trouble." Many of these reasons obviously are based on the schemas about liking and similarity, liking and interaction, and others, that were discussed in Chapter 6. Some subjects obviously assume that they might be rejected if they are different.

Interpersonal Relationships

Nevertheless, these types of reasons for conforming to the group are not the whole story. It is obvious from Asch's descriptions that the relative power of the group and the self source of information about the world is a potent factor. Additional evidence comes from a study by Deutsch and Gerard (1955), in which they presented subjects with the problem of judging the relative lengths of curved lines. Some of the subjects made their judgments anonymously; that is, they learned which judgments were being made in the group, but did not know which person made which judgments; likewise, the subject knew that the other subjects would see his choice, but would not know who had made it. This was accomplished by having the subjects sit in stalls, each facing the screen on which the lines were projected, but unable to see the other subjects. The subjects indicated their choices by pressing buttons on a panel in the booth; these buttons presumably lit lights on the panels in the other booths, thus signaling the choices. The subject, in turn, learned of others' choices by observing the lights on his own panel. In point of fact, the lights on the panels were controlled by the experimenter so as to give bogus information to each subject about the judgments made by other subjects. Each subject was led to believe that he was the last subject to make his choice, so that the experimenter could lead him to believe that the others were making erroneous choices. (This procedure was used to economize on the use of subjects, since all the subjects' conformity behavior could be studied; in the Asch types of study, only one subject out of, say, 12, could be studied, since the others were simply helping the experimenter.) To return to the main question at hand, Deutsch and Gerard told the subjects after they were in their stalls that the order in which they were to respond was randomly assigned, and had no relationship to the arrangement of the stalls. Thus, the subjects were led to believe that the other subjects would not be able to identify them as the nonconformist, if they should choose to be independent of an erroneous group. Nevertheless, the level of conformity to erroneous group judgments did not drop to zero. Thus, the subjects conformed to the erroneous group responses even when the type of motive concerned with interpersonal relationships with others was highly unlikely to be very important.

Size of the Group

If, then, we can be fairly well assured that conformity to the group is related to the subjects' perception of the group or the self as the expert, an important question then has to do with the factors which determine which way the individual will turn. Let us first turn to those factors which enhance the perception of the group as expert. Very small groups do not appear to have much power as experts. If the individual is confronted with only one person who makes erroneous judgments, then it is easy for the individual to explain the discrepancy away by simply perceiving the other person as a bit "nutty," or as "fooling around." After all, once in a while one does run into a person who is "peculiar." Thus, Asch and others have found very little shift to erroneous judgments if the "group" consists of only one other person. If there are two other people, it is a bit harder to explain away their erroneous responses, but it still can be done: "I happened to be in a group with two 'nuts'!" Thus, the per cent of conforming responses increases somewhat. However, if the number increases to 3 or 4, then it is almost impossible for the individual to easily cope with this gross violation of his schemas about the perception of reality. The number of conforming responses begins then to approach the level achieved in larger groups—30 per cent. The increase of conformity which results from increasing size of group is quite small or nonexistent as the group increases in size from 5 to 6, or 6 to 7, and so on.

There are some data to suggest that the per cent of conformity drops off when the size of the group goes much beyond 12, but the data are somewhat inconsistent and inconclusive on this score (cf. Allen, 1965). If such a drop-off is found to be reliable, the reasons for it are a bit difficult to comprehend.

Unanimity of the Group

Not only the size of the group determines its influence as expert; its unanimity also does. After all, the group originally created problems for the person because it was unanimous in perceiving reality so as to contradict the evidence of his own senses. Unanimous perceptions are the hallmark of reality. Suppose, then, that this unanimity is broken, even by only one other person. In some experimental sessions, Asch instructed one member of the otherwise unanimous group to give the correct answers in all cases. Subjects were quick to respond to this break in the solid front against them and the per cent of conforming responses was much lower than when there was no break in the uniformity. It is very interesting that the break in the unanimity of the group does not have to be in the direction of correct answers in order for the individual to feel free to be independent of the group. If the individual is confronted by a group in which one of the members makes errors that are different from the errors made by the other group members, then even this break in the group's unanimity increases the independence of the individual. Notice that the individual does not conform to this deviate from the group; he states the truth as he sees it (Allen and Levine, 1968).

The psychological power of the break in the unanimity of the group is also illustrated by an ingenious device of Asch's: He prearranged matters so that a "subject" who had been "breaking the unanimity" in a given session of the experiment suddenly shifted to conforming to the group about halfway through the session. The naive subject then perceives that the group is now "whole," that the other deviant member of the group has "given in." The outcome is a great rise in the per cent of conforming responses, even higher than it would be under normal circumstances. Perhaps this great rise results from perceiving that the other deviant has been convinced by the group. This perception may enhance the subject's perception of the group as expert. However, this cannot be the whole answer, since Asch showed that it results even when the group's unanimity is restored without the deviant changing; this magical feat was accomplished by simply having the deviant leave the experimental room in the middle of the session, pretending to have forgotten an appointment with the Dean. The restoration of unanimity under such circumstances also greatly increases the number of conforming reactions. But not as much as the case in which the deviant switches to the majority. In the latter case, the increase in conformity appears to be a result of the newly established uniformity and the group's perceived "expertness" in converting a former deviant.

The power of even a small break in the unanimity of groups has been used by some to underline even more the importance of free speech. The one lonely person who publicly shouts "The Emperor has no clothes" may lead others who also saw the absence of clothes to publicly affirm their belief in the nakedness of the Emperor. Without freedom, neither the one lonely person nor his potential followers would have been able to point to the truth. Even more: the one lonely person did not have to actually proclaim the truth in order to permit or encourage the second to do so; all the former had to do was publicly disagree with the majority position, even if his own judgment was incorrect! Q.E.D.: Any public disagreement helps lead to the truth!

Objectivity and Expertness of the Group

Of course, the expertness of the group can be increased by other information that the individual has about the group. For instance, if a particular group has had a good record of judging reality in the past, then it is more likely to be perceived in the present to be expert (cf. Kidd and Campbell, 1955). Hollander, Julian, and Haalund (1965) had groups of subjects make a series of 20 judgments about which of three lights went off first in a sequence. Each subject thought he was the first to communicate his choice to the others, and that he would then learn the choices of the other subjects. Some subjects were led to believe that the others agreed with them, i.e., saw reality veridically, on all 20 tasks; other subjects were led to believe that the group unanimously agreed with reality only a portion of the time. Next the subjects were all led to believe that they would be the last to communicate their choices, but would learn of the choices of the others before they were to communicate their own. The others' unanimous choices were now always wrong. The subjects who had previously been led to believe that the group made accurate judgments of reality conformed more to the group in these later tasks than did the other subjects (Julian, Regula, and Hollander, 1968). Di Vesta (1959) and L. A. Rosenberg (1963) showed that if subjects were led to believe that their co-subjects had been making obvious mistakes in judging reality, then there was less conformity to the group. Likewise, Allen and Crutchfield (1963) found that the experimenter's telling the subjects that the group was right in making their judgments increased the number of conforming answers. Another, more subtle, way of increasing the perceived expertness of the group is to lead the individual to believe that the members of the group are motivated to tell the truth. For example, if the subjects are led to believe that the other members of the group will gain some money for giving true answers, the amount of conformity will increase (Krech, Crutchfield, and Ballachey, 1962; Becker, Lerner, and Carroll, 1964).

Self-Confidence

On the other side of the street, any factor which enhances an individual's perception of himself as an expert in judging reality will increase the degree of independence of the group. Hochbaum (1954) showed that the individual's previous successes in judging reality decreased his conformity to the group judgment. L. A. Rosenberg (1963) found that leading a person to believe that he had made many errors in judging reality increased his degree of conformity to the group. Sometimes the individual's overall evaluation of his abilities may lead him to feel that he is more of an expert in confronting the group. Asch (1952) found that the subjects who did not conform to the group were people who tended to have generally high evaluations of their own abilities. Likewise, Janis and Field (1959) and Janis (1954) found that people who feel generally adequate in social situations are more likely to be independent of the group.

Sometimes it appears that an individual is independent of a group, is not conforming to it, when it would appear that there is little basis for him to judge that he himself is expert and that the group is non-expert. One explanation for this is that the individual is, in fact, conforming to a group, but it does not happen to be the present one. The group might be one that made judgments about a similar bit of reality as the present group; or it might be one which the individual perceives to be more expert than the present one; or there may be other factors leading him to accept the absent group's judgments, such as a strong desire to be a member of the absent group. The question of whether the individual will conform to the absent group or the present one is answered by examining all of the factors just suggested, as well as others, and by determining their relative strengths.

Consequences of Conformity

Now that we have examined some of the factors which determine how much an individual will conform to obviously false group judgments about reality, we need to ask what the consequences of such conformity are. Since one of the motives for conformity was to reduce the anxiety caused by the exception to the schema about unanimous perception of reality, the individual's anxiety is reduced by his conformity. Hoffman (1957) not only found that people showed less anxiety physiologically after conforming, he found that this reduction was found especially in people who appeared in general to give much weight to the opinion of authorities, i.e., experts. Those who conform not only have lower levels of anxiety, they also feel more confident of the choices they make (Allen, 1965). Thus, people who remain independent do so at a cost. They still are troubled by the discrepancy between themselves and the others. Since conformity tends to increase confidence in the choices made and to reduce (but not eliminate) anxiety, it is not surprising that once an individual begins to conform in a situation, he will tend to continue to do so (Asch, 1952; Gerard, 1961). He has worked out his solution to the problem of the discrepancy and sticks with it.

As we saw above, the individual is more likely to accept the judgment of the group if the group is unanimous. This also applies with respect to the degree to which the individual continues to accept the group's definition of reality after he has left it. Gerard (1954) had subjects discuss a labor-management dispute in groups, but arranged the groups so that in some there was a high degree of agreement, while in others there was little. About a week later, the group members were confronted with a trained, skilled "arguer" who tried to change them from their original judgments about the dispute. Subjects who had been members of a group of high agreement were more resistant to this arguer than were those who had been members of a group of low agreement.

The resistance to change of schemas that are agreed upon by most, if not all, of one's peers has also been found with respect to schemas about oneself. Backman, Secord, and Peirce (1966) had college students rate how much they felt a need to attain certain values in life, such as success, friendship, and wealth. They also indicated how they thought each of five of their friends would rate them on these needs; i.e., they guessed what their friends would say about them with respect to these needs. Then the subjects received a psychologist's evaluation of how important these needs were to them—this evaluation differing from the subject's own. Finally, the subjects rated these needs again for themselves. It was found that those subjects who guessed that their friends agreed with one another in their guesses about them were less influenced by the psychologist's evaluation than were those who judged that their friends disagreed.

On the other hand, if the information the individual receives after he has left the group is patently true and unequivocal, then the effects of the group tend to dissipate and the individual is free to react to the evidence of his own senses again. Luchins and Luchins

(1963) found that if the individual is no longer in the presence of the group, he no longer misjudges the level of lines. The schema of the group's definition of reality is no longer aroused, as it is likely to be in the physical presence of the group, and thus the individual may avoid having that schema aroused, since it is associated with so much anxiety. Nevertheless, it might still be the case that if an individual undergoes a long series of experiences like those in the Asch-type experiments, he would be reduced to the state of the protagonist in Orwell's *1984*, who sat alone and exclaimed, "Good is Bad, War is Peace."

We have just examined at considerable length the individual's reaction to blatant discrepancies between the evidence of his own senses and the knowledge that others, similar to him, do not report that their senses give them the same evidence. We have pointed out that one attempted solution to this problem is for the individual to perceive either that he himself is more expert than the group or that the group is more expert than he. This "solution" to the problem appears to be predicated on the schemas about experts: that because of their special abilities, experiences, and so forth, they can know things about the world that non-experts do not know. This schema about experts appears to be of quite low probabilism in many cases, lower than would have been guessed. In fact, the power of this schema has been shown in research in which extreme viewpoints have been advocated by peers and by experts. While these viewpoints are rejected if they are attributed to peers, they are accepted if they are attributed to an expert.

EXPERTS AS SOURCES OF CONTRADICTIONS

If experts, communicating in the area of their expertise, tend to be so well accepted, it is small wonder that so little research has been done on the problem of how an individual reacts when an expert makes a statement which is at variance with the evidence of his senses. This absence is in sharp contrast to the considerable research that has been stimulated by Asch's classic studies. Of course, in this discussion, we are assuming that the expert is communicating in the area of his expertise, and that his audience has previously accepted him as an expert. As we pointed out earlier, the reason for this power of the expert is no doubt that so much of what we know about the world is really secondhand information. The information explosion has left us at the mercy of the experts.

Nevertheless, there are some cases in which an expert may be perceived to be a little less expert because he communicates an

The Governor and the people: conflict between experts. Photograph by Irwin Nash.

idea which is quite inconsistent with his audience's conceptions of reality. Notice here that the communication is one which is so un- equivocal, so clear in meaning, that it cannot be reinterpreted to be consistent with other schemas one has about the expert's beliefs. The expert must clearly be saying, e.g., that "*all* people need no sleep," not just a few exceptional people. We saw earlier in this chapter that if the communications are in the least open to reinter- pretation to be consistent with other schemas, the audience will rein- terpret. Another characteristic of the case in question is that the audience does not doubt that the expert actually made the statement. If the statement is sufficiently contradictory to schemas one has about him and about reality, one might resolve the discrepancy by guessing that he did not actually make the statement. This possible "solution" to the problem of the discrepancy sometimes is difficult because the expert is actually seen making the statement. In some research, this possible disassociation of the statement from its alleged source is reduced simply by making the statement not quite extreme enough to violate schemas about him or about reality. Thus, the cases we are talking about are those in which an expert makes an unequivocal statement which is contrary to the schemas about reality held by his audience, but not so contrary as to lead to disbelief that he made the statement.

Osgood, Suci, and Tannenbaum (1957) studied such situations using a rather special technique for measuring the subjects' evaluations of the statements and of the experts. The details of the technique are described in the box which later follows. Osgood *et al.* measured the subjects' evaluation of various political leaders, i.e., measured the degree to which they were presumed to be reliable sources of ideas and information about political issues. The researchers also measured the subjects' evaluations of various statements about political issues. Next, they passed out statements which were attributed to the various leaders, so that in many cases statements that the subjects evaluated poorly were attributed to esteemed leaders. These statements were quite clear in meaning; and it still was plausible that the leader had made the statements. Finally, the researchers had the subjects evaluate the statements and the experts again. In line with our discussion up to this point, the statements were evaluated more positively after they had been attributed to the expert than before; more specifically, the subjects shifted their evaluation of the statements toward their high evaluations of the expert. However, in addition, they tended to lower slightly their evaluation of the expert; he was a bit less expert than before. Thus even experts are not invulnerable, although they are obviously not nearly as vulnerable as peers.

Osgood *et al.* also found that the less highly evaluated an expert was, the more likely was he to lose some of his expertness as a consequence of having made a statement in which the subject had indicated earlier he had little belief. Not-so-highly evaluated experts thus are easier to reject than "real" experts.

The reader will recall that the schema we have been concerned with here is that experts make true statements about the world. As we have seen in other cases of schemas, the individual tends to perceive the world as consistent with the schema, regardless of which dimension of the schema he perceives first. Thus, if we perceive that a person who is only somewhat of an expert makes a statement with which we strongly agree, we will tend to think of that person as being even more of an expert. Thus, Osgood, Suci, and Tannenbaum (1957) found that if only moderately evaluated experts ostensibly made statements with which a person strongly agreed, the expert was evaluated more highly than before. Although the individual tended slightly to disparage the statement because it was made by a not-such-an-expert, he raised his evaluation of the expert considerably. All these types of changes shift evaluations of the situations in line with the schemas: experts say true things, non-experts can say false things.

The technique that Osgood, Suci, and Tannenbaum (1957) used to measure a person's evaluation of a statement or of a person is called the semantic differential. On top of a page the subject finds the name of the expert or the statement. Beneath are a series of 7-point rating scales, which have at their poles such adjectives as good-bad, wise-foolish, dependable-erratic, strong-weak. The particular set of adjectives can vary from study to study. The subjects then rate the name or statement at the top of each of these scales, even when there is no logical or realistic basis for doing so. The subjects are instructed to react in terms of their first impulses, not their thoughtful replies. The researchers' procedure is to elicit a series of such sets of answers from a number of people. They then compute coefficients of correlation between all possible pairs of rating scales; i.e., they measure statistically how much relationship there is between people's answers on one of the scales to their answers on other scales. By means of a highly complex statistical procedure called factor analysis, the researcher is able to determine which scales seem to be getting at the same underlying dimension. Among the dimensions that typically emerge from this procedure is one called evaluation, which seems to reflect the general level of esteem with which the expert or statement is held. Obviously, this technique can be used to measure evaluations of many other things besides statements and experts.

DEVIANCE FROM ESTABLISHED PATTERNS OF GROUP ACTIVITY

Earlier in this chapter we described the way that people acquire schemas about one another's behavior in groups and how people interact with one another. We pointed out how the acquisition of such schemas reduces anxiety. But we also pointed out that, because of the complexity of the behavior of other people in such face-to-face groups, contradictions of the schemas are frequently not perceived. Nevertheless, contradictions are sometimes perceived if they are sufficiently obvious or repeated frequently enough.

Resistance to Role Change in Groups

As in the case of other schemas, blatant violations of the schema cause anxiety, that is, violations which are so obvious and clear that they cannot be perceived as fitting the familiar schema. And, as we have seen many times, the violation of familiar schemas causes anxiety. Thus, the clown who begins to take himself seriously, the information giver who remains silent, the solution giver who dries up, all will generate anxiety among group members, including themselves. "It bothers me that Joe can't be funny anymore." Thus, there are strong pressures to minimize deviation from the predictable, stable ways of acting in the group.

There are, however, in addition, more practical reasons for minimizing the amount of deviation of actions from the schemas about actions. In some groups, the time and energy taken in acquiring the skills involved in new actions may be very great; this source of pressure against change is especially salient in work groups. Or, in some groups, the individual members may have found that they can satisfy their needs by behaving in certain ways. Changes in the actions of other people may sometimes be perceived as threats to the individual's ability to satisfy his own needs; the other person may be perceived as trying to feed at the same small trough. These practical types of motivation for reducing deviations from schema-guided behavior simply add to the general motivation against deviation from schemas mentioned in the previous paragraph.

The dislike people have for changes in the organization of their social relationships is well illustrated in studies in which the pattern of communication between four, five, or six people working on a group task is experimentally varied. That is, in such studies, the subjects are allowed to communicate only with certain other members. For example, they all might be allowed to communicate with one other person; or the pattern of communication might be so organized that it forms a circle, with each person communicating only with his neighbor. Lawson (1965) did a study in which all the subjects first worked on a group task, with each subject being able to communicate with each other subject. He then shifted them to a pattern of communication in which all the subjects but one could communicate only with this one subject. Thus, the subjects could not maintain their previous organization of work, and accordingly reported that they disliked the second organization more than the first. However, if the second organization permits them to retain their first organization, they don't feel negatively about it. In another part of Lawson's study, he shifted subjects in the reverse order, so that they had the possibility of continuing the same pattern of communication. The subjects felt more satisfied with this arrangement. It is not surprising, then, that people who have developed a way of relating to each other in a given way will attempt to retain that way, even when other circumstances do change. A. M. Cohen (1961) had subjects first work on a group task so that communication was centralized in one person. Then, they were shifted to a pattern in which communication was organized in a circle, as we described above. On their own, the subjects retained the more centralized form they had developed in the first pattern.

Maintenance of Group Action Schemas

There are many ways by means of which members of groups attempt to minimize the deviation from schemas about actions in the group. These ways are established in groups on the basis of schemas the members bring to the group and on the basis of efforts made within the group. One way is simply to bring strong pressure to bear on a person to adhere to the schema held about him. If he deviates, other members may ridicule him, reject him, directly communicate their expectations, or show in other ways their disapproval. Since a group member tends to be anxious when his own behavior deviates from the schema he has about it, he will tend to avoid such actions, even without the sanctions of other members of the group.

Membership Stabilization

A second way in which deviation from a schema is avoided is simply by keeping the same membership in the group. In addition to the reasons we mentioned in Chapters 5 and 6 for feeling anxious about strangers, the group members may try to close the group because each new member at least potentially may refuse to adhere to the schemas of the group, and may even try to change them. Thus, there often is a preference for continuing a group with those people who have acquired the schemas and behave according to them (Ziller, 1965). Marwell (1966) demonstrated this process by having students first participate in a series of three two-person groups, each group containing different members and working on different tasks. One task required that the members cooperate very closely, one reading instructions, the other carrying them out. The other tasks entailed only discussions. When the subjects were asked which other subject they would pick to work with them on a new cooperative task, they tended to choose the one with whom they had previously cooperated. They had worked out schemas together as to how to cooperate, and were attempting to protect these schemas from change. When given a choice, they kept the group closed. No doubt if Marwell had asked them with whom they would prefer to "discuss," they would have chosen one of the other people.

Formalization of Rules

A third way in which deviation from schemas is sometimes avoided is by making the schemas quite formal—by writing them down. Some groups develop their bylaws, the table of organization, their rules. These written rules make it easier to educate new members of the group to its schemas. Thus, written rules are more likely to be developed in "open" groups. Furthermore, the writing down of rules makes it easier to bring sanctions to bear on a member who deviates from the rules. "You've broken Rule three: never smoke on hikes."

There no doubt are other means employed by group members to minimize the amount of change, the amount of deviation from the member schemas. The list above is not meant to be exhaustive. The main point is to give some idea of the ways that members of groups attempt to support their schemas. But life will not always leave groups be. Change is sometimes forced upon a group. The reasons that change can be forced on a group are numerous: It may be subordinated to another group; the front office or the home office may simply order a change. Or, it may become obvious to the group members that their present ways of doing things are inefficient; new technologies may develop; the physical means may be exhausted for doing the old, such as when a teenager's car breaks down. The members in a group may begin to lose their ability or skill. New members may come into the group as a matter of necessity, and so forth.

Resistance to Imposed Changes

One of the implications of the above discussion is that the members of the group will tend to resist such changes imposed on them by the physical and psychological realities. Although this point has not been demonstrated through highly rigorous research, it has been well documented by students of change in organizations such as Mann and Neff (1959). There often are refusals to accept the new technologies, to recognize that old timer X is out of tune with the times, to accept the ideas of the new members. People who are in the business of getting organizations to change have often noticed the degree of resistance to change. To them, these re-

Suicide prevention through communication of concern and hope.

sistances often appear senseless and irrational, because the demands of reality are so "obvious." But, as we see, the roots of such resistance go deep. In fact, group members may develop a variety of techniques for minimizing change from these sources, or reducing the amount of anxiety the changes may engender. However, change does occur, despite these resistances.

If the source of potential change is the influx of new members, then the members of the group may attempt to "educate" the new members to the schemas. An old member may take a new one aside and tell him how "we do things." In formal groups, actual classes may be held, such as at Police Academies, or orientation lectures in the military, or Freshman orientation on campuses (cf. Ziller, 1965). Thus the amount of change is reduced, although probably not eliminated.

If the change is minor or slow, the old timers in the group may perceive that it really is not much of a change. They may perceive only that the change is superficial; that nothing is really changing; that "it's all a big hoax." Sometimes, of course, these perceptions are accurate, sometimes not. In either case, at the time the group members do actually perceive the change as minimal, their anxiety is low.

If the change is, however, inevitable and clearly not minor, then the group members' anxiety will be lower if the change itself is clearly perceived (cf. Mann and Neff, 1959). If the nature and purpose of the change are clearly stated, if the implications are sharply defined, the amount of anxiety resulting from the change will be reduced—not eliminated—because new schemas are being communicated to the group members. If the old members of an organization know something about the new recruits, if they know exactly how the new regulations are going to work, if they know something of how the new boss is going to act and what he will demand of them, anxiety will be lower. Thus, the anxiety resulting from the absence of specific schemas is avoided; the old schemas are replaced with a new set, so to speak, and the level of anxiety resulting from the absence of L.O.S.s is reduced.

Of course, groups and organizations differ in the amount of anxiety their members experience. Some groups have already developed some of the techniques for reducing anxiety indicated above, so that the group members face the new with little difficulty. Furthermore, we have already pointed out from time to time that people find the new less negative and even attractive if something in the situation remains unchanged, familiar, or well-known. The same applies to people when they are in groups. Thus, some groups may face change and newness with little anxiety because much of the organization, much of this way of doing things, much of their setting, of their membership, rules, insignias, and so forth, do not change. Better established groups, with long histories which have given rise to many familiar traditions, may therefore be better able to face change than relatively new groups, all other factors being equal. Before the reader gets the impression that we are arguing that groups of long white beards will soon be seen plunging into the unmapped terrain, it should be noted that those aspects of a group which are stable and familiar may become even more precious to the members because they have an anxiety-reducing effect. The members of a well-established group with much stability may value its stability with respect to certain aspects of the group's activities so that they can face the new in other aspects with equanimity. Other factors which we will set forth later also have important effects on the degree to which group members face change and newness without anxiety, so that the reader is asked to bear with us until we can explain these factors in their proper order.

One type of stability which enables a group to face change more readily is the very stability of the process of change. For example, the rules of parliamentary procedure for enacting changes, the traditional aspects of the hazing or educating of new members, the predictable times when new members will arrive, all minimize anxiety, since the change itself occurs in a familiar way. The almost contradictory tone of the last sentence bespeaks the subtlety of this process. Often group members will be very strongly motivated to leave the rules of change fixed, even to the point of opposing changes which they otherwise might favor, because the rules have this anxiety-reducing effect. Part of the resistance of the "establishment" to the changes demanded by "militants" stems from the fact that the militants are trying to bring about changes in new ways; they reject the familiar rules of change. Why the militants themselves feel capable of facing such changes will become more clear later on.

References

Allen, V. L.: Situational factors in conformity. In L. Berkowitz (Ed.), *Advances in Experimental Social Psychology*, Vol. 2. New York, Academic Press, 1965.
Allen, V. L., and Crutchfield, R. S.: Generalization of experimentally reinforced conformity. *Journal of Abnormal and Social Psychology*, 1963, 67:326–333.
Allen, V. L., and Levine, J. M.: Social support, dissent, and conformity. *Sociometry*, 1968, 31:138–149.
Asch, S.: *Social Psychology.* Englewood Cliffs, New Jersey, Prentice-Hall, 1952.
Backman, C. W., Secord, P. F., and Peirce, J. R.: Resistance to change in the self-concept as a function of consensus among significant others. In C. W. Backman and P. F. Secord (Eds.), *Problems in Social Psychology.* New York, McGraw-Hill, 1966.
Baron, R. M., Robinson, E. L., and Lawrence, S.: The effectiveness of social reinforce-

ment as a function of changes in rate of reinforcement. *Journal of Experimental Social Psychology*, 1968, 4:123–142.

Becker, S. W., Lerner, M. J., and Carroll, J.: Conformity as a function of birth order, payoff, and type of group pressure. *Journal of Abnormal and Social Psychology*, 1964, 69:317–323.

Brock, T. C.: Communication discrepancy and intent to persuade as determinants of counter-argument production. *Journal of Experimental Social Psychology*, 1967, 3:296–309.

Brock, T. C., and Balloun, J. L.: Behavioral receptivity to dissonant information. *Journal of Personality and Social Psychology*, 1967, 6:413–428.

Canon, L.: Self-Confidence and selective exposure to information. In L. Festinger (Ed.), *Conflict, Decision and Dissonance*. Stanford, Stanford University Press, 1964.

Clarke, P. and James, J.: The effects of situation, attitude intensity, and personality on information-seeking. *Sociometry*, 1967, 30:235–245.

Cohen, A. M.: Changing small group communication networks. *Journal of Communication*, 1961, 11:116–124 & 128.

Cohen, A. R.: The effect of volition. In J. Brehm and A. R. Cohen (Eds.), *Explorations in Cognitive Dissonance*. New York, Wiley, 1962.

Deutsch, M., and Gerard, H.: A study of normative and informational social influences upon individual judgments. *Journal of Abnormal and Social Psychology*, 1955, 51:629–636.

Di Vesta, F. J.: Effects of confidence and motivation on susceptibility to informational social influence. *Journal of Abnormal and Social Psychology*, 1959, 59:204–209.

Freedman, J. L., and Sears, D. O.: Selective exposure. In L. Berkowitz (Ed.), *Advances in Experimental Social Psychology*, Vol. 2. New York, Academic Press, 1965a.

Freedman, J. L., and Sears, D. O.: Warning, distraction, and resistance to influence. *Journal of Personality and Social Psychology*, 1965b, 1:262–266.

Gerard, H. B.: The anchorage of opinions in face to face groups. *Human Relations*, 1954, 7:313–325.

Gerard, H. B.: Disagreement with others, their credibility, and experienced stress. *Journal of Abnormal and Social Psychology*, 1961, 62:559–564.

Hochbaum, G. M.: The relation between group members' self-confidence and their reactions to group pressure to uniformity. *American Sociological Review*, 1954, 19:678–687.

Hoffman, M. L.: Conformity as a defense mechanism and a form of resistance to genuine group influence. *Journal of Personality*, 1957, 25:412–424.

Hollander, E. P., Julian, J. W., and Haalund, G. A.: Conformity to process and prior group support. *Journal of Personality and Social Psychology*, 1965, 2:852–858.

Janis, I. L.: Personality correlates of susceptibility to persuasion. *Journal of Personality*, 1954, 22:504–518.

Janis, I. L., and Field, P. B.: Sex differences and personality factors related to persuasibility. In C. I. Hovland and I. L. Janis (Eds.), *Personality and Persuasibility*. New Haven, Yale University Press, 1959.

Jones, E. E., and Aneshansel, J.: The learning and utilization of contrasalient material. *Journal of Abnormal and Social Psychology*, 1956, 53:27–33.

Julian, J. W., Regula, C. R., and Hollander, E. P.: Effects of prior agreement by others' on task confidence and conformity. *Journal of Personality and Social Psychology*, 1968, 9:171–178.

Kidd, J. S., and Campbell, D. T.: Conformity to groups as a function of group success. *Journal of Abnormal and Social Psychology*, 1955, 51:390–393.

Krech, D., Crutchfield, R., and Ballachey, E. L.: *Individual in Society*. New York, McGraw-Hill, 1962.

Lawson, E. D.: Change in communication nets, performance, and morale. *Human Relations*, 1965, 18:139–148.

Lowin, A.: Approach and avoidance: alternate modes of selective exposure to information. *Journal of Personality and Social Psychology*, 1967, 6:1–9.

Luchins, A. S., and Luchins, E. H.: Social influences on judgment of descriptions of people. *Journal of Social Psychology*, 1963, 60:231–249.

McGuire, W. J.: Inducing resistance to persuasion: some contemporary approaches. In

L. Berkowitz (Ed.), *Advances in Experimental Social Psychology*, Vol. 1. New York, Academic Press, 1964.

McGuire, W. J.: The nature of attitudes and attitude change. In G. Lindzey and E. Aronson (Eds.), *Handbook of Social Psychology*, 2nd edition, Vol. 3. Reading, Massachusetts, Addison-Wesley, 1969.

Mann, F., and Neff, F. W.: *Managing Major Change in Organizations*. Ann Arbor, Foundation for Research in Human Behavior, 1959.

Marwell, G.: Types of past experience with potential work partners. *Human Relations*, 1966, *19*:437–447.

Miller, N., and Campbell, D. T.: Recency and primacy in persuasion as a function of the timing of speeches and measures. *Journal of Abnormal and Social Psychology*, 1959, 59:1–9.

Mills, J.: Avoidance of dissonant information. *Journal of Personality and Social Psychology*, 1965a, 2:589–593.

Mills, J.: Effect of certainty about a decision upon post decision exposure to consonant and dissonant information. *Journal of Personality and Social Psychology*, 1965b, 2:749–752.

Mills, J., Aronson, E., and Robinson, H.: Selectivity in response to information. *Journal of Abnormal and Social Psychology*, 1959, 59:250–263.

Osgood, C. E., Suci, G. J., and Tannenbaum, P. H.: *The Measurement of Meaning*. Urbana, University of Illinois, 1957.

Rosen, S.: Post decision affinity for incompatible information. *Journal of Abnormal and Social Psychology*, 1961, 63:188–190.

Rosenberg, L. A.: Conformity as a function of compliance in self and confidence in partners. *Human Relations*, 1963, *16*:131–139.

Sherif, M.: *The Psychology of Social Norms*. New York, Harper, 1936.

Steiner, I. D.: Galvanic skin resistance and responses to interpersonal disagreements. Unpublished progress report, U. S. Public Health Service Grant M 4460. University of Illinois, 1964.

Watts, W.: Relative persistence of opinion change induced by active compared to passive participation. *Journal of Personality and Social Psychology*, 1967, 5:4–15.

Wilson, W., and Miller, H.: Repetition, order of presentation, and timing of arguments and measures as determinants of opinion change. *Journal of Personality and Social Psychology*, 1968, 9:184–188.

Ziller, R. C.: Toward a theory of open and closed groups. *Psychological Bulletin*, 1965, 64:164–182.

CHAPTER 10

THE SENSE OF COMPETENCE

OVERVIEW

Throughout the previous chapters frequent reference, directly or indirectly, has been made to the most pervasive of types of human activity—motivated action, initiated and maintained in the interest of goal attainment. Most of our waking hours are spent engaged in behaviors designed to satisfy needs, to achieve goals. The goals can range in significance and extension from those that take a lifetime to attain, such as professional or artistic eminence, to those that may be achieved in the space of an eye blink. Often there is a mixture of goals, the immediate and the long range, as the attainment of immediate goals is often instrumental to the attainment of ultimate goals. The preceding discussions of motivation and its effects on persons' relationships with others and with themselves did not cover a most important aspect of motivated activities. This has to do with an individual's perception of his probability of attaining goals, with his schemas concerning the likelihood of achieving desired end states. In the present chapter, these schemas will be dealt with especially as they are relevant to our relationships with other people.

First, the manner in which an individual acquires schemas about his acting to attain his goals will be examined. This acquisition is based on his observations of his own actions, on his observations of others, and on communications from others and groups of others.

Sense of competence in the face of ordeal. Photograph by Irwin Nash.

We will then see how these schemas come to involve a conceptual dimension of evaluation, so that he evaluates more positively those schemas which hold that he is highly likely to attain his goals. His evaluation of himself will then also be shown to be a function of communications from others about him. Finally, the effects of these schemas on the person's actions and his ability to face strange and new situations, such as negative communications from others and persuasive communications, will be discussed. Now, to begin:

Obviously, an infant begins life almost completely dependent on others, typically parents, for assistance in the attainment of goals. However, even from the beginning, the child is not a completely passive organism, lying like a vegetable and hoping to be nourished, warmed, and held by others. He is born with some "wired in" tendencies to act in certain ways, and these ways frequently lead eventually to the attainment of goals. The most obvious example is crying in response to hunger cues, which often brings a nurturant mother more or less quickly. Or, a child's restlessness when upset by cold, wetness, or pain will attract a mother's attention and lead to warmth, dryness, or relief. Thus, in the beginning of life, the individual experiences some mixture of passively having needs met and of acting to meet them.

On the basis of these experiences, most individuals develop a schema which indicates that their own actions can lead to the attainment of goals, to the satisfaction of needs. Notice that this schema does not imply that only one's own actions lead to need satisfaction; schemas will also be developed to the effect that relating to other people leads to goal attainment—to need satisfaction. The individual is both dependent and independent.

However, as a child acquires new competencies, learns to do more and more difficult things to attain his various goals, he acquires more and more L.O.S.s which support and are subsumed by the H.O.S. about his actions leading to goal attainment. He learns to walk, to talk, to hold, to manipulate, to throw, to pick up, all of which help him to attain such goals as eating, drinking, seeing. The child's own observations of the connections between his actions and their consequences support both the lower order schema about each of these actions and the H.O.S. about actions in general. To use White's (1959) very apt term, the child develops a sense of competence.

For purposes of exposition in this chapter, let us use this term, the sense of competence, i.e., the degree of competence the person "senses," to refer to his perception of the probability that his actions will attain his goals. In some cases this sense of competence will refer to goals in general; in other cases, it will refer to specific goals. The context in which the term is used will make it clear which type of goal is referred to. Obviously, this term can be "translated" into schema items: the person's sense of competence refers to the nature of the schema which indicates that his actions lead to the attainment of his goals at a given level of probability.

SOURCES OF VARIATION IN THE SENSE OF COMPETENCE

Individuals obviously vary along this probability dimension. Because of its significance, this variation is one of the central themes of this chapter. Therefore, we need to turn to an examination of the sources of such variation. There are a number of these which are related in complex ways. We will take them up one at a time.

The view from "competence hill."

Perceived Effectiveness of Own Actions

A most obvious source is the degree to which the individual's own actions are perceived by him to lead to goal attainment. There are many factors which lead a person to attend to his own actions and their consequences. For instance, the fact that actions entail movement or change attracts our attention to them. Because of this attraction, an individual will perceive how effective his actions are and will therefore acquire schemas about how competent he is. De-Soto, Coleman, and Putnam (1960) showed that a person's pre-dictions of his probability of attaining a goal of making the "right" associations to stimuli were a direct function of how successful he'd been up to that point in making the associations. The same type of effect has been found by Feather (1962) and Rychlak and Eacker (1962). However, the sense of competence may not be limited to the goals of the same type as the individual had been successful (or unsuccessful) in attaining up to that point. His sense of competence may generalize to other, similar goals, as determined by the con-ceptual dimensions of his schemas and the relationships between different orders of schemas. Whiting and Child (1949) asked people about their reactions to their successes in life. Many of them said that these successes led to greater confidence that they would be able to achieve other goals in the future.

To turn to the child—the above evidence implies that if chil-dren have ample opportunity to do things, and do them suc-cessfully, they will develop a high sense of competence. At a very mundane level, Coopersmith (1967) found that boys who started to walk earlier had a higher sense of competence when they were 8-10 years old. Their early start at walking opened up many other possible activities, e.g. taking things from higher places, such as the tops of tables. Furthermore, if the parents did not impose themselves physically on the boys through caressing and fondling, thus restricting the child's freedom to act, the boys' sense of com-petence tended to be higher. Also, if the parents controlled their sons more by rewarding desirable activity than by punishing un-acceptable behavior, the boys had higher self-esteem. And the more that the parents involved their children in family discussions, and let them "have their way" sometimes, the higher was the boys' sense of competence. In short, the more that children are able to act effectively in their environment, the higher is their self-esteem. The wide range of activities in which such children engage success-fully increases the likelihood that they will develop an H.O.S. of a high sense of competence, which is based on and subsumes these activities.

Coopersmith refers to the sense of competence of the boys as their self-esteem. However, his measure of self-esteem consists of a series of questions, about half of which concern how well the boys think they can cope with various everyday situations. For instance, questions are asked concerning how dependable they are, how sure of themselves they are, and how sorry they are for the things they do (scored negatively). Certainly, such questions refer to what we are calling the child's sense of competence. In addition, some of the other questions refer to the boy's overall evaluation of himself, such as his wanting to be someone else (scored negatively), wanting to change things about himself. As we will see later, there is good reason to assume that these overall self-evaluations also reflect the sense of competence. Therefore, close to ⅔ of the questions in Coopersmith's self-esteem questions can be considered to be measures of the sense of competence.

This process of success generating a higher sense of competence has been vividly described by Murphy (1962) on the basis of her observations of three-to-five year olds:

". . . each experience of mastery and triumph sets the stage for better efforts in the next experience. Confidence, hope, and a sense of self-worth are increased, along with the increase of cognitive and motor skills . . ." (p. 367)

The Repertoire of Goal-Oriented Actions

One of the most important aspects related to the sense of competence is the ability to choose—having at one's disposal a series of alternative courses of action from which to select ways to attain goals. Unless an individual is in a position to choose in this manner, he will often not be able to take the course of action which minimizes work, sacrifice, or pain involved in the attainment of his goals. If the alternative courses of action are too few, he is, on the whole, more likely to find that the price of attaining his goal is too high. In addition, in many situations of everyday life, problems can be solved, goals attained, only if the person varies his actions. A child might not be able really to enjoy a toy unless he can handle it in many ways. Or, he might not be able to open a candy box unless he tries several different approaches. Or a person might not be able to repair something unless he can try alternative techniques. On the basis of a variety of such experiences in which such freedom leads to success and pain avoidance, and its absence leads to failure and pain, an individual is highly likely to acquire a schema which suggests that his sense of competence is higher when he has this sort of freedom of choice. It should be noted that an assumption is made here that the individual conceives that he is capable of acting on the options open to him. In other words, freedom to choose courses of action that are beyond one's ken is not what we have meant here by freedom.

Availability of Specific Schemas

Another determinant of the sense of competence concerns a person's schemas about a situation. As has been pointed out a number of times, an individual's having well-articulated, specific schemas about a given situation may reduce his anxiety partly because such schemas will better enable him to act effectively. He is better able to achieve whatever goals may be relevant in the situation when he has detailed, specific schemas. Thus, Coopersmith (1967) found that boys with a higher sense of competence came from homes in which the standards of behavior were made very clear to the children. They were then able to know just what would happen under specified circumstances, just how their parents would react to their behavior, and could thus guide their behavior accordingly.

An individual is more likely to have lower order, more specific schemas, about situations or entities with which he is familiar. Accordingly, an individual will feel more competent in familiar settings and surroundings than in unfamiliar ones. We have all heard ourselves and others say, "At least I understand these problems; they're the ones I'm used to."

Observations of Others

Another source of variation in individuals' sense of competence, especially among children, is information derived from the observation of other people. There are several ways in which others can influence a person's sense of competence. One has to do with schemas which involve perception of similarity between oneself and another person. The many factors which lead to an individual's acquiring schemas which suggest that he has traits like those of other people and to his overtly imitating these other people have been presented earlier. Schemas relating similarity to liking, to interaction, to group membership, and to physical closeness, can all lead people to conceive of themselves as possessing some of the attributes of others. The schema that similarity is general, that similarity in one trait or aspect implies other similarities, also leads persons to perceive that they have traits similar to others'. In some cases, the similarity which the individual acquires in this manner involves the other person's level of competence; an individual may come to conceive of himself as possessing the same level of competence as that which he infers a similar other person to have.

Parent-Child Relationships

In a child's relationship with his parents, many of the sorts of schemas mentioned above operate simultaneously and in conjunction with one another, all thereby leading the child to become similar to his parents. Thus, children tend to acquire a sense of competence similar to their parents' overall sense of competence. The parents may, in a wide variety of ways, indicate that they believe that the world is a place that can be coped with, rather than something that is overwhelming them; and their children will tend to come to share these beliefs about the world.

The effect that parents have on a child's sense of competence has been well documented by Coopersmith (1967). The high competence boys' mothers were more self-assured and self-reliant, more confident in their abilities as mothers, and more likely to make day-to-day decisions themselves than were the mothers of less competent boys. Coopersmith found that the fathers of the boys with a high sense of competence tended not to have ever been unemployed and tended to relate well to their wives. (The findings were less extensive with respect to fathers, because Coopersmith did not conduct in-depth interviews with them as he did with mothers. No doubt Coopersmith's results would have been even stronger had he been able to study the fathers. Also, they would no doubt have been even stronger had he related the senses of competence of girls to those of their mothers. The fact that the relationships he found were as strong as they were becomes, in this context, even more striking.)

A child often acquires a schema to the effect that he will be able to act as effectively (or as ineffectively) as his parents when he finally grows up and finds himself in the same situations as they are in presently. Thus, as we will see, the effects of the acquisition of a schema about competence may in some ways not be evident until much later.

Perceived Similarity

One of the schemas about interpersonal situations which appears to have important influences on a person's sense of competence outside his family is that of the generality of similarity. It has already been shown, in the experimental studies by Stotland and Hillmer (1962), Chapman and Volkman (1939), and Hertzman and Festinger (1940), that an individual will tend to assume that he has the same level of ability as do others who are similar to him in other respects. The same process apparently occurs quite widely in everyday life. The reason for its widespread occurrence probably lies in the fact that an individual does not have to interact with or communicate with another person or group in order to perceive his similarity to this person or group. Even similarity to nonexistent or deceased people can be involved in the functioning of this schema. Thus, the possible applications of this schema are very wide indeed.

Information Concerning the Range of Competence

Still another way in which the perception of other people influences a person's sense of competence concerns the individual's conception of the range of the dimension of competence. The individual may have acquired the conceptual dimension of level of competence without having a clear idea of what its range is. A child might learn that his I.Q. is 115, and yet have no way to interpret this information, to know how "good" such a score is. Any student who has received a grade on an examination without knowing how well or poorly his classmates have done will know what is meant by a lack of knowledge of the possible range of competence. An individual's sense of competence can then be strongly influenced by what he learns about the ability or performance level of other people. Obviously, if a student learns that he has the highest grades in his class, he will have a greater sense of competence than if he finds he is lowest. Thus, what the individual learns about the range of performance of other people can also have a strong influence on his sense of competence, since this range influences what the person perceives as an effective or ineffective level of performance (cf. Lewin, Dembo, Festinger, and Sears, 1944).

In some instances, an individual may perceive only one other group of people who "work at" the same tasks as himself. The performance levels of people in this group then will be the primary determinant of the range of the person's conceptual dimension of competence on a task. However, in some instances, an individual may perceive that there are several different "groups" which work at some given same task; he may recognize that there are competitive skiers, expert skiers, intermediate skiers, and beginners—and the "kids" on the "bunny tow." He may perceive that within each of these groups there is a range of performance levels which, in fact, is often the case, given the variation of human beings. The question then arises as to how the range of competence will be defined under these circumstances. One answer is indicated by the schema about the generality of similarity. Having this schema will lead the individual to generalize in a special way described below, more from the group to which he is most similar. The similarity involved here can concern experience, background, size, sex, or any other characteristics which are relevant to performance of the task. Such groups with similar relevant backgrounds, etc., are often termed reference groups.

The term reference groups also sometimes is used to indicate groups to which an individual conforms, to which he is motivated to make himself similar. This meaning is different from the one implied here in which reference groups are those that provide a person with knowledge about the range of the dimension of competence.

If he has practiced skiing as much as most intermediate skiers and finds himself possessing skills typically associated with this level of skiing ability, he will generalize from that group to himself more than from groups of experts or beginners; that group will be his reference group. However, since all members of even this restricted group do not perform at the same level of expertise, he cannot simply acquire a schema to the effect that he can perform at a specific level simply because he shares some of the relevant attributes of this reference group. Instead, he will acquire, as part of his schemas about his competence, a conception of the range of possible levels of competence at which he can perform the task; he will come to believe that as an intermediate skier, his range of possible performances starts at effective stem christies and ends with smooth, linked parallel turns. He then evaluates his competence in skiing relative to this range; it is the range of the dimension of competence for him. He will believe he is a good or poor skier relative to the range for intermediate skiers. Of course, he will recognize that he is better than beginners and worse than experts, but, if queried, he'd probably say those groups don't matter—now.

Communications from Others Regarding Competence

Thus far in our discussion of the way that other people can influence a person's sense of competence, we have been concerned with the way that a person's perception of the performance levels of other people influences his sense of competence. We have not yet discussed the influence on the sense of competence which communications from others concerning their evaluation of the person's abilities may have. Since schemas can be acquired through communications from others, the person's sense of competence can be influenced by such communications. However, it was established earlier that an individual is more likely to acquire a schema from others he believes to be expert about the area of concern of the schema than from someone identified as a non-expert. Thus, if an individual receives an evaluation of his abilities from an expert, he will be more likely to accept the evaluation. Videbeck (1960) had subjects read poems aloud to an expert in poetry reading. The latter either approved or disapproved of their performances. Subjects who were disapproved of shifted their self-ratings of their abilities downward, although the approved of subjects did not change their self-evaluations. Maehr, Mensing, and Nafzger (1962) had boys rate themselves on various athletic abilities. Then an audience of experts watched them dribble, do calisthenics, and other athletics, and gave them either high or low ratings. Finally the boys' own ratings of their athletic abilities were obtained and were found to reflect the experts' ratings. Haas and Maehr (1965) found that the effects of the experts' ratings were still evident six weeks later. Even though these studies did not involve a variation in the degree of expertness of the judges, the data cited in the chapter on the communication of schemas make it very doubtful that non-experts would have as great an influence as would experts.

However, if the area of ability in question is a new one for the person, it does not appear to be very difficult to establish someone as an expert. Zander, Medow, and Efron (1965) had groups of college students work as a team on a game involving motor skills. While they performed a series of trials at the task, the group was observed by another group of subjects, whose job it was to agree on how well they expected the team to do on the next trial. These expectations were communicated to the team, which, in turn, had to agree about its own expectations. It was found that the team was directly influenced by the level of the observers' expectations.

Self-Esteem

We have now examined a range of factors which influence a person's sense of competence—his perception of the effectiveness of his own actions, his perceived freedom to select among a number of possible actions, the number and specificity of the schemas he has about a given situation, schemas about his similarity to other people, his comparison of himself with relevant others, and communications from others about his sense of competence. All of these factors may directly affect a person's sense of competence. However, the sense of competence is usually related to another schema, one which is of higher order than the sense of competence. This H.O.S. is usually termed self-esteem. It involves some very broad self-evaluation, such as "I think highly (or poorly) of myself." Let us turn to an examination of the relationship between self-esteem and the sense of competence, since self-esteem affects and is affected by the sense of competence.

In schema theory terms, self-esteem refers to the evaluation the person makes of the H.O.S. he possesses which refers to all of the attributes, possessions, experiences, and abilities which he conceives as being his own. This H.O.S. emerges partly as a consequence of the conceptual dimension, "selfness," which is part of each of the schemas referring to these various attributes. For instance, the person may have the schemas "I own that; I can do this; I am a quiet person." The commonality of "I" in all of these leads the person to develop an H.O.S. based on the common conceptual dimension of self as "I." This H.O.S. referring to the self is also acquired through communications from others. The individual is referred to by others by his proper name, by "you," "he," "that guy," "son," "Mr. _____," etc. All of those communications imply that there is a unity, a totality which corresponds to self—the same unity or totality referred by the H.O.S. which the individual develops out of his own L.O.S.s about himself.

In addition to acquiring an H.O.S. referring to the self, the individual acquires the conceptual dimension of evaluation as part of this H.O.S. There are several factors which lead to the acquisition of this dimension. First, many of the lower order schemas out of which the H.O.S. emerges entail evaluation. In some cases, the evaluation is the result of association of some object, entity, or activity with the satisfaction of needs, the attainment of goals. People, situations, objects, which are associated with need satisfaction are liked, are evaluated positively; those which are associated with frustration are evaluated negatively. For present purposes, it is important to notice that the individual will tend to make a positive evaluation part of a schema of "I can do this useful and desirable thing" and a negative evaluation part of the schema of "I can't do that, when most people can." This is because, in general, the ability to act is associated with the attainment of goals, the satisfaction of needs. Thus, an individual who is generally capable of doing things, of acting in many ways, will tend to evaluate his total self more positively, to have high self-esteem. "I like myself because I can do things."

General Self-Evaluation

The reader may have noticed that in discussing the emergence of an overall dimension of self-esteem an assumption was made that the individual can either be generally competent or at least sense that he is, or generally incompetent, or sense that he is. On what basis can we make the assumption of overall, uniform competence or incompetence? In the first place, there is a general trend for people to perceive themselves to have roughly the same level of competence in many areas of life. Once even a quite probabalistic evaluation of the total self is acquired, the individual tends to bring the L.O.S. subsumed under this H.O.S. in line with it. If the individual begins to establish some very general self-evaluations which may at first be replete with exceptions, a person will be motivated to minimize these exceptions, to develop a schema of low probabilism about himself. One way he can do this is by making the L.O.S.s consistent with the overall evaluation. The consistency between the overall evaluation and the person's sense of competence for specific tasks and goals is illustrated in the work of Morris Rosenberg (1965), who asked adolescents to evaluate how satisfied they were with themselves in general and found that the levels of these overall evaluations were correlated with the person's sense of competence in many areas of his life.

Secondly, the individual receives communications from others in which he is evaluated as a totality, as a unified entity. Early in life he is told, "You are a good (bad) boy (girl)." Later, "You're a great guy" or "You're a bum." However true or false these statements are, the person is being evaluated as a totality. This evaluation by others has the conceptual dimensions of a self and an evaluation in common with the H.O.S. which emerges from the person's own L.O.S.s regarding his own attributes; and thus the two sources of self and of evaluation form a new H.O.S. which incorporates them both.

There is, however, a further reason why these two sources of evaluation of the overall self should emerge into one H.O.S. This reason is that the evaluations made by others often are completely consistent with the evaluations the individual makes himself on the basis of his own analysis of the degree to which his activities lead to the satisfaction of his needs. This consistency results from the fact that traditionally in America, as in some other countries, probably the most broadly employed criterion used in the evaluation of others is their effectiveness, their ability to act capably to effect and maintain control over their environment so as to maximize reward and minimize punishment. Such capability and control are typically publicly observable and are manifested in material rather than psychic or personal terms. Thus, the sense of competence and the esteem that others communicate are tied closely together.

In other societies, this tie-in of others' evaluations with personal effectiveness may be less close. An individual may be evaluated by others because of his family background, his birthplace, his school, or other social factors (what the anthropologists call "ascribed status"). Of course, in America the same sorts of evaluations on the basis of such factors are also made, such as race. However, evaluations made on the basis of race are often rejected because they violate the basic tenet that a man is to be evaluated by what he does.

The way a person's self-esteem is influenced by communications he receives from others is shown in a study by Harvey (1962). He had students in a college class evaluate themselves on various traits. At a subsequent session they rated others in the class and received the others' presumed ratings of them. The received ratings were lower than the person's own, but the degree of discrepancy from his own ratings was made to vary. Then everyone rated himself again. It was found that the greater the degree of discrepancy, the lower the person's re-ratings of himself.

Sometimes the opinions others have of a person are communicated by their behavior toward him. If they reject him, they imply that they have a low evaluation of him. Pepitone and Wilpizeski (1960) assembled groups of three students to discuss premarital sex. Two of them had been trained by the experimenter to either agree with the third toward the end of the discussion or to disagree with him, then ignore him or be rude to him by talking just to each other. The subjects then evaluated themselves on a private questionnaire, and the second group of subjects had lower self-evaluations than the first, agreeing with group. Likewise, Jones (1964) found that if a person is instructed to try to present a favorable impression of himself to another and if the other appears to accept this impression, the person's own evaluation of himself will become more positive.

Parents' positive evaluations of their children are communicated either directly or indirectly through the amount of positive, supportive attention which they give to their children. Coopersmith (1967) found that the mothers of high self-esteem boys had a generally higher interest in their sons, even from the latter's earliest years, than did the mothers of low self-esteem boys. The former had more confidence in the boys' abilities, gave their sons more affection, and showed more interest in their children's experiences. Morris Rosenberg (1965) found that the overall evaluations high school students gave of themselves were positively related to the amount of interest the mothers took in their children, as reflected in their interest in the latter's friends and academic performances. The parents of high self-esteem children talked more with them at mealtimes. Further, the fathers of high self-esteem boys were more supportive of their sons.

On the basis of this discussion on the relationship between self-esteem and the sense of competence, we will use these terms more or less equivalently. In describing some studies where limited performances or evaluations are concerned, "sense of competence" would be somewhat more appropriate, although even here "self-esteem" is lurking in the shadows. In describing studies which involve evaluations of a broader nature, "self-esteem" will be used, but again, "sense of competence" is obviously closely involved as well. The interchangeability of the terms reflects the fact that a change in self-esteem effects a change in the sense of competence and vice versa.

EFFECTS OF SENSE OF COMPETENCE ON BEHAVIOR

Now that we have determined the various factors which influence self-esteem, we need next to discuss the ramifications which differences in self-esteem or sense of competence may have. What difference does it make whether a person's self-esteem is high or low?

The Likelihood of Action

In Chapter 7, it was pointed out that schemas can function to guide behavior; this applies also to schemas about the probability of attaining goals. Clearly, an individual will choose to act in the specific way that he believes to be most likely to lead to the attainment of his goals. Furthermore, the individual is more likely to engage in a given action, the more he perceives that this action will lead to goal attainment (cf. Stotland, 1969). A simple example: people who do not feel that they can be effective by voting do not vote in as many elections (Campbell, Converse, Miller, and Stokes, 1960). A person's perception that his actions will lead to goal attainment is in part a function of his general sense of competence.

Thus, the higher the person's sense of competence, the more likely he is to act to attain his goals. A more complex example: Wattenberg and Clifford (1964) measured the self-esteem of kindergarten children by recording their spontaneous comments in response to a picture of their families and by giving them an incomplete sentence test. Their self-esteem scores predicted how well the children had learned to read by the second grade, regardless of their I.Q. The high self-esteem children had evidently made a greater effort to learn how to read. Morris Rosenberg (1965) found that high self-esteem adolescents were more likely than lows to speak up in group discussions, to make friends easily, to be in leadership positions, and to join groups of various sorts. Cohen (1959) found that persons high in self-esteem attempted to influence others more than did lows. The tendency of high self-esteem people to speak up more, and to try to influence people more, evidently leads them to acquire a schema based on this fact (Coopersmith, 1967) playing an active role and prepare for it accordingly; thus, they are more likely to try to gain information about a topic which they expect to be discussed in a group (Clarke and James, 1967). Since the lows don't expect to speak up, they aren't as likely to prepare for a discussion in this way. Seeman (1963) found that reformatory inmates who believe more that they are able to control their environment have more knowledge of parole procedures than do those who indicate a belief that fate or chance factors control what happens to them, even when such factors as educational level are controlled statistically. The former group apparently sought out such knowledge more since they believed more that they would be able to use it to their own advantage. These groups did not differ in their knowledge of other aspects of their environment. Seeman and Evans (1962) likewise found that tuberculosis sanitarium patients who perceived more that they could control their fates knew more about T.B. than did other patients who were low in this belief.

League and Jackson (1964) found that people with high self-esteem did better at a task which required them to count or estimate the number of rapid-sequence clicks they heard in a given period of time, presumably because they attended better to the task at hand. Leventhal and Trembly (1968) showed movies of auto accidents, some gory, some not. High and medium self-esteem people said they would think about the film and take action, with respect both to themselves and others, to stop the slaughter on the highways. They were more likely to indicate these intentions if they had viewed the movie from close up, so that the emotional impact was greater. Low self-esteem people, in contrast, indicated that they would not try to do anything except to avoid thinking about the movie and the problems of accidents. Zimbardo and Formica (1963) found that people with high self-esteem think they will be better able to cope with a severe electric shock then do lows.

Success and Future Performance

The person's sense of competence is in part an outcome of his previous levels of success or failure, as pointed out above. Since a high sense of competence leads to a higher probability that a person will act to attain goals, success leads to more action to attain goals than does failure. Gebhard (1948), Gewirtz (1959), Cartwright (1942), and Nowlis (1941) all found that an individual will make much less effort to work on tasks at which he has failed than on tasks at which he has succeeded. For some tasks, the person's level of performance, of goal attainment, is directly affected by the amount of effort he expends. On such tasks, a person who has succeeded will be more likely to continue to succeed, since his first successes lead to a higher sense of competence and thus to greater future effort. Sears (1937) gave subjects a card-sorting task and led them to believe that they were either succeeding or failing. The "failing" subjects went on to perform worse on the succeeding tasks. Similar effects have been found by McClelland and Apicella (1947), Osler (1954), Rhine (1957), and Feather (1966, 1968). An individual's sense of competence applies to goals and tasks in addition to the original one on which either success or failure has been encountered. The sense of competence applies to other tasks on which the individual works in the same setting. The common setting makes it possible for the person to develop a schema, "I do well at tasks in this setting." Thus, Hutt (1947) found that if children take an I.Q. test with the easiest types of items first and then go on to the harder ones, their I.Q. score will be over 10 points higher than if they start on the difficult items and move on to the easy ones. Lantz (1945), McClelland and Apicella (1947), and Moshin (1954) also found similar results. This type of effect of success or failure has also been found with respect to an individual's effort in reading a difficult passage. Gollob and Dittes (1965) led subjects to believe that they had either succeeded or failed on a test that was supposed to measure the ability to abstract. The subjects then read a message, part of which presented a very difficult, complex, somewhat contradictory message regarding the nature of research on cancer. The subjects who had been led to believe that they were high in abstracting ability were more likely than other subjects to understand the message and therefore to come to accept the points it made. Their greater understanding most likely occurred because of their greater efforts at comprehension of the complex message, in line with their expectation that such an investment of effort would pay off.

Later in this chapter, we will learn that persons with high self-esteem tend to be resistant to attempts to persuade them. The study by Gollob and Dittes may appear to be contradictory to this tendency. However, a closer inspection reveals that such resistance of persons with high esteem is a result of the higher credibility that they place on their own beliefs as compared to other people's. Low self-esteem people tend to attribute greater credibility to others' beliefs. However, this difference between high and low self-esteem persons is predicated on both groups' having equally good knowledge of other people's beliefs; they differ, then, primarily in their evaluation of these beliefs. On the other hand, what Gollob and Dittes (1965) show is that this equality of knowledge of others' beliefs may not occur if there is some difficulty in understanding these beliefs. This point has been made very cogently by McGuire (1969).

One strong implication of this set of results is that people who early in life encounter many successes will tend to continue to succeed; people who start out in life with high self-esteem will be likely to continue to succeed and their very success will tend to keep their self-esteem high. Silber, Hamberg, Coelho, Murphy, Rosenberg, and Pearlin (1961) studied highly competent adolescents, those who were excellent students and active in extracurricular affairs. In interviews, the students indicated that an important way in which they maintained their high sense of competence was by recalling the ways in which they had coped with difficult situations in the past.

Freedom to Select an Appropriate Response

In the earlier discussion of the influence a person's perception of the effectiveness of his own actions has on his sense of competence, the importance of his perception that a variety of possible actions are available in his repertoire of abilities was mentioned. To carry this point further, it can now be seen how the higher sense of competence which results from having freedom to make a choice from a number of possible behaviors leads to a higher level of performance in many situations. Mandler and Watson (1966) had one group of subjects take a series of tests in any order they chose, and had another group take the same tests in a fixed order. Each person in the fixed order groups was matched with another subject in the free choice groups, so that the former persons were actually given the tests in the same order as was their free choice counterpart. The freely choosing group, however, did better on the tests than did the others who encountered exactly the same sequence, but who had not chosen it.

Similar findings have come from industrial settings. Coch and French (1948) studied a pajama factory in which there had always been an immediate and marked drop in production whenever new equipment was introduced, and the long period of recovery and ultimate rise in production was considered to be not very satisfactory. The researchers came upon the scene just when management was considering the introduction of new machinery. Coch and French divided the workers into three groups. One group had the new equipment introduced to the workers as it always had been in the past—a notice from management with an explanation of why the machinery was better, etc., etc. A second group met in discussion groups with a management person present in order to come to a decision as to whether or not to have the new machinery introduced; all the discussion-decision groups decided to have the new machinery. A third group elected representatives who met with management and then reported back to them in a discussion group in which they made a decision about the new machinery. In other words, the second two groups felt considerably greater freedom with regard to the changes which took place than did the first. Not surprisingly, these latter groups showed less of a drop in production and a more rapid regaining and surpassing of the previous levels of production than did the traditionally treated groups. No doubt other factors than the freedom to choose were involved, but there is little doubt that it did play a role. Kahn and Katz (1953) report that foremen who allow their workers freedom to work out the details of their work have better production records than do those who do not allow their workers this freedom.

Not all tasks are subject to this type of influence. Sometimes the task is so organized that the higher sense of competence of the workers which results from this sort of freedom can make little difference in production (cf. Morse and Reimer, 1956). On other occasions the very freedom itself leads the subjects to change their goals in working on the task from, say, quantity to quality (cf. White and Lippitt, 1960).

Task Structure

In addition to previous successes, and freedom of response selection, another factor which was shown above to increase the sense of competence was the clear structuring of the situation, so that a person would be better able to determine precisely how to act in order to attain his goals. Thus, if an individual's sense of competence is increased because of a clear structuring of the task, he is more likely to engage in the task-relevant behaviors to achieve some goal (cf. Cartwright, 1949).

This enhancement of the sense of competence may be one of the factors involved in a series of studies which show that people are more likely to act if they are given specific information regarding an appropriate set of actions than if they are not. Of course, this effect of giving information also results simply from the fact that if a person doesn't know what to do to attain a goal, he is unlikely to attain it. Leventhal, Singer, and Jones (1965) experimentally aroused considerable fear of tetanus infections in a group of subjects. Some of them were then given very specific instructions as to how they might obtain anti-tetanus shots—where, when, how—while others were only given vague information on this point. The subjects who received the more specific instructions were more likely to actually go out and get shots. The researchers also found that if they did not arouse sufficient fear, neither type of information had any effect on the likelihood of persons obtaining the anti-tetanus injections. These results were essentially replicated in another study by Leventhal, Jones, and Trembly (1966). Likewise, Leventhal, Watts, and Pagano (1967) found that giving people specific rather than vague instructions on how to stop smoking led to their expressing a greater intention to stop smoking, provided that the subjects' fear of cancer had been sufficiently aroused. Leventhal and Singer (1966) found that if people were frightened sufficiently by a film on the consequences of inadequate dental care, they were more likely to plan to brush their teeth better if they were given explicit instructions on how to do so than if they were not.

The knowledge that a person has in a situation does not have to concern the task directly in order for performance to increase. Neale and Katahn (1968) gave subjects a series of tests, telling some of them in which order they would take them, and not telling others what the order would be. The former group did better on the tests.

The reader may get the impression that the discussion of the effects of freedom of choice on action is somewhat contradictory to the findings about the effectiveness of L.O.S.s in increasing competence. On close inspection, this apparent disparity disappears. An individual can have freedom of choice between clearly defined alternatives or between rather fuzzily defined ones, His sense of competence would be higher in the former case.

Communications from Others

Earlier in this chapter it was pointed out that a person's sense of competence could also be affected by communications from other people. Accordingly, if a person's sense of competence is raised in this manner, then he would be more likely to try to attain goals, to work at tasks which might lead him to succeed at them. If an individual's sense of competence is lowered by communications from others, then his performance on tasks would be expected to deteriorate. Thus, Sarason and Sarason (1957) had persons work on a standard learning task which required them to associate pairs of nonsense syllables. At the end of the first 15 trials, the experimenter told some of them that they were doing very badly, that, in fact, they were doing worse than anyone else ever had, and that the experimenter wondered what was the matter. Other subjects just chatted with the experimenter at the end of the 15 trials. When all of the subjects were given an additional trial, the discouraged group did worse than the others. Crandall (1963) found that children whose I.Q.s increased from one testing to another had parents who were very interested in having their children achieve highly in school and who were emotionally close to their children, so that they might be expected to have communicated in a competence-enhancing manner with them.

Sometimes encouraging communications can even overcome the effects of failure. Zeller (1950) first gave his subjects a task of associating nonsense syllables. Then, he demonstrated for them a task in which they were to tap the same colored block as he did. In the relevant part of the study, the subjects were then given one of two different treatments. In the first, the tapping tasks which were given were easy and the experimenter told the participants that they were doing well. The second group was given a difficult version of this task at which they were told they failed, but the experimenter also told them he was surprised at this because they had done so well at learning the pairs of nonsense syllables; he told the subjects to "get hold of themselves." Persons in this second group were then observed to improve their performance. Although no research is available to illustrate this point, it would also be expected that if an individual succeeds on a task and is told by an authoritative person that in the future he would fail when he attempted this task, his performance would deteriorate.

There can be little doubt that part of the reason that the high self-esteem children and adolescents studied by Coopersmith (1967) and Rosenberg (1965) performed so well in school and in all sorts of activities was that their parents encouraged them. Rosenberg reports that the high self-esteem adolescents had more supportive fathers than did the lows. Coopersmith (1967) reports that the mothers of the high self-esteem boys had high estimates of their sons' abilities. No doubt some of these high estimations were an outcome of the parents' perceptions of the actually superior performance of the high self-esteem boys, but it would be hard to deny that some of the effect on performances resulted from encouragement, especially in the face of failure.

Observers' Influence on Performance

There are situations in which two of the factors which influence the sense of competence work hand in hand with each other to magnify their separate effects. Take the case of an individual who is working on a task before an audience. If he is doing poorly on the task because, for example, it is new to him, he will be likely to assume that his audience will perceive that he is doing poorly, and will also expect that he will continue to do poorly. After all, the audience has little evidence on which to base their judgment other than what they have just observed. His perceptions that the others do not expect him to do any better will then tend to depress his performance. Thus, Quarter and Marcus (mimeo) had 8th grade children take a digit span test either alone or before a silent, serious-looking group of teachers. Not surprisingly, the pupils thought that the teachers were judging them rather negatively, especially since digit span tests are not easy and they themselves felt they were doing poorly. Consequently, they did more poorly if they were before the group than if they were performing in isolation. When an individual is learning a difficult task, he is not likely to do well at it. If he is learning it in front of a group who are in a position to evaluate his performance, his perception of the group's expectations will further inhibit his performance. Zajonc (1965) cites data to show that people learn to do such unfamiliar tasks as finger mazes and learning to pair nonsense syllables better if they are alone than if they are watched.

On the other hand, if an individual expects to do well before

An audience with effects.

an audience, and, in fact, is quite competent at the task in question, his perceptions of the audience's expectations should enhance his performance. Consequently, if an individual works at a task which is well learned and easy for him before an audience, he will do better than if he works on these tasks while alone. Thus, Zajonc (1965) points out that people do better before audiences than alone on such tasks as multiplication tables and word associations; in both cases, the associations have been well learned because of frequent repetition.

Zajonc's own interpretation of the research on social facilitation, as this area is called, is based on the idea that people become more aroused and more highly driven when in the presence of other people. This high state of arousal presumably has the effect of increasing their tendency to perform their dominant, i.e., well learned, habits, rather than less well learned ones. If these dominant responses are "correct," then the person performs better before the group than alone; if they are incorrect, as is likely to be the case in the early stages of learning a new task, he does more poorly before the group than alone.

Zajonc's explanation is wanting, in part because he does not distinguish between the mere presence of others and their being an audience. In all of the work he cites to support his view, the groups were audiences, spectators, observers, and thus potential evaluators. Therefore, the subject's perception of the audience's expectations is a relevant consideration, which Zajonc ignores. In fact, Cottrell (1970) has assembled data from several experiments that show that the presence of others who are ignorant of one's performance has less of an effect than if the others are spectators. For instance, the presence of blindfolded people has little effect. Secondly, we have seen how the communications from others can have either salutary or negative effects on performance, depending on whether the communications are positive or not. Thirdly, Zajonc's explanation of why the presence of others increases arousal or general drive level is not completely clear. If this effect is a consequence of the individual's experiences with others, whether arousal occurs or not, its magnitude should be a function of the particular experiences a given individual has had with others and not a general, across-the-board effect, similar for all persons. In fact, Paivo (1965) has documented very well the fact that the degree of anxiety aroused by audiences depends very much on a person's previous experiences with them.

We have just seen the effects on actual performance which others' expectations about a person's level of performance may have. There are, in addition, other ways in which persons can influence another's performance by influencing his sense of competence. Data presented earlier established that the schema concerning the generality of similarity between people led college students to perform at the same level on clerical tasks as did another person whom they observed who was similar to them in some rather arbitrary ways (Stotland and Dunn, 1962). Furthermore, a person's actual performance on a difficult syllable-counting task was shown to be directly influenced by the performance level of someone with whom he had previously interacted (Stotland and Cottrell, 1962). The ways which have been discussed earlier by which the perception of other people influences a person's sense of competence obviously also indicate ways in which a person's actual performance on a task can be influenced by others.

General Effects of Sense of Competence

Thus far, we have examined the effects which the sense of competence may have on an individual's expected and actual performance on tasks which are the same as, or similar to, a task on which the individual's sense of competence is based. However, a person's overall sense of competence or his self-esteem is not just a reflection of his performance on these specific tasks. It is also an H.O.S., and, as such, it has a range of applicability beyond its roots in specific performances. The individual conceives of himself as a generally competent or incompetent person. If he has succeeded at a variety of tasks, part of his schema about his own competence may include the notion that he generally succeeds at all sorts of tasks. Furthermore, the communications he receives from other people may entail the idea that he is a generally effective or ineffective person. Similarly, any of the other sources of influence on the sense of competence can have had the effect of leading to general conceptions of competence.

Self-Competence and Approach to Novelty

One consequence of the broad or abstract notion of self-esteem or the overall sense of competence is the influence it may then have on a person's approach to, and behavior in, new or different situations in which he has few relevant L.O.S.s to guide his behavior. Thus, Coopersmith (1967) gave his seven to eight year old boys a test of creativity in which they were asked to list a number of new and different uses for common, everyday objects. Boys with higher self-esteem performed better at this task, were more creative. Starbuck (1965) cites data which indicate that in large organizations the least resistance to change comes from the more competent employees. In fact, Wispé and Lloyd (1955) report that when a salesman is being successful, he is more willing to have an unstructured, more spontaneous discussion with his supervisor. Canon (1964) showed that persons who had recently experienced consistent successes in solving complex problems were more inclined than were those who had done poorly to seek out information which opposed their own point of view.

Persons' willingness to face the new or unknown can be shown to be an outcome of the same sorts of factors as is increased self-esteem. Getzels and Jackson (1962) divided above-average students into two groups. One group was higher in creativity than in I.Q.; the other group was higher in I.Q. than in creativity. The test of creativity demanded that the subjects list new uses for everyday objects, think of different meanings for words, think of different types of endings to stories, and so forth. It was found that the students who were higher in creativity than in I.Q. came from homes in which there was much less criticism of the children's ideas. The parents of the creative children were therefore less nonsupportive or, by implication, more supportive, of them. Likewise, Watson (1957) studied the creativity of children from well-to-do homes on the basis of the imaginativeness of their free play. He found that the more creative children came from more permissive homes.

The effect of the sense of competence on the person's tendency to approach the new, the different, and the unknown adds to our knowledge of the conditions under which a person will make such approaches. In Chapter 3, we pointed out that a familiar context increases the likelihood that a person will pursue the new, and this was explained in terms of the person's inability to process more than a given amount of information. Here we are saying that there are additional factors that enter into the situation, such as the person's sense of competence. However, the effect of a familiar context on the reaction to the new may be the result of the relationship between familiarity and the sense of competence, as well as of the ability to process data. An individual will tend to conceive of himself as being more competent in the presence of the familiar than the unfamiliar. Thus, if part of a situation is familiar, this familiarity will tend to lead the person to perceive that he is more competent in that situation. This higher sense of competence would be relevant not only to the familiar parts of the situation, but, since the sense of competence tends to be general, also, to a greater or lesser degree, to the new aspects as well. When a person meets a stranger in the company of an acquaintance, his sense of competence in relating to the acquaintance will enhance his sense of competence with respect to the stranger; he will then be more likely to feel that he can relate easily to the stranger. Consequently, he will be more likely to talk to him, to try to strike up a conversation and perhaps befriend him.

Self-Esteem and Conformity

The high sense of competence of persons with high self-esteem is not limited to their evaluation of their ability to act. They also are more confident of their ability to perceive the world accurately, to make valid judgments about reality (Morris Rosenberg, 1963). In fact, there is evidence that, in the face of disagreement with others, high self-esteem persons become even more confident of their opinions, while people with low self-esteem become less certain of their own positions (Worchel and McCormick, 1963). As a consequence of this difference between high and low self-esteem people, the lows attempt more than highs to prepare for situations in which they will have to confront a disagreement, such as in a debate (Clarke and James, 1967). One major consequence of the greater confidence that high self-esteem people have in their perception and interpretation of reality is that they are less prone than lows to conform to the judgments that other people make about reality. This negative relationship between self-esteem and conformity has been found in a wide range of studies—with old people and young people, with respect to judgments of length of lines, with judgments of who will win a race, almanac type facts about the world, judgments about other people, and others (Wicklund and Brehm, 1968; Coopersmith, 1967; Crutchfield, 1955; Rosenbaum, Horne, and Chalmers, 1962).

The greater tendency of persons of low self-esteem to accept the judgments of others extends even to judgments about themselves. Diggory (1966) found that when two people were performing a series of trials on the same task and were asked to indicate how well they expected to do on subsequent trials, people of low self-esteem were more likely than highs to base their expectations on the other person's degree of success or failure.

Rosenberg (1965) reports that low self-esteem adolescents say they feel that they are more sensitive to the opinions others have about them. Stotland, Cohen, Thomas, Thorley, and Zander (1957) conducted a study in which they first formed subjects into groups by having them work on a task together. Then, each person in the group was to work on an individual task which was sometimes described as relevant to subsequent group tasks, sometimes as not relevant. Before working on these tasks, the subjects voted on whether to have strong expectations that each person complete his individual task or to expect only that each person try his best. In half the groups the subjects were led to believe that the group voted for the strong expectations; in the other half for the lenient decision. The subjects then worked on the task, a variation of a jigsaw puzzle, and half of them were given insolvable puzzles. The subjects then judged how well or poorly they had done. It was found that low self-esteem subjects who were given insolvable puzzles judged their failure to be greater if the group had high expectations rather than lenient, provided the task was relevant to the group. High self-esteem people were not affected by the group's expectations. No differences were found when the subjects succeeded on their puzzles.

Despite all that we have said about the greater sensitivity of low self-esteems to influence from others, some exceptions to this trend have been found. Among females, Gergen and Bauer (1967) found that for easy and moderately difficult tasks, both those with very low and very high self-esteem conformed less than did those with moderate self-esteem. However, self-esteem was unrelated to conformity on a task which was both more difficult and more subjective. Silverman, Ford, and Morganti (1966) also found that women with very high and those with very low self-esteem conformed less than did those with moderate self-esteem. However, these curvilinear relationships were somewhat unreliable, since both Gergen et al. and Silverman et al. did not find them in all the substudies they conducted. Nevertheless, these findings do raise a question as to why females with low self-esteem sometimes conform less than those with moderate self-esteem. One possible explanation stems from the general tendency for women to have lower self-esteem than men (Wylie, 1961). Thus, women identified in various experiments as having low self-esteem are probably extremely low, lower even than are the men selected as low self-esteem. As we shall see in the next section, low self-esteem is often associated with rather negative feelings toward others. In this group of extremely low self-esteem women, such negative feelings may have overcome any tendency to turn to others as more competent than oneself, which is the process at the heart of the general trend for low self-esteem people to conform more.

At the other extreme, Silverman (1964) found that among a group of residents in a V.A. domiciliary—a home for older war veterans—the greatest conformity was found among those with the very lowest and very highest self-esteem, with the moderates conforming least. A clue to the reason for this peculiar finding comes from the fact that the high self-esteem veterans were in fact higher than high male college students who had taken the same measure of self-esteem. Thus, the high veterans were extremely high, while the moderate veterans were much like the high male college students in level of self-esteem; and both the moderate veterans and the high college students conform less. The question remains as to why the extremely high veterans conform so much. The answer might be that in order to describe oneself in sufficiently laudatory terms to obtain such high scores, the respondents may have been either deliberately or unconsciously distorting the picture they presented. One reason for generating so desirable a picture of oneself might be to gain the approval of the researcher. A person who is motivated to gain the researcher's approval might also be motivated to gain other people's favor, and therefore might conform more.

One general implication of these findings is that extremely high and extremely low self-esteem are manifestations of somewhat different processes than those which occur in moderately high- and moderately low-esteem people.

The H.O.S. self-evaluation not only has an influence on people's view of their ability to achieve but also on their confidence in the validity of their own perceptions. This schema has also been found to influence other lower order schemas which pertain to the person—as if a person with high self-esteem will think better of all aspects of himself and his actions than will a person of lower self-esteem. Thus, if a person with high self-esteem perceives that he has decided to do something morally wrong, he will attempt to reconcile this discrepancy between what he has chosen to do and his high estimate of himself. Thus, Buss (1961) led students to consent to inflict electric shock on another student. Some of the former students had previously received information which raised their self-esteem, while others had received information lowering it. The subjects who had had their self-esteem raised resolved the discrepancy between their high estimate and the "immoral" behavior of inflicting shock by tending to derogate the shocked student, as if he might even be deserving of the shock because of his presumed negative characteristics. The subjects who had not had their self-esteem raised did not engage in similar derogation of the other. This study was essentially replicated by Glass (1964). Likewise, Gerard, Blevans, and Malcolm (1964) found that subjects who were told by the experimenter that they were good at making choices between paintings were more likely to enhance their evaluation of a painting they had chosen than were subjects who had not had their self-evaluation raised by the experimenter's communication.

An ingenious example of the effects of an H.O.S. on perception of specifics about oneself comes from the work of Bramel (1963). On the basis of personality tests, a randomly selected half of the subjects, all males, were told that they were very well adjusted people, while the other half were told that they were poorly adjusted. Then, all of the subjects were shown pictures of nude men, while attached to an instrument which presumably recorded their emotional reactions. Half the subjects were led to believe that their emotional reactions indicated that they had hidden homosexual tendencies, while the other half were not given this generally very unacceptable information about themselves. Finally, all of the subjects were asked to judge the amount of homosexuality in another person like themselves. The group that had been led to have high evaluations of their adjustment and had been led to believe that they had homosexual tendencies was more likely than any other group to judge this person as being high in homosexuality. By doing so, these subjects were saying, in effect, "I'm still a relatively well-adjusted person, since 'everyone' has this tendency anyway."

References

Bramel, D.: Selection of a target for defensive projection. *Journal of Abnormal and Social Psychology*, 1963, 66:318–324.

Buss, A.: *The Psychology of Aggression.* New York, Wiley, 1961.

Campbell, A., Converse, P. E., Miller, W. E., and Stokes, D. E.: *The American Voter.* New York, Wiley, 1960.

Canon, L.: Self-confidence and selective exposure to information. In L. Festinger (Ed.), *Conflict, Decision and Dissonance.* Stanford, Stanford University Press, 1964.

Cartwright, D. O.: The effect of interruption, completion, and failure upon attractiveness of activities. *Journal of Experimental Psychology*, 1942, 31:1–16.

Cartwright, D.: Some principles of mass persuasion. *Human Relations*, 1949, 2:253–267.

Chapman, D. W., and Volkmann, J. A.: A social determinant of the level of aspiration. *Journal of Abnormal and Social Psychology*, 1939, 34:225–238.

Clarke, P. and James, J.: The effects of situation, attitude intensity, and personality on information-seeking. *Sociometry*, 1967, 30:235–245.

Coch, L., and French, J. R. P.: Overcoming resistance to change. *Human Relations*, 1948, 1:512–532.

Cohen, A. R.: Some implications of self-esteem for social influence. In C. I. Hovland and I. Janis (Eds.), *Personality and Persuasibility.* New Haven, Yale University Press, 1959.

Coopersmith, S.: *The Antecedents of Self-Esteem.* San Francisco, Freeman, 1967.

Cottrell, N. B.: Social facilitation. In C. G. McClintock (Ed.), *Experimental Social Psychology.* New York, Holt, Rinehart & Winston, 1970.

Crandall, V.: *Achievement in Child Psychology.* Chicago, National Society for the Study of Education, 1963.

Crutchfield, R.: Conformity and character. *American Psychologist*, 1955, 10:191.

de Soto, C., Coleman, E. B., and Putnam, P. L.: Predictions of sequences of successes and failures. *Journal of Experimental Psychology*, 1960, 59:41–46.

Diggory, J.: *Self-Evaluation: Concepts and Studies.* New York, Wiley, 1966.

Feather, N. T.: The study of persistance. *Psychological Bulletin*, 1962, 69:94–115.

Feather, N. T.: Effects of prior success and failure on expectations of success and subsequent performance. *Journal of Personality and Social Psychology*, 1966, 3:287–298.

Feather, N. T.: Change in confidence following success or failure as a predicter of subsequent performance. *Journal of Personality and Social Psychology*, 1968, 9:38–46.

Gebhard, M. E.: The effect of success and failure upon the attractiveness of activities as a function of experience, expectation, and need. *Journal of Experimental Psychology*, 1948, 38:371–388.

Gerard, H. B., Blevans, S. A., and Malcolm, T.: Self-evaluation and the evaluation of choice alternatives. *Journal of Personality*, 1964, 32:395–410.

Gergen, K. J., and Bauer, R. A.: Interactive effects of self-esteem and task difficulty on social conformity. *Journal of Personality and Social Psychology*, 1967, 6:16–22.

Getzels, J. W., and Jackson, P. W.: *Creativity and Intelligence*. New York, Wiley, 1962.

Gewirtz, H. B.: Generalization of children's performances as a function of reinforcement and task similarity. *Journal of Abnormal and Social Psychology*, 1959, 58:111–118.

Glass, D. C.: Changes in liking as a means of reducing cognitive discrepancies between self-esteem and aggression. *Journal of Personality*, 1964, 32:532–544.

Gollob, H. F., and Dittes, J. E.: Effects of manipulated self-esteem on persuasibility depending on threat and complexity of communication. *Journal of Personality and Social Psychology*, 1965, 2:195–201.

Haas, H. I., and Maehr, M. L.: Two experiments in the concept of self and the reaction to others. *Journal of Personality and Social Psychology*, 1965, 1:100–105.

Harvey, O. J.: Personality factors in the resolution of perceptual incongruities. *Sociometry*, 1962, 25:336–352.

Hertzman, M., and Festinger, L.: Shifts in explicit goals in a level of aspiration experiment. *Journal of Experimental Psychology*, 1940, 27:439–452.

Hutt, M. L.: A clinical study of consecutive and adaptive testing with the revised Stanford Benet. *Journal of Consulting Psychology*, 1947, 2:93–103.

Jones, E. E.: *Ingratiation*. New York, Appleton-Century-Crofts, 1964.

Kahn, R. L., and Katz, D.: Leadership practices in relation to productivity and morale. In D. Cartwright and A. Zander (Eds.), *Group Dynamics*. Evanston, Illinois, Row, Peterson, 1953.

Lantz, B.: Some dynamic aspects of success and failure. *Psychological Monographs*, 1945, 59:No. 1 (Whole No. 271).

League, B. J., and Jackson, D. N.: Conformity, veridicality, and self-esteem. *Journal of Abnormal and Social Psychology*, 1964, 68:113–115.

Leventhal, H., Jones, S., and Trembly, G.: Sex differences in attitude and behavior change under conditions of fear and specific instructions. *Journal of Experimental Social Psychology*, 1966, 2:387–399.

Leventhal, H., and Singer, R. P.: Affect arousal and positioning of recommendation in persuasive communications. *Journal of Personality and Social Psychology*, 1966, 4:137–146.

Leventhal, H., Singer, R., and Jones, S.: Effects of fear and specificity of recommendation upon attitude and behavior. *Journal of Personality and Social Psychology*, 1965, 2:20–29.

Leventhal, H., and Trembly, G.: Negative emotions and persuasion. *Journal of Personality*, 1968, 36:154–168.

Leventhal, H., Watts, J., and Pagano, F.: Effects of fear and instructions on how to cope with danger. *Journal of Personality and Social Psychology*, 1967, 6:313–321.

Lewin, K., Dembo, T., Festinger, L., and Sears, P. S.: Level of aspiration. In J. McV. Hunt (Ed.), *Personality and the Behavior Researchers*. New York, Ronald, 1944.

McClelland, D. C., and Apicella, F. S.: Reminiscence following experimentally induced failure. *Journal of Experimental Psychology*, 1947, 37:159–177.

McGuire, W. J.: Personality and susceptibility to social influence. In E. F. Borgatta and W. W. Lambert (Eds.), *Handbook of Personality Theory and Research*. Chicago, Rand-McNally, 1969.

Maehr, M. L., Mensing, J., and Nafzger, S.: Concept of self and reactions of others. *Sociometry*, 1962, 25:353–357.

Mandler, G., and Watson, D. L.: Anxiety and the interruption of behavior. In C. D. Speilberger (Ed.), *Anxiety and Behavior*. New York, Academic Press, 1966.

Morse, N. C., and Reimer, E.: Experimental change of a major organizational variable. *Journal of Abnormal and Social Psychology*, 1956, 52:120–129.

Moshin, S. M.: Effects of frustration on problem-solving behavior. *Journal of Abnormal and Social Psychology*, 1954, 49:152–155.

Murphy, L.: *The Widening World of Childhood: Paths Toward Mastery*. New York, Basic Books, 1962.

Neale, J. M., and Katahn, M.: Anxiety, choice, and stimulus uncertainty. *Journal of Personality*, 1968, 36:235–245.

Nowlis, H. M.: The influence of success and failure on the resumption of an interrupted task. *Journal of Experimental Psychology*, 1941, 28:304–325.

Osler, S. F.: Intellectual performance as a function of two types of psychological stress. *Journal of Experimental Psychology*, 1954, 47:115–121.

Paivo, A.: Personality and audience influence. In B. Maher (Ed.), *Progress in Experimental Personality Research*. Vol. 2. New York, Academic Press, 1965.

Pepitone, A., and Wilpizeski, C.: Some consequences of experimental rejection. *Journal of Abnormal and Social Psychology*, 1960, 60:359–364.

Quarter, J., and Marcus, A.: Drive level and the audience effect: a test of Zajonc's theory. Mimeo, University of Toronto, Ontario Institute for Studies in Education.

Rhine, R. J.: The effect on problem solving of success or failure as a function of cue specificity. *Journal of Experimental Psychology*, 1957, 53:121–125.

Rosenbaum, M. E., Horne, W., and Chalmers, D.: Level of self-esteem and the learning of imitation and non-imitation. *Journal of Personality*, 1962, 30:147–156.

Rosenberg, Morris: Parental interest and children's self-conceptions. *Sociometry*, 1963, 26:35–49.

Rosenberg, Morris: *Society and the Adolescent Self-image*. Princeton, Princeton University Press, 1965.

Rychlak, J. F., and Eacker, J. N.: The effects of anxiety, delay, and reinforcement on generalized expectancies. *Journal of Personality*, 1962, 30:123–134.

Sarason, I. G., and Sarason, B. R.: Effects of motivating instructions and reports of failure on verbal learning. *American Journal of Psychology*, 1957, 70:92–96.

Sears, R. R.: Initiation of the repression sequence by experienced failure. *Journal of Experimental Psychology*, 1937, 20:570–580.

Seeman, M.: Alienation and social learning in a reformatory. *American Journal of Sociology*, 1963, LXIX:270–284.

Seeman, M., and Evans, J. W.: Alienation and learning in a hospital setting. *American Sociological Review*, 1962, 27:772–781.

Silber, E., Hamberg, D. A., Coelho, G. V., Murphy, E. B., Rosenberg, M., and Pearlin, L. I.: Adpative behavior in competent adolescents. *Archives of General Psychiatry*, 1961, 5:354–365.

Silverman, I.: Self-esteem and differential responsiveness to success and failure. *Journal of Abnormal and Social Psychology*, 1964, 69:115–119.

Silverman, I., Ford, L. H., and Morganti, J. B.: Interrelated effects of social desirability, sex, self-esteem, complexity of argument on persuasibility. *Journal of Personality*, 1966, 34:555–568.

Starbuck, W. A.: Organizational growth and development. In J. G. March (Ed.), *Handbook of Organizations*. Chicago, Rand McNally, 1965.

Stotland, E.: *The Psychology of Hope*. San Francisco, Jossey-Bass, 1969.

Stotland, E., Cohen, A. R., Thomas, E. J., Thorley, S., and Zander, A.: The effects of group expectations and self-esteem upon self-evaluation. *Journal of Abnormal and Social Psychology*, 1957, 54:55–63.

Stotland, E., and Cottrell, N. B.: Similarity of performance as influenced by interaction, self-esteem, and birth order. *Journal of Abnormal and Social Psychology*, 1962, 64:183–191.

Stotland, E., and Dunn, R. E.: Identification, "oppositeness," authoritarianism, self-esteem, and birth order. *Psychological Monographs*, 1962, 76:(9, Whole No. 528).

Stotland, E., and Hillmer, M.: Identification, authoritarianism, and self-esteem. *Journal of Abnormal and Social Psychology*, 1962, *66*:334–342.

Videbeck, R.: Self-conception and the reactions of others. *Sociometry*, 1960, *23*:351–359.

Watson, G.: Some personality differences in children related to strict or permissive parental discipline. *Journal of Psychology*, 1957, *44*:227–249.

Wattenberg, W. W., and Clifford, C.: Relation of self-concepts to beginning achievement in reading. *Child Development*, 1964, *35*:461–467.

White, R.: Motivation reconsidered: the concept of competence. *Psychological Review*, 1959, *66*:297–333.

White, R. K., and Lippitt, R.: *Autocracy and Democracy*. New York, Harper, 1960.

Whiting, J. W. M., and Child, I.: Effects of goal attainment: relaxation versus renewed striving. *Journal of Abnormal and Social Psychology*, 1949, *45*:667–681.

Wicklund, R. A., and Brehm, J. W.: Attitude change as a function of felt competence and threat to attitudinal freedom. *Journal of Experimental Social Psychology*, 1968, *4*:64–75.

Wispé, L. G., and Lloyd, K. E.: Some situational and psychological determinants of the desire for structural interpersonal relations. *Journal of Abnormal and Social Psychology*, 1955, *51*:57–60.

Worchel, P., and McCormick, B. L.: Self-concept and dissonance reduction. *Journal of Personality*, 1963, *31*:588–599.

Wylie, R. C.: *The Self Concept*. Lincoln, Nebraska, University of Nebraska Press, 1961.

Zajonc, R. B.: Social facilitation. *Science*, 1965, *149*:269–274.

Zander, A., Medow, H., and Efron, R.: Observers' expectations as determinants of group aspirations. *Human Relations*, 1965, *18*:273–287.

Zeller, A. F.: An experimental analogue of repression. *Journal of Experimental Psychology*, 1950, *40*:411–422.

Zimbardo, P. G., and Formica, R.: Emotional comparison and self-esteem as determinants of affiliation. *Journal of Personality*, 1963, *31*:141–162.

CHAPTER 11

SAFEGUARDING SELF-ESTEEM

The previous chapter took up the determinants and certain of the direct consequences of an individual's level of self-esteem or of competence. The ramifications of a given level of perceived competence which were examined were generally straightforward, direct expressions of self-esteem—greater or lesser effort, industriousness, openness to new information, resistance to influence, and so forth. However, some of the effects of self-esteem are more indirect and subtle—but extremely important nevertheless. We will turn to them now, in this chapter.

SOURCES OF MOTIVATION TO MAINTAIN POSITIVE SELF-EVALUATION

The major source of these less direct effects is the individual's motivation to keep his self-esteem as high as is feasible, within the limits of his understanding of what his actual traits, abilities, and liabilities are. In this chapter, then, the primary focus will be on the various and sundry ways people have of protecting and enhancing their self-esteem. But first the question, "What are the

478

sources of this motivation to keep the sense of competence as high as possible?" must be dealt with at least briefly. One of its bases is simply that an individual is highly motivated to possess those traits, attributes, and qualities which he has come to evaluate highly. The positive evaluation of these traits arises, in part, as a result of communications from others. However, once the schema corresponding to their evaluation and their desirability has been acquired, it is no longer necessary for the individual to communicate back to those from whom he acquired them that he has, indeed, come to possess them. As is the case with any schema, those which indicate that it is desirable to achieve high status, to be honest, and to have wealth, for example, become stable parts of the individual's cognitive structure, independent of their roots in communications from others. As was noted earlier, in our particular culture a high value is placed on attributes which imply that a person is competent, that he is able to achieve his goals. The evaluation that an individual comes to place on keeping high his self-esteem in general and his sense of competence in particular stems in large part, then, from schemas acquired from others.

Expectation of Successful Goal Attainment

In addition, a high sense of competence is valued simply because it leads to the perception that relevant goals can be attained. This basis of the motivation to keep the sense of competence high has been termed "efficacy motivation" by White (1959). It is important to note that an individual may acquire a sense of competence without yet having attained any goals. For example, a young girl might develop a sense of competence about her ability to be popular simply on the basis of positive comments made to her by her family, but before any real test of her popularity outside the home. Even more broadly, a person's overall sense of competence, as an H.O.S., becomes relatively independent of the attainment of any particular goals. Persons, then, come to value, to protect or enhance a high overall sense of competence. With a high sense of competence, they expect to attain goals in general, all sorts of goals, broad, long-range and specific short-range ones. The person is therefore motivated to enhance his sense of competence with respect both to high order and low order sense of competences, those dealing with goals in general, and with specific goals.

A third factor, rather closely related to the second, involves the fact that an individual tends to be in a state of anxiety when he perceives that he is unable to attain important goals. As was mentioned in Chapter 3, it seems generally to be the case that anxiety results when the organism is unable to function in some important way. At that time, an inability to process more than a certain amount of information was emphasized as a basis for such anxiety. Here the more general proposition that individuals become anxious when they perceive that they are unable to attain important goals is being stressed (cf. Stotland, 1969). Thus, people with low self-esteem would be expected to be more anxious than would those with a high estimate of their general competence and ability to cope. Coopersmith (1967) found that boys with low self-esteem tend more than do highs to be viewed by others as less happy, and to report a higher level of anxiety in response to a questionnaire. In addition, they are more likely to be insomniacs, to bite their nails, to lose their appetites, and to exhibit other such responses which may be taken to be signs of anxiety. Likewise, Rosenberg (1965a) reports that they suffer from insomnia, hand trembling, "nervousness," irregular heart beating, headaches, finger biting, sweaty hands, nightmares, and shortness of breath even when not working. On the basis of this relationship between low sense of competence and anxiety, then, attempts to keep sense of competence high would be expected because anxiety may be avoided by doing so.

Variety of Behavioral Options

It was pointed out above that a person's sense of competence depends in part on his perception of his freedom to choose among a variety of possible coping responses. Thus, if an individual loses this freedom, he should become more anxious. The eminent social psychologist, Lewin (1951), pointed this out by saying that when an organism loses its space of free movement, it becomes more tense. Stotland and Blumenthal (1964) told subjects that they were about to take a series of tests to measure important abilities, and that previous studies had shown that the order in which the sub-tests in the series were taken would have no influence on their scores. Half the subjects were told that they were to take the tests in a fixed order, the other half that they could take the tests in any order they chose. The former group showed more palmar sweating, a frequently used index of anxiety, than did the latter while they were being given these instructions—in fact, they never did work on the tests. (Studies on animals also show this relationship between loss of freedom and anxiety [cf. Stotland, 1969]). This association between anxiety and the loss of freedom no doubt leads many people to acquire a corresponding schema. In turn, this schema adds to the motivation to keep the sense of competence high, partly through keeping freedom of this sort high.

EVALUATION OF EVENTS ASSOCIATED WITH VARIATION IN SELF-ESTEEM

One effect of the motivation to keep sense of competence high is a positive evaluation of those situations in which the person feels competent and a negative evaluation of those situations in which he feels incompetent. Evaluations of other people who are instrumental in raising or lowering self-esteem are similarly affected.

Negative Evaluation of Goal Blocking Circumstances

If an individual suffers a lowering of his sense of competence because of his perception of his inability to attain certain goals, he will come to dislike the situation, and the people, if any, who were felt to be instrumental in leading to the loss and to the consequent anxiety. In plain language, people don't like situations in which they have been blocked in their efforts to attain their goals. This experience is obviously very common; we have all been annoyed when we have failed to complete some task that we have started on, when we have been unable to act effectively to attain our goals. And we don't like the experiences or the people who have caused this blockage. Despite the universality of this experience and its apparently commonsense nature, it will be profitable to examine in some detail the reasons for our dislike of such situations, because often the extent of the consequent annoyance is greater than should be expected simply on the basis of the importance of the unattained goal. Thus, there may well be more to this relationship than is at first apparent. We have all had the experience of being very greatly annoyed with someone who stops us from completing a simple task, from attaining a relatively unimportant goal: someone takes the last candy in the box; an elevator door is closed just before you are able to get to it, and so forth.

Obviously, one reason for the annoyance at such trivial interferences is simply that goal attainment was indeed blocked. However, another basis for the reaction, and one likely to be more directly responsible for the overly negative reaction, involves the fact that the sense of competence is involved by such experiences. But how can such frequently trivial and transitory experiences be important enough to involve the sense of competence? The answer stems from the fact that an individual can have a sense of competence about a limited task as well as an overall sense of competence. As was mentioned above, the different orders of schemas involved in self-esteem are related to one another. To some extent, the overall level of sense of competence evolves out of the L.O.S.s;

and the overall schema influences the relevant L.O.S.s. One way in which this influence of the H.O.S. occurs concerns the motivation to keep the sense of competence high. This motivation is generalized throughout all levels of the schemas concerning the person's competence and esteem. In other words, the individual places high value on his ability to do specific things, to attain even limited goals. Have we not all, at one time or another, found ourselves completely immersed in even the most trivial of tasks, say, a puzzle or a game of some sort such as Monopoly? Lewin (1935) pointed out that we often find that we have a "quasi-need" to complete tasks that have been started, even when there is no particular payoff for doing so. For example, a worker who is paid by the hour may still feel badly if he is unable to complete a particular unit, or if he finds that he has to go back to it to correct it. In other words, even tasks which have never been involved in the attainment of any particularly important goals, or any goals at all, may become significant because the sense of competence is involved.

However, in some instances, the situation may be perceived in such a way that the connection between the goal blockage and the sense of competence is severed. For example, a person might be told that a particular task is one which is in no way a measure of ability to do anything other than complete that specific task. Or, the task may be so different from any others which the individual has experienced or expects to meet in the future that its relevance to his sense of competence is dubious. In such cases, failures are not likely to be particularly bothersome and little annoyance will be associated with such situations.

One illustration of the way in which an individual devalues people and situations which he perceives as being associated with a loss in the sense of competence comes from the work of Janis (1953, 1967) on people's reactions to viewing films about topics such as tooth decay and automobile accidents, which were gory and designed to arouse fear. Janis reports that when the recommendations given regarding ways of preventing decay and accidents were not readily accepted by the viewers, they expressed very negative feelings toward the people who presented the film. These people made them experience anxiety as well as showing them the unpleasant pictures. When the same material was presented in less gory and frightening ways, the subjects felt less negative toward the presenters of the films.

Janis has argued that one of the effects of presenting strong fear-arousing material depicting the consequences of failure to

follow a recommended course of action is rejection of the recommendations made in the film. He assumes that, because of
the extreme fear and discomfort aroused, the subjects became so
hostile that they rejected the advice given in the film. The present argument indicates that the causal sequence might also occur in the reverse direction: the anxiety and hostility result from
the failure to accept the recommendations. Of course, it is possible for both processes to occur; nevertheless, Leventhal and his
associates (Leventhal, Jones, and Trembly, 1966; Leventhal and
Singer, 1966; Leventhal, Singer, and Jones, 1965; Leventhal and
Trembly, 1968; Leventhal, Watts, and Pagano, 1967) have found
that if the recommendations involved are easy, clear, specific,
and feasible, subjects are more likely to follow them if they are
presented with high fear-arousing films than with milder ones.
Thus, the recommendations that Janis finds subjects rejected
may well have been too difficult or unspecific.

Enhanced Self-Esteem and Liking

The relationship between perceiving that one is effective in a
situation and liking the situation or people in it is illustrated in a
study by Aronson and Linder (1965). Each subject had a series of
sessions with another subject (actually a paid assistant) in which
they were to try to get the latter to increase the frequency with
which he spontaneously used certain words. Periodically, the paid
assistant would meet "privately" with the experimenter to evaluate
the subject's effectiveness at this task, but the subjects "accidentally"
overheard these evaluations. Some subjects heard the paid assistant
make positive evaluations of them during the first meetings, while
others heard her make negative evaluations (e.g., dull, stupid). Later
in the series of evaluations, some of the initially positive assistants
continued to be positive, while others drifted to negative evaluations. And some of those who were initially negative became more
positive, while others remained negative. Finally, the subjects themselves had an opportunity to rate the paid assistant. Among other
things, it was found that those who heard the paid assistant shift
from an initial negative to a subsequent positive evaluation perceived that this was the result of their own efforts to impress the
paid assistant. Accordingly, they rated the paid assistant quite positively; more positively, in fact, than did those who heard her make
and retain an initially positive evaluation. Thus, it appears that
another person is liked more not only when he likes you, but also
when he has been involved in your enhancing your sense of com-

petence by making him like you and think positively of your abilities. (The implications of this relationship for what happens in courtship are obvious, and have certainly not been unknown to some "coy" young men and women who play "hard to get." The effectiveness of such a strategy receives considerable support from these results.) No differences were found among the other groups of subjects.

A similar relationship between enhanced sense of competence and liking was found by Sigall and Aronson (1967). Here an experimenter evaluated the reasons given by subjects for their opinions on a variety of issues. In one condition in which the experimenter shifted his evaluations from initially negative to positive, the subjects showed a more positive evaluation of the experimenter than when he made an initially positive rating and stuck with it over the sequence. The positive evaluation was shown in the subjects' willingness to be influenced by a speech by the experimenter which they subsequently heard. Similarly, Berkowitz (1960a) also found that an individual likes another more if he shifts from a negative to a positive evaluation of the individual than if he simply makes an initial positive evaluation and persists with it.

Diminution of Self-Esteem and Liking

On the other hand, if a person experiences a lowering of his sense of competence, he will react negatively to the person perceived as being responsible for it. Horwitz (1958) conducted a study in which a teacher told his students that they would vote on whether or not to continue classroom discussion of a given topic. He told half the students that his own vote would count for more than theirs (presumably, a teacher's prerogative), and the other half that their vote would count for more than his. The actual vote was against continuing on the topic, but the teacher continued with it anyway. The students then were given a chance to inform the teacher of what they thought of him. They were found to be more hostile toward him if he had previously told them that his vote would count less than that of the class than if he had told them it would count more. He had created options for the second group of students and then had taken them away. Horwitz' study is also very instructive because he examined the effects of returning power to the students after their votes had at first been apparently ignored. He had the teacher sometimes correct himself and defer to the wishes of the class by moving to another topic after he had started to continue with it. The students' hostility toward him dropped to zero in this case. Thus, the restoration of the sense of competence restored good feelings even toward the person who originally had taken it from them.

The same general effect was shown in a study by Rothaus and Worchel (1964). The experimenters administered tests to students, insulting and badgering them throughout the administration. Then they left the testing room, leaving the students in the charge of an assistant. Trained assistants also pretended to be student-subjects. In some of the groups, the assistant accepted, repeated, and restated whatever spontaneous feelings the subjects had about the experimenter and experiment. In other groups, the assistant not only did as he did in the first set of groups, but he also was very supportive of the students. In the third set of groups, the so-called instrumental, the assistant did the same as in the second, but one of the "pretend" students said he would tell the experimenters when they returned not to insult them anymore, and in fact, did do so. In a fourth set of groups, the subjects just filled out questionnaires. When the experimenter returned, he no longer insulted the students, but only in the instrumental condition did his cessation appear to be the result of the students' action. Finally, all of the subjects rated this experimenter. Only in the instrumental condition was their hostility to the experimenter less than in the control groups which had just filled out the questionnaire while the experimenter was gone.

Interpersonal Relations and Level of Esteem

In his everyday life—where meeting other people and relating to them are involved—the person with high self-esteem perceives that he can be effective, that he can relate appropriately to others and meet his needs in his relationships with them (cf. Rosenberg, 1965; Coopersmith, 1967). And, by satisfying needs through interaction with other people he comes to feel more competent than do low self-esteem people, who are likely to anticipate that they cannot relate easily with others. As a result of these differences between high and low self-esteem people, highs find that relating to others is a positive or pleasant affective experience, so that they are likely to come to like other people in general. Others are associated with need satisfaction. For the lows, on the other hand, relating to others is associated with frustration, since they do not expect to be able to meet their needs related to others or any other needs that might involve others. Therefore, they come to evaluate other people relatively more negatively.

There are, however, additional reasons why high and low self-esteem people differ in their evaluations of others. As was pointed out in the chapter on the perception of others, people tend to perceive others as having the same characteristics as they themselves do. Thus, a person with high self-esteem would tend to view other people as possessing more positive traits than would people with low self-esteem. Accordingly, highs and lows will differ in the degree of liking of others because of the traits they see in them. Still other reasons for the relationship between self-esteem and the liking of other people will emerge when we discuss hostility and aggression later in this chapter.

And, Rosenberg (1965) did, indeed, find that high self-esteem adolescents had a more positive view of other people, in contrast to the lows' tendency to be misanthropic. The highs are more likely to join clubs and to make friends. This relationship between self-esteem and liking can even be observed in parent-child evaluations. Medinnus and Curtis (1963) found that mothers who felt that there was less discrepancy between the sort of person they would like to be and the way they perceived themselves actually to be also evaluated their children more positively than did mothers whose self-evaluations fell far short of their ideals. Furthermore, some of the factors which lead to high or low self-esteem have been found also to lead to a more positive approach to other people. Thus, Hoffman (1961) found that if a boy comes from a home in which his primary model (i.e., his father), is dominated by his mother, then the boy has a lower estimate of himself, and tends to be less friendly to other children. Baldwin (1949) and Peck (1959) found that if a child's parents give him an opportunity to actively cope with the world, that is, if they treat him in a democratic fashion, and thus encourage the development of high self-esteem, the child tends to be friendlier to other children. It is small wonder then that children with high self-esteem tend to be more popular (Ziller, Hagey, Smith, and Long, 1969; Rosenberg, 1965). And, this greater popularity enhances the person's self-esteem or, at worst, keeps it from dropping, while the unpopularity of the lows tends to keep their esteem low. Thus, the process tends to become circular, in a benign or a vicious way, as the case may be.

Again we need to qualify our statements. Despite the evidence we have just cited, Reese (1961) found that children who are very high in self-esteem tend to be unpopular, as well as those who are very low. Perhaps this exception is also a matter of the complex motivations of persons who manifest extremely high self-esteem.

Response Freedom and Situational Evaluation

When the sources of the sense of competence and of self-esteem were discussed earlier, it was pointed out that freedom to make choices, to determine one's own actions leads to a rise in self-esteem. By this token, then, a person who feels this sort of freedom to choose would, on the whole, evaluate people and situations involved in his choice more positively than he would were a variety of behavioral options not open to him. This is well illustrated in laboratory studies of groups working on problems together under circumstances in which the pattern of communication among the members is controlled. For example, in some groups all of the members but one can communicate only with that one central person. In other groups, all of the members can communicate with all the others. In still others, the communication permitted is only between neighbors—and so on. Generally, it has been found in these investigations that the more people with whom a person can communicate, the more positively he feels about his job. Shaw (1964) comments in his review of this experimental literature that the underlying reason for this greater satisfaction is that the individual who sends and receives information from more people has a higher "degree of freedom", has more independence in doing his job in the group.

This pattern is also observable in "real life." It is illustrated, for example, by the relationship between an employee's perception of his ability to influence the course of work in his part of a firm and his attitude toward his job, his supervisor, his firm. Morse and Reimer (1956) studied two divisions of clerks who performed more or less the same type of work. In one, they trained the supervisors to give more autonomy to the clerks; in the second, they trained the supervisors to reduce the amount of autonomy given the workers to an even lower level than it had been. After several months, it was found that the clerks whose autonomy was increased were more satisfied with their jobs, their bosses, and with the company, both as compared to what they felt before they gained autonomy and as compared to the clerks who lost autonomy. The latter also became more negative than they had been before the loss of autonomy. Smith and Tannenbaum (1963) compared workers who felt that they had much or little control over the way they did their work and found that those who perceived that they had more control evaluated their jobs more positively.

Freedom and Interpersonal Evaluation

Not only will an individual evaluate more positively total situations in which he has more freedom to act, he will also

No kind thoughts for the jailers.

evaluate more positively those people who grant him more freedom when they are in a position to do so, and will devalue those who limit his freedom. Thus, Kahn and Katz (1953) and Likert (1959), in reviewing many studies conducted in industrial settings, found that workers evaluate more positively those foremen who give them more freedom in working out the details of their job.

Sometimes the negative reaction to a reduction in freedom occurs even when the person responsible for it apparently means well in bringing it about. If a well-intentioned action places an obligation on a person so that his freedom in a situation is reduced, he will tend to feel negatively toward the actor. For example, Brehm and Cole (1966) arranged for two subjects to arrive at the laboratory at about the same time. One of them, actually a trained assistant, then left the room momentarily. During his absence, the experimenter asked that the true subject, for purposes of research, give his first impressions of the other "subject" while the latter was out of the room. The experimenter explained to some of the subjects that his reason for obtaining these initial impressions was that another professor was interested in gathering data on first impressions. The remaining subjects were told that a graduate student was doing such research. The other "subject" (the trained assistant) then returned. For half the subjects, he brought a soft drink for the true subject, but none for himself. For the other half, he came back empty-handed. This unsolicited favor—bringing a soda—clearly set up an obligation on the true subject to be nice to the donor. The experimenter then asked the subjects to rate one another on a number of traits. It was found that the subjects lowered their ratings of the attractiveness of the other person after he'd done them a favor, but did not do so in the condition where no unsolicited favor was involved. However this result was obtained only when the subjects had been told that the initial ratings were being made for a study being conducted by a graduate student and was not found when they were presumably being made for the professor. Perhaps the subjects felt under a stronger obligation to adhere to their actual first impressions when the ratings would go to a professor. In any case, this study implies a very interesting limitation on the proposition that persons evaluate more positively those who help them more. Apparently, this proposition does not hold in situations in which the other person limits one's freedom in some way through his being nice.

The negative evaluation of someone who restricts one's freedom may sometimes be so great that an individual may avoid coming to an agreement with this other person even when such agreement would be mutually beneficial in a concrete, monetary way. Deutsch and Krauss (1960) had pairs of college students work at a game in which each was in charge of a toy trucking company. Each student could make money by directing his model truck across a replica of some trucking routes from his garage to a delivery point at the far side of the replica; the faster he got his trucks across, the more money he would make. Each player's garage and delivery points were on opposite sides of the playing area. Each participant could use either a long or a short route, but the short route for each included a common road, where only one truck at a time could pass. Thus, in order for both players to make the maximal amount of money, they had to reach an agreement as to how this common road was to be used. In one third of the pairs, each player was given control of a gate which he could close to prevent the other subject from making a delivery; thus, each restricted the other's freedom. In one third of the pairs, only one of the players was given control of such a gate, and for another third, neither was given control of a gate. The negative feelings that each player felt toward the other when the other could control the gate were so great that it was difficult for them to reach an agreement on how to share the use of the common road. Thus, the average level of earnings was greater when neither had control of the gate, and least when both had control of the gate. This study provides experimental evidence for the old political adage, "Don't work your opponent into a corner." Another example of the same sort of process comes from a study by Horowitz (1968), who had subjects come to the laboratory for a particular study. After they arrived, half of them were told that they would have to participate in an additional study, while the other half were given a choice as to whether or not to participate in it. All of the subjects were then asked how much time they would give to the additional study—and the free choice subjects offered to give more.

Over-valuation of Lost Response Alternatives

In addition to de-evaluating a situation or a person associated with a loss of freedom, persons may react to such a loss by over-valuing those possible options of action which have been lost. These objects are not only valued in their own right, but are given additional value because they represent "freedom." This type of reaction to a loss of freedom has been documented by Brehm (1966) in a series of studies. In one, he first had subjects rate the desirability of four phonograph records. Next, he told some of the subjects that they could choose to keep any one of the four records. Others were told that because of shipping difficulties, one of the records would not be available, so that they would have to choose from among the remaining three. (Each subject was told that the record they had initially ranked third most attractive was the one which was unobtainable.) Then everyone was asked to re-rank all of the records. Those in this second condition raised their evaluation of the third or lost option; it represented greater freedom to them, even if it was not one of their preferred records.

Brehm's studies concerning the loss of options which we describe in this chapter were related by him to his theory of psychological reactance. Reactance refers to the state of the individual after he has lost an option which he previously could choose, if he so desired. In the account we are giving here, we refer to this state as another instance of anxiety, and relate it to more general theorizing. Aside from this terminological difference, Brehm's approach and the present one do not differ in any essential way.

When freedom of choice was discussed earlier in this chapter, it was noted that one basis for the psychological effect this variable has is that through possession of freedom of this sort, the individual's sense of competence is enhanced. However, freedom of choice obviously increases the sense of competence only to the extent that the available response options are ones which can in fact be exercised. That is, a person will not feel that his sense of competence has been diminished simply by being confronted with restrictions on actions which he had not previously perceived as open to him. This point is also illustrated in Brehm's study just cited, as some of the adolescent subjects were simply given one record in return for their assistance as subjects and had no choice in its selection. Since the absence of choice in such a matter was not out of line with what would be expected in a setting of this sort, these subjects did not increase their evaluation of any of the records.

In the Deutsch and Krauss (1960) study described above, the subjects must have seen the importance of the gate as an elimination of an option they expected to have, since such gates are not expected in normal trucking operations. It is interesting to speculate how this study would have worked out in another context, say, in the Dark Ages when highwaymen and lords commonly controlled bridges or their own section of the highway.

Evaluation of Others

In the previous chapter we saw how a person could have his self-esteem raised or lowered by his perception of his similarity to another person, their interaction with one another, their membership in the same group. Thus, if a person perceives that another person is the cause of some change in his sense of competence because of the functioning of one of these schemas, his evaluation of this other person will be affected. Sometimes we become very annoyed at the quarterback of our college team when we perceive him to be responsible for the team's loss; we have both groupness and similarity relationships with him and, thus, our self-esteem is affected. Likewise, we adulate the astronauts, who help us raise our self-esteem; "We're prouder to be Americans now."

For these schemas about interpersonal relations to have an effect on evaluation of other people, it is necessary for the person to perceive the connection between what he observed about the other person and the changes in his self-esteem. The functioning of some of these schemas may often be so subtle that the individual may not perceive the connection. In the examples we have given, the connections are sometimes explicitly verbalized by the people involved, since they were so apparent. In other cases, this relationship might not be so apparent (cf. Stotland and Hillmer, 1962).

GOAL-SETTING BEHAVIOR

The general motivation to keep self-evaluation as high as possible and to avoid experiences which migh lead to a decrement in it has some very direct ramifications for the selection persons make regarding the particular goals for which they will strive. If an individual sets his goals too high, if he strives for a very difficult goal at or close to the limits of his abilities, he may guarantee failure and, consequently, anxiety and a loss of self-esteem. If he works toward only very easily obtainable goals, he may avoid failure and anxiety, but may at the same time make no gain in self-esteem. Under these latter circumstances, he will not have an opportunity to heighten his sense of competence by achieving new goals. Thus, there is a tendency to avoid both extremes—goals that are too high and goals that are too low—and instead to set goals which are just moderately higher than the level of difficulty which has most recently been successfully attained.

It should be noted that the differential effect on self-esteem which the attainment of difficult and easy tasks have represents a qualification on the overall assumption which has been made about the relationship between goal attainment and the sense of competence. Though probably an obvious point, we did not make explicit in our earlier discussions that the attainment of some goals has a more significant influence on self-esteem and competence than does the attainment of others. This relationship has been thoroughly examined by Lewin et al. (1944) in their review of research on the level of aspiration. The level of aspiration is the level of difficulty of goal which the individual sets for himself. Broadly stated, the findings in this area indicate that if a person fails at a task, he sets his goals lower for the next attempt; if he succeeds, he tends to raise his goals.

Level of Aspiration and Self-Esteem

This process of adjusting one's goals downward in order to avoid failure is doubly motivated: it may eliminate a threat to the sense of competence as well as a futile expenditure of energy. Thus, to avoid the anxiety which might result from both of these sources, an individual who has failed a number of times may "pull in," stop aspiring at all, give up goals. In its extreme forms, the avoidance of goal-striving activity can lead to apathy and depression, even to the point of a person's giving up his motivation to live. Nardini (1952), Bettelheim (1960), and others have commented on "apathy deaths" among American prisoners of war in North Korea and the almost voluntary march to the gas chambers among concentration inmates in Germany during World War II. At a less extreme level, this same phenomenon may occur among whole groups of people, such as the poverty-stricken, who give up aspiring toward a wide variety of goals. This "withdrawal from motivation" is further enhanced by the fact that attempts which are made to achieve goals are often doomed to failure. Their attainment often demands a persistence and a mobilization of energy of which the apathetic and the poverty-stricken may be incapable for psychological as well as physiological and material reasons.

The tendency to give up unattainable goals, to "sour-grape" them, may sometimes clash with the tendency found by Brehm for people to overvalue alternative courses of action which have been lost. Persistent overvaluation of the lost alternatives will generate anxiety. Research by Mann and Dashiell (in press) suggests that people cope with this anxiety by shifting, over a period of time, from the overvaluation to an undervaluation. They measured the evaluation college students placed on various non-draft-exempt occupations three times, once before the draft lottery, once immediately after the lottery, and once ten days later. Immediately after the lottery, students with low draft numbers, i.e., ones which made their induction very likely, tended to increase their valuation of these particular occupations, since they were likely to be lost to them. However, ten days later, they shifted to a derogation of these occupations as compared to their evaluations before the lottery.

The apathy of the downtrodden often has the effect of making it sadly easier for any of their persecutors to maintain the relatively deprived position they hold. Even more sadly, it presents serious obstacles to those who would attempt to improve their lot. This hopelessness on the part of the poor may be part of the reason that anti-poverty programs are so difficult to consummate.

Rising Expectations Following Success

On the brighter side, the process of raising goals after successes can lead to an upward spiraling of aspirations, to the seeking of new goals. This process is often observed: "driven man" whose very successes lead him to strive for even more successes; a group of people on the move which has just overcome some difficulties and now attempts to achieve even higher goals. This latter phenomenon has recently been popularly dubbed the "revolution of rising expectations." Downtrodden, persecuted people, such as black Americans, people in economically underdeveloped parts of the world who have just started to make gains may aspire to even greater and more rapid advances. Trade unions started with the goal of a 45-hour week and now are considering guaranteed annual wages. These rising expectations are in part a function of the rise in the sense of competence resulting from previous successes. However, the interpersonal schemas which change a person's sense of competence can also have a parallel effect: e.g., the person may observe similar other groups do well and assume that similar successes may be his. Or, the person can receive communications from others which raise his sense of competence. All of these can lead to rising expectations.

Poverty and apathy. Photograph by Irwin Nash.

The process of rising expectations also has the effect of making the person more vulnerable to anxiety. He is striving toward difficult-to-achieve ends and thus leaves himself open to set-backs and failures. Of course, his own self-esteem and rising sense of competence may tend to mitigate this anxiety. Nevertheless, failures are part of life and often they are of sufficient magnitude to overcome the high sense of competence of the individual. In such cases, the individual might resort to some of the anxiety-reducing, self-esteem-restoring actions that we will describe later in this chapter. Among these actions is aggression or violence. Thus, ironically, a group which is "on the move," which has rising expectations, is often the more likely to engage in violence. As we will see later in the chapter, the downtrodden and unaspiring are unlikely to be violent, or really do anything much to improve their lot.

REACTIONS TO DIMINISHED SELF-ESTEEM

Much of the rest of this chapter will be concerned with an examination of other ways in which the motivation to protect self-esteem influences an individual's actions. More particularly, we will see how people attempt to restore their self-esteem after it has been jolted or threatened in some way. In attempting to restore their self-esteem, schemas about the other factors which influence self-esteem will often be employed. For instance, a person who has suffered a decrement in self-esteem because he has been insulted by someone whose opinions he values might try to restore his self-esteem by working very hard at a hobby of his at which he is quite good.

Effectiveness of Substitute Actions

Implicit in the description of the program just set forth for the rest of this chapter is the assumption that substitute actions or experiences can indeed influence self-esteem. But how can such substitute actions accomplish a restoration of self-esteem? After all, the man's working at his hobby does not eliminate the fact of the insult. Part of the answer stems from a tendency of these substitute actions to arouse H.O.S.s which themselves imply generally high competence or esteem. For example, the person in our example knows he is good at his hobby; his effective work at it then arouses a schema relevant to his general level of competence. In turn, this schema can arouse a still higher order schema about all sorts of actions leading to the attainment of goals. Once such an H.O.S. is aroused, its effects will dominate lower order schemas and information about self-esteem. Thus, pressures will arise to somehow reduce the incongruity between the insult and this higher order schema which implies competence and esteem as attributes of the person in question. He may come to believe that the insulter was incompetent, did not know what he was talking about, spoke in anger, didn't mean what he said, and so forth. Notice here that this sequence of events depends on the person's having an H.O.S. which indicates that he can indeed attain goals through his actions. For most people this schema is well established by their everyday experiences, but there are obvious individual differences in the extent to which this schema has been acquired and therefore can be used.

Another reason why substitute actions can serve to keep self-esteem high is simply that such activity tends to distract the person. By engaging in these substitute actions, he arouses schemas that were dormant at the time of the insult. Their arousal may then lead the schemas about the loss of self-esteem to lapse back into dormancy; accordingly, anxiety is reduced. When the man is giving a great deal of attention to his hobby, he may hardly remember the insult.

Still another basis for the functioning of substitute actions in reducing anxiety is an outgrowth of the first two reasons mentioned. The individual may have observed many occasions in which he has survived a threat to his self-esteem by such substitute actions. He may then develop an H.O.S. to the effect that they work. "When I'm 'down' working at something else really makes me feel better." This schema will then guide his behavior toward this substitute action. The first time that an individual experienced a restoration of his self-esteem through a substitute action might have been an accident. However, if such accidents occur a number of times, the individual will acquire the corresponding schema, which will then guide him to such compensatory action on future occasions. Furthermore, he will tend to act in a manner consistent with this schema: he will tend to exaggerate the degree to which his hobby helps him restore his confidence. These substitute actions may sometimes have a more material effect than just raising a person's self-esteem and lowering his anxiety. Since they also raise the sense of competence, they may have the effect of increasing the person's persistence in attempting to attain his original goal—the goal which he failed to attain in the first place. Thus the substitute action may not act as a complete substitute, but as an encouragement to persistent striving toward the initial goal. However, this return to the original problem may not occur if the substitute action is so involving that the person is completely distracted from the problem, as we pointed out above (cf. Berkowitz, 1962).

There are many types of events or experiences which can constitute a threat to a person's self-esteem, to his sense of competence. He can fail at a task; his freedom to choose among a variety of behavioral options may be restricted; he can be confronted with a situation that he finds himself incapable of understanding; he may perceive failure in a person who is similar to him, or with whom he has interacted, or who is a member of the same group, or whom he likes; he can perceive that other similar people are much more competent than himself; he may hear himself derogated by someone else, and so forth. As was pointed out above, it is not necessary for a person to restore his self-esteem by acting directly on the source of the loss, nor by using the same type of experience that was directly associated with the lowering of his sense of competence. That is, an insult does not necessarily have to be balanced off by a compliment. The deleterious effects of the insult can be made up by, say, just plain hard work, and it is this fact that is most interesting and worthy of further examination.

As we saw early in the chapter, one way in which the sense of competence is determined is through the individual's perception of the effectiveness of his actions. The person can thus restore his self-esteem by acting effectively in some way, even if the action is not directed toward attaining the goal the person originally had. Dittes (1959) assembled college students in a group for a discussion. Some of the subjects were led to believe that they were being rejected by the other members of the group, while others were led to believe they were accepted. Thus, some of them had their self-esteem lowered by the group's reactions. The subjects were then given a series of tests in which they were presented with ambiguous stimuli and were asked to draw conclusions about them, with no time limit set. The stimuli consisted of a vague story, an inconsistent picture of a person, and an ambiguous speech by a person. The subjects who were rejected by the group took less time to draw their conclusions. As Dittes points out, the rapid drawing of conclusions increased their sense of adequacy, their sense of competence. Dittes also found that this reaction of drawing quick conclusions was more characteristic of people with low self-esteem than of people with high. The reason for this difference is probably that the lows' self-esteem was more affected by the rejection they had experienced earlier.

Lowered Esteem from Limitation of Freedom

Let us now turn to the situation in which an individual suffers a loss of self-esteem because his freedom has been limited. His first reaction might be simply to try to restore his freedom. Obviously, in many instances, the person cannot simply re-establish this freedom. There are often practical, real limitations on this variable. Nevertheless, if an individual is given an opportunity to do so, he is quite likely to take advantage of it. A striking example of this comes from another study by Brehm (1966), who told some subjects that their opinions on a topic would be influenced by learning of the opinions of other subjects. This was a direct assault on their freedom to react to the others in any way they chose. The information they were then given about others' opinions indicated that these persons held opinions which varied from being close to to being quite different from the subject's own opinions. The more discrepant they were, the less the subjects actually changed in response to this information. The more their freedom had been threatened, the more independent of the threat they became. In contrast, Brehm told a second group of subjects that they were to look at the opinions of others simply to be better able to understand these other subjects. The second group, when measured later, gave evidence of having changed their opinions more, the greater the discrepancy from their own opinions had been. In part of a study by Wicklund and Brehm (1968), subjects read the applications of two people for a job as a student advisor and rated the applications in terms of their merit. The subjects then received a message favoring one of the applicants from another subject who was described as someone skilled in making such judgments. The message was either one which implied that the subject still had the power to make his own independent judgment, e.g., "Paul is the best advisor . . . ."; or the message implied limited freedom of judgment for the recipient, e.g., "There is no question about it; Paul is the best advisor. . . ." The subjects then made additional ratings of the two applicants. It was found that when the threat to the subject's freedom was great, he accepted the judgments of the purported experts less and even tended to reject this information. The implications of these two studies by Brehm and his associates are vast—that people value their freedom greatly and will go to considerable lengths in an effort to maintain it. Notice that in both of these studies the subjects, normal college students, would be likely to expect that they would not be easily influenced by the opinions of others— thus, they perceived the pressure being put on them as representing an attempt to take away options which they believed they would and should have. If other groups of subjects who did not have such expectations had been used in the study, they might well have reacted differently.

Restoration of Esteem via Positive Action

Needless to say, in many situations in life, an individual may attempt to overcome the threat to his freedom of choice and self-esteem by making a direct attack on the person who is threatening this freedom. Such a direct attack would accomplish two purposes. First, it would, if successful, obviously eliminate the threat. And second, it would help to restore the person's sense of freedom and competence in that situation not only by eliminating the threat, but also, and more subtly, because the individual would find himself acting in some effective way in the situation.

In some cases, the substitute action may take place in the same physical context as the original unsuccessful one, and thus the individual may be more likely then to return to and attempt once more to attain his original goals. Some of the most dramatic examples of the ways in which substitute actions can restore a person's sense of competence come from reports of behavior in prisoner of war camps. Here the prisoner's sense of competence is very severely threatened, since so few of his goals are attainable through his direct action. Sometimes, the sense of competence drops so low that the individual does not even seem willing to take actions which will help insure his very survival. He lies down and dies a so-called apathy death. However, Stressman, Thaler, and Schein (1955) report that apathy deaths among American prisoners of war in the Korean War could be prevented by getting them to engage in some activity, no matter how unimportant, or getting them interested in some current or future problem.

If an individual has experienced a number of occasions on which a reduction in anxiety and a restoration in self-esteem occurred after he had taken some positive action, had done something, anything, effective, he would be likely to develop a schema encompassing this observation. This schema would then guide him to engage in such actions when he was in a state of anxiety. Thus, frustrated people are sometimes hyperactive, nervous, and jumpy, as they fight to restore their sense of competence.

Aggression Toward Source of Frustration

At times, this action may take a particular form, that of aggression or violence. A person's sense of competence and self-esteem may have been based at least in part on the results of aggressive, if not violent, actions. Furthermore, he may have experienced situations in which he has attained a goal after having been frustrated by aggressing against some person who was blocking its attainment. Or, he may have perceived other people to do so, either directly or through mass media; or he may have received communications about the effectiveness of violence or aggression. He thereby acquires a schema that attacking the source of frustration often leads to goal attainment and raises his sense of competence. Thus, when a person has been frustrated and his sense of competence lowered, aggressing against the source of his frustration may be seen as an effective compensatory action.

It is important to note that this reaction can occur even when the goal can no longer be attained. The schema may be of such a high order that the failure of aggression to lead to goal attainment in a given instance will not materially influence the operation of this schema. This process has been demonstrated in a series of studies by Hokanson and his associates (Hokanson and Shetler, 1961; Hokanson, Burgess, and Cohen, 1963; Hokanson and Burgess, 1962a; Hokanson and Burgess, 1962b). For example, Hokanson, Burgess, and Cohen (1963) instructed subjects to count backwards from 100. Half the subjects were allowed to complete the task without interruption; the other half were badgered and interrupted by the experimenter while they counted. Next, some of the subjects were told that they were now to participate in a study of the effect of pain on guessing. Some other person was to guess what number the subject was thinking of; if he was wrong, the subject was to shock him; this procedure was repeated a number of times. The person doing the guessing was one of the following: the experimenter who had earlier interrupted their work, a graduate student, or another student. After the subjects shocked the experimenter for his "errors," the subjects' blood pressure dropped, indicating lowered emotional arousal; it did not drop if the shocked person was one of the others. Other subjects did not play this guessing game, but turned on some lights with the same motion as was used to inflict shock. These subjects did not show a decline in blood pressure.

Obviously, people differ in the degree to which they have acquired a schema which indicates that aggressive action overcomes or compensates for the consequences of frustrated goal striving behavior. This association between goal attainment, sense of competence and esteem, on the one hand, and aggression on the other, is obviously more likely to exist for males in American society than for females. Thus, when frustrated, males are more likely to lower their anxiety by aggression than are females. Hokanson and Edelman (1966) had some male subjects inflict shock on another person on a pretext in the laboratory. Some of the shocked subjects were then given an opportunity to administer shocks to the person who had previously shocked them. As a consequence of this aggressive action, their blood pressure dropped, indicating lowered arousal. If the subjects were not given an opportunity to retaliate in this fashion, no such diminution in blood pressure was found. However, this drop in blood pressure did not occur among females who had a chance to return the shocks (cf. Holmes, 1966).

This restoration of the sense of competence through aggressive and, at times, hostile action, is a frequently observed phenomenon in recent American history. For example, much of the violence in the urban ghettos of this country has been directed at the restoration of self-esteem by people whose self-regard has been assaulted in many ways by their experiences in this country. In the ghetto environment there is ample opportunity to acquire a schema indicating that aggression overcomes frustrating circumstances. It is not the most downtrodden, disadvantaged, and poverty-stricken who would be expected to be the most likely to strike out violently, however, even though their plight might seem to best justify such a reaction. As was pointed out earlier in this chapter, these people tend to have given up the pursuit of many goals, to have forsaken striving, and, in so doing, have avoided the anxiety which would accompany failure. Thus, they are less motivated by failure-induced anxiety and consequently, less likely to require esteem-bolstering compensatory behaviors such as violence. Of course, there are other, more direct, reasons for their nonviolence: preoccupation with basic survival needs and physical exhaustion, to name only two. One consequence of this finding is that the participants in urban riots tend on the average to have gone farther on the educational ladder than have ghetto residents who do not participate in riots, and to have somewhat better jobs (Berkowitz, 1968; Bowen et al., 1968; Cohen, 1967; Endelman, 1968; Gurr, 1968; Lang and Lang, 1968). The attainments of the relatively more successful group lead them to aspire to even higher goals; and the societally imposed barriers to the achievement of these goals lead to frustration, anxiety, and ultimately, violence.

As we have seen a number of times already, few, if any, forms of overt action are caused by only a single process. Sometimes a particular instance of a given form of action has several different determinants, and different specific instances also may have different causes. The same principle applies to aggression, and a number of writers have pointed out (e.g., Feshbach, 1964;

Kaufmann, 1965) that there are multiple motives for aggressive behavior. We have discussed aggression primarily in terms of the role it may play in maintaining or restoring self-esteem, but in so doing implied an additional motivational base—being aggressive in order to attain goals. Even lower animals can learn to be more aggressive than they typically are if there is some payoff for being aggressive. In some conceptions, such as Kaufmann's, such "aggression without anger" is simply described as a distinct category of aggression, separate and distinct from emotionally laden aggression. In the presentation here, it is held that the two are intimately related: the learning to be aggressive in order to attain goals is the basis for an individual's exhibiting aggressive behavior in frustrating situations where anger and anxiety are likely and where such aggression will serve only to reduce anxiety, and will not further the attainment of the blocked goals. It should not be assumed that we have exhausted the possible causes of aggression in our discussion; more will be described below and even these may not complete the list of possibilities.

The relationship between frustration and aggression which is being described here has long been postulated on the basis of common sense, and by writers such as Dollard, Miller, Doob, Mowrer and Sears (1939), and Berkowitz (1962). Such approaches have typically rather simply asserted that there is a relationship between frustration and aggression, without attempting to explain why this relationship exists. They have maintained that frustration causes tension, or, in Berkowitz' terms, anger, and that this tension or anger can be "drained off" through the expression of some sort of aggression. The present approach goes beyond the simple assertion of the relationship and shows why it is that such aggression takes place. Worchel (1961) and Feshbach (1964) have analyzed aggression in much the same terms as those used here. In addition, the present approach provides a basis for an understanding of why some people are more likely to react aggressively to frustration than are others; the approach of Dollard et al. in particular has been criticized for not taking into account differences in the tendency to aggress and the possibility of other reactions to frustration besides aggression.

The increase in self-confidence which may result from a person's aggression in response to goal blockage can have the effect of leading him to renew his attempts to solve his original problem, unless his aggressive actions have distracted him completely (cf. Berkowitz, 1964). Thus, he might try even harder to attain blocked goals after having shown some hostility, even if the hostility has gained him nothing. (Recall that the hostility is based on an H.O.S. which is not highly vulnerable to change as a consequence of one failure.) One consequence of this process is that the expression of aggression does not necessarily have a "cathartic" effect, i.e., an effect of just having the person "blow off" steam until he feels better and will aggress no more. The expression of aggression can lead to greater efforts and purpose in his actions, some of which themselves might be aggressive in nature. The upward spiraling of violence in the ghettos of America in the late 1960s may have been, in part, a result of this process. It is not surprising, then, that there is very little evidence, if any, that catharsis occurs; that is, little evidence that a person will be drained of his hostility toward the original source of his frustration, and become quiescent and placid (cf. Berkowitz, 1964) following overt aggression. He may become less anxious, but more confident. Or, he may become exhausted physically, but that is a different type of process than that which is usually referred to by the term catharsis.

Displacement of Aggression

The higher order schema which mediates aggression and hostility is one which indicates that being aggressive will foster goal attainment, especially if the aggression is directed against a perceived source of goal blockage and frustration. Suppose, however, that it is not possible for a person to direct his aggression against the source of his frustration. The source might be viewed as too strong, too powerful, too high in status, or too well protected by other people. Or the person may not perceive himself to be competent enough to express hostility directly at the source of his frustration. Worchel (1958) and Veldman and Worchel (1961), for example, found that high self-esteem people are more likely than are lows to express hostility directly at a person who insults them. Or the individual may simply not have sufficient opportunity to be directly aggressive. One way in which residual anxiety can yet be reduced and self-esteem raised involves the expression of aggression toward some other target, especially one which in some way is similar to the original source of the frustration. In this way, by means of a sort of psycho-logic, the individual will tend to feel as if the original source of frustration has been battered. The similarity that is sufficient to make some substitute target an appropriate and acceptable one may involve nothing more than the fact that the substitute also frustrated the person at some other time or place, or is also disliked for some other reason (cf. Berkowitz and Holmes, 1959; Berkowitz, 1960). Or the target of the substitute aggression could simply be seen to be of the same category of people as was the person who caused the blockage (Berkowitz, 1959).

White and Lippitt (1960) conducted a series of meetings of boys' clubs under adult leaders who enacted their roles in either a democratic or authoritarian way. In the authoritarian condition, the leader did not allow very much freedom to boys as they worked on the task of making models; he told them when and how to do what; also, he was cold and somewhat rejecting of them. All of these actions on his part led to a threat to the boys' sense of competence. The democratic leader, however, had the boys decide as a group how to go about their tasks, and each boy had considerable freedom; further, the democratic leader was supportive and warm. The researchers report that the boys under the authoritarian leader were more negative and hostile in their actions toward each other. Furthermore, when a janitor entered the clubhouse, the boys under the authoritarian leader were much more likely to throw spitballs at him and to be otherwise hostile to him. The researchers interpret these expressions of hostility as efforts by the boys to restore their sense of mastery over the world.

Regardless of what we have just said about substitute targets, the expression of anger at a substitute target does not appear to have the same value in reducing anxiety as do direct expressions; it does not fit the schema of direct attack on the source well enough. People do not appear to blow off steam at substitute targets and then feel fine about the original source. As was pointed out above, they may still devalue the original source of their frustration. In fact, their restored sense of competence may lead them to be even more aggressive toward the original source of frustration.

Notice that the aggression or hostility is directed toward the person who is perceived to be the frustrator or insulter; in fact, he may not have been the true cause of the frustration. Thus, if an individual is led falsely to believe that a given person is the source of his frustration, the latter may become an innocent victim. This process is sometimes called scapegoating, and probably underlies much racial and ethnic prejudice.

Perceived Relative Competence

Yet another way in which the individual can restore his sense of competence following some goal blockage involves manipulation of the range of the dimension of evaluation which provides a frame of reference for gauging self adequacy. If that range can be extended downward without changing the individual's position on the dimension, he can assume a higher relative position on it. In plain

English, if one can perceive that there are people much more incompetent, much less estimable, than oneself, one can evaluate himself rather well. Therefore, a person can regain some of his lost self-esteem by reducing the evaluation of other persons. The very same kinds of events or experiences which an individual perceives will lower his evaluation of himself will be assumed also to lower both his own and other people's evaluation of another person. Relevant actions here might take the form of humiliating another person, insulting him, frustrating him, restricting his freedom, or perceiving that he has undesirable traits. All these processes appear to occur in race prejudice, when one group of people comes to see itself as superior to some other group. Cowen, Landes, and Schact (1959) led some of their subjects to believe that they had done much more poorly on two puzzles than had other people. Other subjects were led to believe that they had done well. After these experiences, the "failing" subjects became more anti-Negro than did the succeeders. A study by Campbell (1947) showed that people who were less satisfied with their jobs were more anti-Semitic than were other people. Bettelheim and Janowitz (1950) discovered that World War II veterans who were worse off economically and socially after the war than before it were more likely than were other groups to be anti-Semitic.

Comparison of Self with Others

Or, in a perhaps more simple operation of this principle, a person may seek to find others who are worse off than himself in order to raise his evaluation of himself. Darley and Aronson (1966) told subjects that they were going to participate in a study involving a high degree of pain. The subjects no doubt were concerned about how well they would be able to "take it"—how well they would be able to attain the goal of showing up well in the study. They were told that they would have a few minutes to wait before the experiment itself started. They were told that they could choose among waiting with another subject who was just as fearful as themselves, with someone even more fearful, or with someone less fearful. They tended to avoid choosing the person who was less fearful than themselves. Likewise, Hakmiller (1966a) did a study in which he told some subjects that the psychological tests which had been run on them showed that they had a great deal of certain undesirable traits. They were then given an opportunity to learn the specific scores on these tests of other subjects; the true subjects were told whether to expect the scores of these others to be high or low on the test. The true subjects chose to find the specific scores of others who probably had much of this undesirable trait.

In another condition, this trait was not described as being so un-desirable; in this condition, the subjects were not as interested as in the first condition in learning the specific scores of someone who had much of this trait.

Another way in which an individual might seek to restore his self-esteem is to seek out people who are similar to him in one respect, but who are evidently more competent in some other respect. Darley and Aronson also had a condition in their study in which the subjects were told that it was uncertain as to how much pain they would receive, since this was the first time the study had been run. The subjects were thus uncertain as to how fearful to be. To reduce the amount of fear, they sought to wait with another subject who was calmer than themselves, rather than more fearful.

The question then arises as to why this schema did not function to make the subjects more frightened than in the condition in which they were certain that they would experience severe pain and they chose to be with someone who was more frightened than themselves. The answer is that they were certain that they were quite frightened; this schema was unlikely to lead them to change their degree of fright. On the other hand, they sought to be with another, more frightened, person because they could then evaluate their degree of fright as not being quite so "shameful." "It can't be that bad to be so frightened—after all, the others are even more upset."

Needless to say, the individual might attempt to do the same thing by reading about "heroes" who were similar to himself in some respects other than his area of incompetence, watching them on TV, or on the football field. These "heroes" are those whose areas of competence are the same as the areas of incompetence of the person. Likewise, a person might attempt to establish a friendship with someone who is more competent, to gain his liking, to try to interact with him in some way, maybe even to join the same group with him. By doing these things, the individual is using some of the social schemas about interpersonal relationships in a way that we discussed in Chapter 8.

COMMUNICATIONS FROM OTHERS AND SELF-ESTEEM RESTORATION

We have not yet examined one of the most important ways in which other people can help an individual restore his diminished self-esteem. It involves direct communication from others of their esteem for him, or indirect communication of their esteem for him by means of expressions of liking and affection. A number of studies have shown how individuals work to gain the good will of others after they have lost esteem because of actual or expected failure on some task.

Attempts to Gain Approval of Others

Freedman, Wallington, and Bless (1967) led some people to suffer a loss of self-esteem as a result of their having told a lie, or because they "accidentally" upset a set of cards. As compared to others who had not done these things, the "guilty" subjects were more willing to comply with a subsequent request made of them by the experimenter. Lanzetta (1955) assembled groups to work on tasks together. The members of some of the groups were given no time limit and were allowed to work at their own pace. Other groups were given a strict time limit. Still other groups were not only given a time limit, but also were confined to a small space, and were badgered by the experimenter. As compared to the first two groups, the last group was rated by observers as being less confident in themselves. They were more friendly and less aggressive toward one another, argued less and agreed more, helped one another and cooperated more, and were less selfish. The effort to perceive oneself as a more likeable person may underlie the findings of a study by Smith (1960). He gave subjects a success or a failure experience on a test. Next, he provided them with copies of the Allport Vernon Scale of Values, half of whose items had been completed ostensibly by another subject. The subject's job was to predict how this other subject would have filled out the rest of the questionnaire. The subjects who had failed the test in the first part of the experiment were more likely than were those who had done well to predict that this other subject would fill out the scale the way that they themselves had previously filled it out. The failing subjects apparently tried to establish similarity with others in order to make themselves more likeable.

If an individual loses self-esteem because he is rejected or negatively evaluated by someone, one possible recourse is to turn to still other people for support. Thus, Snoek (1962) found that people who were rejected strongly by members of a group were much more interested in joining another group. Walster (1965) had girls take a series of personality tests. While each girl was waiting in an anteroom for the experimenter's report on their performance, an attractive young man came in and asked her to take a word-association test for some of his research. He also flirted with her and made a date with her. The original experimenter then gave the subject either a very flattering or a very negative evaluation on the basis of the earlier tests. The girls were then asked to evaluate the young man, since he was associated with the psychology department. The girls who received the negative report from the experimenter liked him more than did the others. Supportive, positive evaluation from another is particularly welcome following a diminution in self-regard and leads to greater liking for and attraction to the supportive person.

In some cases, an individual might attempt to regain the esteem of the very person who appeared to reject him. Thus, Baron, Robinson, and Lawrence (1968) led some people to believe that an experimenter thought poorly of them because they had failed at a task involving the labeling of depicted emotions, while others were led to believe that they had succeeded. The failing subjects were then more likely than were the successful ones to comply with the experimenter's request to participate in another, rather unpleasant experiment. A child will no doubt feel rejected by an adult who simply tells him to wait in a room by himself while the adult goes to do other things. One way the child can restore himself to the good graces of an adult is by being particularly careful to do the "right" thing in subsequent interactions with the adult. Walters (1960) took preschool-age children one at a time into a room, treating them very warmly, kindly, and supportively. At the end of five minutes, for half the children, he left the room for five minutes, saying he was busy, and then returned. In the other half of the cases, the experimenter stayed in the room during that five minute period, while continuing to treat the children warmly. Then all of the children played games with the experimenter in which they were to guess what the experimenter was thinking of and in which they were to copy an arrangement of blocks he presented. The children who had been left alone for five minutes learned the right answers and actions in the two games better than those who had not been isolated. Gewirtz and Baer (1958a; 1958b) had an adult ask children to leave their classroom in order to help him with a study. Half the children were then told to wait in a room by themselves and were left there for some 20 minutes before they were brought into the experimental room. Here they were given a simple two choice game, one choice being "right." Other children were brought directly from the classroom to the experimental room where they played the same game. The "rejected" children, i.e., those left alone initially, were more likely to make the right response than were the others. A question might arise as to whether it was the time *per se* which the children were forced to spend in isolation which was responsible for these effects. That time was not the key factor is indicated by a study by Walters and Parke (1964a and 1964b), who had the experimenter act in a cold, rejecting manner or in a warm manner to children. Half the time the experimenter took the children to the room and immediately started playing a game with them. In this game, they were first shown a picture of twin boys and asked to name one Bill. They then were shown a series of pictures of the twins, and had to try to name the same one Bill as they had on the first card. In the other half of the cases, the experimenter had the child wait in the room for ten minutes before starting the game. The cold experimenter gave no explanation for their having to wait alone, while the warm one indicated that she had to go "fix the machine" and thus they would have to wait for her return. The children gave more "right" answers to the cold experimenter, regardless of whether there was a wait or not. The waiting in isolation, then, had no effect on the dependent variable in and of itself. This outcome, then, strengthens the interpretation that the critical variable here is the sense of rejection or acceptance which the experimental manipulation generates in the child. If he interprets the enforced period of isolation as an indication of rejection by the adult or is otherwise made anxious by cold treatment, he will then be more influenced by, and responsive to, subsequent indications of approval on the part of the adult. By eliciting such approval and doing what he is told is right he may regain the approval and support which is so important for the redemption of his lowered feelings of competence and esteem.

The results of the Walters and Parke study might seem contradictory to some of the effects of liking on conformity which were found in earlier chapters. There the relationship between liking and conformity was emphasized. The difference would appear to lie in which motives are aroused, a desire to restore self-esteem, or to act in conformity with a schema. Different situations will arouse different schemas and therefore different motives. For example, the cold experimenter in the Walters-Parke study might have implied that she would be pleased by the child's doing well on the task. In the cases cited earlier, this instrumental use of the schema might not have been made salient.

Derogation of the Source of Negative Evaluations

The important role which others' evaluations may play in the restoration of self-esteem points to still another way in which a person can overcome a loss. The power of derogatory evaluations by another person depends in large part on their credibility and the perceived expertise of their source. If the individual can come to discredit the derogator's credibility, then he can eliminate the threat to his self-esteem. Harvey, Kelley, and Shapiro (1957) found that the more negative the rating an individual received from a stranger, the more negatively the stranger was evaluated in return. And, further, Harvey (1962) found that if a person disparaged a source of negative ratings of himself, he was then less likely to accept the implications of these ratings as part of his own self-image. Moreover, some of the instances of negative evaluations of frustrating or anxiety-arousing people which were discussed earlier might have been motivated by this sort of effort to discredit, as well as by the general tendency to negatively evaluate sources of threats to positive self-evaluation. Furthermore, some of the aggression and hostility which occur in response to frustration may also be motivated by a desire to reduce the credibility of the agent perceived to be responsible for the failure to attain goals.

THE SEARCH FOR FAMILIAR QUALITIES

A final way of restoring the sense of competence that we shall examine involves a search for familiar elements in the situation. As was mentioned earlier, a person's sense of competence is higher in a familiar environment than in an unfamiliar one. Haggard (1964) has reviewed the journals and reports of people in extremely hazardous and strange situations, such as those having to do with arctic explorers and shipwrecked people, and found that those in such extreme circumstances either perish in the first few days of their exposure to the danger or they survive for a much longer period. Whether a person survives or not appears to depend on whether he can find something familiar in his environment or even in his hallucinations—something predictable to him. In a much less dramatic setting, Hall (1959) points out that people often feel more comfortable at a series of lectures if they sit in the same place at each session. Every instructor must have noticed how students tend to sit in the same seats they happened to sit in the first day of class. Obviously, there are other reasons than an enhanced sense of competence for this behavior, but there can be little doubt that a greater feeling of competence is one of the reasons for it.

FAILURE TO ESTABLISH ESTEEM-RESTORING OPERATIONS

An individual faced with a threat to his self-esteem may find, for a variety of reasons, that he cannot make restitution for it through any available means. He may not have acquired the schemas necessary for the effective operation of the esteem-restoring actions which have been discussed; some of these necessary actions may be extremely difficult or costly, such as being aggressive, or derogating a good friend. The individual is then left with a heavy load of anxiety. One way that this anxiety can perhaps be reduced is by escaping the situation physically or psychologically. Other schemas then may become aroused, replacing those associated with the anxiety. Of course, the person is still left with the damage to his self-esteem, since the schemas that were aroused in the threatening situation would only be dormant, and could be aroused later. He may be unavoidably reminded of his failure or humiliation. And the L.O.S. about the loss of self-esteem in the given situation will have at least some minimal effect on the overall level of self-esteem. Nevertheless, if the individual gives up his goal, if he physically leaves the situation, he can perhaps reduce his immediate experience of anxiety. Janis (1967) has argued that one of the reasons that people sometimes do not follow health and safety recommendations is that the threatening manner in which the recommendations are presented is so frightening and anxiety-arousing that people avoid the schemas associated with the anxiety, including the recommendations. Turner and Wright (1965) removed some toys from children's playrooms without any explanation. Some of the children were told that they never would be able to play with them again, others were told that they might be able to play with them again, and still others were told nothing about playing with the toys again. All the children then ranked all of the toys with regard to how much they would like to play with them. The first group of children subsequently lowered their rankings of the removed toys while the others did not. It might then be argued that the first group simply gave up the goal in order to avoid the situation of anxiety. Paivo (1965) measured the degree of anxiety that children experience when performing before an audience by means of a questionnaire on the topic. He then showed that if highly anxious children are told that they are going to have to tell a story before an audience of adults and if they are given a few minutes to wait before they appear before the audience, they spend this time arousing schemas about how anxious they have been in the past in such situations. When they finally do speak before the group, they tell shorter stories—to escape the situation more rapidly—than do children who do not describe themselves as being anxious about public speaking. If the children are not given a few minutes in which to worry, these differences in the length of speeches do not occur. It appears that children's schemas relevant to this situation are not so well acquired that they become anxious immediately upon being told that they are going to talk before adults. Of course, if an individual withdraws from anxiety-arousing situations sufficiently frequently, if he gives up goals in order to avoid anxiety, he may soon become apathetic, depressed, and inactive—in extreme cases, even to the point of not making efforts to live.

SELECTION FROM THE VARIETY OF ESTEEM-RESTORING RESPONSES

The broad array of techniques which an individual might use to restore self-esteem makes for some confusion in ordering this topic. This confusion is in part a reflection of the fact that people do, indeed, shift from one way of restoring self-esteem to another. Persons may attempt to gain acceptance from a group, and, failing that, may reject it in anger and hostility. People may attempt to act constructively, and, failing there, may suddenly withdraw. If people are humiliated by an overwhelming group, they may join the group to share in its competence: "If you can't lick them, join them." Perhaps the most dramatic indication of these shifts from technique to technique is the fact that most murders in America are committed among friends, acquaintances, or relatives—if a person can't maintain his self-esteem by affirmation from other significant acts, he may resort to maintenance of it by hostile acts.

Selection Based on Modeling

Nevertheless, this variability, this shift from technique to technique, is not completely random. As was mentioned above, some actions simply are too difficult or costly; reality can play a direct part in determining the chosen alternative. Different people have acquired different schemas about the effectiveness of these various techniques. In addition, more subtle processes can influence the person's tendency to use one way or another. For example, it was demonstrated in previous chapters that one of the means by which an individual can acquire a schema about possible actions in a situation involves the observation of others' behavior. Berkowitz and his associates (Berkowitz and Geen, 1966; Berkowitz and Rawlings, 1963) have amply demonstrated that people are more likely to become hostile if they have observed a hostile model. Similarly, if something in a given situation arouses a particular schema concerned with the effectiveness of a given way of restoring self-esteem, the individual will be more likely to use that technique.

Berkowitz and Le Page (1967) found that if a gun "happened" to be lying around an experimental room, subjects administered more electric shocks to other subjects who had shocked them previously than if a gun was not visible. The social implications of Berkowitz' findings are obvious and important. A society, a community, a home which abounds in conspicuous weapons, in models of violence, will tend to generate more violent behavior, even in ways which do not involve the use of weapons.

Perceived Social Support for a Given Response

Sometimes social support can determine whether or not a person acts in a given way to restore or maintain self-esteem. The agreement among group members, for example, that a given course of action is right and proper will increase each member's belief in its propriety and thereby increase his tendency to use this action to support self-esteem. Pepitone and Reichling (1955) formed subjects into groups which were either highly attractive and supportive of one another or low in attraction. The experimenter badgered and insulted the subjects in both groups, but the members of the more attractive group were more likely to express hostility to the experimenter. Likewise, Wright (1943) found that children who were frustrated by an adult were more likely to go up to the adult and express their negative feelings if they were close friends with another child and the two approached the adult together. Stotland (1959) had subjects work on an involving task under a frustrating supervisor. If the subjects had a chance to meet privately with another subject who was being similarly tormented by another supervisor in a separate room, they were more likely to fight back verbally against their supervisors. Notice here that the subjects could not help one another. It was the shared and established belief in the propriety of their action and of the impropriety of the supervisors which made the difference.

A person's perception that he has the support of other people for engaging in hostile or violent behavior can sometimes be the result of the operation of some of the schemas about interpersonal relations discussed in Chapter 7. For instance, a person's having the schema that people are similar in many ways may lead him to perceive that people similar to himself who are watching him engage in violence which he believes to be warranted will also tend to believe that his actions are justified. Bystanders in a riot situation may inadvertently, or advertently, lend support to the violent core. Likewise, a person may observe that one member of a group or crowd engages in violence or "talks it up." He may then assume that all the others are about to act violently, thus leading him to be more prone to engage in violence himself as he is a member of that crowd. In addition to violence, other reactions to threatening situations, such as fleeing them or acting constructively, are more likely to take place if others are engaging in these reactions as well. The rapid spread of panic behavior is a well-known instance of such effects.

Level of Self-Esteem and Withdrawal

One factor which appears to determine how much an individual will withdraw from and avoid anxiety-arousing situations is the individual's overall level of self-esteem. People with high self-esteem perceive that they will be able to cope with a threatening situation and be able to protect or restore their self-esteem, should this be necessary, without leaving the situation. Thus, Stotland (1959) found that after having failed to meet a group's expectations people with low self-esteem were more likely to reject the group than if they succeeded in the group. The degree of prior success had little effect on tendencies to reject the group among people with high self-esteem. Dittes (1959a) assembled subjects in groups which were made very attractive by attributing high prestige to them, giving them prizes for their good performances, and so on. After an hour of discussion, the subjects rated one another as group members; then some of them were told that the results of these evaluations indicated that they had been rejected by their peers. Rejected subjects with low self-esteem in turn rejected the group. Rejected subjects of high self-esteem remained attracted to the groups. In addition to perceiving that they will be able to cope with the group situation, another reason for the failure of the high self-esteem people to reciprocate the evaluations made by the rejecting groups is that their own beliefs about themselves are less influenced by the evaluations of others than are the beliefs of persons of low self-esteem. This relationship was described earlier in this chapter. It is not surprising, then, that Morris Rosenberg (1965) finds that low self-esteem adolescents tend to avoid competitive professions and positions of responsibility.

An individual might not only be motivated to avoid threatening situations which immediately confront him; he might also move to avoid contemplated future situations which might be threatening. A person might, for example, anticipate that he will have to face many situations in which he will appear before hostile or evaluative groups, or ones in which he will have to relate effectively to someone of the opposite sex, and so forth. One way he can attempt to

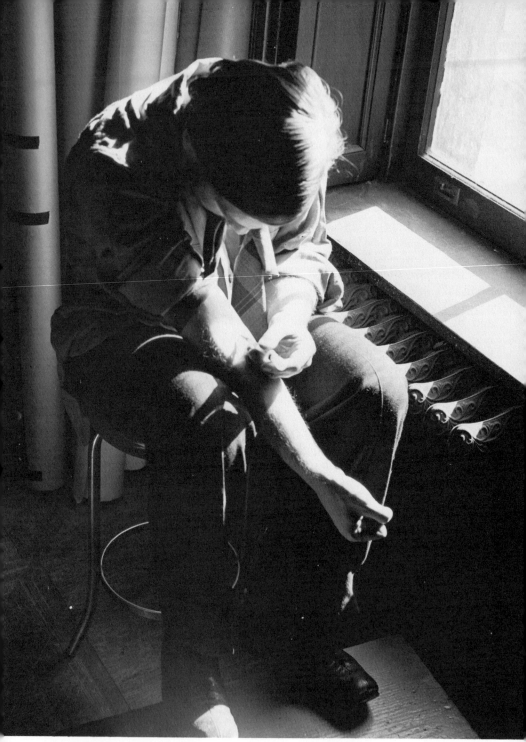

Withdrawal takes many forms.

avoid anxiety, to avoid a threat to his sense of competence when he does encounter these situations is to become as adept, as skillful as he can in meeting his needs in such situations. What he can do, then, is practice acting in such situations in meetings where much less is at stake than the meeting of his important needs. More specifically, he can "play games" which are duplicates or micro-cosms of the more important situations he expects to encounter later. Some of the motivation behind the play of children stems from this source; often children's play consists of practicing adult roles, such as playing "house."

Eliciting Assistance from Others

Thus far in this chapter, we have emphasized a view of persons striving to attain their goals independently, on their own—a picture like that in the poem *Invictus*. Obviously, such extreme in-dependence is not always possible. Certainly when we are young we are especially dependent on other people, on our parents, or on adults in general to help us meet our needs. To be sure, there are many pressures to move away from such dependency. Nevertheless, all of us, to varying degrees, have had experiences which led us to acquire a schema which indicates that other people can help us at-tain our goals.

Let us then consider a person who is in a situation in which he has little expectation of successfully meeting his needs on his own, and in which none of the more indirect ways of raising the sense of competence which have been mentioned in the past few pages are available to him. Such a person would be in a state of con-siderable anxiety, for at least two reasons—the lowering of his sense of competence resulting from an awareness of his ineffectiveness, of self-esteem and the sheer inability to attain important goals. It may well be possible, however, to eliminate at least the second of these sources of anxiety by gaining help from other people in attain-ing goals. A child stops crying when mother helps it find a lost toy, or, more basically, feeds it when it is hungry. To be sure, this de-pendency on others does not enhance the child's sense of com-petence with respect to actions aimed directly at attaining goals. In fact, in many instances among both adults and children, the re-ceiving of help may be perceived as humiliating. However, if the person has called for the help and has directly acted to gain it, he might not only avoid a loss of sense of competence, but might bolster it because of the effectiveness of his actions in eliciting the desired help. Further, the willingness of others to give assistance enhances his self-esteem.

Anxiety Reduction Through Affiliation

In any case, the individual can acquire schemas regarding the effectiveness of gaining help from others in attaining goals, and of the consequent reduction in anxiety. Such schemas can then be aroused by the person's awareness of the presence of another person, especially if this person has been helpful in the past. The arousal of these schemas obviously would have the effect of reducing anxiety. In fact, these schemas about help from others are usually of such a high order that it is not necessary for the person actually to be materially helpful in the situation in order for anxiety reduction to occur. The sheer presence of others reduces anxiety. For instance, children in a strange new situation are less likely to cry when a friendly adult is present than if they are alone (Arsenian, 1943). Vernon, Foley, and Schulman (1967) showed that children were less anxious when facing anesthesia with their mothers present than with their mothers absent. The same process even occurs in adults. Kissel (1965) gave adults a series of unsolvable perceptual reasoning tasks. Some of the subjects worked alone. Others worked in the presence of another subject, a stranger, who worked on an entirely different problem. Still other subjects had a friend present who worked on a different problem. Physiological measures taken indicated that the subjects were less anxious when working in the presence of a friend.

Since people acquire a schema to the effect that they feel less anxious in the presence of others, they are motivated to seek others out when in a threatening situation. Every mother knows this. A number of researchers have found this to be the case among adults, among subjects waiting to participate in experiments which they expect to be painful (e.g., Schachter, 1959; Zimbardo and Formica, 1963; Miller and Zimbardo, 1966). The more frightening the situation, the more persons indicate a desire to be with other people. This wish to await the pain together with others occurs even when the subjects expect not to be able to talk with one another—sheer presence is all that is needed. In fact, Zimbardo and Formica (1963) asked subjects why they wanted to be with others, and the most common reply was simply that it is comforting to be with others in that situation.

Schachter (1959) and Miller and Zimbardo (1966) found that when subjects are given a choice of waiting for a painful experiment with people who are also waiting for this experiment, or with people who are waiting for other reasons or who are of the same personality type as themselves, the subjects prefer to wait with those who are also expecting the painful experiment. The reason for this preference might be that the subjects may have schemas that people who share a problem are rather likely to help one another, if they can. Even though material help cannot be given in these situations, the schema might be so well established as to reduce anxiety.

Needless to say, the reduction of anxiety in the face of threat is hardly the only motivation for anxious people to seek each other out. They may be seeking clarification of issues, distraction, or even a way of constructively solving problems.

When people in a group feel threatened by someone or something outside the group, they will seek each other out more (Lott and Lott, 1965). Torrance (1961) reviewed the reactions of military and other groups when faced with threat and found that one of the very characteristic reactions is a closening of the ties among the men.

References

Aronson, E., and Linder, D.: Gain and loss of esteem as determinants of interpersonal attractiveness. *Journal of Experimental Social Psychology*, 1965, 1:156–171.

Arsenian, J. M.: Young children in an insecure situation. *Journal of Abnormal and Social Psychology*, 1943, 38:225–249.

Baldwin, A.: The effect of home environment on nursery school development. *Child Development*, 1949, 20:49–61.

Baron, R. M., Robinson, E. L., and Lawrence, S.: The effectiveness of social reinforcement as a function of changes in rate of reinforcement. *Journal of Experimental Social Psychology*, 1968, 4:123–142.

Berkowitz, L.: Repeated frustrations and expectations in hostility arousal. *Journal of Abnormal and Social Psychology*, 1960, 60:422–429.

Berkowitz, L.: *Aggression: A Social Psychological Analysis*. New York, McGraw-Hill, 1962.

Berkowitz, L.: Aggressive cues in aggressive behavior and hostility catharsis. *Psychological Review*, 1964, 71:104–122.

Berkowitz, L.: The study of urban violence: Some implications of laboratory studies of frustration and aggression. *American Behavioral Scientist*, 1968, 2(4):14–17.

Berkowitz, L., and Geen, R. G.: Film violence and cue properties of available targets. *Journal of Personality and Social Psychology*, 1966, 3:525–530.

Berkowitz, L., and Holmes, D. S.: The generalization of hostility to disliked objects. *Journal of Personality*, 1959, 27:563–577.

Berkowitz, L., and LePage, A.: Weapons as aggression-eliciting stimuli. *Journal of Personality and Social Psychology*, 1967, 7:202–207.

Berkowitz, L., and Rawlings, E.: Effects of film violence on inhibitions against subsequent aggression. *Journal of Abnormal and Social Psychology*, 1963, 66:405–412.

Berkowitz, L.: Anti-semitism and displacement of aggression. *Journal of Abnormal and Social Psychology*, 1959, 59:182–187.

Bettelheim, B.: *The Informed Heart*. Glencoe, Illinois, Free Press, 1960.

Bettelheim, B., and Janowitz, M.: *Dynamics of Prejudice*. New York, Harper, 1950.

Bowen, D. R., et al.: Deprivation, mobility and orientation toward protest of the urban poor. *American Behavioral Scientist*, 1968, 2(4):20–24.

Brehm, J. W.: *A Theory of Psychological Reactance.* New York, Academic Press, 1966.

Brehm, J. W., and Cole, A. H.: Effect of a favor which reduces freedom. *Journal of Personality and Social Psychology,* 1966, 3:420–426.

Campbell, A. A.: Factors associated with attitudes toward Jews. In T. M. Newcomb and E. L. Hartley (Eds.), *Readings in Social Psychology.* New York, Holt, 1947.

Cohen, N. E.: The Los Angeles riot study. *Social Work,* 1967, *12*(4):14–21.

Coopersmith, S.: *The Antecedents of Self-esteem.* San Francisco, Freeman, 1967.

Cowen, E. L., Landes, J., and Schact, D. E.: The effects of mild frustration on the expression of prejudiced attitudes. *Journal of Abnormal and Social Psychology,* 1959, *53*:33–38.

Darley, J. M., and Aronson, E.: Self-evaluation vs. direct anxiety reduction as determinants of the fear affiliation relationship. *Journal of Experimental Social Psychology Supplement,* 1966, *1*:66–79.

Deutsch, M., and Krauss, R. M.: The effect of threat upon interpersonal bargaining. *Journal of Abnormal and Social Psychology,* 1960, *61*:181–189.

Dittes, J.: Attractiveness of groups as functions of self-esteem and acceptance by group. *Journal of Abnormal and Social Psychology,* 1959*a*, *59*:77–82.

Dittes, J. E.: Effect of changes in self-esteem upon impulsiveness and deliberation in making judgments. *Journal of Abnormal and Social Psychology,* 1959*b*, *58*: 348–356.

Dittes, J. E.: Impulsive closure as reaction to failure-induced threat. *Journal of Abnormal and Social Psychology,* 1961, *63*:562–569.

Dollard, J., Miller, N. E., Doob, L. W., Mowrer, O. H., and Sears, R. R.: *Frustration and Aggression.* New Haven, Yale University Press, 1939.

Endleman, S.: The etiology of the race riot. In S. Endleman (Ed.), *Violence in the Streets.* Chicago, Quadrangle Books, 1968.

Feshbach, S.: The function of aggression and the regulation of aggressive drive. *Psychological Review,* 1964, *71*:257–272.

Freedman, J. W., Wallington, S. A., and Bless, E.: Compliance without pressure: the effect of guilt. *Journal of Personality and Social Psychology,* 1967, *7*:117–124.

Gewirtz, J. L., and Baer, D. M.: Deprivation and satiation of social reinforcers as drive conditions. *Journal of Abnormal and Social Psychology,* 1958*a*, *57*:165–172.

Gewirtz, J. L., and Baer, D. M.: The effect of brief social deprivation on behavior for a social reinforcer. *Journal of Abnormal and Social Psychology,* 1958*b*, *56*:49–56.

Gurr, T.: Urban disorder: perspectives from the comparative study of civil strife. *American Behavioral Scientist,* 1968, *2*(4):50–55.

Haggard, E. A.: Isolation and personality. In P. Worchel and D. Byrne (Eds.), *Personality Change.* New York, Wiley, 1964.

Hakmiller, K. L.: Need for self-evaluation, perceived similarity and comparison choice. *Journal of Experimental Social Psychology Supplement,* 1966, *1*:49–54.

Hall, E. T.: *The Silent Language.* Garden City, Doubleday, 1959.

Harvey, O. J.: Personality factors in the resolution of perceptual incongruities. *Sociometry,* 1962, *25*:336–352.

Harvey, O. J., Kelley, N. H., and Shapiro, M. M.: Reactions to unfavorable evaluations of the self made by other persons. *Journal of Personality,* 1957, *25*:393–411.

Hoffman, L. W.: The father's role in the family and the child's peer group adjustment. *Merrill-Palmer Quarterly,* 1961, *7*:97–105.

Hokanson, J. E., and Burgess, M.: The effects of status, type of frustration, and aggression on vascular processes. *Journal of Abnormal and Social Psychology,* 1962*a*, *65*:232–237.

Hokanson, J. E., and Burgess, M.: The effects of three types of aggression on vascular processes. *Journal of Abnormal and Social Psychology,* 1962*b*, *64*:446–449.

Hokanson, J. E., Burgess, M., and Cohen, M. F.: Effects of displaced aggression on systolic blood pressure. *Journal of Abnormal and Social Psychology,* 1963, *67*: 214–218.

Hokanson, J. E., and Edelman, R.: Effects of three social responses on vascular processes. *Journal of Personality and Social Psychology,* 1966, *3*:442–447.

Hokanson, J. E., and Shetler, S.: The effect of overt aggression on physiological arousal level. *Journal of Abnormal and Social Psychology,* 1961, *63*:446–448.

Holmes, D. S.: Effects of overt aggression on level of physiological arousal. *Journal of Personality and Social Psychology*, 1966, *4:*189–194.

Horowitz, I. A.: Effect of choice and basis of dependence on helping behavior. *Journal of Personality and Social Psychology*, 1968, *8:*373–376.

Horwitz, M.: The veridicality of liking and disliking. In R. Tagiuri and L. Petrullo (Eds.), *Person Perception and Interpersonal Behavior.* Stanford, Stanford University Press, 1958.

Janis, I. L.: Effects of fear arousal on attitude change: recent developments in theory and experimental research. In L. Berkowitz (Ed.), *Advances in Experimental Social Psychology,* Vol. 3. New York, Academic Press, 1967.

Janis, I. L., and Feshbach, S.: Effects of fear-arousing communications. *Journal of Abnormal and Social Psychology*, 1953, *48:*78–92.

Kahn, R. L., and Katz, D.: Leadership practices in relation to productivity and morale. In D. Cartwright and A. Zander (Eds.), *Group Dynamics.* Evanston, Row, Peterson, 1953.

Kaufmann, H.: Definitions and methodology in the study of aggression. *Psychological Bulletin*, 1965, *64:*351–364.

Kissel, S.: Stress-reducing properties of social stimuli. *Journal of Personality and Social Psychology*, 1965, *2:*378–384.

Lang, K., and Lang, G.: Racial disturbances as collective protest. *American Behavioral Scientist*, 1968, *2*(4):11–13.

Lanzetta, J. T.: Group behavior under stress. *Human Relations*, 1955, *8:*29–52.

Leventhal, H., Jones, S., and Trembly, G.: Sex differences in attitude and behavior change under conditions of fear and specific instructions. *Journal of Experimental Social Psychology*, 1966, *2:*387–399.

Leventhal, H., and Singer, R. P.: Affect arousal and positioning of recommendation in persuasive communications. *Journal of Personality and Social Psychology*, 1966, *4:*137–146.

Leventhal, H., Singer, R., and Jones, S.: Effects of fear and specificity of recommendation upon attitude and behavior. *Journal of Personality and Social Psychology*, 1965, *2:*20–29.

Leventhal, H., and Trembly, G.: Negative emotions and persuasion. *Journal of Personality*, 1968, *36:*154–168.

Leventhal, H., Watts, J., and Pagano, F.: Effects of fear and instructions on how to cope with danger. *Journal of Personality and Social Psychology*, 1967, *6:*313–321.

Lewin, K.: *A Dynamic Theory of Personality.* New York, McGraw-Hill, 1935.

Lewin, K.: *Field Theory in Social Science.* New York, Harper Row, 1951.

Lewin, K., Dembo, T., Festinger, L., and Sears, P. S.: Level of aspiration. In J. McV. Hunt (Ed.), *Personality and the Behavior Researchers.* New York, Ronald, 1944.

Likert, R.: *New Patterns of Management.* New York, McGraw-Hill, 1959.

Lott, A. J., and Lott, B. F.: Group cohesiveness as interpersonal attraction: a review of relationships with antecedent and consequent variables. *Psychological Bulletin*, 1965, *64:*259–309.

Mann, L., and Dashiell, T. C.: Reactions to the draft lottery: reactance or sour grapes. *Journal of Personality and Social Psychology* (in press).

Medinnus, G. R., and Curtis, F. J.: The relation between maternal self-acceptance and child acceptance. *Journal of Consulting Psychology*, 1963, *27:*542–544.

Miller, N., and Zimbardo, P. G.: Motives for fear-induced affiliation: emotional comparison in interpersonal similarity. *Journal of Personality*, 1966, *34:*481–503.

Morse, N. C., and Reimer, E.: Experimental change of a major organizational variable. *Journal of Abnormal and Social Psychology*, 1956, *52:*120–129.

Nardini, J. E.: Survival factors in American prisoners of war of the Japanese. *American Journal of Psychiatry*, 1952, *109:*242–248.

Paivo, A.: Personality and audience influence. In B. Maher (Ed.), *Progress in Experimental Personality Research.* Vol. 2. New York, Academic Press, 1965.

Peck, R. F.: Family patterns correlated with adolescent personality structure. *Journal of Abnormal and Social Psychology*, 1959, *57:*347–350.

Pepitone, A., and Reichling, G.: Group cohesiveness and the expression of hostility. *Human Relations*, 1955, *8:*327–338.

Reese, H.: Relationships between self-acceptance and sociometric choice. *Journal of Abnormal and Social Psychology*, 1961, 62:472–474.

Rosenberg, M. J.: When dissonance fails: on eliminating evaluation apprehension from attitude measurement. *Journal of Personality and Social Psychology*, 1965, 1:28–42.

Rosenberg, Morris: *Society and the Adolescent Self-image*. Princeton, Princeton University Press, 1965.

Rothaus, P., and Worchel, P.: Ego support, communication, catharsis, and hostility. *Journal of Personality*, 1964, 32:296–312.

Schachter, S.: Deviation, rejection and communication. *Journal of Abnormal and Social Psychology*, 1951, 46:190–207.

Schachter, S.: *The Psychology of Affiliation*. Stanford, Stanford University Press, 1959.

Shaw, M. E.: Communication networks. In L. Berkowitz (Ed.), *Advances in Experimental Social Psychology*. Vol. 1. New York, Academic Press, 1964.

Sigall, H., and Aronson, E.: Opinion change and gain-loss. *Journal of Experimental Social Psychology*, 1967, 3:178–188.

Smith, A. J.: The attribution of similarity: the influence of success and failure. *Journal of Abnormal and Social Psychology*, 1960, 61:419–423.

Smith, C. G., and Tannenbaum, A. S.: Organizational control structure. *Human Relations*, 1963, 16:299–316.

Snoek, J. D.: Some effects of rejection upon attraction to a group. *Journal of Abnormal and Social Psychology*, 1962, 64:175–182.

Stotland, E.: Determinants of attraction to groups. *Journal of Social Psychology*, 1959, 49:71–80.

Stotland, E.: Peer groups and reactions to power figures. In D. Cartwright (Ed.), *Studies in Social Power*. Ann Arbor, Research Center of Group Dynamics, 1959.

Stotland, E.: *The Psychology of Hope*. San Francisco, Jossey-Bass, 1969.

Stotland, E., and Blumenthal, A. L.: The reduction of anxiety as a result of the expectation of making a choice. *Canadian Journal of Psychology*, 1964, 18:139–145.

Stotland, E., and Hillmer, M.: Identification, authoritarianism, and self-esteem. *Journal of Abnormal and Social Psychology*, 1962, 66:334–342.

Stressman, H. D., Thaler, M. B., and Schein, E. H.: A prisoner of war syndrome: apathy as a reaction to severe stress. *American Journal of Psychiatry*, 1955, 112:998–1003.

Torrance, E. P.: A theory of leadership and interpersonal behavior under stress. In L. Petrullo and B. M. Bass (Eds.), *Leadership and Interpersonal Behavior*. New York, Holt, Rinehart, & Winston, 1961.

Turner, E. A., and Wright, J. C.: Effects of severity of threat and perceived availability on the attractiveness of objects. *Journal of Personality and Social Psychology*, 1965, 2:128–132.

Veldman, D., and Worchel, P.: Defensiveness and self-acceptance in the management of hostility. *Journal of Abnormal and Social Psychology*, 1961, 63:319–325.

Vernon, D. T. A., Foley, J. M., and Schulman, J. L.: Effects of mother-child separation and birth order on young children's responses to two potentially stressful experiences. *Journal of Personality and Social Psychology*, 1967, 5:162–174.

Walster, E.: The effect of self-esteem on romantic liking. *Journal of Experimental Social Psychology*, 1965, 1:184–197.

Walters, R. H.: Some conditions facilitating the occurrence of imitative behavior. In E. C. Simmel, R. A. Hoppe, and G. H. Milton (Eds.), *Social Facilitation and Imitative Behavior*. Boston, Allyn & Bacon, 1968.

Walters, R. H., and Parke, R. D.: Emotional arousal, isolation, and discrimination learning in children. *Journal of Experimental Child Psychology*, 1964a, 1:163–173.

Walters, R. H., and Parke, R. D.: Influence of response consequences to a social model on resistance to deviation. *Journal of Experimental Child Psychology*, 1964b, 1:276–280.

Walters, R. H., and Ray, E.: Anxiety, social isolation, and reinforcer effectiveness. *Journal of Personality*, 1960, 28:354–367.

White, R.: Motivation reconsidered: the concept of competence. *Psychological Review*, 1959, 66:297–333.

White, R. K., and Lippitt, R.: *Autocracy and Democracy*. New York, Harper, 1960.

Wicklund, R. A., and Brehm, J. W.: Attitude change as a function of felt competence and threat to attitudinal freedom. *Journal of Experimental Social Psychology,* 1968, *4:*64–75.

Worchel, P.: Personality factors in the readiness to express aggression. *Journal of Clinical Psychology,* 1958, *14:*355–359.

Worchel, P.: Status restoration and the reduction of hostility. *Journal of Abnormal and Social Psychology,* 1961, *63:*443–445.

Wright, M. E.: The influence of frustration upon the social relations of young children. *Character and Personality,* 1943-44, *12:*111–122.

Ziller, R. C., Hagey, J., Smith, M. D. C., and Long, B.: Self-esteem: a self-social construct. *Journal of Consulting and Clinical Psychology,* 1969, *33:*84–95.

Zimbardo, P. G., and Formica, R.: Emotional comparison and self-esteem as determinants of affiliation. *Journal of Personality,* 1963, *31:*141–162.

12

LEADERSHIP, GROUPS, AND STATUS

Aside from having become a cliché, the old joke about the Martians landing on earth and demanding of the first earthling they meet, who just happens to be a farmer's cow, "Take us to your leader," also indicates that most of us assume that the phenomenon of leadership is literally "universal." In a sense, it is. Parents lead children; teachers lead them, too; some employers lead their employees; lieutenants lead privates; some chairmen lead members; statesmen lead countries; politicians can lead constituents; and this list leads on, too. In the present chapter, social psychological aspects of the process of leadership will be examined. In doing so, it will be seen that many of the findings, conclusions, and general propositions set forth in the previous chapters are relevant to an understanding of leadership. In a sense, then, our concern with leadership is in part an application and extension of what has been discussed earlier in this text. The application of these earlier discussions to leadership is obviously not the only possible application that could be made. Other areas, such as the problems of social change, group conflict, and interaction, could be dealt with in this fashion. Nevertheless, the application to leadership behavior is not arbitrary. Social psychologists and other allied professionals have done many studies of leadership and we shall take advantage of that fact.

524

MOTIVATION TO FORM GROUPS

The study of leadership is different from the concerns of the previous chapters. In the latter, our focus has been primarily, though not exclusively, on one person's reactions to other people and to himself. In the present chapter, we will have to be more concerned than we have previously been with the ways in which people interact, with group processes. For example, some of the changes that take place over time in groups will be dealt with. However, we will still be concerned with the individual members' reactions to these changes, and will, as well, show how some of these group processes are a reflection of the reactions of the individual members.

Since leadership implies "followership," and together they imply the existence of a group, we will start our investigation of leadership by asking some questions about groups. The answers to these questions involve leadership and thus will ultimately return us to the central topic. The first question is: why do people form or join groups in the first place? Notice first that this question implicitly excludes situations in which the individual is physically forced to enter or maintain some sort of group affiliation which he is physically unable to leave, as is the case in which prisons, some wards in mental hospitals, and concentration camps are concerned. The individual in these circumstances has no choice but to stay. We shall ignore such groups and concentrate instead on those in which the individual perceives that he has a choice of entering into or forgoing membership. As we have already seen and as is quite obvious, an individual initially joins or remains in a group because he perceives that he can attain his goals more easily by being in the group than by staying out. Included in these goals is that of minimizing costs to him, to reduce his suffering in terms of work, money, or other sacrifices. Thus, a person will join a group if he perceives that being a member of this group is the least costly way he has of attaining his goals and has the highest probability of any course of action of attaining his goals. The goals that the individual might perceive the group as being instrumental in attaining can be quite varied: money, companionship, status, survival, fun, or others.

Group Activity Fosters Goal Attainment

For purposes of our analysis, let us consider a group of people who have just formed a group, each one of them having joined the group to attain his own goals. These individual goals may all be the same, i.e., having fun and meeting other people. Or they may vary:

making money, gaining prestige, or others. Nevertheless, the members all perceive that the same group activity is satisfying their individual needs. For instance, a group of boys may join a team to compete in an athletic contest; some may do it for fun, some for the money prize, some to make friends, some for the prestige, some for a mixture of these goals. Nevertheless, they are all interested in forming the team. On the other hand, an example of more complete uniformity of individual goals would be a number of passengers of a sunken sailing ship who suddenly find themselves in the same lifeboat. They are all therefore extremely interested in the success-ful navigation of the boat. In either of these cases, the important fact for our purposes is that the members all perceive the same group activity as instrumental to the attainment of certain of their goals. It is important to notice that relevant group activities may in-clude not only such obvious ones as forming a team and winning, but also such things as having a party, just sitting around and "rapping," and so forth.

Involvement of Sense of Competence

Matters are not as simple as all that, however. As was seen in the last chapter, whenever an individual initiates an attempt to at-tain some goal, his sense of competence becomes involved. And this involvement will both influence the degree to which he will anticipate the attainment of his goals and provide additional motiva-tion to attain the goal in order to keep the sense of competence as high as possible. A parallel process occurs with respect to an in-dividual's functioning as a member of a group. His perception of the group's likelihood of attaining its goals will be influenced by his general expectations about his own goal attainment; and he will be motivated to have the group attain its goals in order to bolster his own sense of competence.

Group Success and Individual Sense of Competence

By what means does this occur? How can a member's own personal sense of competence, his self-esteem, be influenced by the achievements—or failures—of a group to which he belongs? In Chapter 6 we pointed out the prevalence of schemas associat-ing felt similarity with physical proximity, with interaction and com-munication, with being part of the same unified group. Since an in-dividual is typically physically proximal to other group members, since he interacts with them, since he, and other people, may come to perceive the group *as* a group, he will tend to perceive similarities between himself and the group. Thus, if he has a high sense of competence, he will tend to assume that the group is likely to attain its goals. The process works in the other direction as well. If the group succeeds, the individual members will raise their own sense of competence; if their group encounters failure, they will lower it. Even the bench warmer on a football team will tend to feel like a better athlete himself if his team wins. An individual may well have had a number of experiences in which his self-esteem was influenced by these processes—and thus will be further motivated to help the group attain its goals.

In addition, there are other processes which strengthen the tie between the person's own sense of competence and the group's degree of success. Other people, in and out of the group, will tend to evaluate the person in terms of the degree of achievement of the group. No doubt the bench warmer on a winning team gets more compliments from other people than the bench warmer on a losing team. The member might see other members of the group receiving compliments from other people, and then assume that, because of the schemas referred to in the previous paragraphs, he too has received or will soon receive a similar expression of adulation. When the quarterback receives a trophy, the bench warmer may feel proud, too.

Still another factor increasing the person's motivation to have the group attain its goals stems from the fact that the individual chose to join the group. If the group succeeds, he perceives that he has made a wise choice; if it fails, he perceives that he has made a poor choice. His perception of his ability to make wise choices, which is a part of his sense of competence, is thus influenced.

All the above processes by which the person's sense of competence is related to the group's success become even more important in light of one general aspect of a person's reasons for having joined a group in the first place—he perceives that he is less likely to be able to attain certain of his goals outside the group than as a member of it. This perception implies that his sense of competence would be threatened if he were not a member of the group. Alone, outside the group, he may perceive that he is likely to fail in his pursuit of some relevant goal, and thus suffer a loss of self-esteem. By being a member of a succeeding group, he may protect his self-esteem.

General Involvement in Group Activity

One implied consequence of this complex set of motives involved when people form new groups is that the members' original motivations for forming the group may become relatively less important than the motivation stemming from the protection of the sense of competence. A person who joins a group simply to find sociable companions may discover that he soon has become involved in other aspects of the group's activities because his sense of competence is now involved. There are, of course, other reasons for the development of new motivations and behavior patterns after the group has been formed, such as doing what is necessary to remain a member in good standing in the group or to keep others actively involved in it, but there can be little question that a person's involvement in the group task may supersede his original motivations for joining.

Fromm (1941), Hoffer (1951) and others have argued that one of the primary reasons that people have for joining groups is their low self-esteem or low sense of competence without such membership. This general statement needs to be greatly qualified. For example, as was just pointed out, a person's expectation that the group will succeed is influenced by his own sense of competence. Thus, people of low self-esteem may perceive that the group "will not make it." This effect then provides another reason, in addition to the ones mentioned in the previous chapter, as to why low self-esteem people are less likely than are highs to join groups. Nevertheless, there may be circumstances under which Fromm's and Hoffer's ideas are borne out; in fact, the groups that Hoffer and Fromm appear to be referring to have certain special characteristics. First, for ideological and other reasons, these groups convey a very strong sense that they are going to be successful. Thus, the pessimism of the low self-esteem person may be overcome. Second, the demands made of new members may be so clearly defined and obviously possible to meet that even a person with low self-esteem will perceive that he can gain acceptance in the group. Third, by implication, the groups referred to are already established ones. Low self-esteem people would be unlikely to try to form new groups, but may be more likely to join already established, "successful" groups. Groups that have all of these characteristics, then, are not common. However, it is probably true, as Fromm and Hoffer point out, that if a low self-esteem person does join such groups, he will be extremely motivated to help the group; he will be a "True Believer," an "escapee from freedom." One implication of this discussion is that people who form new groups will tend to be of high self-esteem. At this writing, however, there appear to be no relevant data available on this general point.

LEADERSHIP IN NEWLY FORMED GROUPS

Now that we have discussed the rather complex picture of the motivations people have in forming a new group, we can move on to examine some of the problems facing such a group. For a variety of reasons, the members are motivated to have the group attain its goals—whatever they might be. However, in the truly new groups to which we are giving our attention here, it will often be the case that the members have not had a chance to acquire or develop many specific lower order schemas about the best course of action to follow. They may have few ideas about what steps should best be taken to facilitate goal attainment: How do they assign men to the various positions on the team? What plays are they to use? How do they train? And so forth. Obviously, this is a situation which generates anxiety.

In the previous chapters, we have seen many other instances in which an absence of L.O.S.s leads to anxiety. The obvious way of reducing this anxiety is to acquire useful and relevant lower order schemas concerning appropriate courses of action. Certainly, at least some of the members will have acquired an H.O.S. that having L.O.S.s in general, and particularly in such situations, is associated with greater behavioral certainty and low anxiety. Thus, a strong motivation to acquire these L.O.S.s is likely. Such motivation is heightened still further by the members' wish to see the group attain its goals both because they are desirable in their own right and because their attainment will bolster self-esteem. In fact, the very working out of the details of the way the members will act to attain their goals is likely to increase their expectation that the group will, indeed, attain its goals.

In fact, the motivation to acquire L.O.S.s which will help structure the group's activities is often so great that almost any reasonable ideas put forth about what specifically to do will be readily accepted. These ideas can quickly reduce that anxiety which was due to the lack of specific schemas about how to act. The act of setting forth such ideas we shall term an act of task leadership; i.e., leadership with respect to the group's task.

Terminological Notes

A point to note is that we have not yet used the term "leader" to designate the person who sets forth these ideas. We are talking about an act, not a person, as yet. One of the reasons for making this distinction is that we need to examine the process whereby a person who engages in leadership acts comes to be designated by others as a leader.

The term "leadership act" is used to designate a pattern of interpersonal behavior in which one person attempts to influence another and the other person accepts this influence. Such a definition of leadership has several implications. The first is that whether an act is one of leadership or not depends in part on the degree to which others accept it. Leadership is not defined here as a quality inherent in a person, nor in an "act" pure and simple. Leadership exists in the relationship between two people. Note furthermore that in terms of this definition the person engaging in the act of leadership must have an intention to influence. That is, he intended to communicate to others, and hoped that they would accept his ideas. Thus, a person who is a "style leader" because other people copy his (or her) dress, when he (or she) has no intention of having this happen does not engage in leadership in the present sense of the term.

A final definitional note: Leadership needs to be distinguished from power. In the exertion of power, the person with the more power is able to do one or both of two things. He can control whether the other person attains one or more of his goals; he does this simply by means of making a decision to allow the other person to attain his goals or not, to give him his pay or not. Or, secondly, he can determine whether the other person can act in a given way: to block off a street or not (cf. Thibaut and Kelley, 1959). Notice that in a very precise sense, all executions of leadership can be executions of power, since the leader also facilitates goal attainment and indicates what to do. What, then, is the difference? The difference lies in the reason for the other person's acceptance of influence. In a power situation, the low power person has the number of his options greatly reduced; he becomes physically able or unable to engage in certain acts simply because the other person has decided to do something or not. The more powerful person may designate certain acts that the less powerful one must engage in if the more powerful person is to act favorably, and the less powerful can decide to act or not. But even in this case, the ultimate decision lies with the person with high power. On the other hand, an act of leadership leaves options physically open to the person. The act simply involves an attempt to convince the others that one course of action is better than another, or attempts to indicate what options are feasible and possible. The other group members still have the opportunity to choose among the several acts proposed. Of course, there are many shades of gray between the two "pure" cases, and sometimes a person may at the same time have power and engage in acts of leadership. We shall see examples of these mixed cases later in the chapter.

Early Acts of Leadership

As should be clear by this point, the ambiguous nature of such a situation increases the likelihood that an act of leadership will occur. In any situation in which members of a group are highly motivated to attain a goal and yet few share any ideas about a specific course of action, there will be a strong tendency to accept the first reasonable ideas offered without much further discussion or critical evaluation. The acceptance of the initially preferred ideas occurs not only in newly forming natural groups, but also in groups that are contrived in the laboratory in which the task given the group is one for which there is no clear-cut solution. Thus, Bales (1952) and Kirscht, Lodahl, and Haire (1959) found that in such groups the person who talks the most is viewed by other members as the one contributing the most to the group's solution of its problems, or as the person best fit to represent the group in talking to outside groups about the group's task. Haythorn (1952) had people work in a series of three different groups; one group worked on reasoning tasks, one on mechanical problems, and one on discussion tasks. Because Haythorn could observe each person in a variety of types of groups, he could determine what each person's "typical" pattern of action was. After taking the nature of these patterns into account statistically, he found that if one member of a group engaged in acts of task leadership by showing initiative, great interest in the solution of the group task, and aggressiveness, the other members were less likely to engage in such behavior. In other words, the problem solutions suggested by the first person to plunge in tended to be accepted by the group.

If the person who engaged in the initial act of leadership continues to behave in such a manner, the members of the group will come to develop a schema about what he regularly does in the group; i.e., he leads. In other words, by the repetition of such actions he will come to be viewed as their leader. We will examine the implications of this process later in this chapter, but meanwhile it is important to note that a person can also come to be viewed as the leader by a quite different means. He may simply be assigned the job of leading the group through some formal procedure within the group or by the action of some external agency, such as the higher levels of an organization. If the person who is assigned this role then actually does engage in acts of task leadership, he can become a leader in the first sense mentioned above.

Groups that are ongoing and which have established leaders can sometimes face difficulties much like those which have just been described as typical of those which newly formed groups face.

For example, an ongoing group may confront a situation which is both new to them and which threatens so basic a goal as the survival of the group, e.g., the crew of a plane downed in the wilderness or a grade-school class in a burning building. Most of the members of the group may have no clear precedent as to what to do under these circumstances. Torrance (1961) has reviewed many reports of members' reactions in such situations and finds that there is a strong tendency to turn to the usual sources of information about what to do—that is, to the established leader of the group. The crew of the plane would turn strongly to the pilot, the pupils to the teacher. There will be more requests for his decisions and greater acceptance of them. This process goes on hand in hand with the greater tendency of people in such stressful situations to turn to one another in order to gain a greater sense that they will overcome their difficulties. Thus, Torrance reports that in such anxiety-arousing, stressful situations, there is a greater tendency to function "by-the-rules," to be more concerned with good communication, to show more concern for doing one's own job to help the other fellow. This tightening up of the group facilitates the acceptance of the leader's directions, since they will be communicated more readily and carried out more effectively. Furthermore, at least some members may have the schema that such tightening up helps the leader communicate his directives; these members may operate in terms of this schema.

Competence and Stability of the Leader

So far in the discussion, we have stressed the way acts of leadership reduce anxiety by providing the group members with L.O.S.s to guide their behavior. The structuring information and proposals communicated by the leader are likely to be accepted by the others because they appear to provide at least some basis of movement toward the goal. However, as the group acts on these directives, their actual utility in moving the group toward the goal is put to test. In many—not all—situations the members of the group can perceive how rapidly and efficiently they are progressing toward the goal. The airliner crew might have little difficulty in finding out whether they are "making it," the pupils will have little difficulty in knowing whether they are getting out of the school building in time. If the leader's directives are effective, the members obviously will tend to keep the leader in his position (cf. Hollander, 1961). Further, they will tend to evaluate him highly. They will accord him high status, and treat him with respect and deference. After all, he is perceived as instrumental to the attainment of important goals. Their positive evaluation of him can be reflected in their motivation to contribute to the group task. Cooper (1966) found that if a foreman is seen to be very able to solve problems and to organize work, then his workers will have relatively low rates of absenteeism and lateness.

On the other hand, if the leader's directives are not effective, if the group perceives that carrying out his ideas does not move them toward the group's goal, then the members will become anxious. Torrance (1961) reports that in such circumstances in real life groups, the members show their anxiety by becoming hostile to one another and by showing general defensiveness. Group members attempt to escape this anxiety in a number of ways. Torrance found that they may become apathetic, reducing the importance to them of the goals of the group; or, if possible, they may quit the group. Another solution is simply to find another leader who has ideas which are effective. Torrance reports that this sometimes does occur to groups in stress whose original leader has failed. Hamblin (1958) had boys work on a group task; after one of the boys had become the leader, the rules of the game were shifted in unpredictable ways, so that the leader was no longer effective. Very quickly, the boys replaced the old leader with one who seemed to know better what to do in these circumstances. Pryer, Flint, and Bass (1962) found that groups that are effective don't change leaders. Crockett (1955) found that in decision-making conferences in government and industry, leaders who did not produce L.O.S.s about how to attain goals, who did not organize the discussion properly, were in effect replaced by other members of the group who began to engage in acts of leadership. Despite these examples of the replacement of ineffective leaders, the process is not always as simple as has been implied. There are many obstacles to changing leaders, which we will discuss at length in this chapter. Meanwhile, we can note that the high level of hostility, apathy, tension, and so forth, resulting from ineffective leadership no doubt occurs more frequently when these obstacles to changing leaders are very great.

In some cases, the leader who is replaced because of his incompetence is a person who is in a formal position, an officially or legally designated position of power. It may not be possible to remove such leaders from their formal positions and in such cases, another person may emerge as the "informal" or unofficial leader. People may pay enough attention to the formal leader not to offend him too greatly, but may really follow the ideas of another person in the group. The official leader becomes a figurehead, a token leader, and the real leadership shifts.

General Ability Level of Leaders

This process of replacing ineffectual leaders is not an automatic or universal process. Yet it occurs frequently enough that those who do remain in leadership positions do tend to have greater knowledge and ability regarding the task confronting the group. If the task is mechanical, they tend to be above average in mechanical ability; if the task is verbal, they are more verbal; if the task is athletic, they are better than average athletes. Some groups which have a number of different goals or tasks will tend to have the same task leader for all these goals, if the same person has considerable ability on all these tasks. Thus, in boys' camps, athletic ability, fighting ability, ability to manipulate adults, are each relevant to different group tasks; and leaders in such camps tend to be high in all of these abilities (Lippitt, Polansky, and Rosen, 1952; Campbell, 1964). In some groups, leaders may simply have better all-around judgment with respect to all sorts of problems. Whyte (1943) in a classic study of a gang of young men in a slum district found that their leader possessed this all-around judgment. In short, the variety of abilities that task leaders need to have to act effectively depends on the variety of tasks that the group faces. However, abilities do not stand in isolation from one another. Abilities tend to cluster, so that people who are high in one tend to be high in others. Thus, task leaders may tend to be generally more able people. Obviously, the level of general all-around ability of leaders is no doubt greater in groups with varied problems than with those with single, highly specialized problems. It is not surprising, then, that the overall drift of many studies of all sorts of groups is for leaders to score somewhat higher than non-leaders on intelligence tests (Gibb, 1969). Gibb points out that the correlation between leadership and intelligence is no doubt higher in groups with non-routine problems, since intelligence reflects in part the ability to solve new problems. However, the fact that the relationship between leadership and I.Q. is not very high indicates that the task leader of a group needs to have the ability required by the specific task at hand. Intelligence as measured by I.Q. tests is only *associated* with these abilities; it is not in itself a determinant of effectiveness of leadership.

However, ability alone does not make a person a task leader. A person with ability who is not motivated to engage in acts of leadership will not often come to be a leader. On the other hand, a variety of motives can lead people to engage in acts of leadership. One obvious source of motivation is the nature of the group task itself. Some potential leaders may be more interested in it than are others; the former would therefore be more likely to engage in leadership acts. Thus, Swift (1964) reviews data that show that some children become leaders of children's groups in part because of their very high interest in the types of games being played. Hollander and Julian (1969) also find that interest in the group activity is related to leadership behavior.

LEADERSHIP STYLES AND ORIENTATION

On the other hand, the sort of interest and involvement in the task which leads to the evocation of leadership behavior may be very general. That is, for some persons success at the group's task, no matter what that task happens to be, may be of very great importance. It may be of such great significance for them, in fact, that other potential satisfactions which might be derived from group activity, such as warm and pleasant social interaction, tend to be ignored in their pursuit of task success. Such people would also be highly likely to contribute what ability they have to help the group attain its goals. Fiedler (1967) and his associates have developed an instrument to measure leadership styles and motivation toward the attainment of the goals of groups in general. It is unfortunate that Fiedler has not yet conducted research which might show the relative frequency of such motivation among leaders and followers. Yet his extensive work does represent a major contribution to the understanding of the complexities of leader-member relationships and demonstrates the importance of motivation in determining the behavior of leaders. The instrument, termed the LPC Scale, consists of a series of semantic differential type items, in which the respondent is asked to evaluate the one person among all of those with whom he has ever worked with whom he would *least* prefer to work, i.e., his least preferred co-worker. This least preferred co-worker is rated on such traits as pleasantness, friendliness, helpfulness, enthusiasm, and so on. Since all of these trait-adjectives are ones which call for an evaluation of the person being rated, the instrument measures how positively or how negatively a person feels toward his least preferred co-worker. The person who indicates that he feels negatively toward his least preferred co-worker, who indicates low esteem for this person (low LPC) is someone who considers this person's presumably poor performance in joint tasks to be so important that he rejects him. In short, he considers task achievement to be very important. On the other hand, the person who rates the least preferred co-worker positively and has relatively high esteem for him (high LPC) is someone who is saying, in essence, the task is not all that important, and thus he does not reject a person who performs poorly on tasks in the group. Accordingly, Feidler reports that low LPC people who happen to be in leadership positions feel much more positively about a group and about themselves when the group has succeeded on a task than when it has failed. High LPC people in leadership positions don't show this difference.

Interaction of Situational Favorability and Leadership Style

More to our central point, Fiedler reports that when a group is faced with a difficult situation so that its ability to attain its goals is very severely threatened, low LPC leaders are more likely than are high LPC leaders to engage in acts of task leadership. When there is no great threat to the group's attainment of its goals, then the low LPC leaders' motivation to assist the group by means of task relevant behaviors is not aroused. This difference is most clearly shown in a study by Sample and Wilson (1965). They conducted a course in experimental psychology in which the students were organized into four-man teams, with one student appointed in each group to be the leader. On the routine laboratory problems in which full instructions and ample time were given the students, no difference was evident in the behavior of low and high LPC leaders. However, at the end of the course, the students were given a laboratory problem with no manual to guide them and with less time to complete it than they previously had had. Furthermore, this last problem counted more toward their final course grade than had the previous problems. In the early planning stages of work on this much more stressful group task, the low LPC leaders gave more directions and attempted more solutions to problems than did the high LPC leaders. During these early stages, when the anxiety was highest and the need for planning the greatest, the low LPC leaders engaged in acts of task leadership, but tended to be less interested than were the high LPC leaders in praising or supporting the other group members. During the later stages of work on the task, the LPC negative leaders became more supportive of the other group members than did the LPC positive, once the group had developed a good tack, all that was needed was a "pat on the back" to get the group through. On the other hand, the LPC positive leaders began in these later phases to make suggestions about the problem, when it was too late. This difference in reactions of the two types of leaders cannot be attributed to ability, since Fiedler finds that there is no difference between the groups with respect to intelligence or any other ability. Not surprisingly, Sample and Wilson found that the groups led by LPC negative leaders performed better on these stressful group tasks, while there was no difference between the two groups on the less stressful tasks. Burke (1966) assembled groups of students to work on group tasks of decoding Morse code into words and sentences. These groups were to compete against each other. However, only the leader was given instructions about the task, so that the other group members did not have L.O.S.s about how to attain the goal. If the group leader was an LPC negative leader, the group members rated the leader as being more effective than if he was an LPC positive leader. In addition, Fiedler cites other data that suggest that when a group is in an extremely difficult position, it is more likely to attain its goal if it is led by an LPC negative leader. If these findings are borne out in further studies, it would be expected that leaders of groups in very difficult circumstances would tend to be LPC negative; the high LPC leaders would have been rejected for ineffectuality, or their groups might ultimately have fallen apart. Obviously, the success of the low LPC leaders would tend to increase the motivation of the members to stay in the group, and, as a consequence, the group might become generally more effective in attaining its goals, independently of the leader's LPC score.

We have so far seen two types of motivation which eventuate in acts of task leadership; the first was interest in the particular task at hand, the other was a general interest in succeeding at group tasks, this latter motivation being especially important when the group is faced with difficulty in achieving its goals. Both of these sources of motivation concern the group task directly. But, of course, there are other sources of motivation to engage in acts of task leadership. Cartwright and Zander (1968) mention a person's "hunger for power" as a determinant of seeking the leadership role. Gibb (1969), in his review of the relationship between personality and leadership, concludes that leaders tend, on the whole, to score higher on measures of dominance. If one assumes that such measures do reflect a desire on the part of a person to be in dominant positions, then we have evidence for Cartwright and Zander's speculation, which is not far from common sense.

Relationship of Sense of Competence to Leader Behavior

We have seen how ability and motivation are related to a person's tendency to engage in acts of task leadership. Another factor is implied by the central concern of the last chapter, the sense of competence. An individual may have the ability to give task leadership; and he may desire to do so. But, if he does not believe that his acts of leadership will be accepted by other people, he will not be likely to engage in them. Or, he would be less likely to attempt to lead if he did not believe that his ideas were correct and effective ones. Both of these beliefs about probable effectiveness are influenced by the sense of competence and self-esteem. Thus, Gibb (1969), in his review of the literature, indicates that one of the most consistent findings in the study of leadership is that leaders have higher self-esteem than do non-leaders.

Another possible reason for the association between self-esteem and leadership concerns the leader's communication of his confidence that the group will, indeed, successfully attain its goals. This sort of communication is especially important in those situations in which the group members do not have any direct way of determining just how much progress they are making. For instance, stockholders in a firm which is making very long term investments may have little immediate basis for knowing how sound the investments are (cf. March and Simon, 1958). In such cases, the members will often tend to rely on the leader's confidence as a way of gauging their progress or ability to attain their goals. Thus, highly confident leaders, leaders with high self-esteem, would tend to reduce the group's anxiety. Torrance (1961) reports that when groups are in stressful situations, the members strongly desire to have their leader remain calm and function "as usual." Stotland and Kobler (1965) found that in a mental hospital, the staff was very sensitive to the degree of confidence the medical director had in himself and in the fate of the hospital. Obviously, leaders of high self-esteem are more likely to show such confidence.

Communication Effectiveness

Implicit in our discussion of leadership has been the idea that leaders and followers are able to communicate with one another. Obviously, without communication, there can be no leadership. But, further, the better able a person is to communicate with others, the more likely he is to be able to engage in acts of leadership. He is in a better position to gain information, to indicate possible ways of attaining the group goal, or to coordinate and organize the group's actions to attain its goals. Sommer (1961) finds that leaders tend to sit at the heads of tables in small discussion groups. The person at the head of the table is better able to maintain eye contact with others, thereby facilitating smooth communication. Sommer also reports that the person who sits at the head of the conference table in jury deliberations tends to have greater influence over the outcome of the deliberations. Shaw (1954) reports that in groups which work on tasks with experimentally controlled patterns of communication, the person who is in the best position to communicate with other members comes to be regarded as the leader by other group members. He is the person who is best able to coordinate the various bits and pieces of problem-relevant information which the individual members have. In addition to such physical factors which control the networks and patterns of communication, there may be more subtle factors which help to determine the effectiveness of communication and thus will influence leadership effectiveness. One such element may be the degree of commonality of schemas between the leaders and others in the group. Runkel (1956) showed that commonality of conceptual dimensions between people increases their ability to communicate effectively with one another. This need for common schemas may be an additional factor underlying the finding that the I.Q. of leaders tends to be only somewhat higher than that of other members of a group. If there is a great discrepancy between the leader's I.Q. and that of the other group members, the leader may simply be unable to translate his ideas into terminology readily understood by his co-workers. This need for common schemas between leaders and followers may also underly Hollander's (1964) finding that naval cadets who are asked to nominate fellow cadets either to be the commanders of their ships or to serve under them if they were commanders, tended to select the same cadets for both types of positions. The ability to communicate made it easier for them to view the other fellow in either position.

Now that we have examined some of the situational and personal factors which are associated with task leadership, it is time to review the assumptions we have been making about leadership. The discussion was begun with an example of a newly formed group having a goal but very few ideas regarding specific methods of attaining it. It was noted that the members typically tend to accept the first reasonable ideas presented in order to reduce the anxiety brought about by this ambiguity. In ongoing groups, a similar process occurs when a group is faced with a new or changed situation in which the most effective manner in which to proceed is not clear to the members. They are especially likely, then, to turn to a leader for guidance. In both the newly formed and ongoing groups, this heightened dependence on a leader can be viewed as an outcome of perception by the members that they themselves do not possess appropriate L.O.S.s concerning efficient means of goal attainment. In other words, their own sense of competence with respect to their group's attainment of its goal is low; and their own sense of competence about the effectiveness of their own particular actions in the group is also low. How can they know what to do themselves if the manner of the group's functioning to attain its goals has not yet been clearly established? Thus, the acceptance of the leader's ideas can only enhance their sense of competence. To the extent that they are involved in the group's attainment of its goal, their sense of competence will be raised by their perception that the group can now move toward its goal. To the extent that the leader's suggestions about the group's actions indicate to a given group member what he can do in the group, the leader's suggestions raise the member's own sense of competence.

EMERGENT LEADERS AND THREAT TO MEMBERS' COMPETENCE

Let us now carry the story a bit farther to examine those cases in which the members are not without ideas about how the group can act to attain its goals or how they can act in the group. The situation faced by the group is similar enough to situations previously experienced by the group members so that they have at least some schemas to guide them in their own activities or in what they believe the group should do. This might involve junior executives meeting with a senior executive about a new labor-management negotiating session; a chef meeting with his cooks to plan a banquet; a committee of social workers having to decide on the treatment to be given to a juvenile delinquent. All of these situations illustrate instances in which the members have some ideas, based on their previous experience, as to how the group should act and how they themselves should act.

In most such cases, the schemas that individual members have differ among themselves because of the sheer variety of human experience. There are a number of ways by which groups move beyond this diversity of points of view to attain some mutually agreed upon, unified way of functioning as a group. Before discussing them, however, a central problem which is involved to a greater or lesser degree in any course of action which a group settles on should be noted. It is that an individual member's sense of competence may well be threatened by the development of a particular mode of operation which the group adopts in its attempt to attain its goals. This threat results from the fact that, aside from the leader, no member is likely to have all of his own ideas about the best course of action for the group accepted. If an individual's ideas are not adopted, a threat to his self-esteem occurs for a number of reasons. First, the rejection of an idea of his implies a rejection of him as a person, since most people have a schema associating liking and agreement. The dislike which is then implied by the rejection presents a threat to the person's self-esteem and sense of competence. Second, the rejection of an idea of his implies also that it is invalid or unrealistic, since agreed-upon ideas are perceived as being more real, more true, than those about which there is disagreement. Third, if the group develops a way of functioning which specifies in some detail just how an individual is to perform his particular job in the group, then an additional sort of threat can develop. If the individual initially had schemas about how he might best contribute and how he should perform his own job, a group decision may not include these alternatives of action which he had envisioned as possible. As was seen in the previous chapter, such restrictions on the freedom of action alternatives tend to diminish the sense of competence and self-esteem. And finally, the person whose ideas are accepted by the group tends to be given higher esteem by the others. The giving of high respect to the task leader indicates to each of the members that they are not as highly respected by the group as they would have been had the group totally accepted their ideas. This too presents a threat to the members' self-esteem.

With all of these factors threatening a diminution in the self-esteem of the members of the group, how can a situation in which such low senses of competence are generated among the members that they no longer can function well in the group be avoided? How do group members avoid the high levels of anxiety which result from a lowering of self-esteem? The answers to these questions depend on the type of group task, on the social organizational context within which the group functions, and most basically, on the way it goes about developing L.O.S.s about how to attain its goals. Let us now examine some examples of how this occurs.

Role of Socio-Emotional Leaders

Let us deal first with groups in which there is a free and open discussion on a group problem, in which no one person has been designated as the leader. To a certain extent, the members of the group will feel anxiety about the lack of a clear path to the goal; the very lack of agreement among the members tends to keep this anxiety high because the lack of unanimity raises questions about the validity of any single solution. To be sure, the anxiety level may not be as high as would be the case in groups in which the members lack any schemas at all about appropriate action, but it is still likely to be high enough to generate a tendency to accept the ideas of the first person who sets forth reasonable solutions. Bales (1953) and Bales and Slater (1955), who studied such groups, found that a task leader soon emerges; the person who talks the most is typically regarded by the members as the task leader, and they accord him a high degree of respect. Typically, at first this person is also well liked by the other group members, although he is relatively less well liked than respected. After all, he has helped the group members to attain their goal (cf. Slater, 1955). However, he also presents a threat to the self-esteem of the group members. It is his ideas which supersede their own. As this becomes evident to the members, their esteem for him quickly drops. Bales reports that at the first of a series of meetings of such groups, the task leader has about a 50-50 chance of being the best liked man in the group. By the fourth meeting, his chances have dropped to 8.5 per cent. Thus, the group members tend to accept his ideas, and respect him, but they probably do not like him.

If matters were to rest at this point, the members would experience lowered self-esteem, cease to be highly active in the group, become anxious, and probably quit, leaving the situation. There can be little doubt that on occasion, groups do break up at this point. However, often another "solution" emerges. Another person in the group sometimes acts to bolster the self-esteem of the other group members. Bales has found that this person is one who listens to others, tends to agree with them, and makes jokes. He communicates to them that he likes them, that their ideas are worth listening to, thus bolstering their self-esteem. He tends to like everyone in the group, not discriminating among the members in terms of their differential contribution to the group's attainment of its goals. As a consequence, he is typically the best liked person in the group. Bales and others have dubbed this person the social-emotional leader, the group leader with respect to taking care of the emotional problems that emerge in the group. The social-emotional leader does not limit himself to soothing the egos of people who have been threatened by the rise of the task leader; he also acts to bolster good relationships between other members of the group, and tends to be generally supportive of the group members. As was suggested above, without this leader, the group is more likely to fall apart. Thus, this type of leader is sometimes also called the group maintenance leader.

Determinants of Need for a Social-Emotional Leader

Since a large part of the social-emotional leader's function in the group is to sustain the self-esteem and sense of competence of the members in the face of the implicit threat from the task leader, the intensity of this threat will determine in part how the social-emotional leader will act in the group. The relationship between the actions of the two types are best illustrated in a study of Burke

(1967). He assembled small groups of students who were then faced with the task of agreeing upon a decision as to what to do about a juvenile delinquent whose case they were discussing. Burke determined who the task and social-emotional leaders were by giving the participants a questionnaire in which they described the behavior of various group members. He also had trained observers rating the group for their interest in the case of the juvenile delinquent. The degree of threat from the task leader was measured in terms of the proportion of group members who were rated by their peers as making many attempts to engage in acts of task leadership. Those in the group who were contributing a large number of ideas independently of the task leader and whose ideas were not being accepted because the task leader's suggestions were, were obviously going to feel threatened by the task leader. The greater the proportion of such people in a given group, the more the group atmosphere could be said to be threatening. In groups with high threat, the task leader was less well liked than in groups of low threat ($r = -.73$). Further, the more threat there was in a group, the less did the task leader act positively and supportively, i.e., less like a social-emotional leader. He was, rather, fending off the competition from the other "idea-men" in the group to such a degree that he tended to ignore the other members' feelings to an even greater extent than he otherwise would. In fact, the more of an idea man the task leader was, the less he was liked. It is not surprising, then, that in the groups with higher levels of threat, the social-emotional leader avoided putting forth recommendations and ideas of his own and acted in a more distinctively supportive, group maintaining way. In fact, the more of an idea-man the task leader was, the more the social-emotional leader had to play his distinctive role. It is very interesting that this interrelationship between behavior of the task leader and that of the social-emotional leader occurred only in those groups in which there was a relatively low degree of interest in the group task. In groups characterized by very high interest in accomplishing their task of deciding on the fate of the juvenile delinquent, the sense of competence of the members was apparently so dependent on the quality of the group's decision that they were not threatened by the rejection of their own ideas by the group. If the leader's ideas were effective, they were quite willing to let them prevail.

Symbiotic Relationship of Task and Group Maintenance Leaders

It would be incorrect to give the impression that the differentiation of the actions of the two types of leaders being discussed here leads to a split in the group. Obviously, in such groups both types of leadership are needed to maintain movement toward the goal. Further, it appears that the two types of leaders recognize that both are needed in the group. Bales and Slater (1955) found that the two types of leaders interacted to a high degree with one another, and tended to agree with one another. It is as if the social-emotional leader absorbs the suggestions made by the rank and file, while at the same time supporting the ideas of the task leader. Since the social-emotional leader is well liked by the group members, his public agreement with the task leader's suggestions helps to gain them acceptance by the group members. In turn, the task leader derives support for his own self-esteem which might be threatened by the almost-dislike which is accorded him by the other members of the group. Thus, Bales and Slater (1955) found that members of groups in which this symbiotic relationship develops between the two types of leaders feel more positively about their groups, are more satisfied with them. One might also expect that such groups tend to attain their group goals more often than do those groups in which the two leaders do not hit it off. Little research has been done on this problem, although Ghiselli and Lodahl (1958) showed that groups did better on a toy railroad if the members were less threatened because few of them thought that their own ideas were as good as the task leader's. If, on the other hand, the two leaders do not recognize or work out a mutually satisfying relationship, then the group will tend to function more poorly and may even break up.

Acts of group maintenance are of course engaged in by others in the group in addition to the social-emotional leader. He happens to be the "specialist," not the monopolist. Others can indicate acceptance and esteem to group members who feel rejected, angry, or tense for any reason. Levinger (1964) has data indicating that in two person groups, such as husband-wife, both members engage in social-emotional acts about equally.

Sometimes such acts can take the form of joking, of just having fun. Such group maintenance actions are often differentiated from actions which are designed mainly to propel the group toward its goals. A number of studies have shown that in descriptions of behavior of people in groups, it is possible to distinguish the two types of actions (Gibb, 1969). Sometimes, however, some actions in groups may serve both functions: "Let's go along with Jim's idea!" (Bales, 1953).

Characteristics of Social-Emotional Leaders

What sort of person tends to become a social-emotional leader? If, as has just been pointed out, any member may engage in acts which help maintain the group, what sort of person is likely to

Leading charismatically. Photograph by Irwin Nash.

emerge as the specialist in this sort of action? Unfortunately, not much research has been done to answer this question since, in most of the research on leadership, little distinction has been made between the task leader and the social-emotional leader. Thus, it is possible that some of the same characteristics which were described earlier as distinguishing leaders from followers also apply to social-emotional leaders. However, it is somewhat doubtful that social-emotional leaders necessarily are better at the group's activities than are the followers; by the same token, they might not have higher I.Q.s. On the other hand, it is probably quite likely that they do have high self-esteem, since it was seen in the previous chapter that such people have more positive attitudes toward other people. Furthermore, Fiedler's (1967) work suggests that people with high LPC scores are more likely to be concerned with the social-emotional and supportive aspects of the group's functioning. This seems quite reasonable as a concomitant of the fact that they tend to evaluate even the "least" of the members of the group positively. This relationship, however, has not been demonstrated empirically. There is indirect evidence that people who turn out to be social-emotional leaders differ from others in stable ways which are sometimes recognizable to other people. Shovel (1960) found that soldiers who knew more about who liked whom in their outfits were rated by their peers as having more leadership potential than were less knowledgeable soldiers. McClintock (1963) determined that ROTC students who had held a number of leadership positions outside of ROTC showed more positive feelings toward other group members during a discussion. Swift (1964) cites data to indicate that some children who are leaders consistently have a high interest both in the games they play and in the needs of other children. However, little is known about what distinctive features of personality or other types of individual differences lie behind these differences. On the other hand, Hollander (1964) found that naval cadets tended not to choose their most liked co-cadet as the person they would select as captain of a ship they were on; the cadets perceived some sort of difference between liking someone and wanting him as a task leader.

Leaders Who Serve Both Task and Maintenance Functions

To sum up the previous pages, we have seen that one way in which groups may meet the problem presented by the threat of a strong, directive task leader is through the emergence of a social-emotional leader. There is no intrinsic reason why such a leader must arise in any given group. Having someone who will fill this role is partly a matter of the accidental composition of the group and of who perceives the need to take care of group maintenance problems. Some groups may fall apart for lack of such a leader. By the same token, it is possible that some task leaders may behave in such ways as to take care of the very problems they create, or even to prevent their arising. Bales (1952) found that if a highly active task leader not only presents ideas about the group task but also takes time to listen to the other members of the group, to indicate that he considers their ideas worth listening to, then he is better liked than other task leaders. In a sense, he is combining to some extent the jobs of the two types of leader. In fact, Burke's (1967) work described above indicates that if the task leader does not specialize to a high degree, the social-emotional leader also does not specialize to a high degree in group maintenance activities. The people who become such combination types of leaders are probably quite mature and substantial people to perform this dual role, but no research has been done to identify factors associated with their distinct roles. In any case, the fact that such combinatory leaders are found does indicate a second way in which the problem of this sort of threat is handled.

Pressures for a One-Leader System

In the situation studied by Bales, the emergence of leaders who took on both task and social-emotional duties was primarily a function of the talents and dispositions of the task leader; if he could not or would not engage in both these types of behavior, a social-emotional leader was likely to arise. However, in some situations there are strong forces to have only one leader. He may be the formal leader; he may have a special position in the group; he may have power, or communications may be directed only to him and so forth. These factors tend to thrust him into the position of being the task leader. For instance, if he is at the center of a communication network, he may be in the best position to know about important details relevant to successful pursuit of the task. When one person is thus thrust into the leadership position, he often has the option of becoming mainly a task leader, or both a task and social-emotional leader in the way that we have just described. He does not usually have the option of becoming only a social-emotional leader because in doing so he would lose status, as we shall see, if he turned the task leadership over to someone else.

However, in some special cases, a formally designated leader might survive in the position primarily as a social-emotional leader.

In many real-life situations, this leader is often a person who has power over the other group members: he is the foreman, supervisor, teacher, employer. He can determine whether others in the group gain their individual goals, such as pay raises and promotions. He can often set up standards which must be adhered to by the group members if they are to be permitted by him to achieve their goals. In such cases, the leader presents even more of a threat to the sense of competence of the members, since he can determine the degree to which their actions are effective in attaining their goals.

This threat to the self-esteem of the group members would also obtain, of course, in a situation in which another person just had power over the group members, even if he did not, in fact, engage in any acts of leadership. In such cases, the threat will be even greater since the powerful person would not increase the members' sense of competence by helping in the attainment of the group goal, with which the members are likely to be involved. However, in most cases in real life, people in positions of power combine leadership with power; the executive, the supervisor, and the foreman usually have power and exercise leadership. More exactly, in the situations that have been researched and are reported below, some mixture of the two is involved. Obviously, one consequence of the threat to the self-esteem of group members under such leadership is that the group members might try to turn to social-emotional leaders. Often in large organizations such leaders emerge through informal group processes, through unofficial friendship groups which spontaneously spring up on the job. In some cases, all the members of such informal groups engage in acts of social-emotional leadership for one another.

Significance of Support from a Powerful Task Leader

Yet, the support that people derive from such informal groups is often not enough to compensate for the threat from the powerful leader. When the leader of the group both exercises leadership and has power, supportive behavior from the powerful leader himself may be extremely important for the group members' self-esteem. There are a number of reasons why supportive actions by the powerful task leader may be so vital to the self-esteem of the members. First, if he has power, not only does his supportive behavior have the usual effect of bolstering self-esteem; it also implies that he will use his power in a beneficial way, thus further reducing anxiety which might result from the expectation that this power might be used to block the attainment of important goals. And, of course, negative nonsupportive behavior on the part of a powerful leader implies that he might use his power to frustrate the members' attempts at goal attainment; this potential blockage may present so much of a threat to the person that supportive behavior by the others may simply be inadequate. Second, in many cases, the powerful leader may be expert in the area of group activities. Thus, his praise, or acceptance, of any of the group members' ideas leads to a rise in their self-esteem. Third, warm social relationships with the powerful leader may lead the other group members to feel more similar to him, to share in some of his power and status, and thus to bolster their self-esteem, since as we saw in Chapter 8, liking, interaction, and communication are all associated in schemas with similarity.

Impact of a Combinatory Leader

Obviously, people who occupy such powerful leadership positions vary in the degree to which they also act as social-emotional leaders. Thus, we are back to our main concern—the variations in the degree to which the foreman, the boss, the supervisor, emphasizes the social-emotional as well as the task role. If a leader in such a position works at both roles, he becomes more popular with his men and they are more satisfied with their jobs. Likert (1959) has reviewed many studies of leadership of foremen in industry which lead to the conclusion that foremen who take the time to develop good personal relationships with their workers, who take greater interest in their workers' personal needs, who listen to them, and praise them, are better liked by the men and have workers who are more satisfied with their jobs. Likewise, Stouffer, Suchman, deVinney, Star, and Williams (1949) found that sergeants were more positively evaluated by their men if they were more sympathetic to them and developed warmer social relationships with them.

Formal, powerful leaders who function as social-emotional leaders not only are well liked, but raise the self-esteem, the sense of competence, of their fellow group members. Furthermore, in some cases, the work is so structured that the high sense of competence leads to a higher rate of production. Likert (1959), for example, found that foremen who acted as social-emotional leaders, who were considerate of their men, tended to have higher rates of production than did those foremen who did not engage in such supportive activities.

Leader Motivation and Group Success

Some further evidence showing the relationship between good social-emotional leadership and the degree of the group's attainment of its goals comes from research using Fiedler's (1967) measure of the leader's motivation to have the group attain its goals. High LPC leaders are those who are relatively more motivated toward maintaining good relations in the group, rather than toward emphasizing the group's attainment of its goals. Thus, formal ongoing work groups led by high LPC leaders would tend to have higher production and do better as a group. This does not contradict what we said earlier about the effectiveness of low LPC leaders, since their presence was associated with better production specifically when the group is faced with a serious problem and the group members do not have clear ideas on how to proceed. Fiedler's investigations disclosed that companies in which the chairman of the board of directors could be characterized as having high esteem for his least preferred co-worker had better profit records than did those which had a low LPC chairman. Research chemists working under a high LPC director had better production records than did those who worked under a low LPC one. Notice that the work of the boards of directors and of the research chemists is of such a nature that it is highly likely that those working under leaders' supervision had some, and perhaps many, ideas about their own roles as well as about how the group should best proceed. A good social-emotional leader would be needed under such circumstances.

Burke (1965) showed this relationship between the social-emotional leadership of high LPC leaders and the effectiveness of groups in an experimentally controlled situation in which the group was presented tasks about which all the group members could feel competent. These tasks involved either decoding a message in Morse code or discussing how best to survive in space. Students formed into groups under high LPC leaders rated their leaders as more effective than did those with low LPC leadership.

Part of the effectiveness of groups working on problems about which many of the group members feel competent stems, obviously, from the fact that the group members are in a position to make unique contributions to the solution of problems. A good social-emotional leader will facilitate this effect, thereby increasing the creativity of the group and the likelihood that it will be able to solve difficult problems. Thus, Anderson and Fiedler (1964) showed that groups who function under leaders who make explicit attempts to elicit participation from all the members turn in more creative solutions to such problems as devising ways to become famous and generating unusual uses for common objects. Likewise, Maier and Solem (1952) have shown that groups are more likely to solve difficult puzzle type problems if the leaders protect the expressions of minority points of view. This reason for the increased productivity of these groups functions in addition to the effects of the increased sense of competence that the group members feel because of the treatment they receive from the leaders.

Productivity, Leadership Style, and Situational Favorability

Fiedler (1967) has also maintained that low LPC leaders, those more interested in the task than in a good atmosphere in the group, generate high production in groups in which they have "everything going for them": where, for example, they have high power over the others; where they are well accepted by the group members; and where the group's task is clearly defined so that the leader has ample basis for expecting his directives to be followed. In fact, there is evidence to support this: it has been found that directors of chemistry labs with highly structured tasks, business managers of companies who are highly accepted by their staffs and by boards of directors, and managers of super-market meat departments who are well accepted by their workers, all have more productive groups if they are low LPC leaders. However, Fiedler (1967) also has evidence that in such situations low LPC leaders act much like social-emotional leaders! On the other hand, the evidence indicates that high LPC leaders in such situations engage in more acts of task leadership than do the low LPC leaders. In other words, in such situations of very high favorability for the leader, the low LPC and high LPC leaders reverse the type of leadership style they exhibit under more stressful, less favorable circumstances. The net result of this reversal is that in such situations, the low LPC leader—who now is acting like a social-emotional leader—has more productive groups than do high LPC leaders, who are now acting as task leaders. Thus, the total array of data appears to be consistent: leaders who are considerate of their workers have more effective groups than do those who are not so considerate.

This analysis raises the further question of just why such a reversal occurs. Here we can only speculate, along with Fiedler. Under very favorable circumstances, the low LPC leader may have his primary need for group attainment satisfied as the group begins to produce well so that he now feels free to relate in a relaxed and open way with the group to whom he probably feels grateful. On the other hand, the high LPC leader now feels that people are relating so well in the group that he can turn more of his attention to the problem of the group task. But, all of this is speculative.

After an individual has been in many groups and has experienced a variety of leaders as well as a variety of forms of power exercised over him, he is quite likely to acquire a schema to the effect that his self-esteem is relatively higher when the leaders like him, are supportive of him, and act as social-emotional leaders. Thus, he may attempt to make the leader feel and act as supportively to him and the others as possible. Such attempts are more likely to occur when the leader also has high power, since under these conditions having the leader exercise his power in a way beneficial to the members is more critical. An additional source of motivation for attempts to induce a powerful leader to increase social-emotional acts is simply that by influencing the leader in this way the individual increases his sense of competence. The very act of influencing the leader is an indicator of competence: "I'm not afraid of my boss; I can wrap him around my finger."

Task Specialization and Threat Reduction

So far, we have taken a look at three ways in which the threat from a task leader can be mitigated: the emergence of a social-emotional leader; the development of informal friendship groups among the members; and the task leader's also functioning as a social-emotional leader. Each of these processes operates to reduce or prevent the lowering of self-esteem which may result from the actions of the task leader through the introduction of supportive social-emotionally oriented actions. However, the threat presented by an active task leader may be reduced in yet another fashion—through the development of a specialization of jobs within the group. Until this point in the discussion, we have been treating the actions of the task leader broadly, as if they had implications both for the general goals of the group and for the specific activities of the individual members. However, it is not necessary that a task leader communicate with respect to both the group's and the individual member's tasks. Often he can restrict his communications and directives to matters having only to do with the group's overall objective or task. In that case the individual members can have considerable freedom of action concerning the manner in which they structure and develop the nature of their own work. In the last chapter we saw that a sense of freedom regarding behavioral options can increase a person's sense of competence and self-esteem. Thus, the leader who gives his workers considerable autonomy can thereby raise their self-esteem. Kahn and Katz (1953) and Zander and Quinn (1962) surveyed a variety of studies of foremen and other supervisors in industry, offices, construction crews, etc., and found that foremen with both the most satisfied workers and the highest producing workers were those who delegated more authority and checked up less on their workers. These successful foremen spent their time doing jobs quite different from those of their workers, jobs that were distinctly their own: planning and organizing the work and working for promotions and other benefits for their group members. Thus, they not only gave the workers greater freedom, but they also concentrated their efforts on the group's attainment of its general goals.

In addition to raising the self-esteem of group members, the effectiveness of these foremen may have been due to the fact that they devoted more time to the technical aspects of the jobs that were distinctively theirs, such as planning the flow of work.

Member Autonomy and Satisfaction

Morse and Reimer (1956) showed that an increase in the amount of autonomy given to workers can increase their sense of competence and make them feel more positive about their jobs, while a loss of autonomy generates changes in the opposite directions. These researchers worked with two divisions in the offices of an insurance company which did more or less the same kind of work. In one, they trained the office managers to give office clerks more autonomy as individual workers, and more possibilities of influencing decisions about the organization of their division's work. After a period of six months, these workers felt more positive about their jobs, their supervisor, and their company, as compared to the pre-autonomy period—and fewer of them quit. On the other hand, in the other division, the supervisors reduced whatever autonomy the workers had. As a result they became less positive about their jobs, their supervisors, and their firm both as compared to the period before the diminution in their autonomy and to the group that gained in autonomy.

However, the two divisions did not show any change in productivity as a consequence of the change in autonomy. The researchers argue that the work was so organized in these offices, and in relation to the rest of the firm, that the workers simply could not have a very great influence on productivity at all. This finding indicates a restriction on the findings reported by Kahn and Katz (1953) which suggest that giving workers autonomy increases production by increasing the worker's sense of competence. In some cases, the work is so organized and structured that its rate cannot be altered.

The specialization of the jobs of the "leader" and the member can sometimes take another form. This form is one in which the leader acts as a chairman, simply indicating who is to communicate at a given time, making sure that the communication process does not break down. People in such roles are often termed chairmen, presidents, although obviously not all chairmen fulfill this function and some chairmen also are task and social-emotional leaders. However, the coordinator of communication is not a leader in the sense that we have been using the term here. Nevertheless, by his functioning, he may increase the self-esteem of the members because he assures them a platform, a voice, an opportunity to try to contribute to the group's activities.

In the previous chapter, it was noted that people attempt to maintain or even to increase their degree of autonomy and freedom from constraint. The same motivation no doubt obtains when the potential threat to the person's freedom stems from a leader, especially from one with power. The rebelliousness, the negativeness of children may in part stem from this motivation. The attempts of all sorts of subordinates, soldiers, prisoners, and workers to find areas of autonomy in their jobs, to find some form of "self-expression," may in part result from these efforts. By acting differently from others or from the powerful person's expectations, the individual may manifest his attempt to maintain or expand his freedom, to enhance his sense of competence and his self-esteem. Sometimes, the effort to establish autonomy takes organized forms, as in the case of strikes or rebellions, in which the individual's quest for freedom is mediated by means of the group's attainment of freedom from powerful persons, both for itself as a group and for its members as individuals.

Democratic and Authoritarian Styles of Leader Behavior

To reduce the threat to his fellow group members which his actions may imply, then, a leader can act with consideration for them, as a social-emotional leader; he can give them much autonomy on their jobs, or he can arrange for them to contribute to the decisions about the group task *per se* by being receptive to their suggestions. In some cases, a given person might engage in all these behaviors. Such leaders could be termed democratic leaders, in contrast to authoritarian leaders, who act in none of these ways. In fact, the latter are often described as inconsiderate and domineering. Thus, a democratic leader is likely to have a much more positive effect on groups than will an authoritarian leader. This is best demonstrated in a study by White and Lippitt (1960), in which boys' clubs were led by adults either in a democratic or authoritarian manner. Under the democratic orientation, the leaders allowed the boys autonomy to work on their group task in their own way, organized the group so that it could come to its own decisions about the group task, and were warm to and considerate of the boys. The authoritarian leader told the boys just what to do, allowed no group decisions, and was rather cold to them. Consequently, when working with a democratic leader the boys were more positive and supportive with one another; they were less tense and hostile, less hostile to outsiders; and worked on the task even when the leader was absent. However, the boys under the autocratic leader produced more than did the others, again showing that rate of production is not simply a matter of high motivation.

THE STABILIZATION OF LEADERSHIP

Our next concern is with the issue of the stabilization of leadership, the factors which will determine whether or not the same person will continue to be in the leadership position. It has already been noted that the more effective, competent leaders tend to be retained, while less competent ones are replaced, either officially or informally. However, there are factors other than evident expertise which are also involved in the stabilization of leadership. Before examining the first of these factors, it will be useful to reiterate some of the effects which the passage of time has on the relationship among group members.

Schemas Regarding Patterns of Social Relationships

It has been seen that as persons interact in groups, they acquire schemas about each other's qualities and characteristics and about the patterns of social relationships which typically occur. Patterns concerning who likes whom, who talks to whom, who cracks jokes, who helps and to what degree, and so forth, are established and learned. The group members come to positively evaluate these schemas with the passage of time, as they become more and more familiar. Further, there are pressures to try to protect these schemas from contradiction, to minimize the amount of change in the pattern of social relationships.

Schemas concerning the person in the group who fills the leadership position can be viewed as just a special case of the acquisition of schemas about the pattern of interpersonal processes. Group members tend to agree on who has the best ideas, i.e., on who is the task leader. For example, Lippitt, Polansky, and Rosen (1952) found that boys in a summer camp had a high degree of agreement as to who their leaders were, and the researchers observed that the agreed-upon leaders actually did lead (cf. Bales, 1953). Likewise, members will come to agree on who is best liked, although the level of agreement may tend to be lower where this judgment is concerned.

Legitimization of Leadership

Just as in the case of other types of schemas about the forms of social interaction among people, the group members will come over time to evaluate positively the schemas which have been developed about who is the leader in the group. This process is often referred to as the legitimization of the leader, i.e., making it right and proper that this person exercise leadership (cf. Verba, 1966). Thus, should an opportunity arise to change leadership, it is likely to be rejected in favor of retention of the current holder of that position, all other factors, such as the leader's competence, being held constant. Thus, Cohen (1961, 1962) had groups work on a task in which the communication links between members were so arranged that one person was central in the communication network. This person became the task leader by virtue of his centrality, since he was the only person who could effectively coordinate the group's work. After they had had some experience with this centralized communication network, they were given a chance to select a leader for a new network. They tended to select the same person who had been central in the previous network. On the other hand, Flament (1956) found that if a group is not allowed to retain the same leader when it shifts from one centralized network to another, the members become dissatisfied with the group. Thus, the process of legitimizing the familiar leader tends to set up forces which operate to keep the same person in the leadership position. Obviously, this process is a self-strengthening one. The greater the familiarity, the greater will be the legitimization, and this will heighten the stability of leader and group which, in turn, makes for still greater familiarity of the leaders. As the old union refrain has it, "Henry is our leader; He shall not be moved, Just like a tree that's standing by the water, He shall not be moved."

Motivation to Maintain a Leadership Position

Thus, any process or event which tends to keep the same person in the leadership position would also contribute to the legitimization of that person as the leader. One such process results from the activity of the leaders themselves in attempting to retain their positions of influence. These attempts are an outcome of the fact that leaders generally find their position need satisfying in a number of ways. They receive support for their ideas from the members of the group who accept their proposals. Secondly, the higher status they have in the group bolsters their self-esteem. They know they are respected by the other members, even though in some cases this respect might be communicated only in subtle ways, such as simply having attention paid to one's pronouncements. Thirdly, since their actions determine in large measure what happens in and to the group, their sense of competence is enhanced through their own acts of leadership. They exert influence over other particular group members, and over the activities of the total group. And, of course, it may often be possible for the leader to direct the group's activities to satisfy his own particular needs; he can slant the manner in which the group's activities attain the group's goals so as to suit his own "style," or to help himself in more material ways. Also, this possibility of guiding the group's activities to suit his own needs implies that a leader has greater behavioral freedom than do followers; to some extent leaders can act when, how, and where they choose to. This increased freedom also has the effect of raising the self-esteem. Obviously, such a list can be extended, but the above examples serve to give a partial catalogue of the benefits which derive from being in leadership positions.

Some people may have aspired to be leaders because they perceived that being a leader would enable them to gain the benefits just described. Others may only discern that they can gain these benefits after they find themselves in the leadership position. In either case, attempts will be made to continue in such a position. The tenacity with which leaders hold on to their positions needs little documentation; the resentment of rivals, the effort to do as good a job as possible, their "communicating" about their achievements, all reflect this desire. In any case, these actions to retain the position tend to stabilize a person in the job of leader, thus increasing his legitimacy.

Method of Attaining a Position of Leadership

There are still other factors in addition to time in office and the motivation of leaders which enhance the legitimacy and therefore the stability of leadership. The way in which a leader emerges in a group may influence the members' perception of his legitimacy. The group members may have H.O.S.s regarding the right and wrong, proper and improper, ways by which leaders may gain their position. These schemas typically have been acquired through general experience and education and observation of the operation of many other groups. The group members' perception of the legitimacy of a leader may be influenced by the degree to which the events which led to his attaining this position were consistent with the relevant schemas (cf. French and Raven, 1959). For instance, in American society, a leader who gains his position by means of an election is perceived as more legitimate than one who simply usurps the job of leader. A leader who is elected fairly is seen as more legitimate than one who has stuffed the ballot boxes.

Legitimization by Another Group

One significant procedure by means of which a person may legitimately acquire leadership status is through the agency of some other group. The latter, legitimizing group is one which has previously been accepted by the group members as a source of information as to what is right and wrong, good or bad. Thus, when this legitimizing group or one of its representatives indicates that a given member of the group in question is the legitimate, rightful leader, then group members will tend to accept him as their leader. A teacher can appoint a student as her "monitor"; an experimenter can appoint one subject in a laboratory group as the leader; the "front office" can appoint a new foreman; and so forth.

Consequences of Leader Legitimization

What are some of the consequences of enhanced stability and legitimacy of leadership? One obvious result is that the members of the group are more likely to accept the leaders' attempts to lead. For instance, leaders who have been in power longer are relatively more likely to be followed. (cf. Hollander, 1960). Leaders who are elected by a group are more likely to have their suggestions followed than those who just usurped power. Raven and French (1958) had coeds work on group tasks under leaders who had been "elected" by them, although, unbeknownst to the subjects, this leader was always a trained assistant and not necessarily the leader actually preferred by the girls. In some cases, this leader continued in that position throughout the group meeting, going around to each coed and suggesting that she either speed up or slow down her work. In other cases, the elected leader "disappeared" and another girl, also a trained assistant pretending to be a subject, just took over the job of leading the group, explaining that the other girl had to leave and that she was simply going to take her place. The usurper then made the same suggestions to the group members as had the elected leader in the other groups. Observation of the groups indicated that the girls obeyed the two types of leaders equally when she was able to directly supervise and observe them, but, when she left and moved on to make suggestions to another group member, only the girls who were operating under the elected leader followed the directives which had been given.

Reduction of Threat Through Legitimization

A second effect of the legitimization of a group leader concerns the degree of threat that the leader presents to the self-esteem of the group members. Legitimization means that the group members accept as right and proper the leader's engaging in acts of leadership, indicating what individuals should do and what the group as a whole should do. By the same token, a given member also must perceive that he himself is *not* engaging in such acts because it is not proper, not legitimate, for him to do so. In other words, the fact that a group member who is not in the leadership position does not engage in acts of task leadership will not be viewed by him as indicative of a constraint on his response freedom or as a reflection on his own competence. Where the leader is seen as highly legitimate this state of affairs will be seen rather as simply a matter of proper and appropriate patterns of behavior. His sense of competence is thus not reduced or threatened by the acceptance of the task leader's guidance. "I could do that, too, but it's not my job"; "I do what he suggests not because he's any better than I, but because he's the boss"; "Oh, he has a right to tell me to do it that way, even though I know of a better way."

The fact that legitimate leaders present less of a threat to the group members than do non-legitimate ones has some very important consequences. First, it obviously increases the degree to which the legitimate leaders' suggestions will be followed, since following them does not threaten self-esteem as much, as the group member will be unlikely to be motivated to raise his self-esteem by defying the leader. Secondly, the group members will have less need for a social-emotional leader. They will not have need for someone who praises their ideas, who affirms them as people, is sympathetic, warm, and friendly. Verba (1966) has pointed out very acutely that this relationship between the legitimacy of leadership and the lack of a threat helps to account for the frequent failure to find social-emotional leaders as very important in well-established groups. As Verba points out, most of the research which shows the importance of social-emotional leadership has been done on groups which are new, which work on new problems, which have no members who are known to each other. In such situations, the degree of threat from the task leader is high and social-emotional leadership is needed. One might even say that legitimization and social-emotional leadership serve the same function in different ways. As a group continues to exist, to attain its goals, to function well under the same leader, the social-emotional leader may become less important to the group.

Inappropriate Retention of Legitimized Leaders

The legitimization of leadership is also a factor which may make the retention of leadership in the face of ineffectuality or incompetence on the part of the leader more likely. Torrance (1961), who examined many reports of groups in situations which severely threatened their survival, found that one of the main difficulties facing such groups was that they continued with the same leader even when the task confronting the group was so new and different that his old competences were no longer relevant. An airline crew downed in a wilderness area may continue to look to the commander for guidance even though he has little if any expertise in tactics of wilderness survival. A Prime Minister of Great Britain, Chamberlain, was kept in power after World War II had broken out even though it was obvious that he showed no aptitude for wartime leadership. Of course, an additional factor leading to the retention of such inappropriate task leaders is that the leaders themselves are highly motivated to retain their positions. Not only because of the reasons we mentioned earlier, but also because of their motivation to attempt to restore their own self-esteem in the face of their failures in the new situation. As Torrance reports, leaders in such situations often attempt to exert more power, to check up more on subordinates, to insist more on the respect of their followers. They may thereby protect their self-esteem, but they do not necessarily help the group. In fact, the leader's altered behavior presents an additional problem to the group, partly because it is changed, partly because his increased exercise of power threatens the group members.

Legitimization and Leader Behavior

A frequently significant consequence of the legitimization of leadership on the leader himself stems from the fact that he no doubt perceives that he is well accepted and regarded as the legitimate leader. This may then lead to a heightened sense of security in his position of leadership. He therefore feels less pressure to demonstrate that he is the leader or to protect his position as leader. Thus, Bales (1953) finds that if a group continues to meet a number of times, the person who is the task leader no longer tends to be the most active participant in the group. He can afford to slack off. Whyte (1943) reports that the leader of a slum gang of long standing did not originate all of the ideas for group activities, although he was the arbiter of their acceptance.

The greater security felt by legitimized leaders may provide yet another factor which will reduce the threat from the task leader. Since there is less need for him to defend his position, he can grant the individual members greater autonomy, and increased autonomy of this sort should enhance their self-esteem. This granting of autonomy to other members no doubt will be more likely to occur when the leader has derived his legitimization by means other than simply having proven himself to be the best task leader. For instance, if the task leader has been appointed by some other, legitimizing group, he may perceive that he does not have to contribute many ideas to the group in order to protect his position. Of course, he would have a strong stake in seeing that he continued to be acceptable to the group that had, in fact, legitimized his leadership. Thus, Carter (1953) found that appointed leaders were less aggressive and put forth fewer ideas than did those who were elected by the group. The latter would see the ideas and contributions of other group members as a threat to their leadership and would try to overwhelm the group with evidence of their own expertise. Of course, if the leader is re-elected several times, he may then "ease off."

Leader Legitimization and Schemas Regarding Group Interaction

The legitimization of a given person in the leadership position is but one instance of the general process whereby members acquire schemas about the interactions of others in the group with one another. In a sense, then, the legitimization of leadership is but part and parcel of the legitimization of the total pattern of interactions among members of a group. However, the term "legitimization" has not traditionally been applied to the schemas which develop regarding the total group interaction, so we will not confuse matters by applying it in a more general way. Other terms, such as social system, institutions, role system, have been used, but none seems to convey the idea exactly.

In any case, regardless of terminology, this analysis raises the possibility that a conflict might arise between the schemas the members have about their established patterns of interaction and attempts at leadership made by a person who has not been legitimized in that position. In such cases, it would be expected that the leadership acts of this person will be rejected. He would be seen as an "upstart," an "outsider," a "stranger trying to take over." This rejection is but a particular instance of the general principle that familiar, valued schemas will be preferred to new, less familiar ones.

The rejection of leadership acts which are in conflict with the group members' social schemas about their interactions is well illustrated in a study by Merei (1949). He and his colleagues observed children in a nursery school to determine which children were the leaders and which were followers. Then for an hour a day for several days running, sets of three or four non-leader children were placed in playrooms by themselves with an adequate number of toys. As would be expected, these segregated children began to develop more or less routinized ways of playing concerning such things as which games to play first, who "owned" which toys, where the toys were kept, and so forth. Once these routines had been established, that is, once the children had acquired schemas about their patterns of interaction, one of the children who had earlier been identified as a leader was introduced into the group to play with them in their segregated playroom. The leaders attempted to assert their leadership through various directive, structuring and controlling behaviors, but these attempts were rejected. The other children tended to ignore the leader's directives. Sometimes, by sheer force, he might impose his will, but such victories "by the sword" were temporary. The message of this study underlines what has been implicit throughout this chapter: leadership is a matter of the group's acceptance of a person as a leader.

However, schemas about well-established patterns of social interaction can be used to the advantage of a leader as well. A group member is less threatened by a directive that comes from a legitimized leader than from one who is not. Likewise, a group member is relatively less threatened by a directive which simply communicates the already established, "legitimized" routines of the group. Not only does the individual value these routines, but also, following such a directive does not lower his status, does not imply that he is less competent than another, that he is losing any of his sense of competence by so doing. Thus, if a would-be leader has some difficulty in getting others to follow his directives, he can arrange for adherence to them by simply indicating that the members are to do what is already routine. Thus, in Merei's study, some of the would-be leaders began to assert their leadership by simply telling the other children to do what the latter were planning to do anyway. By so doing they began to legitimize themselves in the role of leader, since superficially they were "directing" the others. Once the would-be leaders had thus legitimized themselves, some of them went on to suggest slight changes in the routines. They had so legitimized themselves as "order givers" that they could spread out a bit. In fact, some of them went on to become genuine task leaders, proposing new games and new ways of doing things. This "technique" can be used not only by would-be leaders, but by legitimized leaders who for one reason or another may be having some difficulty getting group members to follow their directives. The leader might remind the member that he is urging him to act in a given way "in the name" of the group (cf. Thibaut and Kelley, 1959), rather than as a personal request.

SCHEMAS CONCERNING LEADERSHIP AND POWER

Schemas which are commonly developed concerning leaders are not basically different from many other types of schemas which have previously been discussed. Let us now examine some of the prevalent schemas about leadership and power and the manner in which they function. A prevalent schema suggests that leaders are more competent than are others at tasks relevant to the group activities. As was seen earlier in this chapter, leaders, in fact, do tend to be more competent; therefore, there is ample basis in experience for people to acquire this schema. One direct effect of this schema is to lead those who hold it to expect that a person in a leadership position is more competent than in fact he may actually be. For example, Sherif, White, and Harvey (1955) first determined which boys in a summer camp were leaders by means of systematic observations of their day-to-day interactions. Then they gave all the boys in the camp a test in which the researchers first showed them a target and then covered it. The campers were then to test their pitching skill by throwing balls at the covered target. Under these conditions, however, neither the pitcher nor his audience could tell for certain how accurate any particular performance was. The boys then made estimates of each other's performances. The estimates of the leader's performance were higher than were those of other boys, even though, in fact, they did not do any better than the others. Likewise, Koslin, Haarlow, Karlins, and Pargament (1968) found that boys in a summer camp overestimated the ability of their leaders as riflemen and canoers.

Power and Perceived Competence

Leadership and power are often associated, especially in formal organizations. Thus, people tend to extend the schema regarding competence to include power: powerful people are more competent. The extent to which this schema leads people to attribute competence to more powerful people is illustrated in part of a study conducted by Stotland (1959). Male college students came to the laboratory where they met another subject who was actually a trained assistant. Together they were to plan the layout of a new city, using models. One of them, selected by "chance," but always the trained assistant, was instructed to make no placements of the models, but he did have the right to veto any placements made by the other subject. He actually vetoed placements in a completely arbitrary and random fashion. When the planning was over, most all the subordinate subjects privately described their powerful co-worker as having a high degree of competence in the task and as having made very good suggestions!

The perception of the competence of leaders and people with power adds to the pressure group members feel to continue with their existing leadership. This tendency to perceive the situation in a manner consistent with the schema leads members to overlook errors on the part of the leader, to interpret his mistakes as being the result of factors other than incompetence. Thus, a qualification needs to be put on the earlier findings regarding the replacement of ineffective leaders: they tend to be replaced if their ineffectuality is great, is blatant, or when it is repeated frequently. The blatancy and repetition are needed to overcome the effects of this schema about their high competence. On the other hand, the tendency to keep leaders in their positions may also provide them an opportunity to learn their jobs better, so that the members' perception of the leader's competence begins to have even more support.

This schema even influences a person's perception of his own effectiveness when he is in a position of power or leadership. Gerard (1957) had subjects work on a jigsaw puzzle as a group, with one of the members given the job of recording the moves made and of sending messages as to which pieces should be assembled next on the basis of information at his disposal. Half the subjects given this special job were told they were "bosses," the other half that they were "recorders." Although their actual activities were no different, the "bosses" reported later that they felt more effective in their jobs—and they liked their jobs more. This study points to another reason for the tendency for leaders to have high self-esteem, in addition to the fact that high esteem is needed for the job in the first place. It is simply that a person perceives himself as more effective, more competent, not only as a result of his own prior level of self-esteem, but also of his attainment and retention of this position lead to a further enhancement of his self-esteem. This heightened self-esteem may in turn increase the leader's actual effectiveness, since he perceives himself as more competent, and so the benign circle turns. This increase in his actual effectiveness may then enhance the group's perception of his competence, and the circle spins even faster.

Violation of the Leader-Competence Schema

As in the case of other schemas, people feel negatively about situations which violate the schema about power, leadership, and competence. Exline and Ziller (1959) assembled two person groups to work on a group task, the subjects being told that one of them had more ability than the other, although there was in fact no basis for making this judgment. One of them was given the power to make decisions on the group task. In some situations the person who had been designated as having greater ability was given the power, in other cases the reverse was the case. When the powerful person presumably had less ability, the subjects were relatively less congenial and felt more negatively about each other. In fact, they both tended to see the other as losing in ability through the course of the task. In short, people felt more negatively about a situation which appeared to violate this schema, even when there was no real basis for the assumption that the person in charge was low in ability.

Behavior and the Leader-Competence Schema

This schema not only influences evaluations of situations and perception of leadership and competence; it can also guide behavior just as other schemas do. A person who perceives that he is more competent will engage in more acts of leadership. Levinger (1959) assembled subjects in pairs to work on a joint problem, but led one subject in each pair to believe that he was more expert with respect to that problem. These subjects tended to make more attempts to influence the other, resisted the other's suggestions more, were more generally assertive and saw themselves as having more influence over decisions. Likewise, in the Exline and Ziller study just described, when the powerful subject was the one who was thought to have higher ability, there was a greater tendency for him to engage in acts of task leadership than in situations which violated the schema. Obviously, this tendency of the person who sees himself as competent to act as leader helps to explain the process described earlier in the chapter in which people with ability tend to move into leadership positions.

Instrumental Use of the Schema

Furthermore, this schema also can be used instrumentally by the person. For example, when an individual is in a state of anxiety, he may attempt to reduce it by participating in a group task under a leader, since people tend to involve their own senses of competence with the group task. Of course, there are many instances in which people turn to leaders when they feel incompetent in the pursuit of important goals and when they perceive that the leader can help them attain these goals. Nevertheless, this schema can lead to a reduction in anxiety even when the leader obviously can do little about the actual source of anxiety. Helmreich and Collins (1967) told some high school student subjects that they would be working on tasks while receiving painful electric shocks and having blood samples taken. Other subjects were told that they would receive subliminal or no shock, and were told nothing about blood samples. Then all the subjects were given a choice of waiting alone for the experiment to start, waiting with other subjects, or waiting and working on a task under the supervision of a graduate student. The subjects who had been made fearful were most likely to choose the group-task leader alternative, while there was no particular preference among the low fear subjects.

The implications of this study are very important with respect to the survival of democracy, since it shows that people turn to leaders even when the latter can do little to help them overcome their problems. In some instances, these leaders may be more concerned with their own power than with their followers' welfare, and may thus become authoritarian and totalitarian. The leader does not have to solve the original problems which made the people anxious, but need only reduce their anxiety.

On a more hopeful note: people's exaggeration of the competence of leaders can be mitigated if the former can come to perceive that their own ability is great, that they can make judgments independently of the leader as to the correct course of action. In Stotland's study involving a city planning task, under an arbitrary leader, some subjects were given a chance to meet privately during an intermission in the planning with another participant who was also being subjected to another arbitrary "leader" in planning a city. In their conversation, the two subordinates tended to support one another's ideas about town planning. When they returned to the task, they argued and verbally fought with the arbitrary leader more than did subjects who had not had such meetings. After the planning was over, the former subjects were quite negative in their evaluations of the leader, in contrast to the near adulation of the latter subjects. The political implications are obvious.

Schema Relating Leadership and Behavioral Freedom

Closely related to the schema which suggests that leaders are more competent is the one to the effect that leaders have greater freedom than do others. As was seen in the previous chapter, freedom and the sense of competence are closely associated. Thus, the schema that leaders are competent will tend to imply that they are more free to choose the specific nature of their own actions from a wide variety of options. Furthermore, since leaders often do have more power to determine their own fate, there is ample basis for people to acquire a schema associating leadership and freedom. The schema is well illustrated in a study by Thibaut and Reicken (1955). They had three subjects come to a laboratory at the same time, although two were trained assistants. One was introduced to the true subject as a new Ph.D. college instructor. Another subject was introduced as a freshman college student. The true subject was then told that his job was to send the same messages at the same time to both of the other subjects in an attempt to persuade them to contribute to a blood bank. He could select any ten out of 38 prepared messages to send to the others. After the tenth message had been sent, both of the other "subjects" indicated that they would indeed contribute blood. The subjects then filled out questionnaires and their responses indicated that they thought that the instructor had freely decided to comply with their requests, while they thought the low status person complied only because of the social pressure brought to bear on him. The instructor was perceived as having greater freedom to decide whether to contribute or not, even though his behavior was exactly the same as the other person's. Thibaut and Reicken repeated their study by comparing the subjects' perceptions of an ex-combat commander and a nondescript student, both of whom had complied with the subject's request to lend them a book. Again the leader was perceived to have chosen to lend the book on his own, while the student was seen as having been "forced" into complying. Although Thibaut and Reicken don't make an issue of it, this study would also imply that a leader would be held more responsible for any misdeeds than a non-leader.

Status-Leadership Schema

Another schema which people generally acquire about leadership and power is one which indicates that leaders are accorded more status than are non-leaders. In new groups or groups facing new problems, task leaders tend to gain the respect of other members, tend to have higher status in the group. Further, in ongoing groups, especially in large organizations, the leaders with power tend to have higher rank in the organization, tend to earn more, tend to be older, and so forth (cf. Benoit-Smullyan, 1944). In fact, the association between power and status is so close that the exceptions are noted for their very rarity: the powerless king or queen of Great Britain; or the "man behind the throne"; the political "kingmakers." Thus, status and power are associated sufficiently often that many people acquire the schema associating power, leadership, and status. Like other schemas, this one tends to be self-supporting, since the higher status accorded the task leader is partly a function of the effects of this schema. Violations of this schema are negatively evaluated as would be expected. Berkowitz (1953) found that members of groups of business executives felt dissatisfied when the person in charge of their meeting, who generally was of higher status in the firm, did not act as the leader. In fact, when other leaders emerged in the group to informally replace the person in charge, the emergent leader tended also to be of high status. Another example comes from family life, about which we can assume that in the schemas of most Americans, wives still have somewhat lower status than husbands. Blood and Wolfe (1960) found that families in which the husbands were dominant were happier than those in which wives were dominant.

In addition to the schema about leadership and status being associated, there is evidence that people generally have schemas that different types of status are correlated, i.e., status due to power, age, sex, title. Sampson (1969) reports a study by Brandon in which an older graduate student, an undergraduate male, and a coed were to work on a group task. Presumably, the order of status of these three was in the order which we have just listed them. Despite the current trend toward greater emancipation of women, there can be little doubt that they do yet occupy somewhat lower status in American society than do men. In the groups set up by Brandon, there were three levels of status as determined by the differential contribution of each of the three task-related jobs to the quality of the group project. The subjects reported that they liked the group better if these jobs were allocated in order of status determined by age and sex. In addition, three different levels of status were established by setting up three degrees to which a person could represent the group in meetings outside the group. Again, when the age-sex status levels correlated with the levels of representativeness of the group, the members felt more positively about the group. However, Sampson points out that there may be a limitation on the effects of this schema in the case where different types of status are associated in unexpected ways, in ways that do not fit any schema. Thus, Brandon found that people did not expect the group representative necessarily to be the person with the most responsible job. If this association was imposed on the group, they did not evaluate the group quite so positively. The subjects were quite unhappy with a situation in which the male graduate student had both the more responsible job and the highest level of status in representing the group, while the coed was lowest on both the jobs. The reason Sampson suggests is that the subjects may perceive that this distribution of the desirable jobs was unjust to the coed, who had "nothing." In other words, the schema about different dimensions of status correlating may be limited by considerations of justice.

Verba (1966) points out that the occurrence of status differentials in newly formed groups will often reduce the degree of threat felt by members if the high status person also acts as task leader. On the other hand, he points out that in groups in which the members are of the same general status level, there is little basis for legitimizing the primacy of one person as task leader. Under these circumstances, social-emotional leaders typically emerge to cope with the threat.

Throughout this chapter, we have attempted to show that leadership is a dynamic process in which the leader and the followers interact, and in which the leader attains his position as a result of the actions of the followers and their needs, as well as in response to his own actions. This situational view of leadership stands in contrast to a conceptualization which holds that leadership is a quality which adheres in a person, so that he is a "born" leader, a person with characteristics which will make him a leader in any group he enters. The born leader approach is sometimes called "the great man" theory of leadership. Nevertheless, the great man theory and the situational approaches are not irreconcilable. It was pointed out earlier in the chapter that leaders do tend to have high ability on tasks relevant to the group's functioning. If, however, different groups share some common tasks and problems, then a given person can certainly emerge as a leader in each of them. People with high I.Q.s are more likely to become leaders in any group they enter, presumably because they have a wide variety of relevant abilities. Thus, with respect to task leaders, the situational and great man theories can both hold, the degree to which each is valid depending on the specific nature of the group task. The same analysis applies to social-emotional leadership. The talents which this type of leadership requires no doubt are much the same in different groups. However, the need for such a leader may vary with the degree of threat from the task leader or powerful person in the group. We have seen the great variety of factors which determine the degree of threat; these same factors will help determine the need for a social-emotional specialist.

References

Anderson, L. R., and Fiedler, F. E.: The effect of participatory and supervisory leadership on group creativity. *Journal of Applied Psychology*, 1964, 48:227–237.

Bales, R. F.: Some uniformities of behavior in small social systems. In G. E. Swanson, T. M. Newcomb, and E. L. Hartley (Eds.), *Readings in Social Psychology*. New York, Holt, 1952.

Bales, R. F.: The equilibrium problem in small groups. In T. Parsons, R. F. Bales, and E. A. Shelts (Eds.), *Working Papers in the Theory of Action*. Glencoe, Illinois, Free Press, 1953.

Bales, R. F., and Slater, P.: Role differentiation in small decision making groups. In T. Parsons et al. (Eds.), *Family, Socialization, and Interaction Process*. Glencoe, Illinois, Free Press, 1955.

Benoit-Smullyan, E.: Status, status types, and status inter-relationships. *American Sociological Review*, 1944, 9:151–161.

Berkowitz, L.: Sharing leadership in small, decision making groups. *Journal of Abnormal and Social Psychology*, 1953, 48:231–238.

Blood, R. O., and Wolfe, D. M.: *Husbands and Wives*. New York, Free Press, 1960.

Burke, P. J.: The development of task and social emotional role differentiation. *Sociometry*, 1967, 30:379–392.

Burke, W. W.: Leadership behavior as a function of the leader, the follower, and the situation. *Journal of Personality*, 1965, 33:66–81.

Campbell, J. D.: Peer relations in childhood. In M. L. Hoffman and L. W. Hoffman (Eds.), *Review of Child Development Research*. New York, Russell Sage, 1964.

Carter, L.: Leadership and small group behavior. In M. Sherif and M. O. Wilson (Eds.), *Group Relations at the Crossroads*. New York, Harper, 1953.

Cartwright, D. O., and Zander, A.: *Group Dynamics* (3rd edition). New York, Harper, 1968.

Cohen, A. M.: Changing small group communication networks. *Journal of Communication*, 1961, *11*:116–124, 128.

Cohen, A. M.: Changing small-group communication networks. *Administrative Science Quarterly*, 1962, 6:443–462.

Cooper, R.: Leaders' task relevance and subordinate behavior in industrial work groups. *Human Relations*, 1966, *19*:57–84.

Crockett, W. H.: Emergent leadership in small decision-making groups. *Journal of Abnormal and Social Psychology*, 1955, 51:362–370.

Exline, R. V., and Ziller, R. C.: Status congruency and interpersonal conflict in decision making groups. *Human Relations*, 1959, 16:147–162.

Fiedler, F. E.: *A Theory of Leadership Effectiveness*. New York, McGraw-Hill, 1967.

Flament, C.: The influence of changes in the networks of communications upon the performance of groups. *Psychologie Française*, 1956, *1*:12–13.

French, J. R. P., and Raven, B.: The bases of social power. In D. Cartwright (Ed.), *Studies in Social Power*. Ann Arbor, Institute for Social Research, 1959.

Fromm, E.: *Escape from Freedom*. New York, Farrar & Rinehart, 1941.

Gerard, H. B.: Some effects of status, role clarity and group goal clarity upon individuals' relation to group process. *Journal of Personality*, 1957, 25:475–488.

Ghiselli, E. E., and Lodahl, T. M.: Patterns of managerial traits and group effectiveness. *Journal of Abnormal and Social Psychology*, 1958, 57:61–66.

Gibb, C. A.: Leadership. In G. Lindzey and E. Aronson (Eds.), *Handbook of Social Psychology* (2nd edition, Vol. 4). New York, Addison-Wesley, 1969.

Hamblin, R.: Leadership and crises. *Sociometry*, 1958, *21*:322–325.

Haythorn, W.: The influence of individual group members on the behavior of co-workers and on the characteristics of groups. Unpublished doctoral dissertation, University of Rochester, 1952.

Helmreich, R. L., and Collins, B. E.: Situational determinants of affiliative preference under stress. *Journal of Personality and Social Psychology*, 1967, 6:79–85.

Hoffer, E.: *The True Believer*. New York, Harper, 1951.

Hollander, E. P.: Competence and conformity in the acceptance of influence. *Journal of Abnormal and Social Psychology*, 1960, 61:365–369.

Hollander, E. P.: Some effects of perceived status on response to innovative behavior. *Journal of Abnormal and Social Psychology*, 1961, 63:247–250.

Hollander, E. P.: *Leaders, Groups, and Influence*. New York, Oxford University Press, 1964.

Hollander, E. P., and Julian, J. W.: Contemporary trends in the analysis of leadership process. *Psychological Bulletin*, 1969, 71:387–397.

Kahn, R. L., and Katz, D.: Leadership and practices in relation to productivity and morale. In D. Cartwright and A. Zander (Eds.), *Group Dynamics*. Evanston, Illinois, Row, Peterson, 1953.

Kirscht, J., Lodahl, T., and Haire, M.: Some factors in the selection of leaders by members of small groups. *Journal of Abnormal and Social Psychology*, 1959, 58:406–408.

Koslin, B. L., Haarlow, R. N., Karlins, M., and Pargament, R.: Predicting group status from members' cognitions. *Sociometry*, 1968, 31:64–74.

Levinger, G.: The development of perceptions and behavior in newly formed social power relationships. In D. Cartwright (Ed.), *Studies in Social Power*. Ann Arbor, Institute for Social Research, 1959.

Levinger, G.: Task and social behavior in marriage. *Sociometry*, 1964, 27:433–440.

Likert, R.: *New Patterns of Management*. New York, McGraw-Hill, 1959.

Lippitt, R., Polansky, N., and Rosen, S.: The dynamics of power: a field study of social influence in groups of children. *Human Relations*, 1952, 5:37–64.

McClintock, C. G.: Group support and the behavior of leaders and non-leaders. *Journal of Abnormal and Social Psychology*, 1963, 67:105–113.

Maier, N. R. F., and Solem, A. R.: The contribution of a discussion leader to the quality of group thinking: the effectiveness of minority opinions. *Human Relations*, 1952, 5:277–288.

March, J. G., and Simon, H. A.: *Organizations.* New York, Wiley, 1958.

Merei, F.: Group leadership and institutionalization. *Human Relations,* 1949, *2*:23–39.

Morse, N. C., and Reimer, E.: Experimental change of a major organizational variable. *Journal of Abnormal and Social Psychology,* 1956, *52*:120–129.

Pryer, M. W., Flint, A. W., and Bass, B. M.: Group effectiveness and consistency of leadership. *Sociometry,* 1962, *25*:391–397.

Raven, B. H., and French, J. R. P.: Group support, legitimate power, and social influence. *Journal of Personality,* 1958, *26*:400–409.

Runkel, P. J.: Cognitive similarity in facilitating communication. *Sociometry,* 1956, *19*:178–191.

Sample, J. A., and Wilson, T. R.: Leader behavior, group productivity, and rating of least preferred co-worker. *Journal of Personality and Social Psychology,* 1965, *1*:266–270.

Sampson, E. E.: Studies of status congruence. In L. Berkowitz (Ed.), *Advances in Experimental Social Psychology,* Vol. 4. New York, Academic Press, 1969.

Shaw, M. E.: Group structure and the behavior of individuals in small groups. *Journal of Psychology,* 1954, *38*:138–149.

Sherif, M., White, J., and Harvey, O. J.: Status in experimentally produced groups. *American Journal of Sociology,* 1955, *60*:370–379.

Shovel, M.: Interpersonal knowledge and rated leader potential. *Journal of Abnormal and Social Psychology,* 1960, *61*:87–92.

Slater, P. E.: Role differentiation in small groups. In A. P. Hare, E. F. Borgatta, and R. F. Bales (Eds.), *Small groups.* New York, Knopf, 1955.

Sommer, R.: Leadership and group geography. *Sociometry,* 1961, *24*:99–110.

Stotland, E.: Peer groups and reactions to power figures. In D. Cartwright (Ed.), *Studies in Social Power.* Ann Arbor, Research Center of Group Dynamics, 1959.

Stotland, E., and Kobler, A. L.: *Life and Death of a Mental Hospital.* Seattle, University of Washington Press, 1965.

Stouffer, S. A., Suchman, E. A., DeVinney, L. C., Star, S. A., and Williams, R. M.: *The American Soldier: Adjustment During Army Life.* Princeton, Princeton University Press, 1949.

Swift, J. W.: Effects of early group experience: the nursery school and day nursery. In M. L. Hoffman and L. W. Hoffman (Eds.), *Review of Child Development Research.* New York, Russell Sage, 1964.

Thibaut, J., and Kelley, H. H.: *The Social Psychology of Groups.* New York, Wiley, 1959.

Thibaut, J. W., and Riecken, H. W.: Some determinants and consequences of the perception of social causality. *Journal of Personality,* 1955, *24*:113–133.

Torrance, E. P.: A theory of leadership and interpersonal behavior under stress. In L. Petrullo and B. M. Bass (Eds.), *Leadership and Interpersonal Behavior.* New York, Holt, Rinehart, & Winston, 1961.

Verba, S.: Leadership: affective and instrumental. In C. Backman and P. F. Secord (Eds.), *Problems in Social Psychology,* New York, McGraw-Hill, 1966.

White, R. K., and Lippitt, R.: *Autocracy and Democracy.* New York, Harper, 1960.

Whyte, W. F.: *Street Corner Society.* Chicago, University of Chicago Press, 1943.

Zander, A., and Quinn, R.: The social environment and mental health. *Journal of Social Issues,* 1962, *18*:48–66.

NAME INDEX

573

SUBJECT INDEX

581